REFLEXIVITY AND THE CRISIS OF WESTERN REASON

With superb philosophical, literary and sociological scholarship, he reveals the historical shift from an ecological-ontological grammar of reflection to a socio-dialogical grammar of reflexive practice.

John O'Neill, *Distinguished Research Professor of Sociology, York University, Canada*

To describe the scholarship as outstanding is almost faint praise. I was continually struck by the sophistication with which the author weaves together ideas, references, quotes to present a fantastically assured and polished grasp of his material.

David Chaney, *Professor of Sociology, University of Durham*

In its combination of extraordinary scholarship and patient analysis this book offers a redirection of cultural and social theory which merits comparison with the work of Derrida, Foucault, Habermas and other European theorists of the first rank.

Stephen Crook, *Senior Lecturer in Sociology, University of Tasmania*

This ground-breaking work, the first in a series of volumes, explores the genealogical analysis of the discourses of reflection. Barry Sandywell traces the differences between the traditional discourses of reflection and the experiences of reflexivity in everyday, social and philosophical thought.

The central contention of Sandywell's argument is that in order to begin to address these types of questions we must first explore the force field between the discourses of reflection and reflexivity. To do so requires radical self-investigations of the role of reflexivity in human experience, and more especially of the role of the languages, practices, and institutions of self-reflection within the fabric of Western culture.

Consequently, these 'logological investigations' introduce a method of analysis which traces the epochal movement of thought from a videological to a dialogical conception of the world. In doing so they introduce some of the preliminary work necessary for more detailed studies of premodern, modern, and postmodern forms of reflexivity in the subsequent volumes.

Brilliantly organized and abounding with astonishing insights, Volume 1 offers a fundamental challenge to our normal ways of viewing social thought.

Barry Sandywell is Lecturer in the Department of Sociology at the University of York.

REFLEXIVITY AND THE CRISIS OF WESTERN REASON

Logological Investigations
Volume 1

Barry Sandywell

London and New York

First published 1996
by Routledge
11 New Fetter Lane, London EC4P 4EE

Simultaneously published in the USA and Canada
by Routledge
29 West 35th Street, New York, NY 10001

© 1996 Barry Sandywell

Typeset in Garamond by Michael Mepham, Frome, Somerset
Printed and bound in Great Britain by
Biddles Ltd, Guildford and King's Lynn

British Library Cataloguing in Publication Data
A catalogue record for this book is available from
the British Library.

Library of Congress Cataloguing in Publication Data
A catalogue record for this book has been requested

ISBN 0–415–08756–2

The path to hell is paved with good intentions.

(Proverb)

The light dove, cleaving the air in her free flight, might imagine that flight would be easier in empty space.

(Kant, 1929: A5, B8)

Im Anfang war die Tat (In the beginning was the act).

(Goethe, 1949: 71)

For
Isabel Lavin-Garzón
and in memory of Susannah Sandywell (1908–85)
and James Sandywell (1907–92)

CONTENTS

CONTENTS

Part IV Dialogue

PREFACE
By way of a general introduction

In the following preface I provide an account of some of the central concerns and major themes of Volume 1 and an indication of the content and argument of subsequent volumes. The guiding intention of this multivolume project is to rethink the nature of social and philosophical inquiry in the light of the radically reflexive character of human action, temporality, and discursive self-formation. To simplify a very complex story, my major contention is that existing theories of the *self, action, community*, and *reality* have studiously underplayed and, in many cases, completely ignored the reflexive configurations of human experience, language, and social praxis in world-making processes. This blindness toward the reflexive practicalities of human life-in-the-world has predisposed mainstream theorizing and research in the human sciences to elaborate profoundly reductive images of social existence which, in turn, have authorized uncritical frameworks of inquiry and objectivistic epistemic practices. Nineteenth-century sociological thought, for example, repeatedly tried to secure its status as a science of social formations by laundering its subject matter – structures of meaningful human relations and self-activity – of their ontologically embodied, temporal, and relational properties. Moreover, by identifying with empiricist and rationalist metalogics – especially those taken to be essential to scientific epistemology – the human sciences have facilitated their own cooption for technocratic, instrumental, and social engineering purposes. We might recall that the fundamental idea of sociological discourse – the concept of the social system as a complex structured whole – is the product of a technical metaphor. No doubt a similar case can be made for the limited ontological conceptions of the self, culture, and reflexive existence within the research frameworks of history, literary criticism, and the humanities. While the larger story I unfold concerns the vicissitudes of 'value', 'selfhood', and 'alterity' in everyday life, the substantive focus concerns practices that have developed methods of self-understanding by problematizing their own procedures and presuppositions.

The logological field

The essays which follow are thus presented as explorations in the style of logological investigations. The qualifier 'logological' requires immediate clarification. To constitute a form of inquiry that has, as yet, no settled name, let us say that logological research designates 'foundational inquiries' which take as their theme the whole range of sense-making activities in social life – the cultural conversations, technical systems, and normative institutions of 'signification', 'communication', and 'interpretation' which constitute social worlds from the material structures of objects and object relations. Formulated most simply, logological investigations are 'second-order' inquiries into the foundational presuppositions of first-order discourses. By bracketing the presupposition of the objectivity of the world this orientation allows the will to 'meaning' to appear as one of the most basic impulses of individual and collective life. Human beings are unique in constructing cultural worlds from the material and symbolic media of inherited traditions. The order of the real is created by the structuring activities of social life. But these processes of 'world construction' are typically hidden in the reflective orientations of everyday life. However, once approached critically, 'sense-making' activities are seen to be 'self-making' praxes in which human beings dramatically categorize, theorize, and narrativize their experience in response to prestructured alterities (to emphasize narrative reflexivity, however, is not to privilege action or language over other forms of mediating praxis, but to remind ourselves that the human world is always-already dramatized and that these dramaturgical modes of meaning are presupposed as the collective background for other attitudes and projects). Suitably modified and respecified we can designate the totality of these 'world-making' systems of semiopraxis as the realm of 'culture' (thus social institutions, like human beings, must continuously enact their identity and reproduce their basic forms of selfhood to remain institutions).

In general terms we can say that self-making activities are first evidenced in the organized, public practices which sustain the intelligibility of everyday life. And what a community authorizes as 'experienceable' and 'thinkable' from the totality of being is invariably embedded in both verbal and extra-verbal forms which define the common terms of existence, rationality, and social value for a society (commending a social ontology, we foreground the mimetic dramas of a society as embodiments of tradition antedating the reflective projects of theory). Given the pervasive role of these autopoeic systems in social life, it follows that any reflexive science must first explore the constitutive work of rhetoric and dramatic categories already embedded in its phenomenal field. It is therefore possible to think of logological inquiries as activities of *metacriticism*, given that they take the ontological assumptions and institutional preconditions of discourse formations as their topic. But they are also metacritiques of discourses and ideologies as these have become embedded in social relations and dominant structures. Human beings *think* as they *live* within the fabric of symbolic institutions.

One of the foundational problems of every social order is how to 'manage' the constraints and alterity of reality in the interests of collective identity. How to reduce the unrepresentable realms of otherness to representations of identity? How to make the phenomenal world of being intersubjectively experienceable? How to coordinate action in order to change the inherited forms of mundane life? I will suggest that one of the keys to the ancient problem of consciousness and will-formation lies in the ontological work of social mimesis defining the cultural *logosphere*. Once institutionalized, mimetic culture provides normative maps through which a society affirms its identity by symbolizing alterity and managing difference. Members of a society inhabit a meaningful world by participating in and internalizing the signifying practices of a specific logosphere. In this way the societal objectifications of everyday perception and praxis are routinely concretized in the fabric of day-to-day reality. But the logosphere is much wider than textual or linguistic self-reflection as this is conventionally understood. The primordial reflexivity of ordinary speech for instance, like Walter Benjamin's mimetic faculty, designates powers and capacities of classification, meaning-articulation, affectivity, volitional orientation, and everyday sensibilities which antedate self-conscious totalization. These immensely complex value structures inform the grammar of emotions, lived needs, and affective experience prior to explicit discursive and social structuration. The myriad forms of mimetic culture which we tend to turn into closed 'spheres of action' or reified 'genres' – everyday action, collective rituals, myth, poetry, art, drama, technology, science, philosophy, etc. – can now be respecified as past social experiments in *self-representation* and *self-knowledge* which change the terms of human freedom. We are tragically aware, of course, that such communal experiments risk forgetting their own intrinsic complexity, contradictory origins, and contingent institutional limitations to end up as ossified 'structures' and 'determining forces'. The complexities of everyday social interaction, for example, are perennially occluded by being translated into static and unreflexive ontic frames. Against all forms of empiricism and objectivism we need to speak literally of the social *invention* of reality.

As a transdisciplinary framework, then, logological research takes the whole range of recursive 'reality-work' as its investigative field. From the logological perspective all human practices and social organizations actively constitute experience and should be studied as historical 'meaning formations' imposing 'readings' upon a relatively indeterminate environment. Of course this work of meaning-constitution does not occur in a vacuum – the parameters and constraints of cultural praxis are already fixed by pre-existing material and sociocultural formations. In this context to speak of 'culture' is to refer to the changing technologies and institutions of collective self-objectification that have dialectically shaped alterities into meaningful social orders. The basic theorem here is that embodied practices of interpretation – whether at the level of material existence, folk theorizing, or higher orders of societal praxis – *produce* rather than simply *reflect* the phenomenal order. In this qualified sense we may certainly claim that sociocultural reality is discursively constructed. But 'reality' is also, more profoundly, an alien order of being that resists the will and constrains the projects of historical agents. For example, in day-to-day living we plan and negotiate our ordinary affairs against a relatively fixed background of pregiven relations and structures whose origins and workings are not typically subject to critical reflection. As finite beings we are even unaware that the narratives we use to describe the world actively constitute its otherness as intelligible 'experience'. Yet by virtue of their 'located' and 'embedded' character, forms of world-interpretation are in principle revisable constructs. In contrast with other modes of social analysis, we commend the idea that the prereflective order of semiopraxis functions as a generative matrix in constituting practices and sustaining the terms of identity. 'Common sense in each epoch consists in an astonishingly complex agglomeration of highly sophisticated half-truths' (Heller, 1975: 19). Indeed the extraordinary richness of human experience goes unnoticed in its self-effacing 'ordinariness'. From this point of view, 'folk-theories' of human identity, action, and value can be approached as everyday strategies which agents use in constituting their social life as an intelligible order. Folk-theories enter the process of self-formation as constitutive rhetorics and frequently end up as the forms of objects themselves. Another logological theorem is that existing sociocultural worlds have been fundamentally shaped by the legacy of past representations of 'self and other' (past philosophical 'half-truths' about the nature of existence, metaphysical beliefs about reality and knowledge, implicit theories of mind, self, desire, nature, death, etc.) as these accounts have been woven into the personal and institutional fabric of culture. As one writer has observed:

> Everyday life is not separate from social institutions, but is lived, to varying degrees, in and with such forms of knowledge and habitualized practices. Institutions are built in everyday practices, as much as they provide rules and resources for living one's life.
>
> (Wagner, 1994: 23)

The grammar of human action, the images of collective identity, and the value-orientations of civilizations are founded upon these deep-rooted symbolisms. But if lived experience is intrinsically dialogical – as we will suggest in the following chapters – to avoid 'misplaced concreteness' any systematic reflection upon habitualized forms of life must take a principled interest in the tacit ontologies of preinterpreted consciousness.

Paradigms of reflection and reflexivity

Wherever we try to think about individuals or society fundamentally we see that experience has already been overlayered with the concepts of past modes of reflection. For example, in subsequent volumes we will follow the ways in which theories of knowledge and metaphysical categories have been embodied in the institutional order of European culture. The pervasive nature of existential preinterpretation underscores the importance of exploring the received forms of human self-understanding.

As a provisional simplification we can say that the dominant paradigm of reflection in the Western philosophical tradition includes a wide range of intellectual and cultural discourses predicated on an ocularcentric model of reality and world-orientation. As a heuristic fiction we can define the 'logic of reflection' as a generic term for a family of epistemic attitudes and ontic practices elaborated around videological models of intelligibility (including practical knowledge, instrumental reasoning, technical logics, popular cultural representations, formal rule systems, reflectionist social theories, etc.), while 'reflexivity' designates the act of interrogating these intepretation systems (thus participating in a democratic process is a reflective practice, while studying the dialectical history of parliamentary institutions takes inquiry in reflexive directions). Where the language-games of reflection sustain the procedures of analytic reason and mundane inquiry, reflexive analysis questions the nature and grounds of first-order discourse. Thus in ordinary life we see things, but rarely attend to *seeing* and its history; we *speak* without reflecting on the complexity of language and its rules, we *think*, without 'thinking about thinking'; we appraise others, without thematizing the criteria of valorization; we *act* without exploring the fabric of social interaction; we engage in social research without investigating the vocabularies of inquiry, and so on. Where reflective orientations tend to adopt an empiricist orientation to their world domains and a pragmatic attitude toward their own authority, reflexive perspectives approach first-order reality work as a constructive process. Reflection posits a neutral world of entities, reflexivity reminds reflection of the sociality of all world reference.

It will be readily seen that 'reflection' and 'reflexivity' do not form the terms of a binary opposition. We might even imagine a continuum between prereflective, reflective, and reflexive experience. Existing traditions of reflexive thought have themselves developed from a critical response to reflective and prereflective practices. But we should also not think of 'prereflection' as a neutral sphere of facts or 'data'. Prereflective experience already contains the primitive forms of embodiment, tacit interpretations and imaginary formations which provide the horizon for more reflective systems of action. Human experience is to this extent an interminable dialogue between prereflective experience, reflective practices, and reflexive action.

We need to think of culture as both meaning and praxis: unlike the closed circle of disinterested reflection, reflexive action changes the form of the self: a reflexive practice never returns the self to the point of origin (the fabric of history, we might say, is created from the interweaving threads of reflective and reflexive action). The difficult task for analysis is to trace *dialectical relationships* across the whole range of prereflective, reflective, and reflexive structures which mediate and define individual and collective existence.

In terms of method and simplifying the discussion to bare essentials: logological investigations question the mimetic, asocial, and transcendental assumptions of unreflective systems of thought and world-work by foregrounding the mediations of *logos* in social life, especially the unexplicated verbal formations and presuppositional contexts of lived experience sustaining the sciences, art, technology, literature, and philosophy. From this point of view what is fundamental about the human species is not the truism that human beings *make* culture, but the idea that they *transform themselves and their world relations* through manifold forms of semiopraxis (if we think of 'technologies' and 'organizations' as historical modes of self-inscription constituted through social interaction this prefigures what I call the *technopoiesis* hypothesis – the history of the human mind is inextricably tied to the development of signifying media, information machines, and mind tools).

Given the vast range of phenomena relevant to this enterprise I have taken quite ruthless decisions about the form and content of these introductory studies. One of my primary intentions is to commend an *ethical* redefinition of human praxis as a cooperative, dialogical project of interacting selves. By living its contingent temporal reflexivities, the human species is in principle a self-defining and self-transforming life form. A related objective is to return human creativity to its situated sources in wider technical, political, and institutional processes (prefiguring a social theory of situated liberties correlated to life-world conditions). A third aim is to link the contemporary crisis of the sciences and humanities to the repression of the intrinsically reflexive, temporal, and dialogical dimensions of human experience. And, finally, I wish to begin the task of recovering traditions of radical reflexivity in ancient and premodern culture, appraising their implications for the discourses of the arts and human sciences. Like all critiques, the emerging idea of reflexive inquiry and the foregrounding of ethical community over economic and political order has important pedagogic and policy implications. Because of limitations of space, however, I reluctantly leave these topics for future elaboration. But we should at least observe that as these issues of collectively embedded action, temporality, and dialogical selfhood raise fundamental questions common to all the human sciences, a critique of the transcendental assumptions of pure reflection questions the legitimacy of every unreflexive model of knowledge, society, and politics. The following studies develop this transdisciplinary ambition by criticizing the 'world models' of dominant modes of analysis (and their canonical discursive forms) underwriting quite diverse epistemic projects – excavating, for example, the Cartesian postulates and metaphysical beliefs which inform the modern scientific world-view, the institutional power of instrumental reason, and the political consequences of the unreflexive discourses of existing social sciences.

PREFACE

The question of reflexivity

To distinguish the logological frame of mind from related perspectives I will in general speak of its primary concern with *semiopraxis* as dialogical interaction constitutive of human worlds. Unlike the 'neutral' and 'substantive' orientations of received views of action and culture, however, this conceptualization emphasizes the shared *activities, instruments,* and *procedures* of self-invention through which social orders semiotically articulate and objectify their own internal and external environments (thus the industrialization of consciousness through mechanical technologies and more recent 'cybernetic systems' would form an important field in studying the social invention of modern selfhood). Logological research adopts a *dialogical* conception of being-in-the-world: its central concern is with the discursively embodied nature of mind and selfhood (consider for example the manifold ways in which the logics of scientific reflection and ideals of formal rationality have become institutionalized in our culture). Where the received wisdom of mainstream social science posits an *ahistorical* and *reflective* nexus between language and the phenomenal world it aspires to describe, here we begin from the idea that language has a *constitutive* moral relation to its 'objects'. Thus traditional vocabularies of inquiry – description, analysis, explanation, narration, etc. – are invariably problematic acts of rhetorical *translation* embedded in communal practices, rather than neutral transcriptions of pre-existing phenomena (we will see, for instance, that early Greek ontology actively reproduced an *atemporal, unitary,* and *substantial* definition of Being and rationality as the basis for its ideological operations and imaginary self-conceptions). But if the monologue form has exerted its hegemonic influence, we should recall that the very beginnings of theorizing were couched in dialogical forms.

To gain a preliminary understanding of the logological perspective it is useful to think of 'culture' as a machinery of 'general intellect' and 'translation practices' available to a society. 'Ways of thinking', 'forms of talk', 'discursive practices', 'embedded knowledge', etc. are axiological media of self-representation and selfhood – rhetorical methods which provide a community's basic 'instruments for living'. As such they are inseparably linked to political relations and codes of authority. But 'instruments for living' also involve operations of exclusion, repression, and forgetting. The elisions of a powerful culture can be condensed in the concept of *heteropoiesis* – the rhetorical work invested in suppressing and silencing 'the other'. On one side, selfhood is dialectically related to the order and dynamics of social technologies (consider the history of warfare, structures of social domination, and organized power within everyday life and its traditions). In another sense, selfhood is defined by the 'will to truth', the desire to establish the nature of reality within a field of competing discourses. In principle, then, every manifestation of self-reflection, critical distance, or recursive attention involves a certain doubling of language before the struggle for truth: whose voice, history, discourse is to be transmitted? And this act of doubling involves rhetorical selection, figuration, and metaphoric projection. Different voices can enter existing traditions only through the polemical mechanisms of competition and contestation. Again the deep-seated problems of dialogical pedagogy and its institutional concretization will be deferred for another occasion.

For reflection, objects are simply things *simpliciter*; for reflexivity, however, things are materialized significations, the outcome of social constructions and translation procedures. To speak of selfhood in the logological sense, then, is to thematize the signifying *processes* which disclose domains of truth by discursively valorizing and devalorizing different dimensions of human experience (in Volumes 2 and 3 we will examine the formative rhetorics of ancient Greek culture in these polemical terms). The disclosure-occlusion dialectic is also visible in higher-level translation activities; the so-called 'superstructures' of rationality, ideology, technology, politics and so on also necessarily draw upon an intellectual instrumentarium (in the advanced technological societies this 'instrumentarium' achieves a global reach and becomes a generative source of 'invented traditions', 'imaginary communities', and reflexive organizations in its own right).

Sociologists first confront problems of generic reflexivity, ethical self-reference, and truth in the form of the paradox that the processes and products of social inquiry are social constructs and are themselves subject to sociohistorical determination. Theorizing and research are particular *cultural forms* which embody ideological categories continuous with the categories of everyday life. As Anthony Giddens has observed, social life is '*produced* by its component actors precisely in terms of their active constitution and reconstitution of frames of meaning whereby they organize their experience' (1993: 86). This reflexive relation has been called the *double hermeneutic* reciprocity between lay and professional frames of meaning. The language-games of classical social theory, for example, are indebted to deep-rooted metaphysical codes drawn from Greek and Judaic-Christian traditions. These frameworks in turn reflexively shape the activities of later forms of life. In general, then, the translation devices of theorizing incorporate ideological figurations of experience. Interpretive social science has also made us aware of the importance of seeing 'agents' or 'members' as knowledgeable, intentional, and self-reflexive sources of intelligent conduct and societal interpretation. These insights are, however, frequently disparaged as disabling obstacles to sociological reason or sidelined as purely philosophical objections to the idea of a science of culture. But from the reflexive paradigm they can be viewed as unavoidable consequences of the radical historicity of human environments. Once we understand the presuppositional role of value and language in all social action, the phenomenon of reflexivity can be approached more analytically and constructively as a field of study in its own right. Thus many of the 'topics' of the human sciences turn out to be the sedimented products of earlier *ethical* practices and institutions. To say this simply, every society is an 'answer' to the question 'How should we live a fully human life?'. The manifold recursivities of human praxis make reflection upon the grounds and conventions of knowledge *production* a fundamental possibility of knowledgeable activities (bearing in mind that self-conscious cognitive reflection can *create* novel and unpredictable genres of evaluative discourse). Giddens' distinction between reflexivity as a dimension of human action and *institutional reflexivity* highlights this important dimension of social life. The latter concerns the 'socialized intellect' of a society, the 'institutionalization of an investigative and calculative attitude towards generalized conditions of system reproduction' (1993: 6). The 'colonization' of first-order moral reflection by apparatuses of organized reflectivity is today one of the most critical dimensions of modernizing societies ('The expansion of institutional reflexivity stands behind the proliferation of organizations in circumstances of modernity, including organizations of global scope', 1993: 6).

Logological research is therefore concerned with presuppositional matrices and the dialectics of translation. To express the same point another way, 'acts of speaking' and 'domains of phenomena' are interrelated in the legacy of *methods* for acquiring and using socially constructed knowledge in everyday life. And being immanently recursive both 'terms' of this dialectic are subject to diremption and transformation. Changes in presuppositional rules and methodologies bring concomitant changes in what we call 'the real world'. Like the 'self', 'reality' must be seen as an open-ended process subject to renegotiation and transformation. This is where larger socioeconomic, political and cultural systems intersect with the field of selfhood. Once institutionalized, these ways of thinking, seeing, and being (valuing) can be approached as outcomes of hegemonic discursive matrices in definite social orders (hence the interest of powerful groups in securing such knowledge-institutions as educational apparatuses, literary technologies, and mass media as forms of authority). For example, the dominant languages of social inquiry – the idioms developed by naturalistic philosophy and the methods popularized by the growth of modern science – developed as the organs of particular interests and forms of life. But once in existence such discourses become causal agencies in their own right. Moreover the self-knowledge made possible by their 'presuppositional structure' can be used as an instrument in the phenomenal order which epistemic communities aspire to recover and communicate. From the logological perspective, then, 'knowledge' should be troped as a category of differential social agency subject to complex institutional conditions and historical mutations.

Discursive forms of the self

Where first-order reflection (whether lay or professional) posits its objects as already organized into pregiven categories, reflexive inquiries study the historicity of sense-making activities – the grammar of a social order's founding rhetorics and representations of communality – as techniques of self-articulation. Where 'selfhood' is lost in the object-thematization and universal claims of the positive sciences, it is recoverable as an irreducible resource from the standpoint of reflexive inquiry: every logic of reflection, methodology, and investigative paradigm is thus in principle a translation device and is therefore subject to deconstruction. We then ask: 'What does it mean to speak about the self in this way?' 'What is occluded in so-speaking?' 'What interests are empowered and disempowered?' The socialization of 'general intellect' is of course the reason why we can imagine a history of the modes of reflection and study the changing patterns of self implicated in the social constitution of phenomenal domains (to which we retrospectively append the labels 'art', 'politics', 'poetics', 'religion', 'philosophy', 'journalism', 'media', etc.).

What is taken for granted by mundane cognition – the artifactual character of all classifications, the recursive potential of semiopraxis anterior to theory, the rich material life of epistemic communities, the moral claims of historical traditions, etc. – form the topics of logological inquiries. By approaching social practices as transcriptions we begin to appreciate the profound (con)textuality, revisability, and open-ended character of what we have come to call self, community, and world. In moving from a reflective to a constitutive understanding of knowledge forms we bring into view the ethical grammar of selfhood (and alterity) implicit in different modes of human experience.

To turn very briefly to the focus upon theoretical discourse in the culture of the West or 'the self-construction of European civilization'. The rationale is simply that what we call 'the West' or 'modern European culture' cannot be understood apart from the legacy of its own dominant epistemic forms – modernity has been essentially fashioned by the ways in which it has institutionalized definite ways of thinking and organized systems of 'general intellect'. The hegemonic role of science and technical reason, for example, is one instance of this incorporation process in modern society. In Volumes 5 and 6 we will see that the projection of an eschatological and teleological 'history' and related attempts to control rationally or transcend historicity are themselves irreducible historical gestures. In particular classical Greek modes of thought, the transcendent value orientations of Christian culture, and the rationalizing discourses of modern social theory have been incorporated into the collective sensorium of modern social life (we think of the pervasive hold of the normative ideal of 'truth' derived from classical discourse, linear-eschatological progressive historiography, and the universalizing dynamic of reflexive capitalism as distinctive dimensions of modern societies).

While the normative claims of *theory* have assumed many shapes the phallocentric idea of the *Logos* and its claim to truthfully (re)present the world remains a perennial concern of Western philosophical, scientific, literary, and social thought. By critically questioning the West's foundationalist paradigms of reason, self, history, and society I wish to delimit the legitimate claims of reflection and by this means redefine the vocation of truth and the theoretical life from the perspective of reflexive theory. Traditional subject-centred conceptions of reason as disengaged, solitary, autonomous reflection (*Nous, noesis,* Pure Reason, Metaphysical Logic, Self-certainty, Universal Transcendental Consciousness, Pure Will, Value-neutral Inquiry, etc.) are shown to involve a disabling aporetic structure, a limitation which facilitates a reformulation of truth and rationality as an order of situated rationality. The collapse of the traditional metaphysical subject also facilitates a rethinking of the profoundly dialogical character of human experience. In sum, the life of theorizing is shown to be a fundamentally moral phenomenon with its roots in an 'ethicized' life-world of 'others'. Ironically we have to relinquish the hyperbolic claims of objective Reason and 'rational consciousness' to become more reasonable. Polemically, the critique of reflective reason is one way of reactivating older ideas and themes covered up by the modern idea of objective Reason. The implications of this critique will become apparent in later volumes which examine the development of modern and postmodern modes of self-reflection in societies that are beset with deep-rooted contradictions and social problems revolving around the normalization, exclusion, and repression of alterity.

The history of self-reflection

It is therefore not a question of 'abandoning theory' or leaping beyond 'philosophy'. In fact to examine the history and limits of *theoria* and the *bios theoretikos* I commend a mode of self-reflection which practises a 'discursive reflection upon discourses' – a kind of critical commentary upon the conditions and fissures of *logoi*, tracing the latter to linguistically constituted traditions. In this respect the essays can be regarded as studies in the aporetic textures of existing paradigms of self-reflection and truth-telling. But this is not to posit a privileged standpoint suspended above the practices of art, philosophy, poetics, rhetoric, and the like. Rather we accept the irreducible dialectic of self and other and self and self at work in the history of discourse formations. Hence the recursive term 'logology' – 'discourse studying discourse and its signifying forms' – identifies the text's concern with the social genesis of self-inquiry in cultural spheres anterior to logical and analytical reflection (Volume 2 for example traces patterns of Western self-reflection to the 'self-other' mythologies and poetics of archaic Greek civilization).

I am acutely aware that the words 'logological' and 'investigation' in the general title of this work may misleadingly suggest the closure of an established framework or the promise of a 'postphilosophical' or 'postmodern' resolution of questions first posed within the Western theoretical tradition. Nothing could be further from the truth. In fact the essays composing this work form a constellation of exploratory *questions* selected from a wide range of cultural materials; the primary selective principle is to focus upon periods and historical contexts that have been productive in discourses which explicitly solicit other and different ways of thinking about human being (and these eventful epochs are typically liminal periods of beginnings and terminations where discourse generates internal contradictions and where 'truth-telling' becomes an insistent concern). Thus we will explore the possibility that modern reflection can be problematized by 'premodern' reflexivity, that the dominant paradigms of knowledge and reason today need to learn from the shock of the old. In all these respects these studies are most emphatically *introductions* to logological research and represent more of a personal quest for more resonant languages of reflexion for human inquiry than a prescriptive statement of salutary method or facile resolution of the crisis currently besetting speculative theory.

The plan of these studies

To introduce the logological attitude Volume 1 begins by exploring the generative metaphors and narratives of self-reflection sustaining some of the hegemonic discourses of Western theorizing in its empiricist and scientistic forms. To set the scene we examine the dominant mode of collective reflection which we call 'reflexive capitalism'. But we need to dig deeper into the European cultural grammar which made reflexive modernity a historical possibility. To institute this kind of genealogy of a whole civilization, the chapters of Parts I and II deconstruct the 'root metaphors' of representation (*mimesis*) and reflection (*consciousness*) at work in everyday ways of talking to reveal the figural operations of language in selfhood (Part III) and to suggest principles for alternative dialogical models of embodied reflexivity for social theory (Parts III and IV). Reflexivity as the 'return of the repressed Other' of *mimesis* makes its appearance when reflection recognizes its inherence within particular forms of life and its indebtedness to inherited language-games and traditions – here the dominant institutions of the West. We begin from the fact that many of the basic positions of Western epistemology are variations on the schema of the *spectacle* (displayed in the metaphorics of the *scene, stage, site, structure,* and so on). Moreover the theatre of knowledge is typically construed in egological terms premised on the repression of more complex forms of dialogue. At the most general level Volume 1 tells the story of the 'movement' from an egological-ontological grammar of reflection to dialogical-social paradigms of reflexivity – a transition from visual ontology to dialogic ethics in our ways of thinking (with corresponding reorientations in the politics of self and community). At a metacritical level, I wish to claim that this epochal shift away from ocularcentric grammar entails a fundamental recasting of our frameworks of knowledge in the direction of paradigms drawn from dialogical and participatory models of signification, reality, and community. Thus the abstract 'plot' of Volume 1 takes the form of an internal collapse of the metaphysical principles of 'videological culture' in deference to the intrusion of the occluded life of radical alterity. While the chapters of Part IV review these themes, a full discussion of the dialectical roots of theorizing and truth will be deferred to later volumes.

Here it is imperative to draw attention at the outset to the strategic role and limitation of these initial analyses. The reader should bear in mind the following qualifications. First, as a metacritique of some of the foundational assumptions of Western thought Volume 1 works at a very high level of generality to establish the idea of a fully reflexive ontology of human experience. Second, because of space limitations the chosen level of analysis involves an ahistorical schematism of the 'movement' from reflection to reflexivity. Finally, the links between the general thesis and its specific ramifications for the human sciences and modern culture more broadly is presented through illustrative examples, none of which are explored in the thoroughness required to institute a comprehensive framework of reflexive analysis. These abstract fictions will be dismantled in subsequent volumes which explore the generative presuppositions of poetics, philosophy, and theorizing as intellectual resolutions of problems generated by specific historical formations. Volumes 2 to 4 are primarily concerned with the beginnings of theorizing and the culture of reflection established in ancient Greece, while Volumes 5 and 6 examine the vicissitudes of the *Logos* in the development of modern and postmodern thought, tracing the ways in which classical reflexive positions have informed modern thought, how this legacy has been diffused and liquidated, and how today it is being reappropriated across a range of diverse theoretical projects. By moving beyond this schema I hope to establish the outlines of a reflexive style of inquiry that can be extended to different cultural domains and made more precise as the field of logological investigations evolves its own distinctive instruments and problematics (to borrow William James' famous rubric, we can imagine a range of future studies with the title *The Varieties of Reflexive Experience*). The austere phenomenology and the reduction of complex themes to one or two sentences where book-length treatment is called for are necessary costs of this overall strategy.

ACKNOWLEDGEMENTS

I would like to thank the following for their help and encouragement while writing this book. For his great patience and intelligent and timely advice, Andrew Tudor; Phil Stanworth for his friendship and irreplaceable 'table-talks'; also other friends and colleagues in the Department of Sociology at the University of York. I would also like to acknowledge the editorial help of Chris Rojek and his successor at Routledge, Mari Shullaw. But above all others, I wish to dedicate this project to Isabel Lavin-Garzón.

1

INTRODUCTION
Towards a metacritique of pure reflection

> With the exception of man, no being wonders at its own existence ... With this reflection and this wonder there arises therefore in man alone, the need for a metaphysic; he is accordingly an animal metaphysicum.
>
> (Arthur Schopenhauer)

We live in an age of critical reflection yet our contemporaries dream of a postmodern, postmetaphysical, postspeculative future. Sociologists diagnose the deleterious effects of rationalization processes engulfing every sphere of contemporary life. Philosophers decipher the terminal signs of European nihilism as products of the logocentric pretence underwriting the philosophical spirit of scientific modernity. Critics tell the story of the sublation of Western Reason's grand narratives signalling the closure of utopian thought, the death of the subject, the end of philosophy (*la clôture de la métaphysique*), and, as a corollary, the imminent demise of the legislative intelligentsia. Feminist theorists dismantle the violent patriarchal Logics of Representation and their epistemic, literary, and political equivalents. Post-Marxists revel in the escalating legitimation crises of late modernity (the waning powers of 'Eurocentric rationalism', 'the failed Enlightenment project of bourgeois humanism', 'the dehumanizing logic of scientism', 'postmodernist late capitalism in full crisis', and so on). The *hubris* of foundational Reason – 'the philosophical discourse of modernity' – and Europe's universal mission of rational progress is abandoned for the aleatory pleasures of playful irony, undecidability, and selflessness. To some commentators the return of the apocalyptic genre in postmodern discourse is a symptom of an old culture engaged in terminal self-investigation, deconstructing the constitutive assumptions of its hegemonic institutions guided by its own Cartesian maxim: nothing in principle need be taken for granted. The ethos of universal self-reflection when applied to the axiological foundations of its own discourses generates the corrosive phenomenon of radical reflexivity – authorizing a fundamental self-investigation of its own universal pretensions.

The diagnostic inventory could be continued; from very different points of view some of the most acute observers of the contemporary scene point to

1

fundamental crises and existential paradoxes in the fabric of European culture and its dominant forms of knowledge and ways of thinking about reality. And given the global reach of European power, we must also link these crises to the fate of Eastern bloc societies and the siege economies of the 'Third World'. In fact the questioning of the leading narratives and metanarratives of modern culture and identity has become a distinctive phenomena of contemporary intellectual life (with the accompanying vertigo of intellectual self-questioning). A natural reaction is to castigate this obsessive reflexivity as enervating narcissism, abandon self-reflection altogether and either return to the fold of grounded theory or simply follow the accelerating velocities of change in aesthetic, intellectual, moral, and cultural spheres, wherever these may lead. In recent years a form of 'posthistorical' relativism – if not a nihilistic collapse of value differences – has appeared which embraces the decentred ethos of permanent *deconstruction* as the last redoubt of Western epistemology. A symptom of this trend is the precipitate abandoning of normative philosophy and the politics of democratic transformation for the piecemeal and 'specific' demands of micro and middle-range politics. The 'value questions' of the legislative political discourses are banished into the critical wilderness. The ancient problematics of being, value, and the quest for the good life are recast as ideological topics to be treated by sociologists of knowledge or antiquarian historiography. What began as the 'desire for wisdom' (*philosophia*), *scientia*, and the 'love of logos' (*philologia*) in the service of the good ends in the sceptical deconstruction and criterial anarchy of the *fin-de-millénnium*.

And of course the 'crisis' is not purely intellectual or 'spiritual'. In essence it reaches into the personal, social, and political fabric of modern societies. The manifold pluralism of factional interests and value claims seems to pre-empt a coherent 'framework of value'. The fragmentation experienced in the social systems of modernity thus plays into the hands of intellectual relativism and the loss of faith in critical theory. And perhaps this explains why there has been no successful attempt to construct an ethical or political philosophy for the modern age. In contemporary culture the stakes are even higher; what cultural critics feared as the 'loss of truth' and apparition of nihilism are now inscribed in the central institutions and technological media of modern life. Beyond the gates of academic institutions civil life is everywhere in retreat before a flood-tide of cynicism and forms of social oppression that benignly countenance the use of terror and violence as normal political instruments. This historical confluence of the decay of 'objective Reason', the dissolution of transcendent normativity, and the crisis of the moral and political order inevitably dictates the contemporary agenda: if the enlightened politics of rational modernity has proved illusory how are we to imagine a polycentric society whose principle is that there are no (non-metaphorical) principles? Without grounded moral judgements or a stable mimesis of the Real can theoretical knowledge still claim to be judged as truthful discourse? If the essentialism of modern social research now obstructs fundamental thinking

2

about the social and political order can we responsibly critique predatory institutions without invoking the authority of a discredited scientificity? If the 'postindustrial' order of global capitalism is unmasked as a belligerent network of hegemonic powers and interests can we still maintain a commitment to generalized norms of reasonableness, legality, and justice? Or in a civilization guarded by a dark Angel perhaps we should resign ourselves to the thought that reason has nothing to say before the contradictions of the present – utopian projects to realize libertarian values are over: 'We're on the road to nowhere'? If the sensibility of a civilization can still be gauged in these totalizing categories, are we not faced with the prospect of a radical delegitimation of the 'European idea' and more particularly with the 'crisis of truth' – 'the outdated reality principle' – that appears in many diagnoses of the modern constellation?

Clearly in this aporetic context we need to stand back and take stock of the status and significance of the values and critical traditions enfolded in Western culture. This need not take the form of an uncritical demolition of its metaphysical auspices in the style of popular poststructuralism; we can also proceed by bracketing the assumed unity of 'Western Reason' and attempt to 'work through' and rethink the underlying sources and causes of the contemporary malaise. This is one of the central tasks of any metacritique of knowledge: how have knowledge and ethics parted company, what are the decisive steps which have separated theory and practice, personal and civic existence? How can earlier forms of reflexive knowledge and dialogue be of relevance to immediate social and political issues? How can an understanding of the radically reflexive nature of human life in the world occasion a reformation of the contemporary arts, law, politics, and human sciences? What follows is a small contribution to this metacritical project.

To anticipate later analysis we can define the principles of the paradigm of reflection as follows. Logics of reflection adhere to one or more of the following normative assumptions:

(i) *videological ontology*: a 'specular' definition of the cognitive subject and object of knowledge in foundational categories;

(ii) *specular epistemology*: disembodied conceptions of knowledge and truth troped in subject/object rhetorics (for example, the representational economy of value-neutral cognition, the canonical world-assumptions of positivist science, the empiricist conception of reality);

(iii) *foundationalism*: knowledge and being are legitimated by reference to transcendental or empirical 'grounds';

(iv) *essentialism*: the privileged and non-contingent character of universality, natural legality, or essential truths ('nature-given' absolutes, objective Reason, universal values);

(v) *substantialism*: the primacy of 'substance', 'identity', 'unity' as presuppositional norms of inquiry;

(vi) *axiological atemporality*: the valorization of atemporal world models and interpretation systems;

(vii) *axiological asociality*: the valorization of non-relational, non-interactional, monological conceptions of 'individual' and 'society'.

Practices and institutions which embody these assumptions can be described as 'reflective'. Like all institutions, the empirical forms of the logics of reflection manifest both constraining and enabling characteristics (Giddens, 1990; Craib, 1992). Institutions are made by the actions of persons, but they also shape the form of the self subject to their logics. For purely practical reasons the essays which follow focus resolutely on one single theme in this complex problematic, namely the changing role of *reflection* and *self-reflection* in shaping – and perhaps deforming – the identity and cultural values of the West. But it will be readily seen that the paradigm of reflection is linked with a cluster of problematic grounding concepts – among the most prominent of these being *reason, knowledge, representation, truth, universality, evaluation, consciousness*, and *selfhood*. To find paths in the vast landscape of reflective thought we must first understand why a 'new critique of Reason' has become central to the intellectual polemics of the latter half of the twentieth century. In Section 1, therefore, I begin by examining the sociological thesis that the key dynamic of late modernity lies in the expansion and differentiation of *rationally organized reflectivity* embedded in collective agencies and institutions that have now achieved a global geopolitical importance. Every individual alive today is subject to the global influence of these reflective institutions. Whatever is rational is to be 'traduced' by these instrumental systems. Moreover the dominant structure of 'general intellect' today has acquired a monologic, mathematical, and technical character. Earlier traditions and forms of life are either to be physically reduced to the idealized form of identity or reconstituted as a commodity that can circulate as 'imaginary traditions'. Taken to extremes, however, the claims of technical reflection turn back upon the social order they legitimate, releasing powers of alterity and difference which I gather under the term *'reflexivity'*. I will suggest that the insistent general problematic of reflexivity is the unifying moment in the field of postmodern, poststructuralist, and posthermeneutic thought. Reflexivity represents, so to speak, the resistance of transgressive voices and forms of life in a culture pervaded by the logics of reflection and identity. Wherever the question of human significance, meaning, and change are remembered we are in the presence of reflexivity. Western culture *in extremis* generates a wide spectrum of dissonant discourses, differences, and social movements which contest the terms of universal translation. By focusing upon the dominant *institutions* of modern corporate rationalization we introduce the sociological concept of *technopoiesis* (Section 2) which helps to crystallize important differences between Reflection and Reflexivity (Section 3). The abstract argument commends a conception of 'reflexivity' as the polymodal 'other' of Reason which turns theorizing back from its normal objects to the diverse 'discourses of the Other' – the polyphony of tradition(s), the 'desiring subject in objectivity', the matrices of embodiment, difference, imagination, rhetoric and transcendence that occasion all self-reflection. Where reflection treats the Other as an occasion to consolidate the Self, Reflexivity approaches the Other as a sign for the irreducible movement of dialogue and spontaneity within selfhood. We then see that the metatheoretical distinction between Reflection and Reflexivity operates at various levels of abstraction and across a range of social processes. In epistemological terms, a reflexive position is one which questions the conditions of the (im)possibility of value-neutral reflection. In ontological terms, the recovery of nomadic reflexivity in modern culture underlines the presence of alterity and violence within every project of world-construction – it is only the 'irritant' of reflexive experience – the unrepresentable in presentation as Lyotard says – that seeds the open life of self-reflection in every domain of experience (Section 4). At the level of everyday thinking, reflexivity represents the tacit *semantic* background for every *syntactical* procedure. In sociological and political terms, reflexivity is manifest in the appearance of social movements and dissonant moral currents which question the alienating logics of modernization and globalization (contemporary history has tragically confirmed Vico's insight that we can create a social order proud of the 'barbarism of reflection'). 'Reflexivity', therefore, is not a single, well-defined, or extraordinary phenomenon; it appears in many social forms and has different historical modalities – from the undecidability within 'ordinary' interpretation systems to the revolutionary disengagements and disjunctive transformations on the macrosocial and global stage.

1 PRELIMINARY REFLECTIONS ON THE LIMITS OF THE MODERN CULTURE OF REFLECTION

The very existence of reflection is proof of its deficiencies.
(John Dewey, 1958: 33)

A first and, at this stage, necessarily undialectical paradigm of reflexivity might be constructed by 'reversing' the generative principles of reflection:

(i) *discursive or communicative ontology*: the primacy of discursively mediated ontological relations;
(ii) *praxical epistemology*: knowledge as already embedded in practical formations;
(iii) *anti-foundationalism*: the priority of socially constructed and negotiated processes of 'grounding';
(iv) *contingency*: non-essentialist conceptions of language, being, truth, and selfhood;
(v) *relationism*: non-substantialist conceptions of world-relations;
(vi) *axiological temporality*: the valorization of temporalization;

(vii) *axiological sociality*: the contexture of value-constituting social relations.

In these terms, to trace 'modes of thought', 'knowledge systems', and 'truths' to their generative conditions in pretheoretical social praxis immediately disturbs and sublates the simple subject/object grammar of reflection (and at the societal level, the opposition modernity/tradition). The Faustian apothegm, *'Im Anfang war die Tat'* ('In the begining was the act') historicizes the cognitive ideal of objectivity as 'absolute truth' into genealogical 'truths' correlated to diverse epistemic procedures and discursive formations: each of our epistemic attitudes is a defeasible social construction through which we make sense of a manifold and ever-changing reality. In this context 'scientific reflection' and 'instrumental reason' are viewed as powerful sense-forming machineries. And like all sense-making procedures the idea of science is invariably linked to the imposition of order in cognitive and social relationships (from the reflexive paradigm every form of analytical reasoning can be viewed as a translation procedure indebted to prior semantic systems and cultural codes). In place of the fixed opposition of subject and object or knowledge and world we find a dialectic of experience and cultural forms. The dialectic of empowering and disempowering structures constituting a culture displaces the specular idea of Reason as an extra-social foundation of objectivity: in other words the social *logos* of tradition antedates the logics of reflection; but reflection on ongoing practices also changes the norms of traditional action; a transformation which, in a spiralling movement, gives rise to new modes of reality and reflection.

For many critiques of scientism, the active 'truth-producing' practicalities of everyday communication displace passive contemplation as a generative epistemological figure. Social, pragmatic, and ecological schemes of reasonableness replace the traditional mimetic schema of vision and monologic reflection. In place of the ocularcentric problematics of perception and consciousness we pursue holistic questions of a rhetorical, praxial, and cultural order: how are objects discursively constructed? What prescientific interests and forms of life occasion and delimit different forms of thought (how do different modes of reflection and their truth-procedures relate to the affective fabric of quotidian experience)? What material concerns and practices lead a community to undertake radical reflection upon its ordering principles and through such reflection reconstruct its 'other'? How is the exteriority of mundane world reference imbricated in the politics of discourse and institutions? How is the Other violently reduced to the Same (cf. Deleuze, 1994)?

Four concepts of limit

But there are insuperable difficulties in 'transcending' the paradigm of reflection by a simple operation of symbolic inversion (here it is not a question of replacing consciousness by language or the sufficiency of Reason by the insufficiency of discourse). In this Gestalt change the boundaries set by the instrumental logics of reflection are simply redrawn without radical deconstruction of the metaphysical *terms of reflection*. We thus end up celebrating reflection by replacing it with its mirror image (for example where models of linguistic constitution or social reflection replace cognitive reflectivity). But a whole series of assumptions are left unquestioned in this oppositional theatre. If reflexion is no longer the *cogito* of Western philosophy what is the measure of radical thinking compared with other forms of expression? Whose voice is heard in the past idioms of theory, poetics, politics, and philosophy? What experiences and forms of existence does hegemonic reflection censure, marginalize, and repress? How, for example, has the hegemony of Enlightened reason legitimated the violent exclusion and exploitation of its 'Other'? In sum: an undialectical inversion of the 'philosophy of consciousness' allows the political and institutional workings of reflection to escape a more radical social analysis.

We might try a more dialectical strategy by accepting the life-world of everyday social relatedness – the concrete patterns of individuals, acting, talking, and living – as a limiting horizon for all cultural praxis. Reflection takes its starting point and orientation from definite historical lifeworlds (the world of fifth-century Greece, the early modern period of the Reformation, the age of popular revolution in the eighteenth century, and so forth). But where reflection accepts the gratuitous meaningfulness of objects as 'natural givens', reflexivity theorizes the construction of worlds as the outcome of definite cognitive interests and social practices. In breaking with the indolence of common sense and routinized cognition, superordinate theory wagers upon an underlying *order* and *fullness* of meaning: questions *will* receive an answer, hypotheses *will* be fulfilled, guesswork *will* be confirmed or falsified: the 'truth will out' as the otherness of being is conceptually mastered by knowledge. The *transcendental* faith in the autonomy and intelligibility of reality is implicit in the most rudimentary epistemic activities of ordinary living. Such unnoticed but operative transcendental securities provide conventional theory with a ground and orientation. Where theory's 'referents' are projected as computable phenomenal domains we may speak of Reflection *simpliciter* (the traditional subject-object rhetorics of mainstream 'philosophical inquiry', 'explanatory theory', and 'scientific research'); where its 'referents' are the *intersubjective categories, contextual resources*, and *rhetorical rules* through which universes of understanding are semiotically constructed we encounter a mode of second-order thinking which we can call 'reflexivity'. For reflection in the modern rationalist or empiricist tradition a true theory ideally discovers and describes the natural world 'as it is'; reflexivity, on the other hand, deconstructs the (con)textual formations and aporetic modes of evidence constituting experience as a prior field of practices (for example, where 'language' and 'communicative experience' are unexplicated *resources* for Reflection they are deconstructible *topics* for Reflexivity). Formulated with

7

maximum generality: pursuing the thought that all discourse selects and frames its objects, reflexivity attempts to provide a reasoned account of the social practicalities by which 'reference' to worlds are textually constructed by powerful groups and interests. Reflection and metareflection at the level of methodology or epistemology is 'deepened' by exploring the sociocultural genesis of practices as variant ways of constituting the world.

Accepting some provisional imprecision we can contrast a style of thought concerned to delimit the conditions of the possibility of semiopraxis with forms of reflection that respect no limits and recognize no irreducible alterity. If the reflective style of thought has come to shape the ground-rules of institutionalized modernity, the postmodern themes of *concern, communication, alterity,* and *dialogue* prefigure a dialogical and reflexive paradigm of world disclosure. For the reflexive paradigm 'objects' – whether the three-dimensional furniture of 'real life' or the analytical referents of theoretical research – are *constructa*, value referents created by some investigative community in its sense-making enterprises. From the logological point of view individuals and communities carry a moral responsibility for the 'worlds' they constitute and inhabit. The vicissitudes of object-constitution, of course, are familiar to everyday discourse in an increasingly postmodern culture. But reflexivity reaches deeper than everyday cognition, phenomenological reflection, or poststructural textuality. The experience of reflexivity historicizes all points of origin as artifacts generated by the rules and conventions of inquiry. Reflexive discourses make the rules and conventions of representation their topic by viewing objects as a site of rhetorical work, and thus problematizing taken-for-granted attitudes and intentionalities.

Since the seventeenth century the empire of scientific rationalism has pursued the impersonal ideal of *universal rationality* by redescribing the whole spectrum of cultural experience in the terms of a single algorithm machine – hence the modern fascination with the promise of a 'unified scientific method' to stem the 'vagaries' of everyday alterity and dissolve all 'ideological' practices. By uncovering the laws of nature, scientific reason would detach itself from the matrix of social relations to establish scientificity as the voice of Nature. Science's objective was not simply to discover Nature's intrinsic legality but to *recreate* the Real by reducing Nature to self-certain, repeatable *representations*. When incarnated in the institutional forms of modern technoscience, Reason would unhesitatingly claim to be the ultimate arbiter of knowledge and legislator of social being: only a mathematical method like Newtonian mechanics can serve as a 'true mimesis' of the world and only true cognition can legitimate the ideal of a rationally organized society – establishing a correspondence between language and world that would end the dogmatic conflicts of premodern interpretation. Modern mathematical science, then, constructs the world in its own image of mastery and dominion. Defending a concept of reality as 'objective nature', modernity would then seek decontextualized, replicable knowledge of Nature's laws as an armature

8

of technical progress and material power. Its implicit epistemology – naturalist rationalism allied with representational realism – is founded upon an objectivist conception of experience as a totality of computable object domains and a conception of truth as clear and rational mimesis (for example in Locke's *Essay Concerning Human Understanding* and Hume's *Treatise of Human Nature*, but archetypically expressed in Kant's defence of Reason in the *Critique of Pure Reason*). And, as I will argue below, modernizing organizations aspired to practically realize what the spirit of reflective epistemology had established in theory: the metaphysical goal of regulating the world through technical, standardized rational procedures.

Yet Reason with its 'longing for certainty' and evidential correspondence has to repress a resilient fact. Inquiry, science, and 'the propensity and vocation to free thinking' are themselves social *acts*, discursive *histories* imbricated in material *practices* and institutional locations. The *logos* is 'contaminated' with the mediations of materiality and sociality. When epistemology realizes its own social conditions, we see that scientific discourse and its will to knowledge is itself a *part* of the social world, not its neutral reflection. Mathematical demonstration, for example, is still subject to the constraints of contextual validation and rhetorical legitimation. Like the ghost of Banquo, Reflexivity returns to remind Reflection that even the most technical descriptions of the general structure of the world remain *rhetorics of sociality* – in both senses of the genitive: as discursive formations constructed in a particular time and place and as archives of what was considered problematic by individuals and groups in a given society. Thus every axiomatic theory begins from and presupposes interpretive practices which internally destabilize its algorithmic pretension to map the Real (logic and mathematics are in a deep sense powerful *rhetorical* games, impassioned ways of coding and interpreting the world). And if every act of reflection marks a site of failed illuminations then the voices of past ideas and thought are traceable in the detritus of spent expressions, leached into the fabric of language and everyday traditions. The tragic disparity between the Enlightenment ideal of absolute reflection ('science' in its Cartesian-Newtonian form) and the claims of recalcitrant reality produces what Max Weber once described as 'the perpetual reconstruction of those concepts through which we seek to comprehend reality' (1949: 105). At the level of its deep structure, this is the underlying 'dialectic' of modernity. In this naive and uncritical phase of self-reflection, the order of the real and the conceptual order, the particular and the universal, appear to be incommensurable. 'Subject' and 'Object' fall apart or are forcibly 'unified' by means of speculative categories. In striving to fulfil Kant's imperative, *Sapere aude!*, the

> history of the social sciences is and remains a continuous process passing from the attempt to order reality analytically through the construction of concepts – the dissolution of the analytical constructs so constructed

through the expansion and shift of the scientific horizon – and the reformulation anew of concepts on the foundations thus transformed.

(1949: 105)

Yet even this nascent reflexivity reveals the limit of formalism in the inevitable failure to satisfy its own apodictic ideal. The long history of this 'failure' can be mapped in the transition from objective to subjective conceptions of reflection.

We come to a second concept of limit as the ethical self-delimitation of abstract consciousness. This appears where the dominant paradigm of Western rationality accepts its own finite status. Here thought moves from an extrinsic thinking-*of* the Other measured by the rules of science or an epistemic ideal to a reflective thinking-*about* the Other as an irreducible alterity. The crisis of formal conceptuality and the aporetic dualism of subject and object is 're-solved' in romantic categories of intuition and synthesis. Inquiry traces the margins of the Other without being able to dispel its alterity. The object, as it were, eludes the subject at the point where the Other becomes opaque to technical reason and the faculty of abstract thought. This is the moment of crisis when positivist science realizes that 'even simple descriptive history, operates with the conceptual stock-in-trade of its time' (Weber, 1949: 105) – recognizes, in other words, its own status as an agent of historicity. One response is for reason to accept that it is no more than a part of human cognitive experience, confined by pragmatic concerns and social interests. Another response leads to the relativization of reason: reflection discovers its recursive indebtedness to the cultural categories and social relationships it seeks to describe. The aporia can be expressed in a simplified manner: if reflection is the heart of science, then theorizing cannot be a documentary *observation* of objects; theoretical procedures actively construct reality through their linguistic operations (thus 'genres' like myth, art, law, metaphysics, history, social theory, political thought, sociology, etc. all began life as clusters of rhetorical acts – forms of speech intent upon persuading an audience of the phenomenal validity of their referents and thereby of the legitimacy of a particular way of talking about and experiencing the world). Another step toward reflexivity is implicit in this historicist position: a community can speak through the discourses of its thinkers, poets, theologians, historians, and prophets as it can through the inarticulate ruins of silenced voices, abandoned technologies, rituals, and material traces. But speak it must. Like the material debris of a civilization, ideas are simultaneously witnesses to a society's capacity for *dialogical action* and epitaphs to its wasteful *expenditure of meaning*. To modify a phrase of Sartre, whatever a society may be, it cannot not be meaningful. Before ideas are messengers of the *Zeitgeist* they are the verbal instruments bound by conventional rules by which a collectivity makes sense of reality and shapes itself into an ethical community:

The relationship between concept and reality in the cultural sciences involves the transitoriness of all such syntheses. The great attempts at theory-construction in the sciences of social life were always useful for revealing the limits of the significance of those points of view which provided their foundations. The greatest advances in the sphere of the social sciences are substantively tied up with the shift in practical cultural problems and take the guise of a critique of concept-construction.

(Weber, 1949: 105–6, trans. modified)

In the shadow of the 'tragedy' of theoretical transcendence we are forced to respecify 'reality' as an open product of cultural dialogue, a creative historical magma of life-world practices. The inherent limits of reflection and its discovery of its own subjective grounds thus still nostalgically point in the direction of radical reflexivity.

A third concept of limit emerges here; with the intimation of dialogical reflexivity within Romantic and historicist modes of reflection the responsibility of thought is no longer simply to code 'the spirit of an era' but rather to project praxis beyond existing conceptual boundaries. We have something like a 'flight' from the cognitive apparatuses of Reason and the beginnings of a permanent crisis of representation. Like modern art and technology, theory must now strive to go beyond, to know 'more than' and 'other than', the *sensus communis* of existing discourse. Reflexivity should be critical, transgressive, and emancipative and not merely positive and phenomenological. But in acquiring a deeper self-understanding theory also now understands that the creation of 'truths' is only possible within the linguistic horizon of specific discursive projects bound to particular sociopolitical orders. The risk to the theoretical imagination here is not formal paradox, but melancholy before the insuperable demands of totality and the impotence of belatedness in ever knowing the whole. Theoretical reason now appears to be both an effect and a critique of more active economic, political, or cultural processes. Or, in a more Hegelian vein, reflection is a late gift of the recursive possibilities of ordinary language elaborated and refined by a decaying community. And with respect to the legacy of collective thought, as Durkheim long ago observed,

we stand in the same relationship as Plato's *nous* to the world of Ideas. We never manage to see it in its entirety, or in its reality. We do not know all the concepts worked out by our own civilization.

(1983: 105)

Quotidian reflexivity in other words is a fundamental condition of sociality. From this perspective, science, like myth, is a narrative resolution of the reflexive question 'Who are we?'. But the tension between reflection and metareflection is clearly disclosed. We gain self-knowledge through artificial techniques of simulation, and mimetic desire is now recovered as an irreducible moment of reflection.

A fourth sense of 'limit' is implicit in the axiomatic desire of modern critical

11

and sociological reason to transcend pregiven patterns of meaning and being. The modal declensions 'is', 'might', and 'ought' pervade the realms of human experience: our thinking through the Other leads to a desire to both remember and to think beyond the Other and gain a perspective upon the whole. Recognizing the limits of 'what is' adumbrates the utopian 'might' and the ethical 'ought' of transcendence. But to the degree that Reason accepts the 'Other' thought must relinquish the metaphysical urge to reduce reality to monological categories and accept its involvement in existing heteropoiesis – living practices in which 'the Other' is actively assembled and disseminated. Reflexive experience then appears as a self-recognition of the repressed dialogical auspices of orthodox paradigms of self-reflection (the moment within reflection which makes reflection self-critical). In Foucault's expression, 'the critique of what we are is at one and the same time the historical analysis of the limits that are imposed on us and an experiment with the possibility of going beyond them' (1984: 50).

The modern critique of reason is thus not a matter of codifying the *a priori* limits of language or recognizing the failure of Western rationalism before an incalculably strange universe, but one of grasping the *historicity* of every practice of articulation, accepting the repressed *heteropoiesis* implicit in every mode of self-understanding. Acts of reflection are both supplementary activities of ordinary language and semiotic displays of the social order from which they originate and for which they speak (the pervasively patriarchal form and masculinist content of Western *élite* culture is a salutary reminder of these facts). Human beings *theorize* and they theorize everywhere and about everything, including of course, their own theorizing, its object domains, instruments, and traditions. Theorizing, in sum, reflexively shapes experience. And given the longevity of white, Western, patriarchal civilization it is inevitable that there will be a phallocentric 'physiognomy' to the structure of our dominant forms of perception. In fact the cartographic desire of traditional reflection can serve as a metaphor for community only because existing societies are themselves congealed metaphors (as it were, *mimesis* incarnated in social and political forms). Consequently, what we designate as 'reality' has already been discursively mediated (we cannot prise the history of phallocentric consciousness from its objects, wipe the slate clean and 'start again' from a site innocent of past articulations).

To summarize: in its reflexive phases, reflection becomes aware that it has legitimated epistemic practices that have been used to denigrate and repress the creative possibilities of human experience (the occluded reflexivities of everyday life, politics, and aesthetics). In particular, science and formal reflection overlook their own material inherence, dialogic conditions, and ethical limits, limits which when thematized point toward more fundamental possibilities of decentred reasonableness. In Heidegger's terminology, objective Reason and mimetic Reflection are forms of 'being-forgetting' (*Seinsvergessenheit*). In the language of critical theory, Reflection is part of the instrumentalization of society. One of the products of Reflection's social amnesia is the revolutionary idea that by totally separating itself from the cultural order Reason can perfectly reflect reality – indeed that *only* a universal technique of disengaged representation – deductive axiomatization, formal theory, scientific objectivism, structural *ratio*, and so on – can truly mirror the structure of the Real (Representationalism). A cognate assumption is that universal Reason is grounded in an *a priori* Subject, a 'transcendental Ego' which escapes sociohistorical determinations to found the possibility of knowledge and principled action (Humanism). When combined these two commitments underwrite the modern epoch of progressive Reflection: as truth lies on the other side of language, discourse, and tradition the order of things only surrenders to the 'subject' of pure *theoria* and its instrumental projects.

The universalization of reflection in the era of reflexive capitalism

They do not understand how, while differing from itself, [it] is in agreement with itself. [There is] a back-turning connection, like that of a bow or lyre.

(Heraclitus, DK B 51)

For a number of years I have been intrigued by the way in which the central economic and political institutions of modern societies – and we perhaps should still say the First World capitalist nation-states – have evolved along many fronts in the direction of increasing technical reflectivity in their expansionary practices, rhetorics, and sense-making organizations. Since the end of the Second World War we have witnessed a vast growth of technical-mathematical systems serving the extractive and managerial machineries of 'post-Fordist' accumulation. These achievements were themselves built upon the extended social, political, and technological structures created during the modern epoch of European industrialization. And the networks of interdependence have also involved vast costs in terms of the spatiotemporal extension of systems of exploitation and repression. The effects of these changes can be traced in the development of global capitalism, the growth of the state and military power, the creation of a world-political order, and the hegemony of the culture of the 'Great Powers' during the twentieth century.

Changes in the socioeconomic and political order also have their correlates in the symbolic sphere of signification and communication. It has even been argued that the fundamental divisions between premodern, modern, and postmodern forms of reflection, lie in the impact of new technical modes of production and reproduction upon older symbolic systems. The apparatuses of reflection inherited from the Enlightenment period have been colonized, respecified, and developed by the new global information technologies. Thus despite their commitment to different ideologies and political principles the command structures of the industrialized economies have all embraced the

Taylorist ideology of rational computability, methodic planning, and disciplinary control as the optimum mechanisms by which a society objectifies and reshapes itself. And while social theory agonizes over the principled (im)possibility of generating valid representations of the social world, global organizations have gone about their mimetic tasks of *regulating* and *rationalizing* experience unburdened by methodological constraints or epistemological anxieties: 'Formalization is a way of reinterpreting the world and re-classifying its elements with a view to increasing manageability. The achievements of modern institutions in terms of the extension of reach are regularly based on such kinds of formalization' (Wagner, 1994: 26). It is perhaps not surprising that a hyperreflective civilization proud of its autonomy and technological power should construct a world in its own likeness and generalize its image in the form of the data-processing organization. In this way the 'mastery of the world by means of calculation' is embedded in advanced technoscientific systems (Wagner, 1994: 26)

Of course reflection on human nature, 'man and society', and political identity is an ancient and venerable pursuit. But only relatively recently has the will to classify and order the world under the categories of instrumental action achieved 'world-historical' and 'geopolitical' dimensions. Less than a century after the transformations of the first industrial revolution the material conditions of societal transformation in modern societies have fundamentally shifted. Modern corporate institutions, in a word, have become chronically self-reflexive by adopting and adapting the instruments of telecommunications, computing and virtual reality technology (this 'fusion' of signification and production is arguably one of the essential features of postmodern economies – creating the characteristic phenomenology of cybernetic modernity). This is also why the sheer scale and organizational complexity of corporate life serves to typify the present world conjuncture. But 'bigness' and 'material transformation' considered in itself is not the essence (cf. Noble, 1977). The essential change lies in the hyperdevelopment of apparatuses of informational reflectivity as directive organons of corporate power. The 'general intellect' of the early capitalist economy has been globally technologized and reorganized into qualitatively new structural forms. Correlated to this expansion of knowledge-technologies is the dissolution and reconstitution of new fields of public and private space (deindustrialization, urbanization, nationalization of landscapes, etc.). In sum: over the past three decades the socioeconomic institutions of world capitalism have fabricated and generalized formal codes of reflection in pursuing their transnational objectives. The 'Fordist' age of mechanical reproduction (what economic historians call the period of machinofacture) and centralized bureaucratization has given way to an epoch of decentred reflexive modernization based on the penetration of advanced communications technologies into every sphere of life.

The new apparatuses have carried the materialization of information and cybernetic procedures into the body politic of advanced capitalism while at the same time providing the counterfinalities of media worlds, the new consumerism, and the 'politics of identity'. We might refer to this era as the age of cybernetic modernity. The revolution in organizational reflectivity is thus *qualitatively* different from earlier mimetic experiments in that global industrialization now affects every social system and lifeworld without let or hindrance. Simplifying brutally we can say that the central functional task of corporate power today is to quantify, commodify, standardize, and manipulate the logosphere itself – to render 'meaning', 'culture' and 'daily life' marketable as *informational commodities* (hence the pervasive dissolution of inherited boundaries and traditional hierarchies which contemporaries not without reason associate with a postmodern epoch). Today the logic of accumulation is increasingly driven by the revolution in the production, control, and application of *information* on a scale which can only be compared with the cultural impact of the first information revolution, the invention of alphabetic script. And the form of modern capitalist organization stamps its style upon the content of information – privileging technical and instrumental orders of knowledge over traditional forms of meaning. Social theorists like Daniel Bell, Mark Poster, Manuel Castells, Scott Lash and John Urry thus speak of the postmodern economy as the era of the mode of information. As Daniel Bell has observed, the 'information explosion' is

> a reciprocal relation between the expansion of science, the hitching of that science to a new technology, and the growing demand for news, entertainment, and instrumental knowledge, all in a context of a rapidly enlarged world that is now tied together, almost in real time (that is, instantaneously), by cable, telephone, and international satellite.
>
> (1991: 53)

I will return to these societal and ideological transformations and analyze their organizational structure and cultural impact in greater depth in Volumes 5 and 6, devoted to the emergence of modern and postmodern forms of institutional self-reflection. In keeping with the schematic objectives of this introduction, I will drastically foreshorten this analysis in what follows.

To risk a simplified, developmental schema, we might construct a typology of dominant forms of societal reflexivity and self-reflection, linking the deep structure of different epistemologies to the dominant social formations they underwrite:

Dominant social form	Epistemology	Rationality	Selfhood
(i) Traditional	Foundationalist	Substantive	Logocentric
(ii) Modern	Rationalist	Procedural	Dualist
(iii) Postmodern	Relativist	Constructive	Heterological
(iv) Reflexive	Critical	Dialogical	Differential

In these terms, the key to the latest phase of the 'civilizing process' lies in the technological possibilities of organizational reflexivity when self-consciously grasped by powerful collective actors to actively generate new object domains and thus new forms of 'historicity', 'sociality', and 'power' (from the mega-machines of contemporary warfare and extermination programmes to international systems of cooperation and aid). And the 'carrier' of this process of *'hyperdifferentiation'* and *societal reflexivity* is no longer the autonomous individual, social group, or class but the global 'agency' of multinational organizations operating within a dense competitive network of geopolitical corporate actors. Such organizations we would claim are in the process of reconstituting and (re)visioning their operations in explicitly reflexive terms (that is, by incorporating reflexive world models, information technologies, and self-monitoring systems into their day-to-day operations). As a consequence of these developments, we witness an exponential growth in organizational size, function, complexity, and reflectivity reinforcing the immense powers flowing from the centralized control of information and electronic media. Transnational capitalism remakes itself in the chrysalis of a truly internationalized form of capitalism, which in turn prefigures the first phases of global reflexive capitalism. The 'self-expansion of capital' appears to have found its optimal reflexive medium in the new technologies of digital programming, virtual commodification, and 'hyperreality' (Baudrillard, 1983; Lyon, 1994; Jameson, 1988a; Heim, 1993): 'Through this kind of organization, companies do not merely benefit from economies of scale, if narrowly understood in technical and economic terms, but they produce a social advantage, namely manageability, on their own field of action' (Wagner, 1994: 81).

Reflective organizations

In the 1970s and 1980s one obvious stimulus for the development of reflective discourse in modern organizations and the academic social sciences was the corrosive impact of rapid social change upon traditional work processes, identities, power structures, and cultural logics. In the wake of advanced industrialization vast swathes of experiences that were once considered 'fixed and eternal' were seen to be defeasible historical formations subject to empirical appraisal and technical deconstruction. One effect of this extensive denaturalization was to encourage organizations to forge their own distinctive managerial rhetorics in the course of coordinating human and non-human resources, creating needs, and shaping consciousness. As an instance of the unintentional consequences of social action, 'agencies' create strategies and rhetorics whose logics empower further processes of societal deformation and fragmentation. By generalizing and disseminating their interests throughout the wider culture, organizations become primary actors in engendering social change. Since McLuhan and Innis we have understood the power of global mass media to transmute information into social forms ('the medium is the message'). But today we see that the private and public bureaucracies controlling economic production have become the privileged locus of sociocultural transformation. The combinatorial character of modern networking systems facilitates vast concentrations of power along with commensurate possibilities of unpredictability and risk:

> Given the complexity of modern society and the multiplicity of interest groups, classes and sources of power, it is not surprising that these societies still exhibit high levels of disorder at certain times. It certainly would be surprising if such disorder were not massively increased if the inner circle failed to reproduce itself and thus carry out its task of co-ordination on a societal scale.
>
> (Morgan, 1990: 194; see also Crook, *et al.*, 1992; Wagner, 1994: 82–5; Lash and Urry, 1993)

Today electronic media in such domains as AI and virtual reality technology enable advanced industrial systems to transcend the constraints of time and space which traditionally confined social action to relatively rigid local and regional sites (social parameters which favoured logocentric and metaphysical paradigms of the subject). In sum: all natural and social life is in principle subject to the new technologies of global industrialization. Here the accent must be placed upon the world-constructive character of the new technological systems and the enhancement of the power of cadres of technical *élites*. With the technopolitical complexes of television, press, and radio appear cadres of salaried experts who service an ever-expanding universe of text-processing bureaucracies (Bell observes that 'it is estimated that under present projections the Yale University Library would need a permanent staff of 6,000 persons in the year 2040 to cope with the books and research reports that would be coming annually into the library' (1991: 57)). Far from becoming a 'transparent society', the new mode of global production encircles the world with elaborate technocratic organizations, control mechanisms, and administrative systems, each intensively processing signs and information. The semiotic formations of advanced economies are thus directly incorporated into the processes of advanced technification and societal reproduction. In other words, global capitalism *institutionalizes* knowledge systems and correlated technical specialists as a routine imperative of its ever more complex operations. We should not, however, be misled by the myth of managerial postcapitalism or the simulacral implosion of mass media – organizations are still concerned with governing the lives of others, dominated by propertied *élites* monopolizing 'cultural capital', and powered by 'premodern' interests in control and profitability. Where these processes have been embedded in social, educational, legal, military, and political apparatuses we have the conditions for what has been called the hegemony of the professional managerial, technical, and service classes of late industrial society.

17

The reflective society

These complex global changes in the social structure of organized capitalism have direct epistemological and existential consequences. One of the singular features of modern *systems of reflection* is their explicit commitment to the rhetorical rules of linear-analytical logics, instrumental-digital codes, and cybernetic models of rational action in pursuing their interests. Technical logics of reflection – rational calculi, impersonal algorithms, formalisms, standardized metrics, etc. – are hardly disguised homologies of societal bureaucratization. And bureaucracies routinely posit the logosphere as a flow of calculable informational 'bits' designed to run the complex machinery of the modern age. Discourses which enter the orbit of this global apparatus are rendered into the canonical form of information quanta. In this way what may have originated as a heuristic strategy – such as a useful algorithm, a new regimentation of traditional practices or computerization of central production functions – usurps the original purposes of the organization and even subverts its primary goals. Once in existence networks of specialists exhibit the well-known tendency of making themselves indispensable to the wider collectivity they formerly served – the multiplication of ancillary businesses, data banks, technical support industries, planning agencies, financial organizations, venture capitalists, and the like with their own in-house terminologies and game rules is symptomatic of this long-term process of professional diversification. But today these systems operate as indispensable networks of communicative relays for the continuous social reproduction of global economic markets. To the extent that technical modes of reflectivity have become institutionalized we may speak of the development of institutionalized reflexivity in modern society (Giddens, 1990, 1993).

The general thesis behind these observations is the claim that modernity as an *epistemological* formation produces and generalizes networks of interdependent 'agencies', 'informational technologies', and 'technical discourses' throughout its operative theatres. Each self-organizing sphere effects a definite, and frequently unpredictable, deformation in the field of power and everyday life-praxis. Each advance of 'reflexive modernization' also includes a destructive process with regard to earlier or premodern social forms. Giddens thus speaks of the detraditionalization of modern culture. Unlike earlier processes of societal destruction, modern organizations can now mobilize extensive information resources to implement their competitive operations. And as a primary resource of power, technical-administrative knowledge – especially the power to coordinate, disseminate, and utilize information to produce more information – assumes a privileged role in the armoury of bureaucratization and militarization. At the level of day-to-day life-world praxis 'spheres of knowledgeable agency' with their varying degrees of generalized reflectivity create a spectrum of specialized interpretive communities each promoting its sectional interests. The emerging 'global society' is thus not necessarily one of a fatal homogenization and death of civil experience; it also creates a network of diverse, interlocking systems, a quilt of new and *hybrid social formations*. These polymodal domains then become available as reflexive instruments for further technical transformations of life – played back into the general culture in projects of societal self-regulation. Indeed so powerful are these 'logicized' organizations – transnational corporations, global military systems, communications industries, etc. – that in controlling the politics of knowledge they dictate the life chances of millions of individuals by redefining the material, social, and symbolic terms of individual and collective experience: if you are to experience the world your responses must comply with the frames prescribed by rationalized techniques (consider the transformative role of digital coding, mathematical logics, and statistical techniques in actuarial institutions as these penetrate everyday life in the modern world). In the millennial conflict between *Logos/Theoria*, *Phronesis*, *Techne/Poiesis*, and *Praxis*, the self-defining forces of *Techne* appear to have eclipsed the 'weak powers' of *Theoria* and *Praxis*. Here the metaphor of *societal programming* which has its roots in the utopian discourses of Greek philosophy finds a material armature and becomes a literal description of the contemporary world.

Transnational formal organizations – from fast-food chains to managed energy networks and organizations of pension fund capitalism – now pervade every institutional sector of global society. To each of these colonized spheres we find an organized structure of 'life programmes' (codes which literally govern the practices of eating, movement, work, leisure, etc. as marketable experiences). Individuals living in cultures dominated by monitoring bureaucracies are quite literally subject to their prescriptive operations from birth to death. This epochal change in the field of societal institutions as knowledge-generating systems is frequently presented in the managerial jargon of 'professionalization', 'specialization', and 'rationalization'. Here, however, we approach the phenomenon by viewing the politics of societal reflexivity as responses to the changing socioeconomic, military, and political imperatives of modern life.

Technocratic rhetorics and 'the colonization of civil society'

> The great challenge of sociological subdisciplines that deal with rhetorically instrumental, and hence rhetorically acultural, realms of modern social life is to transcend naturalized categories, causal designations, and relationships among actors (collective and otherwise) in order to treat their social emergence as objects of study.
>
> (E.R. Dobbin, 1994: 140)

To view institutional systems as 'material rhetorics' also highlights the way reflexive organizations articulate and explain their world-work as 'natural' to powerful audiences and reference groups. From the logological perspective each department of societal regulation consists of a grammar of values and discursive strategies which actively separate organizations from one another as they seek to schematize everyday life in their own preferred technical *imago*. In this way instrumental normativity – the axiology of technocratic and managerial efficiency – is generalized beyond the subfields of particular agencies into the public value-spheres and psychological fabric of a society. The dialectic also indexes the limitations of totalizing ventures in changing environments of great complexity – their conditions of (im)possibility delimited by the inertial resistance of pre-existing historical traditions and systems. The first imperative of actuarial bureaucracies, for example, is to secure their own conditions of existence and marketability in a competitive economy governed by oligopolistic financial institutions. And, although absent from Weber's famous ideal-typical description, the means by which modern bureaucratic structures achieve this is often far from 'reasonable'.

One of the unintended consequences of the propagation of technocratic knowledge systems is the proliferation of new spheres of power/knowledge and a quantitative expansion of specialized information archives (the exponential growth in 'administrative sciences', state-financed research, accountancy, management consultancy, insurance broking, company law, marketing and product development, policy research, systems programming, international law, etc.) is indicative of the manifold ways in which the agent-networks of reflexive capitalism impinge upon daily life – the process which began with the instrumental mechanization of production, distribution, and exchange continues in the progressive computerization of societal institutions. But unlike conventional organization paradigms or rational choice theory we should not forget that technical environments are chronically prone to internal schisms and conflicts at both local and national levels – marked by the variant commitments of purpose and orientation of their personnel and by differences internally engendered by an organization's practical steps to realize its objectives. Individuals who work within these systems do not, without grave personal damage, lose their capacity for moral judgement and critical appraisal. The effect of these 'reflexive loops' is to further pluralize and dialecticize the modern world into a force-field of dynamic, interdependent, global 'knowledge markets'. These infrastructural changes also suggest the importance of reconceptualizing knowledge and information as fundamental dimensions of modern global power.

Among the major causes of the growth of organizational reflectiveness in modern societies is the planning-and-control imperatives flowing from the militarization, state penetration, and bureaucratization of social life in the twentieth century – each agency of instrumental reflection advancing as a calculative mechanism of societal regulation. Another factor is the concomitant expansion of science-based communication technologies and popular media across traditional space-time boundaries. A third related cause is the power of advanced communication systems themselves as agencies of reflexive modernization. In combination these forces have generalized the technical logics of scientific knowledge throughout industrial society and thereby helped consolidate the authority of bureaucratic professions and legitimated the power and influence of professional technocratic groups. As Theodor Adorno observed, whoever speaks of culture today speaks of administration as well (1991b: 93). But despite Weber's and Adorno's dark prognoses concerning the coming winter of mass society, 'rationalization' is not a one-dimensional process or a unified societal phenomenon. Organizations cluster into discrete fields structured by mutually antagonistic interests. It is an empirical question as to whether these fields 'overlap' or 'converge' into a more unitary 'field of power'. Rational-legal bureaucracies, for instance, have frequently been the source of innovative changes in social life – and societal borrowing from religious to secular contexts is a well-known phenomenon (ancient and medieval 'fields of power' are replete with such symbiotic processes). We also know that the intrusion of the state into the spheres of civil society produces countervailing forces – and in different national contexts these have frequently given rise to what we might call the middle ground of 'buffer institutions' – institutions which resist, mitigate, and defuse the centralization of power. The characterization of modernity as the era of hyperdifferentiation has both negative and positive ramifications.

In place of 'mass society' theories it is more fruitful to think of the *dialectic* of social differentiation, normative coordination, and global generalization as these dispositions of power impinge upon persons, subaltern groups, corporations, and larger social structures. For some explanatory purposes it may be important to separate the technical, socioeconomic, political-administrative, and cultural dimensions of organized power. Here, however, we emphasize the fact that 'information' has been progressively socialized and generalized as a semiotic medium to coordinate different administrative systems (the phenomenon of generalized normative coordination within and across national systems belongs in this context – producing such transnational regulative bodies as the United Nations, UNESCO, UNICEF, the Club of Rome, EEC Commissions, the World Health Organization, and so forth). But more importantly we see how these global 'subsystems' create and reflexively reinforce power structures, juridico-political, and other societal arrangements which they claim to merely 'reflect' (thus governmental bodies proliferate along the lines of their own vested interests; judicial systems become closed guilds divorced from popular access and control; policing and law enforcement assume more and more political functions, and so on). The hazardous fusion of global information and centralized power formations is most visible in the emulation of state-centred societies by modernizing nations – imposing *state regulation processes* upon themselves without the benefit of adequate infrastructural resources and democratic traditions. Here the lay theory that the absence of institutionalized coordination mechanisms blocks technological development leads 'new nations' to 'modernize' along Western developmental lines, which in turn further reinforces authoritarian control as a 'temporary' solution to the conflicts between state and civil society.

Reflexive powers

[I]n proportion as the social milieu becomes more complex and more unstable, traditions and conventional beliefs are shaken, become more indeterminate and more unsteady, and reflective powers are developed. Such rationality is indispensable to societies and individuals in adapting themselves to a more mobile and more complex environment.
(Emile Durkheim, 1982: 124, trans. modified)

With Reflexive Capital the dream of pure Reason to create a transparent order is practically deconstructed. Institutions of reflection and the knowledge systems they underwrite are not politically neutral or independent of socio-economic structures. They develop and function as autopoeic agencies of powerful interests embedded in definite material contexts. Highly organized, self-governing professions like the judiciary, the military, governmental agencies, political parties, and the like may serve as paradigm cases of this phenomenon. In respecifying experience such institutions display a reflexive relationship to the social worlds they ostensibly report, designate, and administratively organize. Each textual field shapes new *subjects-for* knowledge as it determines the *subjects-of* knowledge. For example, by commandeering and redirecting resources industrializing organizations systematically liquidate received forms of subjectivity and discourse embedded in earlier social formations (the process of 'de-differentiation' which typifies postmodern environments has modern antecedents). This is the darker side of Weber's observation that objective science claims to be 'the only possible form of a reasoned view of the world' (1948: 355). As in earlier periods of rapid change, the disruption and creativity released by new communication technologies has instructed theory that 'sense-making' activities are inseparable from 'self-making' praxis.

Thus 'homogeneity' and 'massification' are inaccurate images of modern societies undergoing rapid social change. Scientific institutions and the new 'aristocracy of intellect' foster processes of dedifferentiation as well as global structures of differentiation. This tension reflects the dialectic of rationalized systems and life-world institutions in contemporary society, especially in relation to changes in class structure, forms of social control, and political economy (Habermas, 1985 1987; Schluchter, 1981, 1989; cf. Luhmann, 1982, 1989). But the old models of state, civil society, and economy have disintegrated. The magma of symbolic, economic, political, and communicative power creates macrosystems such as transnational legislatures, economic-military conglomerates, superstates, and the like). In a market-led world of hyperspecialization accredited personnel continuously move vertically and laterally between different departments of coordinated reflection across the traditional national 'economic/political/culture' divisions. This is why sociologists argue that the centralization of cultural capital produces a new 'ruling' stratum of administrators, *nomenklatura*, scientists, technicians, and cultural intelligentsia (Blau, 1956; Konrad and Szelényi, 1979; Ehrenreich and Ehrenreich, 1979; but cf. Goldthorpe, 1982; Bourdieu, 1992; Bell, 1991: Part III). It would be more accurate to say that by legitimating sectional rhetorics, discourses actively mobilize and empower larger sociopolitical and cultural networks (in practice skewed toward the wealthy and privileged cadres of the urban, professional power structure).

Consider the nexus of *graphic specialization* and *capital acceleration*. Capital increasingly appropriates all the mechanisms of cultural inscription and turns these into productive 'markets'. Moreover the 'writing' carried out in these locations has important effects in changing our conceptions of identity and the conduct of everyday life – and we rightly speak of 'technocratic management', 'economic production', 'advertising industries', 'media colonization', 'jurisprudence', 'business forecasting', 'civic planning', and so forth, with a praxial inflection (for instance, the active interest shown by private and public corporations in longitudinal economic and political forecasting as an indispensable means of further order-appropriation and self-aggrandizement). Spheres of graphic productivity may also be treated as topics of research by other practices – the exponential growth of the behavioural sciences, research-driven planning agencies, research-and-development organizations, heritage industries, epidemiological institutions, and so forth, illustrates this progressive institutionalization of *graphic reflection* (and, of course, academic social science, literary study, art criticism, and philosophy have evolved their own rhetorics, writing-reading styles, cognitive instruments, official organizations, schooling programmes, and the like – which are themselves possible 'objects' – as 'research programmes', 'traditions', and 'paradigms' – for further acts of intellectual reflection). Accompanying the splintering effects of specialization we have the phenomenon of cultural parasitism where a devolved organization generates congeries of secondary 'service' agencies. We should also emphasize the increasing mobility of cultural capital invested in superordinate systems and then 'exported' to 'non-industrialized sectors'. Frequently all three dimensions occur together. For example, social-scientific paradigms, statistical methodologies, data management, and their accompanying rhetorics have taken root in some of the major engineering systems of contemporary welfare capitalism (or said otherwise, everyday life in the capitalist world has become 'scientized' and 'technologized' to the same extent as it has been *graphically colonized* by powerful regulatory practices). Analogous processes can be seen in the transformation of urban space and architecture, artistic production and marketing, mass-mediated music and video industries, the food and leisure industry, military-science-industrial complexes, and corporate planning bodies. By the 1960s we have what some commentators have called the world of 'organized capitalism':

> [Capitalism] based on a mass consumption mode of economic organization, large-scale technological systems connecting all members of society, and regularly recurring mass expressions of political loyalty to the elites. It had also developed a particular kind of reflective self-understanding as conveyed in its social science.
>
> (Wagner, 1994: 119)

To summarize: as normalizing apparatuses modern organizations rationally reorganize preformed social fields in accordance with the technical logics of specific interests (again with wide variations depending upon the particular system and interests of the organization – medical *subjection* being radically different from the spatiotemporal modes of subjectification flowing from urban planning and redevelopment projects, and these are different in turn from the spheres of educational, military, and engineering systems). Social formations as powerful as multinational corporations and nation-states, however, have the werewithal to *instruct their audiences in the arts of civic existence* implicit in such mechanisms as welfare policies, taxation systems, capital building projects, state insurance programmes, and the like. To foreground the *textual transformations* inherent in the world-work of organizations I refer to such systems as *rhetorical institutions* and their products as rhetorically coded *social knowledges* and *identities*. By symbolically *reordering* experience organizational rhetorics must be approached as world-making agencies in their own right – the languages of powerful organizations being literally *narrative embodiments of social order*.

The globalization of reflective information

> The model of modern Western civilization is the virus: the pure bit of information, which turns its environment into endless reproductions of itself.
>
> (Ursula Le Guin, 1992: 180)

In the process of universalization the gendered epistemes of an earlier period have been mobilized to restructure everyday life (the differential impact of electronic communications upon every aspect of social life, the redesigning of social relations by both authoritarian and democratic states, the effects of an increasingly international division of labour in an economy based on the control of information and simulacral image production, and the unforeseeable possibilities of biotechnology and bioengineering). To this extent Bell's thesis is valid: generalized communications and theoretical knowledge have become central 'structural principles of society'. But the possibilities of hegemonic control also expand with the ever-growing networks of global communication:

rhetoric fuses with power to extend the reach of regulatory authorities, information networks restructure the production process, global media reshape the recipients of commodified 'mass culture' into 'silent majorities'. 'Deterritorializing' processes such as mass telecommunications industries, the transnationalization of corporate capital, and the global reach of technological warfare now give *reflective institutions* a primary role in generating new forms of social change (indeed many of the central institutions of the Western capitalist nations are exclusively concerned with the explicit analysis of information and media markets and the creation of systems to 'manage' risk-prone environments).

Reflexive capitalism also reshapes the topography of 'the real' to its own *imaginary* formats (consider the ideological language of the defence establishment and foreign policy departments of the United States analyzed by Noam Chomsky in *Towards a New Cold War* (1982). Superiority in science, engineering, and technology has, in Bell's words, 'paved the way for the transfer of a large part of the routinized manufacturing activities of the world to the less-developed countries' (1991: 212). The structural displacement of industrial production to low-cost satellite producers creates the asymmetrical power structures of the decentred global economy. Such long-term changes in modes of production, exchange, distribution, and consumption have also had major effects upon the social organization of academic, cultural, and intellectual creativity as these are rearticulated within the cybernetic networks of mass-mediated culture. In the wake of large-scale computer technology contemporaries are forced to redraft the opening lines of Marx's *Das Kapital* to read: 'The wealth of those societies in which the capitalist mode of production prevails presents itself as "an immense accumulation of information"' (1961a: 35).

We live in an age of *information capital* and a world economy increasingly dominated by monetary wealth turned into abstractions and circulated as *simulacra* of abstractions – a consumer-oriented economy in which electronic representations drive the production process, enter military apparatuses, and promote the expansion of the state throughout every department of social life. The formal principle of such a social order is creative disorder. In response to new geopolitical and technological conditions, Capital not only produces new modes of living in the world, but adapts and extends its dominion by *instituting reflectiveness at the heart of its own structures and organizations*. Along with the economic revolution of symbolic wealth the self is inevitably displaced from the traditional sources of identification and forced to identify with more abstract – but no less mythical – social categories. The self as the bearer of pure Reason is deconstructed and put to economic use as a nostalgic myth. Graphic formations – whether at the level of global economic transactions, mass-mediated texts, public institutions, state programmes of surveillance and societal regulation, or popular culture and individual microtherapies – not only provide categories for reflection, but, more importantly, restructure the terms of collective identity by prescribing new forms of corporeal experience. Relatively ancient forms of civil society are ruthlessly dissolved and redesigned by abstract institutions. For example, late modernity transforms 'cybernetic writing' into a generalized commodity-form that lends itself to flexible displacement (information being the most ethereal commodity of all – producing no resistance, effecting no contestation, lodging no wage-claims). In effect, the advanced technologies of capitalism write themselves into every relationship and institution along with 'the penetration of the world of everyday life by electronically mediated language' (Poster, 1990: 82; cf. Harvey, 1989; Bell, 1991: 210–27;Lyon, 1994: esp. Part III chs 9–12, 159–225).

Reflexive capitalism is qualitatively different from its predecessors in explicitly mounting a sustained assault upon 'natural' subjectivity as part of its drive for extended valorization: the logic of global consumerism and the artificial universes of technocracy no longer require an essential, substantial society of coherent selves (the depth grammar of consistent identity celebrated by the sociology and political philosophy of the liberal phases of capitalism); the new ideal is, in fact, the fragmented, heterogeneous, multidimensional desire-machines of a collectivity of unsatisfiable, hedonistic consumers. Postmodern categories of vacuous subjectivity and nomadic dispersion are actively generated by the aleatory logics and technologies of reflexive capitalism (the expansion of advanced reproductive technologies, mass spectator sports, mass tourism, electronically reproduced music and images, for example).

The dynamics of the world economy gives greater salience to the thesis that the reality-work of cultural construction lies in the long-term dialectics of communication, desire, and consciousness as these are shaped by changing economic, political, and cultural formations: *logos, eros, ethos,* and *polis* must be articulated together. The fact that relations are today symbolically mediated by hegemonic practices also means that social formations – including the social formations we call 'personal life', 'sexuality', and 'everyday consciousness' – are actively restructured through the techniques and institutions that have shaped and, in turn, been shaped by the languages of the powerful. It is the vast web of social interdependencies produced by global capitalism which warrants the claim that if we are to consider social facts as things, then 'things' must be approached as reflexively invented objectivities. 'Things' are not autonomous entities, but nodes in social networks, temporary relay-points of meaning in extended space-time configurations.

Reflexive capitalism as an epoch of total representation

[I]n our times the individual is in the process of becoming far too reflective to be able to be satisfied with merely being *represented*.

(Søren Kierkegaard, 1951: 151)

These are some of the most striking tendencies of the accumulation processes of reflexive capitalism. I have suggested that reflection can be viewed as a complex social process, differentially embedded in different object scenes of the body politic. As with the configuration of individual consciousness, different societies not only live and experience the world differently; they represent experience using different semiotic systems relative to their interests, beliefs, and cultural concerns (what Max Weber called *Lebensordnungen* or 'life-orders' (1948: 331–59)). Furthermore local categories of significance meld into the fabric of experiences they articulate, creating 'multiple realities' with their own spheres of relevance and criteria of reasonableness. Different cultures construct their logospheres according to different normative conventions of representation (compare the resilience of the traditional periodization of ancient Greek, Judaic-Christian, and Modern 'stages' as, respectively, *ontological, theological,* and *anthropological* matrices). The connecting thread between the different Western epochs of representation, as I will argue in Part I, lies in the universalizing spirit of *mimesis* – the will to save, schematize, and control experience, and, in the modern period, to bring very different economic, political, and aesthetic 'life-spheres' under a single governing principle. In the postmodern era, however, the logosphere itself becomes the central axis of power and authority in the spread of information technology. Living in graphically complex technological societies we are enmeshed in multiple inscription networks drawn from scientific and technological media which demarcate themselves as 'disenchanted' logics from the 'enchanted' realms of magic, religion, and 'prerational' ethics.

This polymorphous graphicity becomes critically important as we move into technoscientific worlds where specialized institutions methodically articulate identities by constructing and recycling past image systems (for example, the corporate uses of modernist art forms (the international style), the global impact of television and information systems, the corporate rewriting of history). Of even greater significance is the fact that hegemonic *inscriptive systems* have infiltrated the practices of everyday life to transform traditional practices and orientations. One consequence of this implosion of writing is that we can no longer think in terms of discrete subjects facing an undifferentiated object world or understand knowledge as the one true account of the Real, but instead have to approach reality as a contested, polycentric field of objectivities created by multiple discursive articulations.

By highlighting graphic media we do not, of course, neglect the material effects of institutional life or underplay the unequal concentrations of economic and political power in society, but rather draw attention to the interfaces between sectoral knowledge formations, their resource base, and wider political, technological, and ideological relations involved in the production and active 'consumption' of objects. We can then study the local genesis of *forms of knowledge* as historically conditioned *inscriptions of the object* on the understanding that rhetorical formations create the structure of differentiated experience in modern societies. Since graphic praxes prescribe the logological space of what is sayable and experienceable, the dialectic of *Logos*, *Techne*, and *Phainomenai* – the changing technical history of self-representations – emerges as a central concern.

The centred, autonomous, phallic Self (and 'Society') of the premodern era – 'the assumption of a permanent, universal and essentially unchanging human nature' (Williams, 1966: 45) is the first casualty of the processes released by the information revolution. For modern capitalism the rhetorical sites of identity are multiplied and diversified to such an extent that no single cultural sphere or mode of representation has an exclusive or mandatory status. We live in an age where the boundaries between classes, nations, high and low culture, fiction and fact, self and body, public and private, language and experience have become fluid, complex, and increasingly undecidable. Commentators have described this phenomenon as part of a postmodern condition. In an era of multinational organizations, different life-orders compete for the hearts and minds of individuals. 'Being-a-self' is no longer a taken-for-granted state, but something achieved, a construction contingently related to the changing markets where identities are now articulated and consumed. We witness, in other words, an unplanned and eclectic fragmentation and social deconstruction of the bourgeois ideal of the rational sovereign citizen.

The darker side of the modern condition of deindividualization is that the mendacious arts of media manipulation and disinformation have been perfected by state bureaucracies and corporate agencies (the diremption of citizenship represents the reverse side of an encroaching authoritarianism and regulatory ethos in contemporary life). Reflective rhetorics and stylized image systems have migrated from the realms of speculative theory to became part of the institutional order of modern economics and politics. Indeed with consumer capitalism the imaginary ideal of a *'style of life'* as an *'aesthetic of existence'* enters public consciousness as a powerful everyday ideology for ever-larger groups of people. Identity is no longer anchored in a stable societal self, but is conceived as the product of individual, consumerized identity-kits. The claims of 'lifestyle industries' to 'actualize' and 'satisfy' the 'inner self' increasingly displace the moral demands of public life spheres onto consumption processes. And simulacral spheres such as the entertainment, tourist, health, and culture industries self-consciously bring new 'selves' into the world: new ways of being are purposefully promoted by corporate capitalism in its expansionary cycles; the commodification of the self extends the sale of space to the commercialization of time; accumulated capital now fabricates and colonizes virtual spaces as the new open frontier of profit maximization. Stylizing, experimenting with, and consuming 'life' become strategic options in the symbolic economies of the late industrialized world. We witness something like a polymorphous stylization of everyday life across a growing spectrum of consumer industries and globally extended economies of signs and space (Lash and Urry, 1993; Meyrowitz, 1985; Beck, Giddens, and Lash, 1994: esp. ch. 4, 174–215).

'Styles of life' (and their sustaining support systems) are sold as commodities along with the products of advanced engineering and technological inventiveness (in the most powerful sectors of the capitalist economy the production of capital-intensive goods and their symbolic carapaces are inextricably fused in the pursuit of 'material well-being'). In economies with public welfare systems, securing and enhancing an 'optimum quality of life' becomes the main objective of political parties and administrations balanced against the countervailing demands of military and business interests. 'Personnel management' as an indispensable component of 'resource management' motivates large-scale internal and external changes in organizations and bureaucracies (to survive in an increasingly knowledge-based economy business organizations must invest in self-reflexive training programmes for their personnel). With this 'implosion' of cultural categories, a politics of identity increasingly replaces class politics. The struggles to control effective identity-management displace the traditional politics of citizenship and collective agency. In the pursuit of 'lifestyle politics' consumer technologies are projected as powerful social rhetorics and sources of suasive images of statuses and identities. The ever-expanding spheres of manipulated 'imaginary action' encroach upon a dwindling public sphere. Ironically the collective processes of profit maximization and generalized calculability actively contribute to the aesthetic stylization and 'privatization' of social reality. This is close to Daniel Bell's diagnosis of the cultural crisis of capitalism:

> the engine of modern capitalism has taken over these cultural styles and translated them into marketable commodities. Without the hedonism stimulated by mass consumption, the very structure of the business enterprises would collapse. In the end, this is the cultural contradiction of capitalism: having lost its original justifications, capitalism has taken over the legitimations of an antibourgeois culture to maintain the continuity of its own economic institutions.

> (1991: 163–4)

Where these changes have advanced furthest we can legitimately speak of relatively autonomized 'work worlds', 'medical worlds', 'administrative worlds', 'educational worlds', 'consumer worlds', 'leisure worlds', 'tourist worlds', 'business cultures', and so on in the same way that we speak of 'art worlds' and 'science worlds' penetrating what was previously regarded as spheres of social life untouched by expert knowledge and technological systems. But compartmentalization, autonomization, and privatization (deindividualization) should also be balanced by the trend toward increasing dependency and interdependence: one of the most striking tendencies of reflexive capitalism is the *interpenetration* of media and communications industries, advanced electronic technologies, and global economic expansion led by the militarization of society. Today the circuits of consumption and virtual pleasure function to subsume the politics of traditional class solidarity and everyday life as an ancillary domain of reflexive Capital, a dispensation which both fosters and represses the immense potential of human solidarity. Understanding these complex transformations and contradictions requires commensurate changes in our traditional modes of thought – to help conceptualize the dynamic interrelationships between the industrial-state-military complex, the capitalist-technoscience nexus, and the capital-culture-postmodern configuration. We have, in other words, to abandon the one-dimensional reflective categories and dualisms of orthodox social theory and to begin to think dialogically and reflexively.

The routinization of self-managing systems, conscious interventions in and manipulation of economic, political, and cultural environments by corporate organizations, the growth of policy-defining institutions, and the hyperactive search for aestheticized forms of 'authentic selfhood' and 'consumer utopias' within a wide range of private and public institutions are undoubtedly symptomatic of the fragmentation and commodification of identity in the making of reflexive capitalism. But these processes have not led to the 'disenchantment' of the world in Weber's sense. If anything we witness the 'resacralization' of the world under advanced technological auspices. 'Expert systems' acquire an aura of sacrality recognizable from earlier orders of sacred knowledge. The commodification of everyday life and its work-worlds continues its dialectical course freed from its earlier motivational constraints. Popular culture is colonized by multinational media industries. Where nineteenth-century social thought analyzed the interaction of 'power' and 'economics' secure in its assumption of the complete separation of observer and observed, we move in a world where reflexive systems recursively interact to create unstable polycentric configurations of desire and subjectivity. One unintended outcome of these experiments is the repoliticization of everyday life relations, even as these relations are subject to the expansive rhythms of corporate business.

Similar paradoxes and contradictions appear throughout the spheres of civic life – which is also subject to systematic processes of privatization, fragmentation, and spectacularization. Rather than the withering away of the state apparatus according to the free-market ideology of liberal capitalism or official Marxist ideology we witness the disappearance of relatively autonomous life-worlds as state institutions assist private capital in colonizing non-capitalist space. Ironically the 'weak powers' of everyday life and local political action are first fully appreciated in the moment of their fragmentation and destruction (a process which sociologists like Giddens and Lash have called the *commodification of time-space* in conditions of reflexive modernity). Given this new order of 'time-space compression' we have to discount the claims of the postindustrial prophets; capitalism has not been 'tamed', is not 'entering its last phase', is not terminally 'disorganized' or endlessly 'flexible' (Offe, 1985; Lash and Urry, 1987). State power has not withered away nor has it been brought under democratic control. The age is, rather, one of *reflexive accumulation*, *global militarization*, and *state expansion*. As everyday life-spheres are aestheticized or become increasingly 'research-based' and 'knowledge-driven', questions of identity are translated into consumer logics (the rapid expansion and pervasive influence of 'expert systems', the colonization of virtual mindscapes, and the growth of symbolic capital are effects of these structural changes). Heterogeneous expert knowledges and their technical and literate bureaucracies function not only as a key axis in the restructuring process being carried out by the industrialized world but as a critical nexus of subjectification and commodification (correlatively, 'meaning' is no longer anchored in well-bounded, territorially specific associations such as the family, neighbourhood, and village, but is increasingly commodified and controlled by specialists or productively resisted by countercultural movements).

Capitalism in its variegated career has shown little respect for individuals: it has made and remade subjects in the violent maelstrom of its own innovative metamorphoses (Marglin and Schor, eds, 1990). For example, mechanisms of deskilling that were once restricted to Fordist production systems were extended to other social sectors and modes of cultural production. In the process of 'post-Fordist' globalization, older forms of conflict are meshed into new antagonisms generated by the global division of labour. Throughout these epochal – and often catastrophic – changes the core of the emerging 'information society' is still determined by generalized inequalities of wealth, power, and influence – modes of class and patriarchal exploitation which drastically deform the landscape of potential consciousness and democratic aspirations. As traditional class relations have been eroded new structures of inequality have appeared, especially hierarchies of power based on the production and circulation of information and knowledge. But we also witness the return of premodern divisions along ethnic lines, racial and gender divisions. What has been euphemistically called the postindustrial world following the 'end of ideology' (Bell, 1974, 1976) develops parasitically upon an earlier mode of production and will 'function', for many decades to come, as a machine of extended dehumanization in a dangerous environment of increasingly globalized conflicts and universalized risks (Bauman, 1991; Beck, 1992; Beck, Giddens, and Lash, 1994; Fraser, 1989; Perrow, 1984, 1987; Sylvester, 1994; Walby, 1989).

We are, of course, tracing the limits of Daniel Bell's liberal postindustrialism thesis that

> the change in the modes of innovation in the relation of science to technology and in public policy – is the change in the character of knowledge: the exponential growth and branching of science, the rise of a new intellectual technology, the creation of systematic research through R & D budgets, and, as the calyx of all this, the codification of theoretical knowledge.
>
> (1974: 44; 1991: xvii-xxx, 236–7)

Bell's model of post-capitalist trends includes: (i) 'the strategic centrality of information and knowledge'; (ii) 'the new innovative role of *theoretical* knowledge for research and development as well as policy'; (iii) 'the growing importance of the science-based industries in the last half of the twentieth century – electronics, computers, optics, polymers; and (iv) 'the rise of "intellectual technology" as the main feature of these developments' (1991: 150). Yet Bell's Panglossian vision of the future is premised on a repression of the actual chaotic form and content of these 'post-industrial transformations' ('we will be moving towards a "postindustrial society", in which the scientist, the engineer, and the technician constitute the key functional class in society' (1963, in 1991: 89; cf. Stonier, 1983; Lyon, 1988: 150–4). He confuses symptoms of postmodernism – such as the growth of the service class and expansion of the 'information economy' – with the deeper, and more dangerous, structural crises of global capitalism. For example, one of the general trends Bell isolates involves the strengthening rather than the dismantling of the welfare state: 'Most of this expansion in professional and technical employment is due to the expansion of government services, particularly in the areas of education, health, and welfare' (1991: 152).

We can summarize this brief discussion as follows. When approached from the standpoint of the history of discourse formations, questions relating to the origins of theorizing and knowledge, the morphology of the self, and structured social power belong to the same agenda exploring the instruments of reflection and the material conditions necessary for their institutionalization and dissemination. Identities are socially constituted in an interdependent nexus relating institutional processes, semiotic networks, and communicative performances. The latter are embedded in wider social relations of ownership and control. And where these power linkages are larger than 'societal' or the 'nation-state' horizon – as in the generic rules of patriarchal power organizing many different social systems and practices or the increasingly globalized forms of political power and inequality – we require new figurational categories (the comparative critique of the discourses of patriarchy and masculinism may be the first attempt to theorize power in global terms). In studying the vastly extended networks of social interdependence (the universalization of reflexive relationships, global conflicts, and state-induced hazards), however, we still recognize the work of older hegemonic interests in expanding the object-spheres of Western power. Indeed it may be true that the globalization of 'risk', 'contingency', and 'chance' is the defining mark of late modernity (Beck, 1992; Connolly, 1991; Giddens, 1991; Harvey, 1989; Heller and Fehér, 1988).

2 THE TECHNOPOIESIS HYPOTHESIS

It is not so much that we see the objects and things but rather that we first talk about them. To put it more precisely: we do not say what we see, but rather the reverse, we see what *one says* about the matter.

(Martin Heidegger, 1992: 56)

The production systems of reflexive capitalism with its global simulacral machines and telecommunications networks have destroyed the dominant epistemology along with the social and political world it expressed and authorized. But by colonizing everyday life and transforming lived experience, modern electronic media reveal the dialectic of communication and technology as one of the crucial armatures of modernity: we are oriented in our basic ways of seeing and experiencing by technically mediated modes of saying and doing. It is through the expansion of modern technology and its techniques of information processing that scientific knowledge has been 'materialized' in the physical environments, artifacts, and activities of everyday life. The fabric of so-called 'ordinary life', in other words, has been thoroughly penetrated by apparatuses embodying and reproducing advanced technical knowledge. And today these pervasive technological apparatuses function as powerful agencies of social change (the global processing of televisual images is frequently cited in this context, e.g. Kroker and Cook, 1991). I will refer to this as the *technopoiesis hypothesis*: *human beings make representations; but they have first been made by representations*. Simulacral technologies are bound up with the humanization of world experience. Every aspect of human reality – from the shaping of the eye, ear, and other sensory modes, to intimate forms of embodiment, values, literary structures, and social relations – are *historical events* mediated by cultural systems embodied in the stock of available technologies and corresponding interpretation systems. Indeed as a cumulative product of self-communication, consciousness itself arises in the structured intersection of social, semiotic, and technical fields (think, for example, of the impact of machinery upon the evolution of mechanistic forms of thought in the modern world). In short, knowledge systems and technologies must be approached as reflexive media of human evolution (there is, so to speak, a *transcendental* link between technology, knowledge, and human selfhood). At all costs we must avoid technologism or the romanticism which rejects artifacts and instruments as alienating the human spirit. In historical fact we both act and think only by means of implicit or explicit technical logics – understanding that the vast sphere indexed by the Greek word '*techne*' represents a complex history of reflexive self-definition.

This approach to technology reciprocally enfolds the axes of communication (forms of semiosis, talk, discourse, rhetoric, culture), selfhood (patterns of identity, subjectivity, embodied self-consciousness, self-understanding), and sociality (power relations, institutions, technological ensembles) as indissociable elements in the production of human culture. Emphasizing the dialectic of discourse, institutions of reflexivity, and technological media is, I will argue, the key to understanding thought and culture as both socially organized processes of meaning and as strategies of difference and resistance. We come to a major theme of the following studies: language is not a transparent mimetic medium through which 'objects' are privately accessed; rather, *discourse* constitutes the field of culturally sanctioned semiopraxis. 'Thought' – as a social field of intellectual practices – is an agency that actively shapes reality. Said in another way: *signifying practices reflexively articulate the body politic as they codify and distribute thought and meaning*. In particular, the model suggests that *technai* constitute the self-experiences prefigured by their operations: *as techniques are organs of human self-definition, the work-world of technopoiesis shapes the world-work of societies* (consider, for example, the complex institutional changes flowing from the imposition of mechanical technologies for measuring time and coordinating time-space relationships in a given society (Elias, 1992); the introduction of print technology (Eisenstein, 1979; Goody, 1977, 1986; Latour, 1990); the printed text as a constitutive agent in the formation of the modern nation-state (Anderson, 1983); the social transformations wrought by electrification (Schivelbusch, 1988; Nye, 1990); the cultural impact of the railway and ancillary technical systems (Kern, 1983; Schivelbusch, 1986); the effects of new techniques of replication on literary practices analyzed by Walter Benjamin in his essay 'The author as producer' (in Benjamin, 1992); the long-term consequences of factory divisions of labour and technology in changing definitions of childhood and childrearing practices (Bowles and Gintis, 1976)). In a formula: we see the world through the frames of meaning embodied in discourse formations.

Reflexive technologies: techne and technology

If *techne* is approached in something like its ancient sense as modes of production on the basis of practical knowledge we can see that the hypothesis has four fundamental aspects: (1) by foregrounding their physical characteristics technologies can be analyzed as *object techniques* which transform material culture (including physical facilities, utensils, commonsense knowledge, manual dexterities, learnt skills, verbal and intellectual capital, and techniques of representation); (2) embedded in local practices, technologies appear as technical *ensembles* of devices and machines 'engineered' for particular goals and purposes defined in the context of specific *values* and social *activities* (the '*in-order-to*', '*what-for*', '*how*,' and '*why*' vectors of value-laden practical action); (3) when codified and resourced by specific agencies these ensembles form institutional *programmes of embedded knowledge* – informing the unconscious *work-world* of a given technological practice; and (4) apparatuses in use actively (and often unpredictably) transform existing objects, artifacts, practices, and relations and through their methodic operations reciprocally transform their users (see Crary, 1990; Sahlins, 1976; Csikszentmihalyi and Rochberg-Halton, 1981; Latour, 1991; Mukerji, 1983).

The sociological concept of *techne* already incorporates the organized social processes of *poiesis* and *praxis* in organizing experience into meaningful orders. Like material artifacts, technologies are usable social constructs shaped by social interests before they are objective tools (thus a transportation system or coordinated system of work needs to be analyzed as a complex social configuration of *poiesis*, *praxis*, and *theoria*). The powerful effects of such combinatorial operations are particularly evident in the area of intellectual technologies and their 'object domains'. And here, we can scarcely overemphasize the importance of symbolic artifacts and information systems in endowing reality with a specific order of coherence and pattern. By stressing the symbolic and narrative involvements of technology we avoid the materialist prejudice which defines technology wholly in hardware terms and approach *technai* in the older sense as machines of congealed knowledge – productive arts meshed into particular material and intellectual apparatuses and relations. With this change of perspective, the sociological properties of technical systems become paramount: an object technique becomes a technology 'when it is consciously developed for particular social use ... These processes of selection, investment and development are obviously of a general social and economic kind, within existing social and economic relations, and in a specific social order are designed for particular uses and advantages' (Williams, 1983: 129–30; cf. Bell: 'the organization of a hospital or an international trade system is a *social* technology, as the automobile or a numerically controlled tool is a *machine* technology. Every theory or analogous intellectual technology derives from an earlier *form of thought* (an *intellectual* technology being the substitution of algorithms for intuitive judgments' (1974: 29; 1991: chs, 1, 2, esp. 20–6)).

This broader sociological conception of technology as 'the instrumental reordering of human experience' includes instruments of knowledge and communication technologies that extend the reach of language, conceptual innovations in thought, trade routes, sign systems, written texts, 'disciplinary technologies', military apparatuses, administrative techniques, energy and transport systems as media of 'general intellect'. We recall the starting point of logological researches which pursues the axiom that technologies are primarily forms of the self. This is also Bell's point when he notes that 'art and technology are not separate realms walled off from each other'. Everyday consciousness, art, and technological change enter into a dialectical constellation of facilitative action (*semiopraxis*). From the technopoeic perspective 'art', 'science', and 'technology' are interrelated media of thought, concrete embodiments of mind used in particular social environments. The so-called 'force of technology' resides in the investment of imagination and artfulness on the part of particular individuals and groups of people to create new ways of conceiving and doing things: 'Art employs *techne*, but for its own ends. *Techne*, too, is a form of art that bridges culture and social structure, and in the process reshapes both' (1991: 20). 'Mind', 'consciousness', and 'culture' are in fact reified expressions for the effects of world-disclosing machines developed and controlled by powerful groups and institutions. The work of knowledge technologies can be used as a general model: as elements in a living social milieu, *technai* function as active constituents rather than reflections of reality: *signification, societal organization, and technical positioning are interdependent elements of technopoeic systems.* Consider, for example, the organization of an education system as a 'mind technology'; here each process of 'culturation' involves a specific mode of subjectification.[1]

As this admittedly superficial sketch suggests, we need to view the workings of modern technologies as interlocking systems of coordinated *technopoiesis.* But this sociological hypothesis should not be confused with technological determinism. Machinery and technology by themselves do not transform cultural and social structures, let alone public consciousness (Bell, 1991: 20–30). The reverse is nearer the mark. Outside of definite social networks of culturally competent agents technologies are inert artifacts. As John Tagg cautions in his work on photographic technology:

> A technology has no inherent value outside its mobilizations in specific discourses, practices, institutions and relations of power. Import and status have to be produced and effectively institutionalized and such institutionalizations do not describe a unified field or the working out of some essential causality.
>
> (Tagg, 1991: 159; cf. Crary, 1990; Foucault, 1980a; MacKenzie and Wajcman, eds, 1985)

Conceptualizing technologies as situated apparatuses in dramatic life-worlds is central to a more comprehensive critical theory of everyday life. In fact, as we shall argue throughout these chapters, some of the most revolutionary technological instruments have been *cultural technologies* and within the sphere of cultural technopoiesis, novel *forms of thought, textual practices,* and *techniques of selfhood.* For example, at the macrolevel of institutions the state's coordination of object techniques creates 'embodied habits', which, in stipulating programmes for human activities, overdetermines and routinizes forms of behaviour, social relationships, and even moral relations prevalent in a historical period – for example, in the premodern state's mobilization of work organizations that Lewis Mumford called the *megamachine* or the expansion of the modern state into a diverse range of knowledge systems and mass media. But such premodern and postmodern megamachines are only set into motion by the social energies released by linguistically embedded values and beliefs.

Technologies of the self

'Reflexivity' can now be redefined as the recursive workings of dialogue, self-understanding and self-interpretation in their ordinary and extraordinary manifestations, most especially in those modes of *embodied concern* and *self-engagement* we routinely attribute to communicating subjects as feeling, thinking, deliberating, speaking, arguing, contesting, self-monitoring social beings engaged with others in artfully producing and reproducing the endlessly variable routines of day-to-day living. We now see that these reflective dispositions are inseparable from the history of technopoiesis and its *institutional* incarnations in the wider organizational and social environments of human interaction. Given the millennial dialectic of *Techne* and *Logos* – or, as we say, technology and culture – in human affairs there is nothing extraordinary about individuals reflecting on their statements and practices, questioning accepted practices or imagining alternative systems. Reflexive stratagems are found in quite unremarkable forms of verbal repetition: the question, gloss, commentary, critical reminder, rejoinder, reformulation, translation, etc. Individuals routinely display the capacity to self-explicatively analyze and debate the specifics of their practices while simultaneously describing themselves so-describing. In everyday life agents signify their operative worlds and indexically signify that they are signifying: in saying one thing they mean another; in leaving things unsaid they turn silence into an eloquent resource. Speakers wonder about, ponder, meditate, contest, and theorize their activities as an unremarked and thereby unremarkable feature of quotidian life.

More fundamentally, social worlds are technopoeically mediated and subject to reflexive truth conditions before they are describable and reportable as phenomenal orders (or as we would now say, the world can be phenomenal only because of prior reflexive systems). The differential subject positions of everyday talk and discourse are, consequently, transformational achievements of social institutions. If both subjectivity and objectivity are 'effects' inscribed in powerful systems of *différance*, similar considerations apply to the systems which regulate the body and corporeal relationships in a social order. In everyday life we unthinkingly resort to the image of the human body as a biological entity subject to a natural field of forces. But '*the*' body – like '*the*' self – cannot exist independently of the movement of social inscriptions in which it is constituted. And these 'inscriptions' are consequential *collective* formations linked to larger structures. The body 'is constituted only in being divided from itself, in becoming space, in temporizing, in deferral' (Derrida, 1981: 29). The operations of *différance* extend to the structures of microinteraction, the technologies used by a given community and its organizations, and the macrostructures of the body politic. All of these relations are collective forms of 'congealed reflexivity'. This is the reason why a 'critique of reflection' leads to a *social* theory of reflexivity asking three related questions: 'How are we constituted as subjects of our own knowledge?', 'How are we constituted as subjects who exercise or submit to power relations?' and 'How are we constituted as moral subjects of our own actions?' (Foucault, 1984: 32–50).

Once in existence, such reflexive systems form an important medium of historical change. Incorporated into technologies of power, self-figurations can enter the fabric of history as sources of agency in their own right; hence today we spontaneously exemplify human subjectivity by citing Romantic idioms of *creativity*, the Protestant image of the *moral agent* as a reflexive subject using the shifter sign 'I' in judging worthiness and questioning standards of worth, the Humanist rhetoric of the self posited in intentional locutions such as 'I witness', 'I think', 'I believe', 'I feel', 'I understand', 'I intend', 'I fear', 'I dream', 'I desire', 'I love', 'I remember'. Each of these expressive forms is connected to a particular image of excluded alterity as an imaginary obstruction to the telos of free creativity: whatever destabilizes and decentrs the self's purposes, institutional constraints on creativity, the imagined, symbolic, and real temptations of moral existence, the dark horizons of unintelligibility, and so forth. This is one way in which object relations enter the body of the self as the self is progressively enmeshed in organizational practices. It is not that the subject facilitates an outpouring of discourse, but that discourses and technologies engender certain types of subject.

The hypothesis suggests that the sociotechnical processes which constitute the body politic also structure the differential field of subjective experience. Imaginary practices of Self/Othering – what Foucault has called 'modes of problematization' – delimit and codify orders of valued difference, modes of thought, and stylized behaviours as a collective repertoire for their practioners. We can then approach received paradigms of conscience, practical consciousness, technical-calculative reasoning, and the like as the traces of past *institutional struggles*. If inquiry begins from *practices*, it should also explore existing *theories of practices* and be aware that these 'metatheories' create new practices. This kind of complexity presupposes an ontology of sociohistorical life which relates epochal shifts in thought to fundamental transformations of society and technology following the principle that we think the way we do by virtue of living out a dialogic existence within the institutional constraints of particular life-worlds.

By drawing upon the axiological resources provided by institutional arrangements while interacting with others, by creatively imagining, accounting for, reading, and researching themselves – by making sense together – individuals acquire the normative attributes of subjectivity associated with definite communities of value. These 'value matrices' of everyday life (*ethos*) form the conditions for any living-together and acting-together. In other words we are concerned with truth-telling agents pursuing the good in definite historical situations, not asocial mirrors reflecting the Real in abstraction from a collective heritage of selective valuations, contextual technologies, and cultural systems. We learn to 'see' and 'think' within the interpretive frames of existing valuations. But this does not mean that the self is 'merely' virtual or 'superstructural'. By participating in different – and often contradictory – 'accountable-activities' individuals display themselves as morally responsible agents and through those practices acquire the lineaments of conviction and social identity. As R.G. Collingwood once wrote:

Of everything that a mind in the full sense does, it gives itself an account as it does it; and this account is inseparably bound up with the doing of the thing. Thus every activity is also a theory of itself and, by implication, of activity in general; but not necessarily a true theory.

(1970: 84)

Intimate technologies

As a general thesis about the dialectic of discourses, subjectification, and cultural formations the idea of technopoiesis also applies to the local world-work of microsocial techniques. Organised talk and the corporeal dispositions of daily life are examples from the domain of *intimate technologies*. Thus the humblest word or commonsense category can be seen as an information programme anchored within some discursive tradition (think of the dense *institutional* history of the concepts 'zero', 'soul', 'sex', 'race', 'phlogiston', 'periodic table', 'class', or 'God'). A word indexes a conceptual category – a conventional codification of experience (in reality words typically involve compound categories or multidimensional concepts circulating in definite social milieux). Words and statements can be considered as dramatic *instruments* anchored in particular social situations. And emergent concepts within social settings may effect radical changes to participants in local speech practices. As Brice Parain observes 'Any word contains the means to use what it designates' (1971: 27). 'Problematics' appear in ordinary language as unformulated action programmes and 'stocks of knowledge' before they are made explicit by reflection or codified into theoretical frameworks. In written texts the axes of interpretation and instrumentation coincide. Written language is more like a diligent bureaucracy than a translucent mirror.

Acquiring reflexive skills enables persons imaginatively to monitor their experience to create a 'shared world', which in turn facilitates the reproduction of social relationships, practices, and ideologies as collective legacies. In a literal sense the self-understandings of agents reflexively inform the routine processes of everyday world construction. Objects only make themselves manifest and attain a stable identity for that mode of social being which endures as life-in-the-world. In quite ordinary contexts we claim to know that we know, analyze our feelings, formulate moral judgements, monitor ourselves in the light of ethical standards, act responsibly, say 'I am', and expect recognition from other souls who display similar normative capacities. The shared rules of such verbal performances are part of what *we* mean by ordinary knowledge: we 'know' that we exist as named, situated, finite beings – that our embodied 'being-with-others', 'acting-with-others', and 'speaking-with-others' are irreducible horizons of alterity (the world is describable only against a system of descriptions, understandable from the site of shared understandings, valuable in terms of a code of appraisal, and so on).

Such active processes of *rhetorical interpretation* are already embodied in the narrative patterns of everyday discourse: concepts translate experiences into meanings (concepts are nascent metaphors 'condensing' past encounters into anticipatory schemas – not merely 'Tigers are striped, four-legged, feline animals', but 'Avoid tigers'). And the questions individuals find worth asking and thought-provoking are tied to their concrete social definitions of what they find relevant and situationally possible. Categories encode experience into meaningful sequences (routines) and structures (operative schemas), which sediment into behavioural dispositions and body regimes. Ideas are always parts of a larger deferred context of concepts; abstracted for particular objectives they act as 'relays' of useful discriminations evolved in the routinization of daily life.

Categories are also dangerous. In political terms, programmes function as the generative matrices for activities in which they themselves come to be located. Once integrated into 'ways of life' they take over the role of 'conscious deliberation' functioning as unconscious decision procedures, definitions, typifications, algorithms of practical action, and coded behaviours. Hence most of our routine responses and learned behaviours take place 'without thinking' – words also perform their work in selecting, distorting, and misdescribing experience. As Heinrich Böll laconically observed: 'where definitions can mean world-views, world-views can mean wars' (1985: 37). Agents strategically use such motivational scripts and 'knowledge structures' as interpretive resources in assembling their worlds and actively making sense of the ever-changing particularities of social interaction. The patterned outcomes of world-making activities inform the everyday perspectives of our local cultures. But words and the specific modes of reading they prefigure can be withdrawn from circulation, questioned, and replaced. Occasionally new categories and ways of thinking lead their users into novel worlds with an increased capacity for meaningful engagement. These get labelled as distinctive cognitive, aesthetic, or ideological perspectives, new codes and stories through which some domain of experience can be reordered and changed. When this occurs imaginary structures enter the phantasmal body of culture. Consider the difference between the cold *light* of reason and the *light* which symbolizes transcendence (Bachelard, 1987: 111).

In certain contexts matrices may be uncoupled from face-to-face exchanges and relocated in larger networks (bureaucracies and formal associations, markets, weapon systems, military organizations, sciences, automatic mechanisms, robots and automation techniques, telecommunication systems, and the like). In Section 1 I have suggested that the 'deterritorialization' and 'recontextualization' of perspectives by means of reflexive technologies is one of the central dynamics of modern society. And it is hard fully to appreciate that all these arrangements are only made possible by signs and words. Novel conceptual connections foreground different aspects of experience, encouraging new patterns of action which dialectically reinforce the initial idiom to change its status from a metaphoric to a 'real' description: *technologies reflexively modify the phenomenal order they ostensibly describe.* Consider the praxis flowing from two different ways of perceiving the sky: as a vast canopy of elemental blue trailing clouds of glory or as a grid of virtual pathways and communication corridors through which objects, commodities, and messages are networked.

Rhetorics of selfhood

We come to an important conclusion: in a fundamental sense we *are* our ways of perceiving, valuing, and knowing. Each dialogic relation embodies a powerful subscript of subjectivity: *you become the self of your knowing*. Societies articulate their own identity in normative praxes: *this is how we live, this is how we ought to live*. From the logological perspective there is no neutral 'representation' or innocent 'understanding' separate from ongoing social processes of signification, just as there is no interpretation-free description of objects that could transcend every rhetorical framework.[2]

Here 'rhetoric' refers to the historical poiesis of human self-invention – we extend Aristotle's conception of rhetoric as 'the faculty of discovering the possible means of persuasion in reference to any subject whatever' (*Rhetoric* 1.2) to the whole field of social praxis. Unlike the limited rhetoric of antiquity, we commend a broader view of the discursive construction of reality. For this purpose rhetorics are respecified as the strategic poetics of communal self-representation – without which we would not only not have the means to talk and think about ourselves and the world, but would, quite literally, have nothing to talk and think about. Rhetoric is the distinctively verbal form of *semiopraxis*. As *institutions* 'rhetorics' normatively codify and disseminate the suasive articulations of value, imagination, and knowledge implicit in dominant practices. Being etymologically literal we can view rhetoric as the verbal matrix sustaining every *axiology of experience*, following the logological principle that the experienceable is inseparable from the given structures of articulation. We then see that the history of mind is inextricably tied to the technical life of suasive praxis.

This is where logological analysis begins. The rhetorics of selfhood – like a society's technologies, its poetics and scientific paradigms – are historically specific placement strategies (personal pronouns, names, signatures, descriptions, official categorizations, titles, biographies, legal codes, ideological nomenclatures, rites of passage, etc.). Like scientific problems, selves only become thinkable, and hence researchable, through systems of symbols and conventional vocabularies drawn from the ideological archive of the wider culture. But not every social order encourages self-inquiry among its ways of being. Self-reflection in its many dimensions – cognitive, affective, aesthetic, ethical, and political – presupposes a symbolic structuration of time and place which few societies have been able to build into their institutional life. We have repeatedly observed that the history of reflection is indebted to techniques and material systems; it presupposes available technopoeic 'actor-networks'.[3] Add to this the fact that many societies have ill-developed languages of self-understanding and we see why whole civilizations have neglected systematic self-reflection as a primary value – just as they have rigidly controlled subject positions and prescribed mandatory forms of consciousness. In this sense not every society has institutionalized the ethic of dialogue or culture of critical discourse. Cultures have endured for centuries with rigorously sanctioned ascribed role categories in the place of what we consider to be the indispensable organs of self-expression. And frequently where a society does create 'research programmes' and correlated categories of intellectuals these knowledge occupations are typically controlled and 'licensed' in the interests of dominant groups.[4] The phenomenology of such modes of social being consequently assumes the form of histories of the manifold workings of violence. From the shock of violent socialization – exhibited most graphically by the patriarchal institutions of our own society – we envision the radical historicity of subjectivity.[5]

3 TWO PARADIGMS OF REFLECTION

Homo – the species which calls itself *sapiens*.

How do these exploratory observations relate to a critique of pure reflection? We should guard against confusing a critique of Reason with the post-metaphysical rejection of reasonableness. The divinization of Reason from Plato to the Enlightenment needs to be demythologized without abandoning critical inquiry. But all too often postmetaphysical diagnoses tend to embrace a totalizing relativism or scepticism. Only rarely do they question the larger *institutions* of reflection or their own involvements as limited cultural and political strategies within the wider configurations of history. With notable exceptions they tend to follow the ahistorical thought patterns of the tradition of Western rationalism they critique. As a consequence, their antinomial deconstructions are easily coopted by the dominant tradition. Here we approach the logics of reflection as rhetorical 'superstructures' premised upon figural operations – artful achievements of discourse which exist by systematically repressing their own reflexive horizons.

Of course we have already risked binarism by rhetorically contrasting the rationalist culture of Reflection with the subversive energies of Reflexivity. Up to now I have used the term 'reflection' as metonymic shorthand for the pursuit of disembodied, calculative knowledge: 'instrumental reason', 'objective science', 'pure art', 'absolute truth', and so forth. Reflection – whether as an *experience, method,* or philosophical *attitude* – desires an order of necessary truths immune from semiotic, figural, social, and cultural mediation. Self-reflection takes the restricted form of logical and methodological debates concerning the object provenance of concepts and validation procedures. By contrast Reflexivity brackets the logics of reflection to disclose their status as metaphorical, cultural formations. Where Reason pursues the essential, reflexivity sees essences as an index of constructive practices. Where reflection ignores the self implicated in reflection, reflexivity is chronically self-involving and dialogical; indeed for many analytical purposes *'reflexivity'* and *'self-reflexivity'* may be used interchangeably. Reflection is positively mandated by its positive assumptions; whereas Reflexivity examines principles as legitimating a particular way of thinking. In Section 1 I suggested that the roots of reflexivity lie in radicalizing the tensions and contradictions latent in modern reflectivity (to condense chapters into thematic headings: the inherent limits of traditional humanist, rationalist, and idealist accounts of reason, self, and knowledge; the exclusiveness of dominant cultural ideologies of identity and difference; the ahistorical act of instrumental self-reflection delimiting itself *in extremis*; the process of reflexive scientization where 'naive science' critiques its own failures (Beck, 1992); the professionalization of political debate that presents itself as rhetorically neutral communication; the specialization and academicization of radical theorizing; the aporias of modernism as institutionalized *avant-garde* 'art praxis', and so on). Risking gross oversimplification the term 'Reflection' can be used as an index for the hegemonic rhetorics, practices and institutions of representation in modern society. The objects produced by these logics are persuasive (re)presentations of experience – elaborating the manifold forms of a cultural hegemony which can still be designated as the *bourgeois form of life*.

Historically, bourgeois culture invented its own self-image as progressive *Modernity* by imposing its own ideal self-conceptions upon the earlier rhetorical fabric of social life. Of course, the actual history and articulation of these 'technologies of self' varies considerably across different national cultures and is decisively influenced by local structural conditions – the particular form of industrialization, urbanization, demographic growth, religious traditions, and so forth. I have suggested that in modernizing societies organized cultural reflection and its 'knowledges' – whether in the education system, institutionalized medicine, technological, or social and economic spheres – assumes at a societal level the role previously fulfilled by pre-modern doxic institutions. Those who are subject to rationalization are forced to carve out lives within the dominant networks of commodified culture. Those who can appropriate cultural capital effectively incorporate 'reflective knowledge of the conditions and prospects of modernity' and in promoting the techniques of self-knowledge and self-creation become agents of 'reflexive modernization' (Foucault, 1980b; Giddens, 1991; Beck, 1992: 93).

From mimetology to heterology

Despite their disparate origins, a number of shared assumptions inform and pattern the practices of modern reflection. I will refer to this constellation as *Representationalism*. The first principle of Representationalism is the ontological claim that the deracinated Subject has a non-mediated, non-perspectival access to objects. Second, the paradigm of neutral objectivity is supported by the view that the epistemology of reflection – concrete experience and universal Reason – secures a value-free mirror of a unitary 'external World'. A third principle is that knowledge works by reducing the Other to the Same in a specular, homogeneous, linear time frame. A fourth assumption is that knowing the Truth licenses the transformation of the Other in the image of the Same. These generative principles converge in the humanist conception of the identity of Thought and Being, a postulate which helps legitimate diverse programmes of scientization, politicization, and commodification. From the perspective of logological inquiry, these postulates can be seen as the constitutive rules of a pervasive rhetoric – but a rhetoric that is premised upon the repression of rhetoricity.

We should note the irony that the dominant metatheoretical paradigm of Reason in modern Western thought exempts its own concepts and procedures from radical self-reflection. While each practice of reflection – whether in the subsystems of the economy (economic policy, corporate power, global communication networks), polity (government apparatuses, think-tanks, advisers, archival gatekeepers) or culture (the modern university, the academy, pedagogic institutions and teaching apparatuses, mass popular culture) – operates upon the basis of particular frameworks of signification, the violent operations these rhetorics perform in subordinating the Other to Reason are not usually taken as topics for investigation. They are taken for granted as the *mise-en-scène* of reflection (just as an idealized form of scientific discourse denies its own figural and rhetorical construction). This 'blindness' can be found at the level of texts, communities of theorists, social practices, and institutions. Knowledge-based institutions are seldomly seen as ideological structures and even less as political-economic formations *in their own right*. Instead knowledge is thought to follow the contours of the Real like a glove fits a hand. Neither the *social relations* of cultural production (the non-identity and violent othering of Representation and Subject-formation) nor the *rhetorical relations* of the 'objects' to be represented are primary themes in the conspectus of Reflection. In sum: the figure of the *mise-en-scène* of methodic technique represses the vertiginous *mise-en-abîme* of infinite reflexivity. Mimetology thus perpetrates a dual repression with regard to the question of the Other (both in the silence concerning the violence invested in constructing the otherness of the Other and in eliding the destabilizing heterology of self-reflexivity implicit in the diverse stratifying practices of othering). This can be expressed by saying that 'sciences' and 'disciplines' created within the representational mind-set may well be *reflective* but in their truncated ontological and epistemological self-awareness they sponsor a deeply *unreflexive* view of the world.

We can now draw a distinction between discourses *of* reflection (Reflection as the intellectual authority to 'think about things', the games of 'picturing things', 'representing things', 'conceptualizing things', 'knowing things', 'inquiring into things', and 'speaking for things') and discourses *on* reflection (Reflexivity as the subversive counterpower of 'thinking about thinking', dialogic conversations exploring the generative rules of cognitive language-games: 'rethinking the conditions of thought', questioning existing frameworks in relation to their material circumstances, engaging in oppositional criticism, and so forth). Reflection typically avoids questions concerning its own constitution and presuppositions (thus the game-rules of the 'sciences of social phenomena' posit an independent world of objects – 'empirical reality' – which they report as an external exemplar of their mimetic categories). Reflexivity interrogates the assumptions of representational thinking by uncovering the *heterology* at work in (re)presentations. Discourse on reflection reveals a self-reflexive moment inherent in the transitive categories of reflection. Wherever such self-questioning occurs, what was a resource for Reflection – its material base and founding authority, technologies, basic concepts, disciplinary norms, writing practices, characteristic literary genres, presuppositions, rhetorics – becomes a theme for reflexive sociology. We could say that the 'subject matter' of reflexive inquiry is given in the unconscious heterologies implicated in reflective discourse. By means of reflection we can talk and think about the Other and pursue knowledge of things as though we were not productively involved in these epistemic practices; but only reflexivity enables thought to talk and think about reflection as the cultural praxis of 'othering' and to imagine alternative modes of discourse, subjectivity, and social life.

In this sense, where common sense considers 'philosophy' to be a typically *reflective* discipline with its own homogeneous language, it is more accurate to describe the impulse of what has been called philosophy as originating in *self-reflexive* experiences that are older than discursive 'cognition' (the visceral experiences of alienation, wonder, compassion toward the Other, the sense of injustice at suffering, the melancholic passage of time, the will to freedom, and so forth). Or to say this in another way, like poetry the problems of philosophy are typically *reflexive objects*, 'alterities' which occasion self-questioning and disturb the constructions of everyday thought. But the typical fate of reflexive phenomena is to be traduced into the topics of reflective discourse, stripped, as it were, of their subversive intent and subordinated to an existing 'regime of truth'. For instance we may be able to institutionalize the techniques of reflection but not the experience of reflexivity (philosophy can be normalized and taught, but not the life of philosophizing).

Logological inquiries as teratologies

Modern Representationalism privileges universalizable cognition of objects but elides the 'monstrous' appearance of reflexivity in its own practices. To emphasize the gendered character of this system: the master code of world

45

representation is constructed by repressing the non-phallic, heterological re-flexivities which destabilize mastery. Yet the 'weak power' of reflexive experience is older than the phallic desire of reflection. Consider the empow-ering logic of the simple reflection game of the masculine Subject observing and describing the Other as Object. By accepting a Subject/Object phenom-enology – whether in its empirical or transcendental form – reflection characteristically overviews its objects from the spectral security of a universal optic. Not finding 'values' as visible items of 'experience' it embraces cognitive nihilism (in practice this manifests itself as a marginalizing of 'values' by means of the *is/ought* hierarchy and a concomitant sidelining of 'ethics' as of little analytical interest to rational inquiry). Not being able to inspect the Other's soul, philosophy approaches meaning through the schematic vocabulary of 'the problem of Other minds' or settles for a detached description of the body's surfaces and causal mechanisms (the many forms of objectivism are different ways of managing the intrusive reflexivities of human subjectivity). Being apparently independent of material life, the self-reflective subject is construed as an autonomous Ego. All of these doctrines are a grammatical consequence of the game-rules which project the 'Subject' as a unified, centred self and the place-holder symbolized by 'Object' as a unitary, bounded, immobile totality – creating the epistemological equivalent of a voyeur's paradise. The notion of a non-unified, multiple or mobile Self or an unstable, collectivist 'object' of knowledge (for example the observed Other answering back, the temporalized and traditionalized Self which resists sequestration in the name of ascribed rights, the irreducibly multiple voices of the excluded Other) are literally 'monsters' from the perspective of Reflection. Whatever disturbs the limits of reason or transgresses the carefully established categories of reflection is *by definition* the scandalous site of alterity.

The grammatical rules which privilege the spectatorial Subject – in one of its many incarnations: *nous, cogito, tabula rasa,* observer, individual, judge, scientist, legislator, reading subject – spectating the 'external world' generates symptomatic *aporias*. In *authorizing* itself Reflection prefigures its objects as discoverable, computable phenomenal structures 'laid out' like abstract predi-cates for an observing, inspecting self (what might be called the *photocentrism* of Western thought). 'Objects' disclosed in sensory experience are literally visible things which stand opposed to a viewing Subject (*Gegenstände*). 'Knowing' proceeds as the Subject mimetically abstracts the object's essential truth from 'sensory impressions'. Reflection raises the logic of visibility in human relationships to the status of a methodological protocol and philo-sophical rationale for scientific praxis in general. In other words, models of the world informed by the figure of mimesis reconfirm the original metaphysical contract of the Subject/Object polity. The Olympian Subject spectates, ob-serves, categorizes, judges, reflects, and transforms the world as a rational Object. Hence all 'problems of knowledge' are referential or, in contemporary jargon, realist in epistemology, objectivist in ontology, extensionalist in semantics. It is not that the institutional powers of modernity 'apply' these logics to persons, society, and nature; rather, a conception of social and natural order as a timeless structure is already presupposed as a product of modern binarism (subject/object, is/ought, facts/values, science/emotion, literal/figurative, form/content, etc.).

Faced with 'objects' of its own making Reflection theorizes the truth of their otherness across the division of the Subject-Object relation, forgetting that the hyphen is in fact a construct not a natural fact. Hence every logic of reflection simultaneously phenomenalizes its objects and occludes its own phenomenalizing authority. In ethical terms its binary rules allow it to take responsibility only for its objects (as 'objects of knowledge') and not for the textual praxis of prior *conceptualization* which situates these objects as exogenous totalities. As a condition of its (im)possibility spatial videology excludes temporal heterology. From the spatial optic the knowable world bifurcates into two discrete spectacles of interior and exterior consciousness (which are rhetorically made to appear as 'unified phenomena' neatly distributed into logic-sentential forms) – and the metaphorical author within this phenomenal structure must also elaborate 'himself' in either the spatial rhetorics of subjectivity or objectivity (the two extreme positions being the spectatorial omniscience of the transcendental Ego and the radical effacement of the 'absent author': allegories of the older metaphysical polarity of full or empty space). Within the social sciences the 'objects' of sociological knowledge necessarily appear as either objective instances of the identity 'society' or as subjective constructions of the unity 'consciousness' (the only metaphysical pathos which sociological reason admits is thus one of *ambivalence* in the face of a prearranged choice between an idealist subject or a reified object: 'free agency' or 'deterministic structure' or where the metaphysics rises to the surface, the 'duality of agency and structure').

To illustrate: the examined life of classical Reason – whether in the Graeco-Latin, Cartesian, Kantian, Hegelian, or Husserlian variants – rhetorically constructs a universal phallocentric eye (the mind's 'I', a masculine, authorial role as a universal human ideal: 'Man(kind)') which actively occludes the contextual praxis of difference at work in the reflective act of disclosing phenomenal realms of the Real. Once 'in place' phallocentric Reflection can, by sleight of hand, 'uncover' or 'discover' the essence of phenomenal manifestation as an ordered grid of essential predicates. Or, at the opposite pole to classical Reason, the discourses of empirical Reflection phenomenalize experience to produce objects of inquiry as a panorama of 'contingent phenomena' ('facts', 'sensory data', 'material substances') subject solely to empirical specification ('Essences are nominal terms'; 'Only the phenomenal world is knowable', 'We demonstrate geometry because we make it', etc.). But in both forms of reflection the foundational desire of the omnipotent 'I' to reflect 'phenomena' elides the question of the situatedness and finitude of desire; the value of theoretical reflection and Reason evades ongoing processes of *in situ* evaluation; the 'community' of extra-worldly monads ('Mankind') naturalizes itself as a corporation of thinking substances safe in their interested disinterestedness from the violent history of power relations and the temporal dynamics of oppression and violence. Whatever else is dubitable the phenomenal status of bounded objects as a representable world is an absolute presupposition of every logic of Reflection. At the deeper level of epistemological and ontological principles, then, Representationalism schematizes experience into the Representing Self, acts of Representation, and the World captured by Reflection.

Assembling these 'reminders', of course, is symptomatic of a shift to critical discourses *on* Reflection which we designate as the *Reflexive paradigm*. Reflection posits the world as computable 'realms of phenomena' for a legislative, spectating, transcendental Ego; Reflexivity explicates the generative principles making the idea of 'phenomenal representation' intelligible. By bracketing the concept of reflection we see that the idea of reflective knowledge is made possible by the 'alterities' it excludes. We also see that a depth grammar constrains us to think about experience in 'either/or' terms (subject/object, mind/body, agent/structure, etc.). Each of these concepts can then be deconstructed as a complex historical formation. An analogue in contemporary physics is the use of reflexive problematics by quantum theory to 'test' and 'stretch' the limits of non-quantum science (quantized phenomena being monstrous events for the classical Galilean-Newtonian framework). The study of reflexive experience within different practices of reflection is quite literally a teratology.

But this dialectic does not abandon the quest for truth in the style of certain postmodernist positions. On a more positive note the *lacunae* and *aporiae* of representational logic suggest an alternative concept of self-reflection as dialogic reflexivity which no longer takes its own grounding sociality for granted, accepts its provisionality, and becomes self-problematizing *vis-à-vis* its historical limits and material preconditions. Where Reflection divorces subjectivity from structure, Reflexivity articulates the interweaving of self and other, consciousness and world. Reflexivity reminds Reflection that its axiomatic procedures are products of specific discursive practices. Reflexive speech refuses the routinized dilemmas and controversies of dualistic reflection to define its own authority and rhetoricity in textual and scriptural terms. Instead of the exemplary activities of spectating and description, it follows the self-explicating displacements of quotidian talk, conversation, and communicative understanding. Instead of selecting from the family-variants of videological reflection (*noesis, clear and distinct seeing, appearance/essence, phenomena/noumena, facts/theories, opinion/truth, subject/object, form/content, sense/reference, presence/absence, identity/difference, self/other, private/public*, etc.), it opens itself to the 'monstrous' demands of transactional experience.

48

4 CONCLUSION: FROM THE TRANSPARENT MIRROR TO THE HETEROLOGICAL TEXT

We can conclude this preliminary critique of classical rationality by reinscribing the reflective category of the self in more reflexive and dialogical terms. From the logological perspective *l'autre* – the horizon of alterity – antedates and provides the suppressed ground of the subject-object discourses of ego-centric logics. The self is delimited by its reflexive sense of alterity (for example, the self posits versions of otherness in achieving and sustaining selfhood). Said more generically: attributions of selfhood are declensions of the Other. In everyday life what we recognize as the 'self' or 'a life' is constructed like a palimpsest from layers of heterological semiopraxis. Alterity also incorporates the counter-inscriptions of the self in the process of actively becoming 'other' – as 'the Other Self' is presupposed in every identification process. Identity considered dynamically must be approached as a transactional symbolic process. Articulating the manifold forms of alterity would be one of the tasks of a reflexive as opposed to a reflective account of the subject-as-social inscription. The simple expression 'the other' has multiple meanings, perhaps along a continuum from the most concrete sense of finitude toward the irreducible horizons of otherness posited by recent forms of post-structuralist and post-modern theorizing.

What are the first steps in this reinscription? First, as a social process, the self is *materially embodied* – positioned by the manifold corporeal inscriptions of pregiven environments and structures of power. Second, the self is *socially, textually, and technically embedded* and *mediated* through existing economies, institutions, and gendered relationships. Third, the self is radically *dialogic*, linked to the lives of known and unknown others by complex signifying practices spanning the whole gamut of affective, volitional, and discursive relationships – each with their specific temporal rhythms and demands. Fourth, in incorporating the perspectives of the Other, the self is *practically knowledgeable* about its own conditions and circumstantialities, a creative matrix of recursive actions rather than a passive recipient of the play of forces – the subject of its experiences and not merely an object in experience. Fifth, the self endures as a *differential site of dynamic resistance, refiguration*, and *imaginative renewal* occasioned by transactional experiences in the ongoing processes of everyday life. Finally, in moments of enhanced reflexivity the self *(re)inscribes* itself in and as a *textual node* in wider *intertextual networks*, often promoting alternative modes of rationality, conceptuality, and being-in-the-world that transgress the logics of mundane reasoning. The force of these alterities effects a deconstruction of the expression '*the* self' by dissolving the 'natural' boundaries between 'self' and 'other', 'subjectivity' and 'objectivity', 'agency' and 'structure' in concrete historical praxis. This is the 'interface' where the self becomes 'other' to its self-conceptions and shifts its terms of identity.

The word 'self' now designates the whole range of transgressive *auto-bio-graphical processes* at work in reinscribing received interpretations under the impress of changing historical contexts and experiences. Unlike the classical humanist subject, selfhood is always already spatialized and temporalized in and as historically effective signifying practices, and self-understanding is achieved by working within rather than transcending everyday practices and narratives. Reason is a dialogic achievement of a specific tradition, not an *a priori* norm governing all possible traditions. Consequently, when we assume the obligations of selfhood we also accept a definite way of living with its moral and symbolic commitments. But unlike the received models of social closure, selfhood is *essentially* open and reflexive upon its own constitutive principles. In contrast to the pure, worldless Substance of the metaphysical tradition with its tacit community of transparent speechless Egos, reflexivity accepts the prior existence of otherness as its medium, intertextuality as its horizon, and asymmetrical power as its occasion. In sum, the self exhibits a dialectical rather than a specular structure. In weaving culture into a concrete 'life' with others the self networks itself within 'the play of *différance*' as a heterogeneous nexus of sociobiographical praxis.

The 'theoretical self' is no exception to these differential strictures. It can only be 'posited' as a secure axiom or aboriginal foundation for certain limited ideological purposes. In reality selfhood is always 'engaged', 'valorized', and 'dispersed' within a polyvocal medium of prior social practices. The received image of the knower as a 'unified subject' is a cultural ideal to be analyzed along with the spectrum of signifying practices we encounter in everyday life. The place once occupied by 'pure reason' and the 'transcendental ego' is now striated with *reading* and *writing processes*. Experiences that were marginalized during the epoch of Reflection to sustain its fundamental ideological categories now take centre-stage: the undecidable, ambivalent, transgressive, nomadic counterfinalities of everyday reflexivity. Philosophical representations and the different selves (and others) they assemble, for example, presuppose dialogic reflexivities even where they strive to eliminate indexicality, ambiguity, heteroglossia, and intertextuality from their projects and accounts (a history of past theorizing could be written by uncovering the persuasive devices evolved in laundering alterity from experience).

We conclude, therefore, that no experience is self-founding – whether in the realms of everyday experience or in the advanced regions of formal axiomatics. The life of reflexivity unleashes the quotidian equivalent of Gödel's theorem of undecidability in metamathematics. By questioning the ideological assumptions of disembodied reason we may respecify the sites of reflexivity as simultaneously affective, practical, discursive, epistemic, political, and ethical orders. To clear a space for dialogical modes of thinking and action we must first dismantle the hegemonic tradition of speechless Reflection. Where Reflection (re)presents objectivity as external *facts* available for analytic recuperation or – in its Kantian branch – as objects conforming to *concepts*, reflexive writing frames experience as a socially constructed referent in and for specific social orders. Where the supra-historical Ego of Reflection is affectively disembodied, Reflexivity elaborates the incarnate conditions of knowledge inhering in our capacities as affective, intersubjective creatures. Where the soliloquizing self divests itself of language, the reflexive self discloses the sustaining differences of alien discourses. Where Reflection presupposes a stable referential horizon rooted in Eurocentric canons of disengaged 'objectivity', Reflexivity interrogates the changing conditions and practices of European world-work to which it itself necessarily belongs.

Part I

MIMESIS

In the two chapters of Part I I examine the mimetic impulse underwriting the dominant logics of European reflection and representation. Chapter 1 explores the metarhetorics of language justifying representationalist conceptions of the world. Chapter 2 shows how these modes of thought and selfhood function by actively occluding and repressing the contextual alterities of incarnation, historicity, sociality, interpretation, and power. By deconstructing the constitutive rules of modern mimetic consciousness we can begin the task of prefiguring a richer concept of reflexivity that would incorporate these principles of difference and otherness in a more radical 'politics of representation'.

1

RHETORICS OF REPRESENTATION

Here too a basic capacity of the mind becomes apparent: that of separating itself from the ideas that it conceives and representing these ideas as if they were independent of its own representation.

(Georg Simmel, 1990: 67–8)

Chapter 1 introduces the theme of mimesis or representation. Mimesis is in fact a label for a vast field of representations which invites empirical and comparative analysis. The legitimating principles of Western mimesis are identified and analyzed as specular metarhetorics informing some of the basic cognitive positions and orientations of our reflective logics. The temptation inherent in the mimetic paradigm is to believe that language 'maps' the world in representations without thereby constituting or transforming its referents. Authorized by this conception of language and world, the speaking subject may 'forget' the partial and limited character of linguistic action and, in certain circumstances, pursue the project of universal depiction (or absolute mimesis). The aporetic idea of universal mimesis underwritten by a correspondence theory of truth sets the scene for Chapter 2. Chapter 1 is divided into three sections:

1 *Mimetic faculties*
2 *Four metarhetorical views of language*
3 *Language-games*

1 MIMETIC FACULTIES

All knowledge is representation.

(Arthur Schopenhauer 1989: 240–1)

'Representation' (from the Latin *repraesentare*) is a complex, almost mythical, word with innumerable functions in a diverse range of discourses and cultural practices. In the dominant philosophical tradition of the West, however, the concept of representation has been overdetermined by a powerful mimetic cosmology of *original presence* which now defines the word's pragmatic grammar. The hegemony of presence, it should be said, has a complex verbal

55

and social history which we will ignore for the purposes of this introductory study. In varying – and often quite hetereogeneous – ways both the Hellenic and the Judaic streams of European thought privileged the temporal mode of 'present being' and correlatively the paradigm of *existence* as *being-present* and truth as the visible *presence* of existing things: what is actual is lived and experienced in the present (*'Wesentheiten werden in der Gegenwart gelebt'*, Buber, 1970: 64); what has-been but is not-now-present can only be retrieved through semiotic *acts* of imaginary *mimesis* – through the signs and interpretations of belated traces, inscriptions, texts, and graphs; what will-be is projected as a realm of virtualities created by the enigmatic modality of symbolic representation called anticipation. In essence the question 'What is *present?*' is posited as the framing question of all knowledge – 'What *is?*' We thus have a ready-made folk-ontology of lived experience in the tripartite organization of temporal verbs (a schema of 'past-present-future' which orient our thinking toward a linear schema of temporal change in constructing psychological, sociological, and historical models). Once in force this onto-logical schema can function as a deep structure for other discursive representations (and representations of representations – in the shift from 'What *is?*' to the question '*What* is?'). From this point of view representations are artifacts which enable the 'whatness' of what was 'originally present' to speak once again. Thus we might live within the flow of consciousness, but to *say* anything about our experience we must reflect upon and represent its 'contents' through language or an analogous propositional medium. Moreover the very 'desire to say *what-is*' presupposes an older and more opaque 'faculty of mimetic desire' – the desire to recover, symbolize, and stabilize the stream of experience in which anything like an existent might be identified. In contemporary thought it has become conventional to refer to this privileged concept of 'the given' as *pre-sence (pré-sence)* as *logocentrism* (although I will refer more generally to the framework as *representationalism* and its generative motivation as the *mimetic desire* to descriptively capture reality (cf. Girard, 1988).

It appears that logocentric concepts of self, time, world, and reality have *aesthetic* origins: the nature of 'real existence' (*ousia*) is accessed through concrete acts of *perception* just as the 'real existent' is an actually existing thing disclosed to the percipient mind as an intuitive spectacle. We might say that in this seductive ontology the field of the actual is prior to the domain of reality. But upon reflection, we find that the aesthetic 'plentitude' of present meaning is interminably sliding into the past and prefiguring the future. Or, at least, this is what the vital illusion of the schema of presence intimates. Once we accept the metaphorical terms of this 'metaphysics of presence' other 'modes of being' can only be measured by means of 'presentist' existential criteria: what is real or actual is what is present and self-identical before our eyes. In everyday speech, representations are taken to be either true reflections or deformations of the 'nature' of *real presence*. This is where the specular discourse of 'truth' holds its sovereign court. If actuality is a stream of consciousness, and reality is lived actuality and its collective products, then articulations which represent the real as 'object' belong to speech and language. In a more modern idiom, forms of existence – or more generally, modes of existential reference – are knowable only as predicatively *(re)presented* being in truth-making statements (for example, as a cognitive simulacrum in the mind's predicational structuring of the sensory manifold or in the schematic work of the faculty of imagination, *Vorstellungsvermögen*, or even in sentences and propositions which truthfully re-present their 'referents'). But the totality of these mediations do not form a seamless whole or 'mirror of being'. It is evident that ancient mythological images of mimesis – what Jacques Derrida has aptly called the metaphorics of proximity or what Girard terms the mimetic desire – are implicated in these ways of representing representation: a representation is something that stands for an original (the German '*Vorstellung*', 'idea', 'conception', and 'representation' incorporate this world theory in its etymological construction – *stellung* meaning 'position', 'standing', 'rank', 'place', 'referent', etc.), a word is a sign which makes its signifier manifest, art is an imitation of the Idea, Nature, Truth. As we observed in the Introduction this metaphysical model of specular reference and subject-centred reflection, in varying degrees, also invokes a negative model of heteropoiesis: the 'other' and, more abstractly, 'otherness', is projected as the 'agonist' of representation, the unrepresentable beyond the margins of sense (whatever is not *darstellbaren*; we might then speak of things beyond the boundaries of conceivability (*das geht über alle Vorstellungen*)). For many mimetic regimes of desire, then, 'alterity' is simply whatever is construed as falling beyond or resisting the work of mimesis (presence/absence). Thus in the dominant paradigms of modern thought alterity is established by the generative question-grid: *is 'it' a subject, object, or mode of representation?* On the basis of the brief analysis of discursive limits in the Introduction above, we can either proceed within the metaphorical grid of this subject-object framework or, shifting levels of analysis, subject the metaphorics of presence to critical deconstruction. The latter strategy transforms the assumptions of representationalism into a thematic phenomenon for further genealogical investigation.

Understood literally, *representatio* (what Kant called *representation in general*) is a repetition of what was originally present ('presented' for example as the 'data of sensation' or *sensatio* in the terminology of empiricism). In a nutshell: reality as experienced being is a correlate of representation (or of the formal conditions of representation). But Kant also understood that the concept of *representation* displayed several distinct modalities. At a higher or second-order cognitive level, *perceptio* also instantiates a structure of mimetic repetition (videological discourse privileges the intuitive recovery of absent *meaning*). And finally, by further redoubling mechanisms consciousness recovers past objects through strategies of non-intuitive representation (among these 'faculties', the operations of recollective memory and abstract thought are pre-eminent – nostalgia indexing the field of repetitive desire). The work of the *understanding* is thus for Kant a higher-order level of representation a 'metarepresentation' of the structure of perception through concepts; and, finally, cognition deriving from *reason* is the representation of the 'data' of the understanding on the basis of universal principles, to *comprehend* an object or gain an 'insight' into a thing (1992: 466). In the so-called 'Jäsche Logic', the stratification of representation is explicitly explicated as a general model of cognition in general:

(i)   the lowest degree of cognition is '*to represent* something';
(ii) the second degree is to represent something with consciousness, *to per-ceive (percipere);*
(iii) the third level is *to be acquainted* (noscere), defining something in terms of similarities and differences;
(iv) the fourth level is to be acquainted with something *with consciousness (cognoscere) (Kant comments that animals are acquainted with objects, but they do not cognize* them);
(v)   the fifth level, is to *understand* something (*intelligere*), the work of the understanding, subsuming particulars under concepts;
(vi) the sixth level is cognition through reason (*to have insight*) into a phe-nomenon (*perspicere*);
(vii) and the final level, is to cognize something through reason (1992: 569–70).

Yet all of these representational modes are founded upon categories of imme-diacy and presence – a tissue of metaphors represented in German usage by the term for 'actuality', *Wirklichkeit*. What was once actually present can be relived as a virtual presence and where experience plays into the hands of conceptual representation we speak of objective perception (*cognitio*). From this perspec-tive, cognition is mimesis which desires to 'correspond with' its objects, as an image correctly depicts its original. Thus Kant can strip language of its affective horizons and define a valid concept as an objective representation of a repre-sentation (a definition which immediately precipitates the problems of the general 'form' of representation – in Kant's problematic a thought which takes the mind in the direction of the *a priori*, schematism, the transcendental imagination, subliminal experience, etc.) and the generic question of repre-sentativeness. Yet something like a congealed Kantian framework persists in the folk epistemology which predisposes inquiry to identify a *subject* of representation, an *object* represented, and a *mode* of representation: is 'X' a *subject, object*, or *form*? (self/other/relation; ego/experience/representation; subjectivity/objectivity/exchange; agent/structure/structuration). Even with-out philosophical elaboration it can be seen that the conventions of a metarhetoric lure thought to represent 'representation' (and thereby the whole realm of conceptual and non-conceptual representation) in concrete, videological metaphors (the great ontological divide between the knower (imagined as a disembodied eye) and the known (imagined as an external referent) can only be bridged by transcendentally veridical 'representations': Mind and World are transcendentally related).

I will refer to this generative schema as the videological conception of the world: reflection links *consciousness* and *object* by means of *representation* (as both the process of *re*-presentation and the product, intellectual representations) anchored in the cognitive gaze of the knowing subject. In this chapter I will suggest that the philosophical foundations of Representationalism provide the 'depth grammar' of Western reflective consciousness and, to varying degrees, inform all of the theorizing and model-building constructed in videological space – whether 'materialist' or 'idealist' in its self-description (Husserl's phenomenology with its problematics of noetic-noematic correlates is a distant variation of this schema).

From symbol and thing to signifier and signified

[T]he first thing philosophy has to consider must be the *medium* or form in which *experience in general* presents itself; this *medium* is the *representation* or knowledge. For this reason all philosophy must start with an investigation of the cognitive faculty and of the laws thereof.

(Arthur Schopenhauer, 1989: 241)

Kant, of course, was a resolute critic of a simple copy theory of knowledge and its underlying dualistic model of the autonomous subject facing a pre-existent object. Valid knowledge does not mirror or duplicate a self-standing world of objects; rather, knowledge is an active, mediate representation of sensory experience (a way of *forming* experience which constitutes the phenomenal world under *a priori* modes of representation – *Darstellungsweise*). 'Truth' in this context is an attribute of representational thought. And in Kantian philosophy, human cognitive limits are coeval with the limits of *a priori* mental representation. Thus the faculties of *Sensibility*, *Understanding*, and *Reason* can be understood as three complementary mimetic ways of mediating object and its conception – three 'faculties' for grasping the world in sensory, perceptual, and cognitive *Vorstellungen*. *Representation* in this context is an active faculty of the mind in its quest to know *Realität*. But Kant was sufficiently reflexive to recognize that the ultimate nature and origins of *representation* lay beyond inquiry – that the basic fabric of knowledge always already presupposed the possibility of *re*-presentation. In the Jäsche *Logic* he writes that since cognition always presupposes representation 'this latter cannot be explained at all. The doubling of consciousness is simply accepted as a primary truth'. Otherwise 'we would always have to explain *what representation is* by means of another representation' (1992: 545; cf. 'representation is an elementary expression which cannot be further analyzed', 1992: 485).

Three related concepts are in play here: the concept of a *thing*, the concept of an *object*, and the concept of *representation*. Being restricted to knowledge of phenomenal objects we can only imagine the noumenal thing-in-itself as a regulative Idea 'beyond representation' (acknowledging the aporetic judgement that this 'beyond' is also a phenomenal stucture). As naive ontological realists we think that we have immediate access to things whereas in fact we relate to objects as phenomenal domains constituted by means of our cognitive functions (or as we might say today, by the frameworks of sayability). The mind is not imitative (*mimesis* in its literal sense), but representational (*mimesis* in its dramatic, 'productive', image-forming sense). The 'thing' of common sense recedes into the distance with every act of (re)presentation. This effect of 'recession' – the 'precession of the object' as a kind of echo of transcendence – cannot be rationally determined or eliminated from the Kantian system. Interpreted literally, the 'thing' which knowledge aspires to represent becomes a *regulative* Ideal. In this way the videological coordinates inherent in the ancient metaphorics of 'mimesis' create the problem of *original meaning* and promise a form of 'sublime' insight that transcends phenomenal knowledge (the profane equivalent of 'final meaning'). The ambivalence of Kantian mimesis, of course, originated from a contradictory legacy of metaphysical problems – being and appearance, mind and matter, soul and God. The dialectic between the 'imitative' and the 'dramatic' concepts of mimesis pervade the Kantian problematic. This ambivalence in the concept of the structure of representation enters into the fabric of modern discussions of representation and the 'crisis of representation'.

With the exception of his theory of judgement, Kant provided no explicit theory of the linkages between mental representation and discursive thought. However, recently the mimetic model of the regulative *Thing* and its *signs* has been troped into a structural theory of *linguistic* representation – 'language' is viewed as a symbolic order of propositional representations which organizes manifold object domains into frames of structured simulacra (the prevalence of the structuralist idiom of 'frames of meaning' is symptomatic of this latent Kantianism in contemporary critical discourse). The cognitive limits of individuals and cultures are envisioned as linguistic constraints embedded in the grammar of language. But now the signifier-signified-referent-reality linkage functions wholly by way of relaying the absent into presence by means of unmotivated processes of signification. Kant's a priori faculties have been naturalized into differential sign systems in this linguistic respecification. To borrow Peirce's generic formula: a sign is something which stands to somebody for something in some respect. It is as though the Kantian relays of *sensatio*, *perceptio*, and *cogitio* were redescribed as networks of culture-laden sign systems – signifier/signified chains – or, in a more radical turn of this line of thought, as *decodings* and *simulacra* marking the deferal, and perhaps the disappearance, of the transcendent referent. Whatever can be *experienced* and *thought* is prefigured by the differential matrix of linguistic representation or, more generally, by systems of significations (an analogous move can be found in the Fregean analysis of sense and reference). Even the subject of knowledge is now situated within a network of signs. This semiotic reduction, taken to its performative extreme, produces hyperbolic arguments of the type: 'Simulacral systems determine the conditions of the (im)possibility of generic reference and intelligibility' (or its Fregean analogue: 'Propositional "senses" constitute the possibility of "reference"'). Whatever 'we' can know of experience, whatever can be accessed as referential, is always-already mediated by semiotic systems (objects are constituted as meaningful in the context of semiotic structures). Reference to the 'world' is always a shorthand expression for the 'world-as-represented' or the world 'from this mode of presentation'. One of the main differences between Kantian epistemology and structuralist semiology, however, is that for the latter there is no escape from the infinite play of representations – every stable point of origin, including the transcendental subject, being itself a locus of representations (and more complex and stratified 'representations of representations'). 'World', 'Nature', and 'the Transcendental Ego' are now officially drawn into the play of either simulacra or the semantic systems of language: every 'origin', 'identity', or 'referent' is enmeshed in the interminable play of semiotic differences. The Kantian doctrine of sublime transcendence is replaced by the idea of the infinity of signification. Yet in this sea change, the generative metaphorics of representationalism remain intact.

To speak of '(re)presentation', then, is immediately to invoke an antithesis: on the one side the foundational dream of unmediated *presence* (an *'analogue'* pole of mimetic vision, intuition, *Anschauung*, causal knowledge placing the mind in touch with the thing itself as an exteriority unmediated by representation, intention, or social context), on the other side, the recognition of socially productive semiotic mediation in every process of representation (the 'digital' pole of laminated signifying practices, difference in identity, the semiotic in every symbolic unity). Where the former orientation treats mimesis as an unproblematic 'window upon the world', the latter orientation views mimesis as a rhetorical action of world disclosure. To borrow an expression from Hans-Georg Gadamer: 'Being that can be understood is language'. The tension between these two models of representation has been expressed by Jean Baudrillard as follows: 'Whereas representation tries to absorb simulation by interpreting it as false representation, simulation envelops the whole edifice of representation as simulation' (1983: 25). Thus alongside the ancient mimetic paradigm of knowledge as a nexus of necessary causes governing the order of things, we have an alternative model of knowledge as the rhetorical reading, deciphering, and interpretation of text-like formations. We thus uncover a homology between these two paradigms of mimesis and the distinction between unmediated reflection and mediated reflexivity. For the latter paradigm everything original is already a cultural representation (there is no experience that is not 'always-already' organized in and by 'writing' (in its generic sense of inscription); 'objects' are accessed in and constituted by (con)textual practices. Furthermore by making this 'Gestalt switch' from a reflective to a reflexive understanding of language and inquiry we can approach the logics of reflection themselves as limited modes of self-reflection (the idiom of the subject as 'reflective consciousness' is the product of a persuasive language-game).

It would certainly be useful to have something like a unified field theory of simulacral action (a theory of articulations where networks of discursive representation would form subdomains and cognitive 'representations of the world' further subsets). However, in lieu of this Grand Theory of Representation it will suffice here to distinguish four categories of simulation. We can refer to these as *cognitive, symbolic, political,* and *aesthetic* mimesis. In reality, of course, each form is embedded in characteristic clusters of metaphors, narratives, and graphic and verbal practices bearing upon the identity of the self and the question of how thought can be said to reflect the world. And in everyday practices many systems of articulations are typically multi-layered formations (admitting further orders of metarepresentation) and hybrid formations (conflating different media and modes of representation). This is particularly true of linguistic, aesthetic, literary, and theoretical modes of reference where intertextuality and metarepresentation are normal features of 'first-order' praxis (multichannel communications, the play-within-a-play, the interplay of reflexive genres, cultural uses of dramatic irony, etc.).

Cognitive mimesis

First, the idea of cognitive representation presupposed by the so-called *correspondence theory of truth* or more broadly by epistemological models of mental images, appearances, and ideas 'before the mind's eye'. To condense a whole philosophical tradition into a phrase: representation is a process of 'making present', the act of bringing what was absent 'into presence'. Here the faculty of representation is one of *ideational replication* of an original. Thus the representational theory of perception asserts that the immediate object of perception is not 'the real object', but an idea, *idée*, image, or *Vorstellung* of the original thing. Ideas are 'internal simulacra' or, as computational theorists say today, 'internal representations' of 'external objects': ideas are mental replications. And 'object in general' is theorized as 'anything subject to the logic of representation' (a metaphysical perspective generalized from the sceptical schema '*it appears to me that p*'). From the standpoint of this 'philosophy of representation' reality becomes an abstract image, like a photographic 'reflection' (Hume's 'source' of impressions, Locke's 'ideas of things without'). However, the analogy with photographic representation is as misleading as the earlier metaphor of the *camera obscura*. In the photographic image we have a physical process where reflected light from an object is causally 'traced' upon a light-sensitive medium rather than a situation of *symbolic* representation which involves a code or abstract system of simulacral rules. The photograph is quite literally a sensuous *light inscription* (the German word is *Lichtbild* or light-writing) and as such is qualitatively different from both preindustrial and postindustrial forms of visual reproduction.

In the tradition of empiricist metatheory both 'inner idea' and 'external natural thing' are posited as unproblematic referents, original 'presences' without further elaboration or jusification: being is simply the stream of ideas, identified quite literally as conceptions of being. Thus for those socialized into the videological idioms of Renaissance perspective and post-Reformation scientific discourse to speak of 'truth' is invariably to think in quasi-perceptual terms of natural – typically visual – referents and their isomorphic *imagos*: the formal correspondence between name and object, word and thing, statement and state-of-affairs, signifier and signified, Language and World. The depiction of 'Nature' as an external world of 'sensible objects' by methodic means of representation is commended as the sole path to rigorous knowledge. To generalize the essential point: the limits of the possibilities of representation are thought to coincide with the limits of our knowledge of physical objects as privileged referents of the real. Like a photograph, the true mirror of objective knowledge would ideally reflect reality as a perfect copy captures its original. Unfortunately the specular figure of truth as statements which correspond with external reality can only be expressed in symbolic discourse. While the surface rhetoric of representationalism invariably leads research toward psychological investigations, its underlying metarhetoric leads back to logic and language. In fact the generative concept of language as a 'mirror of nature' is only intelligible within the fictional coordinates of deeper specular metaphors. Furthermore, as we have seen, such mirroring 'correspondences', 'representations', 'imitations', 'simulacra', '*Vorstellungen*', 'reflections', 'pictures', and 'iconic images' are all exemplary domains of textuality – indeed the grammatical pictures created by these ancient metaphors constitute the imaginary thought worlds of videological culture.

Where the surface rhetoric leads inquiry upon a quest for ideas within the mind's cognitive processes, the depth rhetoric leads back to the construction of the rhetorical concept of 'idea'. We are reminded that to identify the work of *mimesis* in any mode of objectivity is to disclose the ineradicable work of symbolic relations in the reflexive strategies of selfhood. In more institutional terms, cultural systems and social mediations are banished by Representationalism only to return unacknowledged within the specular rhetorics of scientism.

Symbolic mimesis

We may, of course, modernize the eighteenth-century discourse of cognitive mimesis and think of representation not as a mode of iconic veracity or imitation but as a *symbolic relation*: signs symbolize rather than picture a signified; here *semiosis* involves a *conventional* modelling of some domain of reality utilizing a code of simulation or symbolic notation that has usually been

63

effaced in the positivity of its effects. This critical revisioning of representationalism has preoccupied many of the philosophical traditions of the late nineteenth and twentieth century. The putative iconicity of pictorial, diagrammatic, photographic, and visual representation is abandoned in deference to the cultural conventions and rules of 'semiological realism'. This, of course, might be considered as an internal consequence of the radicalization of Peirce's category of the *symbol* as a sign 'which refers to the object that it denotes by virtue of a law, usually an association of general ideas, which operate to cause the symbol to be interpreted as referring to that object'. In the context of traditional semiotics signs are said to 'stand for' the object symbolized (in the Latin formula – *aliquid stans pro aliquo*: the Father 'stands for' the Law, the Cross 'stands for' Christianity). To represent something symbolically we draw upon salient public conventions and symbolic systems in terms of which experience can be reordered and communicated. But with the discovery of generic simulation in the nineteenth century the specular idea of 'inner representation' (Locke's doctrine of reflection as 'internal sense') is replaced by the dialogic field of interminable semiosis and decoding. The mind no longer 'pictures' the external world; it signifies Being.

With this shift we may speak of mimetic *faculties*, a continuum ranging from concrete analogic perception to abstract digital forms of thought. Each point on this continuum of representational capacities, however, presupposes what Walter Benjamin called 'the phylogenetic significance of the mimetic faculty' – the historical self-humanization of a language-using species through a diverse range of mimetic projects ('On the mimetic faculty', in 1979; also cf. Taussig, 1993). Unlike the tangible icon of traditional thought, symbolic representation assumes different degrees of abstractness or 'constructedness' depending upon the nature of the relation of 'standing-for' and available media of representation – perhaps along the Peircian continuum of Icon, Index, and Symbol. For example, only with the availability of literate technology can the book of Nature be deciphered and read rather than seen and perceived as an originary presence.

We might say that symbolic mimesis signals the decay of the referential view of language in deference to the idea of graphicity and simulacral hyperreality: the fundamental coordinates of all that can be known and thought derive their functions from prior forms of *inscriptive signification* – what Soviet semioticians call *modelling systems* but what might be better termed *textuality*. By reflecting upon the symbolic moment within the referential desire we come upon the hermeneutic problematics of *reading as active graphic translation*: modes of representation, interpretation, and imagination are not sensory facsimiles but productive practices drawn from a general economy of signification. Thus Benjamin speaks of language as an 'archive of non-sensuous similarities, of non-sensuous correspondences' (1979: 162). Marcuse describes aesthetic mimesis as 'representation through estrangement, subversion of consciousness' (1979: 45). McLuhan, Innis, and Baudrillard analyze the modern media as constitutive social processes. And Peirce insists that 'every assertion must contain an icon or set of icons, or else must contain signs whose meaning is only explicable by icons' (1960: 11.158).

One very important group of problems relates to the language-games of *imaginative representation* as *secondary modelling systems* (or as we would say, the fictional strategies and conventions of textual representations engendering the *effet de réel* current in a particular culture). Representations understood as texts index a heterogeneous spectrum of active rhetorical practices and sociotechnical processes constructing what passes for reality (consider the range of 'imitations' which function as representational heuristics: appearances, images, icons, portraits, masks, disguises, dissimulations, caricatures, photocopies, drawings, diagrams, maps, working models, mock-ups, illustrations, typifications, abstract symbolisms, mathematical formulae, musical notation, codes, code books, pictures, money in the form of bank notes, cheques, theories, lures, fictions, texts, recordings, etc.). Analogous complexity arises when we introduce changes in the technical *means* of representation (mechanical, chemical, electronic, analogue, digital, etc.) or when we consider *intertextual* and *intratextual* translations within and across cultures. Each of these categories of symbolic practice and mediated information raises questions that require extended logological investigation.

Once the older, theocentric Word-World relation is grasped as a complex of conventional activities we see that all 'reference' is already structured through complex sociosemiotic media (tactile, visual, verbal, scriptural, kinesic, physiognomic, etc.). Indeed from Aristotle's *Poetics* to the *Modistae* of the Middle Ages and Magritte's '*Ceci n'est pas une pipe*', theorists of mimesis have differentiated between 'means', 'modes', and 'purpose' in mimetic productivity: the material and means available to an artist, the 'angle' or aspect of imitation, and the informing intention of representation. But once these 'material' and 'social' dimensions of mimesis are admitted the creation of knowledge cannot be approached as a simple pictorial relation, but begins to be respecified as the outcome of laminated networks of human appropriation, text processing, and rearticulation. Classical mimesis secretes its own rhetorical metatheory which leads beyond the terms of pictorial depiction to the realm of infinite semiosis. Considered as suasive speech acts (re)presentations are the product of specific symbolic praxis and must be analyzed in rhetorical terms: *who* produced these (re)presentations? Through what *codes*? From *what* media? *How* were the materials organized to communicate their effects? In what *context* and settings did communication take place? For *what* purposes? To *whom* where they communicated? *How* were they interpreted and used? And so on. As Paul Feyerabend observes: 'Imitation is a complex process that involves theoretical and practical knowledge (of materials and traditions), can be modified by inventions and always involves a series of choices on the part of the imitator' (1987: 130)

65

Political mimesis

Third, representation can be defined in the language of *surrogacy* and *consensus*. Here ethical and political meanings are typically conflated in definitions of the space of public representation. A representative Subject in this sense is typically someone standing for, speaking for or going proxy for another person, group, body, society, or nation – someone taking the place of another as his or her deputy, someone reciting another's words, someone performing a script ('no taxation without representation'). Unlike the direct democracy of the classical polis, modern political regimes presuppose double representation: to plead a common cause, a collective grievance or injustice and to pursue remedial action involves (i) a consensual representation of the 'objective situation' and (ii) a shared surrogate voice articulating, speaking for, and leading a collectivity to change its situation within a predefined political arena. In the liberal-bourgeois ideology of representation the delegate must be representative of the group's values, interests, and aspirations. Often the 'political subject' is elaborated in the fictions of a universalizable individual agent, party, or collective Subject (typically these are conflated in the flexible category of 'nationhood' or some functionally equivalent idea of 'populist' identity such as the 'people' or the 'public' as a collective subject defined by the possession of rights or 'freedoms'). In formal terms, citizenship is defined as a community founded upon the universal political equivalence of rational agents. In practice, of course, this abstract rule is given a more specific content in terms of more local *representability criteria*: property qualifications, gender attributes, social status, and so on. Those who fall beyond representation or who are deemed to be incapable of voicing their own desires and interests ('non-rational' subjects, the mad, the propertyless, criminals, children, women, slaves, etc.) are either excluded from the sphere of political responsibility or are 'spoken for' by the principial Subject. In most liberal-democratic systems in the nineteenth century, for example, 'men of property' were seen as the natural representatives of 'their' women, children, employees, and servants. Thus in both theory and practice modern democratic surrogacy involves the universal metaphorical substitutability of 'individuals' in representative forums, their ideal equivalence and generalizability for the purposes of the transfer and use of power (to be 'one of the people', to accept the identity category *citoyen*', 'citizen' as an abstract equality before subsumptive Laws in an idealized Republic). Mimetic metaphor thereby becomes the generative ground-rule of modern democratic discourse and a logological principle of modern political order.

Of course different types of exemplary surrogacy and forms of subjectivity appear in different political cultures – for example, the important differences between delegated decision-making and delegated authority to act independently of those represented; passive and active surrogacy; deferred 'trusteeship'; 'individualist' and 'collectivist' interpretations of representative participation; and so on. Many of the central conflicts in modern political

theory are essentially disputes about legitimate and illegitimate political identification and concomitant power-sharing (debates about the nature and
guarantees of political 'subjectivity', mechanisms for the delegation, division,
and 'transfer' of power, disputes over the precise nature of representation and
representative government, ways of elaborating and changing the selection of
agents of representation and constitutions – the role of written charters embodying civic rights and duties, the status and symbolic embodiment of rights
in civil constitutions, self-images of civic order, systems of 'participatory
democracy' or 'proportional representation', institutionalizing accountability,
national identity, etc., the appropriate organs for defining legitimate interests,
integrating private and public interests, and so forth (Williams, 1983: 110–27;
cf. Held, 1987: Ch.9; Bellamy, 1992; Pateman, 1989: ch. 1; Wagner, 1994:
ch. 6)).

Aesthetic mimesis

If we can speak of the mimetic grounds of representative democracy congealed
in practices and institutions, we can also speak of a mimetic conception of
representation embodied in the institution of art. Both processes involve
violence and wider processes of 'subjection' – as the construction of the
'subject of representation', as incorporation, and as exclusion. In fact the
modern idea of representation is often defined in aesthetic terms as the *imaginary imitation*, depiction, portrayal, dramatic impersonation of pregiven
objects. Two opposed views come to mind. The first holds that art is powerful
because it formally represents the way things are. The second, in the wake of
Platonic aesthetics, holds that the work of art is a secondary, distorting image
of things. The images created by mirrors or portraits (classical mimesis) or by
photographic or electronic processes (modern mimesis) are often cited as
evidence on either side of this debate. Of course the word 'image' is polysemic
and our dominant idea of 'artistic mimesis' is skewed in the direction of literal
depictions of a pre-existing world of things. Treated more generally, however,
we can say that the sphere of artistic representations includes symbolically
coded articulations concerned with the production of aesthetic values – a vast
range of practices drawn from literary, architectural, pictorial, photographic,
musical, and plastic arts. The dominant mimetic ideology holds that imaginary
meanings mirror nature or social life (thus fiction's work is defined as the
picturing of everyday reality, metonymically simulating 'the reality of society
and nature'). To speak of realism in one of its many senses is already to invoke
a binarized adversarial economy – historically rooted in the two-world metaphysics of Greek ontology. Indeed the lexicons of *reflection, representation,
reality*, and *truth* (for example, the powerful ideological connotations associated with the German word *Darstellung* symbolizing both representation and
presentation as an 'unveiling display' or the English words *objectivity* and

67

objective truth) have often been treated as universal, non-specific terms: *objectivity is an impersonal, revelation of Nature.*

Yet it is apparent that even 'light-writing' is not a passive reflection of the facts, but a selective *reproduction* of its original by a situated imitator. The putative objectivity of reflection has its historical origins in the Renaissance universalization of pictorial systems as ideal vehicles of truth and objectivity (Leonardo, Alberti, Vasari, and others). As a metatheoretical rhetoric, however, universal Representationalism triumphed in Western culture as late as the Enlightenment upon the ruins of localized regional practices and vernacular discourses (although mimetic conceptions of reason and understanding have dominated European culture for a thousand years before this period). This is the important point made by Fredric Jameson in emphasizing the changing social functions of the idea of 'representing Nature' in order to 'save the phenomena':

> in different historical circumstances the idea of nature was once a subversive concept with a genuinely revolutionary function, and only the analysis of the concrete historical and cultural conjuncture can tell us whether, in the postnatural world of late capitalism, the categories of nature may not have acquired such a critical charge again.
>
> (1988b: 142)

It might even be claimed that mimetic realism in its different species has become the hegemonic ideology of Modernity against which all other epistemic competitors are measured. The privilege of holding a mirror up to nature is thus not a neutral standpoint of the objective observer, but the ideological outcome of a long and tangled social history. Reflection upon the Real in our culture has become an important criterion of truth, or at least of the concept of *truth* as correspondential fidelity to 'the facts' (or what is thought to underlie and generate the surface facts). In particular the idiom of scientific reflection has appropriated the concept of correspondential truth so that all possible 'non-representational' competitors are predefined as deviations from this norm (the emergence and evaluation of artistic movements is implicitly structured by way of contrast to the Mimetic tradition of representational works of art: Symbolism, Aestheticism, Impressionism, Expressionism, Surrealism, and other *avant-garde* movements, Magical Realism, etc.). And in keeping with this underlying logic, academic social science disciplines invariably present their case in representational metaphors: 'Sociology deals with a factually observable subject-matter, depends upon empirical research, and involves attempts to formulate theories and generalisations that will make sense of facts' (Giddens, 1986: 3). In this perspective, reflection is reduced to our three familiar elements: object (a factual world 'out there'), subject (inductive cognition), and means (causal generalization about the factual order of things).

Representationalism: language, reality, and representation

To draw these disparate observations together. The concept of 'representation' is obviously enormously complex and difficult to condense into simple formulae. However, representationalism can be defined as an ideology that stresses the privileged nature of mimetic depiction in everyday life, art, science, and philosophy. For all of these practices knowledge is a truthful description of reality. As an ideological outlook Representationalism has four essential components: (i) *Foundationalism*, the faith in a secure ground of knowledge articulated on the basis of a valid methodology, (ii) *Correspondence*, where truth is defined as the 'fit' between Language and World; (iii) *Objectivism* (or Metaphysical Realism) which posits the existence of three-dimensional 'solid things' linked by relations of causation; and (iv) *Objective Meaning*, where the stability and coherence of 'objective reality' (including the identity of things, language, and selves) is the ultimate measure of propositional truth and guarantor of the legibility of the Real (the ethic of verisimilitude). These elements are configured in the hegemonic signifying practices of modern cultures that derive their principles from metaphysical codes of realist narrativization (for example, in the valorization of representational works of art). We are, of course, referring to the underlying grammar of reflective world orientations.

'Reason', 'reflection', 'correspondence', 'foundation', 'objective unity', 'being', and 'narrative' are polysemic terms with complex histories and social functions requiring careful deconstruction and empirical specification. A radical questioning of any of these elements destabilizes the other parts of the closely integrated network, revealing their underlying code as a generative metanarrative. *Reflection* has been used in its plain ideological sense of *mirroring*, *picturing*, or *photographing* an independent reality (in a continuum of senses from relatively loose everyday metaphors of language reflecting objects to more technical senses in which language appears as a structure of representations, an assertoric or apophantic machinery – for example in the so-called picture theory of meaning deriving from Wittgenstein's *Tractatus*) and in its more Hegelian sense of thoughtfully *mediating* and even *modelling* reality. When scientific objectivity is understood as a complete description of the world we are invariably subscribing to a representationalist frame of mind. Similar considerations hold for the 'reality machineries' at work in other cultural spheres today. We are well aware of the seductive simplicity of the Tarski criterion of truthful speech and the equally seductive attractions of a truth-functional logical machinery for stratifying propositions into epistemic and non-epistemic statements (in everyday experience we tend to be inveterate Tarskians correlating our speech directly with the world). We also see how close the spirit of modern Formalism is to the ideology of realism as a representational *anagnorisis*. Both are committed to the elimination of non-representational difference, non-cognitive subjectivity, and vernacular sociality from their cognitive projects.

69

The aesthetic reflection of the world: Lukács' 'representational aesthetic'

An illuminating example of an epistemological position playing upon the ambivalence of *mimetic depiction* and *narrative mediation* can be found in Georg Lukács' essay 'Art and objective truth', which begins with the strident claim that aesthetic knowledge of the Real is the exclusive prerogative of the great realist novels within the classical European bourgeois literary canon:

> The goal for all great art is to provide a picture of reality in which the contradiction between appearance and reality, the particular and the general, the immediate and the conceptual, etc., is so resolved that the two converge into a spontaneous integrity in the direct impressions of the work of art and provide a sense of an inseparable integrity.
>
> (1970: 34)

In Lukács' realist aesthetic only the totalizing narrative realism of the bourgeois epoch from around 1830 to 1890 can fulfil the strict requirements of aesthetic objectivity, avoiding the error of 'naturalism' and other 'degenerate' variants of 'photographic naturalism'. Only Realist fiction exemplified by the narrative texts of Balzac preserves the great tradition of classical *mimesis* as the essential framework for a 'rational' and 'total' knowledge of the capitalist epoch and its conflicts. For Lukács, as for Aristotle who inaugurated the tradition, art is a mode of *mimesis*, a mirror of life or reflection of material reality with its teleology of eventful beginnings and determinable outcomes. By definition, 'genuine art' – instanced by the Balzacian novel and the developmental *Bildungsroman* – takes its place alongside science as one of the great organs of epistemic representation transmitted with the bourgeois legacy. Fiction is a mimetic organon governed by objective criteria of cognitive adequacy analogous to science. Ironically the most playful and carnivalesque art-form – the European novel – is appropriated as the vehicle of the spirit of totality in its narrative will to reflect reality *as it is*. Lukács uncritically adopts Hegel's insight that the novel is the bourgeois epic: 'great literature' with its typological fidelity to the facts is one of the indispensable modes of the will to knowledge by which the human mind reflects the different objects and structures of 'external' reality:

> The work of art must ... reflect correctly and in proper proportion all important factors objectively determining the area of life it represents. It must so reflect these that this area of life becomes comprehensible from within and from without, re-experienceable, that it appears as a totality of life. This does not mean that every work of art must strive to reflect the objective, extensive totality of life ... The totality of the work of art is rather intensive: the circumscribed and self-contained ordering of those factors which objectively are of decisive significance for the portion of life depicted, which determine its existence and motion.
>
> (1970: 38–9)

Today, of course, the adjective 'correctly' is tainted with the malign influence of Zhdanovism which, from around 1934 (at the Soviet Writers' Congress), imposed 'socialist realism' as the only 'politically correct' form of artistic 'reflection' of an extra-textual reality. The Party – in practice, the General Secretary – decides what can or cannot 'correctly reflect the intensive totality of life' (and which groups and artistic communities assist or detract from the revolutionary transformation of society). Lukács' idealization of narrative verisimilitude anticipates the authoritarian ideal of politically correct art: 'The objectivity of the artistic reflection of reality depends on the correct reflection of the totality.' The criterion of correctness in this context is both a cognitive and a political ideal: 'the detail ... is an accurate reflection of life when it is a necessary aspect of the accurate reflection of the total process of objective reality'(1970: 42–3). However, beyond citing the endemic struggle between classes as the totalizing economic principle of capitalist society, Lukács cannot supply a satisfactory rule or procedure by which the essential 'particular' can be assembled so that it emerges as an integral part of a whole (ironically the novel's literary conventions and reflexive structuration must, so to speak, be disciplined or occluded in order to follow the fragmented fault-lines of the class struggle); in place of such self-reflection, in works like *The Historical Novel* and *Studies in European Realism*, he offers a tautological principle of homology in the form of the 'objective necessity' of linkages between aesthetic and social 'levels' and an exhortation to totality by resorting uncritically to a principle of organic expressivity ('The detail must be so selected and so depicted from the outset that its relationship with the totality may be organic and dynamic. Such selection and ordering of details depends solely on the artistic, objective reflection of reality. The isolation of details from the general context and their selection on the basis of a photographic correspondence with reality imply a rejection of the more profound problem of objective necessity, even a denial of the existence of this necessity. Artists who create thus, choose and organize material not out of the objective necessity in the subject matter but out of pure subjectivity, a fact which is manifested in the work as an objective anarchy in the selection and arrangement of their material'(1970: 43).

This might be termed 'Lukács' *aporia*': how the novel as a product of a specific set of literary conventions can be both a determined instance of the social totality but also transcend its circumstances to grant concrete universal knowledge of the historical totality to which it belongs. Lukács contradicts his own Spinozan premises by asserting that there is more in the *effect* than in the *cause*: the surplus is called 'art' or 'great literature' and becomes the only source of literary value ('only the major realists are capable of forming a genuine avant-garde', in Bloch *et al*, 1977: 48). Clearly the problematic analogy between the literary text and the perspectival space of Renaissance depiction cannot support such a heavy burden of artistic homology and objective causality (a problem which is 'resolved' by Lukács' sophistical resort to figures of reflection at textual nodes where a more critical analysis of his own presuppositional metaphors and metaphysical principles is required). Without this critique, Lukácsian aesthetics becomes an extension of 'the bourgeois metaphysics of totality'.

From this extreme instance, we can see that Representationalism is not an ideology in a secondary, contrived sense. It has entered the fabric of social reality and informs many of our everyday schemes of interpretation in aesthetic, cognitive, and political spheres. The logic governing the 'reflection of reality' has colonized the material structures and cultural spheres of contemporary everyday life. Realist narrative forms have literally become part of the mythical fabric of contemporary culture – perhaps its 'natural view of the world'. Yet once their rhetorical conventions are recognized as forms of cultural production they become topics for a deeper and more reflexive social critique. To deconstruct the logics of representation, as we propose to do in what follows, is not merely to probe the 'myths of contemporary social reality', but to problematize the social processes by which a specular reality is constructed and reproduced (how 'the real' acquires its quotidian stability and identity as a background resource for a whole range of mundane and professional representational practices).

In the history of knowledge systems we can isolate three levels of reflection on representations. The first is well known in the history of science and occurs when different paradigms are in dispute about their conflicting concepts and interpretive frameworks; the second appears with major cognitive shifts in world-views and metarhetorics of representation – here the basic 'rules of the game' and conventions of representation are placed in question; and the third – and most radical – arises when the project of mimesis itself is questioned, when, for example, the question of the unrepresentable Other becomes insistent. This level of self-reflexivity does not merely question the inductive legitimacy or deductive fecundity of concepts and rules constructed to represent and narrate experience, it questions – as it were, abductively – the value and limits of the sustaining ideology of representation itself (of the hegemonic self-understanding of representational experience). In what follows we shall broach the third level by examining the generative presuppositions and limits of four influential metarhetorics of representation.

2 FOUR METARHETORICAL VIEWS OF LANGUAGE

In the introductory chapter I suggested that every form of theory is a codified desire. And like many realized wishes, a successful theory often forgets its own profane beginnings and assumes legislative and controlling functions. Thus socialized by centuries of metaphysical thought we are uncritically oriented by the desire to explain experience in (re)presentational terms. Sustained by this grammar, the idea of a single privileged representation of the world takes its place in a long history of reality-depicting utopias. But we also know that different representations of self and language are the creative products of social and rhetorical work. Reflection upon a practice creates higher-order categorial objects. And the rhetorics by which language is objectified can be 'looped back' and mapped upon other social practices. It is thus important to distinguish constitutive metaphors from other processes of figuration. This can be indicated by describing the *metarhetorics* of a culture as its *logological matrix* – in the sense that once we have determined the nature of language we are predisposed to accept analogous mapping procedures for other realms of experience. Logological matrices have, as it were, a hegemonic authority over other meaning systems in a society. Each metarhetoric promotes a selective range of linguistic functions as the defining order of communication. As axiologies, of course, these images of communication have no absolute warrants; in fact they are suasive constructs in which social orders conduct some of their most vital concerns and by means of such mappings generate systems of knowledge.

Four such metarhetorical frameworks have been particularly influential, each flowing from a dominant cultural image of language – as Mirror, Instrument, Vehicle, and Energy/Expression. These, of course, are ideal-types and in practice a particular text or practice will be informed by more than one schema of intelligibility. Frequently different metarhetorics will overdetermine different parts of a single text or discourse. In the analysis below I will concentrate on images of language, but suggest that similar considerations extend to the tropes of embodiment and gendered action (images of the Western European body in its social incarnations as Medium/Mirror of the Soul, Vehicle (linking self with self), Instrument (the self as body apparatus, corporeal extension, utensil), or Energy/Expression), the tropes of community licensed by these metarhetorics (for example, the 'representation' of sociation as natural interests, organic order, mechanical system, repressed desire, collective agency, centred action, consensual structure, and so on), and finally the tropes of knowledge and communication (as 'what is knowable and communicable through such figurations'). I leave the full exploration of these phenomena for another occasion.

2.1 Language as mirror

The first metarhetoric gives its conceptual content to the idiom of 'reflection' itself, deriving as it does from the metaphorical image system of mirrors, mirror reduplication, and reflective imitation: *language is a Mirror, reflecting or duplicating antecedent realities (language's work is to name, represent, and mirror the furniture of the world)*.

The presupposed grammatical schema can be stated quite simply: *language reflects the World*. The root analogy here is language (sometimes expressed as 'thought', 'meaning', 'grammar', or 'knowledge') as a *reflector* of an antecedent order of determinant 'real objects' and their essential properties (a view which while stable in its generality, fluctuates considerably in the particular accounts given of the mimetic relation in the Western philosophical tradition). As 'names', words 'mime' the things posited as 'out there' (as modern philosophy says: names designate things). Language is understood as a quasi-spatial iso-morphic nomenclature or *system of names* for things existing independently of speech and human purposes. Speech is conceptualized as a rule-governed sequence of names which identify, designate, and represent objects (and writing is viewed as a system of visible signs that represents vocal sounds – a kind of second-order nomenclature).

Given the monological grammar inherent in this concept of reflection, the problem immediately arises of the relationship between name and object, words and their referents. Classically this is resolved by claiming that while serious speech is a denotative or referential record of things thought, and writing is a facsimile or set of symbols of spoken words, the 'mental life' which these directly symbolize is common to all men (Aristotle, *De Interpretatione* 1.16a3–4). Or in the rhetoric of the text where this idea was first formulated: 'A name, then, it appears, is a vocal imitation of that which is imitated, and he who imitates with his voice names that which he imitates', Plato, *Cratylus* 423B)). Naming as a privileged semantic act becomes the model for all verbal expression (cf. Augustine's *Confessions* and *De Trinitae* for analogous para-digms of the relationship between *'ta en te phone'* and *'pathemata tes psyches'*). Naming is the originary speech act of a solitary self.

Cratylean linguistics: the correctness of names

This double mimesis interpretation of the nature of words and speech is one of the oldest metatheories of communication in the Western philosophical tradition, beginning with Plato's *Cratylus* and the question of whether 'names' are more than conventional signifiers and indeed whether there is 'a kind of inherent correctness in names' that is part of the universal structure of thought or mindfulness (Plato, *Cratylus* 383A–B). At the heart of the Platonic text is the question: *'alla tis an, o Sokrates, mimesis eie to onoma?'* ('but, Socrates, what sort of an imitation is a name?'). Significantly, the *Cratylus* is also the first philosophical text to speak of speech as a mirror of the real (albeit in a playful, ironic manner at *Cratylus* 414C: 'Do you not, for instance, think it absurd that the letter *rho* is inserted in the word *katoptron* (mirror)?' The word *'katoptron'* (from *katoptos*, to be visible, seen), occurs in Aeschylus and Thucydides as a figure for whatever is 'a mere reflection' (equivalent to the Latin word *'speculum'*; see Liddell and Scott, 1964: 423; a *katoptes* is a scout or spy in Homeric Greek). The upholders of the latter view – Cratylus in Plato's dialogue – claim that there is an inherent 'rightness' between signifier and signified, word and object. In a nutshell, the veridical Word (or true speech) is so organized that it reflects the World. True names capture the essence of the Real. Truthful language is a power of descriptive resurrection: it is the medium in which the appearances of the world are mirrored and preserved in a timeless present. Language's vocation – in the idiom of Plato and Aristotle – is to pursue Reality as essence – and formulable essence (*ousia*) is simply the universal unity or Identity which codifies and structures the Real in a tenseless Now. Language is, as it were, not merely significance but nascent science. For

> has not each thing an essential nature (*ousia*), just as it has a colour and the other qualities we just mentioned? Indeed, in the first place, have not colour and sound and all other things which may properly be said to exist, each and all an essential nature?
>
> (Plato, Cratylus 423E)

Behind the idea of the correctness of names lies the concept of truth as the adequation of thought to the order of the real (*realia*). In Socrates' words, since it is possible to say in speech both that which is and that which is not (*estin ara touto logo legein ta onta te kai un*, at *Cratylus* 385B), then 'that speech which says things as they are is true (*logos alethe*), and that which says them as they are not is false (... *os d' an os ouk estin, pseudes*)' (Plato, *Cratylus* 385B). The ontology of this folk-model of language is simple: 'things' (essences) come first; true speech reflects things; writing is a reflection of this reflection; true science corresponds with essence; veridical discourse is an unequivocal, decontextualized, universal algorithm of things. All other speech acts are deformations of reflective discourse.

The language of things

In a fundamental sense an 'Adamic' notion of language as a relation of true naming lies behind the two extreme branches of metaphysical semantics: Platonism and Empiricism. Both tendencies take language to be a truth-telling system that captures original presence in order to (re)present it before the mind's eye. For both Platonism and Baconian empiricism the archetypal modalities of language are *mimetic*: naming, representing, describing, reporting, and judging what is 'the case' that it *is* the case. The elements of the real are reflected in the grammatical elements of language (the underlying metaphor of truth as an *alphabet* of essence can also be found at *Cratylus* 424C–425B). True language contains 'knowledge of things': serious language, in other words, is a literal repository of the essence of things. This Cratylean image of language has often been seen as a product of the Greek alphabet and phonetic writing applied to speech and discourse: 'It will, I imagine, seem ridiculous that things are made manifest *'phainesthai'* through imitation in letters and syllables; nevertheless it cannot be otherwise' (Plato, *Cratylus* 425D). Indeed Socrates concocts a tale about the origins of words in onomatopoeic letters (the letter *rho* expressing motion, *lambda* expressing smoothness, softness, and so on). The theory culminates in the first 'picture theory' of language in the Western tradition: paintings and names 'if correct' picture the objects of the world (Plato, *Cratylus* 430B–E, 431–2 *passim*). The relation between 'names' (language) and 'object' (reality) is one of depiction – names have an 'iconic' relation to their objects (Plato, *Cratylus* 439A):

> if the name is like the thing, the letters of which the primary names are to be formed must be by their very nature like the things ... names can never be like anything unless those elements of which the names are composed exist in the first place and possess some kind of likeness to the things which the names imitate; and the elements of which they are composed are the letters.
>
> (Plato, *Cratylus* 434A–B)

The traditions of Platonism and Empiricism differ in formulating discrepant accounts of how truth reflects the real and on what the 'really real' can ultimately be said to *be* in relation to language. But these are notational variations of the underlying schema of *mimesis* and the pervasive tendencies to break up the real (and language) into its constituent elements using the schema of syntactical relations. The Cratylean account licenses a view of linguistic and philosophical activity as an 'analytic' decomposition of the language of things. In a more modern idiom, language has a constative relation to its subject matter. When true the order of words reflects the order of things. Signs are 'pictures' of things. Once committed to the figures of this metarhetoric instances of language such as statements or descriptions are granted paradigmatic status. Like the dream of Swift's Academicians of Lagado, language's promise is to salvage the thing itself irrespective of the conditions of representation.

Vraisemblance

If we accept the terms of this rhetoric, language is adequate to the extent that it correctly describes the *a priori* order of reality. This defines truth as speech which perfectly reflects 'things as they are': sentences in language are true to the extent that their parts (and perhaps even structure – as in the Tractarian Wittgenstein) correspond to bits of the world. The grounding assumption of this conception of objective representation brings with it other equally fundamental presuppositions about the nature of meaning, self, and truth. For example, consider the implicit ontological commitment of the metaphor of truthful depiction in the correspondence theory of truth: that truth is an account which perfectly corresponds with a static, independent, context-free *In-itself*. Reason demands that we see 'things as they are' separated from all 'contingent' relations and contexts; fiction and imagination formulates 'things as they are not'. Talk about objects and phenomena which actually exist is said to be 'realistic' and 'logical' and this encourages speakers to project modes of speech which thematize objects that 'have no existence' or are 'merely imaginary' as secondary and derivative forms of talk. The amorphous residuum of non-veridical speech is labelled 'fiction' ('fictional reflection', 'myth', 'phantasy', 'metaphor', 'lie', etc.). Only veridical language allows its users to grasp the true order of things.

As a rhetoric Mimeticism elides the irreducible moment of selectivity in the naming/mirroring/mapping image by accentuating the visual ideal of naming as a correct simulacrum of an object. True speech is speech which tells the truth about the Real (or 'nature' as an actually-existing manifold of extended substances) or some subject matter that is accepted as 'real' in this presentist sense; 'the Real' is what all objective observers would accept as existent not by consensus or for pragmatic reasons, but by the force of 'Reality-itself' ('Reality-itself' is what indubitably exists and what knowledge is obliged to reproduce in thought – what actually exists is the totality of facts understood as 'states of affairs' independent of language); and truth's 'aboutness' and 'rightness' can be checked by measuring its fit with the facts by an independent yardstick (independent perceptual evidence, first-person observation statements, expert witnesses, authoritative assessors, verification procedures, and so forth).

Both the enunciator of true statements and the monitor of their verisimilitude is assumed to have a privileged access to the facts of the matter, even, indeed, the undiluted truth of things which enter into protocol sentences as states of affairs. Statements are at base names (however 'complex') and when veridically used, descriptive records of facts. To record facts is to establish descriptions which correspond with phenomenal states. Truth is a property of adequation linking statements and states of affairs. This is also the fundamental reason why the textbooks of modern philosophy – dominated as they are by these semantic and epistemological conventions – are filled with examples of referential truth in the form of physical – preferably middle-size, hard, dry thing-like – entities. Since objects do not spontaneously 'flower' into metaphor, neither should 'plain language'.

In this metarhetoric, representational discourse is talk that can be independently evidenced by reference to facts putatively positioned beyond the operation of sign systems and so independently verified (for example, in the use of eye-witness reports in law courts, in the expert use of scientific instruments, in accepted replicability formulae, etc.). True speech is evidentially warranted speech that fits the structure of the world as accepted by all relevant, competent observers. The in-itself is 'the world perceived', 'external reality', 'the order of nature', 'states of affairs', 'referents', or extensional objectivity assumed to be identifiable and independently referenced apart from human activities of interpretation and temporal practices of discursive constitution. Grasping the truth places the knowing subject in the presence of the world. Constative language is truthful only when it captures the *a priori* truth of things in correct representations. Moreover the in-itself (what talk is 'about') – to function as an absolute term for truthful discourse – must be independent of particular frames of reference and unmodified by cultural mediations and praxial interests. The referential concept of 'aboutness' construed as a trans-

parent relation is a presupposition of this metarhetoric. Typically the fulfilment of this ideal demands that the content of the representation (what speech
is about) be commensurable, that is, translatable from one constative discourse
to another. Fact-stating sentences must be convertible – to use Scholastic
terminology – between languages (or to put this more ontologically, the states
of affairs they depict are valid in all possible worlds). Given these semantic
conditions, true statements are sentences informed by the one true method of
reporting the intransitive objects of the real world. To meet these stipulations
veridical reports must retain their ideality and objectivity whether enunciated
in the verbal conventions of English or Azande. The tropological mediations
of translation and the pragmatic modalities of communication are assumed to
be neutralizable in the same way that contexts can be stripped in preserving
the rule of convertibility. Any incommensurability of translation – in logico-
semantic terms, any lack of meaning synonymy – raises acute problems for this
strong version of veridical representation.

Disinterested speech

The ideal speaker is one who effaces herself from the facts of the world to be
faithful to those facts. Fidelity or correspondence to objective reality is
achieved when the simulacrum captures the truth of the original (when it is
true to reality or, more colloquially, true to the nature of things). Configured
into a universal programme we can derive the unity of speech from the
algorithmic unity of method warranted by the objective representation of the
world. The 'vagaries' of everyday talk are replaced by the rigour of a universalizable method of representation. Today the privileged domain of such
context-free descriptions is expressed by the word 'science'.

Speculation on the Word-World linkage is as old as Plato's *Cratylus* and
brings in its train a complex of metaphysical assumptions which are rarely
explicitly justified or argumentatively grounded; most typically they are presented as the necessary outcome of commonsense realist maxims: 'it stands to
reason that words must be "tied" to things in the world', 'it is obvious that
language captures the real, makes discoveries, assembles findings, references
phenomena', 'we enunciate truthful statements every day of our life', 'I can
only check what I mean to say truthfully by looking at the denotative or
ostensive reference of my meaningful utterances', 'there must be something in
the structure of language which allows it to fit the structure of the world', 'what
else could science be doing but revealing the true nature or deep structure of
reality', and so on. Other metalinguistic paradoxes arise from our reference
above to 'unmediated evidence', uninterpreted 'observation' statements, 'independent yardsticks', 'criteria', 'authoritative observers', and 'consensus' or
conventions acceptable to a community of relevant observers. Each of these
expressions implicitly or explicitly introduces social, hermeneutical, and cultural dimensions of warranted belief which are not themselves justifiable using

the limited resources of the mimetic model of truth. This, of course, is an instance of the aporetic consequences arising when discourse reflects upon its own taken-for-granted assumptions and tries to bring its rhetorical horizon in line with its own stipulative rules: a true representation of the Real would immediately become a universal criterion of absolute speech and thereby undercut its own finite status as one particular figuration of language.

Mimesis and metalanguage

When the order of Reality (Being *qua* presence) is presented as an 'imitation' of some higher order invariance or Essence (as in Platonism), we have a situation of paradoxical double representation: language is a second-order imitation of present objects which are themselves first-order imitations of the really real world of forms and essences. A similar 'Platonic doubling', a mimesis of mimesis, occurs when different 'levels' of discourse are introduced to save the metarhetoric: for example, where 'first-order discourses' literally re-present the world, 'second' and 'third'-order discourses represent the truth of first-order discourse (for example, truthful accounts about the practice of science must fit the ways in which scientific practices capture and reflect their first-level phenomena; mimetic literary criticism must realistically recover the success or failure of literature to reflect and represent reality – metacriticism represents criticism which represents literature in representing the real: 'But true expression, like th'unchanging sun, Clears and improves whate'er it shines upon, It gilds all objects, but it alters none' (Pope, 1878: lines 315–17)). The infinite reticulation of textuality is brought to closure by the terminal light of the Idea, Meaning, or Truth (the unruly reflexivities of figurative language are disciplined by a logic of reflection).

From these vertiginous examples we see that what licenses and animates the stratified figures of language and metalanguage is the founding poetics of this pictorial way of thinking about word and world. Mimetology banishes and yet presupposes metaphorization. Indeed, as we have argued, it is only possible as an ideology of language on the basis of poetic functions ('Language pictures' being its generative poem). But if language is a picture of facts, like every picture it tells a very selective story. Language fulfils its role when it absents itself from the experience it accesses, allowing its users to pass without hindrance through the *metaphoric processes of representing* to the *objects represented*, through *cultural mediations* to a neutral realm of objects, and from these things to their underlying Form or Essence. In this sense, mimetic narrative sustains a mythological view of scientific cognition: *depict the world but on no account disclose the material workings of the language of description and the textual and social conditions of representation.* Apodictic language turns out to be a suasive rhetoric: it strives to place its users in a pure, disinterested relation to objective phenomena but in the process constructs an imaginary realm of facts which satisfy the unconscious semantic stipulations of its grammar.

Perfect speech – an absolutely objective science of a phenomenon – would literally be the transcription of nature's speech; it would be speech which had no need of either a concrete speaker or an audience – let alone the material and cultural mediations of language and textuality; but in enunciating this consequence – from the standpoint of scientific realism – we invoke a position beyond the sphere of representationalism: nature as far as we know does not speak, and a transcription device is necessary for reporting on natural occurrences and events. Language in actual scientific work is an integral part of the work of making sense of observations and experimental interventions. In practice whenever we turn to the facts of nature, we find ourselves reading texts, communicating about complex processes by means of specific frames of reference. The mirror system is itself a product of older diegetic traditions.

By deconstructing mimetic metarhetoric in this way we see that the grammar sustaining this view of language creates a hiatus between word and referent, a void which true statements bridge when they accurately represent the referent. The space between word and thing lends itself to description in visual metaphors – language as *picture, screen, mirror, reflector*, and so on, world as *object, spectacle, face, surface, reality*, etc. Thus to write the history of an event, structure, or configuration is to capture the nature or essence of the phenomena, 'how it really was', 'what really happened', 'how things really looked and felt'. But the worm in the apple appears in the persuasive nature of every account as a 'framed description' within a given system of signs – 'what happened', to be intelligible at all, must be couched in selective semiotic categories, must be coded, narrativized, and told in diegetical terms that are themselves not veridically motivated: living in different communities and universes of discourse means that we choose to make sense of the past by couching our descriptions and explanations in particular discourses structured by definite thematic concepts, schematic orientations, projected addressees, and paradigmatic frameworks. These in turn are indebted to the question-frames and diegetic repertoires available to historical traditions. And, more importantly, the realm of *diegesis* and the rhetorical organization of thought do not remain constant (Genette, 1972; White, 1985). Our vocabularies of explanation change with the changing concerns of our questions and problematics – often in response to revisionary accounts of the past made available by technical and social innovations in our own present. 'World', 'reality', and 'everyday life' no less than 'positron' and 'charisma' are invented categories developed in particular discursive practices.

Thought determines language. And language's essence lies in its translucence before the facts of the world. Language fulfils its vocation when we see the world aright, carving reality at the joints, comprehending the spectacle of things laid out before the sovereign Eye, pinned down with fitting words and propositions. Falsity is a species of error (getting the facts wrong) or misrepresentation (for example, in bias, subjective distortion, failing to 'reflect' correctly the eternal Ideas). Falsity appears where speakers intentionally misstate the nature of the facts. Where an artful misrepresentation defines mendacity, unintentional misrepresentation defines the concept of *error*. The supreme goal of truth-telling discourse (apodictic speech) under this regime is to capture the 'facts', to describe the lay of the land beyond the space of words, to replicate the ways things are in their umediated and pristine facticity. Truthful language – that is, the kind of validated statements found in science – consist of strings of propositions which represent the world as it is independent of inquiry. In achieving true speech the speaker places herself beyond – in our symbolic metaphors, above – the world, occupying a God's-eye perspective toward the facts.

As with a geographical map there are but two orders of relations – one internal to the map, the syntax of its symbols and their inner coherence, and one external, the relation of correspondence between logical and propositional relations and the world of facts (for the nominalist persuasion) or forms and causal powers. In their basic commitment to recover an unmediated reality both nominalist or phenomenalist and realist or materialist versions accept a view of language as world-mapping: whether we formulate the referents in terms of phenomenal data, protocol sensations, sensory particulars, perceptual experience, *Anschauung*, physical things, or real structures makes no difference to the underlying ideal of intelligibility: truth occurs when the facts speak for themselves.

Specularism

The specular world-view posits an Archimedean point of access to the true world, a self-transparent and solipsistic self, and a perfectly translucent social order. In the Platonic and Neoplatonic stratagems which haunt our discourse, truthful language is language which corresponds to a transcendent, otherworldly realm of pure, timeless, eternal Forms. In the Aristotelian tradition, truthful language is language which corresponds to the immanent universality of Forms or natural essences embedded in the different regions of substance (the 'Realism' of the Middle Ages). Both conceptions legitimate the construction of a totalized, impersonal utopia by deferring to the logos of universality – which I will analyze in later volumes under its political equivalent of Logopolis.

Modern reflection revises these ancient tropes as an epistemological infrastructure for its projects of rational scientific description and rational political reconstruction: only science – in its modern sense of methodic research – is considered an appropriate medium for truth since only science incorporates a correct theory of the world. Such practices do not merely 'discover' the world to be real (in the extensionalist sense required by this metaphorics), but more ideologically make the world to be real under the auspices of the descriptive prescriptions of this metaphysical frame of reference. This is the deep reason why modern technoscience is not simply a powerful description of reality, but a powerful institution of the real. Once institutionalized, this way of constituting the world creates the idea of the universe as an independent, extra-cultural domain antedating all praxis. In short, the metarhetoric of reflection sustains the ideological view of language as a mirror of reality informing the social and political practices which make up what we may now call the *videological* conception of the world. Representationalism does not merely authorize scientific practices but more fundamentally legitimates their secular realization (in the civic order of Enlightened Science, the rational Polity, the transparent Society).

2.2 Language as instrument

A second metarhetoric draws its suasive force from an imaginary technics: *language is an organon, mechanism, machine, or instrument of thought.* Subscribers to this view hold that language is a tool of communication and words are its means. Like any other instrument we should not ask, 'Does it represent anything?', but 'How useful is it?' In fine, words are the *tools* of thought. And like tools they should be judged by the work they perform, their functions and role in human activities. The key formulation of this position – like the theory of reflection – can also be found in the Platonic corpus. I refer to the famous statement at *Cratylus* 388A–B where Socrates elicits assent from Hermogenes to the proposition '*organon ara ti esi kai to onoma*' – 'A name also, then, is a kind of instrument': 'Regarding the name as an instrument, what do we do with it when we name? ... Do we not teach one another something and separate things according to their natures?' (Plato, *Cratylus* 388B).

Language machines

Like other instruments – the Platonic text speaks of cutting instruments, boring tools (*trupanon*), and the shuttle (*kerkis*) – language has its range of specialized functions. The instrumental model implies that other tools might work to replace parts of language – and here the criterion for replacement would be largely in terms of utility or use-value (the computer, musical notation, formal languages, image systems, etc. manage certain kinds of information more economically than the resources of natural language). Language is imagined as *an organon of organons*, a mechanism which houses many other instrumentalities, a machine for making machines, a matrix of programmes. And just as older machines and machine parts can be upgraded and replaced, so language is changed and revised by innovative instrumentation. Language is a self-revising machine. In Gilbert Murray's view:

Our language is a biological product for certain practical ends; it is a collection of tools for enabling man to communicate with man [*sic*]. This is not to deny for a moment that in its primary and obvious use, as in prose, language is the greatest of all human inventions, a thing of enormous range and subtlety. But it is capable of a further range of expression, indefinitely wider, subtler, and higher, when used with all its associations and half-meanings and overtones and its accompaniments of rhythm and 'music', as in poetry.

(1927: 255)

As an instrument with a pronounced reflexive capacity language collapses the gap between signifier and referent, consciousness and reality in the same way that a physical tool ignores the dualist *aporiae* of classical epistemology: the person with the hammer, to use a well-hammered example, has no use for the metaphysical oppositions of epistemology. She is intent on the practical work in hand and solves the mind-body problem through the medium of successful praxis. She engages in reflection only when the tool breaks or proves inadequate for the task in hand (incidentally, the figure of the broken tool is Platonic: 'Well then', Socrates suggests, 'if the shuttle breaks while he [the weaver] is making it, will he make another with his mind fixed on that which is broken, or on that form '*eidos*' with reference to which he was making the one which he broke?' (Plato, *Cratylus* 389A–B)).

Before it is a neutral mapping of objects language belongs to human ecology as part of its equipment for living. In Plato's textual imagery it combines both functions: 'A name is, then, an instrument of teaching (*didaskalikon*) and of separating (*diakritikon*) reality, as a shuttle is an instrument of separating the web' (Plato, *Cratylus* 388B–C). Language is a differential organ of reality – differentiating and separating beings (*ousiae*) into their natural orders, weaving webs of significance. In the idiom of Chomskyan linguistics: language is a 'generative procedure that enables articulated, structured expressions of thought to be freely produced and understood'. And language's functions are as diverse as the array of instruments necessary to cope with the world and its multifarious contexts. The tool imagery strongly confirms what we can call the *instrumental-calculative* model of rationality (and rational action). This is close to what Joseph Margolis has called the 'technological self' which admits the praxical functions and constitutive operations of language: 'Wherever we speak of intelligent, purposive, deliberate, rational activity, we speak under the veil of the enabling praxical and technological aptitudes we internalize in coming to be formed as the historical creatures we are' (Margolis, 1989: 61).

Today the perspective which Plato exemplified with shuttles and weaving is most typically given a 'high-tech' gloss by being phrased in the metaphors of the cognitive revolution, computing, and generative grammar. Noam Chomsky provides an example of this way of talking:

The alternative was a computational-representational theory of mind: the mind, using its internal mechanisms, forms and manipulates symbolic representations and uses them in executing actions and interpreting experience. Communication, from this point of view, is no specific function of natural language.

(in Mellor, ed., 1990: 57)

Language's manifestations are simply appearances of deep underlying mental structures and the real object of linguistic study is to uncover 'the inner mechanism of mind' (in Mellor, ed, 1990: 57), in other words 'the inner mechanisms that determine form and meaning' (in Mellor, ed., 1990: 66). It would seem that 'mind' as well as 'language' is an innate tool-like capacity. Linguistic rules are a calculus of functions and linguistics becomes the science of innate mental programmes and genetically determined universals.

Mimetic machines

But despite the pluralism and flexibility inherent in the basic root metaphor and notwithstanding its implicit criticism of purely descriptive models of speech, in its most powerful operations language is still viewed in the traditional conceit of a representational instrument: the paradigmatic 'technology' of language is construed as a mimetic machinery – a propositional calculus or modelling system of the real, a tool that puts its users in touch with the Really Real as opposed to culturally-framed worlds. To return to Chomsky's technical image, language embodies a complex set of skills presupposing innate or at least as yet unknown neural mechanisms (universal grammar). Chomsky is equally clear about the Platonic conception of self presupposed and projected by this view of language. To be a self is to be a person who knows – in a strong universalist sense – language: to know a particular language is to have encoded in the brain a certain generative procedure, an algorithm of the kind that one might program for a computer, which assigns a specific interpretation to every possible linguistic expression. In technical terminology, the encoded computational procedure *strongly generates* an infinite set of *structural descriptions* (in Mellor, ed., 1990: 60). The languaged self is not a subject of desire or *zoon politikon* but a language-acquisition device.

Before language is a *speculum mentis* it is a computational window built from generative structures. While the myth of a pure mirror of the order of things is shattered, the technological myth of a mechanical model filtering the real arises like a phoenix from the ashes. To know a language is to have mastered 'a procedure that determines the structure of that language' (in Mellor, ed., 1990: 61). A mirror – even a cracked or distorting mirror – is, after all, still an instrument of kinds. And once we view language as a tool every act of communication assumes an instrumental aspect.

2.3 Language as communicative vehicle, means, or medium

The third frame of reference models language as *a communicative vehicle, channel, conduit, or transmission system conveying meaning, messages, information, and knowledge: language is a system of signs serving as a means of communication.* In this interpretation, before speech is a mirror of the Real or hammer of facts, it is a medium of *communication* between the speaking subjects. Language is a rule-structured semiotic economy which conveys 'messages' or 'meanings' from speaker to speaker by means of arbitrary signs.

Perhaps the English philosopher John Locke provides the simplest account of this vehicular metarhetoric. In Book III of his *Essay* we are instructed on how words *mean.* 'Words', Locke suggests, are sensible signs invented for the purpose of communicating ideas and thought. Language follows from rather than constituting social life:

> The comfort and advantage of society not being to be had without communication of thoughts, it was necessary that man should find some external sensible signs, whereof those invisible ideas, which his thoughts are made up of, might be known to others. For this purpose nothing was so fit, either for plenty of quickness, as those articulate sounds, which with so much ease and variety he found himself able to make ... The use, then, of words, is to be sensible marks of ideas; and the ideas they stand for are their proper and immediate signification.
>
> (Locke, 1975: Book III, ch. 2)

Words or signs 'stand for' ideas. Signs transfer the thoughts and intentions of one speaker to the mind of a recipient.

In this conception any understanding of language must also involve a range of other complex semiotic concerns: coded 'thought', communication, communicative intentions, grammatical conventions, social practices, institutions, and the like. Metaphorically, language offers itself to the speaker as a neutral medium for transferring messages (Lockean 'ideas') between the minds of sincere communicators. It is a medium for contractually weaving realms of privacy into a public forum. As we now say: sentences *convey* ideas, meanings, messages, intentions, and information between individuals. Language – whether the language of morse code or philosophical prose – is simply another transmission system through which 'sensible' signs and messages are processed and circulated from brain to brain; it carries thought as a pipe conducts water and 'with even less transforming function than is exhibited when a wine-press "expresses" the juice of grapes' (Dewey, 1958: 169). In more hermeneutic variations of the theory language is a persuasive sociosemiotic economy for securing mutual understanding, which is typically interpreted as getting the Other ('individual', 'person', 'brain', 'decoder', 'receiver', 'neural processor') to correctly interpret the intentions 'behind' or 'underwriting' a particular act of meaning, utterance, or symbolic action.

Communication is successful not merely when a message is exchanged but when the sender accurately conveys messages about his intentions to mean, that is, when the receiver accurately interprets the communicative intent informing the producer's ideas, feelings, thoughts, and so forth: communication is as much a metainterpretive exchange of intentions as it is a transmission of discrete, pre-existent messages. The concepts of 'meaning' and 'consciously intended meaning' are closely related in this metarhetoric. Through the sentential strings of language we can formulate and state desires, we can examine beliefs for their coherence, cogency, and truth, we can change our minds through transforming the content of our thoughts. As the slogan has it, language is an arbitrary concatenation of signifiers and signifieds, a rule-governed means of communication and expression, a conventional *medium* of sociality, intentional action, and informational exchange.

Once we introduce the intentionality of symbolic behaviour and the complex coded nature of meaning we leave the world of animal signalling and simple semiotic processes far behind. We move into the convention-mediated world of interpretive interaction and rhetorical practices – which, of course, has no theoretical place in the Lockean paradigm of 'plain language'. Like the mimetic and instrumental concepts of language, the vehicular model entails a definite conception of the self and sociality; in most transmission models, language is simply posited as a homogeneous intermediatory between preformed selves, an economy which circulates information in a pre-established system. Lockean community is composed of individual 'private minds' searching for a transparent semiotic medium in which to articulate and express their private ideas and interests. These conceptions are not usually defended; they perform their ideological work as self-evident premises: 'it stands to reason that communication is the transfer of ideas from one mind (brain) to another'; that 'ideas' are symbols which denote things; and that 'thoughts' are untouched by the colportage of communication. This, of course, is the target of Wittgenstein's criticism of 'private language' theories of meaning and communication in the *Philosophical Investigations*. Its metaphysical character is revealed in the way in which this metatheory of language ignores the prior order of subjectivity, power, and sociality in communication. The aporetic consequences are most apparent in references to unmediated ideas-in-the-head, brains-which-think, reflections-in-the-mind, private languages, neurological processing, and the like. Representationalism continues to live a healthy life within the epistemological frameworks of contemporary linguistics, artificial intelligence research, and cognitive science.

Another variation suggests a more promising hypothesis: speech is the activation of language's semiotic potential, the performative act which translates the rules of *la langue* or the antecedent system of *langage* into actual occasions of signification (*parole*). *Speech acts* are the communicative links between preformed subjects and their meaningful intentions, the *hyphen* connecting self and self, self and world. But even this model of the 'speech circuit' lends itself to the simple diagrams relating abstractly separated Egos in the 'speech circuit' that appears in the opening pages of introductory text-books:

Ego–communication–Alter
Self–signification–Other
Addresser–message–Addressee

Ego transmits thoughts to Alter by translating these into arbitary signs; Alter interprets and understands Ego by reversing the process and decoding the movement from 'sense to reference'. The image suggests a model of communication as transference, conveyancing, transporting, or circulating 'ideas' between two spatiotemporal 'points' in a communication circuit. Like the symbolic equivalent of money in an extended commodity market verbal signs act as a generalized medium of thought exchange. Language becomes the common currency between Ego and Alter, the relay-points in a signifying circuit, where meaning or the creation of understanding is the value flowing through the system. However, the alienation of self and other, self and world, self and language, self and thought still remain constitutive features of this economy: in communicating messages, we translate thoughts from one mind to another, but in no sense do we experience the world through language or have our being in language. Language is social in a derived and superrogatory sense. Like the social contract in the natural law tradition it is an intermediary which conjoins already formed social beings (Ego and Alter are usually supposed to be thinking, feeling, acting individuals *prior* to their entry into the symbolic domain of the language circuitry).

We are faced, in other words, with another fundamentally non-dialogic and dehumanized understanding of language. Language is posited as a formal vehicle for the communication of preformed meanings and pre-existent thoughts. In his Chicago lectures, George Herbert Mead suggested a powerful image for this view of mind and communication. Ego and Alter are like prisoners in solitary confinement:

> The prisoner knows that others are in a like position and he wants to get in communication with them. So he sets about some method of communication, some arbitrary affair, pehaps, such as tapping on the wall. Now each of us, on this view, is shut up in his own cell of consciousness, and knowing that there are other people so shut up, develops ways to set up communication with them.
>
> (1934: 6, n. 6)

The moral of Mead's story is, of course, that this view of communication avoids radical questions of communication even in the act of defining Ego and Alter in communicative terms. It is locked into the Cartesian idea of isolated monads as cognitive atoms faced with the problem of 'relating' to others: 'The process of communication cannot be set up as something that exists by itself, or as a presupposition of the social process. On the contrary, the social process is presupposed in order to render thought and communication possible' (1934: 260). His associate, John Dewey was even more emphatic: the stream of 'ideas' Hume found when he reflected upon the self were a sucession of words silently uttered – 'what made the latter identifiable objects, events with a perceptible character, was their concretion in discourse'. Thus when

> the introspectionist thinks he has withdrawn into a wholly private realm of events disparate in kind from other events, made out of mental stuff, he is only turning his attention to his own soliloquy. And soliloquy is the product and reflex of converse with others ... If we had not talked with others and they with us, we should never talk to and with ourselves.
>
> (1958: 169–70)

The conclusion is inescapable: 'Through speech a person dramatically identifies himself with potential acts and deeds; he plays many roles, not in successive stages of life but in a contemporaneously enacted drama. Thus mind emerges' (Dewey, 1958: 170).

Like the videological model, the economic communicative functions of speech and language presuppose preformed lexical objects and context-independent semantic material (meanings, ideas, communicative contents, intentions, thoughts, etc.) which are subsequently put into circulation in concrete acts of individual communication. To communicate is to *encode, formalize, convey,* and *translate* messages (expressions, thoughts, ideas, intentions, feelings, and so on) to others by means of conventional systems of rules and communicative skills.

2.4 Language as energy, expression, productivity

A final framework derives its inspiration from the magical, expressive, and interpretive powers of language to symbolically articulate, construct, and produce experience: *language-in-use constitutes meaning, thought, knowledge, and reality.* Language is a productive power, a creative energy of expression which predates individual speakers (to borrow the idiom of Wilhelm von Humboldt's Aristotelian term *'energeia'*), a world-creating process in its own right. Human beings communicate their experience only because they have themselves inherited those worlds in acquiring the collective legacy of discourse. Language is an expressive *act* before it is an object. Language precedes human projects and praxis as a prior medium of self-expression and world disclosure. Individuals are primary social creatures who construct meaningful worlds through their symbolic-practical activities. Where other metarhetorics foreground decontextualized reflection and preformed thought, this figure elaborates the figures of *expressive self-production* (Hamann, 1967; von Herder, 1966, 1968, 1969), *authentic communication* (Sartre, 1949), and *hermeneutic praxis* (Gadamer, 1976, 1989; Gillan, 1982; Ricoeur, 1976, 1978, 1981).

One well-known example of this position is associated with the linguistic research of Benjamin Lee Whorf (1897–1941). For Whorf, the syntax of language codifies experience traduced to its distinctive categories and grammatical relations:

> language produces an organization of experience. We are inclined to think of language simply as a technique of expression, and not to realize that language first of all is a classification and arrangement of the stream of sensory experience which results in a certain world-order.
>
> (1956: 55)

It is language which 'speaks' through the utterances of individuals. Another variant of linguistic relativism was popularized by the American linguist Edward Sapir (1884–1939) in his contention that 'Languages are more to us than systems of thought transference. They are invisible garments that drape themselves about our spirit and give a predetermined form to all its symbolic expression' (1971: 221). The combined result is the so-called Sapir-Whorf hypothesis. Language is a realm of unconscious, *a priori* structures: experienced reality is quite literally constructed through the linguistic conventions and verbal habits of a given community. Thus ancient Greek syntax, the Hopi grammatical system, and modern Indo-European languages syntactically position their members in different world-views, definite ways of perceiving and thinking about the world. How human beings experience and conceptualize the world is dependent upon what a community can articulate and grammatically assert, and this is determined by the syntactical and semantic distinctions and constraints embedded in their language. Forms of thought and specific acts of thinking are relative to the lexical and grammatical structures of the 'thinkable' embodied in the webwork of language. Grammar – including the 'grammar' of lexica, morphophonemics, and morphology – imposes very general schemes of interpretation which a community imposes on experience:

> No individual is free to describe nature with absolute impartiality, but is constrained to certain modes of interpretation ... All observers are not led by the same physical evidence to the same picture of the universe, unless their linguistic backgrounds are similar, or can in some way be calibrated.
>
> (Whorf, in Carroll, 1956: 214)

The productive imagery of 'cutting nature up', 'organizing it into concepts', and 'ascribing significances as we do' decisively rejects the mimetic idea of language as a passive mirror of pre-existing objects, a reflective map of independent realities, or a pellucid medium of communication, in favour of a view of language as expressively constituting reality. The deep structures of language predetermine the form and content of world knowledge: 'The worlds in

89

which different societies live are distinct worlds, not merely the same world with different labels attached'. This theory can be called the *linguistic construction of reality: language does not reflect, but constructively produces reality.* For example, as linguistic conventions governing the verbal syntax of 'time' and 'space' interpretively prefigure world experience, so the universe assumes the shape dictated by different tense systems of verbal predication dominant in different speech communities. Literary texts, for example, are not *ersatz* descriptions but articulations of the real organized by the 'schemata' of literary codes and narrative grammars. Taken as a metalinguistic 'hypothesis' the native creativity of metaphoric and fictional language is made continuous with the 'primal' poetry of natural language. Of the latter we can only say 'it thinks'. Yet Whorf's linguistic idealism also risks correcting the reification of existing rhetorics of language as a semiotic mirror, medium, or tool by a 'higher' form of cultural alienation – one in which the links between human reality, consciousness, and language are severed by categorical inflation – by granting language an unconscious expressive logic or one-sided determinism beyond the intentions and purposes of particular users in specific social contexts. 'Thought determines language' and 'language determines thought' are equally undialectical affirmations of a more complex reality. If language's expressive status is left unquestioned we might have to admit the Romantic possibility of a pure or absolute expression or 'productivity' (creating a mirror image of the metaphysical idea of language as pure reflection or absolute representation).

From a more dialectical perspective the framework of linguistic constructivism is typically formulated in the terminology of 'construction', 'constitution', or 'world-disclosure' (and, in more recent rhetorics, 'problematization' and 'structuration'): language is not a mirror of objects existing independently of speakers, it is a productive site of meaning structuration that is already at work prior to the possibilities of intentional action and expressive behaviour. Language absences itself in granting presences. Discourses and textual praxis systematically constitute the objects of which they speak, revealing the world under different descriptive aspects. Objects are always correlates of knowledge, epistemes, or horizons of expectations embedded in linguistic frameworks and universes of discourse. Language both produces and problematizes experience. 'Problematization' being 'the totality of discursive or non-discursive practices that introduces something into the play of true and false and constitutes it as an object for thought (whether in the form of moral reflection, scientific knowledge, political analysis, etc.)' (Foucault, 1988b: 257).

As we might expect, there is also a wide range of variations of this approach, a continuum from the weaker forms of a naturalized Kantian determinism to the more extreme forms of linguistic constructivism and on to genealogy and deconstruction. We can sample several variants from this continuum, relating each 'linguistic turn' to its key expressive orientation and pre-eminent exponents. Language functions as: symbolic form (Ernst Cassirer, Kenneth Burke, and Wittgenstein's *Lebensform*), an arbitrary texture of signifiers and signifieds (Saussure), a second-order signalling system (in Russian/Estonian semiology), semantic fields (Leo Weisgerber and Jost Trier) or grammatical prefiguration (the 'Sapir-Whorf hypothesis'), semiotic structure (structuralism from Saussure to Lévi-Strauss), linguistic codes (Basil Bernstein, William Labov), universal grammar (Noam Chomsky, formal linguistics), vocabularies of motives (K. Burke, C. Wright Mills), definitions of the situation (symbolic interactionism), structures of life-world typifications (Schutzian phenomenology), frames (Gregory Bateson, Erving Goffman, Marvin Minsky), indexical accounting practices (Harold Garfinkel), conversational practices (conversation analysis), constructive work (social and linguistic constructivism, e.g. Berger and Luckmann, 1967; Lakoff and Johnson, 1980), and finally, the Heideggerian notion that language is the 'house of Being', the transmission of tradition (Gadamer, Ricoeur), problematization (Michel Foucault), textuality (Roland Barthes), intertextuality (Julia Kristeva), and *écriture* (Jacques Derrida).

In the strongest programme 'Language' is systematically erased; we cannot identify the essence of language from outside the space of verbally shaped contexts simply because there is no *'hors de texte'*, no vantage point beyond the infinite networks of discourse from which we could approach the essence of language: all articulation occurs 'in' language – especially in the dominant verbal and intertextual practices of different communities of language users. In Heidegger's locution, *die Sprache spricht*. Language constitutes modes of existence by virtue of its intrinsic expressive, semantic, or ontological powers (*energeia*) of differentiation, tracing, dispersion and spacing. In learning to speak we enter a world of objects – whether sensible, perceptual, categorial, or imaginable – that have already been inscribed by signifying practices.

It should also be noted that the older Romantic trope of expression can be given an individualistic, a sociological, or an ontological cast. In some versions it is not individual speakers who 'express' their being in language, but language which expresses and 'means' through human expression. We do not 'use', but are used by our signifying practices. It is not human beings who speak and convey their intentions through language, but language which articulates subjectivity (the Heideggerian, Foucauldian, Derridean, and Kristevan models being notational variants of this general theorem). The realms of discursivity now take centre-stage. The metaphors of constitution and problematization also fault the instrumental and vehicular rhetoric as being still too preoccupied with an ideological dualism of language and pre-existent meanings, intentions and objects, names and things. Rather than language drawing its intelligibility from a pre-existent world of subjects separated from isolated objects or from subjects uniquely informed of their own intentions, our worlds *qua* sociosymbolic worlds become accessible, thinkable, and experienceable only within the polysemic folds of specific languages inscribed in particular modes of social appropriation. This comes close to the logological insight that orders of articulation are correlates of the semiopraxical work of sense-making – that social textuality is the productive site of world-work, and consequently the conditions of truth and reference are to be sought in the dialogical matrices which are typically ignored by reflective epistemology.

3 LANGUAGE-GAMES

Here the term 'language-*game*' is meant to bring into prominence the fact that the *speaking* of language is part of an activity, or of a form of life.

(Ludwig Wittgenstein, 1968: §23, 11e)

At least one other conception of language is presupposed by our schematic itinerary, namely a frame in which these Subject-Object rhetorics themselves appear as topics, the language exemplified in the dialogic work of loosening such paradigms from their concrete instances and textual manifestations, the attitude which appropriates these models as voices in a continuing dialogue about the nature of human reality. This standpoint extends the dialogics of figuration indefinitely: language is the dialogic working of metaphoricity itself (of which Mirror, Instrument, Vehicle and Energy are four influential simulations). The fact that powerful individuals and groups have interpreted the 'essence of language' in the terms of these metaphors leads to a deeper understanding of the role of mimetic desire in society. What sustains the life of inquiry and the open-ended inventiveness of language is the failure of all concepts before an inscrutable world (concepts are constitutively 'inadequate' in their desire to 'name' or 'frame' the nature of the world). The suspicion of the human incapacity to comprehend the world in other than perspectival terms was first formulated by Nietzsche:

Through words and concepts we are still continually misled into imagining things as simpler than they are, separate from one another, indivisible, each existing in and for itself. A philosophical mythology lies concealed in *language* which breaks out again every moment, however careful one may be otherwise.

(1968: 191)

This however, is not nihilism; Nietzsche's remark speaks of the limitation or finitude of our descriptive resources and language-games. But in recent scholarship the argument has been given a more radical and sceptical form by Jacques Derrida who speaks of 'the effect of language that impels language to represent itself as expressive re-presentation, a translation on the outside of what was constituted inside'. It would appear that a powerful metarhetoric leads us at once to think in terms of the correspondence between language and world, but indefinitely defers any such 'consummation'. Derrida regards this paradoxical transposition as one of the basic stratagems of every metaphysical *view* of language:

The representation of language as 'expression' is not an accidental prejudice, but rather a kind of structural lure, what Kant would have called a
transcendental illusion. The latter is modified according to the language,
the era, the culture. Doubtless Western metaphysics constitutes a powerful systematization of this illusion, but I believe that it would be an
imprudent overstatement to assert that Western metaphysics alone does
so.

(1981: 33)

'Language' has no essence – language is no-thing – but contains rhetorical lures
which project essences for itself. On the side of the world: reality is 'posited'
as if it was amenable to our cognitive purposes. But there is no self-standing
'world of truth' independent of discursive practices, just as there is no *being*
of Language, no sovereign Structure or superordinate Function, only more or
less local communicative uses, disparate functions, diverse operations, heterogeneous practices, and historically evolved language-games. Again we seem to
move from a critical analysis of presuppositional metarhetorics to a form of
radical relativism. But even this position is unavailable: we cannot claim
'relativism' as a truth about the world or language. This would lead to the
paradox of imagining a world that was wholly beyond our comprehension –
a thought that is common to the tradition of transcendental inquiry from Kant
to the Tractarian Wittgentsein. Language is neither Mirror nor Lamp, but we
persist in foisting an essence upon the diverse practices of our verbal life and
allowing these images to pre-empt an original experience with language. There
is no 'essence of human language'. All we have are world-disclosing language-
games (*Sprachspiele*) with their disparate 'rules' and 'logics'. It is as if the *Logos*
(like the Heraclitean 'world-play') allows itself to be troped into pictures
which are then turned back upon its workings as naturalized frames, empirical
findings, universal essences. As Hegel once observed, whoever looks at the
world rationally will find that it in turn assumes a rational aspect. The central
idea is that if we are taught to frame experience under such descriptive epithets,
experience begins to assume the hypostatized aspects of the frame's stipulations. Speech is in no respects a *mirror, tool,* or *transmission system* but
ideology would have it so. The institutional effects of these figures, however,
now belong to language's long-durational social history in the sense that they
have been taken up and elaborated in powerful social practices and institutions.

But logological patterns do not 'pattern' without patterning agents in
contexts of semiopraxis. If we act toward our being-in-language *as if* it was an
object, tool, or vehicle then we risk shaping our relationships in these phan-
tasms. Language will continue 'appearing' in such simulacra until we
deconstruct their presuppositional principles. From this perspective what
requires explanation is how and why certain ideals of self-understanding have
become 'second nature': how, for example, it would never have occurred to
thinkers to question the assertions that language is a vehicle of ideas, medium

of communication, or system of differences. Or more prosaically that 'language' is composed of 'words', that every 'word is correlated with a meaning', that 'meanings' are configured into 'propositions', and so on. *Which* groups, professions, and disciplines initiated these self-understandings of communication? *Why* were these interpretations promulgated? *Who* benefited from or resisted these construals? And *what* are the consequences of viewing meaning in these ways? These now become central questions. Analogous questions can be posed of the 'language of nature', 'self', 'community' correlated to dominant metarhetorics. It is not accidental that only Western European culture has systematically interpreted Nature in terms of the indifferent legality of a pregiven order and then projected this putative 'law' upon all other spheres, including language itself (today it has become routine to ask 'What is *the* logic of language?'). To pursue the *nature* of language is to apply one particular ideal of intelligibility to the heterogeneous matrix of sense-making structuration: 'we have a universe in many editions, one real one, the infinite folio, or *édition de luxe*, eternally complete; and then the various finite editions, full of false readings, distorted and mutilated each in its own way' (James, 1978: Lecture VII).

Once institutionalized, such metarhetorical questions and rules operate deep within our signifying practices. Indeed they enter the flesh of social relations, practices, and institutions. They are reproduced through the institutional apparatuses in which *theoretical* knowledge about self, language, and culture is produced, disseminated, and policed. Moreover these institutions are themselves self-interpreting sites where the real is graphically determined. By working with their methods we reproduce versions of life consonant with a specular view of the world. And, to a greater or lesser degree, we forget that these ways of thinking are historical interpretations. The immediate corollary of this criticism is that our ways of thinking about communication and meaning – what we think we are doing when speaking, writing, signifying, and so forth – has a fundamental impact on other social relationships – extending beyond the particular orientations of professional and disciplinary interests to wider societal configurations.

To return to the basic theme of this work: the kinds of talk we engage in and the kind of relationships we develop toward discourse and its institutions shapes the kinds of people we become. Wittgenstein once suggested that when we look for differences we find that many of our philosophical problems turn out to be the occluded consequences of particular ways of speaking and metaphoric idioms – pictures rooted in unconscious needs and desires. Our most cherished images of language are the products of deeply held metaphors which we have forgotten are metaphors. Language is like an ancient city built with figural materials upon which we draw to render our worlds inhabitable: 'Our language can be seen as an ancient city: a maze of little streets and squares, of old and new houses, and of houses with additions from various periods; and this surrounded by a multitude of new boroughs with straight regular streets and uniform houses' (Wittgenstein, 1968: §18). Or perhaps language is the ever-mobile swamp into which the piles of scientific construction are driven (Popper) – only here the 'swamp' itself is constituted from strata of occluded metaphoric practices (Nietzsche's 'there are no moral facts whatever ... [morality] is only an interpretation of certain phenomena' (1968: 55). In place of 'the essence of language' and 'the language of essence' we find layers of reflexive discourses and their conjugate forms of life. The version of language as self-reflexive semiopraxis might, with qualification, also be called dialectical in its understanding of earlier frames of meaning as socially dominant dramatic narratives that still resonate within our canonical ways of talking ('Language is a labyrinth of paths'). Its strategic correlate is the logological principle expressed in Wittgenstein's later philosophy:

> Don't say: 'There must be something common, or they would not be called "games"' – but *look and see* whether there is anything common to all. – For if you look at them you will not see something that is common to *all*, but similarities, relationships, and a whole series of them at that. To repeat, don't think, but look!
>
> (1968: §66)

I will try to show in the following chapter that these persuasive metarhetorics – language as Mirror, Instrument, Vehicle and Constitutive Energy – share common ontological presuppositions and, in variegated permutations, criss-cross the topography of the concept of reflection which structures the forms of self-understanding in Western European culture. But the critique of reflection needs to go deeper than simply 'looking into the workings of our language'. We need to excavate the root metaphors – the principles and motivations – behind some of our most suasive language-games. Second, I will suggest that this *videological* conception of the world is of relatively recent provenance – emerging most emphatically with the bourgeois-liberal form of life in the seventeenth and eighteenth centuries in Europe (in this context the pursuit of pure reflection is still an active element in the ideological matrix of modern bourgeois culture). Third, the modernity of the videological complex suggests that we should reappraise premodern signification, storytelling, and language-games to release critical motifs that were repressed in the triumph of Representationalism. Finally, I will argue that this deconstruction facilitates a dialogic critique of pure reflection – or what I have called the Western European Construction of the World. In this way, logological investigations take their place with other contemporary critical discourses concerned with the history and rhetorical construction of modern subjectivity as part of the long-durational appraisal and dismantling of the founding ontology and thanatonic politics of Western culture.

2

THE EPOCH OF REPRESENTATION

[T]he European spirit has strange roots.

(Frantz Fanon, 1967: 252)

Not only our culture, but the entire philosophical tradition, right from the very beginnings of philosophical speculation ... is inspired by rationalism. If pragmatism were valid, we should have to embark upon a complete reversal of this whole tradition.

(Emile Durkheim, 1983: 1)

In the previous chapter we have seen that in order to relate to and think of the Other we had to resort to similarities, images, metaphors, stories, and speculative theories. To invoke a Kantian image, we necessarily schematize and interpret our experience of the Other. I referred to this interpretive process as the mimetic field, and suggested that the vast sphere of figural thought in the culture of the West had been overdetermined by a profoundly cognitive and epistemological concept of representation. This visual scheme of general intelligibility provided the terms of reference and operative logics for a range of purely reflective ways of thinking about human action, history, selfhood, and society in the modern period. This is also why any immanent critique of the concept of representation – and the broader ideology of representationalism – inevitably returns the logics of reflection to the occluded figural order of mimesis. In this chapter I explore the ways in which the field of representation has been shaped by the patriarchal and phallocentric logics of Western culture. In particular the chapter focuses upon the so-called 'crisis of representation' which subverts the legitimacy of universal representation and suggests ways of moving beyond the dominant forms of rational mimesis in cultural inquiry. The chapter is divided into four sections:

1 *Mimetology: the European construction of the world*
2 *The crisis of representation*
3 *Pensiero debole*
4 *Conclusion: the dialectic of reflection and reflexivity.*

1 MIMETOLOGY: THE EUROPEAN CONSTRUCTION OF THE WORLD

All is Water.

(Thales, 6th century BC)

We can define Mimeticism as the dream of discovering a master code of representation. The pursuit of *mimesis* as a total representation of the real is one of the oldest impulses of the Western tradition, a product of the systematizing spirit at work deep within Western culture which can be traced from Thales' universal insight to Plato's timeless eidetic Truth, the Logos in Judaic-Christian theology, Renaissance aesthetic ideals, down to Hegel's pursuit of Absolute Knowledge and the secular philosophies of History in our own time. As a polemic against uncertainty, mimetology would violently terminate the uncontrollable multiplicity and nomadic diversity of non-mimetic practices and traditions. For this representational ideology all alterity should be subject to the order of the *logos* and *Reason*.

What has been called the spirit of totality has its roots in Greek antiquity. In later volumes we will see that the value orientations of ancient Greek civilization were already defining their own sense of identity around belligerent discourses of masculinist reason and imperial control. By reworking the mimetic desires of earlier civilizations, the civilization of the West – evident even from its first exploratory phases in the Minoan-Mycenaean period around 1400–1100 BC – displays a magnificent obsession with mapping its own nature and ordering its own identity, achievements, and concerns in visual and aesthetic notations, schematic models and binary hierarchical logics – whether in the fields of myth, art, literature, science, religion, politics, and speculative philosophy,[1] or in the behavioural ideologies,[2] ethical codes,[3] and social habitus informing Western institutional life.[4]

Mimetology might be considered as the ideology of ideologies, the prototype of the Western *épistémé* which projects reality as a fixed term of imitation and repetition. The will to banish 'otherness' and uncertainty – the impertinence of events – is sustained by what Nietzsche once called 'our prejudice in favour of reason'. But Nietzsche elided the ideological, political, and patriarchal *content* of the dominant logics of Western representation. In Chapter 1 I have argued that every act of representation involves semiotic construction and interpretation (most graphically visible in its violent *spacing* of its Others and their subjection to pregiven rules and judgemental forms). But the totalizing rationality of the West is unique in pursuing a *form of representation* that would culminate in a master interpretation to end all interpretation – and with it a 'transcendental subject' to allay all indeterminacy (as whatever destabilizes the being and identity of the Self). Typically this terminal representation is associated with an imaginary sphere of rational discourse or *logos* as a universal medium of *objectivity*. Underwriting this ideal of *systematic objectivity* is a nostalgia for a form of life without contradictions, a utopianism of pure presence, an existence removed from 'unreason', contingency and change. It appears that European imaginary culture in its unceasing 'civilizing' quest for ordering experience around the Same has been totalizing from its inception (its 'Other' has thus been variously 'totalized' in the rhetorics of a wide range of essentialist frameworks: 'unreason', 'wildness', 'barbarism', 'infantility', and so on). Of course this totalizing spirit has been locally defined and given particular ideological content in terms of definite material interests and social projects throughout the history of Western civilization. Yet the common core of these variants lies in the essentialist construct of the 'nature of nature' as a unitary identity, substance, being, or material structure. Long before the Christian dispensations of feudal Order and capitalist Progress the West has, to borrow Roland Barthes' term, viewed the world as *lisible*, as a seamless aesthetic totality – a *kosmos* – governed by an intelligible *logos* (*Zeus pater*, Nature, the Kingdom of God, Reason, Form, Essence, System, Law, and so on). Perhaps the earliest appearance of this totalizing logic lies in the ranking of the senses as a hierarchy of organs descending from spiritual 'vision' to the alterity of carnal 'touch' (associated with the feminine Other, materiality, and labour). This ancient scheme of order has functioned for centuries as an unconscious code by which social relations could be projected as hierarchical totalities (male/female; sacred/profane; soul/body; mind/senses; public/private; city/country; rational/irrational, pure thought/experience, and so on). The modern manifestation of the Western search for the Absolute is the post-Enlightenment fascination with the evolutionary 'Laws of History' as the story of Reason's progressive conquest of alterity. This is the metaphysical framework sustaining the limited intelligibility of talk about the 'beginning' and 'end(s)' of history. The ancient *Logos*, in other words, has been transposed from the theocentric dream of recovering the Word of God to the theological quest to decipher the movement of Reason in History. The ideological outcome of this kind of metanarrative is the legitimation of a transcendental ideal of rationality and its correlative activity, pure reflection.

Enlightened utopia

Every culture – every cultural form – is a means of contradicting chance.
(Stanislaw Lem)

The sacralization of *master* categories by the logics of reflection is symptomatic of the longstanding Western obsession with rationalist utopias and depersonalized object cognition. Significantly the first concrete totalities imagined by European culture were *aesthetic*. In the intellectual life of antiquity its exemplary articulation was the apotheosis of the Form as a criterial mode of being (from Parmenides to Plato and Aristotle), in the Middle Ages it was the Church's patrimonial monopoly of literacy, and its archetypal instance in the modern period has been the Enlightenment idea of a linear progression toward enlightenment or the closely related conception of 'universal History' as Reason uncovers the great chain of being underlying Nature, Society, and Spirit. The terminus of these progressive narratives is a state in which those fortunate few at the 'end of history' will know the absolute truth about the universe.

Each of these transcendental discourses has its violent social and political correlates (the Mycenaean citadel, the Greek polis, the City of God, bourgeois civil order). But each hierarchical dispensation spells out the same insistent message. Whether in the form of Platonic cosmology, medieval ontology, or Enlightened epistemology, Reason's guiding idea is the claim that nothing is beyond rational regulating, no experience is incalculable, no object beyond representation. The same metaphysical impulse is already implicit in the promise of magic:

> Regulated word, ordered movement, magic speech, and magic gesture compel the demonic element under rule and order. All primitive tech-nique and all primitive organization are magic; tools and arms, language and play, customs and bonds arise out of magical intentions, and serve in their initial period a magical meaning from which their own life only gradually detaches itself and becomes independent.
>
> (Buber, 1992: 167)[5]

The adjective 'master' is chosen carefully to express the fact that the canonical milestones in the European pursuit of Truth are strung out along a chain of *patriarchal texts* and *phallocentric institutions* (each resolving the questions: what must the structure of the World *be* for it to be perfectly captured by *theoria*, thought, calculation, mind, Reason? What must Being be like for truth-saying to be possible? What is the underlying shape of Nature and History? What is the logical form of Propositions?). Wherever a hegemonic male *élite* has attempted to dominate large and diverse populations we find that the control of mimetic machines has been a primary objective (traced in the ancient power-struggle which stratified society into a three-tiered spatial hierarchy symbolized by the tripartite values of contemplative *seeing* (associ-ated with the priests or *brahmins*), *war* (prerogative of the warriors or princes, *ksatriyas*) and *work* (the working people or *vaisya*).[6] In the West *theoria*, *violence*, and *labour* became the archetypal patriarchal ways of disciplining and regulating the heterogeneous, nomadic, 'feminine' Other (in the Platonic myth, the Rational and Spirited parts of the *psyche* control and direct the sensuous, desiring part; during the Middle Ages, the patrimonial control of the wayward flesh; in Enlightenment ideology, the reduction of heterogeneous histories to an all-embracing philosophy of History which accurately repre-sents the universal course of world history). The dream of dominating heterogeneity by mimetic means is itself a sublimated manifestation of the phallocentric tradition which still describes itself as 'European civilization' (cf. Foucault, 1967). We might even speak of the *logophilia* and *logocracy* at work in the depth grammar of European mimeticism – for, it is claimed, only in the 'reasoned Word' can we (men) *say* what the World 'is in truth' and defeat the disturbing forces of the body, desire, and fate; and where the master word atrophies, so does the 'progressive' vocation of *truth* and the social practices it sustains. Centuries before the epoch of Western imperialism and colonialism the founding desire of the West was seeded in that unlimited faith in the law of aesthetic sensibility which appeared with and presided over the 'mirror-stage' of Indo-European thought.

These well-known theses, of course, do not mean that ancient Greek thought, Judaic ethical rationalism, the reflective philosophy of the Renaissance, or the Enlightenment were wholly dominated by rationalist ideologies or a common mythology of *Truth*; the claim is both weaker and more general – that deep undercurrents of rational self-determination have implicitly shaped the ideological, political, and cultural frameworks of the modern period (analogous to the existence and operation of patriarchal formations prior to classical, feudal, and capitalist forms of social organization). To substantiate this claim in detail would require a fine-grained historical analysis of the construction of the different currents of patriarchal power as these have informed and shaped modern 'white mythology', Western philosophical reflection, and European power structures – how, in the pursuit of their varied projects of 'logification', 'urbanization', and 'systematization', European culture in its imperial ventures imposed schematic grids upon heterological peoples, traditions, and cultures. Like the psychoanalytic *stade du miroir* we are faced with an extremely complex dialectic of self-projection mapped upon and resisted by 'the Other'. In this *Entzauberung der Welt*, the 'other', the 'strange', and the 'alien' are represented in exclusionary categories designed to secure a stable identity for belligerent projects of domination. Recall Freud's Empedoclean insight: 'It is always possible to bind together a considerable number of people in love, so long as there are other people left over to receive the manifestations of their aggressiveness.'[7]

A genealogical analysis of the extended history of Mimeticism as an 'imaginary institution' explains why binary codes, influenced by early forms of alphabetic literacy, were readily appropriated as paradigms in the history of European power and eventually ended up as a mandatory grammar in the narrative logics of philosophical, political, and social theory. At the deepest – and it should be said, most abstract – presuppositional level we find a definite gendered normativity embedded in the hierarchical oppositions of literate technologies (cf. Merchant, 1980; Haraway, 1989, 1991; Jordanova, 1989; Plumwood, 1993). The changing history of these dualisms and hierarchical conceptualizations – especially over the last two hundred and fifty years – forms an important domain in the history of technologies of subjugation as societies move from oral cultures to literate civilizations and as 'modern civilization' spreads its forms of rational ordering around the globe. We also experience the violence of interpretation when dealing with the occlusions and repressions within the master texts and reading practices of the European tradition. Phallocentric governance, of course, first operated in the various realms of social life before it migrated to the world of scientific theorizing, philosophy, and literature. Stratified inequalities of power, wealth, and status antedate the rationalization of these social divisions into 'imagined communities'. In this sense the actual history of power in antiquity, throughout the Middle Ages and during the early modern period is a prerequisite for a full understanding of the institutional embodiment of mimetic ideologies.

The spatial polarization of the otherness of the Other was a conducive ideology for a ruling class with literate aspirations committed to defending the hierarchical order of 'natural society' and extending this structure of domination in space and time. To sustain the binary oppositions of representation, *theorein* hierarchically privileges identity over what it determines as 'its other': the body and the life of the senses, desire, doxa, orality, common sense, outcasts, aliens, etc. Whatever escapes the categorial grid falls to the side of irrelevance or even monstrosity – accumulating like a vast *bricolage* of irrational, unassimilable experience. Consequently, the particular logics of social incorporation (and derivatively, theoretical explanation) were successful when heterogeneous 'appearances' could be subsumed under and redefined by the regulatory categories of various kinds of binary regimes. The idea of theorizing within the terms of reference of this phallic economy was itself troped as a technical translation of experience into the ordered terms of an algorithmic grid. The privileged theorist 'grasps' a phenomenon rationally when he can reduce it to the known parameters of a master code in which it is allegorically rewritten as a token of a type (Jameson, 1988a: 149). 'We' explain phenomena in the physical universe when they can be shown to be necessary 'appearances of' a superintendent *law* or invariant *order* (a reduction to repeatability which is often explicitly justified in aesthetic terms). The pursuit of the universal itself then becomes an allegory to the phallic eros of systematization which may be the dominant psychological motivation of Indo-European thought. In mature forms of this discourse, theoretical rationality and political reasoning coalesce as a machinery for regulating the contingencies of social experience. In the modern period 'Nature' (and societies and civilizations imagined to be 'sunk in Nature') increasingly assumed the role of the Other, the alien antagonist to the humanizing project of objective Reason. Nature's wildness symbolized the sublime *alter* of Reason and Identity – an alterity which was, from the Renaissance onward, increasingly feminized and infantilized by comparison to the masculine rhetorics of universal Reason and the progressive Spirit. As Frantz Fanon observed in analyzing the roots of racism:

> The West saw itself as a spiritual adventure. It is in the name of the spirit, in the name of the spirit of Europe, that Europe has made her encroach-

ments, that she has justified her crimes and legitimized the slavery in which she holds four-fifths of humanity.

(1967: 252)

And since the Enlightenment period the teleological charter for this material and spiritual enslavement has been written in the language of a progressive Philosophy of History whose barely hidden *actant* was 'European domination'.

Within the general libidinal economy of mimeticism, Western science and its generalized rationalism evolved into the paradigmatic utopia – with its triumphalist image of the present conquering the irrational past (as the conquest of orality, myth, superstition, and 'femininity') and teleological image of the future (the progressive revelation of Nature's truth). But behind the algorithmic spirit of Reason lies the master code of *Representation* itself: the will to order and secure 'Nature' in a stable mimetic discourse – a stable Law determining the truth of the phenomenal manifold (and with this figure the homologous oppositions that are basic to phallic culture: Reality/Appearance, Form/Content, Inner/Outer, Sense/Nonsense, Science/Fiction, Male/Female, Normal/Pathological). For modern rationalism abstract Reason stands opposed to sensuous Nature according to the generative principle *Male:Female*. This is the secret dualism that created the space for the imperial idea of Man(kind). In the actual course of Western philosophical speculation the *logic of Logic* (and corresponding images of 'Man') finds expression in four great intellectual systems: the Aristotelian canon, Thomism during the Middle Ages – embodied in the *Summa Theologica* of St Thomas Aquinas, the System of Absolute knowledge associated with Hegel's dialectic of Spirit and, inverted and *aufgehoben*, the totalizing allegory known as Historical Materialism. Each can be construed as an elaborate justification of male power. But today while metaphysics is disparaged, the principles of linear 'totalization' have taken up residence in the spirit of technoscience following the universalization of technical knowledge by an increasingly reflexive capitalist system. This is what Jameson articulates without subjecting the binary logic of totalization to reflexive criticism:

> To affirm the priority of Marxist analysis as that of some ultimate and untranscendable semantic horizon – namely the horizon of the *social* – thus implies that all other interpretive schemes conceal a *seam* which strategically seals them off from the social totality of which they are a part and constitutes their object of study as an apparently closed phenomenon.

(1988b: 149)

We are asked to accept that only Marxism escapes the self-deconstruction inherent in the recognition of allegory by self-consciously denying the 'presence' of its own object:

102

a Marxist hermeneutic can be radically distinguished from all the other types [of hermeneutic codes], since its 'master code' or transcendental signified, is precisely not given as a representation but rather as an *absent cause*, as that which can never know full representation ... that History is not in any sense itself a text or master text or master narrative, but that it is inaccessible to us except in textual or narrative form, or, in other words, that we approach it only by way of some prior textualization or narrative (re)construction.

(1988b: 149–50)

Yet despite the revision of Aristotelian premises, we are still left with a profoundly technical view of theorizing. And in speaking from this discursive matrix, individuals automatically become agents of patriarchal power. The Eurocentric dream of a unitary metanarrative perspective does not disappear; it becomes self-reflective and redoubles its efforts to enfold the unrepresentable in a logocentric code of final *explanation*. Logocracy also has significant implications for social, ethical and political life (politics being 'aestheticized' to form representationalist regimes of 'truth'). If 'others' are to think, feel, act, and experience, they are obliged to do so under the auspices of rational machineries substituting and permutating signs for sounds, laws for experiences. And, as we will see, 'alphabetization', 'logification', 'legality, and 'theorizing' trace complementary histories of violent silencing. All prescribe the phallic position in the realms of the spirit.

The alternative – and more radical – option of subjecting the whole mimetic matrix to fundamental criticism in order to create a space for other forms of rationality, selfhood, and sociality is never seriously countenanced. Let us take this option further by exploring some of the immediate epistemic and political conseqences of mimetic phallocentrism.

The impact of alphabetization or the dream of the algorithm

To dismantle these resistant constellations requires a unitary theory of both 'the technical' in social life and of 'the social' in technical life. We might move in this direction by theorizing writing – in the general sense of social inscription – as an organon of power. It is well known that the European imaginary, with its fascination for machines, constructed its institutional structures in and through powerful normative discourses of self and nature elaborated around changing technological models and subsequently used these imaginary machines to map out diverse projects of social, intellectual, moral, and spiritual self-regulation.[8] We learn a great deal about the ruling images of patriarchal selfhood and political order by uncovering the machine systems that have served as tropes of consciousness in different societies and traditions; the profound impact of the various technologies of reflection associated with concrete practices of numeracy and literacy – for example, graphic functions, algorithms, binary classification, alphabetization, scriptural paradigms, musical notations, print, electronic media of communication, new techniques of (re)production and the technologizing of the word, cyberspace – provides rich empirical evidence of radical changes in our cognitive maps and definitions of 'reality'.[9]

At least since the Middle Ages the machine with its lawlike process of machine production has functioned as a fruitful source of self-representations of human nature and civil order. As a result of this fascination for machines, instrumental rhetorics became part of the restructuring forces of European history itself, entering into the flesh of its diverse practices and institutional logics (cf. Mumford, 1944, 1963). Theory informs institutions by means of the same processes by which speech and language enter the field of power. The 'machine language' of clockwork, pressure, self-moving mechanisms, and regulatory processes already dislays a politics and vision of the social order. A perfect machine would be one that could (re)present Thought and Reality and, by means of a pure algorithm of repetition, capture the truth of their correspondence. The ancient lure of instrumentality, in other words, was given a phallocentric meaning and embedded in some of the central institutions of modern life. Such a polymorphous writing machine would literally allow the word to become flesh.

An apparatus which anticipated every subsequent image of mechanical dominion was assembled at the very dawn of the European theoretical tradition. It appeared in the innocent inscriptive mechanism we know as the alphabet, the first true 'expert system' and symbol of self-regulating totality.

What is the link between mimetic aestheticization, phallocentrism, and alphabetization? Alphabetization provides one instance of how an ancient technology – originating as a 'force of production' – created modes of articulation and mentalities tailored to its own analytic requirements (a contemporary analogue would be the figurative uses of the camera or computer). A remnant of this millennial technophilia is the prevalence of the literary figures of *techne*, *production*, and *praxis* as root paradigms in modern ways of thinking about social experience. The phrase 'in the flesh' should be read quite literally – the 'success' of past technologies of thought is best demonstrated where they have become 'naturalized' ways of thinking, evading scrutiny by even the most critical of radical theorists. What began as an imaginary device ends by being reified as an indispensable grid of perception and thought (we thus have recourse to the language of mechanisms, checks and balances, pressure, information flows, etc. in articulating the nature of the self and society). What started life as a plausible model or phantasmic schema – the alphabet as a technique of mimetic reproduction – completes its life as the only way of naming, grasping, and mastering the world. In this way the natural universe and the world of human action become 'readable' as reflections of one common 'script' – the universal language of nature. And the tenacity of the idea that what we call 'the World' must be so arranged that it lets itself be (re)presented by only *one* canonical description is the distant ancestor of this ancient graphic will to totality.

To return to the Faustian uses of alphabetization. Each instrument of consciousness – and we should not forget that the phonetic alphabet is a tool for translating and mapping sounds, as auditory signifiers, into a limited number of visible, spatial, binary signs – licensed a systematic revision of the self and self-understanding within a visual grammar. The very 'rigour', 'finite', and 'static' qualities of alphabetic analysis attracted groups and societies with an interest in regulating and managing experience. Alphabetic consciousness developed from the first portable machine for translating Difference into Identity: what is apparently heterogeneous, materially inchoate, and flux-like – the sonorous and evanescent phenomena of speaking together – can be shown to be governed by a simple system of elements and combinatorial rules. What is context-specific, sensuous, living, alien, and undecidable can be resolved into a repetitive logic of inert similarities – the phonetic representation of speech embodied in the mechanism of an alphabetic script. Alphabetic scripts may have thus been appropriated as the first 'mind tools' of patriarchal power. Thus in ancient Greek culture the formal symmetry and beauty of the Ionian script and the austere rigour of the Latin alphabet encouraged the rapid dissemination of alphabetic consciousness to other cultural spheres (to say this more precisely, these domains became cultural 'spheres' by being subjected to the logics of literate reflection). Alphabetic script was, so to speak, a mobile aesthetic machine for regulating the polymorphic cultural field of signifiers into an intelligible totality. Hence the birth of the idea of the 'text' as a mirror of the universe as a whole.

On the level of the politics of culture, once in existence alphabetic scripts helped codify experience into ritual rules, commercial tables, law codes, religious texts, classifications, and works of literary art (which, as texts, are all *systems of repetition*); and, lubricating these text machines, the monologic spirit of philosophy and theology. Eventually – and the actual history of these information technologies is of considerable interest and should be researched in depth – the machine of grammar and the grammar of the machine became convertible figures helping to build the vast cultural imperium we metonymize as 'the West'. The 'primary' order of representations – 'living speech' – was colonized and transformed by the analytical and atomizing logic of alphabetization (a process which created the possibility of linguistic reflection, with its obsessive focus on the unitary, ideally repeatable 'word' or semantic 'atom'). The idea of the world as an aesthetic whole could then be literalized as a Book to be Read and Understood.

Given the longevity of mimetic desire in the West, it is not accidental that Europe was the first civilization to claim that the natural world is totally intelligible to non-transcendent explanation – a faith in secular intervention woven from the combined premises of the Graeco-Latin literate faith in a presiding Logos of the universe and the Judaic-Christian idea of eschatological

105

universal History governed by the revelatory Word or Law, both primary instances of subsumptive totalization. Its dominant model of Nature as an external spatiotemporal totality – a Book – was constructed by combining two technical image systems: the mental technology of the printed book and the material technology of mechanical machines (creating an image of Nature as the product of divine artifice – an Object amenable to a systematic description from the unitary perspective of a God's-eye viewpoint). Assured of its 'universal significance and value' the West could then proceed to instruct the 'non-European' world in the certain ways of methodic self-reflection and mathematization, shepherding 'others' along the rigorous paths of absolute truth (in different phases of European hegemony this telos has been variously represented through such mythical symbols as God, Nature, Reason, Politics, *Sophia*, Progress, the Dialectic, Democracy, Freedom, and Truth).

Living in a secular age we tend to forget how much of the vast energy European ideology invested in its own self-representation derives from the literalization of theological fantasies – drawn from the *texts* of selected Greek and Judaic-Christian metaphysics and transposed into practices along with the spread of class rule, imperialism and colonial power. The imperial representations of modern science had a ready-made paradigm in the authority Western culture had already cathected in the sacred Logos, Law, Reason, and the hegemonic Book – those primary Apollonian machines with an inexhaustible potential to be dematerialized, metamorphosed, and extended to different social and political domains. The ur-narrative of representation licensed, as it were, the patriarchal logic of Logic – the primary grid underlying all subsequent narratives, the great source of epistemic storytelling in Western society. The tale Europe tells of its own identity allows it to conflate and displace differences in order to craft an imaginary linear curve of Progress running from Plato to NATO – 'to emphasise certain principles of progress in the past and to produce a story which is the ratification if not the glorification of the present' (Butterfield, 1965: 9–33).

Jameson cites the Nietzschean example of the way in which a myth of Apollonian Greece was substituted for the Dionysian actualities of Greek social, political, and religious life – how a suasive representation of Greece came to be 'Greece'. We also follow those who have deconstructed this image system in order to try to evoke the radical otherness of Greek experience and forms of life:

> an alternative Greece, not that of Pericles or the Parthenon, but something savage or barbaric, tribal or African, or Mediterranean-sexist – a culture of masks and death, ritual ecstasies, slavery, scapegoating, phallocratic homosexuality, an utterly non- or anticlassical culture to which something of the electrifying otherness and fascination, say, of the Aztec world, has been restored ... the content of these new motifs allows us to reevaluate the older vision of the classical world, which now proves to

106

be less a matter of individual taste than a whole social and collective mirror image, in which the production of a new artistic style – neoclassicism – comes to serve as the vehicle for political legitimation.[10]

Perhaps the long-durational project of science (*scientia* understood generally as the rational appropriation of Nature, represented, codified and transmitted in alphabetic script) is the most striking manifestation of the will-to-intelligibility underlying the European construction of the World. Such a perfect *scientia* was itself a work of art. For the course of science is very frequently used as evidence of the desirability and actuality of Progress. European civilization may well be called the first self-consciously reflective epoch – presupposing a cultural matrix of literate technologies of representation more ancient than science from which the project of a 'science-based civilization' – and with it, global Europeanization and technological control – could be imagined as a rational and progressive conquest of space and time. The ground-rule of this ideological dispensation can be condensed in a single imperative: *to conquer the world we must first represent the world as conquerable, that is, as representable, amenable to subsumption under stable categories and classifications.* To do this thoroughly – or as Europeans say, 'radically' – is to imagine the world as a wilderness crying out for civilized development. The conquest of the wilderness of difference then licenses the wholesale destruction of otherness – as whatever evades the logic of mimetic naming and representation. The results of this scorched-earth philosophy is called Progress. The Europeanization of global space–time, secure in its metropolitan centre, reaching out into its marginalized peripheries is a necessary presupposition of the social and cultural history of Western imperialism. If the world could speak it would speak systemically, representing itself in the fixed taxonomies of objective representation connected by universal legalities. Whatever the manifest setbacks to the European ideal and the scientific conquest of Nature, Progress is still an irrefutable value by which we measure other forms of life in preparation for their destruction. This is the point where the sociologics of Modernity and the mimetic idea of History coalesce.

I will assay the limits of the Logos tradition and the logic of rational Identity and absolute Truth in Greek intellectual thought more systematically in Volumes 2 and 3. Here we simply note that the idea of a unitary, encyclopaedic transcription of the Book of Nature is one of Western rationality's greatest – if also one of its most problematic – imaginative achievements. If Nature dictates, Science records the transcription in the form of a rational science (Logos, Reason, Law, Totality) of its appearances and legality. But the modern mythology of Progress-through-Knowledge is one of the first victims of the crisis of Representation in the sense that questioning the notion that 'the World' subsists as a fixed objective reality amenable to a single categorial *mimesis* – exhaustive scientific description, for example – is also to question one of the basic enabling ideologies of Western identity, namely that language is at root mimetic and that truth is adequation to a pregiven state of affairs.

Writing as a technology of reflection

Dichotomy is the source of *the need of philosophy*.
(G.W.F. Hegel, 1977: 89)

From these premises we may define the arts of writing and literacy as *collective inscription techniques*. Inscription devices reorder experience by specifying the world under a definite description – commending different selections, different priorities, and perspectival 'cuts' from the welter of experience. But every act of redescription – whether alphabetic, print-based, or photographic – is belated and indebted to earlier forms of embodiment. The universe that theory aspires to represent is already prereflectively organized through the practical logics of active, intentional agents. We therefore stress the recursive dynamics of 'embodied knowledge' in the production of 'truthful normal environments' just as we admit the possibility of imaginative 'reconstructed logics' which actively change those environments. Inscribed environments are such that novel forms of writing can exert profound changes upon the situations which first generated these practices. A well-known instance of this dialectic lies in the impact of the invention of writing itself.

Writing creates unprecedented possibilities of cultural action 'at a distance' and for this reason may be the prototypical reflexive technology. Moreover the communicative skills literacy creates facilitate self-analysis and self-reflection by enabling human beings to disengage from their immediate involvements and follow more systematic modes of monitored reflection and individualized praxis. New styles of defining and relating to the truth become possible and with these new possibilities of cultural praxis and social life. Something like a 'public sphere' and 'autonomous civil society' is premised upon a society of literate agents (Habermas, 1989; Vattimo, 1992). In this sense literate reflection is the supreme example of a *truth technology*: texts can be stabilized, coded, stored, exchanged, reread, decomposed, analyzed, elaborated, and transmitted across generations and alien cultures. When explicitly developed these new means of information create 'techniques of thinking', ways of critically addressing first-order practices (the first uses of writing appear to have been linked to commodity inventories, agricultural accounts, and the state-monitoring of commercial exchanges).

The reflexive mechanisms of literacy enable subjects to disengage from concrete concerns, 'step back' and refigure their actions. In Durkheim's phrase, human beings cannot exist among things without forming representations about them according to which they regulate their behaviour and monitor their worlds. The primary processes of sociation occur as individuals participate in the communicative practices of significant others. The hypothesis suggests social-informational explanations of how subjectivity and its formations could have developed both phylogenetically and ontogenetically by recasting the traditional 'mysteries' of consciousness in contextual, affective, linguistic, sociological, and historical terms. Institutional transactions are quite literally the ontological matrix for the social emergence of self-awareness which, once in existence, dialectically reinforces their initial conditions and mechanisms. In a 'society of generalized communication' (Vattimo, 1992: ch. 2) we no longer posit 'mind', 'consciousness', or *'socius'* as *ex machina* essences but view the machine as a medium of mind and technology as a matrix of sociality. As the history of communicative 'technopoiesis' provides the key to the development of human self-consciousness, reflections on these processes are definitionally *logological* inquiries. To study the self as the outcome of cultural constructions is one of the first marks of a reflexive inquiry. In this way every *phenomenology of the self* presupposes a prior logological domain of communication: how the possibilities of selfhood are metaphorically articulated, inscribed, and disseminated.

2 THE CRISIS OF REPRESENTATION

The limits of my language mean the limits of my world.
(Ludwig Wittgenstein, 1971: 5.6)

The basic thesis of this chapter can be restated: from its earliest beginnings Europe has theorized itself and dramatically projected its sense of identity in what it assumed to be secure cultural metaphors and binary systems of meaning (the Logos elaborated historically into oral, alphabetic, scribal, manuscript, typographic, mechanical, and electronic paradigms – Poster speaks of oral, print, and electronic modes of information (1990: Introduction)). It directed itself in terms of a definite logocentric vision of human nature – a world picture whose historical continuity makes the idea of a 'history of the Western self' intelligible. The energizing power of these technological projections is still in evidence in the theoretical models that have crystallized along the imperial paths to Modernity – including the triadic 'domains' of reason, morality, and art theorized in Kant's *Critiques*, the exfoliating 'Forms of Consciousness' depicted in Hegel's 'Science of the experience of consciousness' culminating in Absolute (self-)cognition, the empowering apparatuses Karl Marx grouped under the title 'forces of production', the reflective domains Max Weber analyzed as the interrelated life-spheres of Occidental rationalization and disenchantment (*Entzauberüng*) and what Jürgen Habermas today designates as the differentiated value-spheres of cognitive-instrumental, moral-practical, and aesthetic-expressive rational action.[11]

Furthermore each of these models has sustained variant, and often mutually exclusive, answers to the questions of individual and collective identity: 'Who are we?' and 'How should we live?', but all the classical narratives, informed by unified religious and metaphysical world-views, have assumed that a universally valid answer was possible and that the object of this new dispensation could be established as a 'phenomenon for the future' (the undiminished Oedipean passion to allay indeterminancy by solving 'once and for all' the riddle of the Sphinx being itself a symptom of the longstanding Western fascination with the Logos as a primary model of social order – modern answers to the riddle being 'Human nature', 'Science', 'the Universal', 'the absolute System', 'Progress', 'the Revolution'). Paradoxically the utopian impulse of Enlightenment Reason accomplished its work by forgetting the revelatory and historicized mediations which conditioned its own possibility: the presence of the unrepresentable within representation sustains the 'politics of Western representation' as a quest for a unitary picture of the universe, self, and reality.

Those unfortunate 'others' who were defined by the utopian grid in their 'otherness' and subject to the force of its interdiction – rather like the native tribes in Caesar's *Gallic Wars* – were invariably displaced into the peripheral zones of imperial governance. If there was one true *mimesis* of an Objective Reality, all possible candidates for rational speech must be fitted into the Procrustean demands of the Logic of Reason (a way of speaking which comes to obsessive self-consciousness in Hegel's self-involving universalizing rhetoric of 'the Concept' as the self-definition of Absolute Spirit). In this way the incorporation of a foundational ideal of rational reflection within the major institutional regions of European culture displays its most essential and long-lived feature: the will to transparent self-centred knowledge and cultural rationalization (Habermas, 1985: 3–15). The same faith in objective representation also recoiled upon language which was reshaped in metamimetic terms as a neutral mirror of a real topography of objects.

Yet in the wake of postcolonialism we hear that the epoch of the Logos – particularly, the humanist ideology of translucent Representation and expressive Identity – may well be coming to an end. Its supreme strength – derived from an absolute faith in Reason variously expressed in the self's pursuit of rule-bound 'logics of inscription' throughout every sphere of experience (in structuralist thought), in the 'universal values' of enlightened self-determination (whether this is displayed in the *Oresteia*, the Acropolis, psychoanalysis, B-52s, or SDI), its commitment to objective knowledge, emancipatory humanism, and total, salutary critique – is also its greatest weakness (we can conceive of a culture atrophying from hyperreflection as we can imagine a society destroying itself by failing to control its own technological forces – in the middle of the nineteenth century Marx (1818–83) and Engels (1822–95) were already describing capitalist modernization as a process involving 'constant revolutionising of production, uninterrupted disturbance of all social conditions, everlasting uncertainty and agitation').

This is also why questioning the Western ideal of total intelligibility – one cause of what Jean-François Lyotard in *The Postmodern Condition* called the 'incredulity toward metanarratives' (1984) – is more than an isolated intellectual or philosophical crisis. The deconstruction of Eurocentrism by way of questioning the Enlightenment project is today being undertaken by a range of discourses in an extraordinary diversity of political, literary, technological, and theoretical contexts. It seems that the chaotic aftershocks of colonialism are also reflected in the crisis of imperial Representation and the will to rationally organize everyday life. This, however, is no simple crisis of 'superstructural' practices. The semantic vacuity created by the ensuing loss of faith in mimesis – and ensuing tactical retreats from the illusions of rule-governed 'progress', the teleology of the World Spirit, 'Historical Reason' incarnate in the Proletariat, and 'Utopian' social engineering based upon the 'complete self-transparency of society' – threatens to subvert the basic rules and values of the modern project at its foundations. *All* that is solid melts into air. The crisis of universal Representation precipitated by the collapse of a belief in a transcendent 'Reality' accessible to technical reason is deeper than a loss of political legitimacy or decline in sociopolitical leadership, in that it reaches into every sphere of contemporary life grounded on the modernist celebration of autonomous identity and self-centred rationality – touching every practice founded implicitly or explicitly upon the dominant cultural forms of modern representation. For postmodernism untrammelled science and technology are increasingly viewed as the most important causes of contemporary 'risk society' (Beck, 1992; Jameson, 1991).

In these circumstances we should speak of a concatenated crisis braided around the installations of modern science in that the late twentieth century is faced with a singular syndrome of contradictions compressed into the span of two generations: the violent aftermath of global war and imperialism, long-term malfunctions in the capitalist economy, environmental degradation and a deepening ecological crisis, unplanned destructive technological development, mass starvation in the post colonial 'peripheries', bureaucratization and erosion of democratic structures, and cultural fragmentation and spiritual disorientation are among the more manifest elements of the current situation. While we cannot hold 'Western thought' or, more locally, the *maître-penseurs* responsible for this conjuncture of problems (contra Glucksmann, 1977), intellectual traditions as powerful as Renaissance Humanism and Science, Neoclassical Economics, Liberalism, Conservatism, Modern Philosophy, Social Theory and Marxism are not indifferent factors in the complex aetiology of the present crisis. Encompassing structural conflicts and political crises is that hardly nameable phenomena, the radical disorientation of thought and values which has been called the *unheimlich* experience of nihilism – a 'mood' embracing the loss of 'spiritual' direction, meaninglessness, self-alienation, and personal insecurity, the appearance of the unrepresentable in many spheres of cultural representation, the dissolution of a determinable boundary between 'the real' and 'the imaginary', technological melancholia, pessimism concerning truth, and an entropic lethargy seeping from the conviction that all values

111

have a contingent rather than a universal basis. Ironically, as Nietzsche already anticipated, the fracturing and dismembering of Modernity is being carried out by instruments forged by Modernity itself. The global impact of the forces creating reflexive modernization poses the question: how was the philosophical project of imperial Representation originally constructed?

Pursuing this rather grand thought leads to the idea that the millennial project of rational representation recently reassembled as 'the Enlightenment project' is intimately connected with larger socioeconomic and political questions concerning the changing interrelations between self and society and self and nature under the different material and technological regimes accompanying 'the rise of the West'. The unanticipated emergence of the postcolonial epoch and economic globalization are inextricably implicated in this history. Some even see the 'pathologies of Modernity' – its environmental degradations, élitism, sexism, racism – as a sobering historical 'learning experience' which will lead beyond the aporias of universal Reason to a new conception of historicity and reasonableness: there is no necessary 'rationale' to the *Aufklärung*'s promise of universal morality and ethics just as there is no 'foundation' for the project of a universal science of 'nature' and the techno-scientific control it promised; the idea of unlimited rational progress is unmasked as a powerful social narrative – if not an illusion fostered by the European powers in their imperial expansion across the globe; and, of course, the portmanteau imagi- nary phrase 'the rise of the West' (and its variants: 'European civilization', 'the project of Modernity', 'Western culture', 'Western science', 'Western technology', 'Western politics', 'Western organization', 'European selfdetermination', 'Modernity', 'Rationalization', 'Reason-in-history', 'Logocentrism', and so forth) is to be reappraised as one of the potent myths that European culture forged in legitimating its adventures from the time of the ancient Greeks to the age of modern Imperialism. To the extent that post-Renaissance Europe pictured itself as a self-originating project it could read its own contingent achievements as necessary way-stages of a linear narrative leading inexorably to an advanced capitalist world and competitive market society.[12] The fiduciary rhetorics of Progress – the mythology of Reason as the pursuit of Truth – helped to constitute a world which could believe itself to be progressive and, thus self-assured, continue to pursue the systematic colonization of non-European space. But this faith in rational mimesis has been progressively eroded over the thanatonic decades of the twentieth century. It has been replaced by a darker, more apocalyptic sensibility.

The generic crisis of Representation precipitated by global war, ecological degradation, and the threat of the total extinction of nature undermines the credibility of such stories – whether as narratives or metanarratives governing knowledge, morality, art, or society. Said in another manner: developmental narratives of heroic Identity are seductive language-games tied to special social interests and particular social conditions. The Cartesian faith in the *cogito* or

Kantian Reason are not *Wertfrei* accounts of a superordinate destiny but allegories of the forcible reduction of difference to unity elaborated by powerful groups and interests. After the critique of colonialism and neocolonialism we are no longer persuaded that the empirical realization of civilization is somehow enfolded in the idea of the West or in the inexorable tendencies of the Capitalist Mode of Production – or, indeed, that there is any kernel of self-identity guaranteeing the universality of the West's civilizing mission.

Reflexivity in the streets

The European age – the age which extended from 1498 to 1947 – is over, and with it the predominance of the old European scale of values.
(Geoffrey Barraclough, 1990: 268)

The technopoiesis hypothesis proposes an alternative, less deterministic theory of the vicissitudes of consciousness. It suggests that we should approach the complex morphology of the European spirit as a socially constructed edifice of discursive practices elaborated in definite historical contexts by specific historical groups and classes. Rather than examine thought as a timeless capsule, a culture's privileged modes of communication should be regarded as intellectual inventions inseparable from power relations and forms of domination – involving class, ethnic, racial, and gendered valorizations of self and nature. Collectivities must first produce the concept of history as unilinear, 'homogeneous' time before they proselytize in its name. Whole communities must be first taught to see the world and think of themselves in terms of linear narrative structures and vocational journeys, salutary movements from scarcity to abundance as conditions of ideal membership. And, as we have seen, Western colonialism, capitalist expansion, and imperialism have violently imposed narratives of identity and cultural self-definition upon marginalized groups and peoples.

The critique of generic representation has the merit of thematizing questions of how and why concepts of order were constructed and circulated. By bracketing the ahistorical subject of traditional rationalist or empiricist epistemologies we may examine the mobile nature of *identification* as a normative process elaborated by different epochs of sociopolitical production in material, historical, and sociological terms. Put simply: different programmes of the polity, the societal, and ideological order incorporate different axiologies of the self, different evaluative 'narratives of identity' providing the repertoires of selfhood available to a given society. In the particular civilizational complex under discussion the central rhetorics of identity have been profoundly influenced by religious self-images of privileged membership and historical necessity. In attending to the mutations of meaning in different social formations we no longer assume that the term 'self' has an univocal referent or that it functions as a self-explanatory sign separated from larger social relations of

113

communication (in fact, *that* influential commonsense assumption is a phenomenon with a long history and indexes a structure of desire which should form a topic of metarhetorical analysis). The first step is to place essentialist and ahistorical views of 'human nature' and 'necessary development' in question and to approach every mode of subjectivity – whether in philosophy, politics or technology – as a historical construction. Happily this societal interrogation is being practically effected by the very organizations created by the instruments of capitalist modernization, especially by the shifts from centric to decentred modes of production and from traditional structures of meaning and expression to new systems of electronic writing, scientific representation, and mass-mediated culture.[13]

While traditional humanist and Cartesian images of the soul are dismantled by mass consumerism, existing forms of theoretical analysis and philosophical understanding lag behind the criticism of circumstances (unprecedented mutations in marriage, sexual arrangements, and family structures run ahead of sociology; transformations of political life, groups and classes make traditional political discourse redundant; revolutions in modern technology defy our inherited models). Theory today, in other words, is being instructed by reflexivity in the streets – or rather by the implosion of derealization processes across all the occupations, social systems, and institutions of modern life (Lyotard speaks of capitalism's inherent power to 'derealize' familiar objects, Habermas speaks of the erosion of the communicative infrastructure of everyday life, and Vattimo emphasizes how the contemporary world is being consciously 'pluralized' and 'fabled' by the very communication media and social sciences which both articulate and express modern consciousness). The existing paradigms of social and philosophical theory – grounded as they are upon archaic metaphysical oppositions – no longer prove adequate before these tumultuous changes. Only by incorporating these derealization processes – unexpectedly accelerated by the collapse of the 'really existing' authoritarian polities in Central and Eastern Europe, the dismantling of masculinism, and major advances in global communications media in the late 1970s and 1980s – can we try systematically to explicate the different modes of individuation – 'identities', 'subjectivities', 'modes of self-production' – as life-forms specific to different societies. To put the point in another way, the existence of some of the most dynamic transformations of contemporary history enables us to study the ways in which earlier and other social orders constructed modes of subjectivity.

The standpoint of rapid societal changes (what the ancient Chinese feared as living in interesting times) is thus a productive environment for sociological and historical investigations of the construction and reproduction of a society's enabling rhetorics for managing selfhood, embodiment, and cultural identity. The unanticipated dialectics of historical change in what has been called reflexive modernization acts as a forcing ground for new modes of difference and forms of life. From the perspective of late twentieth-century global industrialization and the commodification of the mind we begin to appreciate how earlier discourses concerned with the tasks of self-regulation – notably religious-ethical discourse, the agenda of classical Greek political philosophy, the Latinate culture of the Middle Ages, the thought of the quattrocento, the vocabularies of modern social theory, the problematics of Marxism, and the recent upsurge of 'postmodern' literary theory, cultural analysis, and posthistoricity more broadly – were themselves comparable historical responses to complex sociotechnical mutations (cf. Niethammer, 1992).

We see that the crisis of representation – the 'fate of the Self' in its totalizing metaphorical guises as Ego, Agent, Subject, Identity, Consciousness, Author, Reason, Spirit, Totality, Narrative, Utopia, History, and Truth – is inextricably tied to social changes precipitating a loss of faith in the traditional universalist vocabularies of reality and self-reflection. Those who chance their hand have spoken of the present moment not merely as a socioeconomic or political crisis, but as a 'civilizational turning point' and a 'crisis of the old European scale of values'. But defining a unitary 'crisis' or 'terminus' of Modernity is as problematic an enterprise as uncovering an autonomous self untouched by historical and cultural mediations: we can neither bid farewell to European history, its knowledges, technologies, and utopian obsessions (A. Weber, 1947) nor resolutely conquer nihilism by fiat (Baudrillard, 1984; Levin, 1985; Rosen, 1969; Vattimo, 1988, 1992). Rather, the critique of Modernity requires something like a 'working-through' or critical deconstruction of the hermeneutical modes of self-definition characterizing the European project in its ancient Greek, modern Enlightenment, and postmodern incarnations. In its largest compass it necessitates something like a self-critique of the occlusions and silences of Western humanism in its insistent phallogocentric forms (including theory's silences about its own affective, material, metaphorical, linguistic, political, and technological preconditions). We displace the egological question, 'What is the Self (the "I", Subjectivity, Reason, Science, Rational Utopia, Class Consciousnes, etc.)?' with the logological question, 'Where is the Self?' (how is the self constituted in mobile semiopraxical processes and differential sites?). A similar question-shift is therapeutic in debates about essences and objective entities: where *is* consciousness, music, literature, the text, intentions, beliefs, attitudes, and so forth with respect to the 'real world'? While the traditional quest for the *whatness* of things presupposes a strong traditionalist notion of necessary location (*locus*) and truth as referential correctness; the question 'Where?' suggests translations, displacements, and more constructive discursive models of truth. To this end it is necessary to abandon the totalizing imagery of 'decentring' and 'deconstructing' and speak of the dynamic truth-work of discourses in different knowledge regimes (or 'regimes of truth' as Foucault says).

On these grounds, understanding the aleatory flux of the present historical situation cannot be framed as the imminent 'End of Representation', let alone the 'End of History' or the 'Age of the Last Man' – the exhaustion of a certain type of social theory or philosophy of history is not equivalent to the relinquishing of critical reflection – just as subject-centred 'Reason' is not synonymous with rationality or literate thought with thinking *per se*; it can also be approached in the dialectical spirit of imagining new possibilities of reflexive individuation and sociation, anchored in emergent social movements and collective projects, transcending the restrictive models of individualism and community created by the apparatuses of modernization and coded in the dominant theoretical traditions associated with industrial Modernity. Indeed the institutionalization of 'reflexive questioning' (the truth-games of critical *argumentation*, the self-conscious stylization of life, the active production of biographical positions) embodied in different literary, aesthetic, political, scientific, philosophical, and moral practices of interpretation prior to the industrialization of the word may be one of the unique features of Western culture – its first 'consciousness industry' – whose concrete achievements have instigated some of the major mutations of self-conception in the history of European intellectual life.

This, then, is the aporetic historical context in which we ask: what has Western civilization intended by the terms 'self' and 'self-reflection'? The intrinsic complication of optical metaphors indexed by the word 'reflection' imparts a fugue-like structure to any analysis which aspires to trace the historical constitution of the mirror-game; a hint of this complexity is already present in the spectacular semantics informing English usage of words such as 'look', 'glance', 'gaze', 'stare', 'view', 'observe', 'perceive', 'scrutinize', 'speculate', and 'contemplate' – ocular words which seem to carry with them the idea that the intentional attitudes they name and the spatial objects they reveal escape simulacral mediation – as though faced with the vividness and immediacy of perceptual objects conceptuality becomes dispensable. In ocular language the exclusion of 'otherness' in the name of universality came to be criterial for the dominant European definition of 'knowledge' as cognitive correctness and founded certainty. Thus many of the canonical videological rhetorics of rational reflection oscillate between the dream of translucent identity and the desire for absolute transcendence – both imaginary states positing a 'pure' realm of envisioned meaning and truth 'beyond writing' as they are 'beyond alterity'. Yet this transcendence is still elaborated in figures derived from space-constituting traces and suasive rhetorics. As a viable paradigm for theory and politics the *transcendental pretence* – as it has been called (Solomon, 1980) – disguises its own interests in figures of universal salutary emancipation. The Cyclopean spirit gazes out upon matter as a prelude to mastery and domination. Hence our central thesis: the *mimetic logics of reflection play into the hands of technocracy*.

As this example suggests, many forms of European self-invention trail back to ancient desires now incorporated into our modern discourses of visuality: Western culture envisioned its own identity in and through systems of videological desire as old as the narratives of the Pentateuch – *Genesis*' 'Let us

116

make man in our own image and likeness' (1.26), Hesiod's *Works and Days* and the Homeric epics, where the patriarchal stirrings of the dream of absolute self-determination are already adumbrated in the protoforms of the masculine gaze (from Yahweh's name, 'I am that I am', and the imperative to 'speak so that I may see you' to the image of the 'all-seeing' Zeus supervising the affairs of mortals, the Platonic vision of the Forms, down to the Cartesian quest for self-certainty and the emblematic psychoanalytic ruse: 'where Id was, there Ego will be'). It is this dialectical interplay between seeing and signification, visual and textual metaphors of self-regulation, dating from at least 800–750 BC which calls for genetic analysis (of course, one basic difference between phallocratic modernity and its historical precursors lies in the fact that pre-modern civilizations did not have the technological werewithal to concretely implement and practically realize their optical fantasies and simulations – the social media disseminating ideas remained particular, local, and fragmentary whereas the characteristic media of Modernity are universal, global, and systemic). Where earlier theorists and poets of the envisioned Totality remained prophets crying in the wilderness, modern visual totalization is supported by government apparatuses of technocratic future planning: we now live in this Potemkin world. The unique confluence of videological knowledge, centralized state power, and global economic and political domination is what warrants a description of capitalist Modernity as a 'patriarchal', 'phallogocentric', and 'videological' culture: 'phallogocentrism' designating a structure of thought which prioritizes the logos and voice, the *phone*, and the masculine position in philosophy. In the concise inventory of Ursula Le Guin: utopia has been Euclidean, it has been European, and it has been masculine (1992: 88).

In the light of recent theories of patriarchy it may turn out that there is no form of desire which is not already discursively organized – despite the fact that we imagine realms of vision and affectivity as radically untouched by semiotic media or textual relays. Whatever the complex relationships between desire and writing, the everyday sites where they intersect articulate unconscious modes of rhetoric. What if peception and vision were themselves rhetorics, signifying practices, modes of writing which position and subjugate 'subjects'? In everyday perception word and affect – *Logos* and *Eros* – seem to melt into the substance of 'ordinary experience'. Or said more precisely, in becoming habituated with the terms of visual desire we live unaware of the rhetorical media of their articulation – we forget that every value and every perspective is ineluctably rhetorical – a *momento mori* to anonymous others who once lived, worked, felt, perceived, experienced, desired, and talked in this manner. And where the dominant readings of experience have been phallocentric, the ideological shards of these forms of life still bear the inscriptions of gendered power. The point assumes greater political urgency when we recall that the traditional fictions of normative identity (based on the self-centred subject of modern epistemology) have been actively complicit in generalizing ontological amnesia, shaping a static idea of reality inscribed in dominant frameworks and instrumental projects, and occluding the 'non-specular' plural reflexivities of vernacular experience, popular memory, desire, and corporeal life. Memory is one of the first victims of hegemonic power (technocratic knowledge transcends the sphere of the memorable). We do not need to invoke the authoritarian personality or repressive regimes to appreciate the pervasive presence of exclusion, persecution, and authoritarianism throughout social life: the logic runs like a zero-sum game – 'I (We) achieve my (our) identity at the expense of all others'. If 'the logos' – the regime of rational discourse, the pursuit of Identity – is one of the symbolic haunts of patriarchal power, reflection upon the vicissitudes of this power structure gives logological inquiries an important critical role in contemporary culture. A political economy dominated by this model of identity inevitably generates a politics of identity with its concomitant psychic and collective costs. Citing Walter Benjamin on the anamnesic power of reflection Habermas writes:

> Certainly we cannot make good past suffering and injustice done; but we have the weak power of an atoning remembrance. Only our sensitivity towards the innocently martyred, from whose inheritance we live, can generate a reflexive distance from our own traditions, a sensitivity to the profound ambivalences of the traditions which have formed our own identity.
>
> (1992: 242–3)

3 PENSIERO DEBOLE

We are almost certain that fire is precisely the first object, the first phenomenon, on which the human mind reflected.

(Gaston Bachelard, 1987: 55)

One of the paradoxes of modernity is that as Western societies become more self-reflective and individualizing (self-organizing, self-monitoring, self-critical and, of course, self-centred) they also degrade and repress some of the transgressive impulses of earlier forms of incarnate reflexivity native to everyday reality. A dominant culture of instrumental practices will project an image of everyday life and intersubjectivity in purely technical terms. One of the victims of modern reflective culture is the repression of the authority of prescientific modes of knowledge and non-instrumental relations between the self and other. This long-durational process of occlusion has been deepened further by the very technical success of modern formalism and organized technological power. Thus the multiple destructive-constructive impact of new technologies of symbolic representation (print, electronic media, photography, digitalized mass communications, computer imaging, global information networking, and so on) upon tradition-oriented, non-Western forms of life initiated a complex dialectic of consciousness and cultural experience whose consequences for the self and social structure range far beyond the imagination of those who first experimented with these techniques of communication (for example, the vast extension of memory made possible by alphabetization was followed by the destruction of traditional oral techniques of memory, recollection, and storytelling (Benjamin, 1969); the reification of dialogical language into 'information' and 'symbolic goods' carried out by modern communications technologies (Illich and Sanders, 1988; Schiller, 1970); global computerization threatens the creative autonomy of human reasoning and social rationality (Weizenbaum, 1984); interlocking commodity markets, by means of computerized communications networks, introduce both 'risk-detecting' and 'destabilizing' mechanisms into the heart of the global capitalist economy: 'the simple, utilitarian advantage of efficient language transmission becomes, through increased speed alone, a new social phenomenon, as quantity "dialectically" transmutes into quality' (Poster, 1990: 4–5)). Some critics of Western rationalization follow this repression of premodern reflexivity and knowledge forms to its ultimate conclusion:

> The knowledge possessed by non-Western civilizations and by so-called primitive tribes is truly astounding. It aids its practitioners in their own social and geographical conditions *and* contains elements that exceed what the corresponding elements of Western civilization can do for us. As the discoveries become more widely known, blind admiration for Western science and for the 'rationalism' that goes with it gives way to a more differentiated and, I would add, more humanitarian attitude: *all cultures* and not only the cultures connected with Western science and rationalism have made, and despite great obstacles, are continuing to make contributions from which humanity as a whole can benefit.
>
> (Feyerabend, 1987: 185–6)

Thus what has been described as the end of modernity and its idea of progressive history (Vattimo, 1992: ch. 1) – presents an unprecedented occasion for us to reflect upon the nature and extent of what we have lost in spreading the material, political, and technological powers of Western civilization across the globe. Complex problems of defining consciousness sociologically and questions relating to a decentred sociology of meaning, embodiment, and culture inevitably arise as a consequence of the increasing rationalization of modern life – 'the relentless expansion of Western civilization' in Paul Feyerabend's expression (1987: 185). The imminent threat not only to the fabric of human and non-human life-worlds, but also to the basic conditions of existence on a planetary scale have produced a vast range of oppositional voices both within and without the human sciences. The return of 'grand theory' and more global and ecological speculation is one index of this crisis situation. What were the cultural conditions for the era of global wars? How could the great institutional creations of modern rationalism – societal interdependence, material abundance, liberalism, democratization, humanism, the promise of universal literacy, emancipatory knowledge, communications technology, civil government, an international order of law, and so forth – preside over decades of mass destruction in which subjects were quite literally dismembered? What is the nature of modern 'embodiment', 'perception', and 'selfhood' which facilitated or, at least, conspired with the destructive forces unleashed by nation-states in the twentieth century? What is the fate of the self and identity in an epoch enriched by the thanatonic reality of genocide and extermination raised to an almost unimaginable scale of ferocity and technical precision (what E.P. Thompson has called 'exterminism' (1982))? What kind of 'theorizing' or 'science' is adequate to formulate, let alone comprehend and explain, the enormity of the global destruction and military concentration that has taken place toward the end of the second millennium of the Christian age?

The radical social, political, and ecological agendas instituted by the crisis of late modernity all point to the revival of fundamental reflexivity within the arts and human sciences. Again these polemical voices and discursive formations are the product of a larger historical *dialectic*. Generations lucky enough to be alive today are the first to witness the total objectification of the world orchestrated by the dominant armatures of Western reflection. What began many centuries ago as utopian visions of life today culminates in the programmatics of unlimited surveillance, panoptical visual domination, and a potentially global system of state violence. In these circumstances it makes no sense to separate 'experience', 'rhetoric', and 'politics' – their material nexus and variable interfaces need to be studied within a unified theory of reflexively embedded societal processes – including state structures, economic institutions, educational apparatuses, military and propaganda machines. In terms of its historical preconditions, a science-based 'surveillance society' presupposes the existence of societal specularity tied to powerful public and private power installations: the 'society of the spectacle' with the necessary 'public' systems of communication, legitimate apparatuses equipped to manage large groups of 'deviants', the availability of legal instruments of coordination and control, literate communications systems, etc. antedate the panoptical ideal of modern surveillance technologies (Elias, 1978b, 1982; Foucault, 1977b; Habermas, 1989). Apparatuses of panoptical social regulation are not unique to modern societies – witness the centralized bureaucracies of Ancient Egypt, Meso-America, and the militarized power structure of ancient Greece. In these ancient empires the crucial dialectic occurred between the expansion of economic power and the control of military technology (McNeill, 1982; Mann, 1986, 1988; Feyerabend, 1987). The striking difference between earlier megamachines lies in their vastly extended media and spatiotemporal scope. Thanatonic societies capable of mass extermination are only possible on the basis of well-coordinated mass communications, military, and information technologies – typically anchored in integrated state, science and military systems.

Ironically, what we have called the Crisis of Representation calls for more not less reflection on the world-making powers of discourse and ideology (or what today is being increasingly described as the information reshaping of postmodern space-time.[14] In the last analysis it is the global realities of politicized mass destruction and ideological deformation within the modern state system which require us to reappraise the fundamental place of narrative fictions and rhetorics in human affairs, especially in the unprecedented evolution of a global state-military system. What has been described – albeit at a very high level of generality – as the collapse of 'Identity theory' and the 'theoreticism' of total Representation lends a renewed vigour to the study of the dialectics of mediated representation in contemporary society and history. To remind ourselves of the rhetoricity and contingency of even our most objective forms of thought and 'scientific' discourses is not to get lost on 'the spiral staircase of consciousness' (Elias, 1992: 35) or to conflate every mode of speech as 'mere rhetoric' but is, more positively, a powerful way of keeping alive the spirit of vigilance and suspicion essential to the continuing life of inquiry in modern and postmodern conditions. Here the reflexivities of social power and the power of reflexivity must be researched and developed together.

Reflexive universes

Philosophers ... often fail to recognize that their remarks about the universe apply also to themselves and their remarks.

(Alan Watts, 1992: 103)

To loosen the grip of videology upon our orthodox interpretation systems I will risk a tentative ontological commitment by proposing the idea that 'reflexive phenomena' (the experiencing dialogical life of selves, human interaction, intelligent artifacts, social practices, institutions, rhetorics, histories, and the like – the vast field of material semiopraxis) are not 'self-relational' merely by virtue of our choice of description or mode of discourse, but that human experience in the material contexts of everyday life may be best understood and described as intrinsically recursive; or, said more cautiously, that the universes of human reflexivity are vitally implicated in the reflexivities of a creative, material universe. Moreover in developing within local traditions and environments, human cultures are inherently multiple and heterogeneous. The existing worlds of human experience form an open-ended symbol for this universal conversation. Human beings live in a natural, materially complex universe; but in comprehending that they live in the material world and in constructing diverse representations and simulations of such a universe they begin to inhabit a reflexive universe – they activate and transform the world as a reflexive universe of emergent recursive networks. Where the concept of a 'universe' or 'world' involves the idea of system and network, the concept of a 'reflexive universe' of social worlds presupposes the decentred idea of recursive networking (this hypothesis is related to what some physicists have called the 'Strong Anthropic Principle'). While nothing resembling a 'proof'

121

or 'demonstration' of this position will be attempted here, in Chapter 3 I will try to validate the idea by mapping the different levels and appearances of reflexive phenomena across a range of disciplines and discourses – constrained, of course, by my limited knowledge of fields beyond my own. Like other 'fundamental presuppositions' I would include this generic claim concerning the form of a non-mechanistic, non-reductive universe in what the Italian philosopher Gianni Vattimo (1988) has recently called 'weak thought' ('*pensiero debole*'). It is not an axiom in search of a discipline or a postulate designed to effect a paradigm shift, but a heuristic orientation to encourage further thought and inquiry in the realms of self-invention and the arts of human freedom antedating the modern schism between 'theory' and 'practice', 'consciousness' and 'reality', 'words' and 'things', 'science' and 'world'.

By investigating the situated practices and categories of premodern, modern and postmodern reflexivities as *social* phenomena we will try to reorient our thought to the notion that as social selves in our day-to-day ways of being we already inhabit a reflexive universe of endlessly looped conversations; otherwise expressed, that reflexive universes contain networks of practice that have uses for such selves and that any such universe – as a situated *world-of-reflexive-praxis* – only discloses its workings through critical reflection on the institutional conditions and material possibilities of selfhood, consciousness, and cultural praxis. Rhetoric, dialogue, and selfhood are thus indispensable concepts in detailing the institutional dynamics of reflexive universes. By stressing rhetorical praxis we may help dispel 'the illusion of unmediated action or speech' and 'restore' the antiphonal relation between text and text, text and context, text and commentary (Hartman, 1991: 8, 88–9). But by foregrounding dialogical experience prior to social systems we avoid the trap of viewing language, communication, and culture as incidental 'spheres' of social life divorced from the institutional workings of power; to counter all modes of reductionism and scientism we adopt the hypothesis that the public field of significance is constitutive of what different social orders create as 'reality'. 'Consciousness' and its 'worlds', in short, are socially constructed in definite networks of embodied practice – again the matrix of everyday life is preeminent as a source of examples of these prereflective processes.

To pursue this idea radically would entail a complete revolution in our habitual ways of thinking about the social order of knowledge, community, and political experience. But we are obstructed in this revisioning by what has been almost universally accepted as paradigms of mindfulness and self-understanding in the European canon – asocial and immaterial models of passive specular reflection associated with a fixed Subject-Object dualist view of reason (associated today with a positivistic image of modern physical science coupled with an idealized conception of objective scientific description), and a one-sided paradigm of theoretical consciousness as the privileged bearer of 'pure reflection' (*theoria, eidos*, universal theory, transcendental knowledge).

Another caution is in order: by recognizing that we already inhabit a

122

dialogical, reflexive universe woven from heterogeneous logics I have no wish to reverse or subvert the obvious gains made by reflection at the expense of unthinking praxis – how would that be possible other than as a conceptual game using 'theorizing' and 'practice' as abstract counters? – but aim instead to open provisional strategies for a reasoned critique of reflection's traditional rhetorics and self-projects which are already at work within the self-contested language-games of our culture. If a practice of reflection successfully works to elucidate and deepen our knowledge of social experience and cultural artifacts this is justification enough; we learn from the likes of Marx, Weber, and Foucault that hypotheses and theories are cashed in practice. But some of these inherited ways of thinking have become so restrictive that they have, Lear-like, lost their own patrimony within the institutions and everyday practices from which they originated. The hegemony of technoscience and its political appa-ratuses is a well-known instance of this dialectic of knowledge and power. But neither totalizing social science nor technocratic scientism can provide an account of the creative rhetorical work necessary to motivate the coordinate praxis of scientific research. As ideological practices, the inherited paradigms are silent about their own affective conditions, material armatures, and hetero-glossial involvements. Science's concealed 'alterity' – its tacit view of society and politics which prefigures definite ecological effects for example – falls outside the optic of its own field of objects, displaced as part of the necessary 'unconsciousness' of its rational strategy. Its own founding presuppositions are covered up and rendered immune from critical reflection. Organizational scientism is even more unreflexive about the applications and consequences of its methods and policy ramifications within the logics of modern societal rationalization. Of course it might be said that no science contests the society which provides its resources and directives. Lack of radical reflection – as this extreme example suggests – may have enormous consequences once the prod-ucts and procedures of scientific reflection are institutionalized. From past experience it seems to be the case that if a mode of reflection obfuscates and reduces the freedom of creative thought and action it will be invariably seconded to the service of conservative and totalitarian interests. The transfor-mation of Europe into a technological slaughter-house during the first half of the twentieth century is one of the fruits of this silence – as are the systems symbolized by the names 'Chernobyl' and 'Three-Mile Island'. Although modern science and its associated technologies are no laughing matter, where practices of reflection reify and destroy their objects as creative human projects this is an occasion for the criticism of laughter. Humour is still a most powerful technique in appraising the vicissitudes of reflection and exploding the psy-chosis of 'absolute knowledge'.[15]

Subverting reflection: reflexivity for what?

There is a certain ironic asymmetry here: the purest forms of theoretical reflection – for example the advanced domains of theoretical physics and its technological armatures – still appear as fallible, embedded practices – the concerted activities of vital, eroticized, deliberating, representing, model-building, acting, imaginative, communicating agents pursuing their interests with other 'actors' in definite social locations and actor-networks (Callon and Latour, 1981; Callon, 1991). As Adorno once observed, the purest concept 'cannot be thought except in relation to facticity' (1991a: 10). We acquire concepts in learning particular rules and practices, in negotiating the spatiotemporal, causal fabric of everyday life. In recalling the experiential and social origins of categories, however, Adorno forgot to add that the guano-like 'facticity' of taken-for-granted ways of seeing and acting were originally sedimented as the unintended consequence of visionary, affective, utopian activities animated by both secular and sacred interests in self-definition. And guano, once broken up, reprocessed and reused, can have a second life in fertilizing new growth and creativity. The immense historical impact of technoscience as it has spread tendril-like through modern institutions is not a social fantasy that can be 'reversed' or 'abolished'. The 'loss of the life-world' is itself a recursive power which deforms and shapes our definitions of experience and life in the late twentieth century. We cannot 'will away' or 'decommission' the institutional workings of science and technology, any more than we can dissolve the state and its apparatuses into 'discursive formations'. But the existing networks and armatures of technoscience can be defamiliarized and reflexively transformed. The passing of the age of comprehensive metanarratives does not leave a vacuum, for we will continue to speak in terms and symbolisms drawn from these hegemonic discourses. The idea of science and its cognitive authority are still rooted in imaginative human praxis and thus connected with earlier 'impassioned' projects of the self as agency and self-assertion. We may end up 'speaking for praxis' – or practical philosophy as a 'space of engagement' with the problems of late modernity – against what passes for theoria in the critical conversations and institutions of contemporary culture. But this does not mean impugning the ontological integrity of reflection, let alone abandoning traditions of speculation, contemplation, and self-critical science; to the extent that these discourses and practices have had a fundamental material impact in shaping European institutions of reflection and selfhood they are to be approached as powerful institution-making rhetorics. But to reground the project of science in the life-world of occluded libidinal impulses and social networks is also to countenance a transformation of the meaning of 'science', a subversion of the aims and objectives of reflection.

I have come to refer to this critical dialogue with existing theoretical discourses and modes of self-understanding in modern society as 'logological investigations' (setting into play the multiple meanings of the Greek term 'logos' – given that the analysis, criticism, and theoretical discussion of 'what appears' (*phenomena*) and is seen (*eidos*) is mediated and shaped by words and 'words about words' in complex textual laminations). Any phenomenology of human experience must self-critically address its own rhetorical possibility, and this will inevitably take the form of a logological inquiry into forms of affectivity, speech, verbal praxis, writing, and inscriptive technologies norma- tive for a given community of inquiry: the 'facts' of even the most reductive sciences are only intelligible against a background of discursive and non-dis- cursive practices grouped under such disciplinary practices as as 'philosophy', 'science', 'research', 'experimental praxis', and the like. Our practices and institutions are literally embodiments of reflection; they can be nominated as 'realities' not in spite of but rather because of reflexive processes – since whatever has been shaped into a historical and social world has passed through the semiotic media of reflexivity: 'To engage in a political practice is already to stand in relation to theory' (Sandel, 1984: 81). Something akin to an axiological schema is embodied in every human practice: techniques represent the fixation of value-oriented consciousness; technologies are society made durable (La- tour, 1991). In one of its many senses, reflexivity is self-experience which enables thought to undertake the *Aufhebung* and deconstruction of reflection and its foundational rhetorics. But in another sense it is also the experience of difference and dissonance which impels thought to question the existing social embodiments of theory and interpretation. It is our involvement in heteroge- neous fields of concrete social practices which helps us see that the phrase 'pure reflection' is an oxymoron, which, like the notions 'absolute science' and 'certain knowledge', has the status of a self-negating expression (*a contradicto in adjecto*). But this is not an incitement to abandon theory and reflection; rather the sublation of monological, imperial theory by concrete practice is an ironic insight which transforms and deepens our understanding of the situated reflexivities of praxis, helping us to imagine more creative orientations to the praxis of theory. Understanding the past excesses of the reflective imagination is an invitation to renew the experience of reflexivity in anticipation of a post-thanatonic culture.[16]

4 CONCLUSION: THE DIALECTIC OF REFLECTION AND REFLEXIVITY

One day (they were riding, I think, on a train) when Wittgenstein was insisting that a proposition and that which it describes must have the same 'logical form', the same 'logical multiplicity', Sraffa made a gesture, familiar to Neapolitans as meaning something like disgust or contempt, of brushing the underneath of his chin with an outward sweep of the finger-tips of one hand. And he asked: 'What is the logical form of *that*?'
(Norman Malcolm, 1958: 69)

What I have called 'Reflexivity' is not simply reflection squared, another 'level' of 'reflection upon reflection' in an endless Shandean retreat of postscripts – the interminable 'thinking about the self thinking about the world' (cf. Merton,

1965); rather it denotes another domain of desire antedating the traditional practices of reflection and yet still alive within reflection's totalizing rhetorics – precisely the dynamic 'phenomena of desire', *jouissance* (Barthes), transgressive excess (Bataille) or 'the *semiotic*' (in Julia Kristeva's sense, e.g. 1980, 1984, 1989), the irreducible 'Other' (Lévinas, 1969, 1987) or even the 'nomadic' pulses of everyday life theorized by Gilles Deleuze and Félix Guattari in their *Anti-Oedipe* (1972) which fail to comply with the self-imposed strictures of essentialist metaphysics or foundational and positivistic rhetorics, whether these be in moral, symbolic, societal, aesthetic, literary, political, scientific, or philosophical spheres. The enormous effort to reappraise ancient and modern science in terms of their founding desires, to review them as modes of affective experience as well as epistemic intentionality illustrates the difficulties in distinguishing between reflection and reflexivity.

The dialectical tension between Reflection and Reflexivity can also be illuminated with the analogy of 'the relation that a map sustains to the explorations and surveys of which it is the outcome' –

> The map is the product. After it is constructed, it can be used without any reference to the journeys and expeditions of which it is the fruit, although it would not exist if it had not been for them. When you look at a map of the United States, you do not have, in order to use it, to think of Columbus, Champlain, Lewis and Clark, and the thousands of others whose trials and labors are embodied in it.
>
> (Dewey, 1933: 73)

But the rambling processes of guesswork, first drafts, false starts, erasures, risk, and so forth necessary to the vital process of original exploration are effaced from the finished product – the map, like a chrysalis, sheds its own prehistory. Where the voice of Reflection intones: 'Live according to rule (obey the strictures of structure)', Reflexivity whispers with its relentless antinomian tautology: 'We want to live as we want to live.' The clash of these two principles disrupts hierarchies, dissolves binarisms, subverts carefully drawn limits, and in a hundred different ways primes the engines of cultural innovation.

More positively, the occluded pulses of reflexivity – in the form of a tradition's transgressive modes of desire, non-verbal beliefs, *écriture*, expressive and interpretive strategies – provide the conditions of existence of specific practices of reflection and structuration (even where the act of reflection denies its own inscriptive conditions in mundane experience – thus inaugurating a tradition of self-occlusion having its earliest prototype in the Platonic exclusion of the 'Other' in deference to Absolute Knowledge and the ensuing millennial temptations of legislative *prima philosophia*). Ironically Platonism, that most erotic, ludic, and poetic of philosophical movements, promulgated the suasive idea of knowledge as a disinterested, 'master' vision of formal objects (while pursuing what Hegel was the first to recognize as the purest form of playful, speculative reflexivity in texts like the *Parmenides* and *Sym-*

posium). As I will show in detail in particular studies of the genesis of ancient Greek theorizing in Volumes 3 and 4, the subversive reflexivities of tradition – the 'spontaneous outreaching for the new which is the essence of the open mind', the risk-taking constitutive of novel theorizing and practice, the poetics of reflexivity – always precede the deliberate activities of intellectual reflection, a dependency analogous to the priority of everyday talk and interpersonal communication over the explicit production of textual artifacts and cultural actions or, more pertinently, to the force of the semiotic over the symbolic as Kristeva has used these terms or, in more sociological terms, the dialectic of *communitas* and *societas*. The polemical relationship symbolized by the dialectic of Reflection and Reflexivity might be drawn by contrasting Plato's *Laws* and his *Parmenides*. The former expresses the spirit of closure, while the latter evokes the poetics of unbridled speculation.

To return to the main theme of the critique of the ontological foundations of knowledge paradigms. The environments of dialogical reflexivity function as the truth horizon and sustaining matrix of second-order reflective praxes, a dependency which reflection forgets at its peril. Reflection's existential source and temporal matrix is not something controlled or authorized by reflection (this we will see is one of the basic errors of the post-Enlightenment rationalist conception of theory and practice). It is rather the always-already operative world of everyday experiences and quotidian comportment toward the being of things, the rich chaos of everyday language, the contradictory pulses of lived history. Techniques of reflection – whether in the sciences, in ethics, politics, or technological practices – are still historically grounded in practices of self-activity. In one respect the rigours of theory evolve into instruments to protect the mind against its own contingency and histor(icit)y. But as forms of writing they are also indebted to traditions of past speculation and – by definition – transgressivity.

Because of this existential dependency an irreducible structure of self-diremption is always presupposed by the rigid boundaries of a projected ego or the idealized tableaux of identity projected by a dominant social order:

> This means that the Ego is *essentially* dispersed or distended because it is essentially withdrawn from and can never be exhaustively caught up with by its own power of self-objectification. It is the temporality of reflection which makes self-objectification possible and adequate self-objectification impossible.
>
> (Prufer, 1965: 168)

Classical and modern paradigms of self-knowledge – with their organizing centre in egological structures and metaphysical principles – necessarily elide the ambivalent surd of temporal existence: everything temporal is already eroticized – to *be*, to *exist*, to *feel*, to *relate*, to *endure*, is to live within a nexus of relatively opaque relations and processes without origin or end. And 'opacity' is the mark of finitude and situated reason. Reflexive interaction is a transient complication of ambivalent processes delimited by contingent, mobile horizons. But this is not simply to restate the platitude of the priority of historical context over text, of meaning over structure, diachronicity over synchronicity: 'the primacy of praxis' is a phraseology which is prone to deconstruction; it is, rather, to table for investigation the prior structuration and dialectical interplay of 'context' and 'praxis' as a rich system of interpretive experience, the contingent product of earlier processes of desire, sedimented action strategies and textual reflection still at work in everyday life. We have uncovered a 'knowledge prior to knowledge', a 'discourse within discourse' that has fallen through the grids of dominant theory. What follows, therefore, will not be merely exercises in 'thinking about' the historical shapes of reflexive experience but will try to concretely exemplify the living experience of self-reflection itself, turning our representations of reflection away from the siren-songs of pure reasoning and metaphysical securities to their own occluded history in concrete sociocultural experience – self-understanding neither begins nor is exhaustively described in practices which make their primary business the understanding and explanation of human action.

In its active role as everyday semiopraxis reflexivity engenders worlds of human experience which professional reflection imperiously ignores. The disregard of the ephemeral, the temporal and 'unconsidered' fabric of inter-subjective experience is symptomatic of this forgetting in mainstream social science. This is one of the reasons why the modes of thought and perception of earlier 'immobile' or 'traditional' civilizations have to be worked through, loosened, and dismantled by reflection before they can become effective in unhinging our dominant conception of inquiry and knowledge. The cosmologies of classical antiquity – for example, the *noesis* of a Thales or Heraclitus, the *eros* in Plato or Aristotelian *episteme zetoumene* – are not cadavers of forms of life grown cold; the texts of these earlier phases of European civilization still contain powerful transgressive forces and fomenting possibilities. Logological research takes an active interest in the unredeemed alterities of the ordinary, the pragmatic, the marginal, and the rhetorical (traditions of poetry, as we have observed above, preserve the open spirit of reflexive discourse). The mutual involvement of self, signification, and society prior to theory returns our thinking to the older meaning of 'analysis' (Greek *analusis* meaning unravelling and loosening but also, more positively, enabling and *releasing* suppressed possibilities – like the Hegelian *Auflösung*). By loosening some of our most sacred intellectual myths we may help liberate the unremarked codicils of history.

Part II

REFLECTION

Like the word 'representation', 'reflection' is also an expression with diverse roles in contemporary discourse, varying with different theoretical perspectives and forms of inquiry. A comprehensive survey should begin by exploring the history of the term's irregular conceptual, semantic, and cultural functions. Because of space limitations, however, I adopt a more schematic strategy, limiting my analysis to an overview of the metaphorics of reflection. Initially I will be guided by two interrelated questions: what are the conditions of the possibility of generic reflection prior to intellectual praxis? and what are the limits of such a generic characterization when faced with the more complex realities of self, identity, mindfulness, and culture? Pursuing the first theme will lead us into the vicinity of the second question. Chapter 3 thus begins with a simple question: why are reflexive processes found everywhere in nature?, while Chapters 4 and 5 examine the rhetorical grammar of consciousness and reflective thought.

3

GENERIC REFLECTION

[A]ll of nature is full of life.

(G.W. Leibniz, 1989: 206–13, §1)

In this chapter we develop the category of 'generic reflection' by exploring the conditions of the biosocial genesis of self-reference. The main intention here is to specify some of the fundamental aspects of self-organization and autopoiesis prior to the emergence of distinctively human reflexivities. We conclude with observations on the place of self-referential processes within an emerging ecological paradigm of world-orientation. The chapter is divided into four sections:

1 *Generic self-reference*
2 *The biogenesis of self-reference*
3 *Autopoiesis*
4 *Toward an ecological paradigm*

1 GENERIC SELF-REFERENCE

None of us knows what living creatures really are.

(Adolf Portmann, 1958: 320)

Hegel's lexicon provides a useful point of entry into the generic category of reflection by subsuming the category of *Being-for-self* (or *Relation-to-self*) under the general concept of *self-relation* as follows:

> If I say I am for myself, I not only am, but I negate in me all else, exclude it from me, in so far as it seems to me to be external. As negation of other being, which is just negation in relation to me, being-for-self is the negation of negation and thus affirmation; and this is, as I call it, absolute negativity in which mediation is indeed present, but a mediation which is just as really taken away.[1]

He clarifies the distinction by observing that the idea of real being – of Reality – presupposes the category of self-relation and therewith the categories of identity, difference, and contradiction. Every finite being – everything that can

131

appear as an entity or identifiable 'unity' – 'is essentially a unit of distinct and distinguishable moments, which by virtue of the determinate, essential difference pass into contradictory moments. This contradictory side of course resolves itself into nothing, withdrawing into its negative unity' (1969: 442, cf. 439–40). In other words, the criterial 'sameness' of entities entails difference. But entities do not thereby have the property of recursiveness, let alone 'self-relation' or 'the power to endure immanent contradictions'. Objects are related and frequently interrelated in complex forms and patterns without being 'self-related'. We may speak of substances and organisms as 'related' to their environments or environing worlds (*Umwelten*), but only human existence consciously relates itself to its world. Only entities that relate to their own relatedness, so to speak, can be considered to be subjective beings in the full sense of this word; and only such auto-referential existences can be described as possessing a *self*. Hegel turns this elementary individuation condition into an *a priori* feature of living 'objects': opposition and contradiction are implicated in the category of relation (*Beziehung*). Reflexivity as *self*-recursion appears as the zero-degree of concrete mediation – the prephenomenal site where difference begins its dialectical work. Objects determined by their causal and physical relations may be contrasted with 'objects' that are aware of their relatedness ('objects', that is, which relate to their own process of *being* and to which we attribute predicates such as 'living', 'animation', and 'sentience'). The latter class of conscious entities or organisms experience their relatedness as a condition of their existence (they begin to relate to their relations). They are 'objects' which turn back upon their own conditions and 'become conscious' of their limitations and finite freedoms. While the spectrum of 'organisms' to which we might apply the term 'consciousness' or 'mental life' is very wide, it is the world of human beings, according to Hegel, that provides the paradigmatic case of self-relating beings. Only the human world produces reflection and agents that are capable of self-consciousness and meaningful conduct. The problem for thought is how to give conceptual expression to these differences. The epistemological term 'reflection' provided one means to this end.

Re-flection (Latin *flectere*, *re-flectere*, *reflexio*, meaning 'to bend back' or 'turn back') literally means to bend back on itself – as we describe *self-consciousness* as consciousness in the act of reflection: 'What is it to see the blue of the sky?', 'How did I come to know this?', 'Who is the "I" of this knowing?', etc. We now know that the eighteenth-century model of the reflective mind deliberately turning back to the object of previous thought or to the act of thought itself helped to sustain the whole project of transcendental philosophy. Hegel, however, understood that before we can explain the 'life of consciousness' we first need to have some conception of the 'consciousness of life'. Consciousness and self-consciousness should be clearly separated and the difference located in its natural, historical, and cultural matrices. Consciousness in its fully explicit, wide awake forms, is a product of deeper forms of embodied awareness, the tip of the proverbial iceberg of conscious life

(*Bewusst-sein*). Thought and self-consciousness are *developmental* or *emergent* phenomena. Thus many organisms are described as possessing the rudimentary forms of consciousness, but are incapable of self-consciousness. Hegel appears to have set himself the task of specifying the ubiquity of *consciousness* and *self-consciousness* as realms of recursive intelligence emerging from a self-developing, dialectical universe of lower life forms. But the first problem in this expanded concept of consciousness is how to enter the circle of prereflective objective consciousness without privileging subjective, self-conscious life? How to avoid the faculty mythology of *Reason* which dominated the *Reflexionsphilosophie* of his contemporaries?

Hegel's preferred solution lay in the speculative thesis that Reason – what he called the abstract appearance of Spirit – is already implicit in the developmental logic of natural life (that the Real is synonymous with the Rational when viewed developmentally). Hence, rational self-determination is one form of Spirit, one shape of the Idea or, in a theological terminology, one manifestation of God. As he wrote in the *Logic*:

> For as against contradiction, identity is merely the determination of a simple immediate, of dead being; but contradiction is the root of all movement and vitality; it is only in so far as something has a contradiction within it that it moves, has an urge and activity.

> (1969: 439)

In ordinary language we speak of 'self-consciousness' as the mind reflecting back upon itself in a thoughtful relation of self-reflection. Speculative thought takes this figure of speech literally: *consciousness* is the mind's capacity of mirroring self-reflection (Hegel speaks of thinking and its correlative modes of self-awareness quite literally as *Spekulation*, from *spekulieren*, 'to speculate', 'spectate', or 'envision'). A reflexive mode of being is one which not only separates itself from its environment but speculatively turns upon itself, relates to itself as a consequence of not being 'identical with itself' (or perhaps more enigmatically which '*relates itself to itself*'). The attribute of active 'non-identity' or 'negative self-relation' belongs to every finite 'creature' as an organism whose essential nature is to change as it 'refutes' its earlier 'forms of consciousness' as inadequate embodiments of its '*project-to-be*' (recall that for Hegel Reason actualizes itself by 'moving' through a sequence of necessary *Gestalten von Bewusstsein*). The ontogenic emergence of this capacity for *retrospection* presupposes prior systems of temporal relations – or, if we are to avoid prejudging the phenomenon, a prior temporal field. Something like a primitive order of temporality may even be present in the earliest forms of organic self-differentiation (the time-phasing related to the satisfaction of organic needs and vital relations). But this is qualitatively different from the temporal consciousness of human existence. Here the 'turning back' of thinking in recollective desire, for instance, both 'takes time' and 'makes time' ('time' being the paradigmatic medium of 'non-identity' and difference implicated in every form of life) and is confined to existents that contingently endure in the temporal manifold – finite creatures exist, develop, and die as contingent processes (they 'come to be' and 'cease-to-be' in accordance with pregiven spatial and temporal regularities). Self-conscious creatures, however, become aware of 'living finite lives', existing 'in' time as definite identities of meaning over time. The gathering and re-collecting of experiences as 'mine' is thus one of the most basic conditions for the emergence of reflection and its associated self-concept. An operation of temporalization (*temporalisation*), then, is presupposed as a boundary condition in the most elementary acts of self-organization.

But if every lived relation implicates *processes of active meaning* then logical categories such as 'objects in space' or the thing as a 'being-in-itself' already presuppose the relationality of a prior field of meaning. Categories exist and function in a categorial network of relations. In a speculative sense the recursivity of relational existence and self-consciousness (*Selbstbewusstsein*) is prior to the *nachdenken* of abstract thought and the 'higher superstructures' of art, morality, religion, and science. This, of course, was also the conclusion of Heidegger's 'Dasein analytic' in *Sein und Zeit* (1927: Part 1) – that the situated preunderstanding of Being by Dasein is only possible on the basis of temporality as active, embodied 'differentiation' (1982: 16). Generic reflection is not a phenomenal 'domain' or 'realm' of entities, but a relational difference presupposed by any theory of objects – a *function* of ontological differentiation, not a *substance*. Of the entities which populate the known universe only those 'beings' gifted with the possibility of self-reference can be 'agents' of conscious activity, behavioural change, and wilful action. Organisms as 'living beings' temporalize their field of activity in relatively predetermined, species-specific ways. But even for such minimally reflexive beings time is as significant a parameter of existence as space.

Systems that can recursively monitor their environments and situate themselves within their environments, create more complex temporal formations. The time framework of an enduring self is radically different from the temporal cycles of organically preprogrammed needs. This is no longer the homogeneous time of common sense or classical physics. Neither is it a pure form of intuition. Time is plural, situated, and reflexive. This time-space envelope follows from the thesis that organisms are relationally contingent as 'needy', 'desiring', 'incomplete' existents. Different species 'endure' by creating and colonizing different spatiotemporal environments – developing their *typical* capacities within specific spatiotemporal worlds. Hence the parametric structure of time-space bearing upon 'organic life' is radically different from mathematical and physical concepts of time. Heidegger touches on this fundamental point in his inimitable terminology:

> Time-space now is the name for the openness which opens up in the mutual self-extending of futural approach, past and present. This open-

ness exclusively and primarily provides the space in which space as we usually know it can unfold. The self-extending, the opening up, of future, past and present is itself prespatial; only thus can it make room, that is provide space.

(1972: 14)

As time is the universal medium of unconcealment (*Unverborgenheit*) we necessarily 'interpret being by way of time' (1982: 17).

What we designate by the expression 'generic reflection', then, is the 'time-spacing' or *archi-écriture* which discloses a *situation* as a field of relationships in which significant 'location' and 'orientation' can occur. Recursivity is the 'giving in the sense of extending which opens up time-space' (1972: 16). We should note with Jacques Derrida – in this respect Heidegger's disciple – that this phenomenal possibility presupposes temporization in the generic form of *writing* or inscription as whatever 'opens space':

> Temporization, to temporize, means waiting or expecting (*attendre*), postponing or delaying. Temporizing is spacing, a way of making an interval, and here again with the idea of difference the ideas of spacing and temporization are inextricably linked. So time is not given priority over space.
>
> (in R. Mortley, ed., 1991: 100)

Derrida's point is that '*différance*' (in the twofold sense of differing and deferring) is always-already at work in the prethematic event which 'opens' the possibility of presence and representation: '*Différance* temporizes' displaces Heidegger's '*Being* presences' by the idea of the openness of 'spacing' as the horizon of the presence of beings. The manifestation of 'phenomenal events' is now grounded within a more primordial inscription (*écriture*) which discloses the space of representation prior to all positivity ('*le texte en général*' that Heidegger had earlier called 'language'). In the terminology of this study: 'spacing' opens a place of recursion – prior to concrete place and space, a purely indifferent reflexivity which is necessarily presupposed by all 'higher' modes of reference and self-reflection. These schematic descriptions are, of course, oversimplified and misleading. They are not intended as a comprehensive phenomenology of spacing or writing, but as a way of rethinking reflexivity more primordially. In this context the open reflexivity of experience is already enmeshed in prior mediations.

This is one of the meanings of 'mediation' as it bears upon generic reflection: mediation is the site of non-presence prior to all mimesis but is not, thereby, itself 'present' or 'presentable' ('presencing' does not comply with any entitative ontology). Objects and organisms have their own placement in series of differences (*d'une trace différentielle*) but these 'places' cannot themselves be abstracted from the 'spacing' which enables the differential 'inhabiting' of space. This presencing 'non-site' antedates every act of mimesis in space and

135

time. To speak with Heidegger, the opening up a clearing presupposes the prior openness of beings in Being. Moreover this 'spacing' which illuminates the order of the visible is not itself a visible phenomenon, but the accompanying horizon of every visible object.

Unlike a universe of inert objects, the world of self-experiencing organisms invites description in temporal, self-referential concepts. A graphic universe, so to speak, countenances beings that are both subjects and objects of their own experiences. In 'deferring' and 'anticipating' they attend to their own 'presence' and to the specific modalities of 'absence' (lack, need, anticipation, etc.) determined by their organic inscription. The seminal idea is that consciousness accesses reality only within an older system of relationality, that is, only within a horizon of 'open relations' – an openness that both sustains and is disclosed by generic reflexion. We might say, borrowing a formulation of Marx, that *reflexivity-in-general* is certainly an abstraction, but a rational abstraction insofar as it isolates and articulates a moment common to all reflexive systems – the element of self-recursion invariant across different modalities of reflexion. The more general the mode of reflexivity (relationality, temporality, presencing, spacing) the more that mode will be found in all species, societies, and historical periods. Something like this archetypal reflexivity is presupposed in viewing the history of human consciousness as an emergent configuration from the darker background of 'nature' or antecedent modes of precategorial praxis. But once in existence emergent structures actively respecify earlier patterns of reflexivity – consider for example the evolution of the opposable thumb and first finger as an elementary paradigm of generic reflection which evolves from the field of human praxis and in turn actively transforms and revolutionizes that field: the origin of the human hand is simultaneously a cause and consequence of strategic changes in the field of embodied consciousness. A creature with an ability to coordinate hand and eye to create new domains of manipulatory praxis lives in a radically different world from an organism without this capacity (and today we might approach other evolved 'organs of praxis' in modal terms as species-specific cognitive functions).

Like the slippery word *consciousness*, 'reflection' is an essentially contested concept in every discourse with a concern for the constitution of meaning and selfhood.[2] Each reference to *mind, self, self-consciousness, sentience, awareness, thought, meaning* (sense, signification, intention, intentionality), *symbolism, belief, discourse, knowledge, culture*, and so forth, bears witness to the unavoidability of such contested notions – intrinsically self-referential concepts simultaneously referencing and displaying meaning processes. Self-reference might equally well be understood as the generic category of *Meaning* (Latin *prae-sens*, French *sens*, German *Sinn*) – if we accept that the minimal 'conditions of the (im)possibility' of meaning are founded on the generic temporizing structure of significant differentiation we have metaphorically termed 'spacing'.

We are close to Heidegger's idea of the 'preontological' understanding of Being:

> It is understanding that first of all opens up or, as we say, discloses or reveals something like being. Being is given only in the specific disclosedness that characterizes the understanding of being. But we call the disclosedness of something truth ... Being is given only if there is disclosure, that is to say, if there is truth. But there is truth only if a being exists which opens up, which discloses, and indeed in such a way that disclosure itself belongs to the mode of being of this being.
>
> (1982: 18)

As Heidegger observes, 'we ourselves are such a being', caught in the openness of Being in beings. But we are also conscious of being 'such a being' within the openess of beings to Being. Objects, animals, and human beings subsist within the operations and functions of a field of differential mediations; but their 'presence' as 'objects' is constrained by the fixed capacities of organisms and agents constituting such fields; these are patterns of intelligibility which elude conscious reflection and are simply taken as the self-evident starting point of mundane activities. By contrast human beings refer to beings, inquire into the truth of things, formulate the relationships between different categories of being in judgements, and, occasionally, ask reflexive questions about the grounds of these elementary capacities.

Heidegger designates the Dasein of human being with the term 'Existenz' – literally that being which 'stands out' from being (ek-sistent, from the Greek term ekstasis), the being which says 'I am', reflects upon its inscriptive status, thinks, and conceptualizes its existence. Only reflexive creatures can be said to exist, to stand forth reflexively from within the horizon of the world. In a formula: Existenz is the mode of being of human being which makes every other distinctive cultural and linguistic practice of human praxis possible. The Dasein, by virtue of its ecstatic nature, is 'in truth', and only because it is 'in truth' does it have the possibility of being 'in untruth'. Being is given only if truth, hence if the Dasein, exists (1982: 18–19). It is Dasein which mediates beings as beings-already-disclosed, which attends to and investigates the different forms and modes of being-disclosed. Things are disclosed as existing things only for Dasein. But their ready availability hides, in Heidegger's words, the 'event of Appropriation' which first discloses spatiotemporal objects. The event of 'spacing' draws away from the visible phenomena it makes possible. For instance, the horizon of enduring perceptual objects ('real physical things') is taken for granted as a working premise for most forms of mundane praxis. In general the possibilities of perception and action are grounded upon the prior field of prereflective spacing. As we have suggested in Part I, the ontological field of Western thought is already temporalized in the mode of past, present, and futural 'presences'. Any particular experience occurs within the horizon of the perceptual zone and this horizon itself presupposes other unnoticed background horizons of appropriation. Yet the conditions of the possibility of elementary perceptual acts are not themselves 'perceived' or 'perceptual' (just as Appropriation is not to be identified with the spatiotemporal field it assembles – for example, with the field of three-dimensional sensory manifolds).

But is 'being-there' simply another way of saying that human consciousness with its distinctive conceptual and imaginative modalities is indebted to more primordial modalities of reflexivity prior to acts and modes of reflection? The 'taken-for-granted world of perception' is founded upon prior articulations which are not themselves perceptual. In our ordinary, reifying talk of experiences, physical objects, relations, etc. we continually assume mediation or 'significance' prior to meaning (the 'granting' of language which conceals itself in *a-letheia*, in Heideggerian terminology). Prior to the question of *de facto* perceptual objects is the question: how is anything like 'a perceptual field' possible? What is the 'giving' (in '*es gibt*') which founds the possibility of the world of perceptual presence? How are the structures of presence shaped by language and culture? One solution is to accept the recursivity of Being as a primary datum – Being literally folds back upon itself. As a recursive matrix it opens sites where beings may becomes manifest. There is no 'being as such', only recursive folds – from which arise the different spheres of embodiment, symbolism, and sociality in human life. Human beings think and conceptualize being, but only by first existing as beings-in-the-world. The 'being-horizon' is prior to all conceptuality and cognitive comportment.

2 THE BIOGENESIS OF SELF-REFERENCE

[T]he primal loop that seems somehow deeply implicated in the plot of consciousness

(Douglas R. Hofstadter, 1982: 283)

The self comes into being at the moment it has the power to reflect itself.

(Douglas R. Hofstadter, 1980: 709)

These positions are close to the perspective – if not the philosophical language – adopted by George Herbert Mead. Mead traced the higher functions of self-representation to the social field of kinaesthetic meaning: 'reflection presupposes the immediate world as given and that the self arises within social conduct within this field' (Mead, 1938: 17). Symbolization, for example,

> constitutes objects not constituted before, objects which would not exist except for the context of social relationships wherein symbolization occurs. Language does not simply symbolize a situation or object which is already there in advance; it makes possible the existence or the appearance of that situation or object, for it is a part of the mechanism whereby that situation or object is created ... Meaning is thus not to be conceived,

fundamentally, as a state of consciousness, or as a set of organised relations existing or subsisting mentally outside the field of experience into which they enter; on the contrary, it should be conceived objectively, as having its existence entirely within this field itself.

(Mead, 1934: 78)

Mead's analysis of generic meaning as a field of dramatic action complements Heidegger's view of Dasein as a primordial 'spacing' of the world. Both point toward a dynamic theory of the biogenesis of self-reference.

In generic reflexion, self-recursion provides a matrix for significance; the looped field of temporalization antedates the practices of signification; here the category *meaning* or *sense* is indifferent with respect to the differences it gathers and organizes. 'Meaning' is a synonym for the recursivity of difference (biologically, the plural systems of 'meaning' in play in different forms of life). The oriented acts of an experiencing organism anticipate their completion in the temporal process of being-oriented; such acts disclose future states of completion or consummation in practically deferring their goal as a realizable 'objective'. The unnoticed 'background' of object differentiation is what is left unexamined by modern philosophy, just as it ignores the fact that every mode of consciousness presupposes a prior 'site' of disclosure. Heidegger, as we have seen, ofen speaks of this as simply 'openness' (*das Offene*), comparing the event of Being to the ubiquity of light:

Only by virtue of light, i.e., through brightness (*Licht, Helle*), can what shines show itself, that is, radiate. But brightness in its turn rests upon something open, something free which might illuminate it here and there, now and then. Brightness plays in the open and wars there with darkness. Wherever a present being encounters another present being or even only lingers near it – but also where, as with Hegel, one being mirrors itself in another speculatively – there openness already rules, open region is in play. Only this openness grants to the movement of speculative thinking the passage through that which it thinks. We call this openness which grants a possible letting-appear and show 'opening'

(1972: 64–5)

In viewing objects we ignore light, in attending to things we are oblivious to the 'openness' (*Lichtung, das Offene*) which facilitates their illumination. In living with and manipulating beings we ignore the ultimate context of existential intelligibility.

These simple ideas have radical consequences for the question of the biogenesis of self-reference. An organism that can project itself in an 'anticipative' manner begins to operate in a temporal as well as a spatial universe. Here, of course, we can only note that the theme of the purposiveness of animate organisms leads to a vast and complex field of philosophical research. We simply note some elementary observations from the phenomenology of organic teleology.

Compare the relatively 'static' repertoire of an insectivorous plant like the venus fly-trap and a mobile insectivore like the mantis. The latter 'spatializes' and 'temporalizes' its world in response to distinctive zoösemiotic capacities. An insect alighting upon the 'trigger' cells of the venus fly-trap chemically activates the 'jaws' of the plant; but a more complex organism like a preying mantis tracks its victims across a semiotic zone. Organisms which can scan the movement of their prey, anticipating the point where they cross the zone of edibility are engaged in something akin to hypothetical action. Presumably the world of the fly-trap is one in which the larger part of its effective environment, being stationary, has no significant existence; yet a critical difference appears between this form of life and creatures with the capacity to trace semiotic trajectories – the waiting jaws of the mantis are 'tuned' for 'things' which move in characteristic ways across the screen of edibility. Whatever triggers its jaws to snap closed becomes 'prey' – in this case other insects of a certain size, motility, and edibility. The success of the mantis' recursive sensory systems are confirmed by this primary contact experience – here, devouring whatever fits the grid of edibility.

Contemporary biology speaks of nature in a self-referential idiom. At the macrolevel the word 'nature' designates the evolutionary chain of animate organisms and their diverse forms of life. Indeed, if we follow the 'Gaia hypothesis' of James Lovelock, the earth and its ecosphere can be viewed as a living organism governed by a quasi-purposive logic (Lovelock, 1979, 1988, 1991). At the microlevel neurologists conceptualize neural networks as diagnostic, self-repairing software necessary for self-learning systems to survive and extend their organization in chronically unstable environments. In the language of seventeenth-century 'organic rationalism', Nature is a vast interconnected system of unities (*monads* is the word the philosopher Gottfried Wilhelm Leibniz (1646–1716) coined after the Greek philosophical term signifying 'unity' or 'what is one'). For Leibniz – perhaps consciously appropriating the Aristotelian idea of natural teleology – the totality of nature manifests itself as a stratified field of mirroring, interacting substances, a hierarchical community of monads: each body acts on every other body, more or less, in proportion to its distance, and is itself affected by others through reaction; consequently 'each monad is a living mirror or a mirror endowed with internal action, which represents the universe from its own point of view and is as ordered as the universe itself' (Leibniz, 1989: 206–13, §3). In an analogous fashion, for a Leibnizian like Lovelock today, the earth with its living biosphere behaves like a system of mutually adapting, interacting monads – not merely an ultra-complex system, but a *living* unitary organism bringing 'deviations' of climactic change and chemical imbalances back into unity.

Nature as a dynamic, composite totality of self-relating, self-referential systems can be understood as a field of meaning-relations or objective perspectives, without any presumption of intentionality or self-conscious purposiveness. The ancient theme of the *vis viva* is still basic to what is today called zoösemiotics – Nature 'experiences itself' in manifold differential modes through its myriad forms of life. Hegel conveys a similar understanding in his discussion of the category of *reciprocity*: 'In reciprocity ... the straight line movement from causes to effect and from effects to causes, is bent round and back into itself and thus the progress *ad infinitum* ... is ... really and truly suspended' (1969: 217). In Leibniz' idiom 'all of nature is full of life' – in the sense that monads are 'free' to move, behave, and act in the clearing that antedates their being and specifies their species-specific orientations. 'Life' and its continuous struggle against disorganization and disintegration then becomes the supreme ordering principle for scientific reflection (or 'natural philosophy'). For Lovelock, as we have seen, the biosphere of Mother Earth is to be interpreted as a living organism situated in a fragile ecosphere, a reflexive loop within the larger clearing of its encompassing environment. These simple thoughts disclose what has been covered up in the modern conception of nature as a physical mechanism: in this context what is fundamental is the delicate manifestation of the being of nature in relation to its enveloping horizon. As Heidegger observes: 'This means: the phenomenon itself, in the present case, the opening, sets us the task of learning from it while questioning it, that is, of letting it say something to us' (Heidegger, 1972: 66).

> Accordingly, we may suggest that the day will come when we will not shun the question whether the opening, the free open, may not be that within which alone pure space and ecstatic time and everything present and absent in them have the place which gathers and protects everything.
> (Heidegger, 1972: 66)

The idea of natural self-reference *qua* openness (*das Freie, das Offene*) encompasses a diverse range of life forms, particularly organic systems living and restoring themselves through transactional relationships with their relevant ecologies (for example through species-specific *perceptual* systems and *learning* programmes which are coded into the conditions of existence of an organism in its relevant environment or *Umwelt*). While many of the higher sentient, living organisms subsist in complex processes of energy and information exchanges – that is, they engage in communication in the broadest sense of the word – only certain species seem able to reproduce their structural organization by abstracting self-referential models of the world from the flow of material existence and information networks. This may have been the insight behind Leibniz' distinction between *perception* and *apperception*:

> it is good to distinguish between *perception*, which is the internal state of the monad representing external things, and *apperception*, which is *consciousness*, or the reflective knowledge of this internal state, some-

thing not given to all souls, nor at all times to a given soul ... it is because they lack this distinction that the Cartesians have failed, disregarding the perceptions that we do not perceive, in the same way that people disregard imperceptible bodies. This is also what leads the same Cartesians to believe that only minds are monads, that there are no souls in beasts, still less other *principles of life*.

(Leibniz, 1989: 206–13, §4)

When we reach the level of human culture with its 'second nature' of reflexive systems, self-organization raises the adaptive capacities of sentient self-regulating creatures to its ultimate conclusion by creating differentiated nesting structures many times removed from the elementary world-testing relations of less complex semiotic species. An organism that can disengage from its immediate physical environment, experimentally enact and test its world relations prior to acting has a greater adaptive capacity than a system that is governed by a closed circle of immediate behaviour. Such creatures enjoy a greater degree of freedom from their material, physical, and organic preconditions. Without assuming any kind of anthropomorphism we may say that they have a greater capacity to 'transcend' their material constraints and engage in *autopoeic* behaviour. Reflexive circuitry now functions on a qualitatively new plane of semiotic behaviour.

This, of course, is the great evolutionary step made by organisms that have the biological capacity of coding information in neural networks and evolving differentiated subsystems of such networks specializing in complex modular tasks and functions. The evolution of species with such 'networking capacities' appears to be a basic condition of self-reflexive experience (while many organisms 'see' their worlds, only certain species 'see that they see' their worlds). In these emergent forms of life we witness the *radical* interconnectedness of the material infrastructure of life, organic functions, and environmental possibilities as a fundamental condition for the relative independence of the organism. In Leibnizian terms a monad that has the capacity to *apperceive* – by reflecting upon its perceptions and representations – also has the ability to engage in intelligent action toward its environment and neighbouring monads. Such an organism is no longer 'life-driven', but 'life-experiencing'. When we reach the human species, *reflexive* praxis in the form of conceptually mediated activities, purposeful behaviour, and cultural action becomes a normal adaptive condition of action-in-the-world, a background presupposition for concerted action-on-the-world. And the thought naturally arises that whatever is the ultimate meaning of 'nature' (in such expressions as 'living nature' or 'animate nature'), it must contain the principled possibilities for such self-regulative, self-referential ecologies.

This picture of higher-order metarepresentation need not involve any anthropomorphic attribution of 'sentience' or 'consciousness' to nature (any more than the wiring of the human brain is 'conscious' in producing intentional states and events). The self-monitoring properties of human self-activity need have no implications of design or teleology. But it does seem to imply that whatever our final description of the universe may be, it must contain the necessary complexity to generate organisms that have the principled structure of being aware and becoming reflexive in their world encounters. An adequate 'philosophy of nature', in other words, must provide a principled concept of the *person*. The insight goes back to Giordano Bruno and Leibniz, and may be as old as the Presocratic Greek thinkers. But, as Heidegger observes,

> philosophy knows nothing of the opening. Philosophy does speak about the light of reason, but does not heed the opening of Being. The *lumen naturale*, the light of reason, throws light only on openness. It does concern the opening, but so little does it form it that it needs it in order to be able to illuminate what is present in the opening.
>
> (Heidegger, 1972: 66)

To explore the biosemiosis of organic life we can focus upon the following dimensions of world-openness: self-differentiation, disengagement, self-steering, and self-organization.

2.1 Self-differentiation

Generically every self-referential system can be described as *reflexive* to the degree that it possesses the capacity to *turn back* upon its own organization and operations in order to perform work on itself as a routine practical feature of its functioning. In Scholastic philosophy it was thought that only *rational animals* were capable of such reflection – objectifying themselves as 'I', 'soul', or 'mind' (*intellectus*). Hence such monads were called *minds* (Leibniz, 1989: 209). Minds routinely engage in ordered forms of reflexion and self-reflexion. Systems which are capable of self-directed movement are today described as *behavioural systems*. Unlike inert objects they engage in *behaviour*, acting upon and changing their environments. In Dewey's terminology, organisms *act* to satisfy needs: 'By satisfaction is meant this recovery of equilibrium pattern, consequent upon the changes of environment due to interactions with the active demands of the organism' (1958: 253). The governing mode of intentionality is one of fulfilling species-specific needs by means of functions which are usually grouped under the generic heading 'metabolism'. Organisms 'behave' in order to survive and flourish. But they are also 'subject to' definite environmental constraints. The environment must play into the hands of the organism's needs. As we say, rather anthropomorphically, the environment must be favourable for life and, more particularly, for *this particular life form*. A wholly unresponsive environment would not sustain any life forms and we know that small external changes can lead to the disappearance of plant and animal life on a vast scale. The transformation of the effective environment for such organisms further impinges upon the system itself. This frequently elicits ascriptions of 'consciousness'; we feel like saying: only an organism that is in some sense 'conscious' can *behave*. In the phenomena of self-governance we have prima facie evidence of 'conscious systems' – life forms with organic needs acting toward their environments through repetitive cycles of *need-action-resolution*. Inert objects – having no needs or sensibility – do not 'relate', and particularly do not 'relate to themselves'. Only an organism that can relate to itself can be described as a 'psycho-physical' existence (Dewey, 1958: 254–5).

'Self-regulating', 'self-monitoring', and 'self-organizing' systems display a basic reflexive feature we can term *self-differentiation*: 'The project (*conatus*) wherewith each thing endeavours to persist in its own being is nothing more than the actual essence of the thing itself' (Spinoza, 1986: Part III, Proposition VII, 91). As Jorge Luis Borges once observed, 'the stone eternally wants to be a stone and the tiger a tiger'. Self-relational capacities emerge as a correlate of organic organization. 'Consciousness' as self-awareness would then be simply 'the last and latest development of the organic and consequently also the most unfinished and weakest part of it' (Nietzsche, 1974: §11). It is an emergent capacity grounded in 'preconscious' constellations of meaningful orientation. Spinoza, for example, defines the term *conatus* in terms of entities desiring to persist in their being (*behaviour* as integral parts of nature as *natura naturans*: *conatus esse sui conservandi* – 'Each thing strives, as far as possible, to persist in its own being' (Spinoza, 1986: Part III, Proposition VII, 91)). Beings display a 'desire' or 'interest' to maintain themselves in their being and self-identity (cf. Mead's definition of 'organisms' as 'emergent events whose nature involves the tendency to maintain themselves', 1959: 24; also Dewey, 1958: 248–97, esp. 252–4).

In human reality this 'persistence in one's being', this striving for *existence* – as Schopenhauer describes the will-to-live (*der Wille zum Leben*) – takes the paradoxical form of a creative journey through the life forms of others. In an analogous fashion Leibniz transformed the Spinozan insight into an ultimate metaphysical principle accounting for the fact that 'something rather than nothing exists': 'there is a certain urge for existence or (so to speak) a straining toward existence in possible things or in possibility or essence itself; in a word, essence in and of itself strives for existence'. In the medieval Latin image of the chain of scalar Being: 'it follows from this that all possibles, that is, everything that expresses essence or possible reality, strive with equal right for existence in proportion to the amount of essence or reality or the degree of perfection they contain, for perfection is nothing but the amount of essence' (Leibniz, 1989: 150). The stone, the tiger, and man are different realizations of essence – different stages in a fixed scale of perfectibility and rationality. Leibniz, like many metaphysical thinkers before him, believed he could read the *a priori code* of creation out of the configured character of monadic composites. The philosopher is set the task of decoding the apodictic plan of Providence from the dynamic stratification of living systems. This theological claim, of course, presupposes a number of dubious speculative assumptions. As Dewey pointed out, 'he omitted to note that metaphysically the case was begged as soon as an affair, no matter how elaborate in structure, is regarded as *being* composite. To *be* a composite is one thing; to be capable of reduction to a composite by certain measures, is another thing' (1958: 143, n. 3).

Here the basic metaphysical continuity with the Parsonian idea of social systems is also evident: such systems are self-monitoring to the extent that they differentiate themselves from their operative environment through symbolically mediated structures of anticipated action. Social systems no less than biological systems exemplify the universal tendency of organisms to maintain themselves in their being – and as 'cultural systems' they perform this feat by means of complex processes of self-representation and normative regulation. We might even consider modern Systems theorizing as a secularized variant of the language of *conatus* and possible *essence* (systematicity *qua* essence being the foundation of existence). Metatheories of complexity continue by other means the project of Aristotelian metaphysics – to grasp the telic structure and ends of beings in their being, of systems in their 'systemness'. We can understand the moderns' *system* as a notational variant of the seventeenth-century's intelligent *monad* or the medieval reflective *substance*. Mead, for instance, certainly has Leibniz in mind when speaking of the structure of the self as a reflection of the organized social process as a whole. He explicitly invokes Leibniz's famous image: the self is a microcosm of the social whole 'just as every monad in the Leibnizian universe mirrors that universe from a different point of view, and thus mirrors a different aspect or perspective of that universe' (1934: 201).

2.2 Disengagement

Auto-differentiation cannot be restricted to personal, social, or even living systems (in that self-differentiation is a general, criterial property of plant species and servomechanisms). But we can say that organic systems that are self-differentiating and self-monitoring are more accurately described as 'living' when reflexivity takes the form of structural disengagement, permitting the system a degree of autoregulative freedom and projective anticipation (boundary-maintaining metabolism, nutrition, growth, creative feedback, sensory responsiveness, self-repair, spontaneous adaptation cycles, etc.). Thus the simplest unicellular organisms incorporate particular strategies of self-differentiation and self-monitoring in their chemical codes. More complex organisms can be regarded as evolutionary strings of such adaptive networks. With increasing organic complexity systems may develop self-causing *autopoeic* capacities and dispositions and can then be described as 'environment-conscious' or 'aware'.[3] In Schopenhauer's vivid description of the continuum of life:

the more varied and versatile an animal's needs are through the more

145

complicated organization, the more manifold also are the properties of
the objects capable of satisfying them, and the more tortuous and distant
the paths for arriving at them, all of which must therefore be *known* by
the animal; consequently also the more perfect and many-sided must its
representations be, and the more exact, definite, manifold and varied the
knowledge which the animal provides for itself of things, and finally the
closer, more persistent and excitable its attention to the things represented, and hence the more developed its *intelligence*.

(1989: vol. III, 269)

For example, organic systems 'test' and 'negotiate' their relevant environment
– 'colonizing' a niche of the experienceable universe by relating themselves to
their correlative worlds. Such organisms are not 'in' their relevant environments like an object in a box, but reflexively as a transactional exchange. From
the perspective of a living organism the world is a network of pathways created
by its own activity. A relation of double contingency links the system and its
environment: as a result of reciprocal interaction what is a system from one
selective point of view may be treated as an environment from another. Indeed,
every open system is a relatively organized whole, depending upon a range of
encompassing systems and contextual environments. No living system can
ever secure total closure of its defining membrane. In Adolf Portmann's phrase:
organisms 'reveal the merely relative self-sufficiency of their systems in that
they are always found in a relation to the environment as a whole, including
all the realities that we cannot perceive directly with our senses and therefore
seek to comprehend by indirect means' (Portmann, 1955: 344).

Each natural system obeys a parasitical logic of growth and development
(every living system being a parasite upon wider systems and sources of energy
and information). The phenomenon of parasitism is more general than is
usually supposed. In parasitical systems, one organism treats another organism
as its sustaining environment (a virus would thus be a perfect parasite in the
sense of not only treating its host as its resource base, but in transforming its
host's cellular structure in its own image – 'taking over' by 'destroying' the
host configuration but in the process propagating its own form). In principle
every 'natural being' is parasitic upon the body of Nature.

Organic systems functioning as 'parts' of larger systems display the parasitical pattern most clearly:

The root-tips of a plant interact with chemical properties of the soil in
such ways as to serve organised life activity; and in such ways as to exact
from the rest of the organism their own share of requisite nutrition. This
pervasive operative presence of the whole in the part and of the part in
the whole constitutes susceptibility – the capacity of feeling – whether
or no this potentiality be actualized in plant-life. Responses are not

merely selective, but are discriminatory, in behalf of some results rather than others. This discrimination is the essence of sensitivity.

(Dewey, 1958: 256)

As a consequence of parasitism the 'laws' of evolutionary biology rarely assume the form of mechanical predictability or unilinear determinism. The evolution of life is possible only as the genesis of systems which transcend their initial terms of reference to develop new strategies of adaptation in an ever-changing universe. Here the categories of 'possibility' and 'serendipity' are more appropriate to the life-worlds of living beings. Temporality enters into the life-process of the organic system: 'Every form of life appears to us as a *Gestalt* with a specific development in time as well as space. Living things, like melodies, might be said to be configured time; life manifests itself as configured time' (Portmann, 1958: 312).

Life is configured time, an organization of events. Each life form unfolds in and as a possible structuration of experience. The operative environment of an organism is thus not a static given, but emerges as a response to the empirical complexity of organic functions. More complex organisms, as it were, 'elicit' different world possibilities from their environments. In Portmann's words:

The development of animals in time is more than a mere undergoing of the temporal process; it is a resistance to time, a mode of formation provided in the protoplasm of the particular species, which works counter to the merely material processes studied by physics and chemistry.

(1958: 313)

They come to 'appropriate' their worlds, shaping and 'protecting' what is 'proper' to their being (*Ereignis*, appropriation). The organism, in sum, is a dialectical agent within an environing field of agents, part of an actor-network.

This symbiotic intermeshing of two or more orders of complexity is a relatively common feature of many forms of organic existence. Different degrees and levels of disengagement are consequently reciprocally related to emergent forms of experience. Karl Popper describes this dialectic in the following terms:

In extant cells the pathways are controlled, step by chemical step, by enzymes which are highly specific chemical catalysts, that is, chemical means of speeding up specific chemical steps; and the enzymes are partly controlled by the genes. But a genetic mutation, and the synthesis of a new enzyme, will not lead to a new step in the net of pathways unless the new enzyme accidentally fits into the extant net; it is always the existing structure of the net of pathways that determines what new variations or accretions are possible. It is the existing net that contains the potentiality for new inventions.

(Popper, 1990: 44–5)

147

2.3 Self-steering

Disengagement creates a *chiasmus* or space of manifestation between an organism and its environment and by opening a life-space frees the system to act upon and orient itself within its ecology (to steer in the direction of positive stimuli, to selectively relate to other organisms of the same species, to relate to itself). The organism can then be said to 'feel' its environment. Many simple organisms 'sense' their ecologies, sensitivity being understood as a prototype of information-gathering – in Popper's terminology, a process of obtaining knowledge with the help of the organism's sensitivity to the momentary state of its environment (1990: 45). It is one of the constitutive features of a living system to be constantly 'in transition'. The idea of permanence, identity, or absolute homeostasis is a metaphysical fiction: organic life involves transformation, a transitive process or permanent change of state. Indeed any organism that tried to secure permanent homeostasis would rapidly perish. In structural disengagement and boundary-maintenance we find the germ-form of a system's sense of self, the prototype of an organized relationship between the system and its effective world (evidenced by self-testing movement, an organism's learning ability, and its capacity to create novel behavioural strategies when confronted with obstacles or adversaries – to move toward a source of light or sustenance, to remove itself from a threatening environment, to prepare its behaviour by anticipating problems and 'imaginatively' generate alternative solutions and perspectives).

Systems that are capable of self-correcting operations are described as self-steering or *cybernetic* systems (after the Greek expression for 'governing' or 'steering', *kubernetes*). They are typically living organisms with sufficient degrees of complexity to learn from their encounters with their environment, and utilize this knowledge in structuring further cycles of feedback-informed behaviour. Organisms with locomotion or equivalent self-steering capacities become sentiently proactive and act to disclose further potential aspects of their environments: 'susceptibility to the useful and harmful in surroundings becomes premonitory, an occasion of eventual consequences within life' (Dewey, 1958: 257).

The most primitive learning responses of self-steering organisms contrast markedly with the fixity of mechanically programmed systems, systems that are definitionally incapable of disclosure, pattern innovation, and situational change. This is captured by everyday speech which pictures living organisms 'interacting' with their environments, actively determining the conditions of their existence, and tactically using ecosystemic resources to survive and reproduce. Living systems are thus not absolutely fated to live out preprogrammed destinies; they enjoy margins of creative adaptation and change some of the material constraints of their worlds. They live by becoming engaged 'problem-solvers' rather than 'reactive machines'. But this 'knowledge' is not a cognitive possession: it is *embodied* in the system's structural solutions, genetically transmitted from one generation to the next. In evolutionary terms, organisms are complex systems operating to reduce contingency. Schema evolved to reduce undecidability may be incorporated into the species-specific structures of the organism to form 'programmes' which a species brings to the problem of constituting its relevant universe ('Organisms and their organs incorporate expectations about their environments; and expectations ... are homologous with our theories ... So I suggest the hypothesis that adaptations and expectations are homologous even with *scientific theories* and *vice versa* theories with adaptations and expectations', Popper, 1990: 47). This was anticipated in Mead's conception of the *problematic situation*:

> Consciousness is involved where there is a problem, where one is deliberately adjusting one's self to the world, trying to get out of difficulty or pain. One is aware of experience and is trying to adjust the situation so that conduct can go ahead. There is, therefore, no consciousness in a world that is just there.
>
> (1938: 657)

These descriptions trace the biogenesis of reflection to problematic situations: 'Reflective thinking arises in testing the means which are presented for carrying out some hypothetical way of continuing an action which has been checked ... The problem is always a stoppage of something one is doing ... The solution of the problem will be some way of acting that enables one to carry on the activity which has been checked in relation to the new act which has arisen' (Mead, 1938: 79; cf. Dewey: 'As life is a character of events in a peculiar condition of organization, and "feeling" is a quality of life-forms marked by complexly mobile and discriminating responses, so "mind" is an added property assumed by a feeling creature, when it reaches that organised interaction with other living creatures which is language, communication. Then the qualities of feeling become significant of objective differences in external things and of episodes past and to come. This state of things in which qualitatively different feelings are not just had but are significant of objective differences, is mind' (1958: 258)). In an earlier work, Dewey stresses the role of obstacles or the 'blocking' of ongoing situations as a vital stimulus to thought and reflection:

> Deliberation is a dramatic rehearsal (in imagination) of various competing lines of action. It starts from the blocking of efficient overt action ... Deliberation is an experiment in finding out what the main lines of possible action are really like ... thought runs ahead and foresees outcomes, and thereby avoids having to await the instruction of actual failure and disaster.
>
> (Dewey, 1922: 190)

While explicit reflection occurs routinely in 'thinking beings', world-testing or *hypothesizing* should not be exclusively tied to cognitive thinking; 'puzzle-solving' is common to many other species: 'The problem itself ... is antecedent to thinking and may be solved without thinking. Thinking is a certain way of solving problems. The importance of correct thinking is simply the importance of solving our problems' (Mead, 1938: 79, 657–8; Dewey, 1922: 258ff.).

The antiquity of this model of cybernetic intelligence is evidenced by the fact that Aristotle's review of his predecessors' theories of the soul singles out their agreement on this single point:

> the same tendency of thought is shown by those who say that the soul is that which moves itself. For a feature of all these theories is the supposition that the production of movement is the most characteristic feature of the soul and that while it is through the soul that all other things are moved the soul's movement is produced by itself. And this is based on our seeing nothing move that is not itself moved.
>
> (*De Anima* 404a)

This became the basic premise for Aristotle's teleological view of mind as the functional form of the living organism. 'Movement' is the essence of every mode of life (hence the celebrated differentiation of the *psyche* of vegetative, animal, and human existence).

If we adopted Aristotle's entelechial perspective we can view complex forms of disengagement and functional integration as evolutionary developments of more elementary reflexive feedback relationships and conjectural responses. Each order of animate existence articulates a commensurate form of 'animation' or *psyche*. These orders are integrated into the functional roles or 'tasks' of a given order of life (sensing, digesting, reproducing, perceiving, etc.). Popper offers an Aristotelian example of this process in the evolution of the archaic eye:

> its invention incorporates new discoveries, new theories, new knowledge about the environment and also the possibility of new values. For the first bacterium that not only achieved the new chemical synthesis, but went with it to a layer near the surface of the sea and survived, after millions of its brothers had succumbed, proved by its survival that it had solved a *problem* of adaptation; and in solving a *problem*, it introduced a new theory about new *values*. The invention was incorporated in the structure of the organism; in new, inheritable knowledge and therefore in new *a priori* knowledge.
>
> (1990: 48)

Where the modern speaks of 'inventions' and 'hypotheses', Aristotle would speak of *psyche* and *telos*. The light-sensitive organ we know as the primitive eye changed the life-world of its 'host' organism – allowing the 'organism to feed on sunrays without destruction', but also leading to radical new possibilities of interpretation and development:

The invention of the eye is thus an invention of new theoretical *a priori* knowledge, of an adaptation to the environment. It was from the first an adaptation to a long term environmental structure: to the existence of potentially edible sunlight; it thus incorporates knowledge of this environmental structure. It is theoretical knowledge of a high degree of universality, almost like the Kantian knowledge of space and time.

(1990: 49)

While every living species must remain in continuous contact with its ecosystem, reflexive systems exist by relating to their relations, adapting, modifying, maintaining, integrating, and transforming those relationships. Reflexive organisms are able to utilize their own reactions to their ecological conditions as information to advance other forms of activity and disclosure. They not only act upon their environment – advancing or retreating from danger, say – but are *able to monitor and act toward themselves*. If conscious systems map their worlds into operative schema, self-conscious systems manipulate their representations of the world to create higher-order self-representations and models of models. In evolutionary terms some such reflexive process may account for the remarkable differentiation that produced the modular networks of processors in the human neocortex.

Reflexive life forms inhabit phenomenal life-spaces or, to borrow the phenomenological concept, *Lebenswelten*. They not only test their responses to their relevant worlds, but also test their modes of testing and creatively adapt these modes in response to changing circumstances. But if the emergence of meta-testing marks a major step toward higher forms of life we should note that this is not without cost; there is also forgetting. Popper illustrates with the archaic eye's discovery of 'edible sunlight': 'And yet, we – in common with all animals – have forgotten the knowledge that sunlight is edible, and how to eat it. And to this day we have not fully regained this knowledge' (1990: 49).

2.4 Self-organization

Pain is the eye of the spirit.

(Helmuth Plessner)

By abstracting from these phenomena we see that self-differentiation and disengagement create a prototypical figure-ground structure which functions as the most elemental process of *figuration*: the crystallization of a contrastive field between an emergent and its background of emergence, a system and its environment, an organism and its ecology. Recall the example of the archaic eye whose evolution precipitated the radical distinction between life-destroying and life-sustaining sunlight, and how the 'difference' could then be exploited by 'higher' species of bacterium and planktum. The eye as an adjunct of organic adaptation marks the difference between the world of sunlight as an undifferentiated backdrop to organic life and sunlight as a thematic source of

151

energy (and hence of further evolutionary experimentation). A figuration crystallized by the archaic eye becomes the incentive for further differentiation which, in feedback cycles, stimulates the growth of the light-sensitive organ in more complex and responsive directions. Both features are basic to the concept of *self-organization* (in what follows 'organization' should be understood in its active, *verbal* sense).

A living system actively colonizes its ecology by creatively modifying its mode of organization and boundary conditions. The dynamic interplay of form and meaning can be simply summarized by the principle that *systems define their own boundaries* (Luhmann, 1989: 6). In complex systems the work of boundary maintenance is made an explicit task of self-figuration (organisms maintain their boundaries by causally interacting with relevant objects, transforming objects, and routinely monitoring their metabolism to counteract boundary-destroying events – supervising, as it were, the 'between' which integrates while differentiating the organism from its relevant ecology (*Umwelt*)).[4] In Luhmann's terms, by differentiating themselves systems 'constitute the environment as whatever lies outside the boundary'.

Organic systems have both a material and an informational relationship to their species milieux. Plants and animals are complex physical systems with properties similar to the material fixity of an inert thing. But they also possess an additional range of properties we summarize with the adjective 'living'. Each species selects its environment and functions within that environment through species-specific information schemata:

> Its own condition determines the objects and influences to which it will respond. The conscious animal carries selection into the field of its own response ... Living processes include active relationships with objects in an environment, and conscious living processes also include such objects.
> Mead, 1959: 71–2; 1934: Section 32; 1938: Sections XVII, XVIII)

Phenomenologically, the species can even be said functionally to *create* its relevant world on the basis of its functional models of its environment. Unlike 'inert' objects, a living entity is environment-constituting:

> The organism goes out and determines what it is going to respond to, and organizes that world. One organism picks out one thing and another picks out a different one, since it is going to act in a different way.
> (Mead, 1934: 25; cf. von Uexküll, 1957: 5–80; Levins and Lewontin, 1985: chs 1–3)

The basic pattern of organic reflexivity is not one of form and content (or the Aristotelian 'form-of-content') or a microcosm 'in' a macrocosm. It is better described as a *reflexive spiral of information processing*: the self-relating difference created by the system's codes in actively determining its milieu (Mead, 1934: 25–6; Luhmann, 1989: 7). The more complex the organism and its

152

information transformations, the more complex is its corresponding environment (and dialectical relations with other *Umwelten*).

In evolutionary terms, new species weave different possibilities of existence – and in this sense the universe is a different place after the emergence of new orders of relationality and complexity. Emergence, information and complexity are interrelated keys to the phenomenon of reflexive systems. A reflexive species marks a difference which makes a real difference. In Mead's apt formulation of this dynamic relativity, 'the world is a different affair for the plant and for the animal, and differs for different species of plants and animals' (1959: 38). Organic processes

> constitute the objects to which they are responses; that is to say, any given biological organism is in a way responsible for the existence (in the sense of the meanings they have for it) of the objects to which it physiologically and chemically responds. There would, for example, be no food – no edible objects – if there were no organisms which could digest it.
>
> (1934: 77; also 129–30, 214–16, 245–52; 1938: Part II)

In sum, every reflexive species has a *dialectical* relationship with its habitat.

> This intimate relationship of environment and form is something that we need to impress on ourselves, for we are apt to approach the situation from the standpoint of a pre-existing environment just there, into which the living form enters or within which it happens, and then to think of this environment affecting the form, setting the conditions under which the form can live.
>
> (1934: 246)

Each self-conscious life form does not simply exist in the world construed as a closed, physical universe governed by remorseless legality, but actively colonizes its unique *Umwelt*, constrained, of course, by the particular information-programming systems available to the species to which it belongs:

> The appearance of the retinal elements has given the world color; the development of the organs in the ear has given the world sound. We pick out an organised environment in relationship to our response ... We see things in their temporal relationship which answer to the temporal organization which is found in the central nervous system ... Our world is definitely mapped out for us by the responses which are going to take place.
>
> (1934: 128–9)

The colonizing of specific universes represents a unique compromise formation between the possibilities offered by the world and the constraints of the organism's semiotic capacities. Mead expresses this important point in the following way: 'the only environment to which the form responds is the environment which is predetermined by the sensitivity of the form and its response to it' (1934: 246). What determines the operative field of species' worlds is not predetermined by the laws of nature; rather the dynamic field of organic life is produced by the organism's own self-organizational capacities. Different ecologies are the outcome of different *cognitive mappings*:

> The structure of the environment is a mapping out of organic responses to nature; any environment, whether social or individual, is a mapping out of the logical structure of the act to which it answers, an act seeking overt expression.
>
> (1934: 129, n. 32)

It follows that there are potentially as many universes as there are organisms with a distinctive 'attitude' or 'perspective' toward the world. There are an infinite number of possible perspectives, each of which will give a different definition to the parts and reveal different relations between them. The organic responses of different species are 'responsible for the appearance of a whole set of objects which did not exist before' (1934: 129). Nominal referents such as 'Thing', 'Substance', 'Form', 'Matter', or 'Idea' are grammatical hypostatizations of reflexive transactions. Against this naive view we see that with the evolution of a new type of organism – and even more so with the development of a new species of organic life – the universe itself is transformed; this has to be understood literally, not merely that a species has 'added to' the forms of species life. With more complex neurobiological structures species literally change the world to which they belong. New worlds are '*brought forth* in the process of knowing' (Maturana and Varela, 1980).

This can be briefly illustrated with the phenomena of *pain* experience. Ordinary language would have us think of pain in nominal and substantive terms. But from the perspective of this discussion, we should think of pain verbally, relationally, and dispositionally. In living organisms pain functions as a self-referential operation mediating system and environment. At one level the human response to boundary-threatening experiences is just as involuntary and reactive as less complex organisms; pain is the common denominator between human existence and non-human creatures (reflexive withdrawal from painful stimulation is the general rule for people as it is for amoebae). Hence the continuum of 'pain-like experience' which connects all forms of life: 'The physiological or sensory structure of the percipient organism determines the experienced content of the object' (Mead, 1934: 130). Occasionally more complex organisms actively search out and enjoy boundary-threatening experiences: they assume a reflexive attitude toward their own figuration; and in the human species the experience of pain is subject to a degree of redefinition and symbolization which both transforms the phenomenon and creates new socializing possibilities (for example, in the suffering caused by symbolic disintegration, anxiety, fear, anomie, and alienation, and in the symbolic pleasures of distantiation, risk, danger, imagination, and innovation).

Creatures that adopt a symbolic attitude toward hazard and anticipated pain have an enhanced chance of survival; they disengage from their environing world to negotiate life-threatening situations. Something akin to creative adaptation appears to be built into this type of pain orientation. Perhaps consciousness in its intentional senses has its genesis in the mute consciousness of pain common to human and non-human forms of life (the contracting and expanding rhythm of the amoeba's pseudopod is the true intellectual hero in the history of life). Certainly a large and frequently unacknowledged overlap of sentience and intelligent behaviour is shared by all sentient life. It may even be that the temporal structure of reflective anticipation in phylogenetic terms – the what-happens-next structure of lived anticipation, the pain of separation from friends, the root anguish of bereavement or imagined separation – derives its sense from the corporeal economy of pain as reactive avoidance.

The fuzzy borders around pain experience raise the issues as to whether animals can suffer or be in pain in the same sense as human beings, whether or not important categories of pain experience are identifiable in animals, the applicability of the category of 'suffering' to other species, the extent to which 'pain' is socially constructed and culturally variable, and so forth. It seems probable that the phenomenon of disengagement (involving as it does, distan-tiation, figuration and self-organization and, occasionally, loss of self-identity) is causally related to the evolution of pain strategies in more complex organ-isms; the threat of boundary dissolution is a recurrent problem for all living systems; and an organism's functional capacity to uncouple itself from its vital operations appears to be the basic prerequisite of reflexive behaviour. Once more the dialectics of nature are evident: 'since organism and environment determine each other and are mutually dependent for their existence, it follows that the life-process, to be adequately understood, must be considered in terms of their interrelations' (Mead, 1934: 130). An organism that began life as a *tabula rasa*, devoid of all figuration, would not survive to interrogate its environment further. From this perspective living systems should not be approached as totally isolated, autonomous entities, but as figural processes with definite degrees of freedom: an organism *lives* or *suffers* its reflexive relations, experiencing its effective ecology in and through world-experiencing activities. In Mead's terms, the conscious animal not only selects objects, but senses them as well.

Generic reflection, in other words, is not a possession but a function. Inversely, where an organism's pain strategies fail, where they atrophy or malfunction (through damage, age, or other entropic processes) we find a 'disengagement from disengagement' manifest as a dissolution of figuration: the general environment begins to intrude, dissolving the relevant environment and reclaiming the system; the organism's boundaries can no longer be rou-tinely maintained and eventually we say that the organism has disintegrated as an individual centre of functional processes.[5] Destruction of the figural process reverses the structuration inherent in reflexive disengagement. Pain, in Hegel's idiom, is 'the prerogative of living natures'. Sentient existences are an actuality of infinite power such that they are within themselves the negativity of themselves, that this negativity is for them, and that they maintain themselves in their otherness. It is said that contradiction is unthinkable; but the fact is that in the pain of a living being it is even an actual existence.

(1969: 770)

3 AUTOPOIESIS

To see the organism in nature, the nervous system in the organism, the brain in the nervous system, the cortex in the brain is the answer to the problems which haunt philosophy.

(John Dewey, 1958: 295)

While the cybernetic sciences (Computation, Artificial Intelligence, Robotics, etc.) presuppose elementary reflexivity (self-diagnostic and self-monitoring programmes), only living systems appear to have the ability to creatively reproduce themselves as relatively self-contained systems. Perhaps the classic description of this aspect of living organisms appears in Aristotle's *De Anima* 2.415a26–415b8:

> For any living thing which has reached its normal development and which is unmutilated, and whose mode of generation is not spontaneous, the most natural act is the production of another like itself, an animal producing an animal, a plant a plant, in order that, as far as its nature allows, it may partake in the eternal and divine. This is the goal towards which all things strive, that for the sake of which they do whatsoever their nature renders possible. The phrase 'for the sake of which' is ambiguous; it may mean either (a) the end to achieve which, or (b) the being in whose interest the act is done. Since the nonliving thing is able to partake of what is eternal and divine by uninterrupted continuance (for nothing perishable can ever remain one and the same), it tries to achieve that end in the only way possible to it, and success is possible in varying degrees; so it remains not indeed as the self-same individual but continues its existence in something *like* itself – not numerically but specifically one.

We have seen that organic systems create and solve problems within the web of life – in Popper's words:

> All organisms are problem finders and problem solvers. And all problem solving involves evaluations and, with it, values. Only with life do problems and values enter the world. And I do not believe that computers will ever invent important new problems, or new values.

(1990: 50)

As axiological beings, organisms exhibit the basic attitude of self-reference which Popper calls 'self-criticism'. Only such value-creating structures can be said to live together socially. The idea was already a commonplace for the earliest Greek thinkers. Aristotle writes:

> For all living things as well as plants have the nutritive faculty which is the first and most general faculty of the soul, in virtue of which all creatures have life. Its functions are to reproduce and to handle nourishment. For this is the most natural of the functions of such living creatures as are complete and not mutilated and do not have spontaneous generation, namely to make another thing like themselves, an animal producing an animal, a plant a plant, so that in the way that they can they may partake in the eternal and the divine.
>
> *(De Anima* 415a)

Unlike artifacts or constructed objects, 'things existing by nature' display 'a principle of movement (or change)'; natural creatures are self-moving substances having an inherent tendency to change or transformation. No artifact 'has within itself the principle of its own making' (*Physics* Book II, ch.1, 192b8–35). In particular no artifact possesses the unique property of being able to reproduce its form ('it is this incapacity of reproduction that makes a thing art and not nature', 193b10ff.). Living beings have the remarkable capacity to replicate themselves by creating other living beings. We may be able to copy artificial systems or construct systems with the possibility of self-replication, but no known machine can be described – other than metaphorically – as naturally reproducing itself. Life copies itself. Routine natural replication is a criterial feature of living organisms. In recent biological research this simple evolutionary principle has been reemphasized as the principle of the differential survival of replicating entities (see Dawkins, 1976).

After the Greek word for 'making' or 'creativity' (for example, as used in the context of the contrast between natural and artificial entities at *Physics* Book II, ch. 1, 192b), the logic of such systems has been termed *autopoiesis*.[6] Aristotle may be regarded as the first European theorist to construct an autopoeic definition of nature and, conversely, to think of mind as a natural emergent in dynamic terms: 'as the ultimately underlying material of all things that have in themselves the principle of movement and change' (*Physics* 193a28–30). A few lines later Aristotle reformulates the definition to emphasize the dynamic operation of form in autopoeic processes: 'Nature is the distinctive form or quality of such things as have within themselves a principle of motion, such form or characteristic property not being separable from the things themselves, save conceptually' (193b1–6). And the form 'has a better claim than the matter to be called nature. For we call a thing something, when it is that thing in actuality, rather than just in possibility' (193b5–10). The *psyche* of a creature 'inhabits' its body as form 'informs' its matter. A living organism thus contains the possibility of its formal replication. An 'animal' (from the Latin for *psyche, animus*) – a being animated by its '*psyche*' or life principle – is thus definitionally a creature which can potentially replicate itself. For this hylomorphic framework, replication is one of the defining characteristics of an autopoeic system. Literally meaning 'self-creating', *autopoeic* systems have been recognized and to some extent described and theorized from the time of Aristotle; they display a number of distinctive features which we can outline as follows.

3.1 Self-monitoring

Like cybernetic mechanisms, autopoeic systems are self-diagnostic; contemporary biology has had to ignore accusations of vitalism in order to rediscover Aristotle's insight into the teleological nature of life forms as self-organizing systems:

> anything that has in itself such a principle as we have described may be said to 'possess a nature' of its own inherently. And all such things have a substantive existence; for each of them is a substratum or 'subject' (*hypokeimenon*) presupposed by any other category, and it is only in such substrata that nature ever has her seat.
>
> (*Physics* 192b30–5)

3.2 Self-development

Unlike cybernetic mechanisms, which retain their designer's pattern as a fixed programme, autopoeic systems are self-developing forms – they move and act by their own nature; in Aristotelian terms, they contain an entelechial principle which actualizes the telos of the substance: they display natural processes of growth, dispositions toward integration, self-repair, self-realization and, in certain species, formal replication. In Aristotelian language the form of a substance is the end or goal for the sake of which the entity exists: 'if any systematic and continuous movement is directed to a goal, this goal is an end in the sense of the purpose to which the movement is a means' (*Physics* 194a25ff.). Unlike the predetermined algorithms of a machine, living systems are self-elaborating processes. Systems which resist entropy through aim-oriented activities (the degradation of bound and free energy, information and organization) are termed *negentropic* – they accumulate information, develop, and differentiate into more complex, if fragile, formations; such systems typically flourish by inducing changes in their organization and biospheres; the appearance of life involves organisms which deviate from the laws of homeostasis, entropy, and equilibration by organizing their environment in order to creatively manage energy transfers in their own interests; and as Aristotle endlessly reminds his readers, the *telos* or *form* of a living system

158

is not empirically (or materially) detachable from the living processes of that system.

3.3 Synergic coordination

As open structures autopoeic systems possess *synergic* capacities (*synergy* referring to the cooperation of two or more systems) to achieve a goal unrealizable by a single system – from the integration of atoms into a more complex molecule to the dynamic interdependencies of the human cortex and nervous system: 'There are groups of relatively simple reactions which can be made indefinitely complex by uniting them with each other in all sorts of orders, and by breaking up a complex reaction, reconstructing it in a different fashion, and uniting it with other processes' (Mead, 1934: 241). Living systems are not only teleological or aim-directed (in Aristotle's sense), but they also involve the social structure of cooperation in realizing their goal; in general this indexes the presence of synthetic orchestration or symbiosis in nature from the cellular world to the emergent complexity of macro-organisms and ecologies.[7] Synergy indexes the emergence of social coordination and cooperation within and between monads (cells, genes, organs, plant ecologies, animal systems, etc.). In some species synergic achievements introduce adaptive creativity in member systems, which in turn enhances further spiralling levels of synergic development (social animals first acquire communicational skills in the context of such cooperative interaction). An example from ego psychology is the synergic hierarchy of three processes of human organization: the hierarchic organization of organ systems constituting a body (*soma*), the psychic organizing individual experience by ego synthesis (*psyche*), and 'the communal process of the cultural organization of the interdependence of persons' (*ethos*) (Erikson, 1985: 25–6).

An animal can be variously described as a complex of entelechial substances (Aristotle), a colony of interdependent monads (Leibniz), a society of organisms each of which 'prehends' the world according to its own capacities (A.N. Whitehead), or, in Mead's terms, an organization of objective perspectives (the Aristotelian, Leibnizian, Whiteheadian, and Meadian formulations all resonate in Mead's important essay 'The objective reality of perspectives', in Mead, 1959: 161–75; see also his 'Perspective theory of objects', in Mead 1938: 159–65: 'There arise, therefore, perspectives not only in respect to the sense susceptibilities of different organisms, and to their spatial relations, but also in respect to the simultaneities which the organisms select and hence to the succession of events', 1938: 165; cf. Section XIX 'Mechanism and contingency' and the fragment on 'Relations' in Section XXXI, 639); the *leitmotif* of these different approaches is the emergence of the qualitatively new from the quantitatively differentiated and mutually organized patterning of events and systems:

The distinction between physical, psycho-physical, and mental is thus one of levels of increasing complexity and intimacy of interaction among natural events. The idea that matter, life and mind represent separate kinds of Being is a doctrine that springs, as so many philosophic errors have sprung, from a substantiation of eventual functions. The fallacy converts consequences of interaction of events into causes of the occurrence of these consequences – a reduplication which is significant as to the *importance* of the functions, but which hopelessly confuses understanding of them.

(Dewey, 1958: 261–2)

3.4 Self-stratification

The internal structure of autopoeic systems is frequently described in terms of a stratified or hierarchical system of interacting events. Hierarchical programming of more complex systems is often explained as an evolutionary adaptation to the requirements of increasing interdependence; even the simplest forms of organic life are regarded as stratified systems whose different 'strata' emerge under the exploratory techniques and technologies available to the 'sciences of complexity'. Laminated complexity governed by structural regulation thus suggests itself as a basic schema for integrating the objects of numerous inquiries from molecular biology to physiology and the social sciences:

> The conception of a world that is independent of any organism is one that is without perspectives. There would be no environments ... the object exists in its relation to the aspects of the world to which it is related – the form and its environment.

(Mead, 1938: 165)

3.5 Multidimensional complexity

The principle has been most economically stated by Joseph Campbell: 'All life is structure. In the biosphere, the more elaborate the structure, the higher the life form' (1973: 44). The term 'system' should always be understood as a shorthand expression for transactional processes recycling energy, matter, and information within an organism and between organism and ecosystem to create temporary system-environment equilibria. Vertical complexity has its correlate in networks of horizontal complexity both within systems and subsystems and across system levels. We know that what classical science – under the influence of Newtonian mechanics and nineteenth-century thermodynamics – accepted as closed, irreversible systems must now be viewed as dynamic, unstable processes of relational complexity ('relations of events', processes, and 'configurations' become new objects of knowledge). The language of physical states is replaced by quantum concepts (fields, interaction of events, space-time singularities, processes, relative complexity, configuration, transformation, instability, stochastic singularities, irreversible structures, and the like) and universal causal laws by corresponding probabilistic categories.

3.6 Metacognition

If the amoeba could think it would consider the world to be uniquely its own possession and take its pseudopods for instruments of truth. Such is the temptation of systems displaying metacognition. Consider the concept of 'representational system' elaborated by Douglas Hofstadter and Daniel Dennett: 'By "representational system" we will mean an active, self-updating collection of structures organized to "mirror" the world as it evolves ... a good representational system will sprout parallel branches for various possibilities that can be reasonably anticipated' (Hofstadter and Dennett, eds, 1982: 192–3). Open reflexive systems function by incorporating and utilizing information either self-generated or constructed through some intelligent transaction with an information-rich environment ('a representational system is built on categories'); information processing is obviously constrained by the array of senses and correlative field of sentience available to the system ('it sifts incoming data into those categories'); typically information controls energy not only in simple negative feedback loops, but in constructive, and often unanticipated forms of positive feedback ('when necessary refining or enlarging its network of internal categories'); open systems are also typically *irreversible*, by contast with reversible cybernetic, logical, and formal systems: they act toward the future as they live, processing meaning and information into sense and significance ('its representations, or "symbols" interact among themselves according to their own internal logic'). Without invoking some type of operative metacognition we have no way of accounting for the creative capacities of animals to alter their behaviour, delay responses, learn new behavioural repertoires, work cooperatively, and voluntarily control their activities and communicative repertoires:

> A many-layered system can have programs tailored to very specific needs ... at its most superficial level, and progressively more abstract programs at deeper layers, thus getting the best of both worlds. Examples of the deeper type of program would be ones for recognizing patterns; for evaluating conflicting pieces of evidence; for deciding which, among rival subsystems clamoring for attention, should get higher priority; for deciding how to label the currently perceived situation for possible retrieval on future occasions that may be similar; for deciding whether two concepts really are or are not analogous; and so on.
>
> (Hofstadter and Dennett, eds, 1982: 201)

3.7 Emergent reflexivity

As the physicist Ilya Prigogine has argued in several important works, 'we are living in a world of unstable dynamical systems' (see Prigogine and Sengers, 1984; cf. Prigogine, 1980, 1988). Randomness, bifurcation, irreversibility, stochastic instability, indeterminateness and general fragility are emergent phenomena which set definite limits to the prospects of algorithmic theorizing; this follows from the insight that the term 'system' does not designate a fixed and unified entity or substance, but a dynamic network of relations in which each of the 'terms' of relationality are *events* or *interactions*. A general rule here is that increasing complexity produces greater degrees of freedom, differentiation, and flexibility, but also introduces greater dependence, fragility, and multidimensional instability (emergent networks are subject to abrupt, unpredictable, qualitative, and often catastrophic transformations – leading several theorists to develop 'chaos' and 'catastrophe' models of systemic change as a rejoinder to the earlier theories of cumulative development by natural selection and adaptation (the chaos-mathematics of René Thom and Ralph Abraham; see Thom's *Stabilité structurelle et morphogenèse* (1972), the catastrophe-prone systems called 'dissipative structures' and in general 'the constructive role of irreversible processes' by Ilya Prigogine (1980) and James Gleick (1987). The unpredictability of complex systems has led to major revisions of the earlier causality-dominated systems theory of Ludwig von Bertalanffy, Norbert Wiener and their students, pointing in the direction of a more general ecological theory of configurations which reject the classical concepts of physical causality and mechanical determinism (the implicate order of David Bohm, the whole-field universe of Ervin Laszlo, neofunctionalist stress on unstable functional differentiation and dedifferentiation, infinite recursivity of parts and wholes (the fractal geometry of natural processes developed in B. Mandelbrot's *The Fractal Geometry of Nature* (1983)), and even speculative attempts to construct a reflexive model of the universe as a self-relating, self-evolving, self-differentiating whole).

4 TOWARD AN ECOLOGICAL PARADIGM

It is now a commonplace that reductionist explanations drawn from physical, mechanistic, monocausal, and linear-deterministic models of life are of little value in understanding the logic of complex, information-rich, communicative systems; if the objects of research are constitutively reflexive non-linear patterns it follows that unreflexive paradigms of the kind associated with the dualistic frameworks of Aristotelian substance, Newtonian physics, and Cartesian metaphysics will actively distort and falsify experience. As Gregory Bateson observed, we 'have this massive addiction to physical metaphors which ... are completely inapplicable to the life and epistemology of real organisms living in a real world' (Bateson, in Wilder and Weakland, eds,

1981: 354). Bateson's suggestion is that the life sciences should develop a framework of reflexive concepts adequate to ecological phenomena. The logic of the Thing has no purchase on the logos of Life. To avoid reductionism the life sciences must overturn centuries of metaphysical thought and adopt a reflexive paradigm sensitive to the complexity of order-generating autopoeic systems. We can conclude by isolating some of the principal domain assumptions of such a 'deep ecology'.

4.1 Holism

Holism is the principle that a comprehensive account of any phenomena must be given in terms of the structure inherent in that phenomenon and the context in which the phenomenon belongs as a part, phase, or interactive moment. In its most general meaning holism – a term related to 'making whole' and 'healing' – expresses a preference for organic and continuous over mechanical and discrete metaphors and conceptual schemes. In the history of epistemological frameworks it takes as its adversary the mind-body dichotomies of Platonic thought, scientist discourses of part-reductionism, eliminative atomism, and 'dustbowl empiricism'. The emergent properties of self-organized wholes are to be studied rather than their disaggregated parts or components (because of the interaction of system 'parts' a configuration is more than the sum of its components). Holism might be considered as the generalized philosophy of context.

4.2 Context

'Context' is a key term in every holistic perspective, emphasizing the principle of seeing phenomena and significance from the perspective of the system as a whole. But we should speak of *contextualization* and *recontextualization* given that 'context' does not name a fixed object or privileged space-time frame that remains stable for every order of existence. The context of a system is its effective environment – one which may induce spasms of disorder and change. But every 'mapping' of a context implicates further contexts implicated by the initial map. Context, as it were, recedes as we try to describe and articulate its 'nature'. More positively it follows that there will be an indefinite number of relevant contexts (and 'maps') depending upon constraints both of the form investigated and of the interests of investigation. In principle there can be no canonical map of any event, object, or process.

4.3 Process

Holism stresses the understanding of *life* as a contextual interaction between open systems and their ecosystems. Emphasis is placed on the transactional processes flowing between organism and environment, ecological interdependence, and functional processes. In general, the ecological stand-point rejects static, determinist, and functionalist modes of thought in favour of the dynamic emergence of complexity through temporal sequences or phases of a system's evolution (what we have referred to as *contextualization*). From this perspective organic life is viewed as a continuous process of *recon-textualization* occasioned and stimulated by external conditions and environmental changes.

4.4 Emergence

Phenomenological emergence is irreducible to material, chemico-physical lev-els, experienced throughout the orders of life. The spontaneous development of new systems and structures occasionally takes unpredictable and erratic directions (emphasized most emphatically by recent catastrophe models of change, development, and disorder). Emphasis is placed on the unpredictable dialectic of events rather than the unfurling of telic rationality inherent in systems:

> The possibility of the organism being at once in three different systems, that of physical relation, of vital relation and of sensuous relation is responsible for the appearance of the colored rough shaft and foliage of the tree emerging in the interrelation between the object and the organism.
>
> (Mead, 1938: 85)

Self-referentially autopoietic systems are endogenously restless and con-stantly reproductive. They develop structures of their own for the continuation of their autopoiesis.

> (Luhmann, 1989: 13)

4.5 Stratification

'Stratification' refers to the reflexive 'layering' of self-transforming systems capable of qualitative variations and changes of behaviour. In living ecologies the norm is one of open systems operating through multiple levels of functional organization, coordination, and integration. In principle we have to accept the idea of living systems as the product of an *indefinite* number of levels and processes – a paradoxical aspect of ecological structures that is impossible to include in any existing reductive epistemology (for instance, a system that can be described as self-healing necessarily presupposes a laminated interaction of many different physical, chemical, and environmental contexts). The constel-lation of different levels and different situational exigencies gives to each species a definite structure of place and time – animal species, as it were, inhabiting different time structures dictated by their structural properties and contextual relationships. The analytic unit of the ecological paradigm is no longer the isolated individual part, mechanical component, or structure, but the *reflexive configuration* itself: processes of relatively autonomous, hierarchically integrated systems of *relations*).[8]

From the ecological paradigm every system is also an environment and every environment is equally also a system. In this way the idea of the 'individual unit' as a basic term for any kind of scientific description is deconstructed. The more speculative exponents of this ecological vision of nature speak of the whole universe as a system of reflexive configurations. Perhaps we are witnessing a fundamental paradigm shift away from a digital-molecular representation of the universe as a mechanical, deterministic aggregate of isolated items, parts, and elements toward an ecological universe of interpenetrating relations, recursive configurations, and interlocking reflexive processes? But in our practices we still tend to think of these phenomena in the rigid conceptual frameworks of earlier world-views. To overcome this inertia the emerging paradigm requires that we think of life in other terms: that we have the imagination to take the role of the other – where *alterity* embraces forms of life hitherto excluded from our inherited conceptual frameworks.

4

CONSCIOUSNESS AND LIFE-WORLD

My intention in this chapter is to explore the ways in which the concept of consciousness has been thematized in recent Western thought. In keeping with the linguistic and rhetorical emphasis of logological method I explore the underlying 'grammar' of subjective experience (Sections 1 and 2). This discloses the constitutive metaphors and rhetorics of egological reflection in the ways we talk and think about consciousness and self-consciousness today. Finally, I reconstruct the implicit 'stratified' model of consciousness in these 'idealist' ways of conceptualizing the self (Section 3). This reformulation of one important part of our conceptual geography of subjectivity prepares the way for an analysis of philosophical positions that have elaborated these ideas into more systematic theories of consciousness in Chapter 5.

1 *Introduction: the structure of subjective experience*
2 *Consciousness and subjectivity*
3 *The stratification of consciousness*

Understanding is, to use general concepts, *the faculty of knowledge*. This knowledge consists in the determinate relation of given representations to an object; and an *object* is that in the concept of which the manifold of a given intuition is *united*. Now all unification of representations demands unity of consciousness in the synthesis of them. Consequently it is the unity of consciousness that alone constitutes the relation of representations to an object, and therefore their objective validity and the fact that they are modes of knowledge; and upon it therefore rests the very possibility of the understanding.

(I.Kant, 1929: B137)

1 INTRODUCTION: THE STRUCTURE OF SUBJECTIVE EXPERIENCE

In this element of the will is rooted my ability to free myself from everything, abandon every aim, abstract from everything. Man alone can sacrifice everything, his life included; he can commit suicide. An animal

166

cannot; it always remains merely negative, in an alien destiny to which it merely accustoms itself. Man is the pure thought of himself, and only in thinking is he this power to give himself universality, i.e. to extinguish all particularity, all determinancy

(G.W.F. Hegel, 1967: 227)

In their vernacular uses first-person expressions of 'feeling', 'awareness', 'thinking', and 'consciousness' are rough-and-ready synonyms (someone who is rendered insensible – for example, under a general anaesthetic – is routinely described as unconscious). I sit at my desk 'mindful' of both the purpose in hand and 'conscious' of my immediate surroundings: the pen lying obliquely across a sheet of white paper, the light from the lamp illuminating the work-space and my hands; sounds from the traffic and voices in the street beyond my office window ebb and flow as 'background noise'; at any time I can break from writing and consider other projects: I leave the room to answer the telephone, ponder the conversation I have just had while returning to my office, consider my work schedule for the next few days, and so on. All of these first-person 'conscious activities' are routine features of my 'wide-awake life'. They are forms of sentience that are cancelled by sleep or more extended 'non-conscious states'. In sleep we go on living but are disengaged from our vital contexts (although research on the complex processes of sleeping suggests that peripheral sentient awareness and subliminal conscious states are never completely absent); however, a person who loses her reasoning capacities on a more permanent basis has 'lost her mind' – she is no longer capable of intentional conduct, no longer responsible for her actions. In such cases we say that she has lost her identity (a situation which has manifold social and cultural repercussions for the individual); and this state of affairs is typically taken to be a situation that can only be expressed in the language of the self or person.

Each of these ways of speaking suggests that 'consciousness' is centred in a personal existence or a *self* which 'enjoys' and 'entertains' private states of mind: in being asked to think about some topic, we are urged to attend to the task in hand, deliberately to focus our thoughts and achieve a more thematic consciousness of a topic; personal agents are thought to 'know from the inside' what intense concentration feels like – say, in solving a difficult mathematical problem or in struggling to recall a forgotten name or date. To this extent the spontaneous philosophy of common-sense has been enriched by the vocabularies of philosophical idealism. Yet unlike idealism as a defensible epistemological position we do not customarily require a theory of 'inner knowing' or a reflective knowledge of our conscious states or selfhood to appear to others as an agent or person. All that is required is that we display the canonical properties of 'conscious agents' and that we continue to work in a community which shares these tokens of consciousness (the grammar of the 'self-concept' in other words overlaps with the grammar of the word 'person'). Despite the fluctuations of personal awareness and the vicissitudes of self-understanding we continue to represent our everyday experience of selfhood in the language of autonomous consciousness.

The family of everyday terms radiating from the word 'consciousness' overlaps with an equally dense network relating to 'self-consciousness'. In many of these figures of speech *consciousness* is likened to an inner light that can be switched on or off, dimmed, focused, heightened, or enhanced. While ultimately foundational and sovereign, its evident intermittence has been at the root of theological temptations to think of 'consciousness' as a spiritual substance which enters and leaves the body – a 'soul', 'essence', or 'vital spirit' inhabiting the material body. A creature can be said to be conscious without possessing a 'self' or 'personality'. The latter terms, however, are typically thought to be unique identifiers of self-conscious experience as 'mindful': to possess a 'mind' is to be included in the singular society of 'human beings'. Only human beings consciously attribute mental states and self-images to themselves and others. Only human beings describe their lives in the idiomatic vocabularies of selfhood. And being socially consequential such attributions are freighted with personal, cultural, and political consequence. Not surprisingly, the tacit logics of reflection underwriting these folk-ascriptions tenaciously endure in both our everyday talk of selfhood and personal identity and in the sedimented philosophical vocabularies that have shaped talk about the self. How, then, should we deconstruct the language-games of subjectivity?

2 CONSCIOUSNESS AND SUBJECTIVITY

What we are supplying are really remarks on the natural history of human beings; we are not contributing curiosities, however, but observations which no one has doubted, but which have escaped remark only because they are always before our eyes.

(Ludwig Wittgenstein, 1968: §415)

As in previous chapters we take our direction from everyday rhetorics and their grammar. Surveying the extensive range of terms relating to 'consciousness' confirms the fact that we are dealing not merely with family resemblances within a single conceptual array but with interconnected families of concepts organizing the tropes of mental life. '"Consciousness" is most certainly a word of unsettled and unsettling signification' (Dewey, 1958: 298). In everyday usage the functions of 'consciousness' are very different from the uses of 'self-consciousness'. We are naturally drawn to Husserl's description of *consciousness* as a 'wonder' – the perpetual Heraclitean flux – that makes all reference and significant expression possible. Let us not leap into these dark realms too precipitately. Instead, we ask, how do we normally speak of persons as 'conscious beings'? What is the semantic field indexed by the term 'consciousness'?

Standard dictionary entries supply a wide range of glosses, most of which provide a cartography or representational system of disembodied consciousness: *apperception, attention,* and *attentiveness, care, carefulness, cognisance, concern, conscience, consideration, feeling, heeding, introspection, intuition, knowing, knowledge, memory, mind, notice, observance, observation, perception, recognition, reflection, regard, remark, self-consciousness, sense, sensible* (as in 'inwardly sensible'), *sensibility,* and so on. Moreover each term branches out into more complex attributional and propositional networks, creating intertextual filaments which run through our cultural vocabularies of mindfulness: *states of consciousness, forms of consciousness, modes of consciousness, temporal consciousness, sensory consciousness, intentional consciousness, spiritual consciousness, conscious awareness, 'wide-awake consciousness',* and so on. The abstraction from the body goes even further in many European languages. We know, for example, that the French language uses one word, *conscience* for both 'consciousness' and 'moral awareness' (hence *avoir toute sa conscience,* 'to be fully conscious', *être sans conscience,* 'to be unconscious', *perdre conscience,* 'to lose consciousness', *reprendre conscience,* 'to regain consciousness' but also *avoir bonne conscience,* 'to have a clear conscience', *il a mauvaise conscience,* 'he has a guilty conscience', *par acquit de conscience,* 'for conscience' sake', *la conscience psychologique,* 'psychological consciousness', etc.). While the German language has evolved a composite concept from 'conscious' and 'being' in *Bewusstsein* – literally, 'conscious being', the personal mode of existence of the self (*Selbstbewusstsein*).

We also have the evidence of folk-psychology, with its myriad ways of speaking about the mind and body. A similar deep-rooted dualism appears to preoccupy the grammatical schemata of ordinary language. Here terms designating 'consciousness' and its cognates have played a fundamental role in creating cultural images of selfhood and identity. A full survey of the field of folk-psychology would have to be historical and comparative. We defer this for another occasion. But in passing it is important to note that many cultures have complex vocabularies to articulate pretheoretical concepts of identity, belief, desire, intentions, and the like (even accepting that these folk-theories often differ radically from Eurocentric paradigms). Many of these terminological systems valorize the mind above the body, treating consciousness as a privileged term in a hierarchical couplet. As we have already observed in Chapters 2 and 3 this is one of the most fundamental tendencies in European thought about human reality.

Despite the diversity of beliefs about 'conscious life', many metaphors of consciousness reappear in different narratives of selfhood. Thus many societies conceptualize the total destruction of consciousness in death – or at the moment of death (Ariès, 1979) – in terms of the flight of the soul as the animating source of a person. When the 'soul' leaves the body, all corporeal and personal integration collapses. The 'soul' might then be said to be the 'essence' of the body, its 'animating' core. Such a belief has frequently sustained radically dualist accounts of the mind and body. We know, for example, that ancient Indian metaphysics, the metaphysical psychology of Greek antiquity, and ancient Judaic culture thought of the soul in the imagery of 'breath' and 'breathing' (the Upanishads speak of breath, '*prana*', as the life principle; we speak of a person who has died as having 'given up the ghost' and philosophers persuade us of the folly of considering subjectivity as a 'ghost in the machine'). The unconscious body, the body *in extremis*, and the dead body are stages along the terminal path of breathlessness – of the disappearance of *anima* and consequent loss of 'animation'. Spirit – like 'breath' – resides in the corporeal frame, the heart, thorax, or brain (the contemporary 'brain death') and dissolves into the ether at the moment of death. Such is the poetry of mortality (cf. Gonzalez-Crussi, 1985, 1986). Human beings have thus frequently represented themselves as *centred* creatures who breathe, reflect, think and, if we include the idiomatic models of the mind following in the wake of Freud, 'possess' unconscious states, libidinal impulses, unrequited desires, neuroses, 'inner conflicts', and so on. Drawing upon folk-models of selfhood, individuals consider themselves to be self-organizing feeling, sentient, thinking, willing subjects – ignoring philosophy's requirement that 'inner processes stand in need of outward criteria'. Common sense resists the idea that 'consciousness' can be explained or replaced by material causes – or, as we say today, by events in the neural wiring and computational mechanisms of the brain. In the pretheoretical 'natural attitude' we appear to have an instinctual antipathy toward physicalist self-conceptions (cf. Christensen and Turner, eds, 1993). The spontaneous philosophy of everyday life gives rise to the well-known dualist schema of the 'body and mind', underwriting the quest to study 'the mind and its place in nature' (to borrow C.D. Broad's phraseology).

The dominant metaphors for 'consciousness' and its subjective cognates in everyday usage are invariably *spatial*: the mind is like an inner space, enclosure, or *camera obscura*. More dynamically, consciousness is represented as an *inner process* or a *stream* of mental acts occurring in a private, disembodied 'mind-space'. The paradigm case here is a variant of the Middle English term 'inwit' (in-mind, the mind-inside, the 'contents of consciousness', the internal structures of *subjectivity*, the 'stream/field' of consciousness, 'mental representations', 'the mind's faculties', higher and lower mental functions, localization, the mind 'in' the body, phenomenal consciousness correlated to neural 'events', and so on). This way of talking, of course, derives from a metaphysical model of 'thinking matter' that has been shaped over several millennia. It might be condensed in the videological schema of *insight/outsight*: the 'Subject' looks outward toward 'Nature' and inward toward the Self.

Given the tenacious hold of these metaphors of the mental and the physical, reflection is naturally compared to or identified with a 'turning' or bending of the intellectual ray upon the springs of understanding, a 'turning back' of life upon life, a 'retrospection' of thematic acts of the subject *upon* the processes *of* private subjectivity. Thus most paradigms of contemporary psychology account for the emergence of the self by way of a theory of internalization or introjection of the symbolic order. In a culture pervaded by religious beliefs in the immaterial soul, the introspective, reflective ray is frequently given a 'spiritual' inflection. The mind understood as the locus of the immortal soul is given primacy in European definitions of the soul. Reflexion is a 'consciousness of consciousness', the 'turning' of the soul or spirit upon its own inner experiences. In a more extended study we would need to explore in a comparative and sociological manner the 'history of the soul' and its correlated 'discourses of the psyche' as this has shaped a society's practices and institutions. We defer this important project for another occasion (cf. Rousseau, ed., 1990 for exemplary studies).

Like 'perception', 'consciousness' has both a verbal and nominal sense, referring to a process (the 'act' metaphor of awareness) and its Gestalt products ('the objects and contents of consciousness'); but while everyday usage enables us to speak of 'a perception' as though it possessed the attributes of an entity, we are more restricted with the expression 'a consciousness' (ignoring artificially invented paradigms such as 'she experienced a most peculiar consciousness of being observed'). Nothing, however, hinders us from using the metaphysical term 'subject' in this way. Human beings seem to be self-evidently centred 'subjects' – unified proprietors of their sensations, perceptions, and thoughts. They live in the world as subjects and 'posit' entities as 'owned' objects. They exhibit the criterial properties of persons. But the term 'subject', like the term 'consciousness', has many different meanings flowing from a complex and tangled history (it is a sobering thought that for a long stretch of medieval speculation about the mind and knowledge the contemporary Cartesian meanings of 'subject' and 'object' were grammatically reversed: objective having the sense of 'thing thrown before the mind'; hence *ob-ject*, or the German *Gegen-stand*). The spatial metaphors for conscious life and lived experience deserve a much more extended investigation than space allows here.

'Subjectivity', then, is a capacity-term with a long and convoluted social history. In the mainstream Christian-Cartesian tradition persons or agents are *conscious* when they display a capacity to feel, act, think, dream, speak, signify and understand, even if they are not actually engaged in such activities. Wide awake, I am yet still aware that I have the capacity to dream, even though I cannot initiate or control the mental state we refer to with the term 'dreaming'. We do not, so to speak, lose our civic status when asleep or day-dreaming. I remain a subject even if I have the misfortune of falling into a trance or coma. My 'subjectivity' falls dormant, but is still citable as an agentless capacity – a controlling disposition reactivated with the return of normal consciousness and intellectual functions. Typically we use the polysemic word 'knowledge' in speaking of such diverse capacities ('B can swim, play the piano, and speak Spanish' translates 'B knows how to swim, play the piano, and speak Spanish', but not readily into 'B is conscious of being able to swim, play the piano, and speak Spanish'). The term 'self-consciousness' is not restricted in this way; we can, without incoherence, speak of a singular 'self-consciousness', for example,

171

in describing the heightened awareness of art or poetry or even in more mundane contexts in describing embarrassment (and 'self-consciousness' does very humble work in picturing the state of embarrassment); but we cannot say 'B runs, swims, etc. self-consciously' and still less 'B dreams self-consciously'; we can, however, say that 'B acts self-consciously' – in the sense that a bad actor is one who displays this failure to identify with the character, inviting judgements about his 'theatricality' or stilted performance.

Many of these usages overlap with standard uses of the word *awareness* (in the sense of *object-attentiveness*). In innumerable ways ordinary language practically acknowledges the fact that subjects are centres of awareness who routinely monitor their feelings, situations and environments 'without explicit reflection upon consciousness'. I am 'aware' – and thus conscious – without turning my awareness into a topic of self-reflection. For large parts of my conscious life no explicit exercise of reflective agency is either possible or required. It would seem that living a conscious life, being attentive to the course of experience, and monitoring my own behaviour in relation to objects and others do not presuppose self-reflection in the mirroring sense we have inherited from the Cartesian tradition of philosophy.

One of the most striking features of this semantic field is the relative modernity of locutions for 'consciousness' and the particular way in which spatial and quasi-mathematical metaphors have been borrowed from modern science to conceptualize the life of consciousness. This is even more apparent when we trace the history of the expression, 'self-consciousness' to its proximate ideological and semantic fields in early modern European culture. Anticipating this analysis here, we can simply note that it is only within the past two hundred years or so that we have been able to speak of *forms of consciousness, changes of consciousness, structures of consciousness, altered states of consciousness, national consciousness, false consciousness,* and, more especially, of consciousness as having an *ontogenesis* and a *phylogenesis*. The post-Enlightenment language-games of mind and self have developed the vocabulary of 'self-consciousness' as an indispensable resource. Earlier philosophy – say in the seventeenth and eighteenth centuries – thought in terms of 'mind' and 'the understanding'. Even earlier theological traditions spoke of the soul and the spirit. Undoubtedly these linguistic changes are linked to cultural and ideological configurations accompanying the rise of capitalist modernity. While self-examination is a common theme in Hobbes, Locke, Adam Smith, and Rousseau, prior to the nineteenth century speculations about the precise *sites, evolution,* and *alternate* forms of consciousness are relatively rare. Perhaps the crucial date for speculation on the origin and evolution of consciousness is 1859, with the publication of Charles Darwin's *Origin of Species*.[1]

Today, of course, it has become commonplace to locate the roots of consciousness and self-consciousness in the functional systems of the brain just as everyday speech anchors 'mind' and 'personality' ('mental events' and

172

'mental acts') within the neural circuitry of the 'brain' (or more colloquially expressed, 'in the head'). But it is only in the present century that we have come to summarize whole 'universes of discourse' by means of expressions such as 'scientific consciousness', 'moral consciousness', 'political consciousness', 'environmental consciousness', 'religious consciousness', and 'aesthetic consciousness'.

In spite of their evident modernity, the words 'consciousness' and 'self-consciousness' have played a central role in frameworks of modern European thought as diverse as the perspectives of Enlightenment science, German Idealism, European Romanticism, and positivist Evolutionism. In the wake of the Cartesian revolution many forms of European philosophy celebrated the certain 'fact' of human cognitive self-consciousness – not the *existence* of things, but our *consciousness of the existence* of objects as the starting point of knowledge. The rational subject – the knowing self or *cogito* – is posited at the heart of things, and reflection is the subject's privileged cognitive form of life. Theoretical reflection as *Wissenschaftslehre* and, later in the century, as *Erkenntnistheorie*, takes its orientation from this 'truth'. But it is only from around the decades 1820–50 that philosophical and sociological usage began to promote the salutary and even world-forming capacities of 'self-consciousness' (the Hegelian *Selbstbewusstsein*, Fichte's philosophy of the Ego, Wilhelm Joseph von Schelling's *Naturphilosophie*, Neo-Kantian theories of the unity of self-consciousness, and so on). And in the wake of this mid-century historicist generation intellectual culture increasingly described itself as living in an age of reflection, a world of inner sensibilities – to the flux of things and institutions is added the 'flow of inner consciousness' (a text like Hegel's *The Phenomenology of Spirit* is a powerful index of a sea-change in philosophical terminology which provided the terms of art for later philosophical discourse). To overview briefly some landmarks in this cultural tradition it is convenient to begin with the German Idealists from around 1780–1830. As in earlier studies we begin by asking a grammatical question: how did 'the human' and 'human knowledge' come to be defined in the rhetorics of inner 'self-reflection' and reflective transcendence?

Although the problematic of reflection and self-understanding dates back to René Descartes, Francis Bacon, John Locke, and David Hume and is extensively elaborated in the writings of the Abbé Condillac (1715–80), A.N. de Condorcet (1743–94), Pierre Cabanis (1757–1808), and Maine de Biran (1766–1824), the most influential paradigm of the self is found in the writings of the German philosopher, Immanuel Kant (1724–1804). Kant's Copernican Revolution in philosophy was to invert the relationship between mind and world by theorizing human consciousness as the constitutive formal nexus of all possible objectivity and knowledge. In this respect Kant developed the transcendental theme of an 'underlying' unitary consciousness already posited by Descartes (Bader, 1979–83; Husserl, 1960). By radicalizing the *cogito* Kant was responsible for making the self and self/body dualism the central topic of subsequent German philosophical thought. The seminal text is the *Critique of Pure Reason* (*Kritik der reinen Vernunft*, 1781) with its account of the mind's intrinsic forms and categories – and *a priori* self-knowledge of its own categorial capacities and limitations. For Kant, the entire world of perception, memory, and imagination exists only as phenomenal appearances given in conformity with *a priori* conditions of experience (the doctrine of transcendental synthesis and schematization). Mind and reason provide the controlling tribunal of the senses and sensory knowledge. Thus the fluctuating modes of consciousness – the 'rhapsody of sensations' – must comply with the universal formal structure of human understanding which orders all appearances into a world of objectivity:

> For in what we entitle 'soul', everything is in continual flux and there is nothing abiding except (if we must so express ourselves) the 'I', which is simple solely because its representation has no content, and therefore no manifold, and for this reason seem to represent, or denote, a simple object.
>
> (Kant, 1929: A 381)

The 'empirical I', moreover, is a transcendent clue to the ultimate source of rational self-determination – the Transcendental Ego. As Arthur Schopenhauer (1788–1860) correctly observed, 'Kant revealed the subjective and thus the inadequate element in knowledge from knowledge itself, and therefore his philosophy is rightly called a criticism of the faculty of reason' (1989: Vol. III, 660). In the second *Critique* (the *Kritik der praktischen Vernunft*, 1788) Kant traced the moral ideal of the person and the categorical imperative of duty to the 'inner sphere' of rational consciousness in which human praxis transcended the determinations of physical constraint and natural law. Here centred consciousness is a necessary ground for autonomous agency – the self as an *autonomous, wilful moral person* – the 'male position' in ethical life. The resultant aporia between causal nature and moral order culminates in the dualism of the determining and reflective judgement which forms the centrepiece of the *Critique of Judgement*. The regulative Idea is what allows the self to transcend the boundary between the legality of the phenomenal to the freedom of the noumenal realm.

Kant's self-appointed successor, Johann Gottlieb Fichte (1762–1814) fused the transcendental unity of apperception with the moral ideal of *autonomy* to define the transcendental Ego or *Ich* as a universal, non-personal self-determining 'consciousness' that posited not only the form, but also the substance of cognition – the 'not-I' as the totality of the forms of consciousness of objective reality (the move from Kant's formulation in terms of 'conditions of the possibility of the synthetic unity of experience' to the wilful 'creation of possible objects of experience' can be traced in Fichte's *Grundlage des gesammten Wissenschaftslehre* of 1794). In the sphere of practical philosophy human beings become persons in the full sense of the word by attaining a reflexive knowledge of the world-work of the Transcendental Ego. This culminates in a foundationalist conception of philosophy as a consciousness of consciousness (the 'doctrine of *science*' or *Wissenschaftslehre*). The philosophical defence of personal freedom is also central to the practical actuality of self-consciousness which Fichte calls the infinite desire for freedom. From this point onward the epistemological vocabulary of objectivity and subjectivity, 'sense' and 'reflection' became mandatory for German idealist thought.

The philosophers Georg Wilhelm Friedrich Hegel, Arthur Schopenhauer, and Karl Marx would follow similar lines of inquiry by reformulating the doctrine of self-consciousness and moral self-determination in historical, existential, and material categories – in the process laying the foundations for a fundamental anthropology of human praxis as self-reflexive action. The crucial shift is contained in an important paragraph from Hegel's *Philosophy of Right*. Hegel is distinguishing the figure of theoretical consciousness from the wilful 'attitude of praxis':

> the theoretical is essentially contained in the practical; we must decide against the idea that the two are separate, because we cannot have a will without intelligence. On the contrary, the will contains the theoretical in itself. The will determines itself and this determination is in the first place something inward, because what I will I hold before my mind as an idea; it is the object of my thought. An animal acts on instinct, is driven by an inner impulse and so it too is practical, but it has no will, since it does not bring before its mind the object of its desire. A man, however, can just as little be theoretical or think without a will, because in thinking he is of necessity being active. The content of something thought has the form of being; but this being is something mediated, something established through our activity. Thus these distinct attitudes cannot be divorced; they are one and the same; and in any activity, whether of thinking or willing, both moments are present.
>
> (1952: 227)

Where Kant underlines the self's rational faculties as the basis of moral self-determination, and Fichte and Hegel emphasize the faculty of absolute reflectivity, Franz Brentano (1838–1917) singled out the 'intentional inexistence' of the 'objects' and representative 'contents' of consciousness as the decisive mark of mental life (in his *Psychology from an Empirical Standpoint*, 1973), claiming that '*every psychic phenomenon is itself either a representation or is based upon representations*'. Here 'representation' – particularly 'sensible representations' – are functionally equivalent with the empiricist theory of ideas disclosed to us by the senses. In proposing this kind of revisionary empiricism, Brentano confirmed a basic conception of Schopenhauer's thought, modulating the latter with the genitive particle to read '*representations-of*': the life of consciousness is organized by its act intentionality, a structural characteristic unifying the stratification of 'representations'. Where thinkers like Maine de Biran (e.g. in his *Essai sur les fondements de la psycholo-gie* of 1810), Schopenhauer (in *The World as Will and Representation*), and Brentano clearly separated the reflexive life of 'inner perception' from the empirical, psychological processes of 'inner observation', this important dis-tinction was conflated in later, more empiricist accounts of sense consciousness. E.B. Titchener (1867–1927), for example, grasped the inten-tionality of inner sensory awareness but tried to establish an empirical science of inner experience upon the *factum* of 'self-evident' introspective data (a constant theme from his *Outline of Psychology* in 1896/7 to the posthumously published *Systematic Psychology: Prolegomena* in 1929). In a more rationalist vein the Würzburg School of Oswald Külpe (1862–1915) reworked the tasks of idealist epistemology into an empirical psychology of the self-conscious subject, taking as its object the experimental study of perceptual *Gestalten* and thought processes. Alexis Meinong (1853–1920) and Christian von Ehrenfels (1859–1932) prefigured the Gestalt psychology of Kurt Koffka (1887–1941), Wolfgang Köhler (1887–1967), Max Wertheimer (1880–1943), and Kurt Lewin (1890–1947) with the notion of 'Gestalt qualities' (*Gestaltqualitäten*) as an organizing principle of mental life – a theory already implicit in the Kantian-Fichtean doctrine of transcendental schematizing. In fact a whole tradition of European Gestalt psychologists would trace mental functioning to the lami-nated *act structure* of consciousness following in the wake of the intentionalist act psychology of Franz Brentano (1838–1917) and Edmund Husserl (1859–1938). Wilhelm Wundt (1832–1920) – the first great exponent of experimental psychology as a 'science of consciousness' in Germany – following Moritz Lazarus and Hermann Steinthal invented a new discipline to study the empiri-cal forms of everyday beliefs – 'folk-consciousness' – embedded in the 'objective spirit' of language, myth, customs, and cognate phenomena. In the pragmatist tradition William James spends hundreds of pages describing the dynamic, flux-like configurations of the 'stream of consciousness' in his *Principles of Psychology* (1890: ch. IX (condensed in his *Psychology: The Briefer Course* of 1892)) and John Dewey defined conscious reflection as the reflexive movement of the mind which '*converts action that is merely appetitive, blind, and impulsive into intelligent action*' (1933: 17; italics in original).

But despite these later empiricist and pragmatic redactions, the original Kantian problematic of autonomous and heteronomous consciousness held its fascination for some of the leading theorists of the self in German philosophical thought. Georg Simmel's *Lebensphilosophie* ('philosophy of life') respecified the traditional theory of knowledge as a phenomenology of meaningful *Forms* as these organize the objective contents of experience; the Form-Content correlation was even adapted as the basic framework for an interactional sociology studying 'forms of sociation' (*Formen der Vergesellschaftung*). In a related field the seminal hermeneutical thinker Wilhelm Dilthey in his project for a *descriptive and analytic psychology* (1894) and *Einleitung in die Geist-eswissenschaften* (1883; see 1976) urged his readers to relive the inner life of consciousness (*Erlebnis*) and meaning-bestowing 'mind' (*Geist*) which locates every 'external' action and artifact in a 'context of meaning' (the revisionary Hegelian concept of *objektiver Geist* or 'objective spirit' is central to his seminal essay, *Der Aufbau der geschichtlichen Welt in den Geisteswissenschaften* and thereby to the encyclopaedic project of spiritual interpretation Dilthey called the *Geisteswissenschaften*). In this way, *Lebensphilosophie* added 'affective', 'volitional', and 'sociological' annexes to the structure of post-Kantian Idealism.

Following analogous hermeneutic directions, Phenomenology – in the rigorous disciplinary form given to this ambitious programme by Edmund Husserl, Max Scheler, Alexander Pfänder, Martin Heidegger, and their students – offered its services as a transcendental science of pure consciousness 'reduced' through a rigorous reflexive methodology of self-reflection (a radicalism exhibited most clearly in Husserl's *Lectures on the Phenomenology of Internal Time Consciousness*, 1905); but in pursuing its initial descriptive radicalism, phenomenology uncovered the fact that prereflexive temporalizing consciousness already implicates an opaque, pretheoretical *Lebenswelt* as a realm of differential structures. The phenomenological desire to return to the roots of knowledge leads beyond the empirical theory of 'ideas and reflection' to a renewed transcendental theory of lived experience.

An ambitious synthesis of hermeneutic and causal perspectives was also attempted at the same time in German sociology: both Max Weber and Alfred Schutz, for example, began to conceptualize the subject matter of *verstehende Soziologie* (as a *Kulturwissenschaft* based on 'understanding') as 'human behaviour when and in so far as the acting individual attaches a subjective meaning (*Sinn*) to it' (Weber, 1964: 88). As with the German Idealist tradition, phenomenal knowledge is logically derived from the forms of consciousness and representation available to cognition (embedded in the social values and beliefs of social agents); the principle of representation is carried over into the definition of human action itself: action is social when it takes into account the behaviour of others and is thereby oriented in its course (Weber, 1964: 88; Schutz, 1967: chs 1, 2). German sociology in its classical phase thus committed itself to 'the interpretive understanding of social action' by thematizing subjective beliefs, states of mind, and motives as analytic objects.

The French vitalist philosopher, Henri Bergson (1859–1941) in his *Essai sur les données immédiates de la conscience* (1889), *Matière et mémoire* (1902), and *Creative Evolution* (1907) invited his readers to turn their thoughts to the continuously flowing stream of lived time or duration (*durée*) consubstantial with the stream of consciousness and existential life-activity: the 'inner' mental life of consciousness arises as the recollective mind casts its conceptual nets upon the pure continuum of temporal flow – a theme explored to great effect by Marcel Proust in his *A la recherche du temps perdu* (1919). In metaphysical terms, Bergson prioritizes intuition over intellect as the master theme of his philosophical anthropology. Even the positivist sociologist Emile Durkheim advocated the interpretive understanding of the *'conscience collective'* as the fundamental theme of sociological analysis (in *Les Règles de la méthode sociologique*, 1895). Durkheim in fact provided a powerful rationale for studying the role of consciousness in the collective formations of social experience: 'Consciousness is not a function with the role of directing the movements of the body, but the *organism knowing itself*' (1983: 82). Forms of individual intuition and collective consciousness are to be studied by the new discipline of sociology. Consciousness is not reflective and egocentric, but productive and collective: 'Consciousness, far from having only the role of directing the movements of beings, exists in order to produce beings' (1983: 83). Other social theorists during the same period divided the emerging field into 'individual' and 'collective consciousness' (consciousness of an individual agent and consciousness ascribed to a group, collectivity or whole society: 'The development and status of the individual, his imagination and reflection, his feeling and conduct, are largely determined by the group' (Durkheim, 1983: 84; Jerusalem, 1920: 277; cf. Simmel, 1971; Parsons on the *voluntaristic* dimensions of social action, 1937). In the German historicist tradition 'con-sciousness' literally means a 'knowing together', a holistic fusion of apperception, feeling, and volition which helped to popularize the idea of *culture* as the moral values, evaluative ideal orientations, existential attitudes, and world-views of a society – the medium for 'the reciprocal relations of society and the individual in the various spheres of life' (Wundt, 1916, 1973; Jerusalem, 1920: 277; cf. Parsons' conception of 'normative order' in *The Structure of Social Action*, 1937).

During the same period Sigmund Freud created the discipline of psychoanalysis by exploring the dynamic processes binding conscious life to unconscious processes. From the *Studies on Hysteria* (1895) with Joseph Breuer (1842–1925) to writings such as *The Interpretation of Dreams* (1899/1900), *The Psychopathology of Everyday Life* (1904), *Three Essays on the Theory of Sexuality* (1905), *Five Lectures on Psycho-Analysis* (1909), the *Introductory Lectures on Psycho-Analysis* (1915–17), *Beyond the Pleasure Principle* (1920), and *The Ego and the Id* (1923), Freud explicitly attacked the dominant empiricist and rationalist images of the self-centred psyche as either a machinery of sensory association or a translucent domain of self-consciousness – the conceptual effects of this polemic can be traced in the functional terminology Freud crafted over these two decades: *inner drives* (*Triebe*), *dream-work, repression, infantile sexuality, libido, wish fulfilment*, the *dynamic unconscious, unconscious processes*, the *Oedipus complex, narcissism* (the primary narcissism of consciousness), *displacement, defence mechanisms, sublimation, regression, fantasy, projection, transference* and *counter-transference*, the topography of *id, ego*, and *superego*, and so forth. The conceptual shift from 'substance to function' culminates in the great 'social essays' toward the end of this period – *Group Psychology and the Analysis of the Ego* (1921), *The Future of an Illusion* (1927), and *Civilization and its Discontents* (1930), with their stoic recognition of 'the superior power of nature, the feebleness of our own bodies and the inadequacy of the regulations which adjust the mutual relationships of human beings in the family, the state and society'. It is important to note, however, that the guiding intention of psychoanalysis was to augment a richer conception of consciousness through the analysis of unconscious mental states by means of self-reflective procedures; and to this end the psychoanalytic concept of the *psyche* was increasingly interpreted as a dynamic product of civilizational forms and cultural restraints. In the works of Freud's last period the culture-forming capacities of independent self-knowledge emerge as a major theme of his reflections on aggression and war (expressed in the maxim 'Where *Id* was there shall *Ego* be').

Each of these variations on the theme of human self-formation and self-understanding can be seen as attempts to isolate and conceptualize the distinctive dimensions of human existence in a culture pervaded by evolutionary materialism and reductive positivism (Social Darwinism, utilitarianism, mechanistic positivism, behaviourism, etc.). The common motif behind these rhetorics of reflection combines the idea of teleological development (whether in the form of Kantian transcendentalism, Hegelian historicism, or the 'philosophy of life' (*Lebensphilosophie*)) with that of naturalistic evolution of self and society (stemming from the many popular forms of Social Darwinism). Darwin's own speculations on the origins of consciousness in *The Descent of Man* (1871) and *The Expression of the Emotions in Man and Animals* (1872) deeply influenced the work of theorists as diverse as Nietzsche, Wundt, Durkheim, Mead, and Freud. And often the theorists of human subjectivity at the turn of the century resorted to positivistic means to overcome positivism – exemplified by the early contributions to the *Année Sociologique* (*circa* 1888–1900) or the first efforts to define the psychoanalytic process (see Parsons, 1937; Rieber, 1980; Lukes, 1975; Schorske, 1980; Sulloway, 1979). These gestures in the direction of a naturalistic and evolutionary theory of conscious life were, in effect, crisis responses to modernity and the 'bureaucratization of the world' articulated within the specific vocabularies of academic philosophy, psychology, and sociology. They are also not unconnected with the wider political 'crisis of culture and morality' in the last decades of the nineteenth century, itself intricately linked to the impact of Darwinism throughout European culture and political life. Durkheim rightly diagnosed this condition of extreme egoism with the term *anomie*, literally 'lawlessness' or normative disorientation leading to insecurity and deracination (*The Division of Labour in Society* (1893) and *Suicide* (1897)). To engage in sociologically informed criticism during this period was almost invariably to appear as a critic of modernity and its moral and social pathologies – or what Simmel called the tragic conflict in modern culture (Simmel, 1968; cf. Burwick and Douglass, eds, 1990).

One ironical consequence of this anomic situation is that a historicized, dynamic, and temporalized conception of *consciousness* in its rich social modalities of desire, recollection, memory, and experienced life appeared high on the list of essential predicates of human reality: *historical reason* appears as a paradigmatic mode of human experience, even where it is now approached as a decentred, relational phenomenon subject to non-conscious determinations and social aetiologies. As we have noted, Freud still remained faithful to the powers of scientific reason to bring unconscious processes within the realm of self-conscious control. It is as if the so-called 'collapse of meaning' and the legitimation crisis of the early decades of the twentieth century recalled the intellectual *élite* to the simple fact that human existence is a *process* of 'meaningful interpretation' through which historical societies create the complex web of social coexistence in the face of fundamentally irrational phenomena (the underlying dualisms in Karl Lamprecht's *Die Kulturhistorische Methode*, (1900), William James' *Varieties of Religious Experience* (1902), F.H. Bradley's *Appearance and Reality* (1902), Durkheim's *Suicide* (1897), and *The Elementary Forms of the Religious Life* (1912) are symptomatic texts reflecting this crisis sensibility). Durkheim would later trace the origins of the pragmatist movement in modern philosophy to the period of the 'turning point' between 1895 and 1900 (Durkheim, 1983: Second Lecture). Human becoming has its characteristic medium in acts of sacred identification and 'solidarity' exemplified by the material and ideological vicissitudes of the self regathering the experienced worlds of 'past experience' and projecting values and projects into the future. One consequence of this paradigm shift in theorizing the self and society as a dialectical relation was to displace atomic, monadic, and ahistorical categories by dynamic sociocultural, semiotic, and interactional concepts. The work of these revisionary thinkers at the turn of the century also situated the 'consciousness of the sacred' as a major theme of philosophical reflection (a tendency that would later be revived in the Collège de Sociologie (1937–9) founded by Georges Bataille, Michel Leiris, and Roger Callois).

Fin-de-siècle social and cultural theory discovered that consciousness as a *durational* reality is only one element of a larger psychic system governed by unconscious impulses, irrational forces, and prestructured value systems: 'Not ideas, but material and ideal interests, directly govern men's conduct' (Weber); 'The life of the individual is an endless struggling for constantly renewed efforts of the will, necessary and semiconscious' (Schopenhauer, 1989: vol. III, 122 – Herbert Spencer would later coin the phrase 'survival of the fittest' in a related context). Reason and self-interests are tied to passion and erotic attachments (for example in the work of Eduard von Hartmann (1842–1906)); the formative work of intellect and rationality is driven by libidinous forces ('the sexual relation is always the central and main point in all the doings and actions of man' (Schopenhauer, 1989: vol. III, 400–1); rationality is a product of historical conflicts and unconscious powers ('it is obvious that only the smallest part of our essential nature descends into consciousness and that the rest remains in the obscure background of the unconscious and yet is just as much our own essential nature', Schopenhauer, 1989: vol. III, 621). Not surprisingly, many historians have seen the period in terms of the resurgence of irrationalism against the project of Enlightenment optimism, capitalist modernity, and 'liberal' modernization (the adversaries of Le Bon's *The Crowd* (1895), Julien Benda's *La Trahison des clercs* (1927), and José Ortega y Gasset's *La Rebelión de las Masas* (1930; English translation, *The Revolt of the Masses*, 1932)). The anti-modernist decades between 1880 and 1900 witnessed a remarkable resurgence of interest in the work of Kant and Schopenhauer and, toward the end of the century, the writings of Hölderlin, Nietzsche (1844–1900), Dostoevsky (1821–81), Rimbaud, and Lautréamont. In Italian sociology, Vilfredo Pareto began the encyclopaedic project of elaborating a comprehensive sociological system around the idea of the societal effects of non-logical actions (*Mind and Society*, 1963).

Where for Kant the 'I' or 'Ego' was not a citizen of the phenomenal world but its formal or logical condition, *consciousness* in the work of Simmel, Weber, and Freud is presented as a fragile *membrane* marking the boundary between the external world and the spheres of personal and social existence (a duality coded into the *Naturwissenschaften/Geisteswissenschaften* opposition which precipitated the *Methodenstreit* in the human sciences at the turn of the century). In the idiom of Søren Kierkegaard (whose texts were also redis-covered and extensively read during the same two decades), human existence inheres in the committed inwardness of subjectivity. But 'subjectivity' is no longer the pellucid self-consciousness of Enlightenment Reason. It is a product of 'geological' evolutionary changes, anonymous processes of natural differ-entiation and sociological 'selection'. In the late 1920s Ludwig Klages published a work defending the unfathomable 'soul' or 'psychic life' (*Seelen-leben*) against Civilization, Reason, and Rational incorporation (*Der Geist als Widersacher der Seele*). The speculative biologist Hans Driesch popularized a vitalist, neo-Aristotelian perspective in biological research (*The History and Theory of Vitalism*, 1914). For these vitalists human existence is continuous with animal evolution and should be understood by regressing to the darker mutations that have shaped organic evolution. In Schopenhauerian terms, the subject is the *locus* of will, not a transparent consciousness-of-self or Enlight-ened praxis. In psychoanalytic parlance, only a conscious being (an *Ich*) can be said to 'have' an unconscious or to experience the effects of unconscious desires and repressive forces within the libidinal economy of mental life (the Ego is a minor, functional element of the *Id*, a mediator between the demands of the pleasure principle and the reality principle). And in the sociology of the day, subjectivity is subject to the historical dialectics of sociation (*Vergesell-schaftung*), rationalization, and commodification: sociology being the 'science which attempts the interpretive understanding of social action in order thereby to arrive at a causal explanation of its course and effects' (Weber, 1964: 88). It is important to note that a work like Simmel's *Philosophy of Money* (1990) was written as a contribution to a sociological theory of the individualization of consciousness and culture inspired by earlier efforts in this direction in the work of Marx, Darwin, Wundt, and Nietzsche. Each of these speculative theories present different facets of the discovery of *the field of consciousness* and its *structured deformations* by linguistic, social, and cultural forces in the early decades of this century (Ey, 1978; Grene, 1966; Gurwitsch, 1964, 1966, 1974, 1985; Husserl, 1931, 1964a,b, 1970, 1973, 1980, 1982, 1989; Mauss, 1973; Merleau-Ponty, 1962, 1968, 1973; Sartre, 1957a, 1957b, 1964, 1976).

Yet half a century after the attempt to create a dynamic, intentionalist language of consciousness philosophers still prefer to approach subjectivity in terms of such propositional attitudes as *believing, intending, deliberating, referring, hoping, desiring, deciding*, and *fearing*. Psychologists have only tentatively begun to speculate on the invariant structures of consciousness and to examine the phenomenology of alternative states of consciousness (Ornstein, 1986); but recent developments suggest that new paradigms of psychological research have in principle accepted the difficult problematics of consciousness as central to the 'mind/body problem'; research institutes are today preoccupied with the experimental study of bodily sensation, perception, day-dreaming, memory, fantasy, volition, emotion, and thought (Singer, 1993), while phenomenologists continue to study *phenomenal self-experience* and invent new methods to investigate the transcendental field of subjective experience, and even hard-nosed scientific psychologists, functionalists, physicalists, and behaviourists feel obliged to offer arguments to demonstrate that 'consciousness' is merely a brain process, physical event, or behavioural correlate of material events. The unintentional humour of reductive materialism was well expressed by Mead:

> We can say that there are physical things on one side and mental events on the other. We assume that the experienced world of each person is looked upon as a result of a causal series that lies inside the brain. We follow stimuli into the brain, and there we say consciousness flashes out. In this way we have ultimately to locate all experience in the brain, and the old epistemological ghosts arise. Whose brain is it? How is the brain known? Where does that brain lie? The whole world comes to lie inside of the observer's brain; and his brain lies in everybody else's brain, and so on without end. All sorts of difficulties arise if one undertakes to erect this parallelistic division into a metaphysical one.
>
> (1934: 32–3)

If neurologists and materialists reduce the mind to the brain, everyday culture takes an opposite view, portraying the mind as an agent with causal powers over the body (though both accounts draw upon the same mind-brain dualism). A whole commercial sector has grown up in recent years devoted to the arts and techniques of 'constructive thinking', 'T-groups', 'encounter groups', 'sensitivity training', 'body consciousness', 'health consciousness', and 'health awareness', designed to reintegrate 'mind' and 'body', 'consciousness' and 'physiological well-being'. Many of the body's material-physiological processes can be brought under control by the powers of conscious reflection – in 'biofeedback' therapy or what an older tradition would have called 'the will'. Psychosomatic therapies have thus led to a revival of mind-body voluntarism. Orthodox medicine now accepts forms of 'consciousness control' therapy (among the most prominent being biofeedback techniques which exploit the causal powers of phenomenal experience and self-observation in influencing neurophysiological processes – and thus in shaping sensation, perception, emotion, and thought). American medical science and practice has seen the growth of pain clinics involving holistic techniques of pain management and treatment. 'Consciousness-raising' is a crucial force in the so-called 'new social movements' (feminist consciousness, green consciousness, single-issue consciousness, and so on). Even quantum physicists today seriously examine the idea that 'consciousness' – observation, experimental intervention, perception, and theorizing – may have a significant impact upon the 'quantum realities' they investigate (Hodgson, 1991: Part III, esp. chs, 14, 15). 'Consciousness' – in all its forms and modalities – has become a commodity circulating and expanding exchange-value like any other marketable object.

3 THE STRATIFICATION OF CONSCIOUSNESS

> But you will cease to feel isolated when you recognize, for example, that you do not *have* a sensation of the sky: you *are* that sensation. For all purposes of feeling, your sensation of the sky is the sky, and there is no 'you' apart from what you sense, feel, and know
>
> (Alan Watts, 1992: 99)

Many of our folk-theories of subjectivity implicitly assume a nesting structure of terms in interpreting the nature of personal consciousness and phenomenal experience.[2] The most comprehensive of these terms seems to be *experience* or *sensory experiencing*; within experience we then have the field of *awareness*; within awareness, a narrower band of self-monitoring awareness or *'consciousness proper'*; and finally, *self-reflective, conceptual, and 'thinking' consciousness*. A good example of this model can be found in R.G. Collingwood's stipulative definition of *thought*:

> The peculiarity of thought ... is that it is not mere consciousness but self-consciousness. The self, as merely conscious, is a flow of consciousness, a series of immediate sensations and feelings; but as merely conscious it is not aware of itself as such a flow; it is ignorant of its own continuity through the succession of experiences. The activity of becoming aware of this continuity is what is called thinking.
>
> (1993: 306)

We can use this folk-schema of ascending levels of Experience, Awareness, Consciousness, and Self-Reflection to organize the following discussion (in

Wittgenstein's sense we 'remind ourselves of the *kind of statement* that we make about phenomena' (1968: I§90).

3.1 Experience as sensory consciousness

> The past is hidden somewhere outside the realm, beyond the reach of intellect, in some material object (in the sensation which that material object will give us), of which we have no inkling. And it depends on chance whether or not we come upon this object before we ourselves must die.

> (Marcel Proust, 1984: 47–8)

'Experience' in the sense of sensory awareness appears to be the most all-embracing category of 'consciousness': the raw processes of 'felt experience', 'experiences undergone', or 'experiences enjoyed' as the stuff of sentient life. The *data* of preconceptual awareness suggest an image of an anonymous field of experience prior to a separation of subject and object. There are two concepts of experience to be distinguished here. First the notion of experiences 'undergone' or mutely 'felt' by experiencers – a hardly describable 'enjoying' of experience, a 'having of sensations' with a minimum or total absence of conscious awareness (Humphrey, 1992: 180); the second concept evokes a 'field' of sentience that engages or prereflectively implicates the awareness of individual experiencers. Where the Greek word *aisthesis* covers both species, the German words *Erlebnis* and *Erfahrung* express this difference. Where experiences 'undergone' are not necessarily noted by experiencers and accumulate 'unmarked' – rather like Helmholtz's 'unconscious inferences', the latter experiences may be expressed in first-person accounts.

Possessing sensory abilities – the aesthetic modalities of seeing, hearing, smelling, etc. – we 'feel' the impress of qualitative experience and are conscious of what we perceive, even where we have enormous difficulties putting this prepropositional auditory, visual, and tactile sentience into words. This is the primitive world formulated as a sensuous manifold. Alan Watts suggests a description of the former type of experience:

> To be aware, then, is to be aware of thoughts, feelings, sensations, desires, and all other forms of experience. Never at any time are you aware of anything which is *not* experience, not a thought or feeling, but instead an experiencer, thinker, or feeler. If this is true, what makes us think that any such thing exists?

> (1992: 77)

Yet the unreflective and prescientific texture of sensation (sight, hearing, touch, smell, taste) still forms the ever-present horizon for more articulate forms of 'heeding' and attentional directedness. It is, to borrow a Kierkegaardian conceit, the 'aesthetic' stage of human existence. We say that we are conscious of the world 'through' our sensations without being conscious 'of' those sensations, let alone their phenomenological characteristics or psychophysical causes. Once this kind of articulation has appeared we have already left the aesthetic experience of life and are, to borrow Julian Jaynes' term, *narratizing* experience.

The literature in philosophical psychology often speaks of this primitive, raw experience as a stream of timeless and placeless states of experience: 'sensations' are 'had' in an edenic 'here and now'. It is the 'unqualified actuality' or 'sensed existence' described by William James and Henri Bergson – the simple timeless *thatness* prior to the structuration of the perceptual field and more focal forms of consciousness. The primary world of perception thus antedates a coherent self-structure and the superstructures of conceptual thought. Try describing the embodied sensation of the sun's warming heat, the colour red, the smell of lilac, or taste of lemon. Experience-going-on – James', Dewey's, and Husserl's 'general stream of experience' – might be called the horizon of sensate awareness: the bitter of the lemon or the intrusion of a distant sound emerges from a more undifferentiated state of living awareness. As a generic flow 'sensory experience' need not be, and most typically is not, consciously attended to or noted by the experiencer: for most of the time we live in total ignorance of the operative structures and ongoing processes of our conscious states; and certainly as inveterate realists we ignore the neurological, physiological, and organic preconditions which provide the material infrastructure of sensory experience; the modulations of perception, age, and other individual factors are not consciously attended to – the distortions and colourations of sense-perception in illness or under the influence of alcohol are tacitly adjusted to the norm of 'everyday perceptual judgements' and for all intents and purposes discounted; it is unusual – outside of philosophy seminars – to find individuals theorizing about the possible connections between 'outer stimuli' and sensory organs, or doubting the veridicality of their perceptions of the furniture of the world surrounding them. We do not spontaneously espouse Representative Realism, Berkeleyan Immaterialism, or Central State Materialism. The research programme of the experimental psychologist and the speculation of the sceptical philosopher concerning the relationship between the physical and the mental do not usually trouble healthy common sense which accepts the 'evidence of the senses' as proof of their referential validity: 'This pungent odour comes from that citrus fruit over there'; 'I hear the bus coming down the hill'; 'What a remarkable swathe of poppies in the field beneath my window'. Distant objects and sticks bent in water cannot shake the tactile faith in the existence of an extra-human, external world given in immediate, tenseless sensations. However, individuals unfortunate enough to have had direct experience of such 'abnormal' phenomena through physical injury or damage to their sensory organs have an intuitive grasp of the loss of awareness involved in weak eye-sight, colour-blindness, tunnel vision, anosognosia, and similar conditions. Individuals who lose a 'sentient modality' tragically appreciate the fact that they now live in a world whose sensory possibilities have been reduced or significantly modified from what was previously regarded as 'normal awareness' (the study of the effects of impaired vision upon aesthetic awareness, particularly pictorial consciousness, provides important evidence of these phenomenological modifications).

Despite these constraints we nevertheless want to say that we 'experience' the world and are 'conscious' even though we cannot give the experience categorial shape or capture it perfectly in our available verbal nets. We have a sensory consciousness of the qualitative flux of things – of 'ongoing experience' as 'the immediate flux of life which furnishes the material to our later reflection with its conceptual categories' (James, 1912: 93). This is the grammatical background for Dewey's description of consciousness as 'direct apparition, obvious and vivid presence of qualities and of meanings': 'Immediate objects are the last word of evanescence' (1958: 113; also James' essay, 'A world of pure experience', in 1912: 39–91; cf. 1892: 150–60).

But mediation leaks from every account of the 'unreflective' raw presence of experience. As a 'serial course of affairs', wide-awake experience with its characteristic sensory properties, rhythms, and relationships 'occurs, happens, and is what it is' (Dewey, 1958: 232). The *world-qua-qualia* – if we can accept the testimony of modern philosophy – seems to be fragile, mobile, uncertain, unstable, indeterminate. It is not only 'at the mercy of the sequential order', as Dewey says, it is also subject to a range of structural deformations and mutations. Once temporal difference is admitted into the organization of the sensory field, the door is open for a range of other factors which deform 'immediate experience' – from the local mutations in the conditions of awareness to the variations induced by memory, the effects of past experience, the conditions of the body to large-scale psychological, social and cultural influences on perception. By narratively stabilizing the flux of sentience into something like a field we open the phenomenal immediacy of the *qualia* of seeing, hearing, smelling, etc. to the vicissitudes of history and culture which selectively modify, intensify, evaluate, and modulate lived experience. *Actual experience* is necessarily socialized and 'chunked' into public moulds of space-time. We experience the world through social and discursive categories. And these primitive categorialia are already the collective resources of a pregiven social world.

But recognizing the mediation of intersubjective frames is perfectly compatible with an enlarged phenomenological account of 'radical experience'. In James' words, for such a philosophy 'the relations that connect experiences must themselves be experienced relations, and any kind of relation experienced must be accounted as "real" as anything else in the system' (1912: 42, italics in original). The emphasis on the dynamic systems and processes of consciousness eliminates all sense-data atomism as inadequate descriptions of conscious life. The initial assumption of an unproblematic 'norm' of elementary 'experiences undergone' now seems increasingly problematic. Every 'raw sensory experience' is *made* not *found*, shaped by cultural representations that cannot be separated from the experiences they inform and organize. The identity postulate of common sense and empiricist metaphysics is itself created by eliding the manifold ways in which experience is pretheoretically structured to produce the basic 'identity-rule' of normal perception ('Everyone experiences the one-same-world'; 'Individual perspectives are variations from a stable identity "common-to-all" '). We come to the favourite question of every philosophy student: 'Given the innumerable shocks the flesh is heir to, do we see things as they really are?' And if we question the metaphysical postulates of mundane reason, how can we know that *we* experience the same sensations and perceptions? Is it not more likely that my unique biographical situation colours everything that I can possibly experience? And if this is the case, do we not all inhabit different sensory worlds? What we take to be a common and universal waking life – the one sentient world – is a necessary fiction: 'In truth, the universal and stable are important because they are the instrumentalities, the efficacious conditions, of the occurrence of the unique, unstable and passing' (Dewey, 1958: 116).

Let us analyze another grammatical aspect of sensory awareness. Consciousness inserts the mind into the world as a realm of flux and transformation. That is all we seem to be able to say, without 'pushing' sentience into boxes and categories provided by our language-games and cultural categories. But we have questioned the autonomy and integrity of 'immediate sensations' – where the mind and culture are concerned there are no 'raw data', no 'givens' untouched by larger patterns of significance. The question now becomes: why do we feel compelled to talk about sentience in the asocial vocabularies of unmediated data, presence, and the impinging rawness of sensory experience at all?

Here we think we are describing the origins of consciousness, but are simply tracing deeply held grammatical schemes and folk-theories. We might provisionally accept the findings of depth psychology and affirm that the world of consciousness is enveloped in a darker realm of psychic life; we may admit the structuring of preverbal consciousness and *unconscious* experience as the royal road to self-knowledge; we might even embrace the importance of the psychoanalytic archaeology of *unconscious processes* such as object *cathexis* (*Besetzung*) as being beyond immediate conscious retrieval, while still being central to the structuration of personal experience. Research on *subliminal* consciousness, for example, points to similar conclusions: meaningful experience can produce powerful reality effects, shaping responses, attitudes, and frames of reference without any implication of 'conscious' recognition or explicit awareness.

These revisionary pictures have led some theorists – particularly within the tradition of empiricism – to speculate about the emergence of subjectivity from an undifferentiated field of 'feeling-states' where the embodied boundaries of the Ego are blurred in an undifferentiated 'enjoyment' of experienced

sensations and 'adventured finalities'. Feeling is presented as an undifferentiated realm of 'immediate organic selections, rejections, welcomings,
expulsions, appropriations, withdrawals, shrinkings, expansions, elations and
dejections, attacks, wardings off, of the most minute, vibratingly delicate
nature' (Dewey, 1958: 299). Prior to verbal consciousness and linguistic reflection experience is already organized as a topography of lived values. Although
it is dangerous to extrapolate from verbal consciousness back into inchoate
preverbal experience, the 'loss of self' in enjoyment and extreme feeling states
such as grief and anger licenses analogical speculation. 'We are not aware of
the qualities of many or most of these acts; we do not objectively distinguish
and identify them. Yet they exist as feeling qualities, and have an enormous
directive effect on our behavior' (Dewey, 1958: 299). Consciousness in other
words 'begins' with affective value intentionalities situated at the shifting
boundaries of the body.

One exemplary description of prepredicative valorization can be found in
Georg Simmel's description of bodily enjoyment as sensory dedifferentiation:

> Human enjoyment of an object is a completely undivided act. At such
> moments we have an experience that does not include an awareness of
> an object confronting us or an awareness of the self as distinct from its
> present condition. Phenomena of the basest and the highest kind meet
> here. The crude impulse, particularly an impulse of an impersonal,
> general nature, wants to release itself towards an object and to be
> satisfied, no matter how; consciousness is exclusively concerned with
> satisfaction and pays no attention to its bearer on one side or its object
> on the other. On the other hand, intense aesthetic enjoyment displays
> the same form. Here too 'we forget ourselves'.
>
> (1990: 65).

It appears, then, that the image of transparent consciousness is, to say the least,
much exaggerated. In the main we live unquestioningly. We feel our way into
the world 'through our skin' before we sit back and deliberate. Large stretches
of our operative discriminations are carried out 'subconsciously' or, to extend
the current meaning of the word, *emotionally*. Contingency, indeterminancy,
and flux appears to be the rule of pretheoretical sentient life. Events occur and
are *felt* in the depth and upon the surfaces of the body. Undifferentiated
sensations spread themselves across the phantasmal body that is still not a
body-subject; the young child is cathectically 'oriented' towards zones of
sensory satisfaction and pleasurable feelings – a situation Freud captured with
his striking phrase 'polymorphous perversity'. In the idiom of Dewey's home-
spun existentialism: the human individual is a distinctive opacity of bias and
preference conjoined with plasticity and permeability of needs and likings
(1958: 242). We become particular individuals, in other words, by colonizing
the prepredicative field of affective experience. As we are practically instructed
from novels like Dostoevsky's *Brothers Karamazov*, Marcel Proust's *A la*

recherche du temps perdu (1913–27), Wyndham Lewis' *Tarr* (1918), Virginia Woolf's *Jacob's Room* (1922), Hermann Broch's *Death of Virgil* (1945), Musil's *The Man without Qualities* (1930–43) Flann O'Brien's *At Swim-Two-Birds* (1939), and James Joyce's *Ulysses* (1922) and *Finnegan's Wake* (1939), unconsciousness is a Pandora's box of involuntary memories, slips of the tongue, allusions, consummations of inchoate values desired and deferred, uncontrollable chains of signification which take us where they list. In relation to these modes of evanescence the experiencer is relatively passive, a recipient of the material data of sensibility – a perspective reflected in ordinary language when we say that the animate organism suffers experiences. Finally, all of these phenomenological accounts reinforce Freud's image of conscious processes as the tip of the iceberg of an otherwise submerged mental life organized by a fractious economy of desire and governed by repressive defence mechanisms. Consciousness and higher-level intelligent skills are not synonymous with the whole of psychic life. The sentient self is decentred by the same processes which organize self-experience. Self-knowledge as a reflective achievement of transcendence is the product of a long and painful reintegration of unconscious forces within the life of consciousness (Ellenberger, 1970; Klein, 1977; Lacan, 1968, 1977, 1978; Whyte, 1962).

It is a truism that the fascination with unconscious processes, the persistence of the past, memory, and the subjective sources of identity preoccupied nineteenth-century writers like Dostoevsky, Strindberg, and Ibsen, Modernists like Flaubert, Proust, James, Faulkner, Hesse, Gertrude Stein, Djuna Barnes, Robert Musil, Virginia Woolf, and Franz Kafka as well as anti-Modernists such as André Breton, René Magritte, and Louis Aragon. But similar anti-Enlightenment themes and motifs can be found throughout the philosophy and social theorizing at the turn of the century. For example, a similar concern for the 'non-logical' motivation of human action informed the methodology devised by the German sociologist Max Weber to study the consequences of patterns of 'subjective' meaning. In Weber's vision of history 'action' and 'states of consciousness' were not inherently 'rational' or transparently clear, yet the sociologist attempting to construct models of the behaviour of individuals must act *as if* they approximated rational norms. The theoretical concepts of sociology 'are ideal types not only from the objective point of view, but also in their application to subjective processes' (Weber, 1949: 90–107). The interpretive sociologist, like the historian or novelist, constructs heuristic fictions of rationality, rational action and rationalization processes to make sense of the inarticulate beliefs and unintentional consequences of the actions of historical agents:

> In the great majority of cases actual action goes on in a state of inarticulate half-consciousness or actual unconsciousness of its subjective meaning. The actor is more likely to 'be aware' of it in a vague sense than he is to 'know' what he is doing or be explicitly self-conscious about it. In most

cases his action is governed by impulse or habit. Only occasionally, and, in the uniform action of large numbers, often only in the case of a few individuals, is the subjective meaning of the action, whether rational or irrational, brought clearly into consciousness. The ideal type of meaningful action where the meaning is fully conscious and explicit is a marginal case.

(Weber, 1971: 101–2)

Weber, as we know, constructed an epistemology of historical action and its unintentional consequences upon this foundation: 'very frequently the "world-images" that have been created by "ideas" have, like switchmen, determined the tracks along which action has been pushed by the dynamic of interest' (Weber, 1948: 280).

Perhaps the proud conviction that we think we know, that we have access to our own minds and that what we find on inspecting our minds through acts of retentional reflection will serve us as a foundation for our beliefs, values, and projects is a myth? The assumption belongs to the everyday culture of 'as if' (Vaihinger, 1924). In the interest of the dominant social order and its regulative will to control transgression we have imposed fictions upon our own lives. We should again observe the centrality of the thematic of meaning voluntaristically imposed upon a nihilistic world in the great Modernist writers of the twentieth century – especially the exploration of myth in the later novels of Thomas Mann and D.H. Lawrence, the poetry of Eliot, Yeats, and Auden, the artistic *avant-gardes* of the first three decades of the century, the dramatic verse of Lorca and the protoexistentialism of Musil, Simmel, Jaspers, and Weber. The message of modern artists, novelists, sociologists, and philosophers is insistent: in a disenchanted age of momentous change and the titanic bureaucratization of social life we need to be assured that we are still 'centres' and 'masters' of experience; therefore we imagine the self to be an autonomous thinking and personal unity, an ultimate source of meaning and significance; the Kantian *person*, however, is not a '*ding an sich*' but a vital fiction (a common concern in the work of Friedrich Nietzsche, Hans Vaihinger, José Ortega y Gasset as it is with Bertrand Russell, A.J. Ayer, Jorge Luis Borges, or Luigi Pirandello). This is the consoling story modern culture tells to reassure us that we are indeed present at the heart of things and in control of the chaos of history.

We have come to a strange conclusion: our images of selfhood are narrative fictions. The ongoing enterprises of life presuppose a centred order of consciousness and subjectivity. Egocentricity turns out to be a faith or ideological technique for essentializing, universalizing, and necessitating a particular historical experience of the world. These deep-rooted psychic utopias order our lives – which, like any good tale, have a beginning, middle, and an end. The 'self' and 'thinking' are narrative effects of wish fulfilment in the face of an inchoate world. Nietzsche had come to similar conclusions, formulating these

190

in the Darwinian idiom of prereflective 'habits', 'instincts', and 'embodied' knowledge:

> the greater part of conscious thinking must still be counted among the instinctive activities, and this is so even in the case of philosophical thinking ... 'being conscious' is in no decisive sense the *opposite* of the instinctive – most of a philosopher's conscious thinking is secretely directed and compelled into definite channels by his instincts. Behind all logic, too, and its apparent autonomy there stands evaluations, in plainer terms physiological demands for the preservation of a certain species of life.
>
> (1978: 3; cf. §§4, 14, 20)

Other phenomenological evidence points to similar conclusions; for example, the imperceptible changes experienced in 'growing older', the *horizonal* background of perceptual life, selective inattention, culture filtering, the internal experiences and anonymous workings of our own bodies; similar considerations hold for experiences which individuals have had or suffered but which are now submerged beyond the reach of conscious retrieval – the first months of life, the sedimented detritus of memory, *implicit learning*, and the limited information capacities of thought – George Miller's 'Magic Number Seven, Plus or Minus Two', slips of the tongue (*parapraxis*), temporary lapses into incoherence and meaninglessness, dream experiences (for example, reflexive or lucid dreams), and more serious psychopathologies resulting in amnesia, splintered consciousness, loss of identity, dual identity (split-brain pathologies), and so forth.

This can be illustrated by the idea of *petites perceptions*. Leibniz's general thesis is that

> there are a thousand signs which make us think that there are at all times an infinite number of *perceptions* in us, though without being consciously apperceived and without reflection; that is to say, changes in the soul itself, which we do not perceive [*appercevons*], because these impressions are either too small and too numerous, or too unified, so that they have nothing sufficiently distinctive in themselves.

His curious example is the global effect of the roar of the sea, compounded from an infinity of elemental sounds:

> To hear this noise as we do, we must hear the parts that make the whole, that is we must hear the noise of each wave, even though each of these small noises is known only in the confused assemblage of all the others and would not be noticed if the wave making it were only one. For we must be slightly affected by the motion of this wave, and we must have some perception of each of these noises, however small they may be,

otherwise we could not have the noise of a hundred thousand waves, since a hundred thousand nothings cannot make something.

(1968: 148–9, trans. modified)

Compare this with William James' description of forgetting a name:

Suppose we try to recall a forgotten name. The state of our consciousness is peculiar. There is a gap therein; but no mere gap. It is a gap that is intensely active. A sort of wraith of the name is in it, beckoning us in a given direction, making us at moments tingle with the sense of our closeness, and then letting us sink back without the longed-for term. If wrong names are proposed to us, this singularly definite gap acts imme-diately so as to negate them. They do not fit into its mould. And the gap of one word does not feel like the gap of another ... When I vainly try to recall the name of Spalding, my consciousness is far removed from what it is when I vainly try to recall the name of Bowles.

(1981: 243)

James' example might suggest another way of approaching the field of con-sciousness – no longer as a spatial plethora of translucent structures, but as an adventure of significance. Even our most intimate thoughts and memories suffer occlusion; we are readers of our own dark texts which for the main part are beyond conscious control. But the unavoidable structure of the field of experience as 'mine' persists. Even the most particular *qualia* has a shape and positionality within 'my experiencing life': these are 'my' taste experiences, sensations, perceptions. Behind the intrusion of a distinct *qualia* it appears that *self*-conscious experience reasserts itself as a referential network of configura-tions. While not being 'consciously' experienced we still insist that these events and encounters are part of my experience of the world, that they are real and make real claims upon our attention and experience, and may under certain conditions be reactivated by suitable analytic techniques and methodologies (physiological, psychoanalytic, reminiscence therapy, and the like). I can, after all, inform my physician of the flashing lights which prefigure a migraine. Our unshakable commitment to viewing the personal self as a meaningful totality is left unimpaired by Jamesian instances or Borgesian parables. To shake this commonsense axiom we have to turn to more dramatic – indeed epic – instances of intrusive meaninglessness (the staple data for example of psychoanalysis – in the work of Freud, Lacan, or Ey; the neurology of brain-damaged patients (Gardner, 1974); or in a more literary vein, the sad pathologies described by Oliver Sacks in books such as *A Leg to Stand On* (1984), *The Man Who Mistook his Wife for a Hat* (1985: ch. 3) or his *Seeing Voices: A Journey into the World of the Deaf* (1989) or William Styron's self-analysis in *Darkness Visible* (1991). As Mead once observed: 'It has been largely through the pathologist that the importance of the self has entered into psychology' (1934: 200, n. 21; cf. Gonzalez-Crussi, 1985, 1986).

Such experiences, once articulated, call for incorporation into our overall picture of *experience*. Ironically it has been *avant-garde* literary and art movements that have set the agenda for contemporary theory: how would the philosophy of consciousness have to change if it took its starting point from experiences of incomprehension and unintelligibility as models of personal and social existence? How would the subject appear if we began from the ubiquitous experience of nihilism and meaninglessness rather than from the quasi-theological image of an ideal plenum of meaning?

3.2 Awareness

The language-game 'I am afraid' already contains the object.
(Ludwig Wittgenstein, 1967: § 489, 87c)

We turn now to the moment when the process of sentience becomes aware of itself.

Being aware is related to 'feeling', 'sensing', 'heeding', 'noting', 'marking', 'concern', and 'sensitivity'; where 'sensibility', 'feeling', or 'sentience' in general refer to the general openness to sensation, feeling, and affectivity, awareness introduces the moment of recognition in the structure of experience. In being aware we are 'tuned' to the life of things, directed by concern, attentive toward objects (including such 'objects' as toothaches, memories, desires). To distinguish 'thing awareness' from 'object awareness' we can speak in general of *objectual awareness* even for 'things' that have no spatiotemporal properties.

While objectual awareness precedes the conscious articulation of ideas, representations, and judgements it introduces elementary processes of mediation. The primary impulse toward the 'object of desire' is blocked by a reflective relay; the focus of possible enjoyment appears as an *objectivity*, an intentional 'pole' within experience. The unity of sensory enjoyment is disturbed and the experiencer is thrown out of the phantasm of the Now. Differentiation crystallizes the chaos of sensory experience into a nascent field. But we can only explicate sensory experience if our modes of sentience are tacitly structured. The reflexivity of desire provides a paradigm case of this phenomenon.

Following the lead of Hegel, Simmel attributes the dehiscence of the phenomenal field into subjective and objective moments as a product of *desire*:

> In desiring what we do not yet own or enjoy, we place the content of our desires outside ourselves ... Within the practical world ... the origin of the object itself, and its being desired by the subject, are correlative terms – the two aspects of this process of differentiation which splits the immediate unity of the process of enjoyment. It has been asserted that our conception of objective reality originates in the resistance that objects present to us, especially through our sense of touch ... We desire objects only if they are not immediately given to us for our use and enjoyment;

that is, to the extent that they resist our desire. The content of our desire becomes an object as soon as it is opposed to us, not only in the sense of being impervious to us, but also in terms of its distance as something not-yet-enjoyed, the subjective aspect of this condition being desire.

(1990: 66)

'The immediate unity of the process of enjoyment.' Simmel's phrase recalls Freud's fundamental point that the child is first passionately attached to the world through the pleasure-source of the (M)other's body. Simmel's intuitions also correspond with Freud's account of the differentiation of the ego and the object as a violent process of cathexis and fixation of libido on the 'not-yet-enjoyed' body of the Other (for Freud, 'proto-objectivity' begins with the carnal presence of the mother – the Other that is initially the sole object of the child's desire). Awareness of the lack created by delayed satisfaction constitutes the objectual field of subjectivity and objectivity: as Simmel observes, subject and object are born in the same act – the objectual meaning is carried like a cork on a wave of prereflective feeling states.

Genetically, the 'object world' emerges from the life-world of subjectivity understood as a realm of undifferentiated sentience. The nascent forms of subject-object awareness can be traced to the resistance of the object of desire and, for the emerging ego, the necessity of deferring gratification. The beginnings of subjectivity – becoming an Ego in Freudian terms – are grounded in the affective economy of desire – of deferring and 'managing' the impulses of narcissistic gratifications: the child 'discovers' that the body of the Other cannot be 'consumed' like waves of autoerotically induced sensory pleasures, but must be monitored, magically invoked, cajoled, and 'made to appear' through the efforts of the subject. Phantasmal objectification and temporalization is thus constituted in a polemical economy of sexual tensions. Sexual pleasure is, so to speak, a biological lesson in absence and presence. The Other's body signifies the perennially absent desirable object. Pleasure – both on the surfaces of the skin and within the organism – demands the presence of the Other. And the beginnings of autonomous ego functions lie in the awareness that the experiencer must move and act in order to reactivate the equilibrium that flows from sensuous satisfaction; the lost object of desire must be turned into an object of awareness and focused activity: if I am to 'enjoy' the Other I must become subject to the edicts and local legalities of concrete experience, but I must also acquire concrete skills and tactics which help recover the lost object of desire. The child must learn the normative heuristics of a cultural economy of pleasure. In Freudian terms the aboriginal 'repudiation' of the external world has to be abandoned if the self is to survive the phase of primary narcissism. In the earliest phases of reality-testing the nascent Ego learns that the 'object of desire' will only return (in Freud's famous 'Da-fort' case) if it becomes a subject that actively secures repetition by controlling, however minimally, the field of desire. The child acquires the primary lesson of carnal awareness while falling from the Eden of sentient existence: 'the possibility of desire is the possibility of the objects of desire' (Simmel, 1990: 66):

> The object thus formed, which is characterized by its separation from the subject, who at the same time establishes it and seeks to overcome it by his desire, is for us a value. The moment of enjoyment itself, when the opposition between subject and object is effaced, consumes the value. Value is only reinstated as contrast, as an object separated from the subject ... value does not originate from the unbroken unity of the moment of enjoyment, but from the separation between the subject and the content of enjoyment as an object that stands opposed to the subject as something desired and only to be attained by the conquest of distance, obstacles and difficulties.
>
> (Simmel, 1990: 66)

Such an 'objectual world' is intrinsically unstable, giving rise to 'objective' determinations through more complex subjective vectors of attention and activity. It is, to borrow, Donald Winnicott's phrase, a realm of *transitional objects*, a zone of objectual relations between an emerging 'me' and the otherness of the 'not-me'. And, like Freud's phenomenology of this developmental phase, for Simmel, the birth of awareness is striated with anxiety and trauma (cf. Winnicott, *Transitional Objects and Transitional Phenomena*, 1953).

The 'other side' of the dialectic of desire and self-preservation is the emergence of the epistemic possibilities of blocked desire – the most elementary form of which is given as the experience of anxiety and pain (either present pain or the recollected pain of past 'object cathexes'). Objectual structures are 'cathected' with value as a defence against the threat of loss and totalization. And the 'pain of emotional loss' may be the first articulate structure of dis-ease experienced by the child. The traumatic phenomenology of pain is thus the purest index of the presence of unpleasure, otherness, and, ultimately, the threat of death. Value (in psychoanalytic terminology, the libidinal cathexis of objects of desire) and pain are inseparable aspects of the same primary process of objectual dehiscence whereby something like a bodily zone of 'good' and 'bad' referents forms in the flux of experience (the parallels with the pre-Oedipal dynamics of identification between the good and bad 'mother-image' in Kleinian theory should also be noted). The sensory world divides into objectual zones which obstruct or satisfy desire. It may even be that the threat rather than the actual loss of the desired object suffices to start the child on the long path of differentiation and self-development (Freud's explanation of the violence resolving the Oedipal complex follows this type of reasoning). To find an experience 'pleasurable' (to invest transitional objects with affective value or cathect them as terms of affective 'interest') is only possible by way of contrast to experiences that are 'unpleasurable' across the lively spectrum of painfulness – from mildly disagreeable resistances experienced by an organism to the disappearance of the sustaining Other, on to life-threatening phenomena.

The 'researchable' membrane of objectual relationships in early development marking the boundaries of pain and pleasure forms the phantasmal zone where 'my body' will eventually appear (for example, in the unique spatiotemporal zone opened by the rhythms of hunger and satiation in a reflective, social organism). Again, Simmel captures the active aspect of the experience of object dehiscence and object-seeking awareness:

> Objects are not difficult to acquire because they are valuable, but we call those objects valuable that resist our desire to possess them. Since the desire encounters resistance and frustration, the objects gain a significance that would never have been attributed to them by an unchecked will ... Only the repulsions that we experience, the difficulties of attaining an object, the waiting and the labour that stand between a wish and its fulfilment, drive the Ego and the object apart; otherwise they remain undeveloped and undifferentiated in the propinquity of need and satisfaction.
>
> (1990: 67, 71–2)

In general terms, the object of desire is not desired because it is intrinsically desirable, but because such objects resist desire (correlatively the emerging ego which eventually 'incorporates' the object of desire and its accompanying matrix of object relationships also 'destroys' what it consumes).

Pain is the voice of the body

The phenomenology of pain awareness is instructive in bracketing reductive biological and physiological accounts of experiential phenomena. We can begin with the obvious fact that the term 'pain' covers a wider range of subjective phenomena than the expression 'physical pain'. In traditional metaphysical descriptions of the phenomenon the pleasures of the senses are accompanied and countered by the pains of the soul (for example in the work of Hobbes, Malebranche, Condillac, Bentham, Maine de Biran, Mill, and others). We should, then, include the widest spectrum of 'mental' and 'spiritual' dis-ease under this portmanteau term.

We have suggested that all sentient organisms figurate their life-worlds by constituting a contrastive structure of 'value and anti-value': these nascent structurations of 'good' and 'bad' experiences form the life-sustaining and the life-threatening elements braided through every act of awareness. Indeed the protoform of the pleasurable 'feeling of existence' may be the shared bond between animal and human existence. Where pleasure appears to be equilibriating and non-localized, pain indexes points of organic disruption (hence the appropriateness of the metaphor of 'dis-ease'). Pleasure is holistic, pain is differentiating. The more an organism can successfully internalize and 'manage'

these experiential distinctions the more that organism has a chance of anticipating and controlling its environment. Pain indexes the threatening intrusion
of the environment upon the membrane of the organism. Pain is the species-
specific harbinger of dedifferentiation disturbing the organization of lived
experience. Extreme pain presents the organism with an erosion of its integrity.
This may well mark one of the universal anxieties that human beings share with
many other animal species. And, as a corollary, different species evolve different modes of pain reflexivity to manage and 'economize' this necessary
coefficient of anxiety. This, of course, is the motivation behind the religious
idiom of the human being as a finite, suffering creature. An immaterial substance – a being that could not be injured or suffer disease – would experience
no pain, but it would also have no needs, moods, emotions, or desires. A
'soulless' creature would be free from the gamut of 'spiritual suffering'
depicted in the annals of the Christian confessional and grouped today under
the undifferentiated categories of 'depression' or 'nervous illness' (Styron,
1991: 36–9).

The most rudimentary phenomenology of pain awareness suggests that
'pain' does not designate an entity; experienced pain has no 'object' in the
conventional way we think of physical entities or external things (cf. for
example, Ronald Melzak and Patrick Wall, *The Challenge of Pain*, 1983: ch. 1,
David Bakan, *Disease, Pain and Sacrifice: Towards a Psychology of Suffering*,
1968, Elaine Scarry, *The Body in Pain*, 1985, Thomas Szasz, *Pain and Pleasure*,
1957, and William Styron, *Darkness Visible*, 1991). I cannot touch, see, or taste
your pain – but I am intensely aware of my own pain. The 'intimacy' and
'mineness' of pain must be accepted as an irreducible phenomenological
experience. I may find boredom not only intolerable but spiritually painful,
whereas you regard boredom as an occupational norm. Many languages speak
about the sufferer being 'in' pain, of anxieties and fears 'overtaking' the soul,
of 'falling' into melancholy and *accedia*. When I am in pain I suffer; I experience
various degrees of unpleasurable sensations (marking the fact that both physical and 'mental' pain presuppose the disordered working of nerve impulses and
neural processing – as yet little understood by the neurophysiological sciences). Physical trauma tends to be seen as the paradigm of the pain situation:
the bruise on my leg aches and I seek medical treatment; my osteopath
manipulates my limbs and disarticulates vertebrae in my spine to relieve my
chronic condition; as Wittgenstein reminds us, it is unusual to objectify pain
in first-person epistemic reports – a 'queerness' intrinsic to statements such as
'I know I am in pain' (Wittgenstein, 1968: §244; cf. Malcolm, 1958). In normal
circumstances my responses to pain are existential, practical, and functional: I
concretely experience *this particular* back pain and seek the help of an osteopath. I describe the pain to the physician in recognizable terms. I recall the
causal circumstances of an injury (rock climbing), the momentary shock of the
accident, the initial severity of the effect of the blow on my leg, and the causal
consequences of the injury – walking is now painful, I limp, and the pain keeps

me awake at night. My doctor – not being philosophically trained – does not ask me 'What is the sensation *like*?' let alone 'What is pain consciousness like?'; she asks me 'Where does it hurt?' and 'How did you do it?' The language is one of disembedded nouns and abstract descriptions. This is the idiom of medical diagnosis which routinely differentiates the physical point of trauma from the felt locus of pain (a large part of successful treatment depends on my physician being able to correlate my description of the pain state with known aetiologies and syptomatological knowledge).

But if pain is shorthand for 'pain sensed' or 'pain experienced', like all experience it is subject to material, personal, social and cultural variations (Zborowski, 1952; Kleinman, 1986; Benner, ed., 1994: chs 1–2). My description of symptoms typically connects the pain with related changes to my normal body-schema and environmental activities (Fairley, 1980; Gibson, 1982). Pain, like other experiences, is to some degree culturally specific. A child has to be taught the appropriate techniques of localization and pain-accounting practices (although this socialization can never be reduced to abstract formulae). Behavioural responses linked to pain expression are repertoires acquired in definite social situations. In varying degrees pain responses are learned behavioural patterns subject to cultural respecification. It is well known that certain individuals have lower pain thresholds than others – what one person treats as a disagreeable feeling another experiences as excruciating pain; similarly if we are engaged in an activity which requires intense concentration we tend to ignore pain symptoms and even major lesions to the body: our purposes and concerns may modulate and even override pain experience. Different cultures also actively socialize their members to respond differentially to what is ostensibly the 'same' pain-inducing situations. It is well known that certain pharmacological regimes function more effectively in particular sociocultural environments. Yet despite these variations we still accept that all human beings suffer as finite, embodied creatures. Without some innate signal system or message relays of pain 'feedback' the organism would rapidly perish (the loss of pain receptors leads to a chronic lack of self-monitoring and an inability to anticipate local environmental changes). We are suffering animals who live and monitor their existence by heeding and interpreting the insistent semiotics of pain. But surely – we feel like saying – pain is more than the body's biological semiosis; it is a causal power, a force of determination and delimitation within experience. In extreme conditions I suffer severe pain which disrupts the routine pattern of my life. Such chronic pain is a subversive and destructive power. It objectifies my being-in-the-world, freezing my activities and constraining my usual plans. Suffering inhibits my normal capacities and skills; it changes my behaviour, disposition, and attitude to life, often with the sudden force of a Gestalt shift. We all know cases of individuals who are totally transformed, for good or ill, by undergoing a painful experience – often a psychological or social experience such as the loss of a loved partner, unemployment, or some abrupt and permanent change in personal circumstances.

And lay-psychology speaks eloquently of 'mental' and 'spiritual' pain as being among the most formative, long-lasting, and deep-rooted forms of human experiences. In these latter cases the task of removing the 'causes' of suffering is usually immensely difficult.

In extreme pain I can no longer function – a part of my body that was previously silent now urgently calls for attention. It 'differentiates' and 'focuses' itself as an insistent zone of relevance. In naturally occurring pain I am wise to listen to the voice of my body. I am conscious not merely of the isolated 'pain sensation', but of my aching limb and the functional difficulties in walking flowing from this change in the causal nexus of my body. There are good evolutionary reasons why routine pain is one of the most emphatic feeling states that I can experience; evolving as part of the sensorium of human consciousness, it has its own modalities, its continuum of variable aspects, rhythms, intensities, and experiential 'textures': in its most severe forms – for example, in a paralysing migraine or depressive anguish – its causal effects are violently real: my migraine prevents me from working normally, and no efforts on my part, no analgesic painkillers, seem to alter the physical 'grip' of this illness. Such pain inscribes my existence in a new causal relation to the world. It redefines the lines of possible action and activities. In these contexts any action or practice that can remove pain – the popular locution is 'the conquest of pain' – is almost invariably defined as 'a good', and presented in positive, ethical terms (while conversely the infliction of pain and the creation of contexts or instruments that extend the possibilities of suffering are definitionally 'immoral').

We should separate the rhythms of routine or temporary pain from the long-term and perhaps permanent pain of chronic illness. Where instances of the former case have to be controlled and ideally, eliminated, the latter situation has to be incorporated into the individual's personal life-world. William Styron describes the pain of chronic depression in these terms:

> The pain is unrelenting, and what makes the condition intolerable is the foreknowledge that no remedy will come – not in a day, an hour, a month, or a minute. If there is mild relief, one knows that it is only temporary; more pain will follow. It is hopelessness even more than pain that crushes the soul ... One does not abandon, even briefly, one's bed of nails, but is attached to it wherever one goes. And this results in a striking experience ... the situation of the walking wounded.
>
> (1991: 62)

Permanent pain means adapting to a life lived with an alien presence, a stranger in the same body. This is the kind of pain which transforms existence, delimits and defines the horizons of an individual's life-plans. Both categories should also be distinguished from life-destroying pain – the terminal pain which ushers in death. In this direction, routine and managed pain shades into mortal suffering, the pain which sufferers describe as indescribable. Before pain is the eye of the spirit, it is the voice of the body.

In many cases I can objectify and describe my pain when asked 'What's your pain like?' (we might note the difficulties in performing the same lay phenomenology for the forms and modalities of pleasure). I possess a cultural lexicon detailing the intensionality of pain (perhaps the history of the grammar of personal pronouns, especially the indexical signs 'I' and 'me', developed from this prereflective economy of pain experience?). I contrast the sensation of a dull ache with the sharpness of a burn. An old wound occasionally causes me discomfort, it twinges; a cut finger throbs; a backache is mildly discomforting; the inflamed appendix produces a stabbing and 'gripping' pain which bends the body like a seizure. In describing such situations I resort to images and metaphors to convey what I assume to be a shared register of pain experience. I also routinely assume that other people use similar descriptions and give analogous accounts of their sensations and feelings. These symptoms fall into groups and point to known causal conditions. I assume that such indexical pain expressions convey something like a concrete knowledge of the quality of the experience (of course a 'knowledge' that is available only to the trained expert in diagnosis). But this does not mean that the diagnostician can answer the question, 'What is the *essence* of pain?' any more than we can answer the question, 'Where is the *essence* of pain?'

Pain expressions express no *essence*; but they allow a speaker accurately to represent and evoke the particular 'feel' of an aching knee or throbbing headache (but how do such indexical expressions allow another person to empathize with the chronic depressive's 'despair beyond despair' (Styron, 1991: 63)?). I express my experience of pain without mechanically correlating description with sensation. I do not independently check their fit, as it were, adjusting my inner experience of pain to available rhetorical terms. This would raise the possibility that I might be mistaken about the fit between third-person descriptions and first-person experience. If that is possible I may later discover that what I have been calling 'pain' is not in fact pain at all but 'joy' or 'pleasure' or some other feeling-state. But the fallacy here is that such idioms do not so much express a state of mind as codify a configuration of my lived experience. The morphology of pain experience is given with the contexts of its everyday situated, phenomenological manifestations. It appears, then, that the features or aspects of different forms of pain cannot serve to exemplify a stable essence or homogeneous pattern. The diversity of pain sensations is a reflection of the plurality of human activities in particular circumstances – and its forms are as heterogeneous as the manifold forms of our transactions in ongoing social practices. I now experience my leg as an obstacle to movement; the limb obtrudes and obstructs my plans; it manifests itself more like an instrument that refuses to function than a previously unnoticed moment of my spatiotemporal activities. And we can still maintain that the adjectival qualities which enter my accounts refer to sensations localized 'in' my leg (even where in the so-called phantom limb phenomena experienced by amputees there are no pain receptors), not descriptions of 'brain states' or 'mental predicates'. They are not, as it were, 'signs' or 'symptoms' which allow me to become 'acquainted' with my pain sensations. Our everyday concept of awareness prior to philo-sophical doubts presupposes both a phenomenological and a causal nexus of sentience and indexes a more differentiated organization of experience, prefig-uring the radical differentiating powers of *attention*. As Jaynes observes: 'Pain in ourselves is always a complex interaction between the physical stimulus that causes pain behaviour and the conscious reactive component which we might call the conscious suffering' (in Kolak and Martin, eds, 1991: 34).

As this brief phenomenology of pain experience suggests, the sensation of pain already comes inscribed in specific intentional modalities – of perception, belief, and cultural norms, for example. Pain is not simply a 'neural' event, 'input-output' system, or functional outcome of the workings of the central nervous system; it is also a mode of our human being-in-the-world, an integral possibility in a repertoire of practical involvements. We are reminded of Marx's formulation in *The Economic and Philosophical Manuscripts*, 'To be sensuous, i.e. to be real, is to be an object of sense, a sensuous object, thus to have sensuous objects outside onself, to have objects of sense perception. To be sentient is to suffer' (1975: 390, trans modified). In asking how pain functions we see that the phenomenon – like suffering more generally – is not an object for thought but a lived relation (indeed a complex of different relations). 'Man as an objective, sentient being is therefore a suffering being, and since he is a being who feels his sufferings, a passionate being. Passion is man's faculties energetic-ally striving after their object' (1975: 390, trans. modified). And if we were to take our phenomenological sketch further we would have to begin to explore the historical rhetorics, discourses, and institutions which elaborate the rich modalities of suffering as a phenomenon within the human world. Pain is as much a cultural code as a physiological reaction. Pain arises as an existential corollary of embodiment – a sign of the human condition as endemically prone to suffering, a display of human being as 'human natural being'. The hetero-geneous 'grammar' of *suffering, hurt, discomfort, disease, pain*, etc. enfolds a network of social and historical relations as well as coding the evolutionary wisdom of the body's survival mechanisms. For example, the semantics of 'suffering' is closer to ethical and religious vocabularies of motive than to the reductive vocabulary of 'registering pain' or 'responding to hurt'. The appear-ance of suffering invariably marks the time and place where an individual is in greatest need of the help and understanding of others. Pain's grammar is thus specified by syncategorematic configurations of temporality and significance (as in the evolution of an ethic which claims that 'pain and suffering are the greatest of all evils' but also in the bonding communalities of shared suffering). Breaking off this train of thought, we can now return to the theme of lived awareness.

Awareness accompanies routine activities and functions (we are prereflectively aware of our immediate sensory experiences, sensory-motor position, kinaesthetic movements, and so forth without explicitly attending to these). Sensory experience in its different modalities is 'conscious' in an analytic sense (does it make sense to claim that I 'have pain' or 'experience pain' without being aware of it?). To 'experience' pain is, for normal cases, analytically the same as being conscious of pain. The utterance 'I am in pain but I'm not aware of it' invites an incredulous response, whereas in a clinical context the utterance 'He is in pain, but he's not aware of it' (said for example of someone with paralysis) is completely intelligible. It is not merely a case of being able to apply the public rules for using the word 'pain' in appropriate contexts. Pain has an irreducible experiential or, as this is expressed today, *phenomenal* element. Bodily sensations are in this sense 'owned' as part of my ongoing experience. In standard cases, awareness is definitionally an aspect of sensory experience. In general this is what is meant by 'being sensible' or 'having sensations'. I taste the bitterness of lemons, smell the fragrance of violets, feel the coldness of ice, have a painful sensation. We have, however, noted an asymmetry as regards pain and pleasure – where a direct physical pain is 'registered' immediately (I 'undergo' a painful experience), pleasure may well be temporally delayed or mediated. It may also, in psychoanalytic parlance, be overdetermined. But a duality of pain and pleasure remains as a phenomenological invariant: pain's insistence is pleasure's ambiguity. And, as we know, increasing the threshold or intensity of sensation turns pleasurable experiences into occasions of discomfort and pain.

3.3 Attentionality

In general, *attention* is a *tending of the ego toward an intentional object*, toward a unity which 'appears' continually in the change of the modes of its givenness and which belongs to the essential structure of a specific act of the ego ... it is tending toward in realization.

(Edmund Husserl, 1973: §18, 80)

Attention may be defined as thematic awareness. Consider one of the standard psychological conceptions of consciousness as 'the personal awareness of subjective experience at any point in time': 'In general usage, consciousness has meant the individual's total awareness of past experiences and future aspirations, as well as ongoing self-knowledge, and this usage implies active self-reflection' (Brennan, 1991: 327; Murray, 1983: ch. 1). But in the standard literature of modern psychology and the philosophy of mind, attention is presented as a faculty or state of mind which disengages consciousness from action. Attention is the capacity to step back and consciously thematize the stream of conscious life. But active 'thematization' presupposes the larger horizon of unthematized or peripheral experience, the fringe of consciousness which accompanies reflective acts. In phenomenological terms attention is a modality of a more encompassing, and perhaps primitive, order of prepredicative intentionality (intentionality in its broadest sense of affectively oriented awareness – say, in the primordial vectors of painful or pleasurable sentience). In the act of attending to this apperceptive mass I transform a relatively inchoate and automatized awareness ('I have a pain') into a thematic 'object' of my attention ('the chronic stabbing sensation in the lumbar region of my back'). In reflecting upon my experience I 'discriminate' *that* experience as an object or thematic focus of further predicative acts ('belief', 'judgement', 'comparison', etc.) rather than something experientially 'lived through'; in purposefully controlling my anger, for example, I create a new 'attentional object': 'my anger'. And this 'object' may be the starting point for sublimation and displacement activities. Acts of attention and their attentional modalities, then, precipitate a richer division of meaning into the bipolar structure of figure and ground, centre and periphery, focus and horizon:

> The greater part of mind is only implicit in any conscious act or state; the field of mind – of operative meanings – is enormously wider than that of consciousness. Mind is contextual and persistent; consciousness is focal and transitive. Mind is, so to speak, structural, substantial; a constant background and foreground; perceived consciousness is process, a series of heres and nows. Mind is a constant luminosity; consciousness intermittent, a series of flashes of varying intensities. Consciousness is, as it were, the occasional interception of messages continually transmitted, as a mechanical receiving device selects a few of the vibrations with which the air is filled and renders them audible.
>
> (Dewey, 1958: 303–4)

Attentionality is thus an active theme-constituting process in which knower and known are simultaneously disembedded from the ongoing process of experience. Paradoxically, it is only through attentional modes that we gain a sense that we have already lived 'naively' within a more encompassing field of conscious life (of 'ongoing consciousness' in its habituated and routinized structure). We seem to be led by the phenomena themselves to distinguish between predicative-saturated kinds of attentional consciousness ('a belief-laden consciousness') and another more primitive form of consciousness, tied to feeling and experience (cf. Tye: 1993: 35). As a particularly important term of reference for psychological life the word 'attention' would thus repay detailed historical and discursive analysis. As with the rhetorics of other psychological terms we have introduced in this chapter I defer this diachronic investigation for another occasion.

Let us instead return to the synchronic analysis of the metaphor of attention as a trope of conscious life. In the manifold modalities of 'carving out' an object from its contexts attentional acts can be said to 'construct' the patterns of subjective life. Selective attention to the course of lived duration involves a reflective moment, a turning back of the experiencer upon some moment, part, or element of the course of experience, an element which is singled out for some reason by the *ray of attention* and constituted as an 'attentional focus', 'figure', or 'thematic object' rather than something previously 'lived' passively. Each act indexes a site of volitional engagement. Attention becomes distinctively human when another person can direct others to a thematic object and where both can attend to the 'same' experience and thus act in concert.

In moving from parts to wholes and wholes to parts, elementary attentional performances provide the framework for every subsequent act of analysis or practical deconstruction. Here metaphors like 'focusing', 'orientation', 'thematization', 'attentionality', 'directionality', 'purposeful control', 'voluntary synthesis', 'choice', 'selection', 'directive interest', 'active apperception', and 'intentionality' seem phenomenologically appropriate. But the visual imagery of 'attentional focusing' can be seriously misleading. In the 'beam-of-light' metaphor consciousness is figured 'like the eye running over a field of ready-made objects, or a light which illuminates now this and now that portion of a given field'.

> It postulates, even though only implicitly, a pre-established harmony of the knower and things known, passing over the fact that such harmony is always an attained outcome of prior inferences and investigations. It assumes a knowing mind wholly guileless, and extraordinarily competent, whose sole business is to behold and register objects just as what they are, and which is unswervingly devoted to its business.
>
> (Dewey, 1958: 308–9)

The metaphor of attentionality is problematizing in constituting experience as a domain of 'values' or 'relevance structures'. Each *focus of relevance* valorizes experience by drawing out an 'object' from its encompassing environment. What is thus thematized by reflection can then form the attentional nucleus for further acts of consciousness. New contents of experience and objects of awareness are literally created in and by acts of thematic attention. As concern, curiosity, problematization, identification, and thematization take effect, other areas of experience are displaced to the fringes of attention: I turn from one thematic concern to another; I focus my attention upon a new theme; I ignore *this* topic to attend to *that* topic. The shift from *this* to *that*, however, does not involve a complete suppression of the prior thematization (if what was 'loved' is now 'despised' the the new object retains its sense as 'once being loved' – it leaves a 'comet's tail' of intentions which can be subsequently reactivated. Even the simplest acts of practical comparison and mensuration presuppose systems of focused attention. In fact every voluntary action

> is dependent upon the indication of a certain character, pointing it out, holding on to it, and so holding on to the response that belongs to it.

That sort of an analysis is essential to what we call human intelligence, and it is made possible by language.

(Mead, 1934: 95)

Remarkably the overall coherence and texture of attentive consciousness is not torn or disintegrated by these routine shifts of thematization; or to say this in another way, the flexibility of problematization creates no radical discontinuities in the coherence structure of the field of experience. Although explicit concentration requires the expenditure of effort I can shift back and forth at will from heightened attentionality to passive 'inattention' – and this corresponds with the changing phenomenological 'rhythms of consciousness' experienced in day-to-day living. The habitualities of ordinary experience are already organized in terms of past acts of selectivity and attentional judgement sedimented in perceptual *themata*, typical categories and contexts of linguistic usage where they are organized into prepredicative nodal values, aims, and goals. Shifts of experience become routinized and shared – we expect certain 'attentional tensions' in different zones of everyday practice and interaction (reading quietly in a study and reading in front of a lecture theatre are essentially different activities). At a very deep level, then, experience in its configurations of attentionality is thus already prestructured in temporal, social, and cultural terms.

This is the permanent significance of Husserl's description of horizonal consciousness:

> Living wakefully in the world we are constantly conscious of the world, whether we pay attention to it or not, conscious of it as the horizon of our life, and as a horizon of 'things' (real objects), of our actual and possible interests and activities. Always standing out against the world-horizon is the horizon of our fellow men, whether there are any of them present or not. Before even taking notice of it at all, we are conscious of the open horizon of our fellow men with its limited nucleus of our neighbours, those known to us. We are thereby co-conscious of the men on our external horizon in each case as 'others'; in each case 'I' am conscious of them as 'my' others, as those with whom I can enter into actual and potential, immediate and mediate relations of empathy; this involves a reciprocal 'getting along' with others; and on the basis of these relations I can deal with them, enter into particular modes of community with them, and then know, in a habitual way, of my being so related. Like me, every human being – and this is how he is understood by me and everyone else – has his fellow men and, always counting himself, civilization in general, in which he knows himself to be living.

(1970: 358)

Our everyday grammatical expressions reinforce the videological metaphors for consciousness inherited from two or three centuries of psychological speculation. The use of words like *background, context, configuration, fringe, perspective*, etc. suggests something too external or spatially contiguous to express the logological constellations of everyday experience. This fascination with spatial metaphors, in other words, might be corrected with temporal and dialectical images. Experience is not waiting like a fixed terrain of objects to be 'mapped', 'inspected', 'perceived'. We do not have a stable 'core' or 'nucleus' toward which we might adopt an 'attitude'. One possible way of suspending the spectatorial view of awareness is by means of a more comprehensive concept of attentive consciousness. To expedite this move, emphasis might be placed on the transformative capacities of modes of attentionality in ordering an unstable and mutable world. In essence this is the direction taken by modern phenomenological philosophy: attention is much more dynamic than a simple taking-notice or modification of perception, involving as it does corporeal effort, an exercise of will, and a changed attitude toward experience. Indeed some forms of attentional shift can only be described as a complete change in existential comportment (in this respect Husserl and James anticipate the work of thinkers like Heidegger, Bachelard, Canguilheim, and Kuhn). Consciousness, in Dewey's terms, involves a redirection of meanings under the impress of some disturbance to the familiar networks of meaning, of self and its emerging world. We attend to things, for example, when an anomaly appears, when a routine is disrupted or something untoward or unexpected intrudes. What had been stabilized as 'good' is disturbed by impinging events (which the organism must define as 'bad'). Whatever dissolves the structured order is, by definition, an alien Other. Given a problematic situation we have to suspend our current action, backtrack, or at least slow down what was previously executed 'without thinking'. Like organisms tuned to the relevances of their species-specific environment, we tend not to 'stop and think' unless there is a disturbance to our frames of reference. If we have to resort to a rule book to put together the components of action then we have either not acquired the skills to perform the activity in question or we are experiencing the beginnings of a pathological condition. When the customary Gestalt of activities decomposes we are thrown into the mode of attentional awareness. What was a background alterity becomes a threatening Other. The situation itself calls out for reorganization.

By following these paths we return to the insights of the European tradition of philosophical anthropology and phenomenological analysis. We are back with the broken hammer of *Sein und Zeit*, the lost hammer in Mead's *Mind, Self, and Society* (1934: 83), and the 'slab game' which opens Wittgenstein's *Philosophical Investigations*. The simplest modalities of attention involving concrete problematization ('Is this an apple or an orange'?' 'Where did I leave that hammer?'), directive exploration, world-testing, practical manipulation, alteration and change, etc. create new levels of awareness, new attitudinal systems, and more explicit forms of consciousness – usually termed reflective. Unlike many other species, however, human beings actively 'enjoy' the experience of 'hesitancy' toward and 'disengagement' from immediate experience. Achieving distance and dispassionate attention is one of the unique achievements of human consciousness – purposeless looking, speculative enjoyment, abstract thought, etc. The structure of hesitancy, disorientation, and attentional refocusing creates a new order of phenomena – frequently in experiences we do not typically associate with reflection and explicit thought. Such life forms are not merely 'problem-solving' creatures, but creatures who begin to *enjoy solving problems*.

3.4 Reflective awareness

We then understand ourselves, not as subjectivity which finds itself in a world ready-made, as in simple psychological reflection, but as a subjectivity bearing within itself, and achieving, all of the possible operations to which this world owes its becoming.

(Edmund Husserl, 1973: §11, 49)

Reflective awareness is a higher form of attentionality where the thematic object leads the experiencer to turn back upon the act(s) of thematization themselves. This level of recursivity involves both a temporally continuous self and an anticipated project of a future self as the outcome of reflective praxis. We have the beginnings of a 'consciousness of consciousness' and this further assumes a version of selfhood as a *self-referential* and *self-creative* process. An agent is not merely acting attentively, but is aware of so acting (for example, in the sense in which a proficient dancer or actor may 'catch themselves' in full command of a scripted activity – the moment before the virtuosity of training merges into a perfect performance). We think of occasions where we do not merely describe a skilled performance as technically brilliant, but also add words such as 'effortless', 'grace', 'poise', and the like. Here the reflexive 'sense of self' is sublimated into its ongoing realization. The performing self 'forgets' its own finite conditions and becomes 'self-blind'. Intense experience of a 'spiritual' character – joy, happiness, pleasure, and the like also display this 'self-forgetful' characteristic: 'At such times we are so aware of the moment that no attempt is made to compare experience with other experiences' (Watts, 1992: 82–3).

In general, acts of reflection have an explicative relation to their object in objectifying and thematizing complex processes as focal points in the field of experience. Thus Collingwood writes:

To be conscious that I am thinking is to think in a new way, which may be called reflecting. Historical thinking is always reflection; for reflection is thinking about the act of thinking, and we have seen that all historical thinking is of that kind.

(1993: 307)

We naturally think of distinctively human capacities to deliberate, clarify meaning, evaluate evidence, make reasoned choices, and engage in larger chains of ratiocination as exemplary forms of 'reflection'. Each of these activities involves some form of reflexive orientation. This is also the point at which the temporal dynamics of reflection becomes critical for the formation of personal and social identity:

> Intelligence is essentially the ability to solve the problems of present behavior in terms of its possible future consequences as implicated on the basis of past experience – the ability, that is, to solve the problems of present behavior in the light of, or by reference to, both the past and the future; it involves both memory and foresight.
>
> (Mead, 1934: 100)

Reflection in its everyday first-person forms thus interfaces with the reflexivities of discursive thought in that it introduces the prereflexive equivalents of linguistic and logical operations which massively extend and transform preverbal identifications (thematic *abstraction* from situations, *conjoining* of abstract themes, *idealization, schematization, formalization, representation,* systematic *comparison, analogizing* operations and metaphorization, *synoptic* appraisal, representation, inductive-deductive-abductive procedures, *extrapolation, generalization,* and so forth). Often the awareness of criterial properties guiding these projects is cited as a necessary characteristic of reflective thought:

> A reflective activity is one in which we know what it is that we are trying to do, so that when it is done we know that it is done by seeing that it has conformed to the standard or criterion which was our initial conception.
>
> (Collingwood, 1993: 308)

For example, rudimentary forms of analytic and synthetic operations can be found in the operative structures of everyday *problematization*. It is important to underline the point that the protoforms of such verbal skills are already implicit in many of the prereflective practices of corporeal reflexivity (prepredicative contrasts of *qualia*, mensuration, comparison, calculation, idealization, everyday deduction and logical procedures, mundane practical reasoning, recollective synopses, local judgement, and so forth), and that all later higher-order acts of mind insistently refer back to the experiencing subject (and, paradigmatically, to 'my acting self' as *the* experiencing context of subjectivity) cooperating with other subjects. All the elements that we usually take to be unique to discursive thought and action have their prereflective analogues in mundane patterns of prereflective awareness, practical activity, and operative knowledge. Problematization reaches far back into the praxical activities of meaning constitution which serve as the infrastructures for 'higher' acts of thematization and reflective awareness (in the sense that human praxis involves action 'which we are enabled to perform by knowing in advance how to perform it' (Collingwood, 1993: 308).

3.5 Self-reflective awareness

This method now requires that the ego, beginning with its concrete world-phenomenon, systematically inquire back, and thereby become acquainted with itself, the transcendental ego, in its concreteness, in the system of its constitutive levels and its incredibly intricate [patterns of] validity-founding.

(Edmund Husserl, 1970: §55, 187)

A number of figures of self-reflection have become commonplaces under this general heading. They have been typically described using rhetorics of self-perception: to be reflectively conscious involves some form of self-perception by the Ego. The restriction of 'consciousness' to the Ego or an individual's personality has been most influential in non-behaviourist psychology (in the Gestalt, Existential, and 'Third-force' schools of psychology and psychiatry) and, of course, in the rich and diverse literature of psychoanalysis associated with Ego psychology.

3.5.1 Ego-consciousness

Examples of this conception range from lay theories of the 'person' and 'personality' to professional interest in the role of egological structures in the study of the development of a coherent self-concept. Important theoretical positions range from Freud's later reflections on the central position of the Ego (*das Ich*, *'the I'*) in psychoanalytic theory and therapy, to the American Ego psychologists of the 1950s and 1960s, the sociopsychological theories of Ego development (Hans Kohut, Heinz Hartmann, Erik Erikson, Harry Stack Sullivan, Carl Rogers, among others), role theory, and the early papers of Talcott Parsons and his associates on the place of the Ego in functionalist sociology. For this later tradition personal identity and character formation is a product of the values and roles sanctioned by normative culture. The self and its integration or pathological disintegration is viewed within a dynamic intersection of biological, social, and cultural systems. The personality is treated analytically as a sociocultural variable subjected to a range of contingent socialization and institutional mechanisms. Parsons' early formulation was to remain a basic statement of this orientation:

consciousness, according to this analysis, is a phenomenon of the personality, not of the organism; that is, it occurs within the experience system, not the biological one ... [and] personality is a system of action

209

with various levels of differentiation, and different orders of symbolic process integrating the differentiated parts.[3]

3.5.2 Psychic life and self-consciousness

We have seen that Freud distinguishes the structure of the Ego (the *Ich* or 'I') from the wider field of psychic life. For analytical purposes he also separates Ego consciousness from Unconscious processes (*Unbewusstsein*, the psychic dynamics of the Id) on the grounds that the 'psychic' is wider or 'deeper' than self-awareness and self-consciousness. 'Reflective consciousness', in other words, is not the criterial mark of mental life – given that mental processes occur which cannot be described as 'self-conscious acts', but which nonetheless are decisive in structuring Ego processes. Because the human psyche is topographically stratified, explicit or reflective self-awareness (the 'mineness' of my experience) is posited as only one part of a more complex psychic organization or 'economy' (we will ignore the fact that Freud's basic models of psychological organization changed with the development of psychoanalytic discourse). Freud is instructive in blocking a limited view of reflexivity as cognitive 'self-reflection' and consequently positing a radical break between the skills and capacities of the Ego and those prereflective skills woven into the body's corporeal practices and *habitus* (there can be, for example, an unconscious Ego structure). The conscious mind is only one function of psychic life (mindfulness being a much broader category than reflective awareness).

3.5.3 From consciousness to metaconsciousness

To correct the one-sided cognitivism and intellectualism of previous accounts of consciousness should not lead us to ignore some of the unique characteristics of self-reflection, self-interpretation, and self-consciousness, especially those features involving the remarkable ability of a living organism to temporarily transcend and objectify its environment and to relate to its own embodied condition in a disinterested manner; even though the intelligent capacities of human agency presuppose lower-order structures, we need not reduce emergent orders of reflective praxis to lower-level functions.[4]

If we reject Cartesian dualism and 'immaterialist' perspectives for a naturalistic epistemology, it appears that an explanation of the genesis of consciousness must be couched in terms of the evolutionary emergence of metacommunicative capacities of reciprocity and symbolic interpretation.[5] Consciousness in its most culturally consequential sense emerges along with the evolution and development of language and linguistic practices. Emergent forms of reflexive behaviour such as the ability imaginatively to plan, to think, and critically to evaluate the field and consequences of definite forms of conduct are achievements presupposing an integrated stratification of physiological, behavioural, and neurological systems: in this sense reflexive organizations prior to conscious deliberation and planning antedate the emergence of reflective skills. We should also underline the fact that the psyche and its symbolic reflexivities are much older than reflective thought and language. In genealogical terms, these formations are rooted in prereflective systems of practical valuation linked to more universal pragmatic concerns and community-forming imperatives. Moreover the 'higher-order' functions of the psyche must be continuously nourished by the flow of expressive action and interaction with others. The child becomes conscious in acquiring the language of its relevant others, in learning to participate in and speak with his or her significant others. In 'materialist terms', of course, this also presupposes the evolution of the human cortex and complex neurophysiological and organic capacities. In an evolutionary sense human beings have developed definite cognitive, affective, and volitional faculties by constructing cultural worlds through imaginative acts of symbolic identification and communication. The detailed historiography of these symbolic processes as *social formations* now assumes a foundational role in understanding the origins of consciousness and of disciplines that are concerned with the explanation of psychological reality and, perhaps, more importantly, with the discourses of psychological reflection.[6] As an interim conclusion we can reaffirm the finding that the fragile spheres of deliberative thought and theoretical rationality – the logosphere of *consciousness* and *metaconsciousness* – is the outcome and product of a long history of reflexive semiopraxis.[7]

5

REFLECTION AS SPECULATIVE THOUGHT

Thus there really is a sense in which philosophy can talk about the self in a non-psychological way.

What brings the self into philosophy is the fact that 'the world is my world'.

The philosophical self is not the human being, not the human body, or the human soul, with which psychology deals, but rather the metaphysical subject, the limit of the world – not a part of it.

(Ludwig Wittgenstein, 1971: 5.641)

Continuing and building upon the analysis of Chapter 4, I offer a reconstruction of the ideas of reflection and selfhood in contemporary philosophical discourse. Given the emphasis on the speculative or ocularcentric character of videological thought, I use the work of three major philosophical thinkers as exemplars of 'speculative thought': Hegel (Section 1), Husserl (Section 2), and Heidegger (Section 3). Heidegger's analysis of Dasein as primordially being-in-the-world is particularly important in showing the intrinsic limits of the traditional concept of reflection and suggesting radical changes in our basic ideas of subjectivity and world that might suggest other ways of thinking about human being-in-the-world (Sections 4 and 5).

1 *Speculative consciousness: the Hegelian lesson*
2 *The stream of consciousness: the Husserlian lesson*
3 *Transcendental reflection: the Heideggerian lesson*
4 *Dasein*
5 *Intentionality*

1 SPECULATIVE CONSCIOUSNESS: THE HEGELIAN LESSON

The *autonome ratio* [autonomous reason] – this was the thesis of every idealistic system – was supposed to be capable of developing the concept of reality, and in fact all reality, from out of itself.

(Theodor W. Adorno, in Ray, ed., 1990: 64–5)

If generic reflection represents minimal mediation, then the paradigm case of full mediation would seem to lie in forms of self-consciousness indexed by the terms *thought*, *thinking*, *intellect*, and *reason* – the 'one universal self-consciousness' uncovered by Kant (1929: B132–3). To underscore its dynamic character Kant's contemporaries spoke of the faculty of reason (*Vernunft*) as the supreme determining attribute of self-conscious subjects. The transcendental unity of 'I think', the unity of apperception, appears with every empirical subject. It is not, however, to be understood as a thinking thing or substance. In general, then, the subject in idealist thought was presented as an active participant in gaining knowledge of the world. As a constructive source of knowledge, *Vernunft* is the singular locus of human understanding and active intellect (the self is, as Kant argues in the Transcendental Deduction, the *a priori* matrix of the categories of understanding and thus the formal origin of the capacity of rational self-determination – the criterial mark of the *person* as a unitary, continuous, self-consciousness). While criticizing the Kantian understanding of the *a priori*, Hegel frequently uses the terms 'reflection' ('absolute reflection') and 'mediation' ('concrete mediation' or 'mediated unity') as synonyms for the creative life of spiritual existence which antedates explicit reflexive projects (leading him to the notorious postulate of a speculative identity between Mind and World). Like Kant, Hegel also drew the practical conclusion from the transcendental philosophy of the *a priori* that the world of moral life (*Moralität*) and ethical community (*Sittlichkeit*) is impossible without a prior community of self-conscious agents and a prior realm of spiritual existence.

As a human 'faculty' (a concept which is related to the Greek notion of 'capacity' or 'disposition', *dunamis*), Reason is evidenced in its exercise (in the *activities* of practical deliberation, moral conscience, and autonomous interaction). The cultural formation and transformations of self-consciousness are therefore approached as both the medium of the will and the vehicle of the Spirit. In an important 'Addition' to paragraph 4 of *The Philosophy of Right* Hegel explains these linkages as follows:

> Mind is in principle thinking, and man is distinguished from the beast in virtue of thinking. But it must not be imagined that man is half thought and half will, and that he keeps thought in one pocket and will in another ... The distinction between thought and will is only that between the theoretical attitude and the practical. These, however, are surely not two faculties; the will is rather a special way of thinking, thinking translating itself into existence, thinking as the urge to give itself existence.
>
> (1952: 226)

Subjectivity is an abstract term for human self-activity re-collecting its own history (which Hegel calls *Erinnerung*, remembering, but literally 'becoming interior'). In other variants of this Promethean position, thinking and self-

213

consciousness are treated as speculative synonyms (in the German Idealist tradition from Kant to Fichte, Schelling, and Hegel for example, *denken* is one of the exclusive achievements of autonomous, self-centred human beings – a description of human existence which elevates abstract cognition, understanding, and reasoning above sensory experience and perception). *Denken* (the '*Ich denke*' which accompanies all my phenomenal experience, in Kant's well-known formula, the world-positing *Ich* of Fichte (condensed into the abstract tautology of metaphysical identity: 'The Ego = the Ego', 'Ich = Ich'), and the self-contained absolute consciousness of Spirit in Hegel) is the medium of reflexive universality through which human beings create and change their worlds.

For the tradition of German Idealism and the Romantic movement in the first decades of the nineteenth century the experiencing Ego as pure self-awareness is literally the centre of the world (or said inversely, the world is always a world-for-consciousness, a *phenomenal world* for the transcendental self). The only known 'entity' in the universe which has the capacity to 'represent' objects, to recognize their alterity and enter a dialogue with things is the mode of being the Idealist tradition designates with the expression *Selbstbewusstsein*. *Selbstbewusstsein* became the criterial principle of Mind, interpreted as the autogestation of the 'Idea'. Over two or three important decades at the beginning of the nineteenth century 'self-consciousness' was popularized as a term of art for the being of the autonomous person which refers to itself as 'I' (redescribed now as the transcendental source of *autonome ratio*, the unity of subject and substance). The last decades of the eighteenth century were productive years for the emergence of this transcendental idea of the Self. Kant, for example, explores the phenomenon in 'The paralogisms of pure reason' in the *Critique of Pure Reason* and in the 'Anthropological didactic' of his *Anthropology from a Pragmatic Point of View* (1796). In Hegel's metaphysical vocabulary, the universe as objective *Geist* comes to know itself through the dialectic of Subject and Substance (the unity of thought and being). To 'know' anything is to reflect on the processes of objectual cognition created by a self-conscious agency (as Kant says, 'All my representations are my representations', and thus subject to transcendental conditions and rules). But for Hegel cognition itself has a history and develops in a dialectical style from relatively unreflexive forms of consciousness to the self-conscious structures of rational universality. From this staple postulate of 'objective Idealism' the history of philosophical knowledge might be construed as 'the progressive unfolding of the truth' of a universe that is radically informed by 'mind' and 'culture'. There are no longer 'two worlds', the inner world of consciousness facing an inert external world. The critique of faculty psychology and Scholastic metaphysics begun by Romanticism is now elaborated into an encyclopaedic philosophy of the Spirit. Philosophy aspires at last to the venerable title of science or *Wissenschaft* and not merely the love of knowledge. The unitary world is simply the world constituted by Reason (thus

Hegel's *Phenomenology of Spirit* traces the dialectic from Consciousness to Self-consciousness to Reason, Spirit, religion and Absolute Knowledge). And Absolute Knowledge is ultimately to be understood as a process of spiritual self-comprehension – an elaboration of themes that are implicit in Kant's anthropological delimitation of the sphere of moral self-determination in the third *Critique*.

One of the generative schemes of intepretation informing this metatheoretical account of Mind is the grammatical model of Reflection as a specular relation of the subject toward object; stated most simply: *no object without a subject, no knowledge without consciousness*. The anthropocentric Subject-Object schema we might almost say is the ur-metaphor for the whole videological tradition, and leads those who work within this framework to construe reflection in the imagery of subjects mirroring objects, minds reflecting bodies. As we tried to show in some detail in Chapter 2, the specular metaphor of mirror-imaging is the leading idea for this whole style of thinking with a history that can be traced from the late Scholastics to Descartes, the Enlightenment, the German and English Romantics, down to Kant and Hegel. Hegel is the speculative inheritor and ultimate systematizer of this way of thinking. In fact Hegel explicitly defines the ontological nature of Spirit in the language of mirroring self-reflection:

> Spirit, on the contrary [that is, as contrasted with Matter], may be defined as that which has its centre in itself. It has not a unity outside itself, but has already found it; it exists *in and with itself*. Matter has its essence out of itself; Spirit is self-contained existence (*bei-sich-selbst-sein*). Now this is Freedom, exactly. For if I am dependent, my being is referred to something else which I am not ... I am free, on the contrary, when my existence depends upon myself. This self-contained existence of Spirit is none other than self-consciousness – consciousness of one's own being. Two things must be distinguished in consciousness; first, the fact *that I know*; secondly, *what I know*. In *self* consciousness these are merged in one; for Spirit *knows itself*. It involves an appreciation of its own nature, as also an energy enabling it to realize itself; to make itself actually that which it is potentially. According to this abstract definition it may be said of Universal History, that it is the exhibition of Spirit in the process of working out the knowledge of that which it is potentially. And as the germ bears in itself the whole nature of the tree, and the taste and form of its fruits, so do the first traces of Spirit virtually contain the whole of that History.
>
> (Hegel, 1956: 17–18)

To express this rather crudely it can be said that Hegel 'dialecticizes' the ancient videological polarity of Mind and Matter, Soul and Body and 'historicizes' the teleological quest for the unity of thinking and being: where the traditional vocabulary of metaphysics posits a duality, Hegel uncovers a process of interaction. Self-consciousness is thus presented as the truth of the certainty of the self and Reason as the 'realization of rational self-consciousness through itself'. Thus one of Hegel's major contributions to the theory of self-reflection is contained in the thought that we are not born *persons*, but achieve 'personality' by internalizing the objective forms of culture. As an organ of the self-formation of *Geist*, self-reflection is situated and subject to dialectical diremption. The classical mind/body division of epistemology is displaced by the dialectic of matter and spirit. And we should not be surprised that this 'construction' ultimately turned out to be a notational variation of the basic videological metaphors of Western theology and metaphysics. Consider, for example, the well-known text from the Preface to the *Phenomenology of Spirit* (1807). Here Reason is presented as a process in which the Ego becomes a concrete self, a fully actual self-consciousness. Hegel, so to speak, socializes human rationality by historicizing Reason. The Ego develops its selfhood through a dialectical process of negativity and repetitive cycles of mediation. In Hegelian terminology the Ego becomes actual and concrete through the mediation of conflictual oppositions – consciousness is the living unrest and journey of the self as self-objectifying, self-negating, and self-restoring identity. In 'speaking-against itself' (*widersprechen*) the Ego divides itself, to actively unite with its own opposite in order to return to itself as a more complex and, in Hegel's terminology, *concrete* existent. Only subjective self-existence can become an object to itself for the reason that only an intrinsically reflexive process can recover itself as an existence in-and-for-itself. Indeed, in Hegel's metaphysical vision the Absolute as God or Spirit is presented as 'reflectively mediating itself with itself', regathering its unity from its own modes of dispersed alterity and self-alienation. In Hegelese, *Geist* is the essence of mind coming to absolute self-consciousness through acts of recognizing its own self-knowledge. The teleological process of concrete mediation in the realm of the 'I' is appropriately termed *speculation* (*Spekulation* being a species of argument that Kant had earlier proscribed as a transcendent misuse of the understanding). On the plane of objective spirit itself, this process of concretion is called *Bildung* and 'philosophical science' is appropriately respecified as the 'self-comprehension of Spirit' (Hegel, 1976b: Section D, 'Absolute knowledge').

But Hegel takes an even more radical step. The Hegelian idea of Reflection requires us to think of Reality itself as a progressive self-movement of Spirit enlarging and recuperating its empire in the face of resistant worlds of natural facticity and 'objective spirit'. The cosmos 'is more like a great thought than a great machine' in which Spirit (*Geist*) 'loses' itself in its objectifications to return from its alienation through cycles of *conceptual* recuperation. The spiralling dialectic of enlightenment is represented as the necessary self-mediation of Spirit as it cyclically identifies with and negates particular 'forms of consciousness' in gaining knowledge of itself as an absolute source of rational consciousness. History – whether the history of an individual subject or a whole civilization – is relegated to the status of an act in the drama of the progressive unfolding of the Absolute. Its pattern and immanent logic is identical with the autobiography of the Absolute Idea. Philosophical speculation is given the task of grasping this 'unfolding process' in pure thought. As a spiritual process, the 'thinking of thinking' called philosophy necessarily 'forms a circle'; being a reflexive medium of the Spirit 'it circles back into itself' 1952: 225). The first appearances of 'Ego consciousness' are necessarily abstract and unreflective shapes of the Spirit's world consciousnesss; each partial 'consciousness of self' is intrinsically inadequate when compared to the normative Idea of *Reason* (as 'Absolute self-knowledge'). Thus the 'I-exist' of egoistic self-consciousness – the first flickering sign of freedom – must follow the arduous road of alienated consciousness – through the natural determinations of sensory awareness, the vicissitudes of desire, the struggle for mutual recognition, and the vagaries of the unhappy consciousness to more universal – and thereby, more 'spiritual' – forms of self-awareness, to finally consummate its telos in the objective structures of Reason as the rational comprehension of the universal Logos. The *Vorstellungen* of 'art', 'religion', and 'philosophy' are progressively more adequate forms of self-mediating Mind, spiritual vehicles of the Self's pursuit of rational integrity which Hegel calls *'absolute inwardness'*. Self-knowledge as a *zurückgehende Kreis* (reflexive or, more literally, backward-going circle), then, incorporates the triple moments of alienation, recognition, and recuperation which together define the progressive content of dialectical negation. The story has both micro and macro applications:

> In thinking an object, I make it into thought and deprive it of its sensuous aspect; I make it into something which is directly and essentially mine. Since it is in thought that I am first by myself, I do not penetrate an object until I understand it; it then ceases to stand over against me and I have taken from it the character of its own which it had in opposition to me ... An idea is always a generalization, and generalization is a property of thinking. To generalize means to think. The ego is thought and so the universal. When I say 'I,' I *eo ipso* abandon all my particular characteristics, my disposition, natural endowment, knowledge, and age. The ego is quite empty, a mere point, simple, yet active in this simplicity. The variegated canvas of the world is before me; I stand over against it; by my theoretical attitude to it I overcome its opposition to me and make its content my own. I am at home in the world when I know it, still more so when I have understood it.
>
> (1952: 226)

All the classical logocentric themes of European metaphysics are contained in this single passage: the arcane presence of Logos, the passion to understand, the failure of non-rational representations (particulars, sense-certainty, unreflexive scepticism, positivity), conceptual universality as a medium of speculative cognition, and the spiritual will to total knowledge. Hegel's lesson is to construe Reason or Logos both as the inner logic of the historical process *and* as the *inner* Spirit of human consciousness. In 'losing' my self to what is other-than-its-essence (whether as our natural biological heritage, the existence of Others, or the forms of alienated spirit), I acquire something positive which can be incorporated in a richer conception of self – and so the dynamic of cyclical mortification ('negation of the negation') continues until the perfect adequation of form and content is achieved. This is the coded language behind such arcane statements as 'the unity of subject and object', 'Substance is essentially Subject' or that dialectical unity is 'expressed in the idea which represents the Absolute as Spirit (*Geist*) – the grandest conception of all, and one which is due to modern times and its religion. Spirit is alone Reality' (1967: 85–6). If we can continue in this vulgarizing mode it would not be inaccurate to condense the Hegelian paradigm of dialectical reflexivity in the thesis that *Spirit* (or Absolute Reflexivity) *is Reality* – and reflexive knowledge is the full awareness that Reality is constituted by Spirit (quite literally, the 'realization' of divine self-formation as the progressive spiritualization and temporalization of the world).

What can we learn from Hegel's spiritual allegory other than the persistence of the *aporiae* of classical metaphysics? The most striking feature of Hegel's phenomenology is the rich descriptive narrative of human being-in-the-world, historicity, and culture gained despite his grounding in metaphysical categories. As situated, communicative thinking agents, human beings should be viewed as unique possessors of *self-consciousness*. Consciousness and its verbal forms are the fundamental *mode* of human being and becoming. As 'doubled' creatures, human beings are sites of dialectical self-mediation. In infinite reflection consciousness grasps itself in its various modes of self-conscious directedness towards its objects and through the resilient alterity of objects towards itself. Where some animal species may achieve sentient consciousness only human beings are *self-conscious* of their finite, temporal, worldly condition. In short: self-consciousness arises from the time-consciousness of its own finitude and imminent death. We have seen that Hegel's purposes are ultimately metaphysical: to show that there is no radical alterity – that all 'otherness' can be rendered intelligible in the process of spiritual self-recognition and atonement marked by the odyssey from Consciousness, to Self-consciousness, Reason, and Absolute Knowledge. This is best exemplified in the atoning logic internal to speculative thinking. Within the sphere of Reflection thought becomes the immanent form and content of thinking itself – the transpersonality and categoriality of thought is already implicitly present in reflective modes of consciousness – which both Kant and Hegel identified with the activity of the Understanding (*Verstand*). Science (*Wissenschaft*), Understanding (*Verstand*), and Intellect (*Vernunft*) are the characteristic modes of positive, reflective intelligence – the 'pure activity of the self in general'. For Hegel only pure thinking can serve as the authentic manifestation (*phenomena*) and vehicle (*logos*) of the Spirit (*Geist*) understood as the Absolute Idea. Hence Hegel's famous pronouncement that Spirit – the reflexive medium of the Absolute – is both Subject and Substance in the concrete act of reflection (*qua* infinite self-mediation). The telos of reflection – 'the Truth' articulated by Absolute Knowledge (or 'science' in Hegel's usage) as the comprehended Whole in its concrete substantiality and self-identity incorporates both subjectivity and substantiality. To realize this totalization Hegelian *Logik* must repress the finitude of the personal self and deny the radical alterity of natural death. Only if death has a necessary role in the process of Absolute Knowledge can Spirit recognize itself as the essence of Reality.

The personal ego becomes a self in the full sense of the term through the dialectic of self-objectification and self-consciousness. But all concrete self-reflection – whether everyday thought, aesthetic mimesis, or religious symbolism – involves the thinking of Being as simultaneously an alien medium and object of thought. Absolute Spirit has to be grasped as both subject and object of thought. This contradictory path from partiality and abstractness of thought (sensory intuition) toward rational knowledge (Reason) marks the dialectical progress of reflexive thinking exhibited by the *Phenomenology* and systematized in the *Encyclopaedia of the Philosophical Sciences* (1817). Pure thinking is simply the logic of concretely developed reflection in its struggle to become self-reflexive. And for this to be possible the dialectic must follow its meandering path through the necessary moments of polemical alterity – particularly the otherness of nature and the more intractable otherness presented by other consciousnesses, other subjectivities. The self is returned to itself by recognizing the world of the non-self as both nature and intersubjectivity, but most poignantly by acknowledging the alterity of the other self as a self in-and-for-itself. But the dialectic of Master and Servant is only an icon for a larger conflict. Speculatively human self-reflexive existence is an aspect of divine existence. Since finite existence has its principle in a dialectical experience of self-transcendence human freedom is projected, commensurately, as a freedom in and of the Spirit.

Hegel's basic thought-paradigm remained one of dialectical Identity: Divine Existence is refigured as a speculative process of Substance alienating itself and recovering its integrity through the 'instrumentality' of human self-reflection: Substance returns to itself by losing itself, becoming other to itself and negating this alterity through concrete subjectivity. Substantial experience is, as it were, prior to subjectivity – it is the world-already-in-process out of which subjectivity arises in its quest for Absolute Knowledge. The self has a pre-epistemic involvement with this dynamic movement of Spirit before any epistemic relation is possible. Yet the 'knowing' side of this speculative theology is not dispensable. In simple terms, God is dependent upon the expanding horizon of human self-consciousness. In fact without the concrete life of knowing subjectivity, the expressive dialectic of Spirit dissolves into a series of disconnected 'phenomenal forms'. Substance recovers its unity through the mediation of the dialectic of subjectivity in speech and language. Spirit is estranged consciousness returning from its cycles of alienation through the conscious forms of human discourse to a stage of completely rational self-awareness (which Hegel imagines as the form appropriate to absolute discourse). The Science of the Experience of Consciousness – or *Phenomenology* – is consciousness recuperating its essential Being as spiritual life (*für sich zu sein*, hence of *Geist* as *an und für sich sein*). Here the ultimate model is the self-reflective human mind itself – and what else could a rational reflective mind *als denkenden Wesen* be doing but *thinking* – conceptualizing the world in specific forms of consciousness? And how best to characterize the configurations of Spirit (*Gestaltungen von Bewusstseins*) than phenomenologically as manifest forms of thought – indeed the modes of self-manifestation of the Absolute, which Hegel also calls 'the Concept' (*Begriff*)? This 'thinking study of things', to achieve the inherent adequacy of scientific cognition, must be a thinking of the Whole (the Truth, in Hegel's famous formula, is the Whole). But the totality of Truth is historicized as 'the essential nature reaching its completeness through the interactional process of its own development': 'Of the Absolute it must be said that it is essentially a result, that only at the end is it what it is in very truth; and just in that consists its nature, which is to be actual, subject, or self-becoming, self-development' (1967: 81–2). If philosophical rationality posits Being as a unity, dialectical Reason demonstrates this as process and result (*telos*). Truth is Spirit as 'being-in-and-for-itself' (*das Anundfürsichsein*). Only then does Truth 'correspond' with its own intention.

In the terms of the ecological paradigm sketched in Chapter 3, Hegel's fundamental purposes could, without undue distortion, be described as a dialectical holism – as a description of Reason which incorporates all otherness in its quest for the absolute coherence – hence, the *Bildung* or self-formation of the Absolute. Substance – God-as-Spirit rather than Spinoza's *Deus sive natura* – is essentially a reflexive process; it develops itself as a process of self-discovery through the correlated dialectic of alienation and recovery, by negating itself and overcoming its inadequate forms of manifestation, until – via the mediation of subjectivity – it returns to itself as concrete Subjectivity. In place of the *Cogito* we have the speculative concept that the universe is a manifestation of divine Thinking. The circle of Substance and Subject is tied by the dynamic principle of reflexive mediation through which the Absolute attains an existence in-and-for-itself:

> For mediating is nothing but self-identity working itself out through an active self-directed process; or, in other words, it is reflection into self, the aspect in which the ego is for itself, objective to itself. It is pure negativity, or, reduced to its utmost abstraction, the process of bare and simple becoming ... We misconceive therefore the nature of reason if we exclude reflection or mediation from ultimate truth, and do not take it to be a positive moment of the Absolute. It is reflection which constitutes

truth as the final result, and yet at the same time does away with the contrast between result and the process of arriving at it.

(1967: 82–3)

We can now articulate the logological principles underlying the Hegelian concept of mirroring self-consciousness. First, everything I can recognize and know as other-than-my-self is an alterity mirrored in and mediated by that self, an object-for-me or phenomenal structure. This is a 'finding' that is common to Descartes, Kant, and Hegel. Second, consciousness is already imbricated in every act of cognition and to this extent is a universal property of a knowing species. Third, the philosophical '*Ich*' is not an empirical sub-stance. Rather, as Kant was the first to make clear, the 'self' in question here is not fundamentally the concrete, empirical ego, but the metaphysical subject, the Ego that inhabits the noumenal realm of moral action or, as the post-Kantian epigoni would claim, the realms of the Spirit. Fourth – a thesis particularly elaborated by Hegel – *objects* are always given as the correlates of conscious-ness; they are the intentional achievements of distinctive modes of conscious life. Finally, the universality of freedom: only the subject is free to look upon the universe as a totality of objects – containing itself as a spectator subject. As a corollary only the subject may regard itself – and be regarded by other subjects – as an object in principle visible to other subjects within a shared horizon of freedom. The *Ego* is both a subject and an object for itself (*an und für sich*) in sensory self-certainty and perceptual experience, but only themati-cally in the self-comprehending judgements of the understanding and intellect. While sensory intuition brings the mind in contact with Being under its aspect of external reality, the understanding places the mind in contact with itself and the realm of ideas, abstract thought-worlds, moral duty, and culture (*Bildung*). Moreover these are spheres of existence that can be shared with other selves. Reflexivity also names an experience of freedom shared by a community. Reflection may be a fragile superstructure built upon the darker matrix of intentional life. But spiritual self-reflection and the demands of ethical and political life draw the mind out of its solipsistic immanence and into the dynamic processes of '*geistlich*' development and self-formation (for Hegel – influenced in this respect by Schelling's *Naturphilosophie* – the arcane freedom of Spirit as it gathers itself through Nature also constituted the inner logic of European History). The abstract sense of consciousness as the 'egoity' of the 'I think' is enriched and made concrete by the dialectic of spiritual self-devel-opment. Only such a self-explicating and self-educating soul can become a person in the full ethical and political senses of the word (the concrete universal self becomes a particular body-mind-spirit within the context of an emanci-pated totality of civil existence and ethical community). Hegel, in this respect, discovers or rediscovers the communality of rational reflexivity – that beings only become fully reflexive in the context of intersubjective traditions. With this insight we abandon the 'I think' of Kantian rationalism, for the 'I will' and the 'I do' of Fichte and Schelling. In fact all the first-generation post-Kantian thinkers understood their task as overcoming the rigid dualism of Kant's intellectualistic criticism and formalist ethics by respecifying the '*Ich-denke*' as the 'subject of freedom', the Ego of wilful action, moral determination, and spiritual praxis. But only Hegel appears to have understood the extent of the revision of videological metaphysics required to institute a radically social and reflexive phenomenology of intersubjectivity.

Consciousness which objectifies the world as object takes the first step on a long and strenuous ascent of self-development – a dialectic implicit in the fundamentally intentional or directive character of conscious experience: in 'being conscious that x' the 'I' is also returned to itself as the implicit being that is 'conscious-of-x'; and implicitly re-flective moments of difference represent an indispensable link in the chain of self-objectification leading to higher acts of consciousness, moral self-determination, and spiritual self-consciousness. Clearly this framework of free reflection (*Reflexion*), critique (*Kritik*), and freedom (*Freiheit*) – whether in its Kantian, Fichtean, or Hegelian forms – presupposes the *Subject-Object* rhetoric as both its medium and target. But in the post-Cartesian model of consciousness, human experience is not merely intentionally directed toward objects, but more fundamentally is simultaneously a living-toward-self by living-toward-Other in the sedimented horizons of human freedom. Only the person as a thinking human being can be in-and-for-itself. The person is a mind-body unity which spiritually affirms the fact that 'I' *exist* subjectively, 'I' *am* self-consciously a reflexive project within and toward a world of other reflexive beings (as persons existing for me and experienced by me as autonomous *alter egos*). Human consciousness, in other words, generates *universalizability norms*. These norms become explicit in the politics of reflection which informs the German Idealist tradition and the subsequent theorizing of its inheritors. These principles constitute the key to the Hegelian lesson.

2 THE STREAM OF CONSCIOUSNESS: THE HUSSERLIAN LESSON

The world is present in consciousness, and therefore consciousness is the essential starting point for every philosophy. Descartes was the first to recognize it as such, and for this reason he is the founder, creator and starting point of modern philosophy.

(Arthur Schopenhauer, 1989: 266)

If we construe persons as self-positing centres of reflection, thought, and action, as beings who can routinely objectify themselves through various indexical media (the first-person indexicals or *token-reflexives* for example, but also wider self-displays and self-referential patterns embedded in language), we can readily slip into a proprietorial way of talking about the self:

the self as a for-itself is said to 'possess' mental states, thoughts, consciousness (sense impressions, feelings, cognitions, desires, volitions, etc.); selfhood lies in proprietorial capacities ('I can' act, raise my arm, deliberate, plan, think, appraise my actions, accept the consequences of my acts, judge my actions morally, and so forth); these properties are then used as empirical criteria to define rational agency as actions governed by a presiding Ego; the person, in effect, becomes the empirical locus of the totalizing unity of consciousness.[1]

The self-experience of free acting conscious beings – in actively experiencing the world – becomes the criterial mark of personal agency. And this experiential unity of intentional consciousness enters into the spatiotemporal *causal* fabric of events and actions in the world. Indeed some form of lived consciousness of the obstacles to freedom is criterial for any rational change and any project of emancipation. We seem to be drawn inexorably to a picture of the self as a unified, disembodied centre of a manifold stream of acts, states, capacities, and activities, among which is the privileged – as it were, superintendent – activity of reflection. In Husserl's phenomenological view – elaborated over several decades with notable changes from the *Logische Untersuchungen* to *Ideas I* and *II* and the later manuscripts of the *Krisis* – the field of consciousness is immanently meaningful and universally reflective. The transcendental self is the medium of universal meaning formations (the transcendental locus of intentionality, ideation, and universalizability) which is unequivocally a sphere of life that exists in-and-for-itself (transcendental consciousness as a sphere of absolute cognition or, as Husserl says, as a pure stream of immanent data). Selves are beings that not only exist in the midst of other spatiotemporal material bodies, but are capable of '*being-conscious-of*' their mode of corporeal existence and lived experience. Only the self or consciousness can serve as the source of the categorial meaningfulness of reality. But unlike the bare physical entity, consciousness eludes objectification – like the proverbial receding horizon bounding all my activities yet escaping attention as the frame of meaning. Consciousness, in the radical intentional sense Husserl attributes to this word in *Ideas I* and the *Cartesian Meditations*, is the *source* of the world's transcendence.

This is the train of thought which leads to the Transcendental Ego posited by a number of different philosophical perspectives as the constitutive core of personal identity. As William James remarked we are drawn to the intuition that 'consciousness of some sort goes on' or, said more poetically, that we are possessed by a 'stream of consciousness' ('the stream of thought, of consciousness, or of subjective life'). Human beings are creatures that exist in and through processes of immanent reflection upon a prereflective stream of consciousness. In the Kantian and Neo-Kantian tradition this becomes the 'transcendental Self' which undergoes sensible experience, actively attends to the panorama of the visual field, anticipates, recollects, initiates projects, reflects, thinks, and acts – the 'synoptic Ego' of modern mentalistic epistemology, the cybernetic Ego of ego-psychology and psychoanalysis.

However, from Husserl's phenomenological standpoint of transcendental reduction, the Self is not a substantial – if incorporeal and immaterial – Ego along the lines of Descartes' *Cogito* or Fichte's Absolute Self, but a transcendental subjectivity living its meaningful experiences and modes of conscious-existence: immanent correlations of the perceiving-perceived, thinking-thought, willing-willed, and so on. In the methodological constraints of the reduction, Consciousness does not designate another realm of objects, but the intentional matrix of all objectivity (the 'reduced' sphere of immanence as Husserl expressed this in *The Idea of Phenomenology* (1906/7)). As a corollary, reflexive consciousness is not a higher faculty of the empirical Ego, but a functional mode of constitutive consciousness, the centring-decentring praxis of a 'pure Ego' disengaging itself from the comings and goings of everyday life through the 'bracketing' of all natural existence. The transcendental disengagement from worldliness – Husserl's *'epoché'* – practised by consciousness upon its own intentional acts discloses a pure field of 'immanent intentionalities' – the 'object' as a *noematic kernel* elaborated from a wider fabric of noetic meaningfulness. As a realm of intentional objects the 'streaming-life' of consciousness – like the Hegelian *Gedächtnis* – antedates the Subject-Object relation of Cartesian epistemology and all naturalistic and introspective psychology. The 'field' of transcendental consciousness is the universal medium of *meaning constitution* for all possible unities of meaning (and thus, in its ontological sense, for all possible worlds and world-analogues). What was simply accepted as a natural given – the world – now becomes the world as a fabric of meaning. From the phenomenological perspective, the world as an experienced totality is always a *world-for-meaning-bestowing-consciousness*. But this irreducible fact of meaning constitution is not synonymous with radical subjectivism. Husserl's fundamental lesson is simply that there can be no meaningful world – no transcendence – without the self, no object without consciousness, and no concrete consciousness without the sustaining processes of meaning (the phenomenological *epoché* facilitates a 'reduction' of objects to meaning-systems). Moreover this vast realm of intentional correlations tying the self to the world antedates the cognitive determination of worldly consciousness as a personal thinking, self-knowing subject. Paradoxically, the domain of concrete subjectivity presupposes a deeper realm of intersubjective consciousness that is not identical with the physical ego or the formal 'I' of the Kantian transcendental apperception. Consciousness is now less a reflective perception upon the world than an ever-present horizon of world-experiencing-life. Under the auspices of the Husserlian lesson, the heart of radical self-reflection now shifts to a descriptive 'excavation' of the constitutive web of subject-object correlates, the prereflective life of the transcendental ego-sphere of 'pure immanence'.

If the faculty-model of self stems from Descartes (and perhaps Locke, Hume, and Kant), the transcendental view is inseparable from the phenomenological tradition inaugurated by Edmund Husserl. Phenomenology does not locate reflexivity as a higher cognitive faculty of a self-present substance, but rather explores the experiential genesis and intentional operations of lived reflexivity (anticipations, protentional syntheses, corroborations, verifications, negations, etc.) organizing the life of consciousness. This conceptualization of consciousness as a teleological fabric of lived experience explicitly breaks with the cognitivist and introspective view of mental life associated with post-Renaissance Cartesian philosophy. The possession of an inner mental life of ideas (variously construed by Descartes, Locke, and Leibniz), ideas of sense (Berkeley), sense-impressions (Hume), the sensory manifold (Kant), sense-data (Russell) or sense-contents (Ayer) is no longer considered to be the unique descriptive feature of consciousness. These metaphysical and objectivistic pictures of conscious life have started too far upstream in human experience and have committed the fallacy of projecting a one-sided epistemic picture of experience upon earlier modes of conscious being. The Cartesian Self has simply hypostatized one aspect of cognition which is then identified with mind and selfhood *tout court*. Here the Husserlian lesson is manifested in the language of self-criticism: to activate a radical phenomenology of experience we must first critique and abandon all existing models of subjectivity and objectivity.

Unlike the reflective *res cogitans*, reflexivity becomes a *structural* feature of all intentional acts implicit in the self-other polarity of intentional life (for Husserl – as for Hegel – all consciousness is directional meaning experience – an active 'grasping' of meanings, an intending of the world under some 'description' or 'meant' perspective). But if the 'world' is 'for consciousness', it is also, more profoundly, 'before consciousness' as a world horizon of intelligibility. This is the simple, but radical, transformation which Husserl urges upon the whole philosophical tradition of egological epistemology: *reflexive consciousness is fundamentally worldly* – across a vast series of acts consciousness 'intends the world' in a spectrum of different intentional acts and modalities. The philosophical tradition is to move beyond metaphysics not by positing an arcane realm of essences (the earlier phenomenological hypostasis of the *Logical Investigations*), but by describing the universal life of self-experiencing being. The movement of consciousness is located in its life-world imbrications. In the context of the phenomenological reduction, consciousness does not begin with the object. Rather it arises from its worldly correlations. It is already a part of the whole it seeks to know with greater clarity and evidence. The naive dualism of mind and reality, ego and its ideas, subject and object is transcended by means of the thematics of radical intentionality: *all conscious life is consciousness-of-the-world* and as such is immanently reflexive. Reflexive acts of meaning are always-already embodied in the phenomenality of the phenomenon (Derrida, 1981: 30). Consciousness is no longer a thin domain of interiority or radical immanence; consciousness is already 'outside-itself' and as 'lived experience' is structurally directed toward its variegated objectivities (for his analytic purposes Husserl approaches every 'real' transcendent object as originating in *phenomenal transcendence*). In the inevitably misleading vocabulary which Husserl introduced, consciousness 'constitutes' its objects as 'meant objects' (*Sinn, sense*) within the absolute stream of conscious life. Intentionality erases the ancient antithesis of Ego and World, and its underlying picture of an inner self 'observing' its mental contents. In place of an introspective ego we find transcendental subjectivity and the subjective-relational correlates of prescientific life-world experience.

Thus while we may live naively within the 'general thesis of the natural attitude', unaware of the intentional properties of consciousness, structures of reflexivity (understood as active, embodied modes of *intentionality*, '*intentio*' having the literal meaning of '*directing-itself-toward-something*') are nevertheless operative in organizing the coherent fields of life-world consciousness (thus Husserl speaks of the *Lebenswelt* as a vast field of anonymous temporal 'syntheses', each arising as the outcome of 'deeper' layers of genetic intentionalities). The mature schema of Husserlian intentionality is given in the insight that there is no 'meaning' that is not the correlate of temporalizing intentional experience: what can be 'known' of reality is always framed in the prepredicative structures of 'intentional objectivities' – the 'world' is, as it were, always 'the-world-meant' or 'intended' under specific intentional predicates (which, of course, Husserl still insisted on describing as '*cogitationes*' in his generalized Cartesian schema of the *ego-cogito-cogitatum*).

And even more significantly for the critique of Cartesian dualism, praxical intentionalities of the world-as-taken-for-granted in everyday comportment antedate all other modes of predicative consciousness. Human knowledge emerges like a protentional superstructure upon prepredicative configurations of temporal life. In this way the language-games of transcendental phenomenology elaborate a figural discourse to overcome the static, atemporal, metaphysical image of a worldless, translucent self-consciousness by 'incarnating' consciousness within the intersubjective *Lebenswelt* of perceptual experience. The investigative spirit of Husserlian phenomenology commends a radical descriptive ontology of perceptual being-in-the-world (or to speak more phenomenologically, of the noetic-noematic possibilities of being-in-the-world). The egocentric predicament of the Cartesian *cogito* is resolved by 'exteriorizing' lived experience under its diverse modes and contexts of intentional directedness – the notions of 'privileged immanence', 'mental contents', 'contents of consciousness', 'inner observation', and so forth are bracketed as active misdescriptions of incarnate consciousness. In this way two related objectives are addressed: first, the 'ghost in the machine' of Cartesian interiority is abandoned as a metaphysical construct and second, a vast field of transcendence implicit in the expression 'intentional-directedness' is programmatically disclosed. In this way the closure of the Cartesian idea of consciousness marks the disclosure of the phenomenological field as *incarnate being-in-the-world*. These positions are sketched – if only in a prefigurational manner – in the second and third books of *Ideas* (*Ideen II*, *III*). From the genetic-constitutional analysis of the incarnate body, every possible 'super-structure' of reflection can be seen to presuppose prior formations of prescientific reflexivity. With this shift toward the phenomenology of embodiment, radical phenomenology necessarily becomes a phenomenology of the *Lebenswelt* (Schutz, 1973; Sokolowski, 1970; Zaner, 1971).

We have uncovered two basic models of the Ego: the Proprietorial Ego as a cognitive centre steering the body amid the furniture of the world rather as a sailor guides a craft through dangerous waters; and a deeper and altogether darker self lying behind the empirical monad, the logical or transcendental structure of a self-experiencing life – a reflexive structure which makes all reference to 'mind' or 'body' possible, a transcendental matrix anonymously at work beneath the concrete subject of experience (for whom 'the concrete subject' is another intentional referent or transcendent unity: my concrete, spatiotemporally embodied existence in a physical world). This is the outcome of Husserl's phenomenological lesson.

Both views of self-reflection – as proprietorial introspection and as radical reflexivity – have more than a whiff of paradox and solipsism about them – and we will not be surprised when we later turn to examine these traditions and ways of speaking in detail that the threat of radical solipsism and a related clutch of self-destructive *aporiae* have bedevilled these forms of thought. Before we turn to this task, however, we should examine a form of radicalized self-reflection internal to phenomenological inquiry. For this purpose we turn to the metacritique of Husserlian phenomenology begun by his erstwhile student, Martin Heidegger.

3 TRANSCENDENTAL REFLECTION: THE HEIDEGGERIAN LESSON

The world is already presupposed in one's Being alongside the ready-to-hand concernfully and factically, in one's thematizing of the present-at-hand, and in one's discovering of this later entity by objectification; that is to say, all these are possible only as ways of Being-in-the-world.

(Martin Heidegger, 1967b: 417)

Husserl's life-long struggle to transcend the Cartesian paradigm is indicative of the deep-rooted nature of videological rhetoric within the structural impulse of Western metaphysics. In Husserl's conception of transcendental phenomenology, consciousness is no longer to be thought of as an inner substance, entity, or faculty, but is to be construed as a living stream of acts and experiences which constitutes 'objects' – from the perceptual profiles of spatiotemporal things to the categorial architecture of the sciences and cultural artifacts. 'Consciousness' is an index for a vast realm of meaning-bestowing human experience.

Objects and higher categorial regions of objects are the products of acts of subjectivity. In Heidegger's gloss:

> This implies that, in the cognitive possession of its predicates as intentional comportments, the ego also already comports itself to the beings toward which the comportments are directed. Since such beings toward which comportments are directed are always designated in a certain way as objects, it can be said formally that to the subject always belongs an object, that one cannot be thought without the other.
>
> (1982: 155)

The phenomenological term 'consciousness' now includes operative pragmatic relations, categorial activities, prepredicative 'syntheses', propositional experience, signification, judgement, and language – in sum, intersubjective communicative performances which *concretely* implicate the Other – whether a concrete Other or the alterity of the material and linguistic preconditions of intersubjectivity: intentionality constitutes the very structure of comportment itself (Heidegger, 1992: 31).

This important step moves the classical bracketing methodology of Husserlian phenomenology in the direction of the project of logological self-investigation (in the sense that every 'directing-itself-toward', every movement of transcendence, is ontologically already a reflexive self-interpretation and thus presupposes a worldly horizon as a preinterpretive resource). The epistemological horizon of traditional metaphysics and the modern insistence upon the self-certainty of the *ego cogito* give way to a phenomenological ontology of life-world experience or what Heidegger termed the project of fundamental ontology. In logological terms, this shift of attitude reinscribes the fundamental process of semiosis and rhetoric in the heart of philosophical self-reflection. The whole spectrum of prereflective experiential comportment (from the primordial mimesis of bodily comportment to the nascent eidetic syntheses of prepredicative intentionality on to the reflective architecture of theoretical propositions and formalized discourses) now comes into focus as the central topic of a radicalized phenomenological investigation. The insistent field of concrete subjectivity – with its rich contextuality of lived experience – is found to be inseparable from intersubjectivity and its genetic roots in prior structures of sense-formations.

As Heidegger in his major work, *Being and Time* (1927), would later conclude: intentionality belongs to the existence of Dasein.

> For the Dasein, with its existence, there is always a being and an interconnection with a being already somehow unveiled, without its being expressly made into an object. To exist then means, among other things, to be as comporting with beings '*sich verhaltendes Sein bei Seiendem*'. It

belongs to the nature of the Dasein to exist in such a way that it is always already with other beings.

(Heidegger, 1982: 157)

But this prereflexive 'being with' structure of 'being-in-the-world' also implicates other 'prestructures' of understanding constitutive of Dasein's embeddedness and transcendence. Dasein does not *have*, it *is* its prereflexive self-understanding. A scientific praxis such as 'inquiring' or 'questioning', for example, is already bounded by a horizon of pre-existing 'evidential' relations to beings (and thereby, for Heidegger, to the particular self-understanding of this mode of interpreting Being). Moreover the prototypes of these evidential formations are already implicit in the everyday way of being-in-the-world. This insight was already implicitly worked out by Husserl in his later theory of the *Lebenswelt*. But Husserl ignores the way in which 'being' also appears in pretheoretical activities such as idle chatter, curiosity, and the inauthentic enterprises of everyday life. Everyday life and the ontical sciences are thus not neutral or unmediated practices. They also belong to the historical modalities of human existence. Not surprisingly, the central metaphor for this post-Cartesian view is no longer the translucent mirror of inner mental life or representational mental acts, but streams of intentional experience and intentional structures in all their modal forms (acting-toward-a, handling-b, experiencing-c, desiring-d, believing-in-e, positing-f, attending-to-g, thinking-about-h, etc.). The fabric of intentional transcendence forms a field of meaningfulness through which human being-in-the-world is rendered significant prior to all specialized modes of understanding or analytic reason. Thus Heidegger explicitly reformulates 'sense-perception' and mundane observation as a form of comportment or concern. Every kind of seeing implicates an intentional relationship within a referential context of prior activities. In fact, the eidetic or invariant structure of 'directing-itself-toward' (itself grounded in 'concerning-itself-with') can now be generalized to every mode of lived experience: all consciousness incarnates its own form of transcendence toward beings. But Dasein is concerned and 'mindful' in another sense. Dasein is concerned with its own fate; 'to be' here is to ask questions about the ground and meaning of existence. Dasein is the *being who questions about Being*. And this 'questioning' is already indicative of the operative structure of interpretation – the 'hermeneutic circle' that is inseparable from Dasein's existence. Dasein is the being that experiences both the enigma of existing in the world and anxiety before the nothingness of the world.

The ramifications of this radical generalization of Husserl's theory of *Evidenz* and intentionality did not become fully consequential until after the publication of Heidegger's *Sein und Zeit* (around 1927–8) and in the two decades that followed. We can summarize the essential point as follows: consciousness is always-already 'in the world' and explicit reflection upon consciousness is a possibility of returning from the texture of worldly involvements to their 'conditions of possibility' in a range of interrelated 'existential' fore-structures. In a formula, for reflection to be possible we must not only have recourse to an *a priori* realm of categorial relations, but must, more primordially, already live interpretively within the world at the level of corporeal reflexivity and social interaction. Every logic of reflection presupposes a logos of concrete hermeneutical reflexivity – in the most basic and pervasive form of the pretheoretical understanding necessary to exist as a human being-in-the-world. The categories and logic of every form of reflection, in fact, have their roots in lived reflexivity. Reflection is not a product of 'nature', but a definite historical *praxis* within a pre-existing cultural field of historical semiopraxis. In the most generous sense possible we can say that the pursuit of phenomenology as the systematic self-examination of operative intentionality points in the direction of a more radical social or dialogical phenomenology.

Classical phenomenological analysis, as a second-order reflective consciousness, is an active grasping of the world-as-disclosed through *states of intentional consciousness* (to modify a point made by Heidegger, the relations between intentionalities and second-order reflections upon intentional comportment are themselves intentional – our orientations and discourses concerning the structures of subjectivity are reflexive displays of meaning-positing subjective life; cf. Heidegger, 1992: 33). In grasping the pretheoretical life of reflexivity operative within reflection we abandon once and for all the egocentric metaphors and preoccupations of modern philosophy. Radicalized further, these recursive intentional vectors with their different orders of *Wesenschau* are ontologically grounded as modes of being of Dasein's praxis and active comprehension of beings (what Heidegger would call the factical everyday understanding of beings involved in Dasein's situated comportment toward Being). 'Being' or the world-horizon' is the necessary presupposition of all concrete comportment and objectification (again later interpreters would identify this 'dependence' as an index of the ontological character of the hermeneutic circle). Here the classical epistemology of 'theory *and* praxis' breaks down and is turned to the prior 'functional' realms of worldly, incarnate, semiopraxical reflexivity. If we can still formulate consciousness as the transcendence of Dasein, then primordial reflexivity forms a nexus of praxial relations toward beings from within the lived structures of being-in-the-world. Before I am capable of reflection I 'find myself' *thrown* within the horizon of the world as a conscious, affective, embodied existent. I live my world reflexively in such modes as care (*Sorge*) and anxiety (*Angst*) before the reflective mind can interrogate the structures of categorial perception or natural legality. As a worldly existence I orient toward things on the basis of concrete decisions and projects and not through the meaning-frames of formal logic or modern mathematical science. This generic 'fore-structure of comportment', of course, when understood as an ontological theory of situated world-praxis, leads to reflections on the primary nature of instrumentality and ultimately to the operative horizon of intersubjectivity in all existential projects: the functional systems of equipment, equipmental contextures, and the praxical mediation of Dasein's activities in an essentially public world. The self is no longer a proprietorial, substantial Ego within the natural world (a position Husserl criticized two decades before the publication of *Sein und Zeit* as naive naturalism), but a stream of meaning-bestowing consciousness, a heterogeneous field of plural intentional systems with its own rhythms, complexity, and momentum as variable and complex as the constituted correlates it makes possible (in the classical positions taken by both William James and Edmund Husserl, the stream of consciousness is quite literally the *radical source* of all meaning-unities – 'meaning-constitution', which Husserl refers to as the operative-streaming intentional life of transcendental subjectivity and, in his last manuscripts, equates with the life of creative meaning itself as a continuous process of meaning constitution); as a corollary, depth-reflection is itself an emergent feature of the stream of intentionalities we call human life – it is human existence turned back upon its own constitutive accomplishments, human life striving to understand its own mental universes as '*structures of consciousness*'. Husserl's conception of intentionality when radicalized in this reflexive fashion returns the self to the world as an unfinished project and task.

Heidegger's decisive move in this debate was to ground these subjective structures in prereflective incarnate intentionalities as the ontological basis of all understanding and meaning-framing activities: 'When it comes to comportments, we must keep a steady eye solely upon the structure of directing-itself-toward in them. All theories about the psychic, consciousness, person, and the like must be held in abeyance' (1992: 36). To let the phenomena associated with the abstract sign 'transcendence' speak, phenomenological analysis must 'bracket' traditional philosophical accounts of self, reflection, and consciousness; by performing this *epoché* upon every form of Cartesian reflection we may return to the lived comportments of lived reflexivity. Once phenomenology has bracketed out transcendent beliefs concerning the concrete nature and structure of consciousness and its contingent physical causation, we discover the phenomenological *residuum* of embodied consciousness as the Archimedean point of all possible claims to know the world – the universal 'instrument' of cognition, to use a more Jamesian locution. The reflexive act-functionality of the stream of consciousness previously hidden under the natural attitude then surfaces as the integral structure of the stream of experience itself – the irreducible fact, as it were, of existing as worldly, finite, experiencing agents, is now itself experienceable and describable as a grounding feature of everyday experience. Subjects are no longer Egos that mirror the external world but articulated subjectivities emerging from within the universal field of transcendental intersubjectivity. Subjectivity has its ground in a depth community of operative signification and interpretive experience. Understood ontologically, consciousness itself distinguishes within the field both the moment of subjectivity and that of objectivity. In Hegel's terminology:

The experience which consciousness has concerning itself, by its essential principle, embrace nothing less than the entire system of consciousness, the whole realm of the truth of mind, and in such wise that the moments of truth are set forth in the specific and peculiar character they here possess - i.e. not as abstract pure moments, but as they are for consciousness, or as consciousness itself appears in relation to them, and in virtue of which they are moments of the whole, are embodiments or modes of consciousness ... finally, when it grasps this its own essence, it will connote the nature of absolute knowledge itself.

(1976b: 144–5)

But the transcendental Self disclosed by phenomenological reflection is internally fissured by virtue of its finitude, historicity, and mundaneity. The ties that bind consciousness to the world are no longer contingent constraints on a pure freedom; but the constitutive ground of every imaginable dimension of freedom. We have already seen that for Husserl the open possibilities of reflexivity arise from the structural divisions of intentionality known as phenomenological reduction: I (under the bracketing methodology we should signal this as 'I') am not absolutely identical with the various modes of lived experience; experience is differentially organized and perspectively categorized, making disengagement and difference basic features of conscious life. 'I' am not absolutely engulfed by sense-experience, feelings, perception, memories, or any of my other propositional attitudes; these can, in varying degrees, be uncoupled from my ongoing life and explicated in further acts of reflection (the 'I' contains the immanent potentiality of reflection upon its own intentional life as 'I'-constituting-experience, one field of which is that indicated by the personal pronoun 'I'). But consciousness is also 'open' to a range of ontological opacities – from the opaque functions of the lived body to the unconscious structurations of temporal experience and the prepredicative operative intentionalities which form the social and historical substratum for predicative awareness. In these 'darker' formations there is no translucent 'I', but a vague and indeterminate 'directedness', a kind of *shadow-I* that will crystallize as the form of the personal. Experience contains within its dynamics the possibility of self-experience, of an 'I-structure' that is immanently reflexive within the dynamic field-structure of the stream of experience.

We return to the basic axiom of phenomenology: that we are not only aware of the objective correlates and noematic foci of experience, but also of the act-structure of experience itself – not only of the sensed, perceived, recollected, and so on, but of the noetic acts of sensing, perceiving, remembering, knowing, desiring, loving, and so forth – which are also immanent parts of the stream of conscious life. As a thoughtful, relational, experiencing, active Ego the self is immanently disengaged even when living its life – the phenomenological field organizes itself in a dialectic of engagement and disengagement, unity and alterity, sameness and otherness, familiarity and strangeness. As Heidegger in particular stresses, the 'self' is there for the Dasein

> without reflection and without inner perception, *before* all reflection. Reflection, in the sense of a turning back, is only a mode of self-*apprehension*, but not the mode of primary self-disclosure. The way in which the self is unveiled to itself in the factical Dasein can nevertheless be fittingly called reflection, except that we must not take this expression to mean what is commonly meant by it – the ego bent around backward and staring at itself – but an interconnection such as is manifested in the optical meaning of the term.
>
> (1982: 159)

The factical Dasein is always-already *situated*. It is useful to call this type of embodied reflection radical reflection, or simply Reflexivity *per se*. Radical reflection is self-reflection on all possible modes of being-intended and of objective-givenness in the field of the transcendental Ego. The phenomenological perspective still maintains the privileged role of the Subject in our understanding of reality. However this is not a concrete ego, but the reduced subjectivity of radical reflection revealing aspects and modalities of its own historicity: 'This "not going along with" the thesis of the material world and of every transcendent world is called *epoché*, refraining' (Heidegger, 1992: 99).

The phenomenology of reduced consciousness thus adumbrates a pure reflexive science of transcendence: 'This phenomenological suspension of the transcendent thesis has but the social function of making the entity present in regard to its being ... Such an *epoché* can now be performed in principle upon all possible comportments of consciousness' (1992: 99). Phenomenology sets itself the task of studying all possible modes of objectification and reference as these are accomplished through acts of intentional directedness (in this sense it is already metaphilosophy and metapsychology).

> We say that the Dasein does not first need to turn backward to itself as though, keeping itself behind its own back, it were at first standing in front of things and staring rigidly at them. Instead, it never finds itself otherwise than in the things themselves, and in fact in those things that daily surround it. It *finds itself* primarily and constantly *in things* because, tending them, distressed by them, it always in some way or other rests in things. Each one of us is what he pursues and cares for.
>
> (Heidegger 1982: 159)

In Maurice Merleau-Ponty's concise formulation, every *act of consciousness* carries the transcendental within it. This was also the guiding principle of Hegel's *Phänomenologie*:

> Consciousness *distinguishes* from itself something, to which at the same time it *relates* itself; or, to use the current expression, there is something

for consciousness; and the determinate form of this process of relating, or of there being something for a consciousness, is knowledge.

(1967: 139)

But the relation of 'for-ness' is not one of a passive vision of objects on the part of the subject; rather consciousness is actively engaged in the forms (*Gestalten*) of knowing its world – as speaking, acting, interpreting historical subjectivity; as historical Dasein (for example, as personal existence) it is incarnated in the world of things, imbricated in the projects and concerns of everyday existence. Hence Husserl's transcendental idealism: pure consciousness is the sphere of absolute being (cf. Heidegger, 1992: 101).

From this change of perspective we may still designate thinking as 'my consciousness' or 'my pure stream of *cogitationes*', but can no longer speak of this as a discrete set of mental events or mental contents; a theory of consciousness which reduces experience to a physical event or process in the causal spatiotemporal world is, in Husserl's sense, a naturalization of intentionality; consciousness for limited methodological reasons may be treated as a part of the natural world (this indeed is the instrumental heuristic of empirical psychology and, in a modified way, of phenomenological psychology and phenomenological anthropology construed in a naturalistic vein); but the *existence* of consciousness is also the formal presupposition of every possible 'science of psychic life'. Classical phenomenology aspired to become a purely eidetic science of intentional correlates, concerning itself with pure consciousness or 'consciousness from the phenomenological standpoint'. Construed radically, consciousness is operative in every mode of 'meant experience' and it is these correlative structures which are disclosed when we suspend the natural attitude. But ultimately it is only in the radical act of bracketing all forms of naturalism – abandoning the postulate of the world – that we can disclose the constitutive functions of intentionality; once we 'refrain' from positing the world as a transcendent referent we reveal the field of transcendental consciousness and its fundamental insight that reflexive experience is the totality of lived relations binding my subjectivity to the organized structure of possible and actual experience. The 'mineness' that is continually posited by self-experience is displaced into the anonymous experiences which form their condition – recognized tangentially by Husserl in his later attempt to domesticate the 'dark corners' released by radical reflexivity itself: *viz.* the indeterminacies of temporality, prepredicative 'life', existential inscription, historicity, and sociality. Yet all five horizons – of time, life, writing, history, and intersubjectivity – proved intractable to 'pure phenomenology'.

The resolution of these paradoxes seems painlessly simple: abandon the videological rhetoric of mirroring reflection and return to the existential praxes of concrete reflexivity. Refrain from accepting the world, and recover the mystery of being 'in' the world as an *a priori* horizon of relatedness. Reflexivity should not be hypostatized or abstracted from the fabric of lived relations antedating rational awareness. Husserl classically adopted a half-way house between the Cartesian ideal of absolute self-reflection and the self-deconstructive realm of incarnate reflexivity (the latter being disclosed unintentionally in his relentless quest for a self-grounding origin for 'pure reflection'). Said more simply: reflexivity is a possibility of the incarnate *existence* of subjectivity. This is the leading idea behind Husserl's later programme of investigation into the propositional attitudes of intentional consciousness. In his revisionary Cartesianism the Self comes to know itself through the experiences of being perceived and objectified by other consciousnesses; 'I' discover that I am a pole of perception for other self-conscious agents; I am one part of the awareness of another person or society of persons. At this moment the self discovers its own transcendent interactional status: I am one 'pole of transcendence', one entity among an indeterminate range of entities. I am a 'thing' for the other's consciousness. The Other relativizes my existence and my sense of being an absolute consciousness is demolished. In sum: I recognize and am recognized by others. 'I' as a transcendental Ego contain the possibility of radical transcendence, a transcendence implicit in the very first act of perception or kinaesthetic sensation. In Husserl's particular interpretation of transcendence: I (*qua* the transcendental subjectivity of my own experiencing life) am a consciousness-toward-the-world. Consciousness is correlatively situated as a consciousness-of-the-world.

The effect of this procedure is to displace the traditional problem of the existence of the external world and other minds and reformulate these as topics of prereflexive recognition (Hegel), reflexive constitution (Husserl), or preflective ontological foundation (Sartre, Heidegger, Merleau-Ponty). For both Husserl and Heidegger we are 'always-already' inscribed in the historical life-world: Dasein must *be* by *being-with* things (Heidegger); we are interpretively 'thrown' within the world-horizon of concrete projects and instrumentalities; as Husserl came to appreciate this essentially Hegelian point in his later writings, *transcendental subjectivity is equiprimordially intersubjectivity*. In this way we can conceptualize intentionality more radically as a *dialogic relation* between self and other: the language of consciousness is saturated with the voices of others –

> The objective world is from the start the world for all, the world which 'everyone' has as world-horizon. Its objective being presupposes men, understood as men with common language. Language, for its part, as function and exercised capacity, is related correlatively to the world, the universe of objects which is linguistically expressible in its being and its being-such. Thus men as men, fellow men, world ... and, on the other hand, language, are inseparably intertwined; and one is always certain of their inseparable relational unity, though usually only implicity, in the manner of a horizon.
>
> (1970: 359)

This is Husserl's hard-won insight into 'functioning intentionality' (*fungierende Intentionalität*) wrenched from a specular metaphysics grown conscious of its own aporetic limits, yet one whose radical consequences followed through consistently would lead to the self-deconstruction of the programme of self-reflection – here in its most rigorous and self-conscious phenomenological form. Husserlian phenomenology, as it were, forged the instruments of its own deconstruction – the pure phenomenology of consciousness meeting 'transcendence', 'difference', 'materiality', 'sociality', and 'historicity' at the limit of its greatest strengths. Husserlian phenomenology even in its return to the life-world (*Rückgang auf die Lebenswelt*) is still in thrall to a rhetorical construction. Heidegger formulates this in the following terms:

> This idea, that *consciousness is to be the region of an absolute science*, is not simply invented; it is the idea which has occupied modern philosophy ever since Descartes. The elaboration of pure consciousness as the thematic field of phenomenology *is not derived phenomenologically by going back to the matters themselves* but by going back to a traditional idea of philosophy.
>
> (1992: 107)

Historically, it was the great achievement of Martin Heidegger to have grasped the ontological complicity of the ideal of pure self-reflection and to begin to pose the question of another mode of reflexive experience beyond the aporetic confinement of the philosophy of consciousness. As Heidegger had already seen in 1925:

> Intentionality is not an ultimate explanation of the psychic but an initial approach toward overcoming the uncritical application of traditionally defined realities such as the psychic, consciousness, continuity of lived experience, reason ... We shall advance only by following intentionality in its concretion.
>
> (1992: 47)

Husserlian phenomenology acted as a host for the darker problematics of concrete reflexivity – which we have indicated here by the signs 'temporality', 'life', 'embodiment', 'inscription', 'historicity', and 'sociality'. To think the *unthought* of Western Reflection is to foreground these 'marginal' phenomena – time, living, the body, writing, history, and society. But to do so requires the 'parasitic' thematic of incarnate Reflexivity to literally destroy the body of Reflection. The early Heidegger – still shaped by the Husserlian legacy – took the initial step of rethinking intentionality through the paradigm of existential *transcendence*, displacing the pure Ego of Husserlian phenomenology by Dasein as Being-in-the-world. He reverses Husserl's investigations into the intentionality of being(s) to pose the question of the primary *being* of the intentional – what mode of being can be said to incarnate transcendence? – responding

> what *does the transcending*, is not things as over against the Dasein; rather, it is the Dasein itself which is transcendent in the strict sense. *Transcendence* is a *fundamental determination of the ontological struc- ture of the Dasein*. It belongs to the existentiality of existence. Transcendence is an existential concept. It will turn out that intentional- ity is founded in the Dasein's transcendence.
>
> (1982: 162)

Heidegger's lesson sets the scene for the deconstruction of reflection by respecifying the prior claims of ontological reflexivity.

4 DASEIN

> Only a being to whose ontological constitution transcendence belongs has the possibility of being anything like a self. Transcendence is even the presupposition for the Dasein's having the character of a self. The *selfhood* of the Dasein is *founded on its transcendence*.
>
> (Martin Heidegger, 1982: 300)

In a critique of the transcendental concept of consciousness Heidegger respe- cified the problematic of Reflexion within the being-horizon of factical reflexivity. We no longer have a disembodied subject or reflective conscious- ness facing an object-world, but an actively engaged interpretive subjectivity, Dasein as a being related-to-Being – a being in its everydayness already imbricated in relations to mundane beings, equipment, and equipmental con- texts. Reflexivity toward Being is an 'always-already' inscribed structure of interpretation. Heidegger accomplished this paradigm shift by grounding the possibility of transcendence in the hermeneutic mode of being characteristic of human existence (Dasein is, so to speak, the living experience of the *hermeneutic circle* as human being 'interpretively' lives 'toward Being'). Over- simplifying, we can say that the fundamental structure linking *Dasein* and *Sein* is 'in-dwelling' as *care*: 'Dwelling ... as taking care of something in intimate familiarity, being-involved with (*Sein-bei*)' (1992: 158). He concretizes the category of 'concern' with modes of cooperative praxis: working on something with something, producing something, cultivating and caring for something, putting something to use, employing something for something, holding some- thing in trust, giving up, letting something get lost, interrogating, discussing, accomplishing, exploring, considering, determining something. All other in- terpretive practices and relations are grounded in the circular structure of 'in-being': 'Such entering into relations with the world is altogether possible only insofar as Dasein already is being-in-the-world on the basis of its being- involved-with' (1992: 159). What is fundamental here is not merely the unique *relatedness* of human projects as situated, quotidian activities but a prereflective *hermeneutic* relationship to worldly practices antedating the Subject-Object structure, a preontological reflexivity already constitutive of human existence. Knowing, theorizing, and scientific research are derivative modes of being-in-the-world: '*knowing the world is a mode of being of Dasein such that this mode is ontically founded in its basic constitution, in being-in-the-world*' (1992: 161). The existence of the human process of inquiry is itself symptomatic of the mode of being of human existence – a mode of being which exists in and through questioning.

For Heidegger, Dasein's reflexivity is best exemplified in the routine contexts of quotidian world-work and instrumental praxis. But a more primordial relation of reflexive interpretation belongs to the field of temporality (*Temporalität*) which makes any kind of mundane hermeneutic experience possible. As a primary hermeneutic structure 'knowing is always a mode of being of Dasein on the basis of its already being involved with the world' (1992: 161). World-understanding and 'Dasein's transcendence', in Heidegger's terminology, are 'rooted in the ecstatic-horizonal constitution of the Dasein's temporality' (1982: 302). This is where the Cartesian problematic of cognition, self-certainty, and founded reflection is displaced by the hermeneutic problematic of *understanding, language*, and the *historicity of tradition*. All three moments are woven into the horizon of temporality – or what Gadamer would call effective history (*wirkungsgeschichtliches Bewusstsein*).

Considered as reflective practices, every form of knowing displays a temporal or *phased structure* (1992: 163–4). Human experience is literally embodied in temporal relations. This turning away from the problematic of cognitive consciousness and rationalist self-reflection takes inquiry in the direction of a more primordial reflexivity – the ontological reflexivity of worldly projects and through these projects, reflexive relations involving temporality and with temporality the *event* (*Ereignis*) of Being itself. In later writings Heidegger refers to this prior reflexivity as 'the clearing of being', utilizing visual metaphors for Dasein's primary relation to the openness of Being ('*Lichtung*', '*Offenheit*', '*Holzwege*' ('field-paths'), *presence*, etc.). 'World', 'world-horizon', 'equipmental contexts', 'language', 'temporality', and 'human being' are radically interdependent – only an existent that can be 'there' can be said to live within and toward the world, to orient itself in relation to the question of the meaning of that which is, to question the nature of Being – to *understand* things in the world. He also uses the metaphors of 'dwelling' and 'ambient environment' when describing these prior ontic relationships of day-to-day life:

> Existing in an environment, we dwell in such an intelligible functional whole. We make our way throughout it. As we exist factically we are always already in an environing world (*Umwelt*, milieu) ... Dasein exists in the manner of *being-in-the-world*, and this *basic determination of its*

existence is the presupposition for being able to apprehend anything at all. By hyphenating the term we mean to indicate that this structure is a unitary one:

(1982: 164)

'Being-in-the-world' must now be thought as self-projective since the relation of 'being-in' is only possible on the prior ground of temporal ec-stasis: the 'ecstatic-horizonal unity of temporalizing' which Heidegger describes as 'the condition of possibility of transcendence and thus also the condition of possibility of the intentionality that is founded in transcendence' (1982: 318). Dasein exists projectively in an already existing, temporalized life-world. The 'worldhood of the world' or the existence of a world-horizon antedates all conscious subjectivity and reflection. Heidegger stresses the temporal and alethic dimensions in his concept of 'world':

> World is that which is already previously unveiled and from which we return to the beings with which we have to do and among which we dwell. We are able to come up against intraworldly beings solely because, as existing beings, we are always already in a world. We always already understand world in holding ourselves in a contexture of functionality.
>
> (1982: 165)

'World' (the truth of the world) is what is already projected by temporality. Time becomes 'the *primary horizon of transcendental science*, of *ontology*, or, in short, it is the *transcendental horizon*' (1982: 323; cf. 1992: First Division, ch. 2, §21). Only an intentional existent that lives within the world in the mode of temporality described as *ek-stasis* can relate to experience through speech, questioning, thought, and action. Dasein is a questioning being – an existent that poses the question of the meaning of existence. Where the transcendental subject was a field-like source of 'original self-evidence', *Dasein* is the always-already presupposed site for anything like 'evidence', 'object-cognition', 'intentionality', 'transcendence', and 'comportment'. Dasein is not primarily a subject which 'grasps' an entity, but an affective structure of reflexive existence, a prelinguistic 'opening' so that anything like 'grasping', 'moving', and 'thinking' can become possible. *Dasein*, then, cannot be described in the traditional metaphysical lexicon of 'human existence', 'consciousness', or 'the subject', but appears as the ontological-structural possibility of corporeal reflexivity, the 'openness for Being' through Dasein's existential comportment, understanding, and interpretation that is an integral part of Being itself.

Reflexivity now names the temporal difference that makes possible the ontological difference (*die ontologische Differenz*) between Being and beings – the site where this difference becomes actual in the midst of the everyday uncoveredness of entities. Being-in-the-world becomes the 'essential structure of the Dasein's being' (1982: 169). Hence

World is only, if, and as long as a Dasein exists. Nature can also not be

when no Dasein exists. The structure of being-in-the-world makes manifest the essential peculiarity of the Dasein, that it projects a world for
itself, and it does this not subsequently and occasionally but, rather, the
projecting of the world belongs to the Dasein's being. In this projection
the Dasein has always already *stepped out beyond itself*, ex-sistere, it is
in a world. Consequently, it is never anything like a subjective inner
sphere.

(1982: 170)

Temporality, 'due to its horizonal-ecstatic nature, makes possible *at once* the
understanding of being and comportment toward beings' (1982: 325). Temporal disclosedness belongs 'equiprimordially to the world, to being-in, and to
the Self'. It is this ontological difference that is presupposed by all reflective
philosophy (and according to Heidegger's *destruktion*, all modern philosophy
from Descartes to Kant and Hegel have been notational variations of the
Philosophy of Reflection).

Heidegger uses the phenomenological *epoché* against Husserl's own descriptive results as these are expressed, for example, in a work like *Ideas* (1913).
In Heidegger's critique transcendental phenomenology is still grounded in the
rationalist problematics of Cartesian reflection; its Ego is still the subject of
absolute cognition animated by the dream of absolute certainty. Husserl has
failed to radicalize his own phenomenological intuitions and thereby dig
deeper beneath pure consciousness into the existential-hermeneutic structures
of Dasein's praxis. His basic schema of truth and reason remains the thought
of presence exemplified by the at-handness of consciousness and its intentional
correlates. Phenomenological method in Husserl's hands has simply radicalized the Cartesian auspices of traditional ontology, without questioning the
fundamental ontological orientations and historically prescribed tasks of the
metaphysics of presence. The subject as transcendental consciousness is incapable of disclosing its own *a priori* possibility – its 'truth' – which lies in a
different sphere of presence – the ontological structure of being-in-the-world,
world-openness, temporality, and the mode of being Heidegger calls *Existenz*.
Whatever is open to the question of Being displays the reflexive structure
of Dasein (thus 'Poetry, creative literature, is nothing but the elementary
emergence into words, the becoming-uncovered, of existence as
being-in-the-world' (1982: 171–2)). The event of 'truth' arises for that existent
which takes up an interpretive attitude toward existence, a being (in ordinary
German *Dasein* simply means both *existence* and *an existent being*) which
interpretively concerns itself with Being (or as Heidegger says, concerns itself
with the question of the meaning of Being).

In the history of thought Heidegger's notion of the ontological difference
between concrete beings and Being is prefigured by Schelling's distinction
between existence and the Ground of existence or being understood as existence and Being understood as the *Abgrund* of what exists. In the history of

transcendental philosophy it expresses the search for an *a priori* ground of entities. Schelling writes that

> there must be a being *before* all basis and before all existence; that is, before any duality at all; how can we designate it except as 'primal ground' or, rather, as the 'groundless'? As it precedes all antitheses these cannot be distinguishable in it or be present in any way at all. It cannot then be called the identity of both, but only the absolute indifference as to both.
>
> (1936: 87)

In his early work, *The Basic Problems of Phenomenology*, Heidegger formulates an analogous distinction:

> Being is always being of beings and accordingly it becomes accessible at first only by starting with some being ... ontological investigation always turns, at first and necessarily, to some being; but then, *in a precise way, it is led away from that being and led back to its being*. We call this basic component of phenomenological method – the leading back or reduction of investigative vision from a naively apprehended being to being – *phenomenological reduction*.
>
> (1982: 21)

In Schellingian terms, the phemomenological reduction is made possible by the indifference point between being and the ground of Being. *We* are that mode of being that is already in the space of the Being-question, that already ex-sists questioningly (*Existenz* is displayed most emphatically in the temporal process of existing interrogatively). Dasein is the only creature that can be said to *exist* in this sense of the *limen*. For Heidegger human being is the only mode of being which exists in and as diverse questioning activities. Self-questioning – as this is clearly articulated in *Sein und Zeit* – belongs to human being essentially (it is only *Dasein* which can resolutely interpret itself in the mode of *subjectivity* or *objectivity* – can take itself as a purely reflective, metaphysical subject, can reduce itself in self-interpretations as a *res cogitans* sitting in a mechanical universe of *res extensae*, can 'lose itself' in quotidian activities). Subjecthood (whether in the Cartesian, Husserlian, or Sartrean senses) is simply one of the many essential possibilities or ways-of-being of Dasein's hermeneutic mode of being-in-the-world (in that only a being-in-the-world can systematically occlude its own worldliness, finitude, and interpretive social status, a possibility that has become criterial for the modern, Galilean-Cartesian-Newtonian age).

This is the radical twist Heidegger gives to the phenomenological reduction:

> *For us* phenomenological reduction means leading phenomenological vision back from the apprehension of a being, whatever may be the

character of that apprehension, to the understanding of the being of this being (projecting upon the way it is unconcealed).

(1982: 21)

Only a being that is open to its being and the Being-horizon such as Dasein can also, more poignantly, forget its reflexive and linguistic involvements in Being – it can passively or actively alienate itself from the solicitation structure of Being, turning away in indifference from the question of the meaning of Being. It can live, as Heidegger says, absorbed in everydayness, in the pheno-menological involvements of the average, the everyday, and the mundane horizon of entities.

> Being does not become accessible like a being. We do not simply find it in front of us ... it must always be brought to view in a free projection. This projecting of the antecedently given being upon its being and the structures of its being we call *phenomenological construction*.
>
> (1982: 21–2)

To summarize this discussion: reflexivity is no longer a pure intentional project toward objects, a stream of arrow-like intentions toward their noematic correlates, but an irreducible configuration of lived temporal experience prior to reflective activities. Such a being is prereflectively involved in interpreting and understanding experience as a temporal structure of worldhood. *Dasein is radically hermeneutic in its basic modes of temporalizing comportment (ver-halten)*. But it is also hermeneutic in the historicity of its modes of interpretation and 'free projection': 'Because the Dasein is historical in its own existence, possibilities of access and modes of interpretation of beings are themselves diverse, varying in different historical circumstances' (1982: 22). In this way we can say that modes of temporal reflexivity are already implicit in the ontological orientations of Dasein. The world disclosed by Dasein's pro-jectedness (in 'having to do with something', 'producing something', 'attending to something', 'looking after something', 'giving something up', 'undertaking', 'accomplishing', 'interrogating', 'accomplishing', 'evincing', 'interrogating', 'considering', 'discussing', 'understanding', 'speaking-about', 'interpreting', determining', and so forth) is prior to every subject-object relation as an interpreted world in which the body is already anchored by carnal reflexivities antedating perceptual and reflective experience. *Dasein* is the thoughtful practical openness-for-Being – 'the ec-static realm of the reveal-ing and concealing of Being' that is foundational for all subsequent reflective experience. In this sense the prepredictaive and non-conceptual processes of pragmatic reflexivity are prior to other reflective orientations towards things. Dasein's practical-interpretive *ec-stasis* is ontologically presupposed – for example in preontological interpretation – by other concrete relations and reflexivities (in the same way that the notion of 'truth' as unconcealment – *aletheia* – is presupposed by notions of truth as logical correctness, *adequatio*, coherence, or correspondence). As Heidegger indicates, Dasein already lives as a *Seinsverständnis*, within a pretheoretical understanding of Being. Human existence is reflexive in the primordial sense of 'always-already being oriented' to the possible modes of understanding Being. These understandings constitute the praxical structure of Dasein. *Existenz* is thus ontologically oriented prior to all inquiry or explicit epistemic projects. But these 'epochal understandings' of the meaning of Being require deconstruction:

> It is for this reason that there necessarily belongs to the conceptual interpretation of being and its structures, that is, to the reductive construction of being, a *destruction* – a critical process in which the traditional concepts, which at first must necessarily be employed, are de-constructed down to the sources from which they were drawn. Only by means of this destruction can ontology fully assure itself in a phenomenological way of the genuine character of its concepts.
>
> (1982: 22–3)

To conclude this analysis: Being is the project-structure of affective reflexivity prior to all concrete orientation and intentional relatedness. Dasein exists through self-temporalizing processes of being-in-the-world. One such mode of temporality is the specific interpretive disclosure/concealing of 'the meaning of being' in a given epoch. This is articulated in the concepts and discourses available to that epoch, notions which must be subjected to reduction and deconstruction (*Abbau*). In the writings of the 1930s and early 1940s Heidegger simply referred to this ontological structure using the Scholastic term 'transcendence'. Reflexivity is temporal transcendence: an Existence that recoils upon the question of the meaning of Being as the matrix of Existence. In later writings – after the so-called *Kehre* – these formulations will be placed under erasure and subjected to *destruktion* in a quest for a more authentic language of reflexive existence.

5 INTENTIONALITY

Rational conduct always involves a reflexive reference to self.
(Mead, 1934: 122, n. 29)

In so far as Dasein temporalizes itself, a world *is* too. In temporalizing itself with regard to its Being as temporality, Dasein *is* essentially 'in a world', by reason of the ecstatico-horizonal constitution of that temporality. The world is neither present-at-hand nor ready-to-hand, but temporalizes itself in temporality. It 'is', with the 'outside-of-itself' of the ecstases, 'there'. If no *Dasein* exists, no world is 'there' either.
(Martin Heidegger, 1967b: 417)

This brief encounter with phenomenological language raises an important terminological point concerning the terms *intent* and *intentionality* as they bear upon our investigations of reflexivity. Since the 'intention family' has a number of very different usages in the literature on consciousness, it is important to clarify the semantic cartography of intentionality. Some of the most important of these senses can now be distinguished and defined.

5.1 Intent as teleology

This is close to the commonsense equation of intent with vocabularies of *motive*: as purpose, aim, goal, or *telos*; as Mead says, a teleological object is one that defines other things in terms of itself (1938: 301); thus we say that human action is purposive or 'directed toward goals', in contrast to non-intentional, purely reactive 'behaviour'; thus in our folk-psychologies we use terms such as 'interests', 'desires', 'wishes', and 'values' to mark this distinction between purposive and non-purposive activity. In answer to the question 'Why did X do that?' we respond with teleological predicates: 'To achieve A', 'To realize B', 'To ensure that C', and so on.

5.2 Intent as plan or project

Closely related to the everyday motivational usage is the idea of intent as 'conscious' (and thus 'responsible') planning or the purposeful projection of an act (as used in deliberative and forensic contexts: 'malicious intent', 'the intent to harm', and so on): the concept of *lying*, for example, analytically assumes the idea of *purposefully* deceiving another –

> Untruthful talk is only falsehood when deception is intended, and even the intent to deceive, far from being invariably linked to the desire to injure, is often produced by exactly the opposite motive. But for falsehood to be innocent, it is not enough that there be no deliberate harmful intent, we must also be certain that the error into which we are leading our fellow-men can harm neither them nor anyone else in any way whatsoever. It is only very rarely that we can attain this certainty; consequently it is only very rarely that a lie is completely innocent ... To lie without advantage or disadvantage to oneself or others is not to lie; it is not falsehood but fiction.
>
> (Rousseau, 1979: 69)

'Intention' in this sense is synonymous with premeditation or acting purposefully. For example, when Aristotle discusses premeditative voluntary praxis he explicitly separates intentional from merely voluntary behaviour: 'what is done voluntarily is not always done with premeditation; but what is done with premeditation (*prohairesis*) is always known to the agent, for no one is ignorant of what he does with a purpose'(*Rhetoric* 1368b). A contemporary instance is John Austin's distinction between *deliberate*, *purposeful*, and *intentional* action in 'Three ways of spilling ink'(1970: 272–87). Intent as *prohairesis* is the basic meaning of deliction as 'voluntarily causing injury contrary to the law' (*Rhetoric* 1368b); it is also basic to Aristotle's taxonomy of the four causes of voluntary action (Habit, Reason, Anger, and Desire) and the three causes of involuntary action (Chance, Nature, and Compulsion). Clearly a great deal more would have to be said to produce a defensible concept of purposive action, given its fundamental importance for the understanding of social action, rule-breaking, and moral order.

5.3   Intent as semantic property

Intent is frequently used as a term for semantically rich concepts, frequently as the 'intension of a concept' (its connotational 'meaning-content' as opposed to its 'extensional' range or sphere of denotation); in contemporary semantic theory the 'intensional' and the 'extensional' are regarded as complementary descriptions of the way in which words and sentences secure 'aboutness' – the wide range of conventional ways in which words can be used referentially to make statements 'about' the world.

5.4   Directionality

Intention/al/ity occurs in phenomenological philosophy as a structural characteristic of acts of consciousness in their manifold and myriad forms; in this sense, intentionality is a generic word for all meaning-oriented or meaning-bestowing acts; following the seminal work of Franz Brentano (*Psychologie vom empirisichen Standpunkt, Psychology from the Empirical Standpoint*, 1874) and Edmund Husserl (*Logische Untersuchungen* (1900–1) and *Ideas* (1913)), all consciousness is described as an intentional *consciousness-of* something (from *intendere*, 'to reach or stretch towards an object'); thus concrete perception is always a *directing-towards* what is perceived, interest is always an *interest-in* some thematic, thinking a *thinking-of* what is thought, attending an *attending-to*, and so forth; intentional acts can be directed toward 'meaning' or their 'objects-as-meant' but have no sense of 'conscious purpose' or plan about them (objects of consciousness are described, in Brentano's curious Scholastic phraseology, as 'intentional inexistence' – this usage has been further reinforced in current philosophical discussion of the 'aboutness', 'object-oriented' nature or 'referentiality' of mental acts and propositional attitudes – a propositional attitude has a referential dimension but the 'objects' or objective 'contents' of such an attitude do not themselves have an external existence). Philosophers like Dewey, James, and Mead were also engaged by the intentionality of attitudes, dispositions, beliefs, and their kin:

> They are always *of, from, toward*, situations and things. They may be studied with a minimum attention to the things at and away from which

they are directed ... But except as ways of seeking, turning from, appropriating, treating things, they have no existence or significance.

(Dewey, 1958: 238)

The totality of life experience is thus differentiated in terms of these object-
positing vectors of experience. Husserl introduced a complex and subtle
intentionalist lexicon to clarify such terms as 'presentation' (*Vorstellung*),
'meaning' (*Bedeutung*), 'reference' (*Meinen*), 'existence', 'real existence', 'immanent intentionality', 'the intended' (*Gemeinte*), 'noesis-noema', and the
like. And, finally, as we have seen, Heidegger subsumes forms of intentionality
as *modes of comportment* on the part of *Dasein*: 'Comportments have the
structure of directing-oneself-toward, of being-directed-toward. Annexing a
term from Scholasticism, phenomenology calls this structure *intentionality*'
(1982: 58; cf. 1992: 19–23).

5.5 Transcendence

Intentionality also indicates a mode of world-openness or *aletheia*. Here the
emphasis is upon the temporal and affective reflexivities of incarnate intentionality – of both the *whereto of the comporting* and the *toward-which of the
directedness*, as Heidegger puts this (1982: 58). Intentionality designates something like the ontological movement of 'transcendence', the 'opening' of the
world-horizon prior to any objectification, temporal consciousness-of-some-
thing, or concrete modes of intentionality (in the early Heidegger, one mode
of transcendence is produced by *anxiety* arising from the anticipated threat of
death and annihilation, the thought of losing one's being-in-the-world).
Dasein exists by being 'open to experience', by 'being-directed-toward', which
opens up the realm of world-referents. Its 'ecstasis' is ontologically prior to
categorial, logical, linguistic, and intersubjective referentiality. Or to reverse
the relationship: 'it is precisely intentionality and nothing else in which *transcendence* consists' (1982: 63).

Transcendence as the 'ecstasis' of time is a circular hermeneutic structure
presupposed by all modes of temporality, consciousness, and meaningful
action. We might say with Heidegger that transcendence is continuously
displayed as a possibility in the ontic activities of *Dasein*. Transcendence is the
ec-static temporalizing condition of *Dasein*'s basic mode of being as a being-
in-the-world, a being living interpretively toward the world, an existent whose
existence is primordially that of historical understanding: transcendence makes
a discursive 'being-in-tradition' possible. Only by clarifying the primordial
character of intentionality as transcendence can we avoid what Heidegger
regarded as the two basic misinterpretations of intentionality:

> First, against the *erroneous objectivizing* of intentionality, it must be said
> that intentionality is not an extant relation between an extant subject and
> object but a structure that constitutes the *comportmental character* of the

Dasein's behavior. Secondly, in opposition to the *erroneous subjectiviz-ing* of intentionality, we must hold that the intentional structure of comportments is not something which is immanent in the so-called subject and which would first of all be in need of transcendence; rather, the intentional constitution of the Dasein's comportments is precisely the *ontological condition of the possibilities of every and any transcen-dence*. Transcendence, transcending, belongs to the essential nature of the being that exists (on the basis of transcendence) as intentional, that is, exists in the manner of dwelling among the extant. Intentionality is the ratio cognoscendi of transcendence. Transcendence is the ratio es-sendi of intentionality in its diverse modes.

(1982: 65)

From Heidegger's ontological perspective, transcendence enters into and char-acterizes all of *Dasein*'s reflexive possibilities. Hence intentionality as intent, as teleology, as plan or project, as semantic interpretation, and as comportmen-tal directionality are – as possible modes of purposeful human action – dimensions of human experience grounded upon the alethic openness of *Dasein*'s transcendentality. But the superstructures of personal and social action should not be confused with the question of the ontological possibility of semiopraxis. This is the fundamental error of classical and modern philos-ophy – the conflation of praxis and its ground. 'Conscious(ness)' is the ontic term that the metaphysical tradition has developed in its effort to frame ontological transcendence (as the opening which first grants being and think-ing) by bringing it under the terms of everyday discourse. Intentionality radicalized through the notions of ontological comportment and transcen-dence facilitates the deconstruction of the traditional opposition of subject and object:

With an adequate interpretation of intentionality, the traditional concept of the subject and of subjectivity becomes questionable ... We cannot decide anything about intentionality starting from a concept of the subject because intentionality is the essential though not the most origi-nal structure of the subject itself.

(1982: 65)

5.6 Culture as Semiopraxis

Finally, generalizing the definition of intentionality as transcendence to every mode of textual practice and system of action, we can say that in its maximally general sense transcendence becomes synonymous with semiopraxis: the alter-ity of language is productively intentional in creating myriad *traditions*, worlds of meaning, symbolism, cultural objects, and the intangible ideal referents of works of literature, art, or religious forms through which human beings, in definite historical epochs 'dwell among things' (in Joseph Margolis' equation:

the Intentional = the cultural). Margolis provides a useful inventory of the dimensions of radical intentionality. In his terms the intentional is: (i) incarnate, (ii)real, (iii) causally efficacious, (iv) not reducible in physicalist terms, (v) the essential mark of the cultural, and (vi) not, except for finite segments of some domain or as intentionally restricted for a special purpose, open to simulation or generation by some extensional device (Margolis, 1989: 292).

But the expression 'the cultural' here has to be given a more ontological inflection as the dialogical modes of semiopraxis: 'Perceiving is a *release* of extant things which *lets them be encountered*. Transcending is an uncovering. The Dasein exists as uncovering' (Heidegger, 1982: 70). It is the reflexive operations of semiopraxis that make human consciousness, temporality, and historicity possible: '*to understand things historically is to understand how one understands oneself and how one understands one's understanding of other things – including nature, other persons, the phenomena of one's culture – under the constraint of one's self-understanding*'.[2] I will return to the dialogical horizon of transcendence and semiopraxis in later chapters.

Part III

REFLEXIVITY

In Parts I and II we have seen that neutral representation is an aporetic ideal, that reflexivity is implicit in the construction of Self/Other problematics, and that theoretical discourses implicate relations of power and authority. Following the critique of Representation and Reflection we are now in a position to explore ways in which the 'excluded Other' in every project of reflection might be incorporated into a richer concept of Reflexivity. Since the occlusions of representational thinking are manifold we proceed analytically by focusing upon different orders of alterity: discourse (Chapter 6), embodiment (Chapter 7), historicity or praxical reflexivity (Chapter 8), and practical judgement (Chapter 9). This prepares the way for a more radical analysis of intersubjectivity and dialogue in Part IV.

6

THE REFLEXIVE SELF

This chapter has four parts. The first section introduces the concept of the reflexive self by turning to the work of George Herbert Mead. Section 2 emphasizes the verbal or conversational organization of selfhood, while Sections 3 and 4 outline some of the implications of this conception of rhetorical subjectivity.

1 *The reflexive constitution of the self*
2 *Verbal self-consciousness*
3 *Speaking bodies*
4 *Thinking bodies*

1 THE REFLEXIVE CONSTITUTION OF THE SELF

Out of language emerges the field of mind.
(George Herbert Mead, 1934: 133)

Self and world belong together in the unity of the basic constitution of the Dasein, the unity of being-in-the-world. This is the condition of possibility for understanding the other Dasein and intraworldly beings in particular.
(Martin Heidegger, 1982: 298)

Let us begin with the simple observation that what we call the 'self' is a product of coordinated self-relational skills and activities. It is not a closed system, like the mythical Ouroboros eating its own tail, but an open loop of self-awareness, an integrated field of consciousness. In our commonsense ontology of persons the self is a matrix of reflexive capacities and dispositions through which individuals are oriented toward objects – including 'ideal', intangible, and phantasmal objects projected as imaginary values. But prior to all cognitive or spectatorial attentionality, as we have argued in Part II, is the transcendent realm of intentionality and social interaction. I act or intervene within a given environment as part of a coordinated *social* practice. The basic preconditions for this kind of praxial encounter are embodied modalities which provide the

251

self with a sense of being *centred* and *active*, *whole* and *aware* (Erikson, 1985: 86). Consciousness of selfhood, then, emerges in elementary acts of *alertness*, *valuation*, attentional *curiosity*, semantic *inquisitiveness*, reflective *deliberation*, and self-reflective *interpretation*. These are its prototypical modes of comportment. But it also occurs in processes of disengagement which 'release' cognitive consciousness from its habits and embodiments (we have referred to this in Chapter 4 as *reflective* consciousness). How are such everyday acts of valuing, observing, thinking, reading, speaking, and interpreting possible? The solution, we believe, lies in approaching sociality and language as ontologically prior sites of dialogic transcendence: the heteropoiesis implicit in intersubjectivity provides the ontic matrix of agency and selfhood – or in Mead's rather Kantian terms, sociality is the capacity of being several things at once, of merging two different standpoints into one integrated attitude.

Following scattered observations in the works of David Hume (1711–76), Adam Smith (1723–90) was one of the first modern thinkers to pose the question in this way and to proceed to formulate the rudiments of a social image of the mirroring Self, especially in the Third Part of his *Theory of Moral Sentiments* (1759) where he writes that

> We can never survey our own sentiments and motives, we can never form any judgement concerning them, unless we remove ourselves, as it were from our natural station, and endeavour to view them as at a certain distance from us. But we can do this no other way than by endeavouring to view them with the eyes of other people, or as other people are likely to view them.
>
> (Smith, 1963: 189)

For Smith, the self is an intersubjective reality rooted and continuously reproduced in the transactions of social life; it is also the product of civilizing processes in Norbert Elias' sense of this expression: an individual becomes a self (an 'impartial spectator' of the world in Smith's language) only by participating in the civic life and moral world of other persons. Here the faculty of the imagination is fundamental. I become a self by internalizing and generalizing the images others hold of me – whether these be real or imaginary. Smith discovered – or perhaps returned to – the Aristotelian idea of the social self as a product of interpersonal relationships prior to the propensity to 'truck, barter and exchange' theorized in *The Wealth of Nations* (1776). For Smith, as for Aristotle, man is by nature a political being, a *zoon politikon*. The 'humanity' of human beings is grounded upon social relations and social participation. Hence the

> regard to those general rules of conduct is what is properly called a sense of duty, a principle of the greatest consequence in human life, and the

only principle by which the bulk of mankind are capable of directing their actions.

(Smith, 1963: 275–6)

The narrow motives of economic self-interest which appear to govern civil life belongs to a wider range of motivated activities and cannot be considered as innate or universal characteristics of every social order.

Both genetically and ontologically the existence of a field of interpersonal relationships – the sphere of the Other and sociality – antedates personal consciousness and self-interest. Consciousness to this extent is a product of imagination, sedimented in public language-games, and manifest in the ordered forms of social life. The 'fellow feeling' that lies at the basis of community – or, to use the modern expression, intersubjectivity – is empirically and logically presupposed in every reference to other persons. In particular, it is through the rhetorical media of ongoing social life that the self can become the unique locus of disinterested observation, reflective curiosity, and self-reflection. Paradoxically, the disengagement necessary for the solitary pursuits of meditation, thoughtful inquiry, and theoretical thought is an intrinsically social achievement, rooted in the social activities of practical reason and mutual moral recognition.

How can such a self-referential structure of consciousness (or, in the language of the Scottish Enlightenment, the 'moral sense') be explained? How can we account for the elementary act of imagination by which one person reciprocates the meanings, beliefs, and intentions of another person? How can we explain the genesis of self-consciousness? By phrasing the problem of consciousness in terms of its social genesis the Scottish economist had already partially answered his own question. In Smith's idiom, the intercourse of moral life is a process of imaginatively adopting the role of others from the interactional contexts provided by organized civic experience. The roots of moral coexistence are at work in all economic life. Thus Smith's famous 'dispositional' analysis of the origins of the division of labour reads:

> This division of labour, from which so many advantages are derived is not originally the effect of any human wisdom ... It is the necessary, though very slow and gradual consequence of a certain propensity in human nature which has in view no such extensive utility; the propensity to truck, barter, and exchange one thing for another.

(1976: 25)

Or as Mead would later say, the mind 'is essentially a social phenomenon; even its biological functions are primarily social' (Mead, 1934: 133).

This ontology of 'sympathetic' *relations* which perhaps has its proximate source in Francis Hutcheson's *An Inquiry concerning the Original of Our Ideas of Virtue or Moral Good* (1725) would become a central theme shared by the pragmatic tradition (appearing most emphatically in the writings of

253

Josiah Royce, George Herbert Mead, William James, and John Dewey), the American sociological tradition from Cooley to Parsons, and those influenced by German idealism and Romanticism (Dilthey, Husserl, Scheler, Schutz, Gurwitsch, Merleau-Ponty, Sartre, Buber, and Lévinas): the self is possible only as a social structure constituted in ongoing symbolic experience mediated by acts of moral reciprocity. 'We must', Mead suggests, 'regard mind as arising and developing within the social process, within the empirical matrix of social interactions' (1934: 133). The means and ends of sociality – the moral texture of self-awareness and its discursive forms – are themselves bound up with sympathetic self-reflection created and reproduced in social communication: 'to be observed', 'to be attended to', 'to be taken notice of with sympathy', 'to be valued', 'to be loved', 'to be cared for', 'to show compassion', 'to be responsible for the other', and so forth are all founded upon the primary processes of symbolic exchange – and vary systematically across social systems. For Mead, as earlier for Smith, the economic self-interests, needs, and material concerns of individuals do not stand alone, implanted by natural avarice, but arise in the individualizing processes of socialization and moral education which serve as a code for the *organized set of cultural attitudes accepted and shared by a community.*

For this way of talking, the specific field of 'economic relations' cannot be divorced from the moral structures of human sensibility, interpersonal recognition, and sympathetic exchange; economic action arises like a superstructure upon a foundation of earlier *moral* relations, themselves codifying particular solutions to problems in everyday life. As social categories, concepts such as 'luxury', 'emulation', 'taste', 'capital', 'profit', 'competition', etc. presuppose wider sociosymbolic processes. Consequently the problems studied by political economy overlap with the moral constellations of everyday life. In fact the most basic economic concepts are abstracted from prior mundane social and moral relations. Every 'pure' economic category – interest, profit, value, wealth, value, etc. – are indices of moral relationships and genetically refer back to the most fundamental forms of personal and interpersonal relationships. Adam Smith even provides the central metaphor of Mead's social philosophy. We come to know ourselves and acquire a 'consciousness of self' through the 'looking glass' of the other person. The moral judgements of this 'general' other provide the fundamental criteria of evaluation in all human affairs. We view our own conduct from the perspective of the other. All reflective judgement is acquired in entering into the reciprocal exchanges of social life. This is the clue to the sociality of moral life:

> We suppose ourselves the spectators of our own behaviour, and endeavour to imagine what effect it would, in this light, produce upon us. This is the only looking glass by which we can, in some measure, with the eyes of other people, scrutinize the propriety of our own conduct.
>
> (1963: 192)

The unnoticed experience of moral reflexivity is thus at the root of sociality. Smith also provides Mead with the basic dialectic between the 'I' as observer and the 'I' as observed:

> When I endeavour to examine my own conduct ... I divide myself, as it were, into two persons; and that I, the examiner and judge, represents a different character from that other person whose conduct is examined and judged of. The first is the spectator, whose sentiments with regard to my own conduct I endeavour to enter into, by placing myself in his situation, and by considering how it would appear to me, when seen from that particular point of view. The second is the agent, the person whom I properly call myself, and of whose conduct, under the character of a spectator, I was endeavouring to form some opinion.
>
> (1963: 193)

It was the American philosopher, George Herbert Mead, however, who transformed Smith's insight into the axiom of an original sociological theory of mind and self-consciousness. In essence Mead deconstructs the videological schema of Subject-Object by prioritizing the Subject-Subject relation – exemplified in the symbolic communication between two orders of signifying acts. For Mead selfhood emerges from within the social field of communication. Without a prior world of interpersonal relationships we would have no way of explaining the genesis of the self and self-awareness in ordinary experience. A subject's relation to objects and to itself is ontogenetically derived from the integration of subjectivities created by ongoing social communication. For every system of object-reference, primacy must be given to the experiential processes of the ongoing domain of social existence. Mindfulness develops as interactional processes are internalized or introjected by individuals subject to the same process – the individual becomes a person by becoming aware of her relationships to the social process as a whole. Personhood arises in a network of relationships between concretely configurated acting individuals. The emergence of the 'I am' springs from the social 'We can'. The social process understood as a *symbolic matrix of coordinated activities* is thus prior to individual acts of consciousness and reflection. As the critical theorist Jürgen Habermas has expressed Mead's insight: 'persons, as subjects capable of speech and action, can be individuated only via the route of socialization. They are formed as individuals only by growing into a speech community and thus into an intersubjectively shared lifeworld' (in Kelly, ed., 1990: 46).

We can now turn to Mead's specific account of the genesis of self-reflection. His basic thesis can be stated simply: the 'inwardness' of self emerges within the ongoing public conversation of acting, feeling, interpreting agents. Being able to refer to 'my' feelings, actions, and purposes is a skill acquired by participating in the ongoing process of social life. Hence the key to the formation of mind is to be sought in interactional *valuation* and mutual *role-taking*. A child, for example, enters the life of language and community

255

by participating in the ongoing dialogue of significant communication (the explanation of the mechanisms involved in this incorporative communality are given in detail by Mead in 1934: Part III, Sections 18–29). The basic argument can be condensed into the thesis that becoming a self is inseparable from participating in the 'conversation' of communicative interaction and, more especially, that 'the language process is essential for the development of the self' (1934: 135). Children acquire selves as they learn to participate in the rule-guided activities of games available in a given society. Selves are literally conversational structures (Mead, 1934: 254). In playing at being social they actually become social. Achieving selfhood or a definite character structure is the outcome of numberless practical encounters accumulated in participating in the various forms of social life.

In short, human individuation occurs through the reciprocal sociality of role-taking and role-making behaviour. Mimetic play is thus a lifelong preoccupation of the human species. Along with the dialectic of the Other we have to accept the existence of plural environments of heterogeneous selfhood – as rich as the diverse landscapes of role-playing practices. Mead is quite emphatic about the multiple possibilities of identification and societal complexity within the organization of the self:

> There are all sorts of different selves answering to all sorts of different social reactions ... A multiple personality is in a certain sense normal ... There is usually an organization of the whole self with reference to the community to which we belong, and the situation in which we find ourselves.
>
> (1934: 142–3)

The general thesis of the heterogeneous 'other' within the self is stated as follows:

> The unity and structure of the complete self reflects the unity and structure of the social process as a whole; and each of the elementary selves of which it is composed reflects the unity and structure of one of the various aspects of that process in which the individual is implicated.
>
> (1934: 144)

As an experiencing source of relations, I can distinguish both 'I' and 'Me' components in my stream of consciousness. The emergence of an integrated self requires both aspects as indissociable moments of alterity. The 'Me' signifies the self as perceived and addressed by Others in the games of everyday life. The 'I' is the unpredictable moment of choice, voluntary action, and reflexive self-definition. In internalizing the attitudes of the *alter Ego* I learn to situate my own responses in a pregiven social field. By entering the social spaces already defined by existing game-rules I have no option but to assume initially the displacements created by antecedent systems of rules. If I am to play at all I must play by the rules of existing games; but even here the social process is dialectical and creative: 'We are finding out what we are going to say, what we are going to do, by saying and doing, and in the process we are continually controlling the process itself' (Mead, 1934: 140). Each generation of role-learning modifies the existing game system and changes the rules of action. In temporal terms, therefore, there can be no 'Me' without the agency of the 'I'. Pragmatically, they form an reciprocal unity in the stream of personal life.

The movement from play to organized games is fundamental to the genesis of the reflexive self. To enter the play space of the game a participant must be able to assume the attitude of *all* the other players – or at least be aware of their interdependent roles. A social game is one where the game roles have a 'definite relationship to each other'. This public organization, as Mead says, is articulated in the form of the rules of generalized games (1934: 151–2). Complex social games encourage reflexivity by requiring participants to be able to reciprocate imaginatively different functions as a condition of play. In assuming one position in the game I must also act toward others through self-monitoring norms dictated by the specific game-rules. And the reality and structure of these higher-order contexts of normative rules is anchored in the social objectivity of the game itself, rather than being the 'property' of its participants. In the language of dynamic systems, game-rules form a collective schema which distributes the participants into interactional categories of relationality *vis-à-vis* each other as place-holding statuses: 'The game represents the passage in the life of the child from taking the role of others in play to the organised part that is essential to self-consciousness in the full sense of the term' (1934: 152).

Furthermore self-representational game-rules are only fully acquired as the child learns to talk and participate in the web-work of conversational praxis. Dialogic interaction multiplies to infinity the possibilities of displacement, mutuality, and triangulation that are necessary conditions for the higher forms of self-monitoring experience. In grasping myself as 'me' I adopt an attitude toward myself as though observing my person from the vantage point of an external observer (here we might note the striking parallel between the Freudian model of the ego and superego). This doubling perspectivality is also part of an existing repertoire drawn from the generalized reflexive field of social games. The 'me' represents the objectification of my person *as if* I was standing outside my situation and observing myself as I would observe another subject. We might thus say that a structure of transcendence is a constitutive aspect of the social activity of performative games.

Mead's great achievement was to see this basic prerequisite of communicative play and games as one of the fundamental conditions of personality – and thereby of self-reflection and cultural identity. The language of selfhood is quite literally structured by the role-play inherent in language and language-like games (1934: Sections 20–2). I can only become a social self by entering into the asymmetrical neworks of gaming activities – by 'taking the role of the other', in Mead's famous expression. This is why the self-monitoring of linguistic exchange is so crucial to self-formation:

> I know of no other form of behavior than the linguistic in which the individual is an object to himself, and so far as I can see, the individual is not a self in the reflexive sense unless he is an object to himself.
>
> (1934: 142)

Mead refers to the perspective of the game as a whole, the attitude of the community or social group as 'the generalized other': the attitude of the generalized other is the externalized voice of the whole community articulated in its normative discourses.

For Mead, then, social alterity is presented as a sedimented process of normative control internalized in the form of 'regulative inner conversations' by individuals who participate in group life. While the manifest content of games varies considerable, the latent purpose of interactional games is to socialize an individual into the normativity of the generalized other

> What goes on in the game goes on in the life of the child all the time. He is continually taking the attitudes of those about him, especially the roles of those who in some sense control him and on whom he depends ... He has to play the game ... That process is one which is a striking stage in the development of the child's morale. It constitutes him a self-conscious member of the community to which he belongs.
>
> (1934: 160)

Interpersonal or transpersonal relationships – the discourse of the Other – are thus a prior condition of 'personality'.

> A person is a personality because he belongs to a community, because he takes over the institutions of that community into his own conduct. He takes its language as a medium by which he gets his personality, and then through a process of taking the different roles that all the others furnish he comes to get the attitude of the members of the community.
>
> (1934: 162)

Communication with the Other, in other words, is the living matrix of reflexivity. In communication we both respond to the other while simultaneously responding to our self and our own responses to the other. The process is one of reflexive feedback rather than literal mirroring. That part of my person which transcends the objectification of fixed roles and societal types is the aspect of selfhood Mead calls the 'I'. The 'me' is a set of social categories and objects constituted by the Ego's acts of objectification. The 'I' also views these social objects as phenomenal entities (for example, the material 'me' of my body, the social 'me' created by my family relations and everyday encounters). The 'mineness' of personal experience arises as an emergent product of interactional learning and symbolic identification in specific life-worlds. Without the 'I' there can be no 'me', but without the 'me' the 'I' is equally unthinkable. Here the parallels with the thought of Martin Buber, Emile Benveniste, Emmanuel Lévinas, Jacques Lacan, and Mikhail Bakhtin are striking (and, given more space, these different theories of intersubjectivity would be explored systematically).

Mead – a careful student of the German transcendental tradition – was also acutely aware of the emergent character of the reflexive circuitry of organism-in-environment. He argued that life becomes conscious at those points where the organism's own responses enter as part of the objective field to which it reacts (1959: 73; cf. the similar thought of William James, 1950: I: 6). Only through such feedback loops can the organism keep in touch with its own being, and only by reflexively relating to itself can the organism grow and develop its natural capacities and species propensities. Human interaction takes this loop-like reflexive circuitry of self-to-things, self-to-other selves, and self-to-self to a high degree of complexity. 'Minds inhabit environments', but they do so reflexively – by utilizing the environment as part of their transformative sphere of action; purposeful, intelligent organisms are thus found 'in the midst of their concrete relations' (James, 1950). In social interaction, however, dynamic interpretations of the environment and interpretations of the other's interpretation of the environment (including my activities) are routinely incorporated within the spheres of practical action: I act toward the other as I assume she will act toward the meaning of my act and I shape my act so that it will be 'read' as having a particular 'significance' and so prefigure a particular interpretation and appropriate response from her. Such mundane recursivities facilitate symbolic exchange as a normal feature of sociocultural worlds.

If this spiralling structure of mutual reflexivity is fundamental to organic life, it is even more important for communicative animals whose natural milieu is the changing intersubjective worlds and physical environments created by past social transformations. And for Mead these sites of mutually self-affecting behaviour are in principle diverse and manifold: in keeping with his own evolutionary discourse Mead multiplies the occasions that encourage the self to reflect upon the self. Wherever self-reflection occurs the organism's *habitus* – its specific pattern of species dispositions – becomes another focus of orientation and self-action; the process of reflection upon the self is no longer posited as a transcendental invariant of 'interior consciousness'; reflection upon the self and the self-communication it facilitates now become evolutionary discoveries subject to more complex reality claims and performance criteria; for survival purposes the organism may enhance its chance of existence by creatively responding to its own relations as well as to world-relevant objects: 'the organism responds to these organised attitudes in their relations to objects as it does to other parts of its world. And thus these become objects for the individual' (1959: 76). When fully articulated, these reflexive relations may be integrated into a transformed *habitus* as part of the conditions of intelligent, future-oriented, or purposeful activity:

> a living organism has a selective power in maintenance of the life process in the midst of inanimate things, and a conscious individual reacts to his own responses. He thus gains a new type of control in the maintenance of the living organism, and invests with values the objects of his environment.
>
> (1959: 76–7)

In Mead, then, we have something like a dialectical ecological theory of the communicative emergence of mind-brain complexity.

The more complex the network of social relationships a creature enters, the more complex the processes of individuation and self-understanding (and its biological infrastructures). Mead formulates a naturalistic principle of ecological relativity analogous to the perspectivism to be found in the philosophical anthropology of Jakob von Uexküll: 'at its lowest terms any change in the organism carries with it a difference of sensitivity and response and a corresponding difference in the environment' (1959: 4). But the crucial step Mead takes beyond the framework of 'philosophical anthropology' is to transpose all problems traditionally polarized into exclusively causal or volitional categories into topics for a sociological framework of communication and, more precisely, when approaching human reality, in a framework of symbolically mediated reflexive interaction. The dialectical reciprocities of organisms-in-environments define the unique situation of a species' characteristic behavioral repertoires: 'The reflection of the organism in the environment and the reflection of environment in the organism are essential phases in the maintenance of the life process that constitutes conscious intelligence' (1959: 4). And such repertoires are inextricably tied to situational properties unique to that organism and its species activities. What defines an organism from this perspective is the totality of its practical involvements and functional relationships. Living organisms are environment-reading processes surviving by constantly remaining in communication with their relevant ecology; and successful courses of action are organized experiences that have creatively risen to natural semiotic possibilities. To fail to 'interpret' the signs of a specific habitat is to risk failure in the evolutionary struggle (in Gregory Bateson's memorable words, the absence of systemic wisdom is always punished). A successful organism is an environment-conscious organism which has an enhanced chance of passing on its genes to future generations. Here reflexivity, existential interpretation, and genetic inheritance are interrelated evolutionary phenomena.

In this way the Cartesian notion of a pure subject of consciousness is socialized and returned to the stream of symbolic action and ecological interaction. 'Consciousness' is pragmatized and contextualized by being redefined in relation to the instrumental operations and practical situations of social exchange and linguistic interaction. The self is understood as a social relation within a web of ongoing intersubjective relationships. The problematic of reflexivity and self-consciousness is now decisively shifted to the everyday activities and practicalities of living in the day-to-day world of social action. Living-in-the-world may be understood as the pragmatist's equivalent expression for what the phenomenologists term *being-in-the-world*. Consciousness, thus broadened and naturalized, is refigured as a moment of practical activity, itself an evolutionary emergent of self-reflexive life experience. The self is not a substance, a transcendental structure or universal grid which predetermines experience; it is an emergent part of the very experience it organizes, contingent upon the social worlds in which it develops and functions.

The 'I' is not a noun but a verb: indexing interpretive processes shaped by exchanges with other interpretive agents. Its syntax differentiates into the unlimited declensions of social activities. The self, in other words, is an intersubjective achievement, a defeasible symbolic construct logically and sociologically dependent upon the organizing attitudes and cultural responses of other selves. Selfhood emerges as a symbolic formation in a social field, just as society arises from and is dependent upon the coordinated activities and attitudes of self-reflexive members. From the Meadian perspective the concepts of 'individual' and 'society' are abstractions made from concrete social experience, one-sided reifications of a fundamentally relational field. Self and sociation are emergent, *evolutionary* phenomena:

> The self by its reflexive form announces itself as a conscious organism which is what it is only so far as it can pass from its own system into those of others, and can thus, in passing, occupy both its own system and that into which it is passing.
>
> (1959: 82–3)

To summarize: Mead thematizes the dynamic transverse structure of experience – the ability of an organism to occupy at least two possible worlds simultaneously; the difference, contrast and transition across such worlds marks the point of emergence of reflexivity; and in this sense, reflexivity is an emergent structure founded on sociality and social organization. The 'self' arises from the experience of crossing two domains of sense. The paradigm of transverse experience is exemplified in taking the role of another. And while the genesis of reflexivity is a 'natural development within the transverse worlds of living organisms and their environment', the authentic carrier of reflexivity is, of course, the institutionally situated social self. With this paradigm shift Mead approaches the question of consciousness by relating it to the general problem of understanding reflexivity and its institutions sociologically: 'I have presented consciousness as the response of an organism to its own responses, with the corresponding change which the environment undergoes in its meanings' (1959: 78); 'Institution ... is but an organisation of social attitudes' (1934: 211); 'the appearance of mind is only the culmination of that sociality which is found throughout the universe, its culmination lying in the fact that the organism, by occupying the attitudes of others, can occupy its own attitude in the role of the other' (1959: 86).

2 VERBAL SELF-CONSCIOUSNESS

The decisive question ... is who is the other in whose perspective we see ourselves.

(Karl Mannheim, 1992: 92)

No hard-and-fast line can be drawn between our own selves and the selves of others, since our own selves exist and enter as such into our experience only in so far as the selves of others exist and enter as such into our experience also.

(George Herbert Mead, 1934: 164)

The self as a social field is definitionally metaconscious; its emergence presupposes definite species-specific symbolic dispositions and reflexivities: the interlocking of mutual perspectives, the symbolic ability of an organism to take the role of another, the emergence of symbolic action and interaction, and, most important of all, the crystallization of public attitudes in verbal and metarhetorical practices of signification, interpretation, and communication – in sum the 'unstudied talk' of everyday life (Ryle, 1949: 173–7). In Mead's terms 'there is a social process out of which selves arise and within which further differentiation, further evolution, further organization take place' (1934: 164). Every self must be a plural self, responding to the 'attitudes' of different speech communities and reference groups. In a literal sense the model of 'Self-to-Self' is not phenomenologically derived from the data of communicative interaction: in concrete interaction we find a field or network of pluralized selves and processual relations. Self-reflection emerges through the process of role-taking and role-making within the triangulation of interpersonal attitudes. When this interaction is discursively organized we have the makings of an institution – which then becomes an armature of further reflexive processes:

> One of the greatest advances in the development of the community arises when this reaction of the community on the individual takes on what we call an institutional form ... It makes no difference, over against a person who is stealing your property, whether it is Tom, Dick, or Harry. There is an identical response on the part of the whole community under these conditions. We call that the formation of the institution.
>
> (1934: 167)

Like Lacan's concept of the Symbolic order, institutions codify the organized voices of the community, embodied in rules of etiquette, moral censure, religious values, legal proscriptions, and so forth. In one fundamental sense it is true to say that the self is talked into existence within the dialogic and cultural orders in which it is enmeshed. As Mead observes, the self 'does not exist except in relation to something else' (1936: 74).

> The word 'itself' ... belongs to the reflexive mode. It is that grammatical form which we use under conditions in which the individual is both subject and object. He addresses himself. He sees himself as others see him. The very usage of the word implies an individual who is occupying the position of both subject and object.
>
> (1936: 74)

Mead's reflexive self is primarily defined by the *verbal self-consciousness* inscribed by other participants (although we should recall that emphasis is also placed on the *preverbal* dialectics of the 'conversation of gesture' in constituting 'the significant symbol':

> Only in terms of gestures as significant symbols is the existence of mind or intelligence possible; for only in terms of gestures which are significant symbols can thinking – which is simply an internalized or implicit conversation of the individual with himself by means of such gestures – take place.
>
> (1934: 47)

But each relevant Other may itself be understood as a source of transverse experience and dialogic awareness: 'In a mode which is not reflexive, the object is distinguished from the subject' (1936: 74). In being 'seduced' into the configurations of others' talk, the emergent self is positioned as a significant, speaking, categorial being - an agent within the structured relations of the Symbolic Order. Both Mead and Lacan assume that a young child entering the games of sociation is innately responsive to gestural acts, words, and speech events. This condition of 'already being tuned for speech' is never systematically justified or analyzed; it is taken for granted that the primary games of early childhood involve language and the learning of conversational routines; and the putative relationships between games and language-games is never fundamentally clarified. Yet the essential step is taken: selfhood is contingently linked to the social structures and dynamics of an ongoing process of communication:

> The vocal gesture becomes a significant symbol ... when it has the same effect in the individual making it that it has on the individual to whom it is addressed or who explicitly responds to it, and thus involves a reference to the self of the individual making it.
>
> (1934: 46)

Words – the heteroglossia of social conversation – enter into the fabric of the self. The self is literally made from words and the voices which interweave words into social relations. The discourses of others have made me what I am. I am what I am, then, only as the polemical intersection of the categories inscribed in and inscribing the Other's speech. But unlike otherwise similar dialogic theorists like Vygotsky, Bakhtin, Lacan, and Lévinas – who also explored the same fundamental idea – Mead does not devote any attention to the functions of prelinguistic reflexivity and power relations in his social theory of identity formation. Echoing John Donne's thought that 'no man is an island entire unto himself' and Plato's image of thinking as a conversation, Mead is content to simply underline the social-dialogic foundations of reflexivity without examining either the form or content of dialogic processes: 'The final step in the development of communication is reached when the individual has been aroused to take the role of others addressing himself in their roles, and so acquires the mechanism of thinking, that of inward conversation' (1934: 84). As Mead lacked a concept of unconscious signification and structured power in dialogic interaction, the phenomenological dynamics of 'inward conversation' are left unexplicated. In place of a rigorous sociological analysis we are left with a cognitivist account of the emergence of self-consciousness:

> The thinking or intellectual process – the internalization and inner dramatization, by the individual, of the external conversation of significant gestures which constitutes his chief mode of interaction with other individuals belonging to the same society – is the earliest experiential phase in the genesis and development of the self.
>
> (1934: 173)

Let us briefly summarize Mead's basic theses on the dialogic self. Something called 'mind' or 'consciousness' can only arise in an ongoing social process; selfhood is a creative product of the evolutionary order of social communication. If it is only through language-mediated communication that individuality in the full sense of this term arises, then individuation is an emergent process dependent on the creative ability to adopt the roles of others, to assume multiple perspectives and reference points with regard to emergent experience. The term 'self' is Mead's key category describing this play of reflexive reciprocity between behaviour and consciousness. What language reifies as a noun ('mind') is in reality a verbal process (indexing processes of sociation, role-taking, and reciprocal social interaction). The 'facts' of mind, self, and society are thus constitutively relational. More precisely: the complexity of selfhood is contingent upon the heteroglossia of the earliest voices of the Other toward the nascent self. Language – in the sense of concrete acts of talk and symbolic exchange – forms the living texture of consciousness just as it informs the affective environments of social action. This being the case we cannot analyze the voices of the Other without grounding them in the wider patterns of interaction which sustain the larger networks of a society. Language's practical fluidity and ubiquity is the undifferentiated locus of the self's emergence and the basis of the self's solidarity with others who emerge from the same linguistic matrix and, consequently, speak the same language. The self is enveloped in the encompassing signs and voices of significant others. And just

264

as selves change and mutate with respect to the shifting dynamics of reciprocal action, so the 'worlds' and 'realities' created through sociation are more fluid than the schematic concepts of everyday language admit. Language – in its primary form of symbolic communication – appears to be the perfect medium for these multiple universes and symbolic triangulations. It is the voice of the Generalized Other that brings this infinite semiosis to pragmatic closure.

On the basis of these interactional premises Mead elaborated a genealogy of reflexivity as the development of mind in human society, underlining its continuity with earlier ecological reflexivities ('the world of living organisms and their environment') as well as the integral linkages with the fields of everyday praxis and culture (even when his own descriptions of the latter tend to be disembodied and historically unspecific – for example in the rather abstract notion of the 'conversation' between the 'I' and the 'me' phases of social interaction or the genesis of mind from vocal gestures). Mind emerges where organisms can enter the structured possibilities of reciprocal communication, where they can assume the role of the other and, in its most universal form, adopt the attitude of the Generalized Other. As we have suggested above, consciousness as societal practice is prior to human awareness and, for Mead, human activity is not uniquely individuated by consciousness, but rather by the evolution of reflexive capacities, a process inseparable from the development of human sociality, communication, and symbolic action: 'I have wished to present mind as an evolution in nature, in which culminates that sociality which is the principle and the form of emergence' (1959: 85).

The well-known formulations on the emergence of reflexivity from *Mind, Self, and Society* are even more emphatic:

> The evolutionary appearance of mind or intelligence takes place when the whole social process of experience and behavior is brought within the experience of any one of the separate individuals implicated therein, and when the individual's adjustment to the process is modified and refined by the awareness or consciousness which he thus has of it. It is by means of reflexiveness – the turning-back of the experience of the individual upon himself – that the whole social process is thus brought into the experience of the individuals involved in it; it is by such means, which enable the individual to take the attitude of the other toward himself, that the individual is able consciously to adjust himself to that process, and to modify the resultant of that process in any given social act in terms of his adjustment to it. Reflexiveness, then, is the essential condition, within the social process, for the development of mind.
>
> (1934: 133–4)

In fact in Mead's last period sociality (and with it 'reflexiveness') is no longer presented as a singular property of human beings or social systems; sociality and the solidarity it presupposes begins to be encompassed by Relationality itself and perhaps even by an evolutionary ontology of emergent system interaction; evolution differentiates forms of reflexive sociality and their cor-related 'realities' implicit in its earlier stages:

> the appearance of mind is only the culmination of that sociality which is found throughout the universe, its culminating lying in the fact that the organism, by occupying the attitude of others, can occupy its own attitude in the role of the other.

(1959: 86)

'Society' here is a processual term, a 'systematic order of individuals in which each has a more or less differentiated activity' (1959: 86–7). Sociation is simply the universal self-consciousness of an interactive universe, the coming-to-consciousness of nature as self-differentiating life (the parallels between the social cosmology of Mead and Simmel's later *Lebensphilosophie* are striking).

From this evolutionary perspective, sociality now becomes the fundamental form and medium of reflexive articulation, the basis of mind and the matrix of social objects. Mead is thus quite consistent in deriving even our awareness and knowledge of *physical objects* from a prereflective experience of the social field. In *The Philosophy of the Present* (1932) we find one of the first consistently social theories of objects and a sketch of the corporeal constitution of modes of objectivity beginning with the manipulatory area of human praxis (that is, in the concrete experience of touching and handling objects or what Mead calls the sphere of 'the perceptually real thing of the manipulatory area' (1959: 149; cf. 1934: 248–9). The phylogenetic discovery of the opposable thumb facili-tated the 'technique' of exploratory grasping by the coordinated hand and brain – the prototype of the first analytic attitude toward material experience, enabling the human species to 'break up' the world into physical objects as an environment of explorable entities (1934: 249). A species confronting nature by means of a predictive zone of manipulation has greater access to the possibilities of objects than an animal which cannot disengage from natural experience. The coordination of hand and brain enhances different orders of control – ultimately laying the foundation for a form of life that can create a second nature for itself.

We first experience the world in social categories and then abstract from these social matrices concepts of physical or non-social objectivity – 'The child forms social objects before he forms physical objects' (1934: 184, n. 15). Because of the genesis of objectivity in dynamic contact experiences, each subsequent act of consciousness is tinged with the presence of otherness, deriving ultimately from the structure of the generalized Other which pervades all experience. Categories of self and intersubjectivity are thus prior to natural categories. From as early as 1909–10 Mead had proposed the idea that experi-ence in its primary form is social in character. The appearance of independent physical things, forces, causality, and so forth is presented as a process of differentiation and abstraction from the social matrix. 'Objects', in other words, 'are socially constituted from a more primordial field of sociation'.

Physical things and 'objects' of higher symbolic categories arise within the field of action. In terms of Mead's evolutionary naturalism, the word of 'objective nature' arises through communicative processes of symbolically coordinated behaviour: 'Looked at from the standpoint of an evolutionary history, not only have new forms with their different spatio-temporal environments and their objects arisen, but new characters have arisen answering to the sensitivities and capacities for response' (1959: 177).

3 SPEAKING BODIES

We must be others if we are to be ourselves.

(George Herbert Mead, 1959: 194)

The imaginations which people have of one another are the solid facts of society, and to observe and interpret these must be the chief aim of sociology.

(Charles Horton Cooley, 1902: 121)

Thinkers like George Herbert Mead, Charles Horton Cooley, James Mark Baldwin, and W. I. Thomas concur that what we refer to by the term 'self' is not synonymous with reflexivity; the self is a social construction in a field of consciousness and organized societal reflexivities which are already presupposed (in Mead's pragmatic Hegelianism, nature as a self-differentiating reflexive process is the ultimate metaphysical supposition for this standpoint); self-reflection, self-consciousness, and other-orientation are all superstructural achievements premised on the experiential reflexivities of social life. I can only assume a perspective and become an object for myself by means of a detour through the referential perspectives of relevant others: 'It is only by taking the role of others that we have been able to come back to ourselves' (1959: 184–5). The personal 'I' is simply 'the response of the organism to the attitudes of others' which constitute the organized 'me', 'and then one reacts towards that as an "I"'.

To generalize this finding: *intersubjectivity* is a material and logical presupposition of first-person *subjectivity* – 'selves exist only in relation to other selves', and this relational structure antedates the consciousness of self:

It is important to recognize that the self does not project itself into the other. The others and the self arise in the social act together. The contact of the act may be said to lie within the organism but it is projected into the other only in the sense in which it is projected into the self, a fact upon which the whole of psycho-analysis rests.

(1959: 169)

Or said in an even more Hegelian vein: 'Objective consciousness of selves must precede subjective consciousness, and must continually condition it' ('What social objects must psychology presuppose?', in Mead, 1910; cf. 1934: 227).

Only an organism with the biological capacity to coordinate experiential perspectives can acquire the superstructures of conscious thought, belief and moral activities; like the disposition to acquire the rules of language, the *habitus* of reflexivity appears to be a constitutive feature of being human. Only a reflexive creature is capable of entering the cultural worlds of propositional attitudes:

> Our thinking is an inner conversation in which we may be taking the roles of specific acquaintances over against ourselves, but usually it is with what I have termed the 'generalized other' that we converse, and so attain to the levels of abstract thinking, and that impersonality, that so-called objectivity that we cherish.
>
> (1959: 190)

> Since society has endowed us with self-consciousness, we can enter personally into the largest undertakings which the intercourse of rational selves extends before us. And because we can live with ourselves as well as with others, we can criticize ourselves, and make our own the values in which we are involved through those undertakings in which the community of all rational beings is engaged.
>
> (Mead, 1959: 90)

Mead's deconstruction of the Cartesian-Kantian problematic has radical implications for our conventional views of moral reflexivity:

> The child can think about his conduct as good or bad only as he reacts to his own acts in the remembered words of his parents. Until this process has been developed into the abstract process of thought, self-consciousness remains dramatic, and the self which is a fusion of remembered actor and this accompanying chorus is very loosely organised and very clearly social. Later the inner stage changes into the forum and workshop of thought. The features and intonations of the dramatis personae fade out and the emphasis falls upon the meaning of inner speech, the imagery becomes merely the barely necessary cues. But the mechanism remains social, and at any moment the process may become personal.
>
> (1964: 146–7)

It is no doubt significant that the pragmatic tradition of Charles Sanders Peirce, George Herbert Mead, Josiah Royce, Charles Horton Cooley, William James, and John Dewey – influenced as it was by American Hegelianism (especially by the so-called 'St Louis Hegelians') and, more particularly, by the highly individualistic form taken by capitalist development in the latter decades of the nineteenth century – was the first framework to recast orthodox accounts of individual and social experience by introducing an explicit range of social-psychological and communitarian concepts; consider, for example, 'the field of consciousness' (which can be found in Mead's writings from the first decade of the century – undoubtedly influenced by William James' *Principles of Psychology* (1890) and his later conception of a pluralistic universe), the 'community of selves' throughout Ralph Waldo Emerson's essays and in Josiah Royce's pragmatic idealism, 'imagination/imaginary others', 'the looking-glass Self', 'sympathetic introspection', 'we-feeling', 'primary groups' (Cooley, 1902), 'taking the role of the other', 'the "I"-"Me" dialectic', 'the generalized other', 'the inner forum of thought', 'inner speech/conversation', the social construction of selfhood and moral identity, 'self-interaction', 'self-relations', 'self-other orientations', 'play', 'game', 'social rules', 'the social constitution of objects', 'significant gesture', 'the symbol', 'social process', 'communication', 'interaction', 'communication', and 'symbolic action'. The fundamental text for this whole way of thinking remains Mead's *Mind, Self, and Society* (1934).

This richer *rhetoric of reflexivity* evolved, moreover, in an overlapping series of explicitly adversarial contexts – to demonstrate the inherent limits of traditional approaches to social, ethical, epistemological, and philosophical problems ('the mind-body problem', traditional monism, dualism, the egocentric predicament, etc.), to exemplify the superiority of sociological discourse in subsuming and resolving the inherited 'problems of philosophy', and, perhaps even more significantly, to propound an instrumental and reformist approach to political change and democratic social reconstruction. American pragmatism as an intellectual movement thus represents both a critique of earlier social, philosophical, and political frameworks (positivism, utilitarianism, Neo-Kantian thought, Hegelianism, Social Darwinism, *laissez-faire* capitalism, Emersonian romanticism, populist democracy, anarchism, revolutionary socialism, and so on) and a translation of problems previously considered to be uniquely philosophical (selfhood, personal identity, thinking, experience, self-consciousness, free will, and so forth) into explicitly sociological terms (cf. Miller, 1973; Perry, 1912; Thayer, 1981, 1982).

4 THINKING BODIES

Reflexiveness, then, is the essential condition, within the social process, for the development of mind.

(George Herbert Mead, 1934: 134)

Language is never primarily the expression of thinking, feeling, and willing. Language is the primal dimension within which man's essence is first able to correspond at all to Being and its claim, and, in corresponding, to belong to Being. This primal corresponding, expressly carried out, is thinking.

(Martin Heidegger, 1977: 41)

If we accept the theory of the social construction of consciousness it is tempting to identity reflexivity with thought: only self-reflective systems think. But 'thought' and 'thinking' are imprecise terms presenting notorious problems of specification and definition. As products of the culture of Reflection we tend to think of 'thinking' in expressive terms as a mind's way of understanding and interrogating itself – associating thinking with the reflectivity of verbal thought (the activity of asking questions such as 'What is thinking?'). A sociological account of consciousness as metacommunicative praxis may usefully correct this intellectualism: from the standpoint of Mead's social constructionism thinking becomes a verbal or communicative achievement of reflexive interaction. Once liberated from expressive theories of meaning, thinking might also be approached as the living medium of language (*qua* Logos), a decisive mode of being of that mode of being-in-the-world which constitutes conscious existence.

What, then, is thinking? Given this sociological turn how are we now to think of 'thinking'? As with propositional attitudes in general, 'thinking' appears to be a unique *first-person* capacity: a being that can indicate, refer, and speak of itself as an 'I' is not merely an existent, but a thinking social body; but the existence of such pronominal self-indexicals and the ability to use them appropriately ('I am x', 'I feel y', 'I remember z', 'I see that p', 'I love you', etc.) should not be treated as a natural resource; for example, the grammar of pronominal shifters may be restricted to a particular language or language group, the conventions of self-reference, description, reportage may be tied to particular cultural contexts and concerns, and individuals may be complex thinking beings without utilizing first-person pronouns analogous to the English system. While thinking is evidently linked to 'self-knowledge' and 'self-inquiry' we must not elide the rich indexical spectrum of practical activities, routine processes, and reconstructive functions which exemplify and embody 'thought' – but which are typically performed without explicit awareness. We know that many types of habituated activities can, under certain circumstances, become the topic of secondary reflection; a random sample from the English-speaking world would include the following kinds of *communicative* activity: anticipation and expectation; planning; plotting with others; belief and believing; judging; inferring; speaking; deliberating (with oneself or with others); guessing; expressing; realizing; 'taking stock'; wondering; constructing hypotheses and theories; assembling evidence; verifying; contemplating; searching; examining; looking; grasping; criticizing; sketching; making; composing; calculating; 'conceiving of'; choosing; selecting; grading; sorting into categories; ordering; inducing; deducing; trying to understand; remembering; trying to remember; solving problems; 'brainstorming'; refuting; showing interest; collecting samples; 'reporting findings'; mapping; making connections; finding patterns; isolating differences; model-building; arguing; imagining; recognizing; day-dreaming; desiring; enumerating and examining the steps of a proof; making notes; researching; doubting; generalizing; abstracting; analyzing; understanding; theorizing; writing; commenting upon, paraphrasing; writing criticism; etc.

From our own knowledge of their practical contexts we see that these expressions designate many different activities and overt or covert processes which involve heterogeneous kinds of 'thoughtfulness'. These can be roughly sorted into the following groupings:

Thought-as-contemplation

Contemplating, wondering, considering, meditating, considering, 'mulling over', 'thinking to oneself', deliberating, pondering, puzzling, recollecting, remembering, reflecting, day-dreaming, musing, understanding (*Verstehen*, for example, in the hermeneutic methodology of Wilhelm Dilthey, Georg Simmel, and Max Weber), *Nachdenken* (Hegel), *Besinnung* (in Heidegger's sense of 'depth reflection'), *Gelassenheit* as the experience of 'being carried away' in/by thought, being 'lost in the *Sachen* of thinking', meditating, etc.

Thought-as-imagination

Imagination, imagining, imaging, speculating, hypothesizing, expressing, hinting, guessing, revising, reframing, modelling, calling-to-mind, anticipating, projecting, 'brainstorming', 'trying out ideas', lying, entertaining alternative courses of conduct, inventing new patterns, analogies, metaphors, etc.

Thought-as-problem-solving

Computation, problem-solving, asking questions, hypothesizing, investigating, exploring, composing, finding patterns, inferring, conjecturing, judging, assessing evidence, reasoning, defending beliefs, persuading, reformulating, reframing (as in reformulating a problem), redescribing, glossing, summarizing, translating, revising, recasting, reconstructing, combining ideas, synthesizing different ideas and findings, recontextualizing, calculating, criticizing, refuting, proposing analogies and models, etc. Often these usages have a more active or 'resolute' force, as in thoughtful reflection involving 'concentration' or disciplined analysis of some problem.

Thought-as-dialogue

Dialogue, communication, conversation, arguing/argument, dialectic, the 'questioning art of thinking', communing with ourselves (inner monologue, dialogue, conversation), convincing others, deliberative questioning, thinking through, criticizing, achieving consensus, searching for common solutions, revising initial premises and questions, reopening shared positions and solutions, reformulating the account of an interlocutor, requestioning inherited questions and answers, etc.

Thought-in-practice

'Thought-in-practice' unfolds across every mode of praxical involvement shared by human beings and human communities: creatively producing, speaking, making, doing, acting, performing a skill, building models, testing, writing, sketching, drawing, cooperating, working, inventing, playing, etc. This is the fundamental insight common to Wittgenstein, James, Dewey, and Mead: 'it is a mistake to assume that all that we call thought can be located in the organism or can be put inside of the head' (Mead, 1934: 114). For this tradition thoughtful reflection is an *activity* and thus part of a social practice.[1]

Even these admittedly impressionistic groupings strongly suggest that the word 'thinking' covers an extremely heterogenous range of practices recognized by ordinary language; it also suggests that our taken-for-granted ideas about the essence of thinking are profoundly one-sided, intellectualistic and disabling in their emphasis upon abstract cognition and pure theory; we discover that the object of our search – 'the essence of thought' – opens out into a landscape of family variants and closely related language-games (that the language of 'thinking' has evolved historically and is subject to cultural forces and changes); and, perhaps even more significantly, that most of these examples of thinking are woven into a wide range of everyday practices which are not usually considered as tokens of the type, 'thinking'.[2] In this context, to 'think about thinking' means to abandon mechanistic and reductive models of 'thought' and return to the realm of everyday activities which, in their engaged complexity, forces us to question the cognitive model of 'thinking'.[3] Once the inherited objectivism and faculty-models of thought are deconstructed we begin to see that a large part of the field of 'thinking' belongs with the fuzzier rubrics of 'intelligent conduct' and 'cooperative activities'. Intelligent reflection displays a myriad of forms and modes as diverse as the possible social occasions of intelligent conduct. As Dewey observed, in asking 'What is thinking?' the experienced universe must be such that it gives rise to thinking in this modalized, practical, and plural sense. The aleatory field of thinking is evidence for the aleatory and incomplete nature of experience:

> The ultimate evidence of genuine hazard, contingency, irregularity and indeterminateness in nature is thus found in the occurrence of thinking. The traits of natural existence which generate the fears and adorations of superstitious barbarians generate the scientific procedures of disciplined civilization.
>
> (1958: 70)

Reflection

> occurs only in situations qualified by uncertainty, alternatives, questioning, search, hypotheses, tentative trials or experiments which test the worth of thinking. A naturalistic metaphysics is bound to consider

reflection as itself a natural event occurring *within* nature because of traits of the latter.

(1958: 68)

While there seems to be no 'thinking in general' just as there is no 'mind as such', thought-intensive activities appear to be constitutive of human experience – we think of skilled, educated, and highly trained cooperative performances in which public standards of excellence and shared performative criteria are in play. Our central instances of these performances are typically taken from activities which embody intelligent forms of conduct and self-controlled sequences of social action. What this very superficial phenomenological survey of 'reflective intelligence' suggests is that we have to rethink our traditional and commonsense concepts of thought, to revise our notions of human skills and intelligence in line with the complex operations actually carried out by engaged, cooperative persons; and we should also underline the fundamental reflexivity of many of these thinking activities: that their pursuit involves a change of their 'object', a transformative and, frequently, self-transformative relation to a specific zone of the universe. Only a creature that can represent the future can picture the future as different and then invent courses of conduct designed to bring that difference into being. Only human beings are graced and burdened with transcendence.

We must completely abandon the traditional conception of 'thinking' as a single, contemplative attitude (inherited from another dominant polarity of the European self-understanding: *theoria/praxis*) and begin to think of thinking as a heteronomous, differentiated, practical spectrum of *skilled social activities*, tied to public criterial contexts and the future-oriented values posited by human agents. The same conclusion can be reached by following the central recommendations contained in Wittgenstein's later thought. Joseph Margolis, for example, has formulated the central point in the following way:

> The essential clue may be marked casually enough, but its extraordinary force is remarkably difficult to fathom at first – precisely because of its simplicity just at the point of its most radical conceptual adjustment. It may be put this way: we live and function well as the members of a human community – speaking a language, engaging in the ordinary practices of our society, acquiring a store of skills that we exercise spontaneously and inventively without ever having mastered or ever needing to have mastered or even ever having to refer to an official or formulizable set or rules or norms or criteria governing our entire behavior. That's all ... The line of investigation that Wittgenstein facilitates involves, then, challenging any and all presumed fixities of cognitive, calculational, volitional, experiential, actional, habituative, significative sorts.

(Margolis: 1989: 339)

The same idea is said in a more homely idiom by Mead: 'There is some sort of

273

a problem before us, and our statement of the problem is in terms of a future situation which will enable us to meet it by our present reactions' (1934: 119). What passes for intelligent conduct, in other words, is as rich and complex as the range of reflexive institutions and social formations in which its practices are situated and the diversity of organizational contexts in which such skills are routinely exercised. Finally, it makes the *symbolic structuration* of the social field in terms of inequalities of access to knowledge, power, and material resources absolutely central to the study of communication processes.

7

BEING-IN-THE-WORLD AS INCARNATE REFLEXIVITY

The psyche is in a way all the things that exist. For all the things that exist are objects either of perception or thought, and knowledge is in a way the things that are known, perception in a way the things that are perceived. But we must inquire how this is so.

(Aristotle, *De Anima* 431b21–3)

Chapter 7 explores some of the dimensions of incarnate reflexivity. Section 1 is concerned with the embedded, field-character of human agency; Section 2 explores the dimensions of finitude and positionality in human existence; Section 3 reformulates the theme of embodiment as 'carnal reflexivity'. Finally, we argue that the traditional contrast between knowing-how and knowing-that is inadequate as a frame of reference for investigating the praxical realities of human environments.

1 *Embodied knowledge: the habitus of desire*
2 *Positionality: the habitus of eccentric reflexivity*
3 *Embodiment: the habitus of carnal reflexivity*
4 *Knowing-how and praxical reflexivity*

What are the exemplary manifestations of the Other? The phenomenological conception of lived incarnation or lived corporeality, the preontological hermeneutics of *Dasein* grounded in the category of being-in-the-world, Wittgenstein's account of language-games and forms of life and Mead's social evolutionism strongly suggest that the heteropoiesis of lived reflexivity pervades all our cognitive, intellectual, and reflective involvements in the world. Ontological incarnation marks the *locus* of the creation of meaning through my embodied involvement and ongoing life with others; the body in its full social and historical sense becomes a process of praxical inscription within traditions of sociality already organized by the world-work of relevant and generalized Others: I take for granted that I inhabit a particular sociocultural work-world from which I acquire definitions of the significance of things; that I find myself in *this* situation, together with others; that I am related to Others through horizons of affectivity, shared concerns, interests, and needs; that in

275

entering the dialogical processes that are constitutive of life-in-the-world we are faced by a common horizon of problematic situations – structured prior to my individual existence and biographical circumstances; that together we work and transform parts of the world through cooperative activities in definite material relations: we are also conjointly subject to historically specific institutional forces and structural arrangements; we enter a social world that is already mapped by an antecedent cartography of power relations; we speak and for all practical purposes communicate successfully with one another, accepting pregiven fiduciary horizons, acquiring common stocks of knowledge which change in response to changes in our practices.

All of these elements suggest a revision of the phenomenological nature of Dasein understood as being-in-the-world in the direction of a reflexive philosophy of *praxis* as incarnate life-in-the-world. The shift is best indicated by incorporating the dialectic of institutions and embodiment into our basic conception of being-in-the-world (or to say the same thing, by transforming the ahistorical and disembodied category of being-in-the-world by a more explicitly social anthropology of human existence). Here the crucial point is to stop thinking of incarnation as a pregiven 'natural' state and to think of embodiment as an ongoing, dynamic transactional *process*. My *praxial* experience of concrete space, material objects, language, and intersubjectivity – the nascent *logos* of the social world – prefigures and grounds all other orientations and movements I may take towards experience. The subject-body with its subjective vectors is no longer a passive recipient of preestablished meanings or 'puppet' of contingent circumstances (as it still is in Mead's symbolic interactionism or Schutz's social phenomenology). Rather we must respecify 'embodiment' in terms of the body-with-others, the subject-in-the-world oriented toward and organized by a totality of institutional vectors. Human beings are rooted in and inhabit the social world by first orienting to its topography in concrete material activities – we first 'discover' space by walking from place to place, touching and being touched, working upon and transforming objects, cooperatively making and changing environments. In the language of the Czech phenomenologist, Jan Patocka:

> To understand existence as movement means to grasp man as being in and of the world. It is a being that not only is in the world, as Heidegger puts it (in the sense of understanding the world), but rather is itself a part of the world process.
>
> (1989: 179–80)

If we are to understand and trace the coordinates of existential signification, we must, therefore, turn to the world-work of *incarnate reflexivity*, a transactional phenomenon which undercuts the micro/macro dualisms of social theory and the personal/interpersonal metaphysics of Cartesian ontology. Following the account of preontological reflexivity set out in Chapters 5 and 6 we can see that the structures of *positional incarnation* and the historical organization of social space are already regulated by power relations, structured according to prior gender, class, age, and ethnic categories. It follows that the whole range of social relations and forms of life have their roots in these microsociological 'economies' or 'political technologies'. Once we abandon the traditional metaphysical frameworks the 'things themselves' suggest that there is no 'embodiment' without structures of social difference, that the discourse of the Other is always present in 'becoming social', and that life-in-the-world as a *social process* is grounded in the dialogical existence of life-with-others. We already live within the fabric of sociality, just as the order of social experience is embedded in every gesture and action.

The cumulative argument of the preceding chapters strengthens the case for a genealogy of lived experience in its concrete historical locations and diverse sociopolitical variability. In logological terms, it commends a careful study of the anonymous social intersections of power, interests, and divisions at work in every social milieu. Since the theme of incarnation – the 'question of the body-subject' – forms the point of intersection of critical discourse – phenomenological, hermeneutic, psychoanalytic, poststructuralist, and feminist – it is an appropriate *topos* to deepen our investigation of reflexivity.

1 EMBODIED KNOWLEDGE: THE HABITUS OF DESIRE

> The psyche is the principle of living things.
>
> (Aristotle, *De Anima* 402a)

The theme of *embodiment* has both concrete and figurative aspects. At the most concrete level the self is located in a particular 'here and now', a physical location in a historical place and time.

> We are always already somewhere, we are in the world, integrated in an instinctual affective foundation and released by the earth, singled out as individuals, yet still bound, still determined by the natural foundation, retrospectively taken into it. We call this anchoring, or rooting.
>
> (Patocka, 1989: 280)

A person is 'thrown' into a particular nexus of affective relations, shaped by pre-existing historical forces, structures, and technologies of power. The existential locus of human activities is thus always a singular situation in a structured field of interaction: a *hic-et-nunc* individualized by definite material and social constraints. This provides the '*a priori* framework within which all our experience of our possibilities of movement unfolds' (Patocka, 1989: 280). Hence the provocative metaphor of poststructuralism: the individual is individuated through regimes of *subjection*. To say this in a less determinist manner – situational inscriptions frame the historical possibilities of *agency*. In fact the field of social action must now be understood as the reflexive intersection of a range of facilitating projects and praxes. This is the moment Patocka describes as the self-extension or self-projection of incarnate beings. It relates to the Marxist anthropology of self-objectification through the modes of embodiment designated as 'work' or 'labour': 'The realm of self-extension, self-projection into things, is the realm of mediation (abolishing immediacy), of work. It is a world of means in which instinct is replaced by interest, instinctual goals are made conscious, habitual. Here begins understanding no longer as simply immediate but as intelligent, the sphere of intelligence, of understanding both objective relations and personal relations and interests' (1989: 280). This is what the phenomenologist, Alfred Schutz describes as the pragmatic motivation of the work-world.

But the self that is realized or 'emerges' from the mediations of work and social life is also 'embedded' more figuratively in institutional orders and macroinstitutional environments. 'Incarnation' here is both the form and the medium of historical traditions (we can thus think of the production and reproduction of social relationships and meaningful traditions as active dimensions of transcendence and reflexive historicity). This is where the third moment of transcendence becomes effective, the moment in which we seek a more global 'meaning' of existence, a systematic account of our life-in-the-world and its embodied basis. In Patocka's language, the third moment of incarnation makes historicity possible, creating 'the global movement we call history' (1989: 283–4).

The Aristotelian term *habitus* may help to clarify these different orders of praxial individuation and configurations of historical life. We thus begin by viewing discourse (and representations more generally) as a *nexus* of *positional knowledges* (this also conforms to Pierre Bourdieu's definition of the *field* as 'a network, or a configuration, of objective relations between positions' (Bourdieu and Wacquant, 1992: 97).

From the perspective of embodied knowledge or corporeal subjectivity all psychic life interfaces with the material and bodily networks of action and the symbolic orders of social and institutional experience; it is the contingent structure of an individual's *psyche* which marks that individual's inscription in a given place (*situs*) and community (*ethos*). But as we have already argued, the *psyche* is not an aggregate of mental states or fixed faculties; rather selfhood appears as a mobile configuration of functional relations and communicational dispositions (cf. Aristotle, *Nicomachean Ethics* Book 2, ch. 1). And conversely the spatial and temporal *sites* of knowledgeable agency are 'always-already' saturated with cultural differences – as the sedimented products of past activities of signification and lived orientations. Here the local sites of social existence are crucial to the differential formation and transmission of historicity. To the differential concept of the 'sense of place' we must add the 'nomadic' concept of the 'place of sense': 'spaces of objective relations that are the site of a logic and a necessity that are *specific and irreducible* to those that regulate other fields' (Bourdieu and Wacquant, 1992, 97). Both can be incorporated into the concept of life-in-the-world as a differential reflexivity of incarnate spatiotemporal fields in which social systems are practically and symbolically enacted (Massey, 1984; Gregory and Urry, eds, 1985; cf. Bourdieu, 1977, 1984, 1990; Bourdieu, *et al.*, 1991; cf. Benthall and Polhemus, eds, 1975; Lefebvre, 1991b; Mauss, 1972; Robbins, 1991; Polhemus, ed., 1978).

At another level the concept of *habitus* also characterizes the manner in which the beliefs and discourses of agents vary with changes in social divisions and inequalities within and between *cultural fields*. Individuals make sense of their existential situation using the available resources of a particular place and time. But this 'cultural capital' is already embodied in practices and institutions that mediate individual and collective action. From this perspective the 'frames of meaning' available to different agents are critically important resources of further social action. Unlike Foucault's deterministic conception of the disciplinary mechanisms of biopower as individualizing the self through processes of subjection and governmentality we stress the empowering and unpredictable characteristics of human embodiment. Thus different individuals, groups, and classes creatively utilize the possible resources of speech, language, and related semiotic processes in the creation of meaningful environments. But language is only one form of power in a universe of economic, social, and military systems. 'Power' in everyday life is not wholly institutionalized or internalized into the subjective norms and rule-like schemata of traditional social analysis. Rather multiple fields of power are negotiated and transformed through contingent processes of individual and group activity. Moreover these selective processes of symbolic 'enframing' actively change the conditions of interaction. Against the structural model which views individuation as the product of one-directional mechanisms of subjection, here we suggest that there is a more complex, reflexive dialectic between processes of embodiment, social fields, and structural conditions.

By creatively internalizing the object-sites of social, political, and epistemological discourses we are literally inscribed in the ongoing projects of relevant others. This essentially Aristotelian insight has been revived in Foucault's concept of *pouvoir* as facilitative networks, in Norbert Elias' sociology of the body, and more explicitly in Bourdieu's concept of *habitus* as a dispositional system of models of perception and appreciation anchored to particular social and ideological positions. In its dynamic sense *habitus* refers to the prior axiological structuring of social action – 'Habitus is a socialized subjectivity' (Bourdieu, 1992: 126). But we have already noted how this can be assimilated to a social control model of social action. As with Mead's symbolic sociology of the emergence of reflexivity, for Bourdieu 'the human mind is *socially* bounded, socially structured'. Every conceivable social practice is shaped by its constitutive field (in Bourdieu's schematic formula from *Distinction* (1984): (habitus) x (capital) + field = practice). In its reflexive aspect the 'habitus is at once a system of models for the production of practices and a system of models for the perception and appreciation of practices' (1990: 131). Macrosocial analysis is given the task of thematizing structured configurations of *habitus*:

'the durable and transposable systems of schemata of perception, appreciation, and action that result from the institution of the social in the body ... and fields' (Bourdieu and Wacquant, 1992: 126–7).

By combining these dimensions, a phenomenology of lived experience can recover and respecify the central insights of Freudian and Lacanian psychoanalysis concerning the intersubjective character of *desire*. All knowledge – including formal-propositional and theoretical knowledge – is framed by its incarnate and institutional status, anchored in the material activities and historical functions of active, gendered human agents. 'Knowledges' – *epistemes* in Foucault's terminology – are produced within practices consistent with the demands of pregiven institutional fields. Aristotle's entelechial definition of mind as embodied form in *De Anima* was motivated by a similar desire to undercut the division of human agency into mind and body. Today we might speak of the dialectical 'embodiment', 'internalization', and 'appropriation' of structures in *differential fields*.

In principle, then, we can say that every epistemic attitude and knowledge formation is correlated to some affective system of praxis, some prior work of inscription given with a definite spatiotemporal system of social constraints. And each local productive field is bounded by wider social patterns and collective horizons. But the metaphors of control and domination are inadequate images to grasp the dialectics of social life. As a public symbol system, representations made available by such dispositional structures can be used reflexively to comment upon, monitor, and even transform other orientational systems. As Bourdieu observes, habitus 'contributes to constituting the field as a meaningful world, a world endowed with sense and value, in which it is worth investing one's energy' (1992: 127). 'Knowledge' is quite literally the sum total of the various social 'embodiments of mind' available to a given system of action. In this respect, the generative functions of embodied knowledge in everyday human life-worlds – the cultural determinants of reflexivity – demonstrate most graphically the inadequacy of extreme forms of environmental determinism (sensationist empiricism, radical behaviourism, sociobiology) along with traditional formalist and rationalist views of self and action. In positing a one-directional influence from environment to organism reductionism fails to grasp the profoundly reciprocal, transgressive, and dialectical aspects of ecological configurations and how these latter are transformed by wider technological, social, and political changes.

If non-human organisms follow relatively fixed principles, human agents *act* purposefully with other agents within a richly mediated social-symbolic field; this does not mean, of course, that subjects are wholly autonomous agents or absolutely free from situational constraints ('intentionality', as we have argued in Chapters 5 and 6, must not be confused with transparent volition or conscious purpose, nor abstracted from the social structures which it informs and reproduces), but only that the self is first a *habitus* of embodied intentionalities and skills tied to particular physical settings and social positions. In an active sense these forms of affectivity should be regarded as facilitating systems of intersubjective action – the *habitus* provides praxical orientations (for example as forms of *symbolic capital*) which inform and extend the *habitats* of significant interaction. Being prior to cognitive or normative rules, embodied dispositions 'position' agents within a field of practices. As prereflective reflexivities, *life-with-others* in concrete activities antedates spectatorial modes of consciousness and self-consciousness. The praxial experience of being-with-others in organized social fields logically and empirically precedes all other forms of self-awareness.

The analysis of such 'knowledge systems', as a second-order 'knowledge of knowledge', belongs to the programme of logological investigations:

> social science is necessarily a 'knowledge of knowledge' and must priori-
> tize a sociologically grounded phenomenology of the primary
> experience of the field or, to be more precise, of the invariants and
> variations of the relation between different types of fields and different
> types of habitus.
>
> (Bourdieu, 1992: 127)

When approached as a praxial agent, the individual is always already found inscribed in a field of social relations, open to relevant life-worlds and environments prestructured through sexual, symbolic, and cultural praxis; moreover individuals experience their worlds prior to explicit self-consciousness as active intentional agents, orginative sites of cognition, practice, and volition. Praxis, embodiment, and reflexivity are, therefore, interdependent *social categories* and change in different historical epochs. Embodiment and historicity are not 'dimensions', 'media' or 'domains' of free activity for 'desiring machines'; liberties are always intersubjectively situated and structurally delimited by inherited material conditions and practico-inert institutions. From this perspective 'reflexivity' no longer presupposes a pure *self*-consciousness or transparent subject on the model of Cartesian self-reflection, but supports more dialectical models of the interaction of *habitus* and *cultural field* operating 'beneath discourse and representation'. As Bourdieu observes, to 'think in terms of field is to *think relationally*' (Bourdieu and Wacquant, 1992: 96). A fundamental ontology of praxial reflexivity, then, logically antedates all 'theories' of subjectivity, interaction, and institutions.

One immediate consequence of the theory of *incarnate dispositions* is to foreground the widely different patterns of operative knowledge created by different life-worlds and historical institutions. It allows sociological analysis to enter the black box of the category of 'commonsense knowledge' and gives social agents a constitutive role in negotiating the local processes of social praxis. Everyday knowledge is a sedimentation of selected portions of available cultural knowledge – selectivity and limitation flowing from the structuring effects of power and interests that form such a pervasive feature of social life. We can now legitimately speak of a concrete dialectic between forms of consciousness, material history, and social existence – an interweaving of incarnate consciousness and material life which shapes the different systems of knowledge and thought in a given age. Consciousness is not a disembodied faculty or stream of ideas; but neither is existence an unformed mass of sensory impressions or unmediated matter; both moments are imbricated in the knowledgeable processes of social existence – an interpenetration exemplified by the diverse ways in which human agents find themselves creatively orchestrating the practices and organizations of material existence. We can deepen this analysis by examining the concept of positional attentionality as a basic structure of prereflective consciousness.

2 POSITIONALITY: THE HABITUS OF ECCENTRIC REFLEXIVITY

The thickness of the body, far from rivaling that of the world, is on the contrary the sole means I have to go unto the heart of the things, by making myself a world and by making them flesh.

(Maurice Merleau-Ponty, 1968: 135)

A singular dimension of incarnate consciousness appears with the dialectical processes of corporeal metareflexivity where reflection on self-reference forms the substance of the relation (for example Dasein's symbolic and metalinguistic capacities presuppose what Heidegger has called the ecstatic structure of human existence as care (Sorge) and understanding (Verstehen)). We have also interpreted corporeal reflexivity as the body's positional embeddedness within its local forms of world-incarnation and social practices – in the sense that human beings can adopt a conscious orientation, attitude, or reflective stance toward the structures of their sociohistorical worlds, the definition of their fields of interest, and political involvements. Finally, an enlarged phenomenological account of praxial embodiment stresses the emergent possibilities of being-with-others in cooperative work, improvised creativity, and cultural life more generally (the thematics of incarnate praxis form the central focus of Maurice Merleau-Ponty's later writings, from Adventures of the Dialectic to The Visible and the Invisible, although the intersubjective and hermeneutic aspects of the subject-body's incarnate freedom are even more emphatic in the early writings of Paul Ricoeur). Against all determinist models of human reality – including recent theorizing which posits society as a carceral totality – we have seen that human beings are not completely defined by their relationships or determined by the logic of material 'assemblages', but live by continuously remaking, criticizing, reformulating, and existentially testing their worldly orientations. The overwhelming emphasis of orthodox social science upon deterministic processes of social identification and rational calculation must be counterbalanced by models of creative distanciation and appropriation (cf. Deleuze and Parnet, 1987).

Earlier attempts to 'liberate' the distinctively reflexive characteristics of human existence have led some philosophers to claim that the human species belongs to a 'higher' stratum of being emerging dialectically from prior levels of natural existence. Human being in the world is an interlacing of the voluntary and the involuntary (to borrow Ricoeur's title). Creative possibilities of human praxis arise like a superstructure upon prior 'levels' of structural determination ('fields' of inorganic, organic, biological, social, and spiritual life – recall Bourdieu's revision of Hegel – *the real is the relational* (1992: 97)). Important variations on these stratificational and relational *motifs* can be found in the writings of Nicolai Hartmann, Max Scheler, Martin Heidegger, Maurice Merleau-Ponty, Paul Ricoeur, Jean-Paul Sartre, Helmuth Plessner, Arnold Gehlen, F.J.J. Buytendijk, Erwin W. Strauss, Adolf Portmann, and others involved in the project of philosophical anthropology (in the specific German sense of *philosophische Anthropologie* as a comprehensive account of the fundamental structures and constitutive attributes of human life-in-the-world). For these authors creative distanciation and reflectiveness arise from a 'more fundamental' condition of situated eccentricity: being human is definitionally defined by its *transcendence* as existence-toward-being just as human *existence*, for a writer such as Sartre, is a continuous surpassing of practico-inert constraints, a 'going-beyond' by means of freely chosen projects of nihilation (Sartre called this the first principle of existentialism: that man is what he makes of himself, a project possessing a subjective life as a life of self-surpassing consciousness). Here the dominant thematics of the passive 'object-body' are displaced by a phenomenological explication of the affective, volitional, and social vectors of the 'subject-body' (Ricoeur's *Freedom and Nature: The Voluntary and the Involuntary*, 1966 is the classical phenomenological study of this theme).

In the earlier writings of Gehlen and Buytendijk, for example, reflective distanciation is explained as a product of the basic experience of ambivalent positionality rooted in the body's material incarnation. Human existence is suspended ambivalently on the threshhold between nature and culture. The point of intersection of these two 'spheres' is the subject-body. Human incarnation is not radically separated from natural existence in the manner of the Cartesian opposition of subject and object; in patterns of lived or prereflective habitual experience there is no dualism of matter and soul – rather the phenomenology of concrete experience suggests a picture of the universe as a laminated complex of existential modalities created by the humanizing of nature. Following ideas in Husserl's *Ideas II* and unpublished manuscripts, Merleau-Ponty, likewise, makes the phenomenon of existential ambivalence the centrepiece of his phenomenology of prereflective perception. For the human world the universe manifests itself as a stratified nexus or 'knot' of natural emergence: it is a layered structuration in which human consciousness and self-consciousness emerges from antecedent systems of organic life. Human embodiment and the self-understanding it makes possible is a transverse articulation of the levels of nature and spirit. Embodiment – including the whole range of affective life, 'moods', and existential valuing – is the site where natural life and cultural praxis are mediated and intertwined (cf. Max Scheler's non-formalist ethics (1973) and phenomenology of value (1992); similar meditations on the theme of existential ambivalence appear in the work of Gabriel Marcel, in Merleau-Ponty's unfinished work *The Visible and the Invisible*, especially in his seminal reflections on the *chiasm* as 'the flesh of the world' (1968: ch. 4, 130–55), in the *Crisis* manuscripts of Husserl (*The Crisis of European Science and Transcendental Phenomenology*, 1970), in Karl Kosík's *Dialectics of the Concrete* (1976: ch. 2, 36–92); and throughout the pragmatic 'existentialism' of George Herbert Mead and John Dewey)).

Helmuth Plessner, in his work *The Stages of the Organism and of Man* (1928), is the primary source for this theory of organic emergence. In Plessner's terminology, the human species is a realm of situated beings, displaying the characteristic carnal reflexivities of eccentric *positionality* mediating the objective regularities of nature and the subjective conventions of culture. In Heidegger's analysis in the first division of *Sein und Zeit* (*Sein und Zeit* was published one year before Plessner's book), consciousness presupposes ecstatically preunderstood existence (in Heidegger's well-known analysis of the categories of Dasein as *being-in-the-world*). Marjorie Grene has summarized the essential point in the following way:

A body having positionality is a body delimited from its medium by a boundary which it *has*, a boundary which turns back on itself as part of itself and which it nevertheless *transcends* ... in its relation to its medium and in relation to itself. Its relation to its medium, its living in its medium, is necessarily mediated by and through the boundary, and out of this arises an essential mediation of its parts to itself ... [hence] the essential role of mediation in the structure of living things'.[1]

Positionality – embeddedness, location, spatiotemporal inscription – might be described as reflexive liminality, an organism's unique material and biological capacity to stand out from its world and its situational constraints, to objectify its reflexive involvements (the 'opposition to itself', 'otherness of itself' of a boundary-defining existence: organism and positional field as the contrary poles of a structured rhythm of life or *Lebenskreis* – which Grene translates as 'biocycle'). At the centre of Plessner's work is the idea of human existence as self-conscious embodied life: the creative movement of human existence is the central theme of a 'Philosophical Anthropology' that would articulate the interlacing organic, symbolic and historical 'positionalities' of human individuality. And 'positionality' is a generic term which integrates the materially conditioned character of human existence with the situated possibilities of human freedom. Unlike the *sujet connaissant* of epistemology, human positionality is by definition decentred or, in Plessner's terms, *eccentric*: 'life out of the center has, in the human case, become reflexive, has set itself to itself as its own ... This structure Plessner calls *eccentric positionality*' (Grene, 1968: 104). Like the existentially decentred structure of Dasein, incarnate positionality grounds the possibility of the ambivalent reflexivities of sexual, personal, social, and historical existence: 'the ambiguity produced by a centered positionality that has turned back on itself, that holds its bodily and experienced aspects together by splitting them apart (Grene, 1968: 106): 'as a person I am all these at once, my body, in my body, and over against my body' (Grene, 1968: 108), as 'to *be* a body, to *have* a body *and* to take a stand over against both these and the relations between them' (Grene, 1968: 115) become both normal and chronic features of human experience – exemplified in the 'natural artificiality' of symbolic and culture-constructing praxis. The tradition of philosophical anthropology thus concludes that human being is fundamentally existence endowed with the possibilities of transcendence. And human transcendence cannot be reduced to the terms of transparent consciousness or to any other one-sided categories of subjective or objective being (the *en-soi* and *pour-soi* of Cartesian thought, the *Ego* of phenomenology, the acting *subject* of sociology); it would be more appropriate to view the transcendence inherent in eccentricity as an *a priori* structure presupposed by every concrete mode of consciousness. The *ek-sistenz* or eccentricity of transcendence is what makes the concrete encounter, transactional exchange with others, and projection toward the Other possible. It is thus already presupposed by every human orientation and system of praxis. The being typically referred to as 'man' or 'Dasein' is analytically a creature of intersecting threshholds, a liminal being rooted in the context of a world and of others.

Accepting the carnal reflexivities of eccentric positionality, acts of symbolism and cultural praxis such as the human production of meaningful artifacts, tools, and technologies can be respecified as concrete manifestations of a boundary-creating agent (the totality of culture is a universe of semiopraxis: frames, techniques, boundaries, and self-defining fields of human agency). These emergent phenomena can now be interpreted as specific, motivated structures of human self-interpretation. From this perspective the organic and physiological basis of spatiotemporal existence and the creative and cultural dimensions of human freedom are to be regarded as complementary moments of human self-experience. These moments creatively intersect in the life-world structures of active cultural praxis. As a corollary, each 'side' of the dialectic is subject to reciprocal causation and change.

3 EMBODIMENT: THE HABITUS OF CARNAL REFLEXIVITY

We must not think the flesh starting from substances, from body and spirit - for then it would be the union of contradictories - but we must think it, as we said, as an element, as the concrete emblem of a general manner of being.

(Maurice Merleau-Ponty, 1968: 147)

From this perspective positionality presupposes *embodiment* which concretely inscribes my bodily existence in the intersecting meaning structures of material, social, and historical fields, but analogically, includes every form of material and libidinal inscription: we are positioned in the prestructured affective field of perception and sociation, and through our social relations are already libidinally engaged with the orders of language, action, institutions, and history – and these should also be construed as corporeal relationships. These are the basic premises of a radically *non-Cartesian* picture of the embodied mind or libidinal body. Notable among contemporary philosophers, it is Maurice Merleau-Ponty who has most insistently explored the embodied-situated structure of human coexistence, explicitly in his last writings in the context of a carnal philosophy of perception as the chiasmic reality of incarnate being-in-the-world:

> Knowledge is thus founded on the irrefutable fact that we do not exist in the situation like an object in objective space, and that, for us, the situation is the root of curiosity, investigation, interest in other situations as variants of our own, then in our own life as illuminated by others and now considered as a variant of others; finally, it is that which binds us to the totality of human experience no less than that which separates us from it.
>
> (Merleau-Ponty, in Luckmann, ed., 1978: 156;
> see his posthumously published work,
> *The Visible and the Invisible*, 1968: chs 3, 4)

For Merleau-Ponty, the incarnate 'situatedness' and context-bound nature of human being-in-the-world deconstructs the two extreme manifestations of Cartesian dualism: reductive materialism (mechanical materialism, empiricism, behaviourism) and spiritualism (idealism, formalism, voluntarism, intellectualism). Neither materialist nor idealist categories and explanations can account for the dynamic experience of embodied reflexivity in the life of human beings or historical collectivities. The distinctively human is not found at either pole of mechanical *reaction* or pure *rationality*. Rather it is found in the institutions of human *reasonableness* which are implicit in the prereflective social field. Merleau-Ponty had understood that the only way of transcending the metaphysical horizon of social theory was to 'return' to a radical theory of historicity understood as multidimensional embodiment – in the material order, the order of signification, and subjectivity. To escape the constraints of objective reason we must restore the full complexity of human experience as life-in-the-world. For this purpose we require a philosophy (or non-philosophy) of incarnate praxial reflexivity – the 'lived experience' of finite, need-oriented, libidinal human beings within a community of other centres of desire and action. The nascent *logos* of historical structures and reasonable praxis can only be explicated by means of an existential phenomenology of the *bio-logos* of intersubjective historical involvements. This is the precise point where the asocial phenomenology of perception is displaced by a radical sociology of material inscription. And the leitmotif of this reflexive sociology is the concept of dialogue as incarnate *semiopraxis*. As we will see in subsequent chapters the shift toward this radical framework involves something like a cognitive revolution in our ways of thinking about human experience, rationality, and society.

4 KNOWING-HOW AND PRAXICAL REFLEXIVITY

We feel as if we had to repair a torn spider's web with our fingers.
(Ludwig Wittgenstein, 1968: §106, 46e)

In the chapters of Part I we have seen that the dominant epistemological paradigm takes true knowledge to be intrinsically cognitive, reflective, and representational. As we will demonstrate in detail in Volumes 2 and 3 this is one of the enduring Greek theoretical legacies to Europe. 'Knowing' for this tradition is experience objectified in the propositions of reasoned *episteme* to be verified according to the self-imposed demands of *theoria*. In this conception of knowing what distinguishes belief (*doxa*) from genuine knowledge (*episteme*) is not only the putative certainty and necessity of epistemic knowledge but the ability of its possessors to provide a reasoned account of their epistemic claims: we transcend everyday opinions and the level of practical craft knowledge ('practical common sense') by grounding our knowledge claims as evidenced causal propositions – demonstrated, for example, by an ability to teach the basic principles and terms of reference of a domain of knowledge. The acid test of 'genuine knowing' would not merely be a facility with the various techniques and objects of knowledge (practical mastery of a field), but whether or not individuals can provide systematically reasoned accounts of the rules of formation of those objects: and ultimately, an account of the essences indexed by a body of mastered knowledge. Abstractive intellect would thereby be able to formalize the rules governing an epistemic domain and on this basis transmit the resultant conceptual system to novitiates. The formalization of algorithmic knowledge and its pedagogic dissemination become inseparable criteria of authentic knowing.

In this way, the sceptical second-order question 'How do you know what you claim to know?' inaugurates the project of epistemology (whose inquiries into the origins, types, structure, and criteria of genuine knowledge have given a decisive profile to the legacy of thought about reflexive themes and problems). I can only be said to 'know' if I accept this strict definition of formalized cognition. Knowledge must be reducible to formal rules, explicitly defined, and algorithmic in its structure.

More recently, however, we have been taught to distinguish between two fundamental categories of knowledge, which have been called *knowing-how* and *knowing-that*. Obviously each of these terms covers a wide spectrum of cases which should be explored in detail in a more comprehensive discussion. Simplifying, we can say that the first kind of knowing refers to the kind of skilled praxial knowledge involved in quotidian practices (everyday language speaks of 'know-how' – *le sens pratique* as the reflexive resourcefulness constitutive of different practices), while the second type of knowledge refers to linguistic, conceptual, and propositional knowledge. Where the former tends to be concrete and context-dependent the ideal of the latter is an epistemic formation that is abstract and universal. In terms of the above discussion the former belongs to the logological paradigm of embodied reasonableness, the latter to the reflective model of formal rationality. In genetic terms, the acquisition of formal, instrumental, or 'reflective' knowledge is only possible on the basis of sedimented strata of operative knowledge which accompany socialization in a given community or tradition. Where reflective knowledge can be reduced to rules and algorithmic form, the latter resist formalization and objectification.

In one sense, of course, all 'knowledge' is embodied, a product of human praxis incorporated into the structural organizations of everyday life and institutions; but the distinction between knowing-that and knowing-how usefully highlights the relatively unnoticed processes of intelligent conduct and concerted activity that are typical of quotidian rationalities and 'knowledge systems' which operate quite successfully without any kind of 'transcendental' grounding, explicit rules, or 'principled' self-reflection. *Le sens pratique* of practical logics represents, as it were, reflexivity incarnated in systems of quotidian action within the life-world. Thus individuals who can play chess, ride a bicycle, prepare a meal, engage in conversation, change a gasket, perform a ritual, tell a story, participate in a collective project, laugh with others, and so forth definitionally possess the relevant skills and performative capacities – even though they are unable to give an explicit verbal account of their capacities let alone formulate an algorithm or principled account of the procedures involved in skilled activities. While many of these activities can be formalized they are not in themselves determined by formal rules. They belong in the realms of intuitive or 'tacit' knowledgeability explored by Michael Polanyi (1967; and Polanyi and Prosch, 1975) and contemporary phenomenological sociology (Schutz, 1982; Luckmann, 1983; Garfinkel, 1967). The vast practical field of everyday verbal and conversational competences belongs to this category of skilled reflexive performances (and hence can be subsumed in our account of cultured dispositions – recalling the expanded sense of the term 'culture' from Chapters 5 and 6).

Another angle on the ancient Greek stratification of theoretical knowledge above everyday praxis accompanies the claim that *knowing-how* ideally and progressively gives way to *knowing-that*. The humblest appearance of the desire to know begins a process which can only find its resolution in the closure of perfect knowledge. In the process of realizing closure individuals are asked to relinquish or transcend their practical competences and intuitive knowledge in favour of the more secure mastery of theoretical cognition (*theoria*). In this framework *doxa* and commonsense knowledge are almost invariably presented as the poor relatives of algorithmic knowledge systems. The latter remedies and overcomes the putative shortcomings of the former – *theoria* displaces common sense as lower-grade knowledge; in some radical versions of this process, as no knowledge at all, but *opinion*, tied inexorably to the level of pragmatic workaday routines. In this way the millennial-long deprecation of 'knowledgeable praxis' is given an ideological justification and incorporated into the pedagogic and institutional programmes of society. What began as a heuristic *distinction* between theory and practice ends by being reified into an ontological fact about the nature of knowledge and the process of knowing itself. This conflict might be said to be one of the root causes of the preference for dualisms and polarities that appear throughout the Western philosophical tradition. And by capitulating to a one-sided intellectualism or rationalism we lose the dialectical relation between embodied reasonableness and formal rationality. Condensed to a formula: 'If you genuinely know K, you should know the warranting grounds and be able to teach the principles or rules of formation of K.'[2] Anything short of evidentially justified *ratio* is 'opinion', but certainly does not deserve to be graced by the evaluative epithet 'knowledge'. Further along this road and we find the transcendental imperative of Reflection: 'If you genuinely know K, you should not only know the principles or rules of formation of K, but also the necessary "conditions of the possibility" of these principles.' You should not only be versed in the principles and rules of formation of the science of nature, but also of the *a priori* grounding conditions governing the logical possibility of natural science. Knowledge is satisfied only where it delivers the 'things themselves', the very *beings* which saturate the act of knowing.

We are tempted to say that the motivation of every transcendental project belongs on the same continuum as the Greek quest for an explicit and formalizable knowledge of the principles (*archai*), eidetic forms, and foundational structures of epistemic claims. The elision of the difference between incarnate reasonableness and formal rationality is at the root of the lure of pure reflection in all its heterogeneous manifestations. The *Critique of Pure Reason*, although asking the post-Newtonian question 'How are synthetic propositions *a priori* possible?', still shares the same logological space as Aristotle's lectures on First Philosophy with their quest for the grounding causes (*aitia*) governing the various regions of being (understood in its modern sense as scientifically determinable objectivity).

In practice of course, as we have argued throughout these chapters, this simple binary ranking proves to be too restrictive and undialectical to provide a useful cognitive metatheory; where, for instance would we place such every-day epistemic claims as:

(i) 'A has a natural ability (capacity, disposition) to do X';
(ii) 'A knows that X works, but not why';
(iii) 'A knows that X works, and why';
(iv) 'A knows *K* and knows that s/he knows';
(v) 'A cooperates with others in X-ing';
(vi) 'A knows B personally';
(vii) 'A knew that B's conduct was wrong'; and
(viii) 'Adam knew Eve'.

To compensate for the uncritical dualism dividing the domain of knowledge into *knowing-that* and *knowing-how*, some philosophers have recently added the question *knowing-who?*, which is perhaps a useful, if limited, narrative link to the category of 'praxical reflexivity'. But after further reflection it appears that 'knowing-who' is an inadequate attempt to categorize a vast range of 'intuitive knowledge' that does not fit the dichotomy of *knowing-that* and *knowing-how*. It is certainly true that the interrogation of reality in terms of *whatness* (essence) and *howness* (function) has traditionally excluded the legitimate questions of *whoness* (subjectivity). And this occlusion has major consequences for understanding the way we consider subjectivity and the rhetorics of reflection. Yet it is the unique prerogative of a reflexive being not only to be able to ask after the What and How of beings, but also to ask *Who is it?* and, self-inventively, to ask after the *Who* that is questioning. But even this supplement fails to question radically the origins and functions of the basic stratification of theoretical over practical reason implicit in this way of defining commonsense knowledge and everyday reasoning. To advance in this direction we have to abandon these high-altitude categories and return to the pheno-menological topography of experience. In the last analysis the deep-rooted philosophical prejudice against mundane reason and everyday forms of know-ledge as poor cousins of reflective intellect is only reinforced by adding further categories to the original hierarchy without deconstructing the binary oppo-sition itself. The latter deconstruction requires a critique of the constitutive hierarchies of soul/body, inner/outer, *theoria/praxis*, intellectual and manual labour as *social relations*. But to subvert the phallic hierarchy of *Theory* over *Practice* is to pursue logological reflection, moving beyond the terms of reference of this inherited way of speaking and thinking. A major advance in undermining the traditional hierarchization of theory and practice is made with the discovery of the field of praxical reflexivity.

8

PRAXICAL REFLEXIVITY

In the strictest sense, we cannot actually think about life and reality at all, because this would have to include thinking about thinking, thinking about thinking about thinking, and so *ad infinitum*. One can only attempt a rational, descriptive philosophy of the universe on the assumption that one is totally separate from it. But if you and your thoughts are part of this universe, you cannot stand outside them to describe them. This is why all philosophical and theological systems must ultimately fall apart. To 'know' reality you cannot stand outside it and define it; you must enter into it, be it, and feel it.

(Alan Watts, 1992: 103)

Building on previous chapters and the emerging theory of reflexivity as embodied 'being-in-the-world', Chapter 8 examines the field of practical consciousness as a fundamental sphere of semiopraxis (Section 1). Sections 2 and 3 are concerned with the emergence of logics of practical action in recent sociology, particularly with a form of sociological analysis usually designated as 'ethnomethodological studies'. Criticism of the programme of ethnomethodology suggests alternate ways of theorizing mundane reason linking the field of reflexivity with historical, political, and related institutional processes. The chapter is divided into six sections:

1 *Practical consciousness*
2 *Logics of practical action*
3 *Ethnoreflexivity and mundane reason*
4 *Neopraxiology: operative knowledge, techniques, skills*
5 *Institutionalized reflexivities*
6 *Conclusion: mundane thinking as reasoning practices.*

1 PRACTICAL CONSCIOUSNESS

It is one of the ironies of the history of European epistemology that idealized versions of reflection and truth have been constructed by downgrading and, occasionally, dismissing commonsense, literary and metaphoric thought, and

291

practical reflexivity as second-best epistemologies *without systematically examining the delicate organization of mundane reasoning or the history and functions of everyday reflexivities within social practices and organizations.* Orthodox theorizing sustained by a venerable tradition of reflection on the categories of *being* and *substance* has an in-built intellectualistic prejudice against common sense practices, and as a consequence the rich field of praxical reflexivity has remained, until relatively recently, an unknown and unexplored terrain. Even the expression, 'practical reflexivity' carries unfortunate connotations of 'derivative' knowledge – reproducing dualisms and hierarchies which must be abandoned to make way for a more radical assessment.

The repression of 'human doing and acting' – which also accompanies the downgrading of lived embodiment and material relations more generally in our dominant epistemologies – forms a tacit manifesto for many forms of orthodox social and philosophical theory. Traditional accounts of sociological theory, for example, are typically premised on the promissory idea that sociological reasoning will not only remedy the *doxa* of everyday agents and communities but also *replace* erroneous knowledge with the enlightened paradigms of sociological truth. As we know, the remedial motivation of nineteenth-century social thought and modern social theory was grounded in an Enlightenment vision of the progressive work of scientific cognition and a politics of state regulation. A privileged method of knowing – in the form of modern science – functioned as a norm for other belief systems and where these were found wanting they could be dismissed as irrational dogma. Yet the basic premises for this negation of everyday life went unquestioned. This phenomenon can be presented in the form of an enthymemic syllogism:

(i) theory (objective theoretical reason) must transcend the dogmas and prejudices of opinion, subjectivity, and everyday knowledge;

(ii) 'everyday knowledge' is a stock of commonsense notions, already assumed to be selective, distorting, inadequate, perspectival, subjective, and ideological ('commonsense' is synonymous with practical opinion and figuration is banished to the literary ghetto or is treated as a derivative and secondary phenomenon – at best suffered as a heuristic in the process of discovery which can then be dispensed with when the serious work of empirical description and analysis has been accomplished);

(iii) 'therefore' objective accounts of the world must avoid all contamination with common sense, metaphor, and practical reflexivity: 'objective' theory should reject, replace, or remedy commonsense knowledge and everyday social practices.

This reasoning is most evident in the tradition of classical philosophy which has, as philosophers like William James, George Herbert Mead, and John Dewey have pointed out, predefined experience in terms of its own uncritical conception of a trancendent, absolute reality. The actual complexities of experience are then devalued in the light of this preconception. In this way most philosophical programmes have systematically avoided the painstaking work that is involved in describing and recovering the concrete texture of lived experience. In certain intellectual circles this kind of dogmatism has been raised into a honorific principle, embodied in the philosopher's claim to be guided by a method of knowing that is unique to philosophical cognition and completely separated from the procedures of practical experience and the sciences (see Dewey, 1958: Preface and ch. 1 and 1952: ch.1).

The concept of reasonable 'know-how', however, suggests that a sociological study of incarnate consciousness should abandon the traditional syllogism (and with it the dualist presuppositions of Cartesian and post-Cartesian epistemology) and turn instead to the reflexive social skills, figural competences, and practices of day-to-day life, the incarnate knowings and doings tied to specific human activities and life-worlds – to what Herbert Marcuse once referred to as 'human embeddedness in nature' (1979: 29). While investigating what agents say or believe they are doing when engaged in some specific practice – focusing on the agent's own reflective responses and lay theorizing – we should also attend to what they actually *do* when engaged in a skilled activity, social practice, or cooperative enterprise. We move away from the philosophical categories of *being and knowing* toward intelligent processes of *cooperative doing and social action*. This horizon of concrete reasonableness can be expressed by the category of *praxical reflexivity*.

The Pragmatist philosopher John Dewey formulated the basic critique in his Paul Carus lectures of 1929:

> That character of everyday experience which has been most systematically ignored by philosophy is the extent to which it is saturated with the results of social intercourse and communication. Because this factor has been denied, meanings have either been denied all objective validity, or have been treated as miraculous extra-natural intrusions. If, however, language, for example, is recognized as the instrument of social cooperation and mutual participation, continuity is established between natural events and the origin and development of meanings. Mind is seen to be a function of social interactions, and to be a genuine character of natural events when these attain the stage of widest and most complex interaction with one another.
>
> (1958: xiii)

With this reorientation we see why the dogmas of Reflection lead away from a radical understanding of the embodied properties of reflexivity operative in social life. We assume that we already 'know' how some activity is concretely accomplished before examining the activity in question as a complex social accomplishment. *Hubris* about the nature of reality and knowledge forecloses a sociological investigation of the processes of everyday reality construction. By breaking the hold of the cognitivist delusion the key to the problem of consciousness might be found not in escaping from the contexts of everyday experience but by developing an enlarged vision of the quotidian field of reflexive practices as it is enmeshed in objects and forms of material embodiment.

In addition to eliciting agents' accounts or first-person reports about their practices and experience we have literally to enter into social practices and life-worlds as active participants. Of course in practice we can only do this by understanding the meanings agents ascribe to things, the culural functions of objects within social practices and, conversely, the rules governing the use of objects as media of quotidian cultural action. But these understandings and conventions are the first phase of a more radical investigation of the social organization of ongoing communicative life. The preference for methods of non-participant observation and exclusive reliance upon quantitative, decontextualized descriptions of practices must be replaced by an engaged praxical epistemology drawing its inspiration from engaging with others and learning the whys and wherefores of practices as implicit codes of practice. This comes close to the ethnographic ideal of securing a living knowledge of a culture by participating with and, as far as possible, entering the life of the subjects being investigated. We have no other recourse than to enter into the unnoticed procedures which make a routine practice precisely *mundane* and thereby *phenomenally describable* and *recoverable* 'as this practice'. The researcher must bracket his or her commonsense understandings in order to learn the ways in which other groups and cultures constitute their everyday activities and meaningful arrangements. For analytic purposes we should treat the mundane rationalities of others as topics of ethnographic interest rather than as unexplicated cognitive resources.

It is somewhat misleading to speak of a revaluation of the everyday; the mundane world of symbolic interaction has been devalued by almost every philosophical system from Plato to the present; against this work of occlusion we proceed by valorizing everyday life in its own terms; and one way of accomplishing this is by recovering the rich field of praxical alterities implicit in situated practical activities. This is the central theme of any critique of pure reflection as an ontology based on metaphors and principles which overvalue pure cognition compared to the categories of being and acting, doing and communicating. The basic argument was expressed by William James, George Herbert Mead, and John Dewey:

> the possibility of true thoughts means everywhere the possession of invaluable instruments of action ... the practical value of true ideas is thus primarily derived from the practical importance of their objects to us.
>
> (James, 1978: Lecture VI)

> Knowledge is a process in conduct that so organizes the field of action that delayed and inhibited responses may take place. The test of the success of the process of knowledge, that is, the test of truth, is found in

the discovery or reconstruction of such objects as will mediate our conflicting and checked activities and allow conduct to proceed.

(Mead, 1959: 68)

Inquiry is the controlled or directed transformation of an indeterminate situation into one that is so determinate in its constituent distinctions and relations as to convert the elements of the original situation into a unified whole.

(Dewey, cited by Margolis, 1989: 73)

Essentially the same motive underlines the contention of Antonio Gramsci that all men are philosophers in the sense that human beings – as members of a linguistically constituted species – think and act within a framework of complex, antepredicative, sedimented 'spontaneous philosophy' rooted in everyday language with its 'totality of determined notions and concepts', common-sense understandings, inferences and beliefs; further, that this incorporated knowledge is influenced by religiously mediated 'metaphysics', ideological values, and 'the entire system of beliefs, superstitions, opinions, ways of seeing things and of acting, which are collectively bundled under the name of "folklore" ' (1971: 323). Pursuing a 'philosophy of praxis', Gramsci claims that all thought and consciousness is grounded in and responsive to specific economic practices, everyday pragmatic concerns and historical situations. And therefore to make sense of 'consciousness' human self-understanding must be returned to the stream of ongoing practical life: 'efficient practice precedes the theory of it; methodologies presuppose the application of the methods, of the critical investigation of which they are the products' (Ryle, 1949: 31). Expressed more sociologically, everyday consciousness – the spontaneous philosophy of daily living – is rooted in the ideological history and major structural forces of a given society (its specific history of problematic situations, dominant modes of (re)production, power structures, symbolisms, and so on) and practical reflexivities are coded into central rhetorics, paradigms of action, and cultural self-interpretations. Societies develop explicit forms of reflection only when faced with major internal or external problems to their existence or legitimacy.

Gramsci, James, Mead, Dewey, and Ryle all in their different ways advocate widening the concept of social consciousness to include the everyday pragmatic solutions represented by beliefs and attitudes and the unconscious forms of knowledge which are no longer recognized or regarded as 'answers to questions' posed by earlier communities and civilizations. The field of consciousness then becomes coextensive with the domains of human practices and culture. Culture derives its shape and dynamics under the impress and determination of definite systems of social cooperation and exchange. Thought, therefore, is rooted in social and historical exigencies. In their different ways they all attempted to undermine the metaphysical assumptions sustaining the spectatorial view of Self and World. Consciousness is radically situated or embodied and must be understood and studied in the diverse contexts of its incarnation. The role of body relations and changing modes of embodiment now take centre stage. This is evidenced by the way in which the concept of 'the field of consciousness' appeared at roughly the same time – around 1910–30 – in the thought of philosophers such as James, Bergson, Durkheim, Simmel, Mead, Husserl, Heidegger, Lukács, Mannheim, Schutz, Gramsci, and others. Durkheim's observation on the central idea of pragmatism is relevant here:

> Whereas most theorists see thought as a mirror which receives and reflects the image of things, for pragmatists, the opposite is the case: thought becomes a part of things. It is a vital organ, and its purpose is to re-establish equilibrium in a living organism whose functioning has been disturbed.
>
> (1983: 40)

It is also exemplified in the fascination for preconceptual temporal consciousness, the social-symbolic determination of consciousness, and the language-games of generalized 'relativity' in approaching human experience by this generation of thinkers (most graphically in Mead's *The Philosophy of the Present* (1932), *Mind, Self and Society* (1934), and *The Philosophy of the Act* (1938)).

Consciousness and the institutional field of semiopraxis form a dialectical or an implicate order[1] which shapes reflexive practices in decisive ways. From the praxiological point of view human activity is constitutively knowledgeable (rule-constituted, skilled, socially organized, institutionally sanctioned, ideologically determined, and so forth) prior to explicit theorizing; objects and artifacts are integral to the processual field of human praxis and as the product of earlier acts of production they both facilitate and constrain the possibilities of human action; the contemplative notion of 'knowledge' as intellectual cognition is not the primary mode of human comportment; human beings are already temporally engaged in acting, working, and doing before they entertain the idea of a pure timeless project of reflection; 'lived knowledge', as it were, organically belongs to the sphere of human praxis: *all* social practices are symbolically mediated artful accomplishments of specific agents, cooperating in the context of particular organizations and enterprises. In short, *there is no human relationship that is not symbolically configured and linguistically mediated*. In Dewey's words, things are 'objects to be treated, used, acted upon and with, enjoyed and endured, even more than things to be known. They are things *had* before they are things cognized' (1958: 21). To talk of a person's mind 'is to talk of the person's abilities, liabilities, and inclinations to do and undergo certain sorts of things, and of the doing and undergoing of these things in the ordinary world' (Ryle, 1949: 190).

Praxial reflexivity pervades every social practice and consequently may be understood as an integral part of the instruments and artifacts of daily living (the precategorial reflexivity of our everyday knowledge is part of what Kenneth Burke once called 'equipment for living'). It is Dewey's primary world of experience as 'modes of action and undergoing' (1958: 22 – or Ryle's 'doing and undergoing'). Hence the pragmatists' conclusion: knowledge is an organon of action. Intelligent praxis develops from what Heidegger termed the world as *Zuhandenheit* (the social world being 'ready-to-hand' (*Zuhandensein*), contrasting with the *Vorhandensein* of natural things, 'present-at-hand': *es ist vorhanden*). Human being-in-the-world is articulated as a pretheoretical circumstantive absorption in activities constitutive for the 'readiness-to-hand' of a practical ensemble of equipment (1967b: 107ff.). And to some degree each community across the various dimensions of agency and self-interpretation creates its own operative epistemological field of routine work-worlds and practical assignments by means of non-thematic interpretive skills and tacit cultural procedures. Every social world has its own empire of *Vorhandenheit* (the 'extantness' and 'availability' of existing things and instruments with their particular properties and purposes), typically displayed in the stock of cultural artifacts, instruments, and technologies available. The overriding objective of these procedures is given in the 'intelligent administration of the elements of doing and suffering' (Dewey, 1958: 22). 'The self thus arises in the development of the behavior of the social form that is capable of taking the attitude of others involved in the same co-operative activity' (Mead, 1934: 335). Cognitive and intellectual activities should not now be hierarchically contrasted with everyday concerns and praxis constitutive of the life-world; traditional hierarchies of knowledge are replaced by a horizontal field of knowledge-spheres that are already preoccupied with mundane projects and coordinated social activities: the latter are all simply different, specialized forms and superstructures of semiopraxis, everyday skills, and mundane heuristics (organized about the complex of techniques with which people manage and thus understand their daily lives and enter sympathetically into one another's lives). In sum: human epistemic modalities are emergents from the prior field or 'world' of intelligent praxis, toward which they display a dialectical and reflexive relationship. In Dewey's quasi-phenomenological terminology: 'all modes of experiencing are ways in which some genuine traits of nature come to manifest realization' (1958: 24).

The knower can no longer be viewed as a disembodied spectator but needs to be approached as integrally involved in situated, worldly, social practices. The experiencer already belongs to the praxical structure of experience with all its historical and cultural preformations and material mediations. Indeed the particular modalities of knowing operative in a society are themselves cultural achievements relative to the material complexity, technological sophistication, and social organization in question. 'Knowing' is, so to speak, differentially distributed across the topography of agency and embodied activities. The different possibilities offered by the world become actualized in terms of the different forms and modalities of human engagement. There is no 'transcendent knowing' that holds the keys to the kingdom called Reality. Rather we have a complex differential space of prereflective epistemic practices correlated to specific social formations and institutions.

The same characteristics of mutability and difference extend to the identity of the knower. As Gramsci observed, the personality is strangely composite, containing elements and principles from the distant past, mythologies from prehistoric times as well as prejudices from more recent cultures, and intuitions of future possibilities (see 1971: 324). The Self is constituted from diverse reference groups and culturally specific systems of knowledge. Reflective knowledge, pursuing the maxim of ancient thought, 'know thyself', is subject to the same conditions as all knowledge:

> The starting point of critical elaboration is the consciousness of what one really is, and is 'knowing thyself' as a product of the historical process to date which has deposited in you an infinity of traces, without leaving an inventory.
>
> (1971: 324)

Consciousness and self-consciousness can thus only emerge in the practical contexts of social life, traced in the material and symbolic achievements of language and culture. In this context to transform everyday consciousness in the direction of reflexivity is to enter into a radical dialogue with the creativity of past conversations and social discourses. From this perspective, all human knowing and valuing is a dialogical process:

> If it is true that every language contains the elements of a conception of the world and of a culture, it could also be true that from anyone's language one can assess the greater or lesser complexity of his conception of the world.
>
> (1971: 325)

By exploiting the radical shift implicit in this perspective we may see that many of the heterogeneous, multivoiced activities indexed by the term 'thinking' in Chapter 7 are contextually-acquired practical, sociosemiotic skills requiring the active participation of other agents, objects, and artifacts for their successful performance. Many forms of 'thinking' are possible only as the coordinated outcome of ongoing intersubjective work. It follows that modes of reflection are also the product of taking the role of others in the conversation of gestures we call human culture. As a consequence of these praxiological insights, the critical understanding of the origins, functions, and dynamics of knowledge takes a historical and sociological turn. Where traditional philosophy models knowledge upon atemporal paradigms of Being – the specular metaphysics of representation analyzed in Part I – the sociology of praxical reflexivity requires a careful study of the situationally-embedded functions of tacit, local knowledge in specific material, social, and organizational contexts. The emphasis upon coordinated action and social context, the practical situations of skilled engagement, and the cooperative and cultural character of human activities must be preserved in a more differentiated account of the production and reproduction of epistemic practices. The ahistoricity of concepts such as 'symbolic forms', *Zuhandenheit* ('ready-to-handness' accenting the moments of 'presence' and 'utilitarian' value), the pragmatist's 'taking the role of other', or the phenomenologist's 'everyday knowledge' also need to be corrected with a more radically historical and holistic concept of cultural praxis. This is implicit in Gramsci's claim that philosophy *cannot be separated from the history of philosophy, nor can culture be separated from the history of culture.* We need to explore the taken-for-granted strategies of everyday organizations as epistemic processes involving operative intelligence, embodied knowledge, and reflexivity-in-action. And this in turn presupposes a radically *social* ontology of self and society as interactional praxis.

2 LOGICS OF PRACTICAL ACTION

It has become conventional to group the sociological investigation of practical logics or 'logics-in-action' under the general rubric 'ethnomethodological studies'. I will follow this precedent in this section while giving a more radical meaning to the expression 'ethnomethodology'. The following range of research orientations are samples from the ethnomethodological investigation of praxical 'sense-making' activities.

(i) *The reflexive properties of ordinary language in naturally occurring talk and social interaction* (investigations of the everyday semantics of self-reference, reflexive verbal rules, anaphoric reference, referential cohesion, 'shifters', pronominalization, the 'etcetera' structures of everyday speech – descriptions and characterizations, talk's self-recursive machinery of place-work, reference-work, repair-work, the pragmatics of presuppositions, and so on).

(ii) *The investigation of practical sociological reasoning* (viewing agents as practical theorists becomes ethnomethodology's central recommendation and alternative to orthodox sociology's 'cultural dopes' and all other recommendations of constructive analysis (Sudnow, ed., 1972; Douglas, ed., 1971)). In Harold Garfinkel's terminology 'the objective reality of social facts *as* an ongoing accomplishment of the concerted activities of daily life, with the ordinary, artful ways of that accomplishment being by members known, used, and taken for granted, is, for members doing sociology, a fundamental phenomenon' (for ethnomethodology this view of reflexivity constitutes both its central phenomenon for investigation and its practical resource; see Garfinkel, 1967: vii; see also Zimmerman and Pollner, 1971). The programmatic field would include everyday formulating or accounting practices and institutional systems of accountability arising from specific social situations and mundane problems (the original ethnomethodological focus on members' accounting procedures – practices of accountability, describability, reproducibility – in rendering everyday social arrangements intelligible, visible, and reportable preserved something of this focus, for example in Garfinkel's description of accounting methods, everyday categorization and decision procedures faced by jurors and other official decision-makers (in Garfinkel, 1967); see also the generalized form of this programme in the ethnomethodology of 'formulating or glossing practices' (Garfinkel and Sacks, 1970); and cf. Zimmerman and Pollner's programmatic proposal: 'the phenomenon [made available by the ethnomethodological perspective] includes as constituent features the topicalizing of the world, modes of theorizing its order, inquiries into its properties and presentations of analyses about its formulable features by whomsoever, wherever, and whenever that work is done). Social-scientific investigation is itself an integral feature of the order of affairs transformed into a phenomenon by the reduction recommended in the notion of the occasioned corpus' (1971: 99); they conclude by proposing the theme of practical sociological reasoning as the central topic of inquiry: 'we intend the notion of occasioned corpus to organize for study the various practices members employ to sustain the sense of an objective structure of social activities, a society, *exhibited from* the vantage point of particular situations' (in Douglas, ed., 1971: 99–100).

(iii) *The social construction and negotiated ordering of everyday practices and routine activities in organizational settings* (Garfinkel's studies of the artful formal structures available in members' natural language practices (1967); Bittner's study of policing methods on Skid Row (1967); Cicourel's analysis of the use of interpretive procedures in juvenile courts (1968); doctor-patient interaction; interactional uses of typifications, idealizations, and normalizing devices in the practical interpretation of the 'convict code' (Wieder, 1974); norm-displaying local activities in suicide advice centres (Sacks, 1966); procedural devices used in traffic courts as an 'occasioned corpus of setting features' (Pollner, 1974, 1987); schoolroom interaction (Mehan, 1979); the general theory of the 'occasioned corpus' in Zimmerman and Pollner, in Douglas, ed., 1971; cf. Cicourel, in Douglas, ed., 1971)).

(iv) *The situated reflexive techniques of conversational management, turn-taking, and the practical reflexivities of everyday talk as a social accomplishment of specific communities' talking praxis* (e.g. Gricean rules and maxims of conversational exchange (Grice, 1957, 1989); the study of indexical expressions (Garfinkel, 1967); Sacks' technical rules for conversational turn-taking (Sacks, 1972; Sacks, Shegloff and Jefferson, 1974)). Garfinkel and Sacks cite an interesting reflexive practice which they call 'Rose's Gloss' (after Professor Edward Rose):

On a visit to a city he has never seen before, Rose is met at the airport by his host. They are driving home when Rose [looks] out the window – which is to say that Rose, after doing [looking ahead] then does [watching something go by] by turning his head to accord with the passage of the auto. Rose's problem is to get his partner to provide him with what he has been looking at. Doing the notable particulars [looking ahead] and [watching something go by] and their serial arrangement are the crux of the matter, and make up Rose's artfulness. Continuing to do [looking out the window] Rose remarks, 'It certainly has changed'. His host may say something like, 'It was ten years before they rebuilt the block after the fire'. Rose, by having said, 'It certainly has changed', finds in the reply, and with the use of the reply, what he, Rose, was talking about in the first place. Picking that up he formulates further the concerted, sensible matter that the two parties are making happen as the recognizable, actual, plainly heard specifics in a course of conversation: 'You don't say. What did it cost?'

(Garfinkel and Sacks, 1970: Appendix)

(v) *Metalinguistic praxis and the reflexive use of commonsense knowledge in producing orderly social interaction* (the socio-logics of description in ordinary conversation (Sacks, 1963); indexical talk and its local repair work ('the unsatisifed programmatic distinction between and substitutability of objective for indexical expressions' Garfinkel, 1967: 4–7); accountability practices (Garfinkel, 1967: 1ff.); glossing practices; the strategic use of analogues, mock-ups, heuristic definitions, etc. in everyday interpretation and commonsense reasoning (for example, reformulation and respecification techniques in given organizational settings); the pragmatic uses of tacit embedded knowledge and strategic use of presuppositional understandings (Garfinkel and Sacks, 1970; Zimmerman and Wieder, 1971; Polanyi, 1967, 1973; Polanyi and Prosch, 1975; Sudnow, eds, 1972)).

(vi) *Metapragmatics* (action systems and institutions which take their own operations and action as a recursive theme – for instance in self-differentiated technical, scientific, administrative, and expert systems and related diagnostic environments (Garfinkel, Lynch, and Livingstone, 1981; Lynch, 1985)).

(vii) *Mundane reasoning and theorizing* (everyday reasoning as it is organized and distributed in naturally occurring communicative settings within different organizations concerned with establishing the 'normativity' and thus 'accountability' and 'justifiability' of practical action (ascription of beliefs, intelligence, rationality, motivational attribution, interactional negotiation, rhetorics of culpability, allocations of blame, praise, guilt, exoneration, and so forth); cf. Gumperz and Hymes, eds, 1972; Atkinson and Drew, 1979; Atkinson, 1981; Heritage, 1984: chs 5, 6)).

(viii) *Emergent institutions of practices that both facilitate and constrain inter-pretive work and translation* (the specific rules and differentiated organizations of legal, commercial, and cultural institutions for example; the writing activities of ethnographers, sociologists, anthropologists; the constructive work in producing 'official discourse' on social problems:

> The distinctive features of the alternative perspective [of ethno-methodology] ... reside in the proposal that the objective structures of social activities are to be regarded as the situated, practical accomplishments of the work through and by which the appear-ance-of-objective-structures is displayed and detected. The apparent strangeness of this perspective is due to the fact that it introduces a strange and hitherto largely unexplored domain of inquiry - the commonplace world.
>
> (Zimmerman and Pollner, 1971: 103)

(ix) *The study of the reflexive properties of everyday semiotic devices, artifacts, and codes in tactical settings and organizations* (De Certeau, 1984; Gar-finkel and Sacks, 1970 – for example, the practice they call 'certifying an event that you did not bid for': 'You are conversing with another person. The person laughs. You are momentarily surprised, for you had not meant to make a joke. In that you hear the person laugh, you smile so as to assign to the other person's laugh its feature that his laugh detected your wit, but you conceal the fact that the other person, when he laughed, furnished you an opportunity to "claim a credit" you did not seek').

(x) *The sociological study of everyday apparatuses, appliances, and techno-logies as these are practically used, modified, made intelligible, and transformed in the course of social interaction* (Bijker, et al., eds, 1987; Bijker and Law, eds, 1991; Callon and Latour, 1981; Callon, 1991; Latour, 1988, 1991, 1993; Latour and Woolgar, 1979).

3 ETHNOREFLEXIVITY AND MUNDANE REASON

A related way of dismantling the aporetic couplet 'cognitive/practical' (theory *and* practice) is by deconstructing the ranked order which places pure cogni-tion (*theoria*, intellectual knowing, objective science) at the head of reflexive action and social production (the latter understood as 'mere practice', 'ordinary talk', or 'commonsense reasoning'). This can be effected by valorizing ordinary skilled activities, social agents' dispositional knowledge, taken-for-granted assumptions operative in social orders, and 'everyday rationalities' as im-mensely complex, organized, knowledgeable semiopraxical achievements. This directive generalizes the early programme of ethnomethodology and its proposal

that the objective structures of social activities are to be regarded as the

302

situated, practical accomplishments of the work through and by which the appearance-of-objective-structures is displayed and detected. The apparent strangeness of this perspective is due to the fact that it introduces a strange and hitherto largely unexplored domain of inquiry – the commonplace world.

(Zimmerman and Pollner, 1971; cf. Garfinkel, 1967: 6–7; Mehan and Wood, 1975: chs 1, 2)

We find multifarious examples of such self-organizing phenomenal domains in the incarnate knowledge objectified in such ordinary activities of artful membership as intelligent grasping, hand-head coordination, touching, walking, speaking, interpreting, formulating, glossing, and the like; in acquiring bodily skills such as symbolic facial movements, gesture, mimetic capacities, non-verbal communication; in technical skills and work practices; and in such orchestrated performances as conversational ascriptions of motives and action, the moral work of gossiping, dancing, musical performance, acting, the ritualized arts, and so on. Social environments and fields are constructed from these reflexive practices. The clearest examples of 'incarnate reflexivity' (where 'knowledge' is inseparable from the situations of its specific display, performance, or function) occur in the virtuoso skills of musicians, the technical know-how of skilled technicians, the multifaceted skills involved in kinaesthetic arts like ballet, but also in the delicate interweaving of mutually tuned activities in everyday conduct and symbolic interaction.[2]

The study of the *artfulness* and *normativity* of reflexivity-in-action, incarnate skills, verbally mediated activities, logics-in-use (the mind-embodied holistic spheres of human praxis) and encultured practices now becomes central to a more reflexive appraisal of the importance of practical action, everyday reasoning, and the immanent causalities of knowledgeable agents in communicating with one another. The phenomenologist Alfred Schutz (1899–1959) provides a seminal description of the intersubjective prestructuration of everyday life:

Our everyday world is, from the outset, an intersubjective world of culture. It is intersubjective because we live in it as men among other men, bound to them through common influence and work, understanding others and being an object of understanding for others. It is a world of culture because, from the outset, the life-world is a universe of significations to us, i.e. a framework of meaning (*Sinnzusammenhang*) which we have to interpret, and of interrelations of meaning which we institute only through our action in this life-world. It is a world of culture also because we are always conscious of its *historicity*, which we encounter in tradition and habituality, and which is capable of being examined because the 'already-given' refers back to one's own activity or to the activity of Others, of which it is the sediment. I, the human being born into this world and naively living in it, am the centre of this world in the historical situation of my actual 'Now and Here'; I am the 'null point toward which its constitution is oriented'. That is to say, this world has significance and meaning first of all by me and for me.

(Schutz, 1967a: 133)

An important caveat should be inserted here. We should avoid postulating a single function or normative objective for 'mundane reason', just as we should avoid decontextualizing and reifying everyday life and the concerns of daily living as though these expressions referred to one central problem or kernel topic. 'Reflexivity', like 'common sense', is a collective noun for a heterogeneous spectrum of social processes ('There is not just one common sense, for that too is a product of history and a part of the historical process', in Gramsci's words (1971: 325–6)); there is not one canonical structure of Reason, but many forms and processes of practical rationality (and performative 'reasonableness'). One of the great dangers in both orthodox and interpretive sociology is to normalize social praxis by either universalizing social order (reifying it into *'the* Problem of Social Order' or by pluralizing order so that all social practices are seen as 'order fabricating/meaning constructing environments' – as we may see in some of the early work of Erving Goffman or in the exclusively normative direction taken by early ethnomethodological studies). Rather than reify social reality into a single 'commonsense world' or a given domain of 'everyday life' we should emphasize the phenomenon of divergent and heterogeneous 'normative orders' intermeshing within the interactional processes that form the historical sources of mundane reality. From the logological perspective different social orders construct their 'commonsense worlds' from ontological warrants deriving from different systems of cultural typifications and idealizations (creating the everyday symbolic equivalents of Weberian ideal-types formed 'by the one-sided accentuation of one or more points of view and by the synthesis of a great many diffuse, discrete, more or less present and occasionally absent concrete individual phenomena, which are arranged according to those one-sidedly emphasized viewpoints into a unified analytical construct' (Weber, 1948: 90)).

One of the shared limitations of classical phenomenology, American pragmatism, and early ethnomethodology lies in the tendency to overstress the ahistorical, non-temporal order-producing functions of commonsense activities and cultural typification. This tendency generates a mirror image of the atemporal models of social reality underwriting conventional sociology. We not only have an oversocialized conception of the individual and social identity, but an overrationalized conception of everyday reasoning practices and the homogeneous life of 'the everyday'. It would not be inaccurate to see this tendency as part of the inheritance of 'the problem of social order' transmitted into ethnomethodology by Garfinkel's deep interest and involvement with both Parsons' theory of the normative grounding of social action (exemplified by Parsons' *The Structure of Social Action* (1937)) and Schutzian social phenomenology (*The Phenomenology of the Social World* (1932)). The pre-theoretical *Lebenswelt* in Husserl's framework became the central topic for an expansive programme of descriptive analysis, a horizon of proliferating problematics which expanded exponentially under the explications of analytic work. And we have seen that Husserl depicted the *a priori* structures of the *Lebenswelt* as a kind of *ersatz* formation onto which the radical quest of philosophical certainty could be projected. This is what many sympathetic critics of Husserlian phenomenology see as the intrinsic limit of Husserl's last writings:

> Husserl perceived the coincidence of intuition and explication, although he failed to draw all its consequences. All phenomenology is an explication of evidence and an evidence of explication. An evidence which is explicated, an explication which unfolds evidence: such is the phenomenological experience. It is in this sense that phenomenology can be realised only as hermeneutics.
>
> (Ricoeur, 1981: 128)

Like more orthodox paradigms of sociological reasoning, normative ethnomethodology tends to project the putative invariant mechanisms of everyday action and practical interpretive accounting procedures as 'machineries' working unilaterally to secure the naturalness and intelligibility of the life-world for a given – but unspecified – community (typically a local community or some organized sector of the social world, such as the governmental spheres of law and legal settings, educational environments, policing, courts, control agencies, or bureaucratic organizations of contemporary American society). There is a related tendency to assume that the interpretive procedures which 'reflexively order' one sphere of social life will also be valid for all other spheres. 'Action' and 'members' practices' are structurally invariant irrespective of their historical settings and wider institutional contexts. In phenomenological terminology, an idealized model of mundane reasoning centred upon the solitary ego constitutes the taken-for-granted horizons of the natural attitude as an objective, rational, intersubjectively available, causal world – securing the very ordinariness and everydayness of mundane existence as an average expectable environment – the 'paramount reality of everyday life'. At the generative heart of this position we find a dualism of 'self' and 'intersubjectivity' which reproduces the ontological dualism of Cartesian metaphysics. To this extent, the 'phenomenology of the social world' remains a metaphysical project cast into sociological forms.

The project of ethnomethodology might be considered in this context as a radical attempt to overcome the lingering dualism of phenomenological sociology. Consider, for example, D. Lawrence Wieder's variation on this theme:

> The problems encountered in describing and explaining social action hinge in part on the notion that, on the one hand, there is an event in the

305

world, a social action, and on the other, another event which is the description of that action and the method of producing that description. This dualism – which is an instance of the subject-object dualism – generates the issue of the veridicality of the description and, in the context of science, the necessity of literal description. The abandonment of orthodox Cartesian dualism leads to the single phenomenon, an account-of-social-action, or an accounting-of-social action. 'Telling the code', and more critically the work of 'telling the code', is in this view a course of accounting which yields an account-of-resident-behavior which, on the occasion of constructing the account, makes that occasion, the behaviors in it, and the normative order 'behind it' observable and reportable as patterned, recurrent, and connected instances of motivated actions in socially standardized situations.

(Wieder, in Turner, ed., 1974: 144–72)

Yet it should now be apparent that this standpoint is still tied to a metaphysical *assumption* which leads its practioners to overvalue and reify actuality (figured in the categories of *in situ* 'normative order', 'organized patterns', 'recurrent orders', 'motivated actions', 'socially standardized situations', etc.), to the detriment of potentiality (an occlusion tacitly commended in the homogenizing concepts of 'everyday reality', 'mundane reason', 'common sense', and 'life-world'). The atemporality of its leading metaphysical assumption is implicit in Garfinkel's gloss: '[Ethnomethodology] is an organizational study of a member's knowledge of his ordinary affairs, of his organised enterprises, where that knowledge is treated by us as part of the same setting that it also makes orderable' (in Turner, ed., 1974: 18).

Two important features of semiopraxis are occluded in this general perspective. First, the praxical-historical contexts which structurally constrain and socially organize the temporalizing world-work of law courts, juries, policing agencies, bureaucratic administrators, scientific laboratories, etc. to take a bureaucratic interest in the production of social order. Second, the active and transformative processes of human self-reflection as agencies of change in social environments. And related to this an awareness of the *consequentiality* of human action and interaction as a medium of wider systems of power. The elision of these features of social action are connected. Making sense of the everyday functions and strategic operations of official categorization procedures also has its own background conditions – namely, the material and political interests served by such agencies and institutions (which of course, in keeping with the nominalist ontology, ethnomethodology must also treat as emergent properties of members' methods – parts of the scenic display available in members' performative command of the conventions and repertoires embedded in these settings). There is, in other words, more than one way of understanding the idea of 'situatedness' (or 'embeddedness') in admitting that all talk and social practice is situated in everyday realities and rationalities.

Social practices are also situated in the temporal configurations of power and authority which form the initial conditions of action-in-organizations (and these conditions and contexts are forever lost to a sociological vision that concentrates solely on 'the attempt to identify and explicate the workings of the methodic ways in which members collaborate to produce sense, facticity and orderliness' (Atkinson, 1981: 201–23)). Again the critical point is not that such studies are incorrect or selective in some absolutist sense, but rather that they need to be complemented and critically reformulated within the context of a more radically historical conception of social action and inquiry which does not restrict itself to the methodological stipulations of breaching experiments, audiotape transcription, and videotape analysis. We need to stand back from the particular *in situ* reflexivities that accompany and define such bureaucratic settings as 'orderly contexts' and 'normative environments' in order to thematize the dynamics of the contexts themselves. The step from ethnomethodology's normative programme to conversation analysis' concern for the sequential organization of utterances and the micropractices of talk, unless contextualized in this more radical framework of logological reflexivity, is a step away from critical social analysis.

If ethnomethodology tries to escape normative sociology (and its obsessive problematic of social order), it does so by implicitly preserving the latter's notion of 'order', but now respecified as 'members' methods for (re)producing order' or 'the world of daily life known in common with others', thereby occluding its own historical context and structural position within the power structures of American academic life and the wider formations of American society. As it stands the ethnomethodological paradigm has no resources and little incentive to reflect upon its own social context, discursive embeddedness, and ethical-political situation. Certainly we can agree that 'social order' cannot be posited as a resource in the manner of orthodox positivist sociology (and that human beings must not be treated as 'cultural dopes'), but should be studied as a topic of practical sociological reasoning in its own right. But the material structures of world-work, the social categories and instrumental organization of practical theory in the shape of the organizational constraints and forms of rationality of law courts, local state apparatuses, and corporate bureaucracies are themselves crucial parameters involved in framing the kinds of talk and practice encountered within these agencies. A sociology derived wholly from these individualist premises risks reducing its scope solely to a theory of everyday conversational activities.

A deeper ontological sense of the historicity and politics at work in such structural arrangements is absent from ethnomethodological studies (in the principled sense that these concerns are absent from the ethnomethodological understanding of 'situation' and 'embedding' which ignores class, ethnic, racial, and gendered relations and, thereby, the vast field of power relations in society). Furthermore, the basic topics of ethnomethodological interest – commonsense accounts, glossing practices, everyday classifications, membership categorization practices, and accounting talk which produce local orders of facticity, objectivity, or 'reasonableness' – are themselves not unconnected with the 'governmental' structures of reflective organizations and power/knowledge formations left unexplicated by the original programme. There is little sense that social categories and classifications have a complex discursive and cultural history. To remedy these absences we require a much more critical and reflexive theory of the politics of everyday life and the constitutive role of power and knowledge in social praxis – perhaps along the lines suggested by Foucault's theorization of discursive formations or Bourdieu's theory of practical fields ('Practical activity ... is an act of temporalization through which the agent transcends the immediate present via practical mobilization of the past and practical anticipation of the future inscribed in the present in a state of objective potentiality ... habitus temporalizes itself in the very act through which it is realized' (1992: 138)).

Ethnomethodological reflection upon the world-work of practical social theorists, in other words, has no place for the critical anatomy of social organizations, the societal genealogy of discourses, or the microphysics of power. As a consequence of these absences, there is little appreciation of the material and symbolic vicissitudes of the self – and the polemical processes which mediate 'self and society' in the institutional order. Because of these weaknesses ethnomethodology cannot adequately fulfil its self-appointed role as a social 'neopraxiology' (cf. Garfinkel in Turner, ed., 1974: 18). Once again Wieder's concluding paragraph is illuminating as a revealing display of the analytical orientation of ethnomethodological reflection:

> Accountings-of-social-action, for example, 'telling and hearing the code', are methods of giving and receiving embedded instructions for seeing and describing a social order. The interpersonal existence of social orders and their availability to perception and description is the achievement of the various methods entailed in an accounting-of-social action.
> (Wieder, in Turner, ed., 1974: 172)[3]

Garfinkel's recent formulation of the theme of social order in the ethnomethodological programme is also instructive: 'Professional sociology and ethnomethodology agree that the animal they are hunting is the production and the accountability of order* [asterisked terms index topics subject to ethnomethodological scrutiny] in and as immortal, ordinary society.' Ethnomethodological analysis strives to

> show for ordinary society's substantive events, in material contents, just and only in any actual case, that and just how vulgarly competent members concert their activities to produce and show, exhibit, make observably the case*, demonstrate, and so on, coherence, cogency, analysis, detail, structure, consistency, order, meaning, mistakes, errors, coincidence, facticity, reason, methods – locally, reflexively, naturally

308

accountable phenomena – in and as of the haecceities of their ordinary lives together.[4]

4 NEOPRAXIOLOGY: OPERATIVE KNOWLEDGE, TECHNIQUES, SKILLS

Men can be distinguished from animals by consciousness, by religion, or anything else you like. They themselves begin to distinguish themselves from animals as soon as they begin to produce their means of subsistence, a step which is conditioned by their physical organization. By producing their means of subsistence men are indirectly producing their actual material life.

(Karl Marx and Friedrich Engels, in McLellan, ed., 1977: 160)

Philosophers often claim that human beings are unique in using tools reflexively: while many animals utilize tools, human beings use tools to build tools, constructing complex networks in which the human body is hooked up to machines, and finally, even allow tools to take over and transform tasks previously considered to be unique to human beings. For example, human inventiveness produces knowledge-intensive tools (knowledge-processing tools such as the alphabet, print, electronically processed information) which are then used to transform social arrangements. But the functions and applications of these instruments are decisively shaped by the material environment and structural constraints within a given social order. The technopoeisis hypothesis suggests that it is technological formations which shape the diverse forms of human agency and social structures. It also suggests a further respecification of reflexivity which would principally include not only traditional references to consciousness and knowledgeable 'practical action' but also the social and technological media, occupational artifacts, and technosocial embodiments of self-monitoring techniques in the contexts of everyday interaction. These are symbolic formations that provide the operative contexts for members' reflexive talk, 'glossing practices', and artful interaction.

This perspective might be termed 'neopraxiology' given the importance played by a diverse range of human techniques and technologies in shaping the field of praxis. The complex history of the invention and application of technologically extended powers would thus be inseparable from socioeconomic and cultural history. In Marx's words:

The question whether objective truth can be attributed to human thinking is not a question of theory but is a *practical* question. Man must prove the truth, i.e. the reality and the power, the this-worldliness of his thinking, in practice.

(in McLellan, ed., 1977: 156)

In a more generalized praxiology forms of practical consciousness and tacit knowledge are typically sedimented around pragmatic concerns with the production and reproduction of social life. They form part of the immanent 'logic' of a practice, its operative 'sense' as 'just this practice', evolved for 'just these particular problems and goals'. In this sense the operative technologies of everyday life also tend to become 'seen-but-unnoticed' phenomena. Consider the role of replicability in apprenticeship learning (Bensman and Lilienfeld, 1973). Here, above all, the truth or 'validity' of a practice is demonstrated *in concerted activities*. Apprenticeship is learning carried out in a rich context of relevant objects, traditional techniques, work technologies, and locally negotiated objectives; hence the criterion for the successful acquisition of practical skills is not usually whether an individual can reflectively verbalize craft knowledge or technical 'know-how' (formal examinations to elicit such 'knowledge' are a relatively late cultural invention), but whether the apprentice can 'go on' and perform the knowledge in future enactments judged by relevant peers; craft traditions are not primarily reproduced by formal tuition, but through the praxical transmission of embedded skills *in situ* (illuminating instances of reflexivity-in-action are the way in which London taxi-drivers build up a detailed 'kinaesthetic map' of the road system of the city – acquiring 'the Knowledge' through essentially practical, orientational strategies, the incarnate 'zen' skills involved in archery (Herrigel, 1953, 1960), motorcycle maintenance (Pirsig, 1974), physical description (Zukav, 1979), moral judgement, the learning experiences of skilled wine tasters, mechanical *bricolage* (Harper, 1986), and even walking (Ryave and Schenkein, in Turner, ed., 1974). These prereflective criteria may be generalized across the whole field of skilled social practices (cf. Bourdieu on the logics of practical action as the *logos* of tacit world construction and practical reflection).

As pragmatic engagements and self-monitoring judgements determine the shape of everyday knowledge and its institutionalization the criteria governing practices are overwhelmingly context-dependent and pragmatic (does it work?), task-centred (what are the objectives?), tacit ('business as usual'), and subject to local standards of *in situ* calculability and precision. In a given society there will be many different craft traditions and apprenticeship institutions with their different criterial 'discourses' coexisting in the same cultural space (to say nothing of the many different ways of appropriating and interpreting belief systems, moral norms, discourses, and knowledge by different groups and communities). These embodied craft skills are, of course, stripped away with the development of the social relations of capitalist production (cf. Marx, 'The fetishism of commodities and the secret thereof', in 1961a, 1953). But even the dynamics of alienated labour, the extraction and circulation of capital presupposes a larger background of praxiological fields.

The vicissitudes of the self in relation to dominant forms of economic and political power points to a generalized theory of praxial experience. This appears to be close to what Bourdieu has called a theory of social fields. This richer account of embedded knowledge implicit in daily life activities raises acute problems for the descriptive analysis of human action; a frame-by-frame decomposition of human praxis and its underlying rules falsifies the temporal, performative, and negotiated characteristics of emergent social arrangements (just as an analytic disaggregation of a musical performance breaking the flow of the sound into its individual elements and 'grammar' destroys the integrity of the phenomena we experience in listening to music). Analysis always incurs the danger not only of context-stripping activities in order to focus upon them in detail – as it were under the microscope of abstraction and isolation; but also more seriously, of taking skilled performances out of their historical contexts and temporal settings, isolating them from the stream of life which grants them whatever intelligibility they may possess. But these decontextualizing 'disembedding' operations are the routine occupational concomitants of unreflexive approaches to description and inquiry (as we have observed they are routinely and systematically enforced in the capitalist organization of work in assembly-line, Fordist production systems).

We can illustrate these points by means of the causality experienced by the living body in cooperative social action – for example, a child participating in a game with others. Here the child's body is not governed solely by environmental stimuli, but proximally by corporeal intentions observable as intelligible forms of self-orientation, motivation, and volition (habits or sets of habits); the skilful coordination of hand and eye toward a game-object (a ball for example) might be considered as the prototypical situation of corporeal intentionality operative in the child's field of action. Children become members of cooperative communities by participating in the operative schemata of organized games. The problem is not one of abstractly representing the structure of the game, but rather how to produce a convincing performance as a competent participant – how to incorporate the rules of the game in real-time performances without standing out as a novitiate or outsider. Here the mutual orchestration of kinaesthetic skills, of interweaving bodies-in-motion coordinating complex vectors of action provides a useful model for incarnate praxis: not a superintendent Ego moving an inert body or organ toward an object, but the embodied self moving purposefully and intelligently in a causal field of meaningful objects and interpersonal formats. Activities are animated by interests, directed by the enjoyment of the game, by localized pleasures and mobile awareness. But they also probe the limits and tensions of existing practices, transgress existing rules, and anticipate new forms of life.

Moreover the continuous exercise of these unnoticed corporeal experiments *with others* leads to the emergence of a socially significant topography, a structure of known *places* which precedes further abstract operations in time-space. In this way socially organized body schemata and normative forms of spatiality develop together and are integrated into higher-order reflexive dispositions and action systems. Often these systems 'congeal' to form the conditions of further courses of interaction. More significantly, experiential knowledge gained in such spatializing-temporalizing games can be called upon in subsequent conceptual and social learning. It appears that not only are the child's corporeal skills extensively differentiated and intensively developed through semiopraxis, but that the social ordering of place and temporality is cooperatively constituted by mutually coordinated kinaesthetic systems. In training and coordinating the bodies of others the game-rules symbolically reproduce definite spatiotemporal environments. And these structural formations operate without any explicit consciousness or self-reflection on the part of participants. Spatialization, coordination, and temporalization, as it were, inhere in the operative awareness-forms of rule-governed *social* activities. In developing a concrete sense of place individuals indirectly and unintentionally produce particular places of sense.

We can summarize this important point as follows: human beings artfully utilize the body-sensorium as a locus of operative or tacit knowledge. But this 'knowledge' is not superadded to the social form of interaction; in essence it is the performative logic of coordinated interaction. The knowledgeable lived body cooperating with other selves and their comparable corporeal dispositions is the paradigmatic instrument of human praxis. 'The postural model of the body is not the sum of optic kinesthetic and tactile sensations. It is an integration' (Schilder, 1951: 58). 'Analysis of the problem of the bodily scheme is incomplete if we do not appreciate the importance that motility has for the perception of our body' (Schilder, 1951: 62). The emergent field of relational action is naturally subjected to lengthy periods of elaboration and apprenticeship influenced by many levels of social, psychological, and cultural structuration (the colonization of place-time manifolds is thus not neutral *vis-à-vis* a culture's cultural codes and moral practices; different groups and communities inhabit space and time in culturally variable ways: cultures appraise and evaluate specific gestural and performance systems differentially). Prior to the grasp of consciousness we discover the anonymous, praxical operations of the postural body (the 'body schema' or rather the human body as a power of schematizing the world) or what we have earlier called the phantasmal body in its local kinaesthetic, social, and imaginary functions.

The elegance of a perfectly performed dance sequence or musical event suggests better analogies for personal and societal embodiment than the image of the isolated subject dispassionately representing the furniture of the world or 'members' verbally 'accounting' for their order-reproducing practices. Durkheim offers the example of 'a pianist who can play a given piece perfectly' who will make mistakes 'if he thinks about what he is doing'. Here consciousness obstructs action (1983: 79). Or consider the mutuality of dance. Dancing typically orchestrates different spheres of bodily movement, whereas the world of dance viewed by a spectator appears like a field of choreographed rules or objectified set sequences. In genetic terms, no child enters the sociocultural world of games by formal instruction, just as few adults acquire the art of dance or musical performance by algorithmic instruction. We return, once more, to the fundamental importance of negotiated dialogical understanding which antedates and makes 'rule learning' and 'rule application' possible. The unnoticed realms of existential dialogue – the concrete conversations of everyday life – antedate the realm of rules and explicit programmes of self-reflection.

5 INSTITUTIONALIZED REFLEXIVITIES

These simple phenomenological observations corroborate an important logological principle which was introduced without discussion or critical exposition in the introductory chapter to this work – that becoming reflexive is a long and complex socialization process decisively shaped by the institutional order of social practices and historically available techniques of self-understanding. We referred to this point of view as the *technopoiesis hypothesis* in order to underline the fact that technosocial systems are embedded in local practices and social relations. In essence this is Marx's reminder drawn from an analysis of the totalizing nature of the labour process in capitalist society:

> So the general character of the whole movement is a social one; as society produces man as man, so it is produced by man ... The human significance of nature is only available to social man; for only to social man is nature available as a bond with other men, as the basis of his own existence for others and theirs for him, and as the vital element in human reality; only to social man is nature the foundation of his own human existence.
>
> (Marx, in McLellan, ed., 1977: 90)

One methodological consequence of this principle is that a full understanding of the historical modalities of self-reflection and reflexive experience can only be gained by examining their conditions of existence, namely the sociohistorical construction of selfhood as individuals are embedded in definite technical systems, institutional processes, and forms of life. And, further, that the precise temporal and spatial *modalities* of institutional embodiment – the dialectics of institutionalization and the organized work of symbolic self-interpretation – are subject to social change and historical transformation.

Once modes of self-consciousness have been embedded (or consciously and organizationally 'disembedded') in institutional systems they are capable of following a course independent of their original creators and purposes, to some degree pursuing their own logic and development. Techniques and materialized reflexivity – tools, techniques, capital – are 'stored-up labour', congealed 'general intellect'. As 'forces of production' these structural conditions exert a constraining effect upon patterns of power and authority. The emergence of coordinating mechanisms such as property laws, labour markets, or categories of value have a decisive impact upon the social organization of a given society and its dominant modes of subjectivity. In Foucault's formula: the individual

313

is the product of power. Yet social arrangements act dialectically within the field of action they create and deform:

> The way in which men produce their means of subsistence depends first of all on the nature of the actual means of subsistence they find in existence and have to reproduce. This mode of production must not be considered simply as being the production of the physical existence of the individuals. Rather it is a definite form of activity of these individuals, a definite form of expressing their life, a definite mode of life on their part. As individuals express their life, so they are. What they are, therefore, coincides with their production, both with *what* they produce and with *how* they produce. The nature of individuals thus depends on the material conditions determining their production.
>
> (Karl Marx, in D. McLellan, ed., 1977: 161)

Defining the field of consciousness as a semiopraxical formation lends support to neither metaphysical idealism nor metaphysical materialism; rather the perspective shows that consciousness arises as part of the history of the material means and instrument of production; as 'socialized nature' embodied consciousness transcends the dichotomy of mind and matter by means of the concept of incarnate reflexivity and its performative objectifications. In a formula, self and society are mutually constitutive in the differential field of semiopraxis. Mind and body are active partners in the creative extension of 'instruments of production' rather than the terms of a visual relation. This is a useful point to underscore the praxiological concepts of the *instruments* and *institutions of reflexivity*, concepts designed to facilitate a comparative, sociocultural investigation of empirical processes of practical institutionalization, symbolic codification, and cultural structuration of social action. Dewey sketches a related constructivist perspective:

> The invention and use of tools have played a large part in consolidating meanings, because a tool is a thing used as means to consequences ... It is intrinsically relational, anticipatory, predictive. Without reference to the absent, or 'transcendence', nothing is a tool. The most convincing evidence that animals do not 'think' is found in the fact that they have no tools, but depend upon their own relatively-fixed bodily structures to effect results. Because of such dependence they have no way of distinguishing the immediate existence of anything from its potential efficiencies; no way of projecting its consequences to define a nature or essence ... As to be a tool, or to be used as means for consequences, is to have and to endow with meaning, language, being the tool of tools, is the cherishing mother of all significance.
>
> (1958: 185–6)

A related logological principle is that the study of the development of self-consciousness and self-understanding requires an archaeology of the mediated forms of human interaction, particularly of artifacts and objects which embody reflexive properties ('knowledge-intensive' techniques, 'mind machines', information technologies, etc. – what Marx called 'forces of production'). After making the praxiological turn we can no longer approach the question of reflexivity as if it were solely an ahistorical problem of epistemology: 'For other instrumentalities and agencies, the things usually thought of as appliances, agencies and furnishings, can originate and develop only in social groups made possible by language. Things become tools ceremonially and institutionally' (Dewey, 1958: 186). The radical implication of this theory is that the grammar of self-awareness, consciousness, and self-consciousness is subject to processes of social construction and has a definite historical relativity, emerging quite recently – in Europe around the sixteenth century – as problems, and therefore the explanation of this variability should now be framed in sociotechnical and praxical terms. Consciousness and self-consciousness stand in a dialectical relationship to material, institutional, and cultural systems:

> If the real differences between the human being and the animal lies in the multiple aspects of man's essence and powers in contrast to the unilateral activity and life-potential that cages in the animal, then the subject's multiplicity is reflected in the variety and range of pictures obtained from objects. The image of an object obtained by an animal, probably after many trials and experiences, is the exclusive expression of a uniform nature, of typical needs and apperceptions, and, therefore, of a typical relation to given things. Man, however, is a manifold being, which means that his relation to things is presented in the multiplicity of modes of perception in each individual, in the entanglement of each individual in more than just a single series of interests and concepts, of images and meanings. Thus, for man, the object is not only a desired one, but is one of theoretical understanding, of aesthetic evaluation, and of religious meaning.[5]

6 CONCLUSION: MUNDANE THINKING AS REASONING PRACTICES

We have seen that the seminal programme of ethnomethodological studies initiated and described by Harold Garfinkel and his students commends the study of mundane reasoning practices as explicable, organized reflexive phenomena in their own right. Consider the gloss given by Michael Lynch, Eric Livingstone, and Harold Garfinkel on the presuppositions and implications of such praxiological studies:

> In each of the studies there is a unique preoccupation with local production and with the worldly observability of reasoning. This means that reasoning is displayed in the midst of orders of intersubjectively accountable details: the order of spoken utterances by different parties

in conversation, the compositional order of manipulated materials at the laboratory bench, or the transitive order of written materials on a page of text. Ethnomethodological studies attempt to elucidate these structures in reference to their use as worldly domains of 'consciousness'; as mnemonics, temporal 'states' of reasoned projects, and as observable courses of directed bodily movement. One is confronted with streams of embodied action simultaneously identified with 'material' arrangements and rearrangements accomplished by one or more parties to the respective discipline. This provides an entirely different basis for analytically elucidating reasoning practices than would be the case when reasoning is conceived as a stream of consciousness in exclusively 'private experience'.

(Lynch, Livingstone and Garfinkel, in Knorr-Cetina and
Mulkay, eds, 1983: 205–38)

By analogy with the concept of mundane reason and keeping in mind the intrinsic heterogeneity of everyday social practices we can respecify the concept of 'mundane thinking' as the indigenous heuristics, strategies, procedures and rationales used by agents in the course of everyday social activities (cf. Pollner, 1987). Just as there is no unitary, ahistorical everyday life, so we cannot assume that one homogeneous form of mundane thinking can be isolated and ascribed to every form of society. It is safer to assume that quotidian epistemic practices are diverse, local accomplishments, varying considerably within and across cultural contexts and organizational singularities. We must also stop thinking that we already know what constitutes 'ordinary thinking' and turn instead to the real-time experiences and diverse practices constituting the *objects* of different regions of societal praxis.

The sphere of mundane thinking is simply another instance in a wider logological field. Although this is not the appropriate place to argue the case in detail and provide supporting empirical documentation I will later show that quotidian thinking is best addressed using the resources of logological concepts, particularly those drawn from *rhetoric, discourse heuristics, narrative logic*, and the *pragmatic socio-logics of situated accounting practices* (the heuristics, pragmatics, and semantics of thinking-together include competences of the following order: congitive mapping, associative coupling or linking, associative networking, persuasive use of synecdoche, metonymy, metaphor, etc., analogical extrapolation and generalization, ludic framing and reframing, pattern completion (totalizing, Gestalt-coding), conjectural accounting, guesswork, speculation, transcending 'the given', documentary interpretation, retrospection and counterfactual reasoning, storytelling, narrativization, narrative organization, the artful heuristics of *ceteris paribus* reasoning, protomodelling, dramatization, personification (animism, anthropomorphism), and so forth. Examples of these sense-making strategies can be found in the contexts of everyday conversation and political experience prior to the projects of pure reason.

These are some of the directions an enlarged phenomenology of human experience might take once divested of its traditional epistemological and ontological presuppositions. The analysis of symbolic capital developed by Pierre Bourdieu and Calvin O. Schrag's programmatic hermeneutics of everyday life offer important pointers for such investigations:

> An adequate sociology, at once structural and genetic, of language presupposes that we theoretically found and empirically restore the unity of human practices, of which linguistic practices are but one figure, so as to take as its object the relation that unites structured systems of sociologically pertinent linguistic differences to similarly structured systems of social differences.
>
> (Bourdieu, 1992: 149)

> The human sciences as well as the philosophical study of man have their origin neither in a purified region of abstract conceptualization nor in an inchoate, disarrayed succession of sensory facts. Constellations of sense and significance are already established and already understood in the workaday world of practical projects and everyday discourse. The *logos* is already at work in lived experience.
>
> (Schrag, 1980: 65)

9

PHRONETIC REFLEXIVITY: BETWEEN MORALITY AND PRAXIS

What we ought to do depends largely on what we ought to believe, and in all matters other than the basic needs of our nature our opinions govern our actions.

(Jean-Jacques Rousseau, 1979: 49)

Chapter 9 might be subtitled 'Moral reflexivity and practical reason', given its substantive focus upon the role of self-reflection and self-understanding in the context of practical and moral judgement in everyday life. I use the generic expression 'phronetic reflection' for the whole field of moral and ethical self-reflection. The chapter is divided into six sections:

1 *Introduction*
2 *Phronetic reflection*
3 *The concept of judgement*
4 *Moral self-reflection*
5 *Moral relativity*
6 *Dramatic reflection*

1 INTRODUCTION

What is called judgement, in virtue of which men are said to 'be sympathetic judges' and to 'have judgement' is the right discrimination of the equitable.

(Aristotle, *Nicomachean Ethics* 1143a 19–20)

If we follow everyday usage, reflexion often appears in the context of making and utilizing considered judgements. Even without a great deal of historical and philosophical justification it appears that the emergence of something like 'critical judgement' is only possible in acts of critical discrimination which are found distributed across a diverse range of discursive practices and institutions. But thinking in terms of 'judgement' rather than 'reflection' is not, as it stands, an immediate solution to the question concerning reflexive experience – we must still ask the question: how is deliberative judgement possible as a normative activity? What kind of axiological context is presupposed by acts of informed, critical judgement? How should we explain the untroubled production of valid judgements by human beings thinking and acting without recourse to explicit rules, algorithms, or public canons – how to make sense of the unprecedented, but relatively unnoticed, ability to deliver complex resolutions 'on the wing'. A theory of phronetic reflexivity, therefore, should begin with the role of judgement in the practical and moral activities of everyday life.

2 PHRONETIC REFLECTION

Political wisdom and practical wisdom are the same state of mind, but their essence is not the same. Of the wisdom concerned with the city, the practical wisdom which plays a controlling part is legislative wisdom, while that which is related to this as particulars to their universal is known by general name 'political wisdom'; this has to do with action and deliberation.

(Aristotle, *Nicomachean Ethics* 1141b 23ff.)

In ordinary life we typically resort to practical reflection when blocked by an obstacle or resistance to our projects. To paraphrase Wittgenstein, to imagine different kinds of practical judgement means to imagine different forms of life – or at least, different practices which are not rigorously hedged by social rules or formally articulated canons. Our routine evaluations, avowals, appraisals, and discriminatory acts are relative to cultural criteria of success and failure, right and wrong, beautiful and ugly, praiseworthiness or blameworthiness which, for the main part, are left unspoken. Moreover we only learn to make such intuitive judgements by actively *participating* in real-world language-games and social practices. Here 'judgement' is shorthand for a wide range of consequential social acts and modes of interaction. In general we can say that the different modes of quotidian judgement – moral, aesthetic, practical, etc. – are anchored in the pragmatic relevances which inform different forms of life. Or as we have been taught to say today, they frame diverse kinds of knowledge *embedded* in social institutions. And as such these judgement forms are subject to rhetorical structuration and social negotiation. Indeed the terms and objectives of our everyday appraisal vocabularies and beliefs are so many projected 'goods' linked to specifically valued action contexts – and, as Rousseau observed, we live primarily within the ambience of our beliefs or what we think we *ought* to believe. But most of these 'beliefs' habitually accompany social practices and for members of a community are effectively unconscious. Where the objects of beliefs are verbalized 'goods' and rhetorically mediated 'desirables', we can say that intuitive normativity pervades the fabric of everyday talk and social interaction.

When puzzled we 'stop, attend, and reflect'; when we lose our way we backtrack and start again; before making a difficult decision we seek the advice of someone wiser in such matters, we 'consider', 'mull over', 'deliberate on', and 'ponder' questions and options. We surrender to the forked paths of inner conversation, running over in phantasy the possible courses of action open to us. We present ourselves as 'reflective individuals', persons who think things over before acting. We wish to appear in social settings as deliberative agents who act – as we tell ourselves – from the principled grounds of good reasons. Some philosophers have claimed that 'practical judgement' (for example, the sequences of practical syllogisms embodied in trains of social action) is already implicit in our practices: human agency is quite literally organized into orderly sequences of situational judgements carried out during the course of day-to-day concerted activities. In such contexts reflection involves pretheoretical disengagement, prerational deliberation terminating in a more effective definition of the situation. The outcome of practical judgement is gauged by a more successful form of praxis: 'Now we can go on', in Wittgenstein's phrase. Being close to what the Greek philosophers called *phronesis* (and also to what Hegel termed *nachdenken*) we can call this wide spectrum of mundane intelligence, *phronetic reflexivity*. Let us consider some features of reflection considered as *phronesis*.

Phronetic reflection temporarily disengages the self from practical action; the actor 'steps back' or 'refrains' from action: the 'loop' hesitation creates is one in which alternatives can be weighed, principles discussed, means and ends communicatively reviewed, advice sought, problems considered from other angles, and anxieties crystallized after being 'slept on'. What is not in view in such acts of *nachdenken*, however, is the creation of a 'science' of action. Like moral deliberation *phronesis* is an *in situ* praxiological art. In general terms it does not aim at an abstract or formal understanding of everyday life. But it does involve a moment of judgemental analysis wider than the know-how embodied in technical rules and procedures: we break a larger problem into more manageable parts, assemble more evidence, take a more discriminating view of things, gain 'perspective' to see things in their full complexity, exercise discretion by bending the rules. These operations are typically carried out in dialogic situations involving self-monitoring, self-correcting, and self-directing practices. This is one of the fundamental rationales of cooperative discussion of a problem situation.

Strategically, *phronesis* has its roots in appraisal situations in ordinary activities, discourse, and cooperative social projects. Phronetic reflection typically involves reflexive communication in conditions of uncertainty and contingency (precisely the kind of context characterizing the larger part of human affairs – most graphically in non-dilemmatic moral and ethical situations). Such contexts are inherently more complex and ambiguous than the 'possible worlds' projected by the reconstructed logics of algorithmic reasoning. Unlike the invented situations of technical reason they are typically the practical scenarios of cooperative social interaction. Considered judgement is called for in situations where a number of alternative choices, decisions, or interpretations are equally possible or justifiable – where different objectives, for example, present equally strong claims or where different moral demands are interpreted as genuine choices of the self (for analytical purposes we can distinguish between aesthetic, ethical, and epistemic phronesis). We exercise *phronesis* in contexts that are not algorithmically decidable or technically resolvable, where we cannot come to a resolution of problems by mechanically applying maxims of formal reasoning, but must appraise particular situations in balanced and 'reasonable' ways, the outcome of judgement being always open to respecification and revision as contexts change. In many cases both the universal (general rules) and the particular (concrete situation) are subject to negotiation and reformulation. The inevitable disparity between available *rules* and emergent *situations* provides the immediate occasion of phronetic reflection (and, not accidentally, phronetic conflicts are often important sources of aesthetic, ethical, and epistemological change).

Some of the central features of phronetic reflexivity were first explored by Aristotle in the third Book of the *Nicomachean Ethics*, especially the analysis of practical reasoning and its relationship to *techne* and theoretical knowledge. The author of that text writes that

> every class of men deliberate about the things that can be done by their own efforts. And in the case of exact and self-contained sciences there is no deliberation, e.g. about the letters of the alphabet ... Deliberation is concerned with things that happen in a certain way for the most part, but in which the event is obscure, and with things in which it is indeterminate. We call in others to aid us in deliberation on important questions, distrusting ourselves as not being equal to deciding.
>
> (*Nicomachean Ethics* 3.3.112b 1–10)

Since one paradigmatic situation of undecidability and conflicting interpretation is that of judgements made in forensic contexts, the species of judgement we call *forensic* deliberation may serve as a general model. In fact the adjective 'forensic', from the Latin *forensis*, 'pertaining to the forum' or public assemblies and law courts, proves to be a useful model for practical reasoning in extra-legal contexts. It confirms our previous analysis of the normative, circumstantial, and intersubjective processes of discursive reasonableness in everyday life. Forensic judgements presuppose a concrete *locus* of prudential argumentation, definite interlocutors in well-defined social roles, the powerful medium of oratory, and, more generally, the ritualized interaction of rhetorical performances in a pregiven tradition of discourse. Forensic judgement represents an attempt to balance the idealized claims of universality (the quest for an algorithm that would encompass every concrete situation and the legitimate demands of particularity (the irreducible *haecceity* or 'concreteness' of a given case or application of judgmental rules). The metaphor of a forensic discourse matrix thus provides a useful model for the interlaced practical competences, rhetorical skills, everyday knowledge, and social functions of discourse institutions more generally. The metaphor of a discussion *forum* directs analysis away from decontextualized images of pure reasoning toward situational models of dialogic reasoning – the forum being a practical site of dialectical discourse, ideally an assembly of all citizen speakers – in Roman legal theory, the site where the isolated Ego gains the status of a judicial *persona* – and by implication a theatre of commitment, decisiveness, responsibility, and engaged judgement. Thus by analogy *forensic medicine* – involving the intelligent application of semiotic skills and practical reasoning in a specific phronetic context – is a 'science' relating both analytic and synthetic diagnoses to their legal consequences – hence justifying its role as an indispensable part of medical jurisprudence.

We are now in a better position to compare the situated reasonableness of forensic judgement with formal models of rationality. As formalist models the latter project an image of human conduct measured by the rationalist criteria of mechanical rule-following behaviour, typically imagined as a decontextualized 'world' of minimal sociality and material relations. This is the realm of anonymous sociality, the 'generalized Other' which informs many traditions of social theory. By contrast, concrete forensic rationality involves the situated *use* of rules and maxims as multidimensional resources of empirical judgement (two ideal-typical situations being legal adjudication and competent medical judgement in forensic contexts). The paradigmatic schema of occasioned judgement thus stresses the creative, context-specific application of background knowledge and operative rules to generate reasonable outcomes in particular cases and circumstances. The invocation of 'rules' in this context is closer to processes of flexible rule-interpretation, rule-making, and rule-negotiation than to clear-cut situations in which the mechanical 'subsumption' of particulars beneath universal generalities provides a universal decision procedure. How can this model deepen our understanding of reflexivity?

First, we are directed to the social contexts and praxical criteria of skilled arbitration and decision-making in contexts where there are no algorithmic formulae or abstract decision procedures. Typically such situations are found in the everyday judgemental contexts of social transactions. Second, membership of such forensic institutions involves an intensive training in the relevant practices of judgement: acquiring the background knowledge and experience relevant to specific adjudication spheres (commercial law, civil law, law of torts, criminal procedure, etc.), social skills presupposed by the institutional rules of debate and investigative procedure, and most important of all, rhetorical skills necessary creatively to perform and innovate within existing adjudicative organizations. In principle there is no trans-disciplinary set of rules or standards that would enable an individual to function appropriately across these judgemental spheres. Full participating in forensic institutions, in other words, presupposes a lengthy socialization into the 'form of the personal' correlated with specific adjudicative praxes. And the evolution of professional fields resembles the creation of distinctive forms of life (and rational procedure). Third, in this context 'judgement' is no longer a disposition or innate capacity of the isolated individual, but an educated, cultural faculty embedded in the social contexts of informed decision-making; skilled appraisal involves mediated learning, social training, and practical intelligence as well as a sense for the contingencies and flexible particularities of social and moral life. Fourth, each disciplinary or professional institution of reflexivity projects an idealized version of selfhood in the form of ideal types of 'active' membership for their practitioners and of 'audiences' for their respective activities. In practice, of course, the socializing and evaluative work of organizations are intertwined in the day-to-day work specific to an operative field. In this way organizations both produce adjudicative outcomes while at the same time reproducing their particular organizational form. Finally, the praxical 'making' of warranted judgements is a complex function of historical contexts which form an integral part of the *haecceities* of adjudicative semiopraxis (and these contexts change historically). Judgement is a defeasible outcome of competing versions of the truth, multiple claims and counterclaims, a plurality of 'possible worlds'. Of course, the most concrete sense of 'history' is the temporal constraints in becoming a member of a phronetic community – the existential and intellectual work involved in 'becoming a physician', for example, as a sociological paradigm for the acquisition of definite systems of knowledges, techniques, and operative vocabularies: the skilled doctor being one whose technical knowledge integrates the duality of experiential and reflective judgement. Phronetic models of experiential judgement help us reconcile the 'reasoned' nature of skilled appraisal contexts with the ever-present possibility of contestation (the currently accepted paradigms of medical judgement are contestable and change under the pressure of ongoing practice and 'research programmes'). *Phronesis*, in a phrase, is reflexivity which preserves the spirit of *différance* in the face of the lure of abstract universality.

The hermeneutical reasonableness of medical diagnosis provides another exemplary case of praxical reflexivity in a context of competing claims and adjudicative rationales. 'Rational diagnosis' in a situation of *relative indeterminancy* fosters judgements which are neither analytic nor synthetic propositions. Yet medical statements are grounded in and responsive to warrantable evidence: subregimes involving the compilation of symptoms and alternate sources of 'evidence', the confirmation of hypothesis by speaking with and listening to the patient, the trial-and-error method of 'testing' a hypothesis by observing the course of treatment, the recourse to 'second opinions', resort to the norm of concerted judgement, and so on. And while such judgements are eternally *defeasible*, the style of 'triangulated' rationality involving a cluster of related criteria produces appraisals anchored in 'good reasons' and 'sustaining evidence'. Forensic and medical training may even be understood as a moral education in the kinds of practices and styles of judgement that encourage a flexible use of 'polymorphic' judgemental skills in grounding decisions or adjudications. Instead of thinking of *rules* of warranted assertability and universal *standards* as decision procedures imposed from on high, we should think in terms of maxims and strategies or even different *styles* of judgement relevant to particular institutional settings and *intuitive scenarios*.

By analogy with the complex dimensions and defeasible rationalities of 'judicial conduct', judgemental processes in other areas of social life can also be seen to involve a complex combination and permutation of polymodal criteria. Instead of a single norm of rationality governing all appraisals, we should think instead of multidimensional criteria of *reasonableness* and their correlated adjudicative *positions*. And as a legal judgement can be questioned and interrogated along a number of different criterial dimensions (insufficient evidence, contingency of the particular case, faulty symptomatology, bias of reporting, inadequate case history, etc.), so judgements in everyday life may be deemed 'unwarranted' for an indefinite number of reasons. Consider the manifold ways in which decisions and practical outcomes are 'called upon' to ground and justify themselves in everyday settings. In the context of this model of warranted assertability we might even reappraise our earlier image of the mind as a republican forum of forensic dialogues. Historically we think of the Socratic dialogue of the soul examining a topic from all sides, playfully admitting counterfactual variations, questioning modes of speech and *doxa*, testing theories and accounts, and so forth; but it is perhaps the idea of the democratic law court which enforces the idea of establishing warranted evidence for a claim (in the ancient Greek world the concept of phronetic judgement was historically derived by projecting forensic-legal processes as models of the process of reflective thinking in general).

To summarize the discussion: phronetic reflection replaces the videological rhetorics of interior consciousness and rule-subsumption with the polemical discursivity of skilled adjudication – the latter presupposing tacit knowledge of moral awareness, deliberative norms, intuitive criteria of self-appraisal, and ongoing practices of self-criticism as conventional norms embedded in concrete social situations. With phronetic reflection we find ourselves in the richly contingent practices and public contexts of moral, ethical, and political life. The spheres of practical experience summarized by the Greek term *phronesis* represent an intrinsically socialized form of human self-reflection, inseparable from the concrete social occasions of intelligent perception and praxis. What holds these moral, ethical and pedagogic moments together is a richer and expanded concept of experiential judgement – in the German sense of *Erfahrung* – drawing upon the appraisal contexts of everyday experience. To take this brief analysis a step further we need to examine the concept of mundane judgement in more detail.

3 THE CONCEPT OF JUDGEMENT

Conscience in morals, taste in fine arts and conviction in beliefs pass insensibly into critical judgments; the latter pass also into a more and more generalized form of criticism called philosophy.

(John Dewey, 1958: 401)

The central point should now be clear: paradigms of moral, forensic, and phronetic judgement displace the speechless ego of videological reflection and foreground reflexivity as a discursive-institutional process, bound by specific social norms and procedural rules, beset by contingencies of value, and informed by interpretive choice. 'Judgement' – in reality a spectrum of judgemental processes defined in specific rhetorical contexts in day-to-day interaction – is the practical organon of the *logos* of everyday life. From the wider perspective of 'appraisal praxis' judgemental activities are interwoven in the day-to-day activities of individuals and groups pursuing their particular aims and objectives. Like the vocabularies of valuation available to a society, appraisal and judgemental praxes are never found in a social vacuum. They are organized practices linked with particular forms of action and institutional objectives. Reflection accordingly appears within the many different modalities and dimensions of 'forensic media' (practical judgement, dialogue with others, concerted association, appraisals in work situations, judicial processes, trial-and-error practices, routine acts of moral, ethical, aesthetic, social evaluation, and so forth).

The central claim here is that something like a phronetic paradigm of appraisal in everyday life prefigures a fundamentally *social* conception of reflexive processes as the outcome of contingent appraisal strategies and practical rhetorics of value.

The phronetic paradigm, in other words, turns reflection away from the idealized canons of reflective hygiene to the rough ground of language and speechful activities in the organized activities of contested deliberation and normative disputes. More importantly, it connects without conflating the different regions of judgemental appraisal institutionalized in different societies and subcultures (under these auspices we could begin to explore family resemblances between appraisal praxis in moral, aesthetic, political, scientific, and theoretical practices without reducing this multiplicity to one pure canon – each institutional setting developing its own criterial norms of 'reasonableness'). Given the strictures we have placed on the length and level of analysis in these chapters this is not the place to explore the complex and changing meaning-contexts of *phronesis* or to set out a systematic sociological theory of judgement (although I will sketch the basis of this in later historical studies of classical Greek models of the self, arguing that *phronesis* is a fundamental topic for logological research – particularly as a way of linking the work of interpretive communities to concrete forms of consciousness). The central point is that judgement cannot be reduced to procedural legalism or a reified 'rule-following' machinery. In its institutionalized forms, 'reasonableness' involves intellectual openness, disciplined training, applied knowledge, heuristic norms, and specialized standards of interpretation. As such the 'act of judgement' is best understood as a collective outcome of cooperative agents pursuing the practical resolution of organizational problems. In conclusion: the interpretive practices of everyday life are saturated with 'judgemental' activities incorporating everyday criteria of appropriateness, warranted ascription, relevance, practical success, germane evidence, and so forth.

By being respecified in this way *judgement* takes its place with a range of related concepts we use when describing skilled performances (deliberation, craft, grace, poise, balance, sense of proportion, judiciousness, shrewdness, etc.). In the sense of ongoing evaluation, discrimination, and interpretive criticism, *phronesis* provides the mediating link between *theory* and *practice*. To further explore the place of judgement in everyday life would require ethnographies of the differentiated life-worlds and specialized subsystems of legal, scientific, forensic, aesthetic, and normative deliberation in institutional settings. A beginning can be made with the topic of moral judgement.

4 MORAL SELF-REFLECTION

> The identity of the good with the subjective will, an identity which therefore is concrete and the truth of them both, is Ethical Life.
>
> (G.W.F. Hegel, 1952: §141)

We have already observed that the words 'consciousness' and 'conscience' are semantically related in many European languages (for example in the grammar of the French expression, *conscience*; thus William James' essay 'Does consciousness exist?' was first translated as 'La notion de conscience'). 'Con-sciousness' from the Latin *con*, meaning 'together with', and *scire*, meaning 'to know' is literally a 'knowing-with' or *conscientia*, an understanding grounded in the shared sociality of human arrangements (*conscius*; cf. German *Gewissen*). The 'public' sense of *conscius* and *conscientia* has been eroded, leaving a term for the most private form of 'knowledge' – knowledge of the inner moral state of the soul. From being a symbol for public knowledge, 'consciousness' evolved into a term for moral introspection – the 'moral sense' posited by certain schools of sociology and philosophy. Today, however, the term 'conscience' typically refers to an individual's moral consciousness (as in the description 'a good conscience' for a person who harbours no feelings of guilt or sin). The inner conscience of the 'I' has even been used as a criterial feature in defining the singularity of personal existence. Clearly all of these formulations and implicit moral schemas are derived from earlier social ontologies. The discourse of moral consciousness as an egological concern, for example, is rooted in Western religious models of the self. Thus in the context of the Catholic confessional the soul is a self which reflects upon itself in the light of divinely sanctioned norms. Only such an introspective self possesses moral qualities in the strict sense of the term. To follow the obligatory demands of moral consciousness is to place one's conduct under the interdiction of ethical rules and evaluative prescriptions. By this means *conscientia* aspires to the elevated claims of a disciplinarian *scientia* and its guardians elevate themselves to the role of *ethical legislators* of human conduct. Moral discourse could then be approached as a microcosm of larger ideological and 'social' cosmologies.

For many of these traditions, 'moral consciousness' is, in effect, a synonym for moral existence as a life of 'virtue' sanctioned by the authority of powerful groups and communities. Without 'being in touch' with the moral 'mood' of an age we could not imagine acts that could be appraised positively as moral or judged negatively as immoral. This is another variant of the idea that without moral relations and the power to sustain them, without compassionately taking the role of the other, there could be no moral 'experience' or 'normative sensibility'. The leading idea behind this notion of reflection can be stated quite simply: moral self-reflection is privileged in the sense of being a critical correlate of the moral demands of a legislative Other; we learn to act like reflective beings by internalizing the recursive judgements and obligations of a dominant authority – in other words, by modifying our conduct in the light of sanctionable moral codes; by being socialized into moral vocabularies of motivation; inversely, moral experience is possible only for an agent that can utter the word 'I' and feel bound by others who share the same moral attitudes and sensibilities. This is the form in which the paradigm of moral regulation became the central theme in Durkheim's sociology of morality: 'truth is a norm for thought in the same way that the moral ideal is a norm for conduct' (1983: 98). Or in Mead's terminology:

> In our reflective conduct we are always reconstructing the immediate society to which we belong. We are taking certain definite attitudes which involve relationship with others. In so far as those relationships are changed, the society itself is changed. We are continually reconstructing.
>
> (1934: 386)

Moral reflection, in other words, is a dramaturgy of idealized social models of interpersonal conduct.

Rather than forming a restricted 'sphere of reflection', the collective field of axiological reflexivity has often been regarded as the founding matrix of social life: mundane judgement and self-consciousness has its genesis in the *moral* practices of a society (and indeed for most 'traditional' or 'preindustrial' societies there is no 'ethics' or 'politics' separate from the field of collective moral self-regulation and its adjudicative norms and actions). The full exploration of this idea crystallizes the concept of transactional reflexivity which we will explore in the following chapter. For the limited purposes of this chapter the concept of moral self-adjudication discloses the amorphous field of axiological discourse associated with such topics as free will, self-determination, responsibility, compassion, sympathy, obligation, duty, and the like. But as with our previous analysis of phronetic appraisals, 'morality' has to be construed historically, rhetorically, and culturally. With no pretence to an exhaustive description we can begin by noting the important role of techniques of 'self-concern' and 'self-inquiry' as ways of exploring the cultural grammar of moral coexistence.

The field of moral life presents itself as a vast topography of interhuman relations. Diverse techniques of self-reflection are part of the structures of normative construal and social control which a society imposes upon its members. And these programmes of valuation are always informed by particular ideologies of self and community linked to the basic concerns of powerful groups. Thus a geography of the Western soul might proceed from classical antiquity's 'know thyself' as this was variously elaborated by the Presocratics in the sixth century BC, Socrates and the Sophists in the fifth century BC, to Christianity's *Nosce te ipsum*, the Catholic confessional and the applied ethics of medieval *casuistry* (systematized by St Thomas Aquinas in the thirteenth century), the Protestant cult of moral scrutiny arising from the breakdown of medieval Catholicism and the spread of Reformation individualism in Luther, Calvin, and their followers, down to the multifaceted forms of obsessive, alienated, Romantic self-centredness we find in modern guilt cultures (beginning with Rousseau and persisting down to the present day). The selves imposed by these different regulatory techniques evolved into the stock *ideological types* of later moral discourses – as Mead says, representatives of different kinds of social order.

Strong versions of moral reflection and the ensuing punitive voice of conscience are typically related to periods of massive social uncertainty and political and cultural change. These newly figured selves become 'the instrument, the means, of changing the old into a new order' (Mead, 1934: 387), projecting selves 'belonging to another social order which ought to take the place of the old one. He is a member of a new, a higher order' (1934: 386). These are some of the dynamic aspects of historical selfhood that require comparative investigation in an adequate cultural theory of moral reflexivity (a beginning might be made with terms formed with the modern suffix, *self-*, and the syntax of 'self- ' and ' -self' (as in *self-esteem, self-conceit, self-love, self-pity, self-contempt, self-hate, self-abasement, self-regard, self-absorption, self-affirmation, self-probity, self-importance, self-concern, self-delusion, self-estrangement, the alienated self, the melancholic self, the godless self*, and so on). We have seen that the concept of 'conscience' as an inner forum of internalized voices rather than a divine gift is a *social construction* with a complex history, dependent upon the availability of appropriate narrative techniques, 'confessional' rituals, and motivational occasions (the cultural setting and institutional background of the practice of *casuistry* in the Middle Ages is a case in point). It is not a passive *mimesis* of pre-existent moral experience but a new mode of facilitating ethical action in a specific cultural world. Prior to the rise of modern epistemology 'self-knowledge' and 'self-certainty' were primarily sought in the moral vocabularies and techniques of reflexivity associated with confessional self-objectification and the scrutiny of 'cases of conscience'. To locate the 'truth' of the self through confessional practices was part of the social control mechanisms of the dominant religious order. The Church – and religious instruction more generally – was the supreme broker of moral self-certainty and ontological security. Its rhetorics of selfhood formed one instrument in its will to control a recalcitrant population and extend its own authority to ever-larger spheres.

Fundamentalist regimes raise idealized norms of behaviour and self-comportment into an apparatus of mandatory ethics. The task of the moral guardian in these faiths is to bring the individual's thoughts and actions under the canon of general moral regulations. Everyday life must totally conform to the monologic voice of a legislative system of values. Respect accorded the self becomes empirically inseparable from an individual's publicly displayed adherence to imposed codes of conduct and moral principles. This demands a conspicuous display of rule-governed conduct as a mark of social membership. Typically these prescriptions evolve into the doctrinal contents of a literate religious creed. The guardians of orthodoxy might even define and promulgate a single 'rule' of ascribed behaviour for the whole community (exemplified by the 'rule of the Rule' in medieval monasticism – for example, the Rule of St Benedict formulated in the sixth century – or, in more secular contexts, elaborate detailed manuals of instruction for the correct execution of the confessional and casuistic examination). In this way religious interpretations of conduct were disseminated throughout everyday life as the existential concern of the whole community.

The Christian confessional was not simply one part of religious life; it symbolized the 'collective conscience' of the whole community working upon the mind and body of its dissident members. And everything depended upon and was reinforced by ritualized public practices. The machinery of the confessional evolved to become the arm of the generalized other, the means by which spiritual control could be extended into the hearts and minds of individual believers. In other words, the cure of souls became a powerful technology of the self (Foucault, 1988a; McNeill, 1952). Prescribed images of identity were elaborated by objectifying the absolute norms of a community's rigid expectations (today we can see similar practices in the spread of fundamentalist faiths as a way of overcoming what is perceived as the corrupting relativism, anomie, and cynicism of 'modern values'). These are some of the necessary contexts for understanding an institution such as prophecy – as sociologists like Max Weber and Emile Durkheim have recognized. The prophet is both the guardian of moral life and an entrepreneur for a new dispensation of moral consciousness. The role of prophetic charisma in Hebraic culture and history had a profound significance for the subsequent development of the ethical and intellectual culture of Jewish civilization (see Weber, 1966, 1967; Durkheim, 1954).

To return to the main theme of this chapter. Self-knowledge characteristically became a personal and social issue in contexts of ascribed guilt, moral misdemeanour, and litigation to 'repair' ethical transgression. In our ideal-typical theocracy the apparatus of moral normalization is fused with the laws governing other spheres of social life. Failure to live up to the standards demanded by a centric creed would be invariably diagnosed as a pathology of the soul. Deviation from the universal codes is frequently glossed as a transgression of a palpable ethical norm – in breaking the rules the person of the transgressor threatens the 'substantiality of ethical life'; the transgressor falls short of the projected self of the faithful. Civil transgressions might also be couched in religious terms – turning minor misdeameanours into a threat to the purity of the faith itself. Failure to display the correct behavioural response to a community's ultimate values effectively means withdrawal (or forcible ejection) from the community. As sociologists have observed, the models of selfhood for such communities are typically ascribed rather than achieved roles. And 'ascribed selfhood' invariably translates the corporate ideals of a powerful minority into inviolate 'natures'. In this way the guardians of traditional morality become the custodians of substantial selfhood. Moral virtuosos dictate the ideological frames of self-awareness, both at the level of the content and the form of appropriate selfhood – *what* the self ought to feel and *how* those feelings ought to be publically expressed. The codification of affective embodiment is thus one of the invariant features of every powerful religious culture.

Similar responses appear in the reaction of secular guardians to 'deviations' from pseudo-religious ideologies. Here 'deviance' is typically viewed by members as a pathology that must be 'cured' – frequently by the application of rigorous palliatives and regimes of correction. Moral deviance – 'sin' – calls down the apparatuses of 're-education' and moral reform. No conflict of interests can be accepted without implicitly denying the absolute truth of orthodoxy. Hence every variation or difference from the imposed norm must be anathematized as a threat to the purity and very existence of the community – a language of moral 'taint' and 'corruption' obligatory for such fundamental faiths. Frequently the idealized standard licensing reform is a past-oriented ideal of selfhood which is absolutized as a norm of identity for present and future members.

The two most common courses of corrective action are thus expulsion as a 'non-self' (that is, as being no longer 'recognized' by the community as a responsible agent) or recovery – with suitable ritual redefinitions, public dramas of contrition, and symbolic recompense – and eventual return to the *ethnos*. The latter is one of the characteristic strategies of the charismatic prophet calling the faithful to return to the wisdom of the old ways and norms of conduct. The psychological lever for both strategies is anxiety evoked by the threat of non-membership to those socialized into the modes of being of tightly-knit communities (ways of being-in-the-world associated with strong ritual ties of blood, family, locale, religious fraternity, and the like), the paradigm cases here being the social death of ostracism in the ancient *polis* and excommunication in the small, integrated Catholic communities of the Middle Ages. Each of these mechanisms assumes that human beings can only fully exist as moral selves within the sustaining networks of their respective communities of moral reference, and that the anchorage of such a framework lies in a substantial self, a centred 'identity' which the faithful must comply with or emulate (at the heart of every proselytizing faith lies a strong essentialist ontology of the 'true self' and an equally strong animus against the centrifugal forces of *difference*). A life beyond such networks is quite literally experienced in terms of inertia and death – an existence comparable to the status of a 'thing' or inanimate object. This is the sense in which 'alienation' from the sustaining normative activities of a community may, historically speaking, create the basic sensibility of 'world-loss'. If we add to this the view that the constitutive practices for such small-scale traditional communities are primarily oral, ritualistic, and sacred in character, expulsion from the group also means 'loss of self' by being separated from the community's sustaining language-games, cultic practices, and rituals. We do not imply, of course, that these 'spheres' are explicitly differentiated, let alone 'consciously' formulated by those who participate in the activities warranted by them. The primary anxiety experienced by members of such cultures is thus not physical death or punishment, but communal rejection. Many individuals – as Emile Durkheim has shown in detail – choose death rather than the fate of social mortification (Durkheim, 1951, 1954; cf. Douglas, 1967: Part I).

We are equally conscious of the profound role played by violent ethical and religious practices in defining the self's moral possibilities in more subtle languages of *pride, shame, defilement, despair, guilt, redemption, fallenness, vanity, sin, existential insecurity*, and the like. All of these words presuppose a powerful 'generalized other' embodying appraisal standards by which deviation can be recognized and addressed. Without such publicly available norms the 'moral experience' of shame, sin, and so forth would not be possible. With no accepted standards of 'the ought' – with no undisputed axiological standards – moral deviance as a threat to identity becomes unthinkable. In societies with a strong Protestant tradition (or its functional equivalent), the individual is encouraged to return to his or her soul as an examining censor ('know yourself' is then reinterpreted as 'look into your heart, judge the state of your soul, confess your guilt and follow the path of God').

What is at issue here is not cognitive certainty, but the certainty of salvation, the integrity of the soul before the stern aspect of a hidden God, ethical resoluteness, 'authenticity', 'self-redemption' secured by an appropriate use of the available 'techniques of the self' whose job it is to redefine selfhood in the light of prescribed social values and religious norms. We know that such influential premodern figures of selfhood were often embedded in quite brutal regimes of mortification and corporeal discipline (echoes of this linger in

Charles Horton Cooley's notion of the 'looking-glass self' as 'the imagination of our appearance to the other person; the imagination of his judgement of that appearance; and some sort of self-feeling, such as pride or mortification').[1] For a full exposition of these phenomena logological research would have to turn to a more detailed phenomenology of phronetic phenomena such as the social construction of status, esteem, and honour (often figured in the metaphor of 'face' and normative 'appearances'), the 'presentation of self in society', the creation, maintenance, and mortification of moral selves, the dynamic role of mutual self-enforcement, moral reciprocity, consciousness of sin, shame, disgrace, loss of identity in different cultures, the language-games of moral definition, conflicts between different moral codes, the framing of rule-breaking, misconduct, and transgression, the pervasive use of images of 'alienness' and 'otherness' in societal projects of identity formation and so on. In what follows we can only index these phenomena for future research.[2]

5 MORAL RELATIVITY

Tout est dans un flux continuel sur la terre. (Everything is in constant flux on this earth.)

(Jean-Jacques Rousseau, 1969: 88)

If moral knowledge is construed in axiological terms, that is, as *knowledge* of *values* and moral *principles* (Rousseau's voice of conscience, Kant's analysis of the categorical origins of duty and the universalizability criterion of an ethics of duty, 'value intuition' in phenomenological moral philosophy – for instance Max Scheler's material ethics of value (Scheler, 1973), everyday reifications of 'moral facts' and 'norms'), reflection which questions the possibility of moral facts and absolute norms governing human conduct is typically seen as relativizing reflection. Arguments against moral 'knowledge' typically take the form of an attack upon the validity of proposed standards and principles as universal moral patterns. The principles of substantive moral cognition are allegedly subjective preferences, contingent measures of the good, or empirical rules. What appears to be founded moral intuition turns out to be value preferences or interest-based interpretations imposed by particular religions, ethnic groups, ideological communities, and so on. *Ergo*, all axiologies are contingent impositions of local norms, interests, and values. Scepticism toward the 'springs of morality' inevitably presents itself as a negativity that threatens moral order itself – the 'pale cast of thought' which engenders an 'unhappy consciousness' towards ethical traditions and orthodox beliefs. The spheres of ethical intuition (*Sittlichkeit* or the concrete *mores* of a community) and reflection are set in an adversarial relation. Here again we are probably dealing with a continuum of sceptical attitudes – modalized into passivity (passive nihilism acquiescing, as it were, in the non-existence of moral standards), moral curiosity (entertaining an anthropological disengagement from all possible moral systems), moral doubt, anomie, localized scepticism, amoral detachment, world-weariness, *melancholia*, alienation, cynicism, self-destructive scepticism, active nihilism – among the many way-stations of *der sich entfremdete Geist*.

This would be the place for a historical study of these forms of moral consciousness – particularly the syndrome of passive moral scepticism-melancholia-anomie, on the one hand, and the more activist Gestalt of radical scepticism, cynicism, nihilism, etc. on the other (Sloterdijk, 1988). We also need to explore the social rhetorics of moral reflection in different societies and historical periods (*religious* idioms – sin, transgression, guilt, sacrifice, redemption, salvation, etc., *dramatic* idioms – loss of face, role playing, dishonour, dilemmas of agency, envy, malice, pride, etc., *legal* figures – duties, norms, obligations, contracts, rights, sanctions, penalties, obedience, compliance, etc., *corporeal* discourse – courage, moral strength, resilience, resistance, etc., and *existential* idioms – authenticity, thrownness, choice, contingency, resoluteness, will, self-actualization, etc). Unfortunately we have insufficient space to explore these topics here. But possible directions can be briefly illustrated by explicating the reflexive features of the phenomena of 'shame', 'guilt', 'vanity', and 'self-deception'.

5.1 Shame

One of the particular meanings of the English expression 'self-consciousness' has a bearing on the reflexive experience of shame (self-consciousness indicating a state of embarrassment or unease before the gaze of others – typically accompanied by nervousness, blushing, and related physiological symptoms). Embarrassment is undoubtedly located in the sense of ambivalence associated with human embodment: I anticipate the Other's perception of my own body including my own possible response and anticipation of this anticipation. Acute embarrassment collapses the field of action around the self, obstructing the flow of significant interaction and in its most extreme form 'freezes' the individual into impassivity and immobility. Embarrassment is one aspect of the experience of shame. Shame is a mode of moral reflexivity, depending as it does on the constitutive double presence of self-consciousness: the redoubling of the self in terms of actual or potential transgression, and the awareness of a generalized proscriptive self, the superego or reference group before whom we are shamed. I am, as we say, 'overcome' with shame; rendered speechless and immobile, I wish only to withdraw from the gaze of the Other (and therewith to escape the opprobrium of an imaginary community). Recall the everyday idiom: 'At that moment I wished the earth could have opened up and swallowed me.'

The corporeal effects of shame presuppose a strong awareness of values and internalized normative rules. Shame is not produced by the breach of all social rules or conventions – traffic violators are usually immune from the sensation;

rather shame indexes the breach of social rules which implicate the moral self as a primary source of agency and locus of social responsibilities. To fail to comply with a rule of etiquette is not to 'lose face' or bring dishonour down upon oneself or one's reference group. Shame and the sense of defiling a normative self are correlated social phenomena. Aristotle goes to the heart of the matter in describing shame as the real or imagined impression of dishonour (*Rhetoric* 1384a):

> Let shame be defined as a kind of pain or uneasiness in respect of misdeeds, past, present, or future, which seem to tend to bring dishonour; and shamelessness as contempt and indifference in regard to these same things ... it follows that we are ashamed of all such misdeeds as seem to be disgraceful, either for ourselves or for those whom we care for.
>
> (*Rhetoric* 1383b)

In being caught in dishonourable conduct the self becomes the object of a community's sanctions.

Shame presupposes a strong public sense of shared standards by means of which the self's acts and integrity are measured by a normative Other (this is the reason why conspicuous emotional displays of shame are invariably found in cultures which place a great stress on strict rules of bodily comportment – societies with a strong military tradition or honorific aristocratic stratum for example; 'modesty' – the introjection of clearly and rigorously defined norms of bodily comportment – is also a necessary precondition); without a coded, publically ritualized 'generalized opprobrium' shame makes little sociological sense. As a social phenomenon shame is inseparable from a strong communal sense of the good, the appropriate, the required; the life of excellence or 'virtue' and the '*aretai*' (excellences) are embodied and enacted in public performances and practices. Of course, all these thematics – modesty, selfhood, public sanctions, interdictions, and the like, connect in manifold ways with the ritual forms through which a community or society governs the sexual body – how it 'manages' the cultural economy of desire and erotic expression for different groups and classes in the society. And what is regarded as typically 'ignominious' or 'shameful' varies considerably across different societies and in different historical periods – although the existence of a structured economy of desire, sexuality, and moral status is a universal *focus* of institutional life.

Aristotle, once again, touches upon the essential feature:

> It is shameful not to have a share in the honourable things which all men, or all who resemble us, or the majority of them, have a share in ... those of the same culture, of the same city, of the same age, of the same family, and, generally speaking, those who are on an equality; for then it is disgraceful not to have a share, for instance, in education and other things, to the same extent.
>
> (*Rhetoric* 1384a)

The Greek concept of shame (*aidos*; *atimia* is best rendered 'dishonour') has, of course, little in common with the Christian notion of 'conscience' as introspection or with the sexualized discourse of sin found in modern confessional rhetorics. For the Greeks of Aristotle's time and social class the self's normative identity is constructed largely as an object within the public realm of male political actors. Aristotle's paradigmatic instance of shame expresses this androcentric background:

> we are ashamed when we suffer or have suffered or are likely to suffer things which tend to ignominy and reproach; such are prostituting one's person or performing disgraceful actions, including unnatural lust ... those that promote licentiousness are disgraceful, whether voluntary or involuntary (the latter being those that are done under compulsion), since meek endurance and the absence of resistance are the result of unmanliness or cowardice.
>
> (*Rhetoric* 1384a)

In the Greek context shame is a symbolic disintegration of the core political self, not the 'pangs of guilt' tearing an introspective conscience. Experienced shame arises from the dishonouring of the political self. In logological terms shame is the experienced disintegration of what a community valorizes as normative selfhood (decency, dignity, status, 'face'). This is the other-directed moment of shame: 'Shame is not only shame in the presence of others, but can also be shame one feels for them' (Benjamin, 1992: 125–6).

We can illustrate the contrast by means of another reflexive emotion, *pity*. If we distinguish *altruistic* pity, as a characteristic product of the ethics of the New Testament, from *egoistic pity*, then the Greek notion of shame firmly belongs with robust egoism. A consciousness of undeserved pain or misfortune befalling another person creates an acute awareness that the same fate could befall onself (or one's friends and allies). Compassionless pity is derived from the aggrandizing public self, not the interior ethic of fellow feeling: 'generally speaking, a man is moved to pity when he is so affected that he remembers that such evils have happened, or expects that they may happen, either to himself or to one of his friends' (*Rhetoric* 1386a). The Greek discourse of pity operates without a background of universal 'fellowship', compassion, or human communality; it is 'instrumental' in being generated from actual or imaginary threats to androcentric values – those of the *oikos*, the political club or the male participants of a *polis*. The condition of those who suffer is not metaphysically or ethically exemplary in the Christian sense of fellowship as universal neighbourliness – it is simply a source of instructive edification about the precarious status of oneself and one's allies. We pity ourselves and others if we fail to embody one or more of the classical *aretai* – we fall short of the ideal perfection mapped by these 'excellences'. This is not an emotion measured by a universal 'love of mankind' or by a painful recognition that the human condition is condemned to suffering, sin, and error. It derives from the recognition that human beings invariably fall short of what they might become, that they are subject to fatal reversals and the tragic condition of finite beings in a belligerent world order. The classical Greek soul would have found Bergson's dictum unintelligible: 'True pity consists not so much in fearing suffering as in desiring it' (1971: 19). The Greek patrician's experience of pity and the Christian ideal of pity are products of two different ways of being-in-the-world (similar considerations hold for the contrast beteen *eros* and *caritas* and the larger ideological contrast between 'political communality' and 'universal fellowship', a community of solidarity against a community of forgiveness; cf. Nietzsche on Christian pity as a mode of *ressentiment* in 1968: §373 and 1978: §225).

5.2 Guilt

An analogous parallel between the ancient and modern experience of guilt can be drawn. Its oldest meaning involves a sense of defilement, a contamination of sacred acts and mores which a community must rectify by cathartic techniques; these frequently take the form of collective rituals of purification and transformation (echoes of the ancient carthartic rituals form the stuff of Attic tragedy and live on in the confessional practices of Christianity and in modern legal and therapeutic institutions). But the decisive shift to the modern experience of guilt occurs in Judaeo-Christian individualism with its regulatory machinery of interiorization: modern guilt is a reflective experience of conscience, a gnawing sense of transgression that is impervious to atonement or ritual cleansing. The latter experience belongs to a different moral epoch. It can be illustrated by the case of Rousseau's exemplary Lie: 'my first thought on beginning to reflect was of a terrible lie I had told in my early youth, a lie the memory of which has troubled me all my life and even now, in my old age, adds sorrow to a heart already suffering in so many other ways ... The memory of this deplorable act and the undying remorse it left in me, instilled in me a horror of falsehood that ought to have preserved my heart from this vice for the rest of my life' (1979: 63–4; the actual occasion for the lie is graphically described in Book 2 of Rousseau's *Confessions*; it is prefigured in St Augustine's well-known account in his *Confessions*).

In its modern form, guilt may have both an individual and a collective debilitating effect. Whereas classical guilt is essentially reversible, modern guilt is irreversible. The modern Ego – at least the Ego crafted during the Age of Enlightenment – cannot return to a guilt-free state of existence; even acts of moral retribution and repentance are carried within the stream of consciousness as symbolic tokens of earlier acts of unrequited sin; the values lost or 'contaminated' through transgression can never be fully restored. It is as though moral atonement leaves a subscript of guilt in its movement of erasure (hence the archetypal theme of the claustrophobic sense of guilt, the dead weight of past acts which continue to haunt the Ego, the failure of repentance

– expressed in the existential theme of a self which accepts its fallen nature and shoulders the burden of guilt or in the Kierkegaardian drama of the anxious reflection required by every fundamental moral decision (symbolized by the figure of Abraham in Kierkegaard's *Fear and Trembling*, 1983)). Rousseau invokes the modern aspect of irreversibility in his description of guilt as 'eternal remorse'. This fate is clearly a secularized version of the Augustinian account of the orginal fallen condition of mankind. Modern guilt has introjected the culture of sin and self-defilement which seeps from the pages of *The City of God* (1945).

One facile way of escaping guilt appears in the shape of *vanity*. Vanity as an absolute disregard of the voices of tradition and the glorification of the autonomous self is a common form of self-deception, but it is also consciousness's naive attempt to escape from the irreversibility of moral choice.

5.3 Vanity

In its innumerable manifestations *vanity* displays the peculiar reflexive property of desire turning toward others purely as a means of self-enhancement. Vanity is a type of pathogenic self-regard. The vain person only exists in the rays of esteem s/he draws from the gaze of others. S/he acts only to bathe in the praise of significant others. The vain person lives for the admiring glance of the Other. In Hegel's well-known account the self does not merely desire the Other, but desires the Other's desire, desires to see its own fixated desire reflected in the mirror of the Other's desire. The vain self exists in a closed circuit of narcissistic mirroring and self-deception. As such it is a form of 'self-alienated spirit'. In Sartrean and Lacanian terms, the vain Ego is an unredeemed prisoner of the 'mirror-phase'. If the otherness of the Other is admitted it must comply with the petulant *diktat* of the Self since radical alterity shatters the phantasmal mirror of the Ego. The 'generalized other' is not allowed to function as a critical mirror of conscience or proscriptive voice of public morality, but becomes a self-confirming organ of the Ego. In its monadic narcissism the Ego satisfies itself by observing its valorized image reflected in the admiration (or phantasized admiration) of significant others, creating a circuitry of delusional reflections which stave off guilt and radical moral reflection in a spiralling movement of self-centredness. Libido is looped back and cathected upon the Ego's own real and imagined appearances. Hence the traditional epithets of 'baseless vanity', 'empty pride', delusory conceit concerning one's personal attainments or attractions (self-conceit and narcissistic egoism).

In vanity the Master-Slave dialectic is carried on within the pure immanence of the privatized self: autoerotically, the narcissistic soul revolves interminably around its own image, just as 'love-of-self' parodies the genuine sociality of love and self-respect. But vanity's original motivation is perfectly intelligible: to be noticed, accepted, valued, loved, respected by others – to be admired or, more generally, to be 'of standing' in the eyes of relevant others, and perhaps before the gaze of the Other. Vanity – subjective egotism – is the necessary concomitant of the theatrical nature of human communality. Hence the affinity between vanity and those other paradigmatic reflexive emotions, *pride* and *envy* (Rousseau had accurately seen that 'self-esteem' was the strongest impulse of proud souls and that it was invariably dissolved in erotic attachments). But vanity raises subjective self-esteem to an extreme level (where it fuses with its invariant companions, intolerance and indifference to others:

> self-love, with its train of illusions, can often creep in under the guise of self-esteem, but when the fraud is finally revealed and self-love can no longer conceal itself, there is no further cause to fear it, and though it may be hard to destroy, at least it is easy to subdue.
>
> (Rousseau, 1979: 129)

Vanity in the form of intellectual conceit is perhaps the most dangerous temptation of a self-reflexive species (intellectuals, of course, routinely turn vanity into a form of life, an art of self-publicity – perhaps even their patron saint, Socrates, drank the hemlock out of vanity – just as Empedocles is supposed to have thrown himself into the crater of Etna from similar motives – to be eternally on the lips of posterity, to be remembered as Someone, perhaps even as Someone Divine, to be eternally present – consider other family relatives of vanity: egoistic intolerance, the myth of singularity ('I'm indebted to no one'), the myth of the One Truth (the vanity of orthodoxy), the King's New Clothes, Old Wine in New Bottles, Rediscovering America, etc.). Hegel seems to have had this type of egoism in mind when he wrote in the *Phenomenology* of that

> sort of conceit which understands how to belittle every truth and turn away from it back into itself, and gloats over this its own private understanding, which always knows how to dissipate every possible thought, and to find, instead of all the content, merely the barren Ego – this is a satisfaction which must be left to itself; for it flees the universal and seeks only an isolated existence on its own account (*Fürsichseyn*).
>
> (1967: 138, trans. modified)

Pride, with its undercurrent of resentment (*ressentiment*) and inverted envy, reinforces the cardinal sin of conceit, secure in its privatized cycle of self-deception.

Rousseau's phenomenological distinction between self-love (*amour-propre*) and love-of-self (*amour de soi*) goes to the essence of this discussion. In confessing his own adventures in self-love, he narrates the universal pretensions of the self-aggrandizing Ego (here in the figure of the modern self as Author):

> I was never much given to self-love (*amour-propre*); but in the world this

artificial passion has been exacerbated in me, particularly when I was a writer; I may perhaps have had less of it than my fellow-authors, but it was still excessive. The terrible lessons I received quickly reduced it to its original proportions. At first it rebelled against injustice, but in the end it came to treat it with contempt; falling back on my own soul, severing the external links which make it so demanding, and giving up all ideas of comparison or precedence, it was content that I be good in my own eyes. And so, becoming once again the proper love of self, it returned to the true natural order and freed me from the tyranny of public opinion.

(1979: 129)

Naturally, we read Rousseau's artful confession as a dissimulating, reflexive act of *amour-propre* (in that only a vain self puffed out by self-esteem could announce: 'I was never much given to self-love'). Vanity finds its natural home in the delusional syndromes of self-deception (Rousseau's 'alone with myself, contented with myself and already enjoying the happiness which I feel I have deserved. Love of self alone is active in all of this, self-love has no part in it' (*Eighth Walk*) or perhaps even more poignant coming from a father who abandoned his own children in a Foundlings' Home: 'If I have made any progress in the knowledge of the human heart, I owe it to the pleasure I took in seeing and observing children', 1979: 140).

5.4 Self-deception

Vanity is but one species of the innumerable forms of self-deception based on a delusory, inflated view of one's own singularity, importance, qualities, knowledge, worth, or standing. Yet it is a form of egotistical self-deception that has unanticipated consequences for the life of society. Rousseau, in fact, traces most forms of human wickedness to vanity and its sublimated manifestations. *Amour-propre* is the root of conflict, violence, and oppression in human relationships and society at large. Its mythical prototype is the self-absorption of Narcissus in love with his own image, oblivious to the reality of others and the rest of creation (Ovid, *Metamorphoses* III.2.339–510). It is also the ancient Biblical root of Pharisaism or religious self-righteousness and, in the language of existentialism, the ever-present threat of *mauvaise foi* – 'bad faith' or 'inauthenticity' (notably in Heidegger, 1967b: Part 1, Division I, IV, 'Being-in-the-world as being-with and being-one's-self: the "They"; and Part 1, Division I, V, 'Being-in as such' especially §§34–8 and Sartre, 1957a: 47–70).

Vanity estranges the self from its vital matrix and lays the foundation for every system of violence hatched in the long march to civilization. The manifest continuities with the Christian tradition of 'spiritual sin' is evident. As Alan Watts pointed out, the Christian mind

has recognized that the Devil is an angel, and as pure spirit is not really

339

interested in the sins of the flesh. The sins after the Devil's heart are the intricacies of spiritual pride, the mazes of self-deception, and the subtle mockeries of hypocrisy where mask hides behind mask behind mask and reality is lost altogether.

(1992: 116)

Lucifer fell from grace through the sin of pride. But 'pride' is not unconnected with more violent expressions of force on the part of the imperial self – the desire to exclude and dominate the Other might be seen as rooted in pride's egoism. The vain self must ultimately triumph at the expense of the freedom and selfhood of the Other. Our phenomenology of vanity thus connects with the sociality of power. The darker side of vanity prefigures the phenomenology of sadomasochistic relations.

For the existentialist, self-deception or *mauvaise foi* appears as a double duplicity: (i) the occlusion and repression of the existential project of freely chosen action (what some have called existentialism's decisionism in which the gratuitous act of commitment creates the self, Sartre 1957a, Division II, chs 1, 2); and (ii) the rationalization of indecision by projecting the Self, Consciousness, and the Will-to-freedom in mechanical, asocial, unreflexive categories (in its most extreme form the self-deception which reduces the creative possibilities of selfhood and personal transformation to the fixed behaviour of an organism or the frozen objectivity of a thing). In the latter case *mauvaise foi* – the self's weakness of will and indecision – provides the pretext for acts of violence, where the self-deluding sincerity of the Ego is tacitly complicit in acts of objectification.

The Self tricks itself into hypocrisies by its own failure of will just as much as by its own egoistic voluntarism. Human beings evade responsibility and the creative possibilities of risk by treating their actions and life-in-the-world as predetermined facts rather than the outcome of the interplay between *decision* and *power*. Routines, habitual activities, and 'practico-inert' imperatives take the place of free agency – and retrospectively serve as vocabularies of motive for 'sincere non-action'. In Sartre's language, only a consciousness which projects its being can treat itself as an entity or thing subject to the anonymous demands of social authority and political arrangements (1957a: Part 3, 'Being-for others'). These are recurrent themes in existential moral philosophy from the 'unhappy consciousness' in Hegel's *Phenomenology of Spirit*, to the 'fallenness' and inauthenticity of 'the One' (*das 'Man'*), 'Idle talk', 'Curiosity', 'Ambiguity' 'Falling and thrownness' in Heidegger's Dasein analytic (1967b: Part 1, V, §§34–8; 1992: §26, 'The "who" of being-in-the-world' and §29, 'Falling as a basic movement of Dasein'), the 'man without qualities' (in Robert Musil's great novel), to the 'fear of commitment' and bad faith described by such writers as Marcel Proust, Franz Kafka, Jean-Paul Sartre, Alberto Moravia, Virginia Woolf, and Samuel Beckett.

In modernist fiction the tragic capacity for self-deception and self-estrangement almost becomes the sole defining feature of the human condition. 'Man' is the creature lacking the moral courage to 'be' and 'exist' as an irreducibly singular existence. Acts of inauthenticity have the invariant function of unburdening a person's Dasein (Heidegger, 1992: §26, 247). Paradoxically, to *be* is even more terrifying than the imminent threat of death and nihilation. 'Man' as a name for the multiple projects of failed self-creation is irreducibly a 'divided self' vegetating in the past after having lost a vital relationship to the present and the future:

> Everyone is the other and no one is himself. The Anyone, which answers the question of the *who* of everyday Dasein, is the *Nobody*, to whom every Dasein has of itself already surrendered itself in the public being-with-one-another.
>
> (1992: §26, 247)

6 DRAMATIC REFLECTION

Dialogues, whatever their subject matter, are always dramas of self-constitution.

(Vincent Crapanzano, 1992: 130)

These elementary experiences of moral reflexivity and its psychopathologies confirm the central place of situational and intersubjective structures in human life; we are forced by 'the things themselves' to abandon a philosophy of pure consciousness and introduce dramatic narratives from the finite categories of existential selfhood enmeshed in its social, ethical, and political contexts: before it is a cognitive state or formal structure, reflexivity is symbolic interaction, a moral encounter orchestrating identity and difference in human contexts of existential significance. Any adequate framework of social thought must be able to articulate the complex stratifications of reflexive consciousness arising with agents that possess the capacity to develop self-concepts, self-understandings, and metatheoretical discourse. In Heidegger's terminology, reflexivity emerges along with the fundamental 'being-with' of Dasein as being-in-the-world.

Theological and literary explorations of these phenomena focus on the dialectics of transgression, loss of face, self-deception, self-concealment, confusion of identity, moral crises, and other *Grenzensituationen* in which the Self is dramatically 'stretched' and 'tested' (the *Odyssey* is the paradigmatic literary instance, though similar figures occur in ancient tragedy, the *Bildungsroman*, the literary tropes of narcissism (Lasch, 1979), the comedy of manners, and satire). Each of these dramatic genres implicitly rejects the imperious demands of pure reflection by recalling human beings to the interpersonal worlds of finite existence, sexuality, place, time, and fate. The dramaturgical nature of human existence is displayed in the open 'problem' of the 'to-be' and the endless ways in which social beings evade active appropriation, deferring the 'to-be' by accepting existing forms of ontological relatedness as the only 'ways-to-be'. Here topics such as the loss of 'face', the abasement of the self, degradation rituals, and self-deception take centre-stage (cf. Goffman, 1959). Martin Buber speaks of the inauthentic identification with the 'es-Welt', the 'It-world': 'What has to be given up is not the I but that false drive for self-affirmation (*Selbstbehauptungstriebs*) which impels man to flee from the unreliable, unsolid, unlasting, unpredictable, dangerous world of relation into the having of things' (1970: 126).

Dramatic reflexivity 'finitizes' the hyperbolic rhetoric of absolute reflection and returns inquiry to the concrete structures of action and vicissitudes of human engagements. For example, Dasein, as we have seen, is chronically subject to absorption in an everyday type of self-interpretation where the self is reduced to the dominant social order. In following existing understandings of worldliness and accepted definitions of 'human nature' Dasein loses the open possibilities of the 'to-be' – in sum, of self-creative praxis. The self is, so to speak, lost in the world and so 'fallen' loses touch with its authentic possibilities of selfhood.

In this context contemporary fiction is vitally important in preserving a narrative concern for the life of dramatic reflexivity: pursuing the 'dramatic' metaphor, the human world is disclosed primordially as a realm of moral entanglements and complex ethical relationships. Reflexivity has its living site in dramaturgical contexts. Literature instructs philosophy in the primary sociality of human experience. We learn that the fine-meshed reflexivities of human relationships in their affective and erotic orientations have no tangible reality apart from situated performances and local dramatic occasions. The social self is 'always-already' situated in its concrete ensemble of affective, social, political, cultural, and historical relations. From the dramaturgical perspective the vicissitudes of the Self, Other, and World belong together.

Heidegger speaks of the disposedness (*Befindlichkeit*) of everyday life:

> Dasein does not first find itself by itself in order then from there to look around itself for a world. Rather, disposition is itself a character of in-being, which means always already being in a world. The most immediate phenomenal concretion of this structure of in-being in dis-coveredness must, as always, be sought in the everydayness of being with one another.

> (1992: §28, 257)

These 'dispositional sites' constitute the irreducible cultural habitat for those who would explore the moral vicissitudes of self and other in the changing contours of everyday life. By grounding subjectivity in concrete space-time networks, dramatic reflexivity opens the vast field of a *critical phenomenology of everyday life*. And 'everyday life' is not a replacement for 'natural man' or 'unmediated life in the world' (as some contemporary versions of the life-world theme tend to suggest). Everyday life is the rich historical field of understandings, mediations, and cultural formations in which human beings are inescapably enmeshed. It is the ever-present world of ongoing moral relationships, the unnoticed and unexplicated texture of day-to-day living which precedes all theorizing. In Heidegger's language: all knowing, cognitive proving, and the producing of arguments, sources, and the like always already presuppose understanding (1992: 260).

Ironically, the European tradition of pure reflection is returned to the incarnate condition of the social life-world via a long detour through imaginative literature – forms of consciousness which classical Reflection originally rejected as worthless fictions. But, as we learn from transference in psychotherapy, the return of the repressed proves to be liberating and therapeutic. A handful of contemporary philosophers such as Martha Nussbaum and Stanley Cavell have rightly insisted that we must relearn 'the fragility of goodness' by attending to the texts of fiction as much as by reclaiming the occluded insights of classical moral and political philosophy (Nussbaum, 1986, 1990; cf. Cavell, 1979). To 'return' to these older insights is simultaneously to 'advance' toward a more realistic and nuanced understanding of everyday life where the horizons of human action and community are defined from the outset as *transactional relations*.

Part IV

DIALOGUE

From the studies of heteropoiesis in Part III we now are in a position to respecify the project of Reflexivity in non-representational terms. Where Reflection leads to ocularcentric and videological conceptions of the Self and Other, Reflexivity advances a fundamentally dialogical conception of experience and its horizons of difference and otherness. The chapters in Part IV examine some of the implications of forms of thinking that incorporate alterity and a respect for plurality and otherness as an integral part of their discourse.

10

GENEALOGICAL
SELF-REFLEXIVITY

The age of phenomenological philosophy seems to be over ... But in what
is most its own phenomenology is not a school. It is the possibility of
thinking, at times changing and only thus persisting, of corresponding
to the claim of what is to be thought. If phenomenology is thus experienced and retained, it can disappear as a designation in favor of the matter
of thinking whose manifestness remains a mystery.

(Martin Heidegger, 1972: 82)

*Chapter 10 introduces the paradigm shift toward dialogical models of selfhood
and world, by examining various forms of critical self-reflection in recent
thought: psychoanalysis, genealogy, phenomenology, semiotics, hermeneutics,
critical theory, and deconstruction. The chapter is divided into the following
sections:*

1 *Introduction*
2 *Psychoanalytic genealogy*
3 *Genealogical therapies*
4 *Phenomenological reactivation*
5 *Semiotic analysis*
6 *Hermeneutic repetition*
7 *Critique and metacritique*
8 *Deconstruction*

1 INTRODUCTION

The dialogism implicit in the presuppositional logics of practical reason and
phronetic reflection marks an important watershed in the movement away
from videological thought. Simplified to its most basic theme, dialogism
contests the very idea of a non-interpretive theory of human experience,
reality, and representation. In moving toward a radically social account of
human experience it loosens the tenacious hold of Representationalism by
dismantling its foundational rhetorics (we have already seen that the basic
paradigm of egological reflection presupposes intersubjectivity, that

videological culture is a Eurocentric value system, and that individualist rhetorics of self and world lead to contradictions and generate self-negating paradoxes).

From both sides of human praxis – the 'material-biological' systems of autopoiesis outlined in Chapter 3 and the linguistic, praxical, and phronetic formations explicated in Chapters 6 to 9 – the argument leads to the same conclusion: that we should reformulate the problem of knowledge and reality in terms of constitutive dialogic praxis. Dialogism flows into a wide stream of intellectual practices that advocate a return to the experiential and conversational worlds of human interaction as the matrix of all knowledge. We will see that dialogism overlaps with a complex topography of 'hermeneutical' perspectives in contemporary philosophy and social theory. Perhaps this is what Heidegger had in mind in saying that phenomenology – or the phenomenological attitude, has determined the spirit of the modern age in the most various realms, but mostly in a tacit manner (1972: 81). Yet we cannot follow the ontological direction Heidegger gave to the destruction of the metaphysical tradition without qualification and criticism. There is no simple route from the problematics of European philosophy to a radically dialogical theory of social reality. It is certainly not a matter of displacing the category of *subjectivity* with the category of *intersubjectivity*, or of *being* with *meaning* and *Verstehen*. The origin and status of the 'question of Being' must itself be deconstructed:

> The question of Being aims therefore at ascertaining the *a priori* conditions not only for the possibility of the sciences which examine entities as entities of such and such a type, and, in so doing, already operate with an understanding of Being, but also for the possibility of those ontologies themselves which are prior to the ontical sciences and which provide their foundations. *Basically, all ontology, no matter how rich and firmly compacted a system of categories it has at its disposal, remains blind and perverted from its ownmost aim, if it has not first adequately clarified the meaning of Being, and conceived this clarification as its fundamental task.*
>
> (1967b: 31)

From this point onward we will abandon the egological-ontological language of 'the constitutive subject' and 'pure consciousness' constituting intentional objects, and turn instead to the genealogy of object domains as constructed, dialogical social phenomena. But this 'dialogical turn' is not so much a question of abandoning radical reflection as one of turning the phenomenological tradition back upon its own limiting assumptions and metarhetorics: we 'bracket' the autistic, videological universe of wordless, worldless souls to reveal a contested, heterogeneous topography of socially constructed worlds. The richer interdisciplinary problematic which emerges from this deconstruction dove-tails with the foundational question of the cultural sciences – how to reconstitute the praxical worlds of social agents without predefining these *a priori* constructions? How to 'enter' and 'understand' these worlds as complex rhetorical formations? How to allow this 'knowledge of the Other' to transform our own dialogical perspectives? How, in other words, to make sense of the Other in the projects of selfhood?

Under the terms of the logological parenthesis we can explicitly confront a range of difficult questions not merely of the 'social ontology of dialogue' but also, and perhaps more urgently, of the ethics and politics of contemporary reflexivity, examining how the practices and institutions of self-reflection in our culture have been forcibly integrated into the dominant structures of power in modern society. The 'irruption of the Other' into the dominant concerns and discourses of reflection returns as a central theme. The sanitized versions of 'pure reflection' we have hitherto analyzed make no such moral, ethical, and political claims; but from this point onward alternative voices must be allowed to speak through our 'parenthesizing' methodology. This is where our schematic inventory – and its ahistorical methodology – breaks down before 'the phenomena themselves'. It also follows, of course, that the terminology we have utilized uncritically in previous chapters must itself be subject to deconstruction and perhaps discarded for more resonant language-games open to the heteroglossia of different traditions and dialogical commitments. In sum, we need to recover the contestatory voices of excluded others in our language-games and programmes of inquiry.

One theme may help in moving from the videological to the logological framework, and this is the idea of reflexivity as a collective struggle against occlusion and reification in social life. Everyday experience secures its authority by forgetfulness, by repressing and routinizing its own constructed history, moral relativity, and heterogeneity. Like its equivalent in human biography, radical amnesia appears to some extent to be a functional necessity for the 'forward-living' movement of social projects and collective action. Hegemonic cultures can be viewed as ready-made formal 'answers' to petrified questions, questions which were originally animated by the force of desire. It is not that Reason or Being has been forgotten in some global sense, but that the historically contingent possibilities of more reflexive ways of being – the finite possibilities of concrete liberty – have been effaced and occluded. As with semiosis in general, cultural forms appear to follow the cyclical pattern of creative praxis, routinization, and reification. Once domesticated, libertarian projects assume the solid appearance of neutral objectivity. As phantasmal systems they provide an illusory satisfaction to the reflective mind, while actually disabling the self from radical inquiry and a more principled pursuit of radical communality. Asking unsettling questions was, of course, the ancient vocation of philosophical reflexivity. Questioning as a struggle against the forces of dispersion and occlusion may even be coeval with human existence as future-oriented praxis. Following paths opened in Part III we must now ask: what strategies of 'collective remembering' can reverse the processes of reification inherent in social life?

2 PSYCHOANALYTIC GENEALOGY

The unconscious is structured like a language.

(Jacques Lacan)

If we approach the *psyche* in its Aristotelian rather than Freudian sense, the struggle of the self to recollect itself within the diverse 'forms of animation' may be called psycho-analytic genealogy (the difference between ancient and modern analysis can be marked with the 'hyphen'). In the etymological sense 'the analysis of the *psyche*' specifies *psychology* as a quest for the *logos* of the *psyche* – the 'logos' being deeper and more encompassing than the field of verbal activity or conscious thought. According to the author of *De Anima*, self-knowledge as self-interpretation is possible only by virtue of the spirited life of nature predating human speech and language. Selfhood is the 'archae-logical' site of a differentiated subject where desire and logos interweave in and as the self's experience of self – most visibly in the experienced concreteness or 'animation' which contests every form of occlusion and reification. Hence analysis must take the form of an archaeology of unconscious 'sedimenta'. Psycho-analytic genealogy presents itself as the archaeology of the *psyche*. The form of the self is interpreted as a self-experience of the interweaving of forms of life (*bios*) and discourse (*logos*), a living dialectic by means of which consciousness acquires a palpable sense of itself through the struggle of spirited and occlusive forces.

Thus Jacques Lacan speaks eloquently of the linguisticality of conscious and unconscious experience and the mediation of all consciousness by language:

> What I seek in speech is the response of the other ... I identify myself in language, but only by losing myself in it like an object. What is realized in my history is not the past definite of what has been in what I am, but the future anterior of what I shall have been for what I am in the process of becoming.

(Lacan, 1977: 86)

Some of these themes are still preserved in modern psychoanalysis. In Freud's metapsychology, outlined in *The Interpretation of Dreams*, dreaming, recol-lection, and psychic life in general are troped in the figures of a palimpsest and the layers of a buried city. Dreaming places the human subject in touch with the occluded strata and forces of mental life; as a process beyond conscious control, dreaming generates imagery which has the status of an enigmatic cipher in a autopoeic text, a scrambled message and clue to repressed signifi-cance. The opaque texts of dreams are thus the central medium and instrument of psychoanalytic genealogy. Dreaming holds the key to the decentred char-acter of the self – the insistence of an irreducibly alien presence within consciousness – a 'special case of reflexive mental activity, in which the self becomes twofold' (Rycroft, 1991: 45). Dreaming is the trace of a dialogical heteropoiesis at work within the Ego. In a fundamental sense – like the cultural leavings of a lost civilization – dreaming is an oblique communication from the libidinal past of the self:

> Dreaming is thus a form of communicating or communing with oneself and is analogous to such waking activities as talking to oneself, reminding oneself, exhorting oneself, consoling oneself, frightening oneself, entertaining oneself or exciting oneself with one's own imagination – and, perhaps more particularly to such waking meditative imaginative activities as summoning up remembrance of things past or envisaging the prospect of things future.

(Rycroft, 1991: 45)

One crucial difference between talking and the 'inner dialogue' of dreams, however, is that the latter proceeds primarily in the medium of overdetermined non-discursive symbolism. The libidinal semiotics of dream-work (*Traumarbeit*) is more ancient than the codes of verbal discourse and consequently must be 'read' by different hermeneutic rules. As a 'primordial' mode of signification, dreaming resorts to older symbolic systems – drawn especially from the sphere of corporeal images and iconic signs (Freud repeatedly emphasizes the atemporal nature of unconscious processes and their resistance to depiction in spatial and causal terms). Dreaming is an ideography of the mind trying to communicate with itself. The primary medium of *anamnesis* is the affective sign which compresses erotic and phobic 'thoughts' into images that defy the logics of conscious thought and mundane reasoning. Socially proscribed desires and fears thus get deflected and come to rest in comparatively 'safe' symbolisms. The dream is a dynamic 'train' of such past cathected re-presentations. As Rycroft notes, 'dreams tend to resemble moving pictures more than they resemble literary texts' (1991: 46). In short, in psychoanalytic genealogies the ambiguous mindscape of the *psyche* is primarily constituted from apparently inconsequential, prelinguistic symbolic image systems.

As an *archaeological project* self-reflection arises from the vicissitudes of a desiring being becoming progressively aware of its lived, animate, and carnal conditions – a 'becoming-conscious' in self-implicating recoveries of hitherto anonymous functionalities and intentionalities (in Aristotle's account the *psyche* is imagined as a hierarchical substructure of 'erotic' Forms colonized by a reasoning, logos-attuned soul – the active intellect). Self-awareness has its nascent forms in the biological dynamics of the organism. The dialogue within consciousness both conjoins and separates the orders of life (desire) and discourse (language): the orchestrated ecology of biophysiological existence, the rhetorical performances of speech, the rhythms of communicative dialogue.

Psychoanalysis presents itself as a methodic procedure of repetitively 'working through' (*durcharbeiten*) and to some extent reproducing the non-intelligible processes of repressed self-formation. Analytic interpretation is

351

modelled on the idea of a painstaking retrieval and restitution of the repressed 'texts' of unconscious processes. The subject 'in analysis' is assisted in recollecting and explicating repressed contents – encouraged to reread and rewrite the traumatic constellations of the primal scene. In recent forms of psychoanalysis, Freud's project for a scientific psychology has been explicitly reconstructed as a hermeneutic archaeology of unconscious processes (for example in the existential hermeneutics of Paul Ricoeur, the dialogic critique carried out on Freud's metapsychology by Mikhail Bakhtin in Bakhtin/Volosinov, *Freudianism: A Marxist Critique*, the structuralism of Jacques Lacan and hermeneutic phenomenology of Henri Ey and, finally, in the deconstructive reading elaborated by Jacques Derrida – see Derrida, 1972a for example). But throughout these reconstructions the fundamental genetic schema of an analytic reconstruction of a 'depth logos' remains in play.

Indeed, for Ricoeur, Lacan, and Ey it is language and its dynamic operations in communicative situations of person-to-person relationships rather than reductive biology and unmediated instinctual forces which holds the key to the workings of the unconscious. As Lacan claimed, 'the unconscious is the discourse of the Other' (1972). Language is more than a physiological capacity or emergent biological property of human beings. It is the constitutive medium of subjectivity, and site of all conscious and unconscious processes. In this sense it is more accurate to speak of the self as a gift of the field of language. And 'language' here is shorthand for the interplay of signifiers and desire. In fact 'unconsciousness' is articulated in semiotic terms: 'we teach that the unconscious means that man is inhabited by the signifier' (1972: 66). Consequently the 'conquest' of the instinctual forces of the *Id* by self-reflection is everywhere mediated by symbolism and language. 'Desire' is always-already symbolically mediated prior to the genesis of the self and psychic structures. For Ricoeur, influenced by both semiotic and hermeneutic traditions, desire is shaped by mediations from the field of myth, tradition, and culture. In Bakhtin's texts it is the socially accented ideological dispositions sedimented in language's heteroglossia which constitute the field of consciousness. Consciousness has its being in the material reality of sign processes, a differential realm of ideological forms linked to the diverse interests, and signifying practices of different groups and classes. Every sign is thus 'accented' by evaluative preferences and dispositions to constitute the heteroglossial realms of human discourse. From the perspective of Grammatology it is the intertextuality of difference (*différance*) as an allegory of irreducible alterity at work in signification. Yet what is common to all of these revisionary theories of language is the emphasis upon the constitutive character of the *logos* in human experience. These revisionary formulations are perhaps best exemplified by Lacan's famous thesis that the unconscious is the discourse of the Other – where 'alterity' encompasses a multiplicity of factors and material processes.

Each of these theorists, despite important differences, accepts that the linguistically structured nature of conscious and unconscious processes was

Freud's great discovery – but, like many discoverers, Freud did not fully realize the radical nature of his own work as a dialectical hermeneutics of repressed experience: all the 'data' of psychotherapy have a textual organization and are therefore to be decoded as arcane messages. Since the dialogic 'text' of signs is integral to the structure of psychic life, the term 'unconscious' could be systematically replaced by the dialogic thematic of 'the discourse of the Other' – or in later variants, by the 'intertextuality of the Other'. In Lacanian termino- logy, unconscious processes are structured like language – that is, they carry within themselves the alterity of signs, the opaqueness of desire and embodi- ment (Bakhtin had analogously already 'verbalized' the dynamics of the consciousness/unconsciousness topology in proposing a semiotic archaeology of interacting 'consciousnesses'; see his *Speech Genres and Other Late Essays*, 1986). For Lacan the Subject enters the symbolic sphere through the differen- tial mediations of linguistic and social relations. The subject is constituted by the representations embedded in the productive dialogues of socialization and symbolic internalization (it is the shock of leaving the illusory unity of the 'mirror stage' precipitated by the 'law of the Father' that is treated as particu- larly crucial for the construction of subjectivity and further processes of imaginary identification, while in Bakhtin's dialogic theorizing selfhood lies in the genesis of intersubjectivity which is inseparable from the ideological struggles of class recognition and misrecognition).

What is called 'language' is not a 'faculty' of the soul of a rational animal, but rather the dialogical texture and living medium of semiotic activity, a fundamental mode of the self's existence. In the light of this conception Charles Rycroft proposes that we should take the communicative turn literally and interpret the dynamics of consciousness and unconsciousness in expressive, dialogical terms; thus dreaming 'must be communications not between two persons but between two aspects of the same person'; dreams are 'intra-per- sonal not inter-personal communications' (1991: 53). And the domain of 'intra-personal' reflexivity – the site where the topography of psychic life is articulated – will be as rich as the field of symbolic mediations. For similar reasons, Lacan distinguishes betyween the *symbolic* and the *imaginary* orders – psychic dynamics are grafted onto the theory of the child's entry into the symbolic sphere. Henri Ey also redefines the role of symbolism in unconscious processes in dialogical terms:

> the word which dwells in consciousness is a discourse, an oratorical art and not a simple transmission of signals ... the structure of consciousness can be constituted only in and through the dialectic of a being constitut- ing its language. In this respect language is not a contingent superstructure, nor an anonymous structure of consciousness, but is the structure of consciousness in debate with itself.
>
> (Ey, 1978: 17)

Further:

to be conscious is to be capable of grasping one's own knowledge in the categories of verbal communication. Such, in effect, is the conversational structure of speech through which all the phenomena which enter into the structuring of consciousness are grasped. As Janet has insisted, to be conscious is to recount one's experience; language is thus a structural quality of consciousness through which precisely this consciousness can arise in men. Speech is here the locus at which experiences are mediated and placed at the disposition of the subject.

(Ey, 1978: 16)

In other words: the speaking *psyche*, a subject that can discursively articulate desire and experience, is already a dialogic existence dispersed through a laminated network of discourse formations. Reflexive difference – the self-alienation of the subject – is now a vital precondition of dialogic individuation. Without the immanent differences of psychic life no project of selfhood could be undertaken: without the Other, no I; without alterity, no communality; without language, no speaking self. This is perhaps one of the central claims of psychoanalytic genealogy: 'language' arises in the diacritical structure of consciousness in dialogue with itself. Consciousness as self-reflection and self-interpretation is now describable as a dialogue of voices and affective 'positions' exemplified in the living-accounting-intersubjective experience of concrete speaking and acting human agents: 'The subject is born insofar as the signifier emerges in the field of the Other. But by this very fact, this subject – which was previously nothing if not a subject coming into being – solidifies into a signifier' (Ey, 1978: 16ff.). The traditional conception of 'what language essentially is' is broadened to include the prereflective realms of affectivity, desire, and non-verbal symbolism. And these horizons of experience inevitably open out upon concrete historical, political, social, and cultural formations – relations which now demand to be explicitly theorized within any comprehensive reflexive psychology and psychoanalytic praxis.

In acknowledging the opaque 'dialectic' of psychic life as an interface between genealogically prior life forms, historical practices, and institutions (the 'Law of the Father'), and the verbal imbrications of the Logos, contemporary psychoanalysis (in the hands of its most responsible and sensitive critics) confirms the intuitions set to work by the author of *De Anima*: verbal reflexivity shapes itself in the restless spirit of a self-questioning consciousness, the transitional site of human coexistence as being-together-in-language. Echoes of the ancient Socratic art of dialectic live on within contemporary psychoanalytic therapy: 'we' come to ourselves, relate to ourselves, transform ourselves by sharing a common questioning relationship to the ever-questionable horizons opened by language – 'language' now expanded to encompass the diverse affective, moral, practical, epistemic, oneiric, aesthetic spectrum of discourses constituting the genealogical horizon of every moral community. 'Language' appears wherever the body enfolds itself in systems of incarnate significance – the 'body' is another misleading term for the totality of affective articulations. And if 'moral order' – the superstructural sphere of the Superego (*über-Ich*) – is only possible for a norm-relating and value-orienting creature, then moral life has its grounds in the concrete verbal dialectics of Self-Other transactions. Psychic life is not an 'effect' of causally prior structures (biology is not destiny), but is a dialogical product of the field of social experience itself: 'desire is the desire of the Other'.

We initially began these investigations by naively assuming that we could without any principled difficulty reflect on reflection and self-reflection, but now discover that the subterranean correlates of these problems were always already mediated 'structures' of language, sociality, and moral community. Reflexivity as an irreducible mode of social-being-in-language turns out to be a dialogic movement of self-communication. The generic capacity to speak enters into a definition of the human being as a communicative, interpretive agent. This is a 'Freudian' insight won despite the reductive biologism and naturalistic positivism inherent in Freud's original programme. The alterity of 'already existing' practices and social institutions are already functioning to give meaning to the world in which the individuals have to locate themselves as speaking subjects. The founding insight of psychoanalytic reflexivity teaches that there is no unmediated experience accessible to human beings; that every form of the Same is indebted to the circuitry of the Other: that the 'I' and the 'Other' are moments of a Möbian transaction which spirals away into that darker field of desire, phantasy, and imagination which psychoanalysis designates as 'the Unconscious'. Freud seems to have thought of the Unconscious as the threshhold and limit of consciousness – something that could only be evoked by negative and paralogical attributes:

> It is the dark inaccessible part of our personality; what little we know of it we have learnt from our study of the dream-work and of the construction of neurotic symptoms, and most of that is of a negative character and can be described only as a contrast to the ego. We approach the id with analogies; we call it chaos, a cauldron. It is filled with energy reaching it from the instincts, but it has no organization, produces no collective will ... the logical laws of thought do not apply ... contrary impulses exist side by side without cancelling each other out ... There is nothing in the id that corresponds to the idea of time ... The id, of course, knows no judgements of value; no good and evil, no morality.
>
> (Freud, quoted by Rycroft, 1991: 155)

It follows that the struggle to create a 'meaningful world' or 'integrated self' is an interminable project riddled with contradictions – the self is no longer a cohesive 'centre' of experience, but a polemical process of self-construction and self-creation within an already-structured dialogue with other 'consciousnesses'. As Freud correctly intuited, the disengaged subject of Cartesian epistemology – the sovereign Ego of consciousness – is not a monarch over its introspective field, but is thoroughly mediated by the very operations and functions which constitute ego-consciousness, by the 'chaotic' processes of reflexive experience – archaic desires, libidinal energy, non-logical condensations and displacements, the dark dialectic of Self and Other. Our initial orientation to the introspective structure of subjectivity does not lead, as we might have anticipated, to the lonely centre of a personal labyrinth but back to the public, polemical, heterogeneous, transgressive life of collective signification – to the dialogical life of language, familial experience, authority, and power relations incarnated in social practices and materialized institutions:

> We are thus approaching the reflexive structure of consciousness in which language adds its power by constituting itself ... language, interwoven with the intersubjective ties which are its vehicle, forms within itself a heterogeneous space which is the lived and verbally articulated space of the field of consciousness, but which is also the *logos* of the self insofar as the person is formed only in uttering itself. But in and through this double function which incorporates it into lived experience and into the formation of the self, *it enters into consciousness only by positing the Unconsciousness as a dimension of its own discourse.*
> (Ey, 1978: 18–19; cf. Ragland-Sullivan, 1986, ch. 1; Žižek, 1989)

3 GENEALOGICAL THERAPIES

Alternative versions of the 'genealogical impulse' abound in the different schools and traditions of contemporary psychoanalysis, each culminating in a different therapeutic praxis. Nietzsche's 'genealogy of values' might be canvassed as the single most important source of the archaeological self-examination of the unconscious horizons of human experience. Nietzsche's particular version of reflexivity – heir to the ancient injunction 'Know Thyself', the Enlightenment project of self-determination posited by the autonomous rational Subject, and the Romantic discourse of 'self-overcoming' – takes an explicitly historicist and culturally relativizing stance: there are no moral facts, only moral interpretations of phenomena; and since we can only study human arrangements as valorizing processes, the self-analysis of value-positing praxis is itself – in reflexive fashion – a value-commitment ordered by its therapeutic success in uncovering 'unconscious' systems of illusion and misinterpretations through which cultures organize their practices. By removing the sources and structures of illusory 'idols' we can effect something like a personal and cultural 'cure' – we can learn to live without the 'spiritual crutches' of Metaphysics, Religion, and 'bourgeois culture'. Above all we can divest ourselves of the metaphysical ideas of God, Certainty, Unity, and 'two-world' interpretations of life. By means of this 'catharsis' we may once more accept life purely as an immanent realm of value-positing acts and finite projects of meaning. We can then live a desacralized, post-Metaphysical existence. With Nietzsche the ancient directive 'Know Thyself' points toward a genealogy of the axiological self-interpretations founding societies and civilizations, rather than an egocentric psycho-analysis of individual pathologies. The power structures defining the body-in-culture are prior to the individual body-ego. In this his image of the post-nihilistic Self recuperating its history bears comparison to Hegel's *Phenomenology* as a study of the objectifications and valorizations of incarnate consciousness. But the values celebrated by Hegel have, as it were, been reversed. We are to pursue the spirit of self-reflection in its immanent, finite, this-worldly incarnations and by this means cure ourselves from the curse of *Geist*.

But it is also true to say that Nietzsche shares with later analysis – whether Freudian, Jungian, or Adlerian – a view of the therapeutic and emancipative objectives of genealogy, as self-inquiry removing layers of occlusive (mis)interpretations – illusions, obsessions, repressions, fears, neuroses, reification, misrecognitions, myths, etc. – which systematically block or inhibit alternative possibilities of human embodiment. Nietzsche's philological readings even preserve the Romantic hermeneutic motif of uncovering and reintegrating lost worlds of significance. Despite his anarchic reputation Nietzsche also shares a systematic commitment with later psychoanalysis: genealogy is charged with systematically disoccluding the unconscious processes at work in the founding axiological charters of modern society and culture – the 'illnesses' of our existence are ultimately 'depth' pathologies which no amount of surface treatment and therapy can cure. To this extent these nineteenth-century 'therapies' betray a latent Romantic pathos for a 'lost unity'. And not accidentally, they all lead to conceptions of therapy as instruments of heroic individuation. Nietzsche is simply the most explicit and intellectually honest exponent of the promissory ideal of Romantic transfiguration.

Perhaps rather than 'Nietzsche' we should speak of 'Nietzschean reflexivity' to index the way in which Nietzsche's texts have been differentially incorporated into a variety of poststructuralist enterprises which are by no means reducible to a single 'perspective' or 'school': consider, for example, his role in the work of Jacques Deleuze, Michel Foucault, Jean-François Lyotard, Philippe Lacoue-Labarthe, Felix Guattari, and Vincent Descombes. But while the attempt to derail positivism and formalism at the level of method by using Nietzschean 'philology' has proven illusory, the different theoretical possibilities generated by this 'dialogue with Nietzsche' have had productive consequences for contemporary cultural theorizing. The 'genealogical' theme of power-knowledge in contemporary philosophy, sociology, psychology, and cultural studies is one of the most striking products of this critical encounter with Nietzsche's thought. Interest in the 'archaeology' of concepts, discourses, disciplines, and practices has become central to the project of contemporary cultural analysis.

Nietzsche has not been read simply to criticize the methodologies of the human sciences, but rather as a source of positive strategies to circumvent their basic presuppositions and to reconstruct different 'objects of knowledge' and inquiries. Michel Foucault's violent reading of Nietzschean problematics has been the most influential example of this process of appropriation. From Nietzsche Foucault derived a new and potentially more radical reflexive thematic: not the history of the moral self, but the genealogy of the 'knowledges' into which the self is inscribed – a history of the subject as a mutable discursive formation (see Foucault's *The Order of Things: An Archaeology of the Human Sciences* (1970), *The Archaeology of Knowledge* (1972), *The Birth of the Clinic: An Archaeology of Medical Perception* (1973), *Discipline and Punish: the Birth of the Prison* (1976) and the multivolume *History of Sexuality* – for Foucault's reflection on his own methods see his essay 'Nietzsche, genealogy, history' (in 1977a) and *The History of Sexuality, Volume 1: An Introduction* (1979)). In Foucault's view, Nietzschean reflexivity serves as a corrective of the narrowly individualistic archaeology of traditional psychoanalysis animated by the self-evidence of the 'repressive hypothesis'. Yet both therapies are genealogical in construing self-inquiry as the reprieve of repressed unconscious, prepredicative, forgotten experience. They both link the return of the repressed with a strengthening of the Self's powers of reflexive control and affirmative freedoms. But psychoanalysis fails to reflect on the sociality of its own concepts; it resolutely adheres to the individualistic terms of the philosophy of consciousness and makes no effort to ground its own praxis in societal semiopraxis. Freud's account of 'lay-analysis' and 'self-analysis', when compared to the direction taken by the rest of his work, are occasional thoughts or asides rather than systematic attempts to explore the strengths and limits of analysis's own version of self and community.

It is not the least of the many ironies of contemporary psychoanalysis that the most radical horizons of reflexivity – especially with respect to the project of critique and emancipation – have been repressed and excluded in psychoanalytic theory and practice (psychoanalysis's notorious tendency to positivistic closure, to foreclose dialogue with other reflexive disciplines and perspectives, its gender-blindness, and its failure radically to question its own language and moral commitments are well-known expressions of the strength of unanalyzed presuppositions in a discipline that is formally committed to the normative ideal of reflexive emancipation through configurational 'analysis'). One of the undeniable achievements of recent feminist critiques of Lacanian psychoanalytic theory and the practical therapies it has licensed – particularly in the writings of Luce Irigaray, Hélène Cixous, Julia Kristeva, and others – has been to draw attention to the insurmountable patriarchal and phallocentric limits of the basic assumptions and methods of both orthodox and heterodox (e.g. Kleinian, Laingian, Lacanian) analytic practice, and to suggest alternative ways of thinking and conceptualizing the otherness and reflexivity of women's experience (Oliver, 1993: ch. 7 and Conclusion).

4 PHENOMENOLOGICAL REACTIVATION

I must lose the world by epoché, in order to regain it by a universal self-examination.

(Edmund Husserl, 1960: 157)

A profoundly genealogical 'dialogue' with occlusive structures also animates the later writings of Edmund Husserl and those thinkers such as Maurice Merleau-Ponty, Paul Ricoeur, Henri Ey, Alfred Schutz, Thomas Luckmann, and Jean-François Lyotard who were deeply influenced by Husserl's explorations of the *Lebenswelt*. We have already seen that self-reflection in Husserl's earlier phenomenology took a predominantly egological, epistemic, and onto-logical-foundationalist direction: the constitutive Subject or Ego 'lost in the world' wills itself to recollect its own anonymous intentional life by explicating the intentional substructures of cognition, returning itself to the temporalizing experience of transcendental consciousness (often later interpreted as the foundational realm of transcendental intersubjectivity). The radical method of phenomenological reflection revolves around a quasi-Cartesian theory of the subject and subjective self-certainty and never completely abandoned the metaphysical impulse of its original source. The alienation of science from its sustaining life-world is implicitly defined as a problem to be resolved at the level of individual consciousness, precisely as the 'loss of meaning' implicit in the naturalization of consciousness (psychologism, anthropologism, scien-tism, etc.). The ethic of cognitive self-responsibility is particularly strong in Husserl's later historicist account of the self-shaping work of the Transcen-dental Ego that is implicitly present from the beginnings of European philosophy and science. But this 'return to origins' or genealogy is now given a dialogic inflection. The turn in Husserlian phenomenology appears to have occurred around the time of Husserl's lecture series entitled 'The crisis of European sciences and psychology', given in Prague in 1935, but the theme can be found in his manuscripts on the 'Origin of geometry' and in writings dating from the early 1920s (Husserl, 1970: 269–400).

The changed social and political context from the 1920s up to the catas-trophe of 1933 had also rendered the idea of a 'solipsistic' transcendental phenomenology fundamentally impotent to address the 'crisis of European reason' precipitated by the political and cultural crisis of middle Europe. Given the situation of rising irrationality, a more radical 'reactivation' (*Rückfrage*) of reason and experience is called for. 'What', Husserl ask, in *The Crisis of European Sciences and Transcendental Phenomenology*, 'can the mission of radical philosophy be in response to the gathering darkness of unreason and forgetfulness?' Philosophy as the vocation of self-understanding and reason must continue its 'archaeological' work of self-reflection (radicalizing even further the universal-self-examination of the *Cartesian Meditations* to embrace a 'civilizational' horizon), but its meaning and direction is now fundamentally changed. Husserl begins to speak in the Hegelian idiom of the spirit of radical reflexivity and even – if we can accept Enzo Paci's reconstruction – in a Marxist register by advancing toward a critique of alienated science and philosophy in the era of Monopoly Capitalism. Universal self-reflection strives to recover its own forgotten meaning-strata and historicity by bracketing mundane reason and all forms of reductive objectivism, facilitating the recovery of the universal meaning-acquisitions, motivations, and *telos* of a rational humanity (self-reflection is no longer an event within the Self, but a collective commitment of the human species in its pursuit of a fully transparent, universal community of Reason). Philosophical reflection, Reason, and Truth as the 'spiritual' *telos* of humanity now displace the monadic life of the transcendental Ego. The alienation problematic explored by Hegel, Marx, and Lukács reappears at the centre of phenomenological reactivation, a philosophical movement which *places itself* at the heart of European culture as the unveiling and recovery of the *sense* and *telos* of a rational life. Husserlian phenomenology, understood as a genealogical critique of alienated experience, was forced by the crisis of European culture to foreground the utopian moment implicit in the theory of intentional transcendence.

Husserlian phenomenology attempted to 'solve' the problem of Reason faced with universal unreason – the vocation of philosophical reflexivity – by displacing rationality from its traditional site in the isolated Cartesian Ego and the Transcendental Subject and relocating it in the teleological project of an idealized collective Subject – 'Humanity' as an immanent 'carrier' or 'embodiment' of a nascent Reason (of which Husserl's own transcendental phenomenology was an incarnation and partial exemplar). The phenomenological studies of everyday experience and the critique of mathematical science in the *Crisis* can be considered to be an attempted *aufhebung* – supersession as overcoming, transcending, and preservation – of the spirit of his earlier radical phenomenology. Husserlian phenomenology in effect collectivizes the subject as the founding centre of all actual and possible experience, reflection, and analysis. The 'pure Ego' is abolished only to reappear as the suprahistorical consciousness of European Reason. It is apparent that this 'Hegelian' turn within the phenomenological problematic is not unconnected with the political events of 1932–3 and the long-durational crisis of culture dating from around 1880 to the 1930s and beyond.

Clearly here we are faced with one of the most aporetic manifestations of the European dream of a universal legislative reflexivity. But from the point of view of logological therapy it is a symptomatic instance of the crisis of philosophical reflexivity that is still construed in totalizing, metaphysical terms. In the writings of the later Husserl the ties between the field of experience, subjective reflection, and constituting life (*Leistungen*) are even more intimate and more desperately ambivalent. Transcendental Phenomenology redefines its own *telos* as the act of phenomenological reactivation that participates in the universal teleology of 'becoming rational' – thematized as Western civilization's universalistic orientation toward Reason as its immanent, motivational *entelechy*: the interminable criticism of alienating conditions and the unfinished project of emancipated humanity. Husserl rediscovers the twin thematics of experiential reason and concrete freedom. Here the very possibility of radical self-reflection is understood as an 'anonymous' product of sedimented motivations and forms of life articulated by the earliest Greek thinkers (and the immanent movement of Greek language and civilization). Self-reflection now appears to Husserl as the most important *ethical* obligation of the human species in its transformative, collective work to dereify the unreflexive structures of the sciences and their metatheoretical elaboration in contemporary philosophy. The 'unrationality' of the reductive, positivistic sciences are surface manifestations of the irrationalism that flourishes where the practice and institutionalization of reflexivity atrophies and decays. Radical phenomenological ontology thus assumes an ethical and even political significance: a more resolute pursuit of reflexive ontological understanding is called for in the face of the catastrophic situation of European civilization. As the wreckage piled up, the pure philosopher pursued ever 'deeper' eidetic inquiries into the 'fundaments' of consciousness. In this delusional system the millennial 'loss of meaning' could only be stemmed by embracing the pure reflexivity of Transcendental philosophy. It is not merely the fate of philosophical reflection that is now at stake, but the whole movement of European Reason and its sustaining ideal of truth. This, of course, is the famous thesis of the radical 'return' to the *Lebenswelt* as the ultimate source of meaning-practices (including the alienated practices of the sciences and earlier forms of radical self-reflection).

Unlike his earlier commitment to epistemic self-reflection, Husserl's later account of reactivation introduces a historical dialectic of subjectivity and objectivity defining the dialogical character of human existence. In many respects some of his descriptive insights converge on themes earlier worked out by Hegel in the *Encyclopaedia of the Philosophical Sciences* and the *Philosophical Propaedeutic*. But unlike the Hegelian paradigm of Spirit the grounding and horizon of Husserl's dialectic is not concretely explicated and in the last analysis remains firmly within the terminological calipers and logological presuppositions of transcendental idealism. In Husserl's programme philosophical self-reflection – the phenomenological theory of the constitutive transcendental subject – recovers its ancient Socratic role as the midwife of a universal reason 'inborn' in European humanity. European philosophy – in the concrete shape of a society of transcendental phenomenologists, all committed practioners of the radical 'world *epoché*' – is the only saving grace against the waves of unreason and irrationality. Defence of the Absolute Idea of Reason is only possible in the 'shape of reflective consciousness' embodied in a universal programme of transcendental genealogy. Husserl is constrained by an ambivalent and critically undeveloped account of everyday life (*Alltäglichkeit*) as the embodiment of this innate rationality; on the one hand, everyday life is explicitly grasped as the sociocultural domain of the

life-world organized predominantly by pragmatic motivations and constrained by the routinized properties of 'naive', unreflexive, daily living; on the
other hand, everyday life is what emerges when the 'naiveties' of everyday
experience and naturalistic science are transcended and the world-experiencing-life of transcendental consciousness is disclosed as the occluded source of
all meaning and reason. Between these two interpretations we hear little of the
concrete practical, ethical, and social mediations of reflexive experience. The
concrete problems and socioeconomic determinations of reflexivity in its
specific institutional and historical contexts have to be grafted onto the Husserlian project (as the interpretations of Husserl worked out in the writings of
Merleau-Ponty, Enzo Paci, Paul Piccone, Karel Kosík, Jan Patocka, and others
have demonstrated). In this respect Husserl's later phenomenology falls behind the dialectical thought-patterns established in *The Phenomenology of
Spirit* and the seminal ideas contained in Marx's *Economic and Philosophical
Manuscripts*. Consider:

> daily practical living is naive. It is immersion in the already-given world,
> whether it be experiencing, or thinking, or valuing, or acting. Meanwhile
> all those productive intentional functions of experiencing, because of
> which physical things are simply there, go on anonymously. The exper-
> iencer knows nothing about them, and likewise nothing about his
> productive thinking.[1]

This is what the phenomenological *epoché* or transcendental phenomenological reduction is designed to disclose. As a 'functionary' in the vocation of
Reason, the self-reflecting Ego must 'deprive the world which formerly, within
the natural attitude, was simply posited as being, of just this posited being, and
he must return to the living stream of his experiences of the world.' In this
stream, however, the experienced world along with its positive sciences is
retained exactly as a phenomenological residuum with the contents which
actually belong to it. After the execution of the *epoché*, the world in no way
vanishes from the field of experience of the philosophically reflecting Ego. On
the contrary, what is grasped by the performance of *epoché* is taken to be the
pure life of consciousness in which and through which the whole objective
world exists for me, by virtue of the fact that I experience it, perceive it,
remember it, etc. The fundamental change is that in the *epoché* I abstain from
belief in the being of this world, and I direct my view exclusively to my
consciousness of the world' (I have paraphrased from the account of Husserl's
student, Alfred Schutz; see his essay 'Phenomenology and the social sciences',
in 1967a: 122–3). With the aporetic reification of 'everyday life' as the central
theme of phenomenology we elide a richer view of human praxis and with this
foreshortening are denied a more comprehensive understanding of the dialectical relationships and institutions of reflexivity in language, embodiment,
sociality, and history.[2] Because of these intrinsic limitations the notion of 'the
everyday' or the 'natural, pregiven life-world' as a mutable, transformative,

historical horizon of different reflexive possibilities cannot be developed within the existing framework of transcendental or social phenomenology. Rather the crisis of modern reason invites a reflexive critique of phenomeno-logical reason and metaphysical idealism as themselves symptoms of the societal alienation of everyday life in the epoch of modern industrialism and advanced technology (cf. Lefebvre, 1991a).

However, to approach the insights of Husserl and his students dialectically, we can say that the 'amnesic' structure of the world-as-taken-for-granted, once recognized, discloses the possibility of a more radical dialogic reflexivity; but in Husserlian and Schutzian phenomenology this insight is buried again in a one-sided social phenomenology of 'mundane existence'; the subjects of expe-rience become reflexive by remembering that the 'world-as-meant' is possible only as a genealogical achievement of living subjective intentions; as Schutz notes,

> in this universe of the experiencing life of the transcendental subjectivity I find my entire cogitations of the life-world which surrounds me, a life-world to which also belongs my life with others and its pertinent community-forming processes, which actively and passively shape this life world into a social world.

(1967a: 123)

Self-reflection re-collects the living matrix of constitution that has been sedi-mented and lost in creating the provinces of meaning in which human beings move and have their being. Schutz again is unintentionally apposite: 'I can return fundamentally to the originary experience of the life-world in which the facts themselves can be grasped directly.' In this way the Cartesian myth of immediacy secretly returns as a dispassionate method of studying and recovering the 'structures of the life-world'. The fundamental framework remains part of the metaphysical project begun in the seventeenth century: the radical reactivation of primordial experience is thus 'a true science of mind (*Geist*)', 'the only method, which seriously means to be a radical explanation of the world through mind' (Schutz, 1967a: 122–3). But the cost incurred by this recourse to the categories of metaphysical idealism is one of viewing the life-world as an ahistorical and precultural 'stratum' of existence (homologous to the crude Marxist notion of 'the economic' as the base 'storey' of social life and its cultural 'superstructures'). In other words, recidivist idealism blocks a more radical critique of the concrete structures and configurations of everyday life.

Phenomenology has, as it were, sprung without mediation from an archae-ology of monologic perception (the early Husserlian theory of the perceptual life-world) to an idealist teleology of the life-world as the ultimate context of European Humanity and universal Reason. Husserl's deep-rooted Cartesian assumptions concerning 'being conscious' have occluded the more radical possibilities of a dialogic phenomenology of 'becoming conscious' – covering up what I have described as the richer field of logological phenomena which are revealed once the videological framework of classical metaphysics is abandoned. In these respects Husserlian phenomenology needs to be corrected and 'transcended' by a return to the dialectical phenomenology of Hegel. I will return to these themes in more detailed studies of the significant impact of the phenomenological project in contemporary European thought and culture in later volumes of this work.

5 SEMIOTIC ANALYSIS

In self-conscious opposition to the metaphysical philosophy of reflection and more especially to Husserl's phenomenological metaphysics of self-reflection, semiotic genealogy – often referred to more broadly as the structuralist revolution – commences with the always-already existing field of language (*la langue, parole, discourse, signifier-signified relations, signification*, and so forth). *Signification* rather than *perceptual intuition* provides the fundamental *leitmotif* of this paradigm. The seminal orientation is provided by the structural model of language elaborated by Ferdinand de Saussure (1857–1913) in the *Course in General Linguistics*. For semiotics, self-reflection – where it is recognized or admitted as a valid epistemological category – is an emergent property of pregiven structures of signification, the ability of sign users to signify through arbitrary signs and, at a higher level, to self-referentially signify about signs by metacommunicatively examining the forms and conditions of signification itself. Rather than being the still centre of the world, the individual posited by humanism is viewed as an epiphenomenon of prior layers of structuration already embedded in the domains of social order, culture, and even biological systems. The aporetic nature of the central thesis of French semiology – the decentring of the metaphysical subject by anonymous, overdetermining 'structures' – should be noted in this context. Underlying structural logics actively 'pre-construct' the forms of individual experience and selfhood. Intuition, perception, thought, and so forth, are always-already indebted to a prior system of signification. To escape from the grip of commonsense empiricism every project of knowledge must thus descend from appearances to the underlying realm of essential forms by respecifying its 'object field' as the product of depth structures and formal operations. 'Appearances' become the appearances-of underlying systems of signification and structuring operations. In sum: reflective discourse and subjectivity are now considered to be effects of the differential play of signs – *la chaîne articulatoire* – and their syntagmatic-paradigmatic relations as these are defined by the conceptual tools of formal linguistics. The pure realm of consciousness or absolute interiority posited by the metaphysical tradition no longer exists. 'Subjects', 'subjective reflection', and thought are produced by entering the structured field of language. The life-world of human beings is always-already organized by sign systems and discourse formations. Thus the experiential formations postulated by phenomenology and the philosophy of reflection are the derivative 'effects' of underlying depth-codes and generative signifying systems that are anterior to all forms of self-reflection.

The archetypal instance of this type of structural model can be found in Lévi-Strauss' hyperrationalism in his *Anthropologie structurale* (1958) where the underlying symbolic order of mythology, kinship systems, and social institutions – as systems of signification – is traced to the binary codes of 'unconscious reason' tracing the universal operations of the human mind.

Given the self-imposed assumptions of the structuralist project, what has to be accepted are the social codes of communication and most particularly the networks created by language as an objective domain of language-like rules (*la langue, la faculté du langage articulé*: 'Language might be called the domain of articulations') prior to all linguistic performances and social relations. Unlike the 'Fido-Fido' theory of meaning where every sign 'names' or 'refers to' a fixed object or referent, the semiotic perspective introduces the universal mediation of arbitrary signifier-signified networks as coded *forms* ('The linguistic sign unites, not a thing and a name, but a concept and a sound-image (Saussure, 1983: ch. 1)). Language as an objective structuring activity and a supraindividual institution is taken to be the primary model of signifying practice. Language consists of a system of interdependent terms (signfiers) in which the value of each sign arises wholly from its contextual relationships with others. Every present structure of signification thus implicates a system of absent signifiers; every speech expression is possible only as the product of a system of virtual semiotic relationships. Following the directives of Saussurean linguistics and Durkheimian sociology, orthodox semiotics privileges synchronic over diachronic relations, the invariant deep structures of *la langue* over the 'vagaries' of *la parole*, and syntagmatic models of 'interpellation' over experiential concreteness and paradigmatic displacements. In the standard formula, it is the *system* of differences – the *spacing of differentiation* – which creates significance: 'in language there are only differences ... differences *without positive terms*.' Thus 'phonemes are above all else opposing, relative, and negative entities'.

However in its more radical incarnations – associated with the work of Roland Barthes (1915–80), Jacques Lacan (1901–), Louis Althusser (1918–90), Michel Foucault (1926–84), and Jacques Derrida (1930–) – the diacritical chain of differences spreads throughout semantic space and never comes to rest in an ultimate 'signified'. A more radical semiology – for example, the positions elaborated by the *Tel Quel* group of thinkers – including Philippe Sollers, Julia Kristeva, and Jacques Derrida – emancipated the play of signifiers from the grip of 'the transcendental signified' to institute a poststructural framework of discourse. The manifold realms of language, art, and culture are no longer construed as a constraining grid of syntagmatic-paradigmatic coordinates, but are viewed as a vast field of discursive structuration and signifying transformations – a 'galaxy of signifiers, not a structure of signifieds' in Roland Barthes' memorable phrase. Rather than deep *structures* we now find language 'in play' as an interminable intertextual deferral of surface meaning: *reality is the effect of infinitely deferred signification*. The initial monologism and methodological solipsism of semiotic formalism – the science of sign systems functioning in the shadow of metaphysics – is abandoned for the dialogic pluralism of deconstructive strategies of reading and interpretation.

In historical perspective we can see that it is only within the context of the cultural dominance of formal reason and structural modes of thought that something like a poststructural conception of language, texts, the subject, and culture could be established. The post-structuralist view of language as decentred signification is thus historically indebted to the prior epistemology of structural signification worked out in a range of different social science fields during the late 1960s and 1970s. And as we have seen the essential move is to reverse the accent of determination from the order of the signified to the structuration of signifiers – the free textual play of signifiers is privileged over the fixed combinatorial rules of normative syntax and the hegemonic system. The logocentric desire for a unified meaning or concealed knowledge behind signification, a centred knowledge and unmediated 'access' to the referent are delayed by the endless relaying and dispersive tracery of signifiers, desire, and the workings of the unconscious (Derrida, 1967; Barthes, 1975; Lacan, 1966, 1968, 1977, 1978). In fact the very fascination with the idea of a 'final' reference point for significatory activities in an original signified (the *transcendental signified*) is itself grasped as an imaginative achievement and ideology of the 'infinite' relay of signifier-signifier figurations ('the infinity of language' in Barthes' *S/Z* replaces the Husserlian 'infinity of consciousness'). The Western metaphysical dream of closure and totality pursued by early structural paradigms is symptomatic of the impossibility of terminating the open-ended play of cultural praxis. Totality and closure are then seen as illusory attempts to discipline the *imaginary* by excising the aporetic possibilities of *reflexivity* and desire from the sphere of signifying practices. The Platonic war on *mimesis* is replayed as formal reason objectifies and represses its own reflexive background.

But once the intrinsically reflexive dimensions of human action and signification as polymodal desire and multiple coding are accepted, semiosis as an 'infinite' recursive network of traces can be extended to the discursive problematics of selfhood, subjectivity, and the symbolic order (the similarity of themes in Lacan's *Écrits* and Barthes' *Le Plaisir du Texte* is not accidental). The subject then becomes a questionable domain of textual relations subject to the interminable processes of semiotic deciphering and social deconstruction. This principled reflexivity also applies to every semiotic deconstruction of the self, including, of course, the texts opposing structural logics and exemplifying deconstructionist strategies. One outcome of this internal debate within postwar French social science and philosophy is the respecification of the fundamental question of the nature of communication in personal and social life and, as a consequence, the opening of the relatively closed perspectives of semiology to a richer dialogue with other models of social communication and social power (in a deeper sense this continuing 'dialogue' reveals large areas of overlap within Continental European philosophical traditions, particularly in relation to phenomenology, hermeneutics, critical theory, linguistic analysis, and text theory).

Another consequence of the deconstructive turn of semiotic theory is the idea that human semiosis with its hierarchically embedded nesting structures of reference and delicately coded patterns of self-reference makes communication about communication a normal feature of ordinary language, especially in the context of reciprocal dialogic exchanges which have evolved structures to facilitate ongoing semiotic analysis and explication as routine features of everyday communication. Reinscribed as a *social semiotics* focusing upon the nature of meaning, discourse, and communication, this view of self-reflection comes close to the concept of logological reflexivity and its insight concerning the figural involvement of language across every interpretive domain of human culture. But like phenomenological analysis before it, semiotics' emphasis upon the interplay of structuration and destructuration tends to downplay the critical concerns of sociological reflection – historical institutions, social relations, praxis, institution, power, alienation, social change, and so forth. A more productive dialogue with the problematics of social theory and sociology has been pre-empted with the exclusive formal concern for closed formal structures (the structural phase) and the obsession with the instability and undecidability of all meaning (in the 'poststructural' phase of semiotics).

Although many of these themes are presupposed by structuralist analysis, it still remains the case that the application of structural theory in the writings of Ferdinand de Saussure, Claude Lévi-Strauss, Emile Benveniste, Roland Barthes, Louis Althusser, and others, has not explicitly explored the reflexive grounds, the historical institutions, or the intrinsic limits of the semiotic project. The uncritical appeal to the authority of science and objective knowledge that served to legitimate the original structuralist project is not itself grasped as a commitment to a specific semiological code (Umberto Eco's attempt to produce a Philosophy of Semiotics, Roland Barthes' attempt to transcend scientific semiotics in terms of a deconstructive *semioclastics*, and Jacques Derrida's grammatology are notable exceptions to this generalization). We are still justified in applying the same critical reservations we directed against orthodox phenomenology. One possible exception to these strictures lies in the project of a more self-conscious and reflexive form of hermeneutic thought.

6 HERMENEUTIC REPETITION

I should imagine that the name Hermes has to do with speech, and signifies that he is the interpreter, or messenger, or thief, or liar, or bargainer; all that sort of thing has a great deal to do with language.

(Plato, *Cratylus* 408A)

If semiotics concentrates upon the formal conditions of semiosis, hermeneutic repetition proposes to read, retrieve, and reconstruct the occluded signs and texts of human experience in their particular personal, mythic, literary, social, and political contexts. The *leitmotif* of hermeneutics is the irremediably mediated processes of *human understanding* and *interpretation*. The key-words here are *meaning*, *understanding*, and *interpretation*. Hermeneutic analysis strives interpretively to reprieve the lost traces of meaning as expressive documents of subjective life embodied in acts of meaning and communication. Hermeneutic paradigms methodically reinterpret the traces of past acts of meaning as a palimpsest of occluded meanings; at its most radical and expansive – in so-called 'philosophical hermeneutics' – the perspective aspires to reconstruct the 'phenomenal worlds' of alien cultures and forms of life which sustained these earlier acts of significance. By discursive repetition the analyst may enter into the understanding-worlds of other cultures. Hermeneutic self-reflection, then, appropriates experience in accord with the schema of symptomatic interpretive repetition – typically expressed as a linguistic recovery of the hermeneutic rules of a text-like product from an alien way of life. Where structuralism privileges universal codes, the interpretive paradigm stresses local knowledge and 'reading-in-context'; where semiotics uncovers 'deep structures' organizing a given domain of semiosis, hermeneutics looks toward the operative conventions and practical canons facilitating a cultural practice of reading; where structural methodologies strive to decode and demystify cognitive systems, hermeneutics seeks to 'understand' and 'interpret' the 'surplus significance' of beliefs, texts, and actions.

A more recent, revisionary 'critical hermeneutics' has advocated a concept of reading in which texts are seen as dialogical occasions for interpretive recuperation of the self (as possible sites of radical self-interpretation – for example, in the dialogical hermeneutics of Hans-Georg Gadamer, Paul Ricoeur, Hans Robert Jauss, Wolfgang Iser, and Stanley Fish). Gadamer in particular has pursued the post-Heideggerian philosophical programme of an ontological respecification of 'the human condition' as existence-in-dialogue: our very being-in-the-world is to *be* dialogical *beings* (Bernstein, 1991: 49). As Bernstein notes: 'Gadamer's entire corpus can be read as an invitation to join him in the rediscovery and redemption of the richness and concreteness of our dialogical being-in-the-world' (Bernstein, 1991: 49). Modern hermeneutics, or 'philosophical hermeneutics' in Gadamer's nomenclature, situates itself between the field of the preinterpreted life-world and the language-horizons of diverse and heterogeneous traditions.

Of course different strategies of hermeneutic reading (psychoanalytic, ontological, archteypal-symbolic, sociological, reader-oriented, and so forth) have given rise to various programmes of discourse analysis and 'interpretive repetition' linked to what has come to be called post-structuralist and post-phenomenological philosophy. In the idiom of the present discussion, the theory of hermeneutic repetition with its thematic focus upon the diverse uses of language and correlated versions of self clearly points in the direction of logological research (for example, in recognizing the metaphorical roots of videology and beginning the exploration of the rhetorical basis of 'self-reflection' as a cultural achievement rather than an innate impulse of the human mind). This is especially the case for recent work in interpretive critical theory.

Critical hermeneutics invites its practioners to explore the verbal figurations of self and reflective experience as achievements of local cultures and historical traditions – it deepens our awareness of the necessary verbal and textual nature of being-in-the-world and underlines the importance of studying discursive acts in the social and communicational contexts of everyday life. And appropriately the paradigmatic images of knowledge and education are revised in the direction of a pedagogics of reading and interpretation. Becoming reflexive is no longer a matter of world-withdrawing introspection but a disciplined process of careful 'reading' and the active refiguring of self through a dialogue with other reading selves. Education becomes 'educare', a process leading the self to a more comprehensive understanding of its own multiple textual horizons. Hermeneutics foregrounds the non-formalizable contexts that enter into the work of meaning and understanding. Interpretation now consists of a range of active 'reading' and 'rewriting' processes engaged in by social and linguistic agents against an unarticulated network of background assumptions. In this sense, it is not merely a methodology of the *Geisteswissenschaften* but, more importantly, the ontological medium of *all* life-world praxis (see Ricoeur, *Lectures on Ideology and Utopia* (1986); Dallmayr, *Life-world, Modernity and Critique* (1991); Thompson, *Critical Hermeneutics* (1981) and *Studies in the Theory of Ideology* (1984)).

7 CRITIQUE AND METACRITIQUE

Our age is, in especial degree, the age of criticism, and to criticism everything must submit.

(I. Kant, 1929: A xii, n. a)

The evolution of the conceptual grammar of 'critique' warrants an extensive genealogical study in its own right (cf. Benhabib, 1986; Jay, 1984; Koselleck, 1988, McCarthy, 1978; Wellmer, 1983). I will turn to this task in the relevant chapters of later volumes in this work; here only a brief excursus is possible.

If personal existence is only possible within a structure of social relations and social relations are subject to interpretive deformation through asymmetrical structures of power and authority, then social life and its constitutive modes of being are chronically subject to self-deception and ideological

distortion. The production of meaning through cultural praxis is also fundamentally mediated by ideology: the genesis of different forms of consciousness
is inscribed by systems of social subjection and alienation. Concern with the
processes of alienation therefore cannot be a supplementary objective of the
human sciences or philosophical critique – from the perspective of Critical
Theory it is the *central* task of social and philosophical analysis (Adorno, 1991;
Lukács, 1971; Kosík, 1976; Gramsci, 1971; Lefebvre, 1991a, b; Gouldner, 1973,
1980; Thompson, 1984). Of all the human sciences, social science has an
irreducible ethical obligation to question the inequalities and oppression of the
established social order by developing categories and methods that advance the
theory and practice of critique. Societies as complex socioeconomic class
formations are subject to relations of domination and thus to ideological
deformation and reification. Where Kantian 'critique' thematized the universal
formal conditions of possible knowledge, social critique is an activity which
assists specific alienated subjects to emancipate themselves from dependence
on reified relations and ideologically deformed consciousness (in Habermas'
terminology, self-reflection is thoughtful criticism inspired by an emancipatory cognitive interest, an interest in ridding the social world of 'distorting'
and 'constraining' systems of communication and their facilitating institutions
(1972, 1974)). In this way, the idea of critique presupposes but transcends the
order of objective knowledge; critique is inseparable from the metacritique of
existing discourses and philosophical frameworks, and this project in turn
presupposes the emancipative normativity of critical judgement ('these social
arrangements are destructive and alienating for human beings').

Etymologically, of course, 'critique' comes from the Greek verb for forensic
explication (*krinein*) – the separation, delimitation, and judgemental appraisal
of some domain of phenomena. This is the irreducible legislative origin of
criticism. In this sense, the theory and practice of *krinein* is closely bound up
with the ethical work of *phronesis*. In its modern usage, however, critical
reflexivity has evolved in three main directions: as an instrument for restoring
the active character of human projects to individuals and collectivities; as
normative criticism of exploitative relations and systems of domination; and
as a deconstruction of ideological formations inspired by projects of social
transformation in the advanced industrial societies. Yet every form of critical
theory is animated by the ethical task of building a non-oppressive social order,
or at least contributing to a more open, democratic, and non-repressive society
(Marx refers to the 'actualization' or 'realization' of the *telos* of philosophy,
Adorno speaks of critical theory as 'open thinking' which points beyond itself,
thinking which prefigures more humane forms of praxis, while Habermas
elaborates the philosophical foundations for a 'democracy' premised on non-
distorted communication). A project of radical inquiry as critical,
communicative action rather than positive or technical reason must move
beyond both the 'extrinsic' criticism of conventional philosophy and sociology
and the 'intrinsic' structural-genealogical investigations of semiotics and

hermeneutics by advancing an *immanent critical interpretation* of repressive forms of life, motivated by the ideal of promoting practical change through human praxis (Horkheimer, 1972). Critique's version of self-reflection and selfhood is thus fundamentally oriented to forms of sociopolitical existence liberated from systems of domination (a democratic politics coded by the modern ideals of 'the good society' and the 'revolutionary subject'). The 'subject' is no longer the disembodied Cartesian Ego or liberal subject, but a subject-in-the-world productively working, communicating, and acting with others in cooperative, transformative projects. From the critical standpoint, human existence is essentially a society of discerning subjects-in-action – practical, knowledgeable, thinking agents working with others in definite historical *milieux* (Habermas, 1985b: Section III; cf. Giddens, 1993). The cultural spheres of everyday communication and symbolic action are thus inseparable from the practical institutions of social and political existence.

Unlike its etymological ancestor *krinein* and its modern paradigm of 'criticism', critique is driven by an axiological interest in emancipation and the practical removal of alienating practices and the social conditions sustaining domination. It abandons the asocial and ahistorical framework of classical and modern philosophical criticism and pursues the idea of a situated intervention in the discourses of theory and politics. The topics of critique are thus not chosen out of curiosity or academic interest, but are selected in terms of their vital role as obstacles to human liberation – as 'causes of human oppression' ('thinking sublimates anger', in Adorno's laconic formula).

> The happiness visible to the eye of a thinker is the happiness of mankind. The universal tendency toward suppression goes against thought as such. Such thought is happiness, even where unhappiness prevails; thought achieves happiness in the expression of unhappiness.
>
> (Adorno, 1991: 175)

The ultimate objective of critical reason, then, is to empower agents to change oppressive worlds which alienate the possibilities and horizons of human flourishing (which in the historical conditions of late capitalism and advanced industrial societies are theorized by Adorno and Horkheimer in terms of the hegemonic power of mass communications (the culture industry) and manipulation (mass culture)). Philosophical discourses and ideologies which reduce, reify, or essentialize the unfinalizable projects of human praxis are to be dismantled as obstacles to the project of human liberation (Bronner and Kellner, eds, 1989). As Adorno observed, the 'Utopian impulse in thinking is all the stronger, the less it objectifies itself as Utopia – a further form of regression – whereby it sabotages its own realization' (1991: 175).

Another important difference separates Critical Theory from Traditional Theory. Critique necessarily involves a moment of metacritique in which theory defines its own material grounds and visionary sense of alternative modes of human life as a normative guide for practical transformation. This deconstructive moment is indispensable to the degree that Critical Theory understands itself as a situated, historical criticism of the reduced or 'failed' modalities of reason at a particular stage in human history (alienation, ideology, domination, technical-instrumental reason, scientism, etc. assuming different forms in different historical epochs). Critical Theory thus assumes a 'richer' or more 'dialectical' conception of reflexivity than the traditional 'unity of theory and practice'). In postwar Critical Theory, represented in particular by writers associated with the Frankfurt Institute of Social Research (*Institut für Sozialforschung* – Theodor W. Adorno (1903–69), Max Horkheimer (1895–1973), Herbert Marcuse (1898–1979), Leo Lowenthal, Franz Neumann, Erich Fromm, Franz Borkenau, and others – and second-generation figures such as Jürgen Habermas, Albecht Wellmer, Oskar Negt, Clause Offe, Alfred Schmidt, Klaus Eder and others), the deformation of critical rationality is identified with the instrumentalization of rationality subject to the imperatives of global capitalist relations, mass media, and hegemonic technology. These provide new objective constraints as well as opportunities for the pursuit of critical analysis. The vicissitudes of criticism and self-criticism have become inextricably tangled in the rapid spread and penetration of global technics, reification, administrative reason and, in the more apocalyptical visions of the School, in the one-dimensional dissolution of the claims of reason and rational self-determination accompanying the 'totally administered society' of late capitalism (Adorno, 1991; Marcuse, 1966; cf. Merquior, 1986; Anderson, 1976).

The conception of Critical Theory defended in such texts as Marcuse's *One-dimensional Man* and Adorno and Horkheimer's *Dialectic of Enlightenment* retains the ideal of theorizing and theory-informed consciousness as a necessary moment of historical critique and adversarial social movements. In its normative meaning as theoretical praxis, critique is only fully actual when it becomes, as Marx taught, a revolutionary force – a vital reflexivity in the service of emancipative interests and 'progressive social forces'. Traditionally this *promesse de bonheur* was linked to the action of a material 'carrier', a group or class embodying reason as reflection-in-action, as one essential phase of the creation of new values, social forms, and cultural practices. Many commentators thus claim that Critical Theory without a practical-revolutionary 'subject' is impotent, if not a contradiction in terms. The leisure to engage in disinterested reflection is a parody of socially responsible reason under conditions of domination and injustice. Even the criticism of earlier forms of criticism is a mode of praxis – that mode of being-in-the-world peculiar to metareflection divorced from life; and as such it should be judged in terms of its bearing on practical and social questions. Metacritique is a specific form of situated reason – in some societies the only medium of practical-critical consciousness. But even metacritique cannot transcend its vital circumstances or the sustaining contexts of everyday life and concrete social struggles; metacritique is determinate negation raised to self-consciousness:

self-reflexivity as a form of permanent suspicion in the field of theoretical and political praxis.

In the extended framework of Critical Theory begun by Georg Lukács in *History and Class Consciousness* (1923) and elaborated by the work of the early Frankfurt School, philosophical radicalism attempted to renew itself as a mode of radical praxis – practical engagement not passive reflection, a means of social intervention within capitalist modernity rather than a self-enclosed pursuit of academic scholarship (Lukács, 1971b; cf. Marcuse, 1966; Wellmer, 1971). Philosophy would find its authentic place in modern culture as part of a struggle to make the world reflexive (expressed in the idiom of the day as the 'reasonable unity' of theory and life or in Lukács' early image of the proletariat becoming self-conscious of its role as the subject and object of history). Achieving reflexive knowledge is no longer the exclusive prerogative of the individual actor or disembodied thinker, but the work of definite historical subjects faced with particular existential problems and oppressive circumstances. 'Knowledge' and 'self-understanding' are viewed as integral historical moments in the 'practical-critical' project of instituting democratic freedoms, justice, and happiness in a classless society (for example, in Lukács' well-known essay, 'Reification and the consciousness of the proletariat' (1971b: 83–222)).

8 DECONSTRUCTION

When the might of union vanishes from the life of men and the antitheses lose their living connection and reciprocity and gain independence, the need of philosophy arises. From this point of view the need is contingent. But with respect to the given dichotomy the need is the necessary attempt to suspend the rigidified opposition between subjectivity and objectivity; to comprehend the achieved existence of the intellectual and real world as a becoming. Its being as a product must be comprehended as a producing.

(G.W.F. Hegel, 1977c: 91)

For the limited purposes of our inventory Deconstruction (*déconstruction*, from the verb *déconstruire*) might be approached as a radical fusion of semiotic analysis and radical hermeneutic repetition by means of which the process of reading itself is turned upon the subject of interpretation. Deconstruction explores the heterology of signifying practices to reveal the 'infinite' intertextuality of semiosis and intertextuality by which every sign system is inscribed. One effect of this deconstruction is to problematize the underlying assumptions of the structuralist project itself. Where Semiotics tried to establish the formal conditions of structuration, Deconstruction seeks to dismantle signifying practices as defeasible formations. Where Critical Theory pursues an engaged subject of histor(icit)y, and hermeneutic readings uncover occluded

373

realms of significance, Deconstruction pursues a more eccentric path cut primarily by Nietzsche's and Heidegger's 'destruction' of Western metaphysics. The schemes of intelligibility underlying both semiology and hermeneutics are themselves deconstructible (the uncritical voice of science and understanding respectively).

Contemporary Deconstruction radicalizes Nietzsche's genealogical critique of metaphysical concepts (symbolized by his famous account of the 'death of God' in *Thus Spake Zarathustra*) by extending genealogical analysis to any centred theory of absolute origins, presence, subjectivity, or transcendental foundations. In its reflexive aspect it extends the critique of totality and foundationalism to the project of Critical Theory with its grand narrative of emancipation directed by a historical science of communicative praxis and proletarian revolution (Lyotard, 1984). All 'centric' structures – whether texts, narratives, philosophemes, ideologies, or institutions, secrete their (inter)textual genesis in language's play and are correspondingly subject to Deconstruction. In particular, Deconstruction sets to work to 'decentre' the subject in all its forms and manifestations (see Derrida's *Of Grammatology*, *Writing and Difference*, and *Speech and Phenomena* (all originally published in 1967)).

But the idea of Deconstruction also has Husserlian origins. Husserl's discovery of the 'infinite' horizonal character of the meaning-generating field of reduced consciousness has properties that are carried over into the post-structuralist view of language as an endless fabric of signification. Deconstruction generalizes the discovery of the signifying 'field' and turns it against all centred, metaphysical ways of thinking. Its critical rejection of the concepts of the transcendental Ego, Presence, Consciousness, Originality, and Transcendence intersect in the portentous announcement of the 'death of the Subject' – the decentring of absolute identity and the abolition of self-reflective identity – as one of the last acts of the Western metaphysical tradition. The two central categories of metaphysics – Being and Presence – are deconstructed in the name of *différance* and deferment of sense as the *spacing* which simultaneously places and displaces signs and their diacritical constellations. Where Husserlian phenomenology claimed that there is nothing outside of the meaning-generating fields of consciousness, for deconstruction 'Il n'y a pas de hors-texte' – 'There is nothing outside the Text' (for the ultrareflexive consequences of this mode of writing which endlessly interrupts the centre with the counter forces of its own margins, the text by intertextual play, see Derrida's *La Carte postale de Socrate à Freud et au-delà* (1980)). *Différance* is thus to be heard as both *difference* and *deferment*: the security of presence is always delayed (or relayed through intertextual formations).

But one radical implication of this oscillation between presence and absence is a renewed awareness of the place of alterity in consciousness and, more generally, the foregrounding of the question of the Other in textual and cultural formations. Deconstruction introduces an attitude that is similar in function to the transcendental *epoché* in Husserl's last work: the world as text (or intertextuality) is secured by losing the world grasped in the positivity of metaphysical categories. The identity-schemas and totalizing logics of European philosophy and social thought now become topics of a more radical textual exploration of the constitution of centred meanings and stable orders of discourse. Like Husserlian *epoché*, deconstructionist critique also seems to be motivated by ethical considerations, without being able to embrace any form of philosophical anthropology. Some commentators, for example, have interpreted this concern with 'recovering' the horizons of the Other in the Same – influenced as it is by the ethical problematic of Emmanuel Lévinas – as the basis of a deconstructive ethics. Of course Derrida's own use of deconstructive strategies need not be regarded as exhausting the social and ethical possibilities of deconstruction as a reflexive interrogation of experience. The dialogue begun by Husserl, Lévinas, and Derrida concerning the role of *différance*, alterity, and the Other in contemporary life may be expected to outlast the particular philosophemes of these thinkers and to foster a wide and heterogeneous range of philosophical responses (Critchley, 1992: chs 1, 5). Whether or not deconstruction can evade the paradoxical logic of auto-deconstruction and whether strategies of deconstruction can be incorporated within a more comprehensive programme of social and cultural analysis open to dimensions of alterity and plurality remain open questions for further logological research.

11

TRANSACTIONAL
REFLEXIVITY

Self-consciousness has before it another self-consciousness; it has come outside itself. This has a double significance. First it has lost its own self, since it finds itself as an *other* being; secondly, it has thereby sublated that other, for it does not regard the other as essentially real, but sees its own self in the other.

(G.W.F. Hegel, 1967b: 229)

Chapter 11 follows the directives of earlier chapters by commending a radically dialogical and transactional concept of human reality. Given the importance of this 'sociological turn' in the theory of self-reflection, it explores the recent attempts within sociology to address this radical problematic. The limitations of these perspectives provides the point of departure for the final Chapter. Chapter 11 is divided into five sections:

1 *Introduction: sociological reflexivity*
2 *The sociology of reflexivity*
3 *The new sociology of scientific knowledge*
4 *Reflexive sociology*
5 *Beyond reflexive sociology*

1 INTRODUCTION: SOCIOLOGICAL REFLEXIVITY

Relation is reciprocity.

(Martin Buber, 1970: 67)

The interpersonal nature of moral reflexion and the collective claims of gene-alogy suggest that reflexivity in its primary forms is embodied, interactional, and dialogical before it is solitary, individual, and categorial. Thus every act of human speech is always addressed in the context of everyday human relationships and involvements with others prior to all theorizing. Unlike the cool reflectivity of the Subject-Object encounter of Western epistemology, its leading category is that of the reciprocal human *relation* or corporeal *engagement* with Others — most simply expressed in the dialogical life of answerability relating persons in the concrete hermeneutical situations of everyday life. The abstract *cogito* of Cartesian epistemology or the subject 'thrown' in the world of post-Cartesian metaphysics are displaced by persons-in-relation, dialogic agents sustained by intersubjective relationships. Here the scandal of 'other minds' and intersubjectivity is dissolved in the multifarious occasions of concrete communication and organized contexts of 'preunderstanding' and semiopraxis. The horizon of openness toward the Other is, so to speak, a presupposition of active processes of identification and selfhood. In terms of our organizing schema, we move from the individual *cogito* of epistemology and the rational 'agent' of social theory to the embodied, socially situated *person-in-relation*. In respecifying 'reflection' as a limited modality of the wider field of incarnate reflexivity, the concepts of life-activity, otherness, dialogue, and 'belonging-to-language' came to the fore as indispensable ontological themes. And as a consequence of this ontological turn, 'dialogue' can no longer be construed as an extrinsic exchange of symbols or information mediating two discrete individuals (we have seen that the metaphysical concept of 'monadic individuals' pre-existing social involvements is a family relative of the 'discrete entities' of the Newtonian-Cartesian world-view and the egocentric metaphysics of modern thought). Rather than a simple Subject-Object or Subject-Subject specular relation we have a configurational *'moral* loop' or *ethical transaction* between active, embodied selves – what Martin Buber called the living intersubjective encounter between I and Thou (Buber, 1992). 'Subjectivity' is not the meeting of two discrete egos independent of context and shared cultural references – a shared 'understanding' (*Verständigung*) in Gadamer's terminology (1976: 6–7). Rather the order of transactionality designates an anterior ethical world of receptive communality embedded in specific traditions and forms of life. 'Language' is now given a more radical sense as the differential space of potential dialogue defining a form of life and social world (Buber speaks of this intransitive zone of the 'between' as the interhuman (*das Zwischenmenschliche*). Intersubjectivity in all its forms – cooperative activity, coresponsibility, encounter, care, sympathy, patience, humility, concern, mutuality, and so on – forms the irreducible surd of the human condition: if 'living means being addressed' (Buber, 1992: 49), 'being addressed' presupposes communality. As participants in a transactive space are always already part of a social web of discourse we may say that the ethical sphere – the space of ethical conversation – precedes and pervades all subsequent forms of human speech and dialogue. Hence Buber's celebrated definition of sociology, dating back to 1908: 'Sociology is the science of the forms of *das Zwischenmenschliche*' (1992: 94).

Dialogue as a relational realm of coresponsibility (*Antwort, antworten, verantworten*) is the realm of concrete transactionality already at work in our incarnate, everyday life-in-the-world. And, as we have seen in earlier chapters, everyday affective relations are already presupposed by interactional orders involving reciprocal cognitive orientations, formal speech, and more explicit

377

structures of social interaction (*Wechselwirkung*). In this sense even the pheno-menological concept of the 'subject-body' is still a one-sided abstraction when isolated from the primary reality of social and ethical incarnation. We colonize reality as persons-in-relation before we exist as 'material bodies'. This is where the philosophical anthropology derived from Hegel, Feuerbach, and Marx acts as a corrective to the Cartesianism of the phenomenological tradition. To borrow Buber's generous expression, 'we live in the currents of universal reciprocity' (Buber, 1970: 67). Every human being is thus necessarily appren-ticed to the arts of living embodied in material and cultural forms in entering the orders of social life. Here the category of 'social relation' must be given its fundamental ontological significance: *human life-in-the-world is dialectical in all its modalities*. To 'speak to others is something essentially human, and is based on the establishment and acknowledgment of the independent otherness of the other with who one fosters relation, addressing and being addressed on this very basis' (Buber, 1992: 64; cf. Bakhtin, 1986; Lévinas, 1969, 1981 for similar themes). Interpersonal existence is 'dialectical in all its properties, a replica, as it were, of this fundamental dialectic of subject and object' (Bachelard, 1987: 111).

Despite his early involvement with the subject-object metaphorics of epistemology, Heidegger also invokes the transactional dimension of the human condition in his claim that the 'very sense of any discourse is *discourse to others and with others*' (1992: 261ff.). The dialogical matrices of discourse found the possibility of reference, semiotic action, and extended communica-tion:

> Communication accordingly means the enabling of the appropriation of that about which the discourse is, that is, making it possible to come into a relationship of preoccupation and being to what of which the discourse is. Discourse as communication brings about an appropriation of the world in which one always already is in being with another. The under-standing of communication is the *participation in what is manifest*.
>
> (Heidegger 1992: §28, 262–3)

However, from the perspective of existing social structures not all dialogic *claims* are possible; not all imaginable moves in social space are encouraged or honoured by the existing social order. Contra Heidegger, the worlds of interpersonal experience and everyday life experience are prestructured by power relations and material constraints. We thus cannot make an unqualified appeal to an ahistorical 'life-world' or 'horizon of language' as the ultimate context of human practices. We need to think, in Lévinas' words, 'otherwise than being or beyond essence' (1981: ch. 1). At the very least we should emphasize that the life-world is already organized on the basis of power relations which prescribe unequal access to material and cultural resources. We must therefore move beyond the thematics of 'philosophical hermeneutics' by approaching the 'order of transactionality' as a structured realm organized by power differentials. We should also modify the bloodless category of *relationality* (and *intersubjectivity*) to accommodate the structured dynamics of gendered, interpretive, and transactional processes in the day-to-day negotiation of human identities. There can be no 'agency' outside the prestructured fields of interaction. But every sphere of interaction presents itself as an asymmetrical field of organized power relations, struggle, and suffering. We are in the region of Marx's well-known claim that the 'human essence' is the ensemble of social relations.

To make the decisive move to the sociohistorical economy of power relations we must recognize that verbal transactions are only one important species of the structure of human relations organizing the field of social existence. And 'power' in this context refers both to the contingent structures of oppression ('power over') as well as to the ontological event of productive alterity ('power to'). As Buber observed: 'Genuine conversation, and therefore every actual fulfilment of relation between men, means acceptance of otherness' (Buber, 1992: 65). This is the Feuerbachian and Marxian core of Buber's fundamental insight: 'In the beginning is the relation' (1970: 69). Persons are both constituting and constitutive parts of an interaction process, a dynamic network of activities and involvements rather than passive 'members of social structures' or 'individuals interpellated by modes of production' – 'the interdependent play of multiple, articulated, quasi-articulated, unarticulated, and inarticulable role modalities in any transaction' (Crapanzano, 1992: 152–3).

Influenced by the videological predelictions of our Indo-European languages and their obsession with fixed distinctions and unmediated oppositions, we understandably have great difficulties in grasping this prior dialectical field of transactionality in non-mechanical and non-mimetic metaphors. The primary realm of social existence is a sphere of aural/oral face-to-face relationships before it is the optical field of Western visuality, a world of lived dialogical praxis (Marx's 'life activity') before it is a realm of contemplation, theory, and abstract thought. The fundamental claim here is that intrinsically reflexive phenomena – such as 'persons-in-relations' – generate their own metaphoric self-descriptions as a moment of the processes of being-toward-the-Other. Ironically, the hardly noticed forms of ongoing social cooperation and conversational concern present more realistic instances of the primary sociality of transactional reflexivity than structured 'social relationships' or 'organized systems'. Behind every social universe lies the ambiguities and discordant conflicts of biophysiological existence, affective experience, and semiopraxical transactions. Hence the immediate problem posed for classical models of Reason is how to incorporate the dynamic phenomena of dramatic encounter, to approach the self as a 'reciprocity of perspectives', and conceptualize sociality in dialogic, emotional, and performative terms (Marias, 1971; Bakhtin, 1981; Buber, 1992; Burke, 1966; Schutz, 1964, 1970a). From this point of view it would seem that the resolution of the antinomies of Western metaphysics lie in avoiding both the dissolution of the self into a formal 'place-holder' for impersonal structures and forces or reifying the self as a substantial 'carrier' of nomadic interests and relations. Only a radically configurational theory of the field of historicity can transcend the Scylla and Charybdis posited by videological schemes of intelligibility.

Heidegger provides an important lead:

> Discoursing with others about something as a speaking-about is always a *self-articulating*. One oneself and the being-in-the-world at the time likewise become manifest, even if only in having the disposition 'manifested' through intonation, modulation, or tempo of discourse. We thus have found four structural moments which belong essentially to language itself: 1) the *about-which talked over*, 2) the *discursive what* [the said as such], 3) the *communication*, and 4) the *manifestation*.
>
> (1992: 263)

We have suggested that the self is an ethical engagement in an already existing *field of discourse* and moral obligations. The 'individual in society' is a metaphysical expression constructed by abstracting from the primary spheres of natural and dialogical transaction. Before individuals can be construed as 'persons', 'subjects of the state', or 'citizens', they are subject to the indeterminate moral and political inscriptions of (en)gendered social relations. From this perspective, selfhood itself arises within a definite matrix of social relations, framed within an epochal horizon of Being. Heidegger's hermeneutic conception of self is radically historical to the extent that questions of identity are returned to the ontological problematics of social finitude and the historicity of Being (construed by Heidegger as the 'epochal disclosure of Being'). Heidegger formulates this nexus of relations as follows:

> language itself is a possibility of the being of Dasein ... The four structural moments belong together in the very essence of language, and every discourse is essentially determined by these moments. The individual moments in it can recede, but they are never absent.
>
> (1992: 263–4)

Since the term 'intersubjectivity' still suggests a combinatorial relation of two independent subjectivities, it is more appropriate to speak of transactional coexistence in what follows. As a metaphor for the configured processes of social interaction, 'transaction' suggests an ontological emergence of social orders of 'othering' 'between' flesh-and-blood interactants, a dialectical rather than a linear structure of information, and a continuing 'negotiation' of significance by unequal parties within operative semiotic networks of power. The seminal ideas of Buber, Lévinas, and Bakhtin can be adopted as a corrective to the ontotheological thought of Husserl and Heidegger. But conversely, the Heideggerian reminder of the ultimacy of the irreducible 'otherness' of being must also be incorporated in an adequate theory of selfhood and society.

The primordial situation of heteropoiesis for Buber is literally human incarnation as flesh-and-blood (m)othering:

> Every developing human child rests, like all developing beings, in the womb of the great mother – the undifferentiated, not yet formed primal world. From this it detaches itself to enter a personal life, and it is only in dark hours when we slip out of this again (as happens even to the healthy, night after night) that we are close to her again.
>
> (1970: 76–7)

The finitude and conditionality of all human projects is shaped by this irreducible dependency upon a pregiven Other. Whether we call this 'other' *Being* or *Nature* is irrelevant to the ontological thesis of primal dependency. Organic emergence from the (m)other, cooperative 'sense-making' in relation to the Other, and contingent structurations of power are irreducible aspects of human experience prioritized by this metaphor: 'No thing is a component of experience or reveals itself except through the reciprocal force of confrontation' (Buber, 1970: 77). Without these determinant relations of structure coexistence there could be no relationality, reference, or association at all – in this sense the order of moral transactions is both empirically and logically prior to the structure of social relationships. As Heidegger also recognized: 'We now have discourse as the phenomenon which thus underlies language: *There is language only because there is discourse*' (Heidegger, 1992: 265). Or Buber: 'It is not as if a child first saw an object and then entered into some relationship with that object. Rather, the longing for relation is primary' (1970: 78).

The ontological expression 'transaction' also has the virtue of foregrounding the temporal dynamics of dialogic reflexivity as a multifaceted organic, material, and dialectical process. Reflexive existence is a movement of encounter with the other and the modalities of 'movement' all involve a specific form of temporal rhythm. Everything that enters the logosphere of human existence is both temporalized and interactional. Human interaction begins and terminates in temporal exchanges of meaning, in relationships organized through temporal rhythms and dynamics – through biologically fixed patterns, individual temporal schemata, and socially orchestrated engagements. Because human beings are finite creatures of need and organic dependence they necessarily confront the world through the sustaining structures of sociality. Individuals become an 'I' through their ongoing transactions with Others (said in another way, the dramatic rhetorical encounter with the Other is prior to the sphere of individual consciousness). Moreover as we have had occasion to observe in the preceding chapters, the realm of transactionality should not be divorced from the workings of force and power in everyday life.

The pervasive role of violence in social life can be illustrated by the manifold ways in which temporality is imbricated in the fabric of sociality. To control the field of time is the first motive of those who would monopolize resources in pursuit of their own interests (in a fundamental sense time is the common *alterity* and basis of *misrecognition* in every transaction between self-conscious beings). Human beings are pragmatic sources of *phronesis* only as beings experiencing the world through the variable forms of time – cosmic, biological, personal, social, and cultural. Temporality also characterizes the living interchange between self and other exemplified most concretely in the continuing conversations of everyday life. As the Czech phenomenologist, Jan Patocka, observed, the world of our pretheoretical life

> is originally a world within which we *move*, in which we are active, not a world we ascertain and observe. The world and man are in *a mutual movement* – the world includes man within itself so that man, together with others, can carry out within it the movement of *self-anchoring, of self-loss in self-sustenance and of self-finding in self-surrender* ... each of our physical movements is in reality a part of this all-embracing overall movement that we are – our movements are, after all, essentially the movements of a subject-body or are inseparably marked by this body in their meaning – and likewise all givenness is a component of what is essentially a corporeal orientation which we can therefore only designate as a movement.
>
> (1989: 268–9)

Time – here the temporality of movement – is the unnoticed horizon of all human transactions. But emergent forms of temporalized experience – created by powerful acts of decontextualization and recontextualization for example – act back upon the subsequent course of interaction in complex loops of interpretation and self-interpretation – for instance in complex long-term changes in the time structure of personal or social life. Human existence is continuous with the horizon of the life-world, and the leading experience of this 'natural' world is an intersection of pregiven temporal rhythms, historicity, and meaningful movement ('the world is always already prevenient in our meaningful context' and 'we are always set into a world' in Patocka's terminology; Patocka also speaks of the threefold 'movement' of *anchoring* – sinking roots into existence, self-extension or self-projection, and the movement of meaningful existence 'seeking to give those preceding realms rhythms, an overall closure, and a global meaning' . The three moments of existence each belong to different temporal dimensions, the past, present, and future respectively) (1989: 268–9).

If we fully embrace the idea that the reflexivity of human existence is inextricably tied to the communicative forms of language, discourse formations, and ideology, it seems inevitable that a richer understanding of reflexivity will involve some form of sociological, sociolinguistic, or rhetorical grounding. The keynote was struck by Marx in the Preface to *The Critique of Political Economy* (1857) with his announcement that 'it is not the consciousness of men that determines their being, but, on the contrary, their social being that determines their consciousness' (McLellan, ed., 1977: 161). The guiding theorem here is that categories and forms of knowledge are grounded in definite sociohistorical relations and institutions: the human essence 'is no abstraction inherent in each single individual. In its reality it is the ensemble of the social relations'. Here we have to prioritize the pretheoretical movements of human existence which antedate reflective social practices (cf. Patocka, 1989: 274–84).

The problem, however, is that extant versions of sociological reason are themselves products of the same contemplative, videological tradition – and face intractable obstacles in dealing with the existential mutations of knowledge, especially where the historicity of logical reasoning and scientific knowledge as particular modes of praxis are at issue. In other words, the classical sociological project itself presupposes foundational rationalism as a framework for its own empirical and theoretical programmes. Unconsciously working with the metaphysical problematics of contemplative knowledge and empiricist views of inquiry, traditional sociology posited its own discourse as the 'centre' of a new, universalist mimesis. However, once in play, certain critical strains of sociological inquiry began to construe many of the traditional problems of knowledge and truth in a more ontological idiom (the work of Durkheim, Merton, Bachelard, Canguilhem, Cavaillès, Foucault, Habermas, Kuhn, Althusser, Bourdieu, and others has been most significant in this context). Durkheim already parodies the sociologizing of thought in his lectures on pragmatism: 'History begins nowhere and it ends nowhere. Consequently, if truth is human, it too is a human product. Sociology applies the same conception to reason. All that constitutes reason, its principles and categories, has been made in the course of history' (1983: 67).

In the wake of this type of sociological relativism the institutional embeddedness of interest-driven knowledge rather than the Archimedean *ratio* of metaphysics was promoted as the key to an *empirical* resolution of philosophy's frozen antinomies. Yet in spite of this sociological turn mainstream sociology in practice still adhered to empiricist methods and techniques of neutral observation as the optimum way of representing its objects and assimilating the social nature of knowledge to the project of sociological reason. Durkheim once more is instructive: 'This pressure that truth is seen as exercising on minds is itself a symbol that must be interpreted, even if we refuse to make of truth something absolute and extra-human' (1983: 68). As a consequence of this ambivalence toward metaphysical discourse the elements of a 'radical sociology' had to be constructed through a long and difficult interrogation of some of the fundamental presuppositions of rationalist epistemology. In recent years this process of self-questioning has typically appeared in the guise of different forms of social constructivist, pragmatic, and hermeneutical conceptions of knowledge and science. 'The sociological point of view has the advantage of enabling us to analyse even that august thing, truth' (Durkheim, 1983: 68).

Three general strategies have recently taken centre-stage in this 'sociological turn'. For the sake of brevity of presentation these may be called the *Sociology of Reflexivity*, the *New Sociology of Scientific Knowledge*, and *Reflexive Sociology*.

2 THE SOCIOLOGY OF REFLEXIVITY

This mode of production must not be considered simply as being the production of the physical existence of the individuals. Rather it is a definite form of activity of these individuals, a definite form of expressing their life, a definite mode of life on their part. As individuals express their life, so they are.

(Karl Marx, in McLellan, ed., 1977: 161)

In the last analysis, it is thought which creates reality; and the major role of the collective representations is to 'make' that higher reality which is *society* itself.

(Emile Durkheim, 1983: 85)

If Sociology is understood in its current form as the comparative analysis, understanding and explanation of practices, social relations, institutions, and structuration processes, then reflexivity might be treated as simply another topical region of sociological inquiry. Social science extends its empire by including among its inquiries the study of groups, strata, organizations, and classes which specialize in self-reflective work (intelligentsia, *literati*, knowledge professionals, moralists, philosophers, sociologists, scientists, publicists, technicians, and so on): frameworks of knowledge are cultural formations or 'social constructions' with their distinctive characteristics, meaningful organization and purposes like any other organized human activity. Moreover, these cultural structures are bound up with dominant economic and political systems. The focus is not upon the content of knowledge, the construction of theoretical descriptions and predicative structures, but upon the *institutions* and *political ramifications* of knowledge systems. To borrow Bachelard's expression, reflection turns its instruments toward the social formation of the scientific spirit. As its pioneer, Durkheim observed:

We can no longer accept a single, invariable system of categories or intellectual frameworks. The frameworks that had a reason to exist in past civilizations do not have it today. It goes without saying that this removes none of the value that they had for their own eras. Variability in time and variability in space are, moreover, closely connected. If the conditions of life in society are complex, it is naturally to be expected that this complexity and with it many variations are to be found in the individuals who make up the social groups.

(1983: 71)

A metatheoretical approach like the empirical sociology of knowledge might, for instance, move from a focus on the sociolinguistic rhetorics of reflection to their concrete role in society, examining their historical construction, forms, and effects within wider systems of social relations and institutions. Instead of advocating 'philosophical criticism', the utopian premises of philosophical 'critique' are themselves treated as topics of sociological interest: what motivation or causal factors would lead individuals to imagine that they could transcend their social order? What social conditions and 'life-activities' led to the belief in 'value-free' inquiry? How did the utopian impulse to revolutionary thought and practice develop historically? Where did the idea of 'revolution' – in social as well as intellectual realms – originate? How have 'deviant' ideas, beliefs, and ideologies been promoted by different social groups and sectarian interests? What kind of social interests and values foster conservative or radical ideologies? How is 'cultural capital' put to use in organizing social hierarchies and stratificatory logics? And so on. In Marx's well-known summary:

> The production of ideas, of conceptions, of consciousness, is at first directly interwoven with the material activity and the material intercourse of men, the language of real life. Conceiving, thinking, the mental intercourse of men, appear at this stage as the direct efflux of their material behaviour ... Consciousness can never be anything else than conscious existence, and the existence of men is their actual life-process ... In direct contrast to German philosophy which descends from heaven to earth, here we ascend from earth to heaven.
>
> (in McLellan, ed., 1977: 164).

We can characterize the paradigm in terms of its key analytic concepts: *collective representations*, *ideologies* and *world-views* (*Weltanschauungen*), *sectarian social interests*, *intellectuals*, *intellectual leadership*, *social forms of knowledge*, and *networks of intellectual institutions*. We might, for example, follow the lead of Max Weber, Karl Mannheim, Lucien Goldmann, and Antonio Gramsci in constructing a Sociology of Intellectuals – a sociology of those specialized groups who have turned a universal human function (thinking, reflection, practical inquiry, ethical speculation, theology, etc.) into an occupational pursuit, becoming, as it were, specialists in reflexivity for a given society. A constructivist sociology of intelligentsia would then take a comparative historical direction given that patterns of reflexivity assume different forms in response to the different social roles, functions, resource bases, and power positions of the intelligentsia and the ideological orientations of the wider society. An empirical sociology of reflexivity, in other words, would move away from the problematics of normative epistemology and philosophical self-images of knowledge to historical studies of the ways in which ideas, beliefs, and knowledge are *practically* produced, socially embedded, generalized, and disseminated by different institutional networks and social structures (as in Gramsci, 1971; Mannheim, 1991; Bourdieu, 1984, 1992, 1993; Gouldner,

1976). In this respect Max Weber's comparative social psychology of the ethical and ideological presuppositions of the world religions represents one of the most influential frameworks of theory and research in the cultural dynamics of institutionalized reflection. For Weber a sociology of rational reflection takes its place as one part of a wider sociology of culture.

Compare Goldmann's formulation of the programme:

> Sociology of knowledge may study world-views on two different planes, that of the *real* consciousness of the group ... or that of their *coherent*, exceptional expression in great works of philosophy and art, or even in the lives of certain exceptional individuals (the latter corresponds more or less to the maximum of *potential* consciousness).
>
> (1969: 130)

Karl Mannheim inventories the kind of questions a 'sociology of mind' might pose:

> the horizontally specialized student of a certain literary current will have to come to grips with the careers and mobility of the literati who espouse it, the incentive system under which they work, the nature of the public to which they address themselves, the channels of communication available to them, the social orientation of their patrons, and the social and political divisions in which they make characteristic choices.
>
> (1992: 22)

A comprehensive 'sociology of mind' follows from Mannheim's three main theses: the broadening of the Marxist 'particular' concept of ideology into the 'total conception', the thesis that all thought is existentially determined, and the idea of the relative autonomy of intellectual groups and collectivities as the productive matrices of knowledges.

An agenda for such a 'sociology of mind' might include the following topics:

- The determination of the material preconditions and sociological conditions of intellectual production (the *resources* of reflective techniques, technologies, institutions of reflexivity); in following Mannheim's programmatic sociology of the intelligentsia it would explore (i) the social background of functional intellectuals, (ii) their particular associations, (iii) their upward and downward mobility, and (iv) their functions in the larger society with a particular concern for the operation of support and patronage (Mannheim, 1992: 122 and *passim*; see Louis Wirth and Edward Shils, 'Introduction' to Mannheim's *Ideology and Utopia*; also the writings of Antonio Gramsci on similar themes); it is important in this context to distinguish the generic concept of intellectuality (or intelligence) from the functional concept (and social category) of *intellectuals* (as individuals and groups who *specialize* in intellectual activities, influence codes of behaviour, transform the practices of everyday life, and so forth); historically 'intellectuals' in the narrower sense of 'intelligentsia' are a phenomenon of late nineteenth- and twentieth-century culture (Bell, 1991: ch. 6, 119–37).

- The dialectic between the 'instruments' of reflexivity and knowledge creation (symbols, papyrus, pen and ink, print technology, books, typewriters, computing, technical means of dissemination, journals, magazines, etc.) available to intellectual groups and the particular sustaining social environments and institutions of reflexivity (publishing houses, museums, libraries, schools, and the like) (Gouldner, 1976); Bell's concept of 'situses' – 'vertically organized locations of interest-bound activities' is particularly relevant in the context of the growth of 'rule by experts': (i) economic enterprises and business firms, (ii) government (bureaucratic-administrative, judicial), (iii) universities and research organizations, (iv) social complexes (hospitals, social service, community organizations), and (v) the military (1991: 159).

- The changing relationships between reflexive specialists and other dominant groups and classes within larger class and stratification systems:

> The concepts which we have and the universe of discourse in which we move, together with the directions in which they tend to elaborate themselves, are dependent largely upon the historical situation of the intellectually active and responsible members of the group.
>
> (Mannheim, 1991: 77)

- A typology of the social uses and situated functions of different forms of reflexive self-experience (for example in the work of historians of art styles and cultural schemata like Heinrich Wölfflin, Jacob Burckhardt, Ernst Gombrich, Erwin Panofsky, Ernst Cassirer or cultural typologists like Alois Riegl (1858–1905), Eric Auerbach, Ernst Robert Curtius, and Ruth Benedict).

- The range and scope of different expressions of reflexivity – in different media, genres, styles of thought, ideological standpoints, world-views, tropological forms, and so forth – in a given society and historical epoch and comparatively across different societies without appealing to epistemological or metaphysical criteria of evaluation:

> The task of a study of ideology ... is to understand the narrowness of each individual point of view and the interplay between these distinctive attitudes in the total social process ... The problem is to show how ... certain intellectual standpoints are connected with certain forms of experience, and to trace the intimate interaction between the two in the course of social and intellectual change.
>
> (Mannheim, 1991: 72)

- The empirical determination of the relative autonomy or societal interdependance of reflexive groups and their intellectual products (ideologies, propaganda, expert knowledge, technological systems, science, organizational skills, etc.); Gramsci's well-known distinctions between *traditional* and *organic* intellectuals might be mentioned in this context (the latter category dividing into *hegemonic* and *counter hegemonic* intellectuals).

- The nature and degree of intellectual specialization and its specific forms in relation to the wider occupational structure and market conditions for knowledge-based professions (magical, religious, moral, legal, aesthetic, medical, technical, scientific, etc. practices considered as 'worlds' or 'sub universes' in society); the study of 'theory groups', disciplinary matrices (Kuhn) and intellectual networks (Mullins); compare Daniel Bell's classification of the 'knowledge stratum' into scientific and scholarly, technological (applied skills), administrative, and cultural (artistic and religious) (Bell, 1991: 158).

- The degree to which such systems and cultural spheres institutionalize their identity (the dynamics of competition, cooperation, and conflict with alternative knowledge formations – a particular concern of the cultural theorists of the Frankfurt School – Horkheimer, Adorno, and Marcuse – and the tradition flowing from Althusser's seminal essay 'Ideology and ideological state apparatuses' (1971)).

- The extent to which 'knowledge' becomes an axis of status and power in its own right and the way in which contributions to this knowledge act as symbols of group identity and collective definition (the emergence of a 'new class' of intellectuals (Konrad and Szelényi, 1979); processes of professionalization in the production and circulation of knowledge as this shapes the work of scribes, artists, scientists, technicians, and philosophers – research on 'cultural capital' by Pierre Bourdieu and his students might be mentioned in this context (Bourdieu, 1984; Bourdieu, *et al.*, 1991; Bourdieu and Darbel, 1991)).

- The role of marginal groups in promoting critical responses to mainstream systems of knowledge and established traditions: 'The sociology of knowledge ... aims to see even the crisis in our thought as a situation which we then strive to view as part of a larger whole' (Mannheim, 1991: 95–6).

- The role of different types of knowledge and reflexive skills in wider systems of cultural legitimation (aristocratic vanguardism, generation differences, the impact of military and political events, the use of reflexive skills as the currency of modern forms of credential authority and their ideologies (Konrad and Szelényi, 1979)).

- Normative questions concerning the resolution of problems of relativism, relationism, and totalization:

> Totality in the sense in which we conceive it is not an immediate and eternally valid vision of reality attributable only to a divine eye. It is not a self-contained and stable view. On the contrary, a total view implies both the assimilation and transcendence of the limitations of particular points of view. It represents the continuous process of the expansion of knowledge, and has as its goal not

achievement of a super-temporally valid conclusion but the broadest possible extension of our horizon of vision.

(Mannheim, 1991: 94–5)

3 THE NEW SOCIOLOGY OF SCIENTIFIC KNOWLEDGE

Every fact is man-made and, therefore, historical.

(Wilhelm Dilthey, 1976: 192)

If our protocol for a sociology of intellectuals rejects the ideal of value-free sociology by relating ideological practices to material, institutional, and power relations, the so-called 'new sociology of knowledge' – and more especially, the sociology of scientific knowledge – takes a deeper interest in the contingent meaning processes and interpretive practices by which knowledge is socially constructed in microsociological and micropolitical contexts. The questions left unaddressed by the classical orientation of the sociology of knowledge – *knowledge for what?* – are reformulated in microsociological terms: whose science? Who is involved in locally constructing knowledge and how is that practically manufactured knowledge authorized? Here the focus shifts back to the socially constructed characteristics of the forms and content of knowledge claims. An important impetus toward a more radical sociology of knowledge was provided by the impact of the phenomenological criticism of positivist sociology. Although the key texts of this interpretive tradition date back to the 1920s and 1930s, the criticism of orthodox positivism only gained ground in the late 1960s with the impact of the phenomenological tradition in American sociology. The work of phenomenological sociologists like Alfred Schutz (*The Phenomenology of the Social World*), Peter Berger and Thomas Luckmann (*The Social Construction of Reality*), and Burkhart Holzner (*Reality Construction in Society*) have facilitated this change of orientation from an extrinsic analysis of the 'non-theoretical conditions' of knowledge to the social construction of epistemic formations themselves as contingent historical processes. The sea-change from positivism to interpretive logics can also be seen in the renewed interest in the theory of social action, Marxist humanism, and hermeneutics at roughly the same period (the seminal texts inaugurating poststructuralism and deconstruction, for example, date from the 1960s).

The phenomenological programme of social constructionism helped to redefine the questions of the classical sociology of knowledge in terms of the local meaning practices and institutions of knowledge production. The macro-problematics of the traditional approach to 'ideologies and total world-views' was replaced by an ethnographic concern for the microsociological social worlds of knowledge production and knowledge representations in everyday life. From this point of view the field of social action and organized practices becomes available as a realm of negotiated structures drawn from life-world relations and rationalities. The axiomatic assumption behind the new pro-

389

gramme was the idea that *all knowledge formations are to be defined as socially constructed practices and therefore must be studied as empirical-sociological accomplishments*. The transcendental ideal of formal reason and a deterministic conception of normative social order were relinquished in deference to a programme of detailed phenomenological research in the actual processes of scientific research. Mannheim's historicism and 'situational determinism' could now be reoriented in the direction of a phenomenologically inspired cultural relativism, following the maxim: *all knowledge is a social construction* (including, of course, the knowledge that all knowledge is a social construction).

Empirical studies informed by this non-deterministic perspective now took a thematic interest in the internal processes and dynamics of meaning construction and dissemination (subjects' beliefs and attitudes, their occasioned use of disciplinary practices, selective criteria, and local problem definitions, the mutable interfaces between experimentation and existing technologies, the practical ways in which investigators obtain practical results, the local strategies of writing and inscription devices, etc.). In stark contrast to the extrinsic macronarratives of the orthodox sociology of knowledge the new paradigm strives to give an agent's or member's account of the processes of concretely 'doing' science, art, technology, administration, policing, etc.; the privileged 'medium' by which these practices were recovered was located in the everyday talk and discourse of scientists. Hence the emphasis shifts from abstract debates about universal standards of rationality to the institutional nexus of the cultural world in question, and finally to the problem of what it is like to live, practise, and speak within different 'finite provinces of meaning'. As a cognitive ideal, research into epistemic formations should ideally provide an exact ethnographic specification of the local processes of commonsense knowledge production, circulation, and use – how 'facts' and 'findings' are socially constituted in and as context-dependent situated performances in relatively bounded subcultures (Garfinkel and Sacks, 1970; Heritage, 1984; Knorr-Cetina, 1981; Lynch, 1985; Lynch and Woolgar, 1990; Mulkay, 1985).

At the level of methodology other differences are also immediately evident. The instruments of the New Sociology of Knowledge are themselves respecified by the dominant interest in the local norms, taken-for-granted conventions, tacit practices, 'materializations', and 'work culture' of the social worlds of scientific production. In Garfinkel's terminology, 'organized social arrangements consist of various methods for accomplishing the accountability of a setting's organizational ways as a concerted undertaking' (1967: 33). Here the traditional emphasis upon invariant rules and normative method is displaced by a more 'anthropological' focus upon members' situated use of knowledge and rules of thumb. This ethnographic objective makes a replicable description of the cultural representations, discourses, and social relations of scientific production a central analytic concern (as for example in Latour and Woolgar, 1979). From the relativist principle outlined above both the form and content of knowledge are approached as socially organized achievements negotiated in local organizational settings of social action (Gilbert and Mulkay, 1984; Knorr-Cetina and Mulkay, eds, 1983; Lynch, 1985). The relativistic implications of this framework have been condensed in Daniel Bell's lapidary formulation of the sociological 'idea of reality': Reality is a confirmation by significant others (1976: 90) or in Paul Feyerabend's related maxim: 'the knowledge we need to understand and to advance the sciences does not come from theories, it comes from participation' (1987: 284). And one fundamental medium of societal participation is the production and reproduction of discourse practices. Accessing the interpretive work of scientists and other professions is facilitated through the analysis of the rhetorical properties of agents' discourse. Unlike the traditional sociology of knowledge, the New Sociology of Knowledge – especially the so-called 'Strong Programme of the Sociology of Science' – brackets epistemological norms to approach all instructive knowledge claims as worthy of sociological investigation independent of their point of origin, structural determinants, possible functions, or ultimate audiences (Barnes, 1974; Bloor, 1976, 1983; Law, ed., 1986; Mulkay, 1979; Restivo, 1983). As the new paradigm of Science Studies was developed and specified through empirical investigations, everyday knowledge and popular culture were given equal billing alongside the knowledge produced by specialist epistemic organizations and institutions. Since *all* forms of knowledge are subject to sociological determination, causal analysis and empirical deconstruction, the same argument applies in principle to the 'knowledge' produced by the sociology of scientific knowledge studying the social manufacture of science (Bloor, 1976: 5; Woolgar, 1988: chs 1–3; Ashmore, 1989). In principle this universal reflexivity extends to logic and the standards of inquiry:

> scientists are not only responsible for the correct *application* of standards they have imported from elsewhere, they are responsible *for the standards themselves*. Not even the laws of logic are exempt from their scrutiny for circumstances may force them to change logic as well (some such circumstances have arisen in the quantum theory).
>
> (Feyerabend, 1987: 284)

In this relativist climate, 'knowledge' is pluralized and mobilized into a heterogeneous congery of 'knowledge claims', 'knowledge systems', and 'universes of discourse' mobilized by specific groups and disciplines. And these epistemic orders are no longer seen as pre-existing the communal practices and organized environments in which they are specified and used (the metarhetoric of contextually organized 'situated practices' became, so to speak, the master theme of many of these investigations). Even the terms of reference and 'paradigmatic norms' of scientific procedure are regarded as locally negotiated constructs (again there are various interpretations as to how far this 'negotiated' character of logics and methods should be taken and fruitfully researched). In general, however, the programme seeks to avoid the aporias of

391

traditional sociology, empiricism, and rationalist accounts of knowledge by means of concrete ethnographic studies of scientific organizations and communicative practices: *a priori* construals of 'knowledge' are to be bracketed and deconstructed by turning to the interactional complexity of knowledge production *in situ*. To borrow Wittgenstein's terms, the New Sociology of Knowledge advocates a detailed, phenomenological reconstruction of the language-games of a practice as a way of questioning second-order assumptions we may tacitly hold about that practice. Implicitly, then, received ideologies of 'science', 'social order', 'policing', 'medical diagnosis', 'bureaucratic rationalities', etc. are suspended to allow the phenomenal domain itself to appear 'in its own terms' as a contingent interactional achievement: we are directed toward the *practical* self-construction, self-construal, and self-representation of epistemic domains and social arrangements. In the early works of this tradition, the predominant text-orientation of the paradigm tended to exclude an explicit thematization of the material systems, conceptual instruments, and artful discursive work of the research community as an inscriptive process within the wider institutional and societal context. This intrinsic focus also tended to restrict the possibilities of self-reflection and systematic reflexivity to a methodological or epistemological level.

In recent research in the sociology of scientific knowledge, however, a more radical variation of the Strong Programme has emerged which does not exempt itself from further sociological deconstruction or reflexive irony: in principle every 'Sociology of Scientific Knowledge' is subject to further reflexive investigation as a constructed, rhetorical, interpretive project (Ashmore, 1989: ch. 2; Callon and Latour, 1981; Latour, 1987; Woolgar, 1987). These metareflexive developments have been greatly influenced by ethnomethodological concerns, methods, and researches (see Garfinkel, 1967; Cicourel, 1973; Collins and Pinch, 1982; Latour and Woolgar, 1979; Lynch, 1985; Mehan and Wood, 1975; Pollner, 1987). And accepting the same microsociological bias they tend to limit the problem of reflexivity to the 'ethno-methods' of members' sense-making accounts and conversational practices. Despite this limitation the renewed interest in studying knowledge systems as contextually 'produced' and 'negotiated' 'ethno-methods' has generated a great deal of innovative research in areas that were previously thought to be immune from sociological investigation (especially in the physical sciences, logic, and mathematics). The axiomatic principle here is that all epistemic practices (logic and mathematics, no less than magic and folk-knowledge) are subject to essentially the same forms of ethnocontextual determination (Bijker, *et al.*, eds, 1987; Bijker and Law, eds, 1991; Callon, in Law, ed., 1991; Latour, in Law, ed., 1991; Collins and Pinch, 1982; Lynch, 1985; MacKenzie and Wajcman, eds, 1985; Woolgar, ed., 1988).

The general argument can be summarized as follows. The fundamental reorientation implicit in this perspective is to envisage science (including technological systems) as the contingent outcome of systems of social praxis and accounting repertoires (praxical organizations of 'shop work and shop talk', the constructive 'methodic practices' of laboratory speech, activities, and strategic production and use of inscription devices). The recent concern for the textually-mediated nature of scientific and technological practices, when coupled with an ethnographic interest in local knowledge practices, leads to a more fully reflective sociology (or anthropology) of epistemic practices, one in which the investigative methods, cognitive styles, and orientations of inquiry are also recognized as modes of constructive *writing* and *graphic inscription* (Ashmore, 1989; Bazerman, 1988; Clifford and Marcus, eds, 1986; Geertz, 1987; Lynch and Woolgar, 1990; Marcus and Fischer, 1986; Law, ed., 1991; McCloskey, 1985; Mulkay, 1985; Rosaldo, 1989; Shapin and Shaffer, 1985; Woolgar, ed., 1988). Without acknowledging this unavoidably metatheoretical involvement, any sociology of knowledge would deny in practice what it advocates as a principled mode of theorizing: that *all* epistemic beliefs – including those of the so-called *freischwebende Intelligenz* – are articulated in the specific contexts of local institutions and social organizations. Of course the acceptance of 'reflexivity-in-principle' does not mean that the implications and consequences of 'reflexivity-in-practice' are either fully comprehended or concretely implemented. The typical response of established epistemic communities – in both the human sciences and contemporary philosophy – is denial and rejection (cf. Hollis and Lukes, eds, 1982; Pinch, in Woolgar, ed., 1988). However, at least one intellectual tradition within mainstream sociology has tried to conduct its inquiries on explicitly reflexive premises. I refer to the project of Reflexive Sociology.

4 REFLEXIVE SOCIOLOGY

Two kinds of sociology have adopted the label 'reflexivity' as their metatheoretical watchword in recent years. The first is the Reflexive Sociology associated with the work of Alvin W. Gouldner and John O'Neill. Perhaps the seminal event here occured with Gouldner's uncompromising attack on the domain assumptions of functionalist sociology and his diagnosis of the crisis of sociological reason and positivist research in his book *The Coming Crisis of Western Sociology* (1970). Extending the earlier critique mounted against orthodox sociology by C. Wright Mills' *The Sociological Imagination* (1961), Gouldner claimed that the contemporary sociological project had been enervated by the hegemony of empiricist-positivist methodology and the dominance of Parsonian structural-functionalism and value-neutral 'systems theory'. In accepting this positivist orthodoxy in the years following the Second World War sociology had not only lost its roots in a living tradition of critical social theory and sociological analysis (which Gouldner would eventually identify with a self-critical, dialectical Marxist tradition), but had abandoned its original moral and political commitments to transforming the world in the direction of an emancipated society and democratic polity.

C. Wright Mills' call for the unity of sociological craftsmanship and creative imagination had fallen on deaf ears; in fact the framework of normative functionalism committed to an empiricist methodology and a technocratic conception of its identity and role in society became the dominant paradigm of American sociology, producing sociological research bereft of any radical engagement with the problems of capitalist modernity.

For Gouldner, then, positivism is to be rejected on methodological, epistemological, and moral grounds. Gouldner's version of reflexivity requires the sociologist to recognize that sociological discourse is an ideological construction epistemologically continuous with the 'objects' of study – social relations, practices, and institutions. Rather than pursuing a programme of critical intervention in the political processes which supply its material precondition, sociology has become a compliant instrument of state domination. For example, participation in the US government-backed counterinsurgency Project Camelot came easy for those social scientists who had been socialized into the professional-mandarin role model of value-neutrality and political indifference.

Gouldner's call for a new Reflexive Sociology can be seen as an amalgam of two genres, one the moral confessional (sociologists as social beings have an obligation to reflect upon and excavate their own moral, normative, and political 'background assumptions') and the other, ideology critique or 'existential sociology' (without reflection and self-critique sociologists become accomplices of the existing normative order and power structure).[1] The common goal of these two strategies is the moral self-transformation of the reflexive sociologist, rather than a fundamental reorientation of cultural foundations or the transformation of society. In Mills' terms 'Whether he is aware of it or not, anyone who spends his life studying society and publishing the results is acting morally and usually politically as well' (1959: 79). To counter the compliant liberalism of American social science, Reflexive Sociology articulates an agenda of integrated substantive and theoretical research to free the sociological community from the disabling dichotomies of the orthodox consensus and renew not only the sociological imagination but its active involvement in the practical politics of a changing society. Thus the sacred litanies of 'value-freedom' and 'scientific objectivity' are to be replaced by a politically engaged empirical sociology of contemporary capitalism.

Unlike Gouldner's remedy for the 'crisis' of Western Sociology, O'Neill's pursuit of a 'limited reflexivity' is more directly grounded in the phenomenological tradition represented by Maurice Merleau-Ponty's reflections on human incarnation in language, history, and politics. It centres on a critical contrast between the classical tradition's pursuit of transcendental reflection (unmediated opposition to which produces the historicism of Mannheim's sociology of knowledge) and what O'Neill calls *reflexivity as institution*:

By means of the notion of institution we may furnish a conception of reflexivity which, instead of resting upon a transcendental subjectivity, is given in a field of presence and coexistence which situates reflexivity and truth as sedimentation and search. We must think of reflexivity as tied to the textual structures of temporality and situation through which subjectivity and objectivity are constituted as the intentional unity and style of the world.

(O'Neill 1972: 231)

In O'Neill's conception, critical sociology can only escape its parasitical position as an unreflective 'skin trade' if it can return to the embodied forms of an occulted life-world, reintegrating its own partial rationality with the larger claims of emancipative reason at work in tradition. The sociological 'worlds' posited by reductive methods and orientations need to be reanimated and transcended by returning to the prepredicative life of the primary 'social world' of embodiment, perception, and historicity. In practice, O'Neill would have his readers return to the lost traditions of critical self-reflection and emancipative rationality to be found in the texts of Hegel, Marx, Husserl, and Merleau-Ponty rather than have them criticize the *actual* institutional procedures of research and theorizing in contemporary social life (but cf. O'Neill, 1985).

The other response to the 'crisis of Western sociology' has come to be called Analytic Sociology, and takes an altogether more radical approach to the question of reflexivity. Analytic theorists seek to abandon the last vestige of positivism from the descriptive, ethnomethodological programme. The phenomenology of the life-world is displaced by a programme of radical reflexivity. This approach rejects models of inquiry which construe reflexivity as an option, a futility, or narcissistic display of self. The antinomial logics of social science are inadequate – either accept the paradoxical recursivity of all textual practices or reject reflexivity and continue with the old paradigms of positivist discourse. The 'choice' is itself an example of an undialectical rhetoric. In generic terms, the irreducible reflexivity of social practice – whether in lay or professional sociology – is seen as an occasion and opportunity for analysis to reflect upon its own auspices or grounds in a dialogic conversation between Other and Self; no project of analysis or rationality is immune from the conversational logic of self-reflection: every discourse – including theoretical discourse – is a 'form of communication' in a lived world and thus reflexive upon its presupposed practices and underlying form of life. The objectivist idea of a purely disembodied self or spectatorial view of knowledge – as we find in some influential versions of positivism – indexes the involvement of theorizing with a generative form of life linked to a particular society and culture.

The norm of self-reflectivity shifts the thematic concern of the Analytic sociologist away from using reflexivity as a salutary topic (the ethnomethodological investigation of *doxa*), confessing reflexivity as a substructure of value commitments (Gouldner's reflexive sociology), or celebrating the endless regressivity and relativism implicit in the strong programme of the Sociology of Knowledge, to the larger project of recovering a strong version of theorizing as a *praxis* of moral self-reflection within a transformed idea of community and being-in-the-world.[2] From being a cognitive embarrassment of orthodox sociology the field of reflexive phenomena can take centre-stage (in ethnomethodology), occasion a radical renewal of the political implications of sociological theorizing (Gouldner, O'Neill, Friedrichs, Bourdieu, and others), and even suggest the possibility of transcending the sociological horizon altogether for a radically non-empiricist vision of human inquiry. In this process of radicalization 'the question of reflexivity' is transformed from the status of an epistemological and hermeneutic characteristic of inquiry to that of an ontological condition of human being-in-the-world. In either conception, however, we begin to understand the phenomenon of self-reflection as a *collective* imperative to transform the inherited forms of selfhood and social structures.

To return to the project of reflexive sociology. The attempt to carry through a radical criticism of positivism and naturalistic social science more generally can be used as a point of leverage for the construction of a profoundly non-naturalistic philosophy of inquiry, exemplified in selected case studies of reflexive formulations in and of everyday social practices. Such studies encourage the development of more explicit forms of self-reflective description and analysis. This enterprise posits a conception of sociological reason that recognizes its own moral and political involvement in creatively rewriting the social. The reflexive imagination is seen as something to celebrate and creatively implement rather than to deplore or ignore. Inevitably this reorientation has epistemic, moral, and political components – but these only come together implicitly in a call to renew an older conception of theorizing (*theorein*) as self-involving communality, dialogue, and ethical commitment. The critiques of positivism, orthodox social science, and representational epistemology more generally are interpreted as episodes within a larger process of moral transformation – phases of the practical-theoretical criticism of the implicit forms of life which underwrite and reproduce alienating versions of self and inquiry. This is the 'limited' or 'weak' political horizon embraced by Analytic Sociology.

5 BEYOND REFLEXIVE SOCIOLOGY

What do you mean by conceiving, the same which I mean?
What is that?
I mean the conversation which the soul holds with herself in considering of anything. I speak of what I scarcely understand; but the soul when thinking appears to me to be just talking – asking questions of herself and answering them, affirming and denying. And when she has arrived at a decision, either gradually or by a sudden impulse, and has at last

agreed, and does not doubt, this is called her opinion. I say, then, that to form an opinion is to speak, and opinion is a word spoken – I mean to oneself and in silence, not aloud or to another.

(Socrates, in Plato, *Theaetetus* 189E-190A)

One of the indisputable virtues of Reflexive Sociology – whether in the shape of ethnomethodological studies, critical theory, or analytic sociology – is to have foregrounded the interrelated issues of language and moral commitment as both the medium and topic of sociological inquiries. This recursivity has become particularly apparent in work criticizing the lack of thematic concern for symbolic mediation, rhetorical textuality, and radical reflection within the conventional frameworks of orthodox sociology. Opposed to this kind of elision and occlusion, Reflexive Sociology gives voice to the irremedial entanglements of self, language, and community both in the quotidian worlds of everyday life and in the specialized institutional worlds of professional theorists. By foregrounding the *social* character of all organized environments, the problematics and instruments of the natural sciences are also included in a programme of systematic constructionism (cf. Bijker, *et al.*, eds, 1987; Pickering, 1984). Once the hegemony of positivist paradigms of social science had been dissolved, the field was open for a wide range of alternative conceptions of inquiry – phenomenological, interpretive, interactionist, structuralist, ethnomethodological, and so on. But these frameworks tended to accept without further analysis the interpretive and situated character of the language-games of inquiry (of course different paradigms of theory had a greater or lesser awareness of the constitutive problematics of theoretical discourse – a feature of sociological metatheory in the 1970s and 1980s which we ignore here). Whether analysts recognize it or not they necessarily speak from within definite discursive formations and cultural locations, and the textual product of research intervention is enfolded in the canonical representational forms and semiotic practices of particular dialogic institutions. This being the case, self-reflection and the pursuit of social knowledge can be construed as the self's pursuit of a more explicit, dialogical, and responsible relation to the contingent grounds and forms of speech. Given the profoundly social character of knowledge, for Reflexive Sociology 'the ultimate feature of the phenomenological institution of reflexivity is that it grounds critique in membership and tradition'(O'Neill, 1972: 234).

John O'Neill describes the project of epistemic reflexivity as follows:

Human action is essentially the unfolding of a cultural space and its historical dimensions, so that in a strict sense we never accomplish anything except as a collective and historical project. For the individual action involves, therefore, a constant dialogue with others, a recovery of the past and the projection of breaks which are never entirely successful. But this is not the source of irremediable alienation; it is the feature of our experience which calls for its completion through a collectivity, with a history that knows a tradition as well as a future ... And this is a feature not only of human institutions, but of our thoughts, our sentiments and, above all, of human talk. Understood in this way, human institutions are the sole means that we have of keeping faith with one another, while being true to ourselves.

(1972: 234)

This is the point where Reflexive Sociology goes beyond its initial starting points in contemporary sociology, phenomenology, and linguistic philosophy to recover an older, more critical and dialogical relation to experience which the first theorists of this tradition called 'wisdom', and in a future-oriented movement, adumbrates a normative ideal of reflexive communality. At many points these different contemporary forms of reflexive inquiry overlap with the project of critical theory and the ideal of concretely building a culture of critical discourse (for example, Foucault's genealogical history of cultural formations, Bourdieu's 'reflexive sociology', and Habermas' ambitious project of communication-based social research). The critical space it has opened – particularly in relation to phenomenological sociology, ethnomethodology, critical theory, and current poststructural theories of the subject-in-language moves social theory into the field of logological reflexivity. The exploration of the necessary tensions between phenomenological theories of reflection and language-based theories of self-reflection is one of the lasting achievements of this tradition of social theory. As Bourdieu observes: 'Far from undermining the foundations of social science, then, the sociology of the social determinants of sociological practice is the only possible ground for a possible freedom from these determinations' (1992: 214–15). While there is no royal road to reflexive sociology, the guidelines offered by these studies and their insights into the critical possibilities of analytic discourse are indispensable signposts toward a fully dialogic understanding of the changing institutions and instruments of self-reflection.[3]

12

DIALOGICAL REFLEXIVITY

The self is therefore the self only when speaking, when speaking to itself or to others, when it is telling itself what others say, and when, through speech it constitutes itself as the author of its history and of its world. This is so true that the articulation of the self's transcendence and of the immanence of its experience takes place necessarily within the field of experience. Nothing can be 'thought' which is not lived ...This relationship is the radical index of the relationships of the self of experience, the self which is unceasingly present as the integrator of the field of experience, which is itself integrated during the historic unfolding of the self.

(Henri Ey, 1978: 119–20)

In the concluding chapter we return to the point of origin and assess some of the dimensions of a fully dialogical conception of human experience and its investigative consequences. The sections of Chapter 12 lead beyond the traditional logics of reflection toward a historically informed programme of critical inquiry into the genealogy of self and society. The conclusions of Volume 1 also mark the point where the metacritical positions we have traced can be displaced by more concrete logological studies of specific forms of life. This sets the scene for the 'genealogical analysis' of Western cultural formations in the following volumes. The chapter is divided into the following sections:

1 *Introduction: presuppositional analysis or the logic of question and answer*
2 *Culture as a constellation of semiopraxis*
3 *Experience as living-in-the-world*
4 *Forms of life as contextual phenomena*
5 *Logological space as a grid of power*
6 *Logological constellations*
7 *Logological deconstruction*
8 *Conclusion: cultural deconstruction*

1 INTRODUCTION: PRESUPPOSITIONAL ANALYSIS OR THE LOGIC OF QUESTION AND ANSWER

It is in and through language that man constitutes himself as a *subject*, because language alone establishes the concept of 'ego' in reality, in *its* reality which is that of the being.

(Emile Benveniste, 1971)

The word 'logology' insistently appears throughout our inventory of self-reflection. It articulates a project of discourse exploring the historical forms of selfhood, the language-games of understanding and self-reflection, and their sustaining cosmologies. In thinking reflexively we bracket taken-for-granted models of mind, self, and reality to research their dialogical conditions. Clearly 'discourse', 'textuality', and 'dialogue' are both topics and media of every dialectical self-investigation. The concept of discourse in this metacritical context is wider than the sphere of linguisticality in designating the figurational work of dialogue, the 'logics of question and answer' implicit in the metaphors and structures of cultural praxis. The focus is not upon 'discourse in the field of experience' nor 'experience in the field of language', but their intersection in the self's temporalizing *praxes* as they are constructed in different historical periods and social formations. By approaching interpretation in the wider cultural and historical contexts of *semiopraxis* we avoid every form of empiricist and formal semantics; by emphasizing the integration of meaning, experience, and situated praxis in human activities we return questions of meaning to the human context of life-in-the-world; by recalling the dialogical nature of selfhood we are reminded that every structure of meaning arises as the negotiated outcome of transactional processes. We are guided by the logological principle that there is no human practice that is not mediated by dialogue and, therefore, no form of 'being in time' that escapes the mediation of sociosymbolic formations. But we must also transcend the unthoughtful relativism of contemporary discourse theory – whether in its Nietzschean or Wittgensteinian variations: '*Wir hören auf zu denken, wenn wir es nicht in dem sprachlichen Zwange tun wollen*' ('*We cease to think when we refuse to do so under the constraint of language*') (1968: §522).

Unlike the relativist frameworks of modern postphilosophy the metacritique of Western reflection leads to a constructivist understanding of social praxis that is compatible with a dialectical view of human experience. Access to the self – as to the past in general – is facilitated by the particular existential circumstances and verbal repertoires of present questions and problems – which are themselves indebted to local spheres of relevance and interested social *logoi*. But this should not imply that all schemes of interpretation are of equal validity or cognitive value. In stressing the historicity of language we have seen that the thematized past is a medium which includes the historic unfolding of the self. Yet this is no longer the founding Ego or the self-transparent Cartesian *cogito* reading the past from an Olympian vantage point beyond social relations or discursive repertoires. Human selfhood is implicated in the rhetorical forms of its own history and the sedimented discourses that it already presupposes as part of its material preconditions. Like the world of texts, the self is mediated by past symbolic relations and interpretive practices:

> the past is such a construction that the reference that is found in it is not to events having a reality independent of the present which is the seat of reality, but rather to such an interpretation of the present in its conditioning passage as will enable intelligent conduct to proceed.
>
> (Mead, 1959: 29; cf. Lloyd, 1993)

In R.G. Collingwood's formulation of the logic of this mediation:

> For a logic of propositions I wanted to substitute what I called a logic of question and answer. It seemed to me that truth, if that meant the kind of thing which I was accustomed to pursue in my ordinary work as a philosopher or historian – truth in the sense in which a philosophical theory or an historical narrative is called true, which seemed to me the proper sense of the word – was something that belonged not to any single proposition, not even, as the coherence-theorists maintained, to a complex of propositions taken together; but to a complex consisting of questions and answers.
>
> (Collingwood, 1939: see 31–42, 60–4)

Only by way of this kind of dialogical interrogation is the vital 'pastness' of the past made effective in the present. And this process of 'interrogation' involves reflexive readings of the past by selves that are embedded in contemporary interpretive procedures and question-frames. The self, in other words, lives its contingent history reflexively by temporalizing its relations of identity and difference in interminable acts of cultural interpretation. This introduces an inevitable 'plurality' and 'openness' to self-experience: what is called the self is both a site of historically sedimented 'answers' and an unpredictable occasion for new questions. Yet pluralism should not be mistaken for relativism (cf. Milner, 1994: 103–6).

Reflection upon discursive practices – particularly the rhetorics embedded in ordinary speech – is pivotal to these investigations. Logological investigations are not concerned with how language comes to reflect and represent the world as an 'in-itself', but rather with the manifold ways in which multiple 'worlds' come to be constituted in the revelatory practice of discourses and their attendant institutions. From the logological standpoint 'language' is no longer a mirror, abstract form, semantic structure, or combinatorial algorithm but an archive of temporalizations through which 'objects' are first disclosed and constructed in their objectivity. Each of the chapters in Parts II and III pointed to the necessity of moving beyond the traditional mimetic imagery of Western thought and returning to the temporal life of dialogue as the matrix

401

of objects (states of affair, facts, events, descriptions, problematics). We need to generalize Collingwood's insight by radicalizing his dialogic theory of meaning and truth:

> What is ordinarily meant when a proposition is called 'true', I thought, was this: (a) the proposition belongs to a question-and-answer complex which as a whole is 'true' in the proper sense of the word; (b) within this complex it is an answer to a certain question; (c) the question is what we ordinarily call a sensible or intelligent question; (d) the proposition is the 'right' answer to that question.
>
> (Collingwood, 1939)

For Collingwood, the 'value' of the answers formulated in any debate is grounded in the axiological principles informing the original questions (and its underlying scheme of intelligibility). This is a vital point in understanding the nature of logological researches. Collingwood – as Hans-Georg Gadamer and others have pointed out – clearly grasped the notion that *all* descriptions, explanations, formulations, or theories as *propositional interpretations* are metaphorical codifications of value-laden assumptions and, therefore, that any understanding of a text, language, or society requires an 'excavation' of its implicit presuppositional schemata and metaphorical principles. Collingwood's fundamental advance over traditional transcendental arguments is that *discursive problematics*, *question-frames*, and *social paradigms* are relative to the implicit cosmologies of particular communities and societies. To understand an expression or text is to enter the relevant frames of meaning operative in a given culture. Hence the close connection between the processes of understanding, questioning, and explanation (Gadamer 1979: 374). In the particular field of historical research the failure to grasp this constellation leads to what Herbert Butterfield once called *presentism* or 'the Whig interpretation of history' – a particularly deep-rooted form of the 'pathetic fallacy' which frames the situation of the past as in all essentials the same as or similar to problems set by the present. The historian's 'pathetic fallacy' is 'the result of the practice of abstracting things from their historical context and judging them apart from their context – estimating them and organizing the historical story by a system of direct reference to the present' (Butterfield, 1965: 30).

I have used the compound term *semiopraxis* to refer to the full range of signifying activities as situated, intersubjective 'conscious human practices' rather than 'verbal systems' in the narrower sense of this expression. This coincides with what has been called the *transformative capacity* of human action (Giddens, 1993: 116–35). Questions, value systems, and problems sustained by such practices are problematics situated in heterogeneous social practices that bind experience into an intelligible unity. But questioning and dialogue (and the explicit reflexivities it introduces) are not reducible to closed methods or fixed situations. To live 'questioningly' is a universal state description of human experience. And since problems and question-frames change from society to society, frequently what appear to be the 'same' concepts and questions turn out to be rooted in radically different discursive systems (drawing analogies at the level of surface grammar often results in mistaking the underlying depth problematics). This is one of the revolutionary implications of Collingwood's discovery which, if we follow his autobiography, he first made in the sphere of political philosophy:

> I soon realized that the history of political theory is not the history of different answers given to one and the same question, but the history of a problem more or less constantly changing, whose solution was changing with it.

> (Collingwood, 1939)

Different question-frames are embedded in different horizons which predefine the sphere of the sayable. Essentially the same sense of plurality and heterogeneity applies to the logic of ideological and social temporalization. The excavation of changing constellations of question-and-answer – the archaeology of the question-frames of inquiry and sciences for example – discloses a secret history of axiological principles embedded in different forms of talk, correlated to the principled ways in which different groups and communities have theorized in the light of different values and beliefs. These metaphoric principles constitute the cultural foundation upon which all thinking rests (cf. Gadamer, 1989: 302; Lakoff and Johnson, 1980: chs 1–3).

2 CULTURE AS A CONSTELLATION OF SEMIOPRAXIS

> But what we thus desire for ourselves we must also grant to other periods; we cannot understand them from our point of view, we must try to understand them from their own; we cannot measure them by an absolute standard, but by that which they set themselves to attain. Hence our historical judgments are only relative, and man develops the faculty of placing himself completely at the point of view of all past systems, of reconstructing them and re-living them. Life thus gains an immeasurable breadth and unlimited elasticity; whatsoever moves mankind seems also to belong to us.

> (R. Eucken, 1909: 144–5)

As a heterogeneous totality of *sense-making activities*, experienced within the mutable worlds of everyday life, art, science, politics, and so forth, *language* is both an exemplary instance and the living medium of temporalizing *praxis*. Language is continually at work in materially constituting the objects and relations which form the day-to-day practicalities of cultures. But the existing universes of articulation do not exhaust the possible spheres of experience and selfhood. Even the most concrete experience necessarily escapes the complete control of dialogic transmission. Reversing the formalism of contemporary philosophy we grant primacy to the tensions of everyday praxis and the questionable rhetorical repertoires of sayability which often subvert theoretical models and disturb the frames of existing discourse (cf. Rosaldo, 1980).

Language may indeed be called the *Logos* that lies at the source of intelligible experience, but it is a decentred 'logos' of difference and reflexivity. Human beings exist primordially as an unfinished 'dialogue' in and with existing universes of articulate experience – and speech and writing cannot exhaustively describe the limits of experience (if only for the reason that thought is also indebted to specific historical formations of answerability (Bakhtin, 1981; 1986; Gardiner, 1992; Giddens, 1993: ch. 3). It is for this reason that in adopting a language we are complicit with its embedded ways of experiencing and thinking, its 'special ways of dealing with reality that are laid down in the tradition of the language' (Parain, 1971: 91). But language's expressive resources are only one side of a dialectical relation. For what language trawls in its networks is to some extent already saturated with the violence of past acts of anonymous valorization and societal interests. In Mead's phase, a person learns a new language and, as we say, gets a new soul – 'He puts himself into the attitude of those that make use of that language' (1934: 283). The acquisition of linguistic registers and their realms of significance is also correlated with the troubled evolution of consciousness and self-consciousness in social life. An individual

> cannot read its literature, cannot converse with those that belong to that community, without taking on its peculiar attitudes. He becomes in that sense a different individual. You cannot convey a language as a pure abstraction; you inevitably in some degree convey also the life that lies behind it.
>
> (Mead, 1934: 283)

Language, in other words, is no longer to be approached in purely *algorithmic*, *semantic*, or *instrumental* terms: it is not primarily a monological form or structure which thought assumes in seeking to express prearticulated ideas and concepts, nor is it primarily an instrument of expression or a medium of communication. We have argued that 'language' names a plural, agonistic field of prior articulations which prefigures and constitutes human reality as 'reality worth knowing and understanding'. As a 'discourse of discourses' language is a vast historical configuration of semiopraxical events embedded in a definite location and time.[1] Moreover, discourse facilitates the creation of other social worlds. And there are many ways in which talk may be said to 'construct' thought or 'incarnate' worlds.

The idea of thought's dialogical incarnation in language was formulated by Karl Marx in *The German Ideology* (1846):

> Language is as old as consciousness, language *is* practical, real consciousness that exists for other men as well, and only therefore does it exist for

me; language, like consciousness, only arises out of the need, the necessity, of intercourse with other men.

(1970: 44)

The thesis is stated even more emphatically in Marx's notebooks for his work
on *Capital*: 'Language itself is just as much the product of a community, as in
another respect it is the existence of the community: it is, as it were, the
communal being speaking for itself' (1964: 88). Language first exists as a
discursive field of possibilities; it first 'speaks' and only then do we locate our
voice and 'style' of verbal existence. In previous chapters we have extended the
dialogical idea to the temporalized field of the self, history, and society:
selfhood is like a surface event within the infinite 'currents' of anonymous
networks of text-events. Individuation is an achievement of language folding
back upon itself in the thoughtful experience and praxis of specific cultures.
The individual 'is related to his language as *his own* only as the natural member
of a human community' (1964: 88).

But it was perhaps Nietzsche in the nineteenth century who shaped this
insight into a theory of communicative desire. The 'problem of consciousness'
– the dream of becoming conscious of oneself – is rooted in the praxical
processes of language; but the 'strength' of self-reflexivity

> always stands in proportion to the *capacity for communication* of a
> human being (or animal), capacity for communication in turn in propor-
> tion to *need for communication*. ... Supposing this observation to be
> correct, I may then go on to conjecture that *consciousness evolved at all
> only under the pressure of need for communication*.

(1974: §354)

Where Marx grounded consciousness and self-consciousness in the differential
evolution of modes of production and their connected cultural practices,
Nietzsche saw these modes of self-knowledge as the effects of power:

> Consciousness is really only a connecting network between man and
> man – only as such did it have to evolve: the solitary and predatory man
> would not have needed it. That our actions, thoughts, feelings, move-
> ments come into our consciousness – at least a part of them – is the
> consequence of a fearfully protracted compulsion which lay over man:
> as the most endangered animal he *required* help, protection, he required
> his own kind, he had to express his needs, know how to make himself
> understood – and for all that he first had need of 'consciousness', that is
> to say, he needs to 'know' himself what he lacks, to 'know' how he feels,
> to 'know' what he is thinking. For, to say it again: man, like every living
> creature, thinks continually but does not know it; thinking which has
> become *conscious* is only the smallest part of it, let us say the most
> superficial part, the worst part – for only this conscious thinking *takes*

405

place in words, that is to say in communication-signs, by which the origin
of consciousness reveals itself.

(1974: §354)

From a different conceptual framework, Marx came to an analogous configuration of desire, power, and consciousness:

> The act of reproduction itself changes not only the objective conditions
> – e.g. transforming village into town, the wilderness into agricultural
> clearings, etc. – but the producers change with it, by the emergence of
> new qualities, by transforming and developing themselves in production,
> forming new powers and new conceptions, new modes of intercourse,
> new needs, new speech.

(1964: 93)

For Marx, the possibilities of self-consciousness and individual self-determination are historical achievements unfolded in the objective capacities and
operations facilitated by definite modes of production. Human beings are
'individualized' in the diverse processes of societal development:

> Man is only individualised (*vereinzelt sich*) through the process of
> history. He appears originally as a generic being, a tribal being, a herd
> animal ... Exchange itself is a major agent of this individualisation. It
> makes the herd animal superfluous and dissolves it.

(1964: 96)

This is the logological premise behind Marx's famous assertion in *The Eighteenth Brumaire*:

> Men make their own history, but they do not make it just as they please;
> they do not make it under circumstances chosen by themselves, but
> under circumstances directly found, given and transmitted from the past.
> The tradition of all the dead generations weighs like a nightmare on the
> brain of the living.

(in McLellan, ed., 1977: 300)

As a system of self-defining articulations language is responsive to changing
needs, desires, interests, and social acts of valorization. Its history could also
be written as a material repository of values and the powerful institutions
which elaborated and reproduced these values. To modify the existentialist
thesis, *logos* precedes essence: in developing their material production and their
material intercourse, human beings alter along with their actual world, also
their thinking and the products of their thinking (1970: 45). But 'material
production' and 'cultural praxis' are no longer separate categories of meaning-
activity; they are aspects of the same processes of 'humanization' (Marx
generally uses the formulaic expression 'material and spiritual productive
forces'). And thus for human beings the domain of language-in-interaction

('modes of human intercourse') is given primarily as a practical field of values – the 'language of real life' as discourse rooted in evolved needs and new modes of appropriation. Language can never be a fixed object, a semiotic grid or medium but exists as a solicitation of the Other in pregiven relations of power and domination. In this sense it is correct to say that human beings are always *unterwegs* ('on the way') to language:

> the evolution of language and the evolution of consciousness (*not* of reason but only of reason's becoming conscious of itself *as* conversation) go hand in hand. Add to this the fact that it is not only language which serves as a bridge between man and man, but that the glance, the clasp, the bearing do so, too; our becoming-conscious of our own sense-impressions, the power of fixing them and, as it were, setting them outside ourselves, has increased in the measure that the constraint grew to transmit them *to others* by signs.
>
> (Nietzsche, 1974: §354)

'Language' (*Logos*) and 'Consciousness' (*Being*), then, no longer stand opposed as two autonomous domains, but are dialectically related as the medium of power. This has been the universal error of European philosophy since its inception at the time of the Presocratic thinkers. Consciousness arises and subsists within the transactional field of semiopraxis:

> Language is as old as consciousness, language is practical consciousness that exists also for other men, and for that reason alone exists for me personally as well; language, like consciousness, only arises from the need, the necessity, of intercouse with other men ... the animal does not enter into 'relations' with anything, it does not enter into any relation at all ... Consciousness is, therefore, from the very beginning a social product, and remains so as long as men exist at all.
>
> (Karl Marx, in D. McLellan, ed., 1977: 167)

There is, consequently, an irreducible dialectical aspect to human subjectivity and language, and with this dialectic a dialogical structure of contradictions that pervades the field of verbal praxis:

> The sign-inventing man is at the same time the man who is ever more sharply conscious of himself; only as a social animal did man learn to become conscious of himself – he does it still, he does it more and more. – My idea, as one can see, is that consciousness does not really belong to the existence of man as an individual but rather to that in him which is community and herd; that, as follows from this, it has also evolved in refinement only with regard to usefulness for community and herd, and that consequently each of us, even with the best will to *understand* himself in as individual a way as possible, 'to know himself', will nonetheless bring into his consciousness only what is not individual in him,

his 'average' – our thought itself is continually, as it were, *outvoted* by the character of consciousness – by the 'genius of the species' which rules it.

(Nietzsche, 1974: §354, trans. modified)

Speech and discourse – as shorthand for diverse social forms of expression – form the living media of characteristically human configurations of reflexive awareness 'threaded' through the institutional fabric of everyday life; but institutions are themselves woven from strips of semiopraxis and operate effectively only as material processes of textual creation and transformation. We might leave the last word to Nietzsche:

> Finally, increasing consciousness is a danger; and he who lives among the most conscious Europeans knows that it is even an illness. It is, as one will have divined, not the antithesis of subject and object which concerns me here: I leave this distinction to the epistemologists, who have got caught up in the coils of grammar (the metaphysics of the people). It is not really even the antithesis of 'thing in itself' and appearance: for we do not 'know' nearly enough even to be allowed to *distinguish* in this way. For we have no organ at all for *knowledge*, for 'truth': we 'know' (or believe or imagine) precisely as much as may be *useful* in the interest of the human herd, the species: and even what is here called 'usefulness' is in the end only a belief, something imagined and perhaps precisely that most fatal piece of stupidity by which we shall one day perish.

(1974: §354)

3 EXPERIENCE AS LIVING-IN-THE-WORLD

It is experience which is the rationalization of a process, itself provisional, which results in a subject, or rather, in subjects. I will call subjectivization the procedure by which one obtains the constitution of a subject, or more precisely, of a subjectivity which is of course only one of the given possibilities of organization of a self-consciousness.

(Michel Foucault, 1988b: 253)

If we can still speak of 'phenomenology', it is a dialogical phenomenology divested of its metaphysical assumptions, a method in which 'lived experience' is retrievable to the extent that it is articulated in expressive, public, semiotic forms; further, the 'lived' nature of social experience does not entail a radical separation from material, textual, and structural contexts; in fact the logological attitude suggests that the 'lived' is only intelligible within pregiven material configurations of difference and delimitation. Being-in-the-world is primordially experienced as textualized, political life. In a formula: the experienced realities of everyday action are mediated through textual forms in all their contingent and heterogeneous modalities. Anthony Giddens expresses the same thought as follows: '*The reflexive elaboration of frames of meaning is characteristically imbalanced in relation to the possession of power*' (1993: 120).

'Understanding' and 'textuality' may then be redefined radically as material sociocultural processes:

> understanding primarily does not mean a mode of knowing at all, unless knowing itself has been seen as a constitutive state of being for being-in-the-world ... In-being as self-understanding in understanding its world discloses the understanding of its world.
>
> (Heidegger, 1992: 209)

Or in its most generic formulation:

> Worldhood is the specific presence and encounter for an understanding concern. Understanding absorption in the world *discovers* the world, the referential connections in what they uniquely are, in their *meaning*. An understanding concern thus encounters what is understood – *meaning*.
>
> (1992: 209)

Understanding is one of the primary modes of Dasein's reflexive existence.

Being subject to a more fundamental metacritique, phenomenology is subsumed within a more encompassing paradigm; phenomenological analysis is 'sublated' into logological inquiry, a genealogy of the textual mediations, rhetorical strategies, and praxical horizons of mediated experience. (Inter)textuality in this broadened sense is simply 'the structure of being of the world' in the sense that 'the referential whole of the world is a whole of meaningful connections, meaningfulness' (Heidegger, 1992: 209–10). In Heidegger's phenomenological ontology, meaningfulness, and discourse are internally related. 'Dasein is moreover essentially determined by the fact that it *speaks, expresses itself, discourses, and as speaker discloses, discovers, and lets things be seen*' (1992: 210). We might illustrate our discussion with the criticism Maurice Merleau-Ponty directed at the schematic model of sexual experience developed by an unreflective psychoanalysis which practises 'culture stripping' to secure the concept of a universal libidinal economy ('a table of the various possible modes in which the child's bodily orifices can be emphasized'). The logological method returns this abstract, specular table – and the germ of truth it contains – to its place in the world of structured practices:

> a table of this kind tells us *nothing* about the relations with others and with nature that define these cultural types, unless we refer back to the psychological significance of the mouth, the anus or the genital apparatus on the basis of our own lived experience, so as to see, in the different uses that different cultures make of these, different crystallizations of an original polymorphism of the body as vehicle of being-in-the-world. This table provides us only with an invitation to imagine, on the basis of our experience of our own bodies, other bodily techniques. That which

is actually realized in ourselves is never reducible to the status of simply one possibility among all others, since it is on the basis of this privileged experience, in which we come to know the body as 'structuring' principle, that we can glimpse the other 'possibilities', different as these might be.

(Merleau-Ponty, in Luckmann, ed., 1978: 145–6)

4 FORMS OF LIFE AS CONTEXTUAL PHENOMENA

History is the subject of a structure whose site is not homogeneous, empty time, but time filled by the presence of the now (*Jetztzeit*).

(W. Benjamin, 1992: 252–3)

Logological inquiry grants methodological primacy to constellations of language in their semiopraxical contexts. But we have seen that these 'forms of social intercourse' cannot be divorced from structures of power and inequality. Reflexive investigations adopt a form of contextualism in which objects are 'given' as the constructive outcome of powerful signifying practices; hence 'analysis' is probably a misnomer, in that method requires an explication of a dialectical constellation in Walter Benjamin's sense of this term. This is also where the phenomenology of the *Lebenswelt* must be recast in terms of the praxial concept of 'forms of life'. 'Forms of life' can be understood more generously to include all world-making human activities, including the field of quotidian practices and institutions left unexamined by orthodox social science. The source of every form of life is the pretheoretical contexts of vital reason: the primordial '*to-be*' which precedes all thought and reflection as a framework of existential orientation. We might say that forms of life are forms of *life* before they are *forms* of life.

It is a curious fact that in hegemonic cultural formations whatever opposes and subverts meaningfulness – the threat of alterity and transgression – is taken up and used as a medium of legitimation. Hegemonic power dictates the terms of reference and the stakes of what will count as 'meaning' and 'culture'. This is where political struggle is invariably also a politics of culture. Consider Heidegger's way of formulating a similar point: 'Since understanding belongs to its being as being-in-the-world, world is comprehensible to Dasein insofar as it is encountered in the character of meaningfulness' (1992: 218). All 'phenomena' presuppose the being of the world – or, in logological terms, experience presupposes the depth matrices which found and constitute the meaningful contexts of *worldliness* for a specific culture. And these constitutive processes are older than the explicit orientational schemas of reflection. From this perspective 'phenomena' are no longer empirically or logically separable from a corresponding 'world'. Particular phenomenal realms only become intelligible in the context of a prior structure of worldliness. Indeed the very insistence of accessible 'phenomena' is an implicit recognition of their being-for a 'life-in-the-world' ('phenomenal orders' being correlated to different forms of life). Reference to 'phenomena' is shorthand for 'phenomena-in-context' or 'phenomena-constituted-in-discourse': textual systems as 'constructa' within more encompassing 'orders of existence' and political frameworks.[2]

As a macroconcept, 'form of life' is shorthand for the institutional framework of historically specific life-worlds – indexing their singular modes of being-in-the-world; while at the 'molar' and 'molecular' levels it is the totality of interpretive strategies, embedded in acts of understanding by means of which individuals construe and construct experience into intelligible formations. For each of these levels of existence, the common denominator of the sociality of being remains invariant: forms of life are contested *social* formations. And consequently the horizon of 'the Other' (and what is imagined as 'other') must be considered as a foundational characteristic of life-in-the-world (this reverses the orientation of Heidegger's hermeneutic phenomenology which attends to the 'being-with' of Dasein after laying out the basic existential categories of Dasein's singular existence as self-transcendence (*ek-sistence*)). At the microlevels of personal 'life-in-the-world' we are dealing with the culturally mediated dispositions, alter-oriented-pleasures, social motivations, and gendered knowledge systems embodied in agents' routine activities and social practices. At the molar level, life-in-the-world is inseparable from collective structurations of social interaction. And, at the macrolevel we meet the fundamental systems of social life and civilizational configurations. As we have argued in Chapter 11, life-in-the-world is primordially transactional.

Logological researches study the ways in which cultures make sense of reality by elaborating and transforming rhetorics through which experience is inscribed, interpretively processed in propositions, and acted upon.[3] Here, of course, 'reading' and 'writing' are no longer seen as individual acts but as transactional processes negotiated within the central institutions of a society. Societies are thus 'world-making' enterprises. As we have repeatedly emphasized, semiopraxis takes precedence over 'cognition' or 'belief' (indeed, we would now recast the latter in the language of praxis correlated to particular historical periods and cultural formations). But as part of a dynamic stratified formation reflective practices exert a dialectical influence upon the life-world and its ideologies by actively reframing and reshaping its practices. The multifaceted concept of 'form of life' sensitizes us to the fact that we need to develop explanatory forms capable of handling complex constellations of interdependent practices, suggesting that logological excavation should take a configurational form. As a 'quasi-chaos' the constellations of everyday life do not fit the model of an unmediated foundation or a set of harmoniously integrated practices.

La vie quotidienne is a complex intertextual formation of different layers of structure and practical ensembles (ideas, discourses, 'climates of opinion', sensibilities, half-articulated desires, cultural sensibilities, routines, habits, 'people's history',[4] institutions, social practices, 'voices') with their own

411

horizons, rhythms, and dynamics. Integration is never total and non-synchronic discontinuities are more prevalent than 'orderly structures'. The concerns of day-to-day praxis demonstrate the inadequacy of the dualism of subjectivity and objectivity. Everyday life is composed of a network of interlocking cultures and traditions, each of which can be decomposed into disjunctive subtraditions and non-synchronous practices along class, ethnic, age, gender, and other dimensions. The logic here is not a simple predicate logic or a linear structure of cause and effect, but a dialectical logic of unanticipated consequences developing unplanned from the context of given structures; a 'quasi-chaos' is one that operates without foundations, a constellation in which practices are related to one another in complex patterns of family resemblances – for instance, the differential variations of the same 'style' in a culture's art, ethics, religious expressions, political forms, and social relations. This notion of disjunctive semiopraxis has resonances with the *Annales* historians' idea of an archaeology of submerged history, transmitted as the unconscious *mentalités* and ideological frameworks of 'everyday life' for a given society across 'long-durational' epochs.[5]

'Everyday life' can be respecified as a system of changing traditions rather than a unitary tradition (forgers reconstituting a text – painting, artifact, or document – have grasped the essential point that a text must display singular contextual features which stamp it uniquely as a product of a specific form of life (cf. Dutton, 1983); similarly with attempts to recreate the stylistic peculiarities of earlier music, extinct games, ancient art forms, and the like: the 'traditions' of everyday textuality have a tangible structure, resilient enough to be reproduced through an artful replaying of the original rules and cultural codes). By virtue of this ongoing heterogeneity, 'translation' is first a quotidian problematic of everyday life before it is a technical problem of literary transmission and hermeneutic theory. The ongoing sociality of day-to-day understandings must, as it were, elaborate appropriate hermeneutic maxims and orientations as part of the routine texture of action and interaction. And others – particularly 'alien' traditions and forms of life – have been successfully intertranslating for centuries prior to the growth of the philological and hermeneutical sciences. The 'sphere of history' is in this sense a misnomer; there is no such 'domain' divorced from the praxis of everyday sociality and its structural horizons; histor(icit)y is continuous with the creative hermeneutic 'chaos' accompanying the particular constellations of a social formation. Giddens expresses a similar point as follows: 'Processes of structuration tie the *structural integration or transformation* of collectivities or organizations as systems to the *social integration or transformation* of interaction on the level of the life-world' (1993: 131).

5 LOGOLOGICAL SPACE AS A GRID OF POWER

Dasein itself is a self-interpreting, self-articulating entity.
(Martin Heidegger, 1992: 302)

Reflexivity has served as a code word for the manifold impulses of human creativity; for instance, paradoxical and ironic reflexive loops facilitate creativity in all its multifarious modalities, and with these unpredicable recursivities, the possibility of self-transformation and historical development. But we have seen that the investigation of textuality cannot be separated from the analysis of the given social conditions of creativity and organized structures of cultural production. We must therefore approach *texts* as both codifications and concretizations of praxis. Texts in their full materiality within a cultural *mentalité* mediate social discourses and praxis, institutionalized in particular forms of cultural production and reproduction (artistic forms, material culture, scientific programmes, technology, architecture, writing, reading, teaching, and similar 'language-intensive' organizations). Given that we have no suitable term for this concretion of 'text-praxis-institution' we have been forced to speak analogically of forms of life as 'text-producing', 'tradition-appropriating', 'semiopraxical' activities.

Thus if we take a complex social practice like scientific research in a given historical period our general procedure would be to explicate the social infrastructure of textual relations, objects, forms, and presuppositions and, under the terms of the logological reduction, examine how this principled infrastructure is strategically used by communities to constitute 'objects', how such objects' uses are contextually determined, and how they reflexively interface with other interpretive fields. If we turn to an excavation of the meaning-configurations of science, the first step would be to inhibit our everyday 'preunderstandings' of scientific work, to bracket what we already know of science's results, and approach science as a heteroglossial field of material semiopraxis. We view the natural sciences as a system of discourses correlated to particular object domains of determinate natural structures. Genealogically we might then turn to the background systems of scientific production – the instrumental work of language, writing systems, notations, symbolisms set to work by specific communities and reflexive traditions (science's own local semiotics); the changing definition of scientific work, its division of labour, the growing dependence of scientific practices upon non-scientific instrumentation; science's particular organizational conflicts and contradictions; the historical conditions of its institutionalization; and so on. Scientific research is not merely 'socially constructed' work; it is a creative, truth-disclosing process founded upon specific ontological articulations of concrete materials, instruments, and social relations of production; science's product – 'textualized knowledge' embodied in 'scientific texts' and 'archives' – cannot be divorced from the reflexive organization of productive researchers, experimental praxis, technicians, propagandists, publishers, and users, any more than it can be separated from its material, instrumental, or historical complexes. Here the logological perspective confirms the 'realist turn' in recent criticism of constructivist epistemology (cf. Bhaskar, 1991: Section 1).

In 'excavating' such structures reflexive research deconstructs the pregiven formations of ongoing scientific activities – we turn from day-to-day practices and representations to their instituting conditions, from science's multiple – and frequently contradictory and internally self-contested – discourses to constitutive social processes. In other words, reflexive methodology heuristically privileges language as constructive sociality and dialogic action: language and communication are no longer regarded as merely a 'means' in a pregiven phenomenal field, but rather appear as integral aspects of a constitutive formation, as elements in a matrix which 'makes possible' all and any such 'objects' and objective reference. Moreover the relation of founding to founded is not a relation of causal ground and dependent superstructure, but one of reflexive interdependence.

The ontological approach to science suggests that traditions and discourse formations are more than sociological constructs; as modes of world disclosure they change the ongoing structure of lived experience and cultural life. *Forms of thinking* are contextual inventions with specific ontological effects. These modes of effectivity are typically embedded in the procedural structure of their corresponding practices. In fact the concept of 'social practice' requires that participants be able to provide 'theories' or 'working acounts' of their practice as a necessary aspect of those selfsame practices. Members of social organizations typically assimilate ontological models of their own activities and traditions. And failure to produce such formulations when requested is interpreted as a symptom of a fall from membership status. Continuous attention to interpretive framing is not an exclusive feature of juridical discourses, philology, legal codes, the human sciences or philosophy: mundane interpretive reflexivity as a basic first-order aspect of human activities is one of the fundamental features of being-in-the-world. But what is even more significant than the factual presence of interpretation throughout human experience is the crystallization of reflexive logics and the range and direction taken by self-interpretation in different cultures. We may agree that human activity is unthinkable without continuous interpretive praxis, but interpretation is not necessarily formalized and codified into logics of interpretation or logological stratagems. Nevertheless, practices of self-interpretation regularly emerge as a culture's modes of self-construal (the collective equivalent of the way in which individuals reconstruct their experience through the master tropes of symbolisms and ideologies). We should thus anticipate dialectical relationships between everyday and analytic hermeneutic logics.[6] Once this ontological dialectic is grasped, the whole range of reflexive rhetorics, practices, and institutions as they evolve in specific historical periods becomes investigatable – for example as a 'phenomenology of the sense of freedom' (Strawson, 1992: 135), as a struggle between everyday practices and state practices, quotidian morality and imposed legal codes (cf. Crook, 1967: ch. 1), the dialectic of emancipative forms of thinking and modes of explicit self-reflexivity (Ricoeur, 1984–7, 1986; Bakhtin, 1986). The empirical investigation of such 'articulations of articulations' – popular culture, dreams, collective ceremonies, carnivalist rituals, symbolic universes, utopian praxis, traditions of thought, frameworks of aesthetic praxis, criticism, and so on – becomes one of the central recommendations of logological investigations.

6 LOGOLOGICAL CONSTELLATIONS

... in the coils of grammar....

(Friedrich Nietzsche, 1974: §354)

It is an analysis of the relation between forms of reflexivity – a relation of self to self – and, hence, of relations between forms of reflexivity and the discourse of truth, forms of rationality and effects of knowledge.

(Michel Foucault, 1988b: 30)

All these remarks converge in rejecting the founding assumptions of pure theory and its dualistic concepts by questioning the axiomatic presupposition that the 'realities' of experience precede discourse, the 'objects' articulated by language antedate language, the structures of everyday life exist independently of praxical reflexivities and processes of communication. Against this tradition we have argued that *all* views of self and world as 'self-interpretations' are constructed from the available discourses and codes specific to particular societies and civilizations. And that these epochal definitions of human existence are, in turn, conditioned by definite political institutions and historical forms of life.

The logological matrices of a culture – its seed-beds of possible human expression and action – function by orienting and organizing everyday practices and spheres of social action. Clearly we are involved with a dialectical relation conjoining world-disclosing discourse, 'mediated nature', and social divisions in the institutional order. Consider, for example, the widespread impact of the discursive institutions of phallocentric law in ordering everyday life in the Graeco-Roman world. 'Law' in the context of Roman imperial power is more than a legal institution in the modern sense; it is closer to being an apparatus for defining the possibilities of human existence. A masculinist 'legal matrix' assumed an almost mythical autonomy as the 'source' and 'guardian' of moral order and rights. It evolved hand-in-hand with the structure of Roman social relationships culminating during the late Republic with the complete interpenetration of legal, social, and moral categories. Roman law was thus not merely a 'reflection' of social categories but an active interpretive instrument of phallocentric relationships and obligations (Veyne, 1990). We have also argued that this productive process of world construction frequently involves the marginalization, exclusion, or active repression of other cultural

415

discourses and practices. Every field of intelligibility that functions as a generative site activates an economy of exclusions (what we have earlier referred to as 'logics of alterity' or *heteropoiesis*). We thus learn a great deal about a culture by determining what is actively laundered from its practices and self-descriptions. What remains unvoiced, unarticulated, and silenced in a culture's field of operations – for example, in its practical, moral, and legal codes – deserves to be treated as a product of discourse just as much as what is officially expressed and communicated. Once again language acts as the universal mediator of social relations in both constructing and deconstructing categories of identity and otherness. This suggests that we should first investigate the operative sociologics – prefigured by logological practices – antedating second-order 'sociological reflection'. The field of the social is, as we have stressed throughout these chapters, primordially reflexive. We can designate the presuppositional order of relations the *logological matrix* of a form of life.

For analytical purposes a logological space can be conceptualized as a dialogical map or grid composed of figural and rhetorical practices in which specific 'object domains' or classes of object are constructed and transformed. The depth matrix sustains modes of thinking by prefiguring the general form of objects of a discursive field. The concept is analogous to the idea of a *social paradigm* as a constellation of practices, values, and concepts. Once institutionalized as an epochal structure the matrix licenses further ways of knowing, acts of perception, practical operations, and imagination along the fault lines of social interests. Although the logosphere shows considerable variation from culture to culture, every organized society necessarily evolves generative principles which shape their activities and existential priorities. Every individual and collective process of production and consumption, for example, presupposes a prior field of meaningful scripts – a cultural 'vision of reality' predelineating the possible field of recognized social action. And these 'spaces' are typically inscribed and reproduced in and as discourses. In other words, every 'intersubjective order' secures its auspices by instituting symbolisms, narratives, myths, etc. which provide the imaginary architecture by which the central activities of a social order are shaped and reflexively reproduced. In this sense imaginary socialization at the level of communally organized matrices precedes 'society'. We have repeatedly stressed the multilayered nature of social existence – flowing from the laminated dialectics of human embodiment: human life-in-the-world is intrinsically 'levelled' as a transverse articulation of many different orders of structure and system (as Nietzsche observed, we do not realize to what degree we are the creators of our acts of valuations – 'and thus capable of projecting "meaning" into history' (1968: §1011)). Recent history of science (following Thomas Kuhn's seminal work, *The Structure of Scientific Revolutions* (1970) explores analogous processes during periods of crisis in science.

Once institutionalized a logological space works as a depth *ensemble* of knowledge-generating rules for a specific community – remembering that 'it is the differences, not the similarities, between one society and another that call for comment and investigation' (Crook, 1967: 35). Civilizations are congealed systems of meaning, economies of significance as well as material modes of production and institutional structures (Giddens, 1993: 163–70). Of course semantic forms and social paradigms do not exist independently of a society's modes of material work, technologies, juridical interests, and local ideals of self-reflection. These different 'forms of embodiment' *qua* reflexive practices are now objects-for-inquiry left within the space of the logological parenthesis. Simmel's category of 'infinite reciprocity' captures an aspect of this dialectic:

> Every interpretation of an ideal structure by means of an economic structure must lead to the demand that the latter in turn be understood from more ideal depths, while for these depths themselves the general economic base has to be sought, and so on indefinitely. In such an alternation and entanglement of the conceptually opposed principles of cognition, the unity of things, which seems intangible to our cognition but none the less establishes its coherence, becomes practical and vital for us.
>
> (1990: 56)

We come into the vicinity of questions first explicitly posed by Michel Foucault: how and in what ways did the human subject take itself as the object of possible knowledges and discourses? How is the self discursively constituted as the subject of different regimes of knowledge? How do 'social practices' and 'ideologies' define the limits of culturally appropriate praxis, creating a material ensemble of structures, social relations, 'movements', and institutions? How are they instituted to exclude possible speakers from entering their 'problematics'? What are the long-term consequences of different rules and practices of discourse upon the groups and societies they inform? But also, contra Foucault, how do selves actively work upon practices and institutions to appropriate, redefine and change their conditions of existence? How do 'the excluded others' operate strategic counterpractices to resist the language-games of power, science, medicine, art, and the law? We should recall the dialectic of 'infinite reciprocity' and examine the complex interaction between 'self-knowledge-power' formations and their specific material, technical, and institutional contexts of being-in-the-world.

To draw these remarks together we can elucidate a culture's metarhetorical deep structure by distinguishing the following constellations of principles – each of which represents a regime of value inscription in a given society:

Cosmological rules

> The intellectual foundation of every human society is a generally
> accepted model of reality.
>
> (Erich Heller, 1975: 211)

The deep structure of a logological space contains rules by means of which a
community constructs its 'world map', its basic ontological beliefs about the
nature of the universe relative to its strategic activities, its 'activity space' of
interests and desires through which its central societal practices are defined,
mobilized, and distributed (and, correlatively, the rules by which 'marginal'
and 'deviant' practices and discourses are normatively defined and distributed
as 'odd', 'marginal' or, upon some stipulative criterion, 'deviant'). Obviously
no complex society has a single stable 'world model' at its core; the image of a
generative axiological *cartography* is a heuristic fiction. In reality such a
'founding mimesis' operates in the face of numerous countertotalizing forces
and processes (which is why a particular matrix is subject to change and
mutation as the culture's cartography is repeatedly rewritten in being appropriated by different groups and communities). However, many societies
valorize and rank their discursive order in the direction of promoting such an
'imagined space' as its dominant axis of representation, its 'doxic acceptance
of the world' (Bourdieu, 1992: 167–8). To attain the status of a *cultural
dominant* such structures must work, whether implicitly or explicitly, upon
the bodies and souls of concrete individuals by shaping their basic cultural
orientations and moral attitudes. Here we disclose the myths and metaphysics
of everyday life as researchable spheres of intelligibility.

The field of the intelligible and the sayable in a given society is thus
constantly bounded by zones of the unrepresentable and the unspeakable
(accepting that the logosphere is older and deeper than what is currently
articulated and legitimated as 'thinkable'). Implicit cosmological rules prefigure very general answers to pre-empt the insecurity raised by questions of the
order: What exists? What are the ultimate objects in reality? How does 'what
exists' enter the spheres of my practical life?, 'How should we alter our bodies
and souls to bring them in line with what *is*? Typically premodern societies
articulate their responses to these questions in mythological, spiritual, religious, and metaphysical vocabularies. The needs and activities of 'practical life'
are thereby sanctioned by wider cosmological matrices which determine the
given order of things. In the context of these value matrices, 'what is' immediately translates into 'what ought to be', and 'what ought to be' energizes social
life as a facilitating collective tradition (particular orders of reflexive relations
to things, to others, and to ourselves are defined together). As Bourdieu has
observed, of all forms of 'hidden persuasion', 'the most implacable is the one
exerted, quite simply, by the *order of things*' (1992: 168).

The operative cosmology of a civilization is deeply enmeshed in its 'map'
of what it takes to be 'human nature', its prevailing conceptions about the

nature of human beings and society – which of course, cannot be separated from its 'normalizing' religious, axiological, and ethical projects in which a society 'writes itself' in order to square the *is* and the *ought*. As depth logics of cultural significance these graphic codes of communal virtues govern the contextual rationalities operative in the dominant institutions of a given culture – and thereby show considerable variation both geographically and historically. In microdiscursive terms, the prevalent (mis)conceptions about human nature distribute words, metaphors, sentences, and discourses in terms of what can be referred to, desired, expressed, articulated, and thought as discourses of human relatedness. At the level of action, these systems order and prefigure prescribed courses of social conduct and human interdependence. The order of rationality, as Foucault has taught us to say, is thus always relative to a governing *episteme* or, more particularly, to prior *problématiques* which weave desires, needs, and intentionalities into discursive formations.

Ontological rules

A culture's ontology or 'model of existence' forms a particular subset of its cosmological schema, shaping transient world interests into an ensemble of ontological commitments. In this context 'ontology' refers primarily to a dominant, taken-for-granted *interpretation* of the order of things at the level of everyday life (in empirical manifestations we should perhaps think of this as a continuum of 'folk-ontologies'). These ontological commitments typically form the epochal principles governing the central activities of a society or civilization as they constitute the spatiotemporal conditions of embodiment, discursivity, and sociality (Schürmann, 1987). As primary ontological commitments prescribe the nature and order of 'the real', they invariably contain affective and normative components which not only describe 'the case' but valorize it as 'desirable' and 'valuable'. A fundamental account of 'reality' is also a view of 'truth' and thus, inversely, a way of thinking about 'unreality' and 'untruth'. These normative cartographies map a prereflective template of appropriate conduct in a given society. Once codified in practices, such folk-ontologies can be codified and presented as 'theories of existence' and, in this rationalized form, are often explicitly defined and defended by religious thinkers, philosophers, and other concerned intellectuals (cf. Sprigge, 1985). Thus 'As far as Christianity was the representative religion of the Middle Ages, their model of reality was essentially sacramental' (Heller, 1975: 211). Tacit theories of existence provide the 'deep structure' of intellectual orientations, ideologies, and theoretical traditions (for example in their role as theodicies, but also as programmes of *possible* secular action and maxims of future plans – consider, for example, the underlying value shifts in the long-durational change from a sacramental to a consumer culture in the West).

In more mundane contexts the grammar of a world model specifies working answers to questions concerning relevant objects and their relations to the texture of human existence. (With what objects do we and should we have dealings? What is desirable? What are human beings? What is their nature? What governs experience? What form should social exchange take? What are the ultimate referents of human action and activities?) The metacritique we have initiated in the above chapters was an attempt to demonstrate the way philosophical images of self, world, and reality have entered the social order in European culture. Where premodern societies have fused their ontologies with religious and magical doctrines, in modern societies such 'ultimate questions' are typically resolved by political ideologies and secular discourses linked to the exigencies of everyday life.

Question-frames and problematics need not be explicit and formalized objects; typically they appear as the tacit, unarticulated versions of existence accepted by a community as its taken-for-granted world (for example, the ubiquitous place of modern science and its dualist assumptions now inform the 'folk-models' of everyday life in industrial cultures). Folk-ontologies inform experience by specifying networks of relevances, patterns of identity, and criteria of ultimate reference as stencils for practical activities. Explicit theories of 'human nature' crystallize, as it were, against a historical background of unformulated 'know-how', taken-for-granted expectancies, tacit beliefs, and preunderstandings embodied in the routine interactions of day-to-day life. A society's ontological matrix functions like the older idea of a transcendental space; only here the 'frames' which organize the 'flow' of desire are not eternally given or wired into the 'human condition' but are socially constructed schema and symbolic systems defining pathways in and taxonomies of cultural space. Logological matrices are not fixed 'frameworks' – they mutate and change and are subject to a range of empirical vicissitudes. The *a priori* is not anchored in a disembodied mind or the cognitive structure of individual consciousness but imposed along with the dominant collective representations of a social order.

Epistemological rules

Among the most important orientational schemata are those governing the functions of language and the symbolic orders of what passes for rational discourse in a particular society. Empirically these rules specify the privileged modes of communication, forms of rational procedure, semiotic media, and communicative relationships in a society:

> We bring to the simplest observation a complex apparatus of habits, of accepted meanings and techniques. Otherwise observation is the blankest of stares, and the natural object is a tale told by an idiot, full only of sound and fury
>
> (Dewey, 1958: 219)

Behind even the most powerful techniques of objective, systematic, and technical praxis we find as their 'conditions of possibility' systems of figural, imaginative, symbolic, and metaphoric schemata. These experiential frames of meaning have been described as world-views, visions of nature, and social paradigms – but it may be more illuminating to approach them as forms of symbolic power (Bourdieu, 1990). They sustain the kind of discourse which Lyotard has called 'grand narratives', referring to modern sciences which legitimate themselves by means of grounding their 'truths' in a universal metadiscourse ('the mechanical science of nature', 'the dialectics of Spirit, the hermeneutics of meaning, the emancipation of the rational or working subject, or the creation of wealth' (1984: xxiv)).

Ethos

The term 'ethos' designates the fundamental ethical rules through which experience and social relations are normatively coded (typically as institution-alized rules of value, goodness, excellence, moral behaviour, 'worthy' activities, rights and duties, responsibilities, authority and power relations thought best to incarnate larger existential and metaphysical claims in social and political arrangements). We naturally tend to think of *ethos* as a system of moral prescriptions or code of imperative practice (such as divine prescriptions or norms governing the public good). However the term *ethos* is more embrac-ing than the sociological concept of a 'moral code' – which tends to be confined to sexual and affective relationships. Distinguishing ethics from moral order we consider *ethos* as the normative order that defines the nature of human reality. Ethical narratives also contain proscribed images of alterity or trans-gression which a culture must control and perhaps destroy to secure its own normative coherence. Frequently the 'civil status' of human beings depends directly upon the rules which codify an ethical space into more concrete legal and moral terms. The field of the obligatory may also include diagnostic and therapeutic interpretations prescribing regulative courses of action for individ-ual and collective conduct (*nomos*). Legal rules, moral norms, and utopian consciousness in all their variegated manifestations exemplify the interdepend-ence of ethical mandates and organized social action.

Axiology

Every civilized society lives and thrives on a silent but profound agree-ment as to what is to be accepted as the valid mould of experience. Civilization is a complex system of dams, dykes, and canals warding off, directing and articulating the influx of the surrounding fluid element; a fertile fenland, elaborately drained and protected from the high tides of chaotic, unexercised, and inarticulate experience.

(Eric Heller, 1975: 279)

As an embedded structure *ethos* provides the foundations of a culture's every-day axiology (from *axios*, what is 'valuable', 'worthy', hence axiomatic), its basic valorization practices – for example, in the different values, ideologies, customs, and habits that are elaborated from the codes of a logological space; while ideologies understood as the temporary vehicles of values change rela-tively rapidly in historical time, the axiological grammar changes relatively slowly (understood sociologically, '*ethos*' refers to a constellation of disposi-tions that are part of the *longue durée* of a civilizational complex containing rhetorical systems which cross ideological frontiers – patriarchal/phallocentric images of power; linear models of space and time; organic-functional concep-tions of social order; metaphysical presuppositions concerning the 'individual' and 'social order', etc.). A culture's *ethos* predefines human identity, the field of possible interaction, and legitimate structures of domination. Since the 'ethical nexus' of a social order dictates the terms of reference for all other modes of behaviour and activities, periods of axiological change are also times of radical transformation in social, legal, and political relations.

In reflexively constituting the field of social interaction logological matrices function as the system of relays and exchanges between social practices and institutional structures. Unlike conceptual frameworks narrowly conceived they are sites of polemical dispersion and *différence*. This is another reason for speaking of culture as *semiopraxis* and *praxical reflexivity* rather than recycling the objectivistic metaphors of 'structure', 'factors', and 'causal chains'. We have argued that the logosphere institutes the prepredicative ideology for the sym-bolic repertoires and language-games of surface ideologies (thus a logological matrix may generate very different images of human nature and correlated ideological practices and, *vice versa*, what may appear to be alternative ideolo-gies and systems frequently turn out to be variants of the same underlying configuration).[7] If we can still use the slippery term 'culture' in the present context it refers to the depth rhetorics and generative matrices of social action. Fundamental choices at the level of cosmological and ontological inscriptions, for example, will in general have a decisive impact upon the value choices and ethico-legal-political incarnation of values in particular interpersonal arrange-ments. The excavation of the former space of writing is one strategy in deconstructing social and cultural superstructures.

7 LOGOLOGICAL DECONSTRUCTION

The displacement and transformation of frameworks of thinking, the changing of received values and all the work that has been done to think otherwise, to do something else, to become other than what one is – that, too, is philosophy.

(Michel Foucault, 1988b: 330)

We are finally in a position to define reflexivity in dialogical terms. Logological analysis involves the deconstruction of the generative rhetorics, inscriptive principles, codes, and signifying matrices of forms of life. In terms of individual speakers, it is a method by means of which we may disengage from our own habitual ways of talking and acting and see them as 'anthropologically strange' and historically relative. But viewed as a form of cultural self-criticism it is part of a larger attempt to explore the linguistic construction of consciousness and changing forms of historical representation. In logological investigations the accent must be placed upon change and becoming – given that the 'phenomena' studied – even as principled rhetorics or generative matrices – are intrinsically temporalized and dialogical orders. 'Reality' from a reflexive perspective is ontologically 'reality-in-process'.

Logological studies are consequently transdisciplinary – and not merely 'interdisciplinary' – inquiries into the generative principles of discursive traditions. In one sense, Logology is a generalization of the idea of studying and rewriting the presuppositional limits and internal contradictions of a practice, and its sustaining discourses (exemplified in variant ways by Heidegger's *Sein und Zeit* (1927), Foucault's *The Order of Things* (1970), Bakhtin's *Dialogic Imagination* (1981), and Derrida's *Of Grammatology* (1976)); but the idea of excavating and respecifying the presuppositions of theoretical and philosophical discourses must be complemented by a concern for the liminal conflicts, aporetic possibilities, and self-transformations of wider societal practices and cultural institutions (Michel de Certeau, 1984; Schürmann, 1987; Bakhtin, 1986). In our metacritique of the rhetorics of reflection we have underscored the 'sociocultural' turn toward the social praxis of institutions and discourse formations as the fundamental theme of logological inquiry. In a formula – the structuration of 'culture' as the sustaining field of discourse is the primary concern of reflexive investigations. In the most generous definition of its terms of reference, then, logological investigations are explorations of the field of reflexive articulations as these are embodied in concrete ways of life. Earlier articulations thus recoded are taken up and elaborated in and as the texts of their analysis – they are respecified as analytic objects and in this form made available for further acts of deconstruction and rewriting. But as forms of life inhere in social and political patterns a purely cognitive phenomenology or hermeneutics of everyday life cannot advance the project of radical reflexivity.

The metaphor of a logological 'depth structure' underwriting diverse social practices bears comparison with Nietzsche's idea of the subterranean grammatical matrix connecting possible metaphysical attitudes to institutions and forms of domination. Reflexive thought 'turns back' upon its own presuppositions and anonymous values as a springboard to a critique and transformation of these structures. Nietzsche is also the source of the 'family resemblance' allegory toward cultural configurations: ancient Indian, Greek and Modern philosophy all share a common linguistic matrix ('the common philosophy of grammar') in exemplifying the same deep conventions ('the unconscious domination and guidance of similar grammatical functions' – namely those embedded in the Indo-European language system). Philosophical themata and problematics arise from an 'innate systematism and relationship of concepts' dictated by the syntax and morphology of a dominant family of languages. The field of thought with its branching structures is an elaboration of the 'prefigured possibilities' of Indo-European speech patterns. The basic rhetorical patterns of world interpretation, the similar development and succession of philosophical systems, are 'prepared at the outset' and rooted in definite forms of life (Nietzsche speaks somewhat reductively of 'physiological' valuations: 'it is our needs that interpret the world').[8] But the critical implications of this position are clear. Reflection is thus more like a return to the seed-bed from which these ideas and vocabularies were initially developed:

> Philosophers ... have trusted in concepts as completely as they have mistrusted the senses: they have not stopped to consider that concepts and words are our inheritance from ages in which thinking was very modest and unclear. What dawns on philosophers last of all: they must no longer accept concepts as a gift, not merely purify and polish them, but first *make* and *create* them, present and make them convincing. Hitherto one has generally trusted one's concepts as if they were a wonderful dowry from some sort of wonderland: but they are the inheritance from our most remote, most foolish as well as most intelligent ancestors ... What is needed above all is an absolute scepticism toward all inherited concepts.[9]

8 CONCLUSION: CULTURAL DECONSTRUCTION

Difference itself continues to be an immediate element within truth as such, in the form of the principle of negation, in the form of the activity of Self.

(G.W.F. Hegel, 1967: 99)

If by 'radical' we mean returning to the roots of texts, practices, and forms of life, we can now define the idea of reflexivity as a collective project in which individuals and groups transgress their inherited epistemologies in order to gain knowledge of the conditions and historical possibilities of their being-in-the-world. Tactically we can only achieve a reflexive knowledge of self by deconstructing the rhetorical categories and forms of knowledge through which we experience the world. And this 'knowledge' now seems irrevocably finite, local, and embedded in specific existential concerns and orientations. This is the reason why there is no neutral way back into a 'sense of Being' or a self-sustaining *Lebenswelt* other than through the contingent social, political, and gendered *relationships* of reflexive agents utilizing given semiotic materials to make sense of their worlds in particular times and places. And this 'making sense' is now part of a project of self-transformation. What might appear as constraining limits – the traditionally unremarked structures of embodiment for example – are in fact facilitating conditions of human engagement and self-development. The passion invested in traditions of radical reflection does not dry up or dissipate in nihilistic relativism. The imperatives of questioning and self-criticism are even more emphatic once we have dismantled the metalanguage of pure Reason. In essence the incarnate realms of reflexive operations allows the world to be articulated and comprehended in historically specific ways – precisely as the correlate of different modes of writing praxis, different forms of engagement, different commitments. We are returned to contexts of experience and self-reflection as diverse constellations of meaning praxis and societal embodiment. In losing the illusory promises of pure reflection we gain a whole universe of dialogic phenomena.

The postmodern deconstruction of the self can be seen as one of the last gestures of spectatorial reflection. The self – like the repressed singularities of concrete experience – returns in its full-bodied cultural incarnations. Its natural 'habitat' is the dialogic realities and institutions of naturally occurring every-day activities. But 'ordinary activities' or 'the world of everyday life' turn out to be extraordinarily rich and diverse in their material, historical, and semantic dimensions. Everyday existence is primarily the interpersonal world of linguistic, cultured, reflexive agents cooperating in making sense of their activities, reconstructing their projects and ongoing social life through a continuous dialogue with others. And reflection on selfhood and identity cannot be divorced from larger social commitments and political allegiances. If anything the fabric of 'the political' enters immediately into the rhetorics and institutions of concrete reflexivity. Metaphysical notions of 'community' are to be dismantled in favour of the differential and pluralistic processes of self-formation, self-development, and transformation.[10]

Logological studies are not the sole prerogative of academic disciplines.[11] In place of the traditional idea of method, we place the plural and hetero-geneous field of critical dialogue, interpretation, and rhetorical self-understanding: each logological study must invent its own hermeneutic techniques specific to the texts, experiences, practices, categories of existence, and conditions at hand. We cannot be constrained by prescriptive rules or stipulative methodologies. In this sense the discovery that there is no single 'reflexive theory' should cause no more distress than the discovery that there is no sovereign, prescriptive scale of value, reality (or selfhood). The discovery of radical dialogism is the logological equivalent of Gödel's incompleteness theorem in metamathematics: methods (as human artifacts) are themselves cultural constructions subject to practical constitution and determinate speci-fication in different sociohistorical contexts. There are no eternal methods just as there are no timeless questions, formalisms, or impersonal resolutions of human problems. Relatedly, the commitment to self-reflection means that every interpretation, conceptual vocabulary, framework of thought and criti-cal model must be in principle open to inquiry and be subject to dialogical norms of criticism and self-revision. Each act of reflection – like each tradition of self-reflection – is in principle subject to further trials of reflexivity. In this way only reflexive investigations can help loosen the cold hand of closure and totality in our lives and imaginations. But to point this out is only to recall that the findings of logological investigations apply in principle to logological research.

We now understand why reflexivity is interminable, once we have abandoned the false security of method. But abandoning the Absolute does not leave us with nothing. We are left with a rich constellation of reflexive practices.[12] As a commitment to the virtuous circle of dealienating self-reflection these investigations cannot rest content with achieved results and positions, but must be responsive to the experiential call to reformulate basic ideas, accepted values, and results. Beyond and more radical than the sociological and philosophical imagination lies the reflexive imagination. The dealienation of our social worlds is not a discrete achievement of any one individual, discipline, or community, but the task of a whole culture. And as we try to realize this goal we urgently need maps and orientations for journeys in an intrinsically reflexive landscape. The studies which follow are incursions within and explorations of this new world.

NOTES

INTRODUCTION: TOWARDS A METACRITIQUE OF PURE REFLECTION

1 Terminology must be approached flexibly, paying attention to context and the necessary development of terms as we explore reflexive practices. But some very basic indications are necessary. First, *logological disciplines*; these are inquiries concerned with the life of ideas, meaning, symbols, and discourse in society. But *'discourse'* encompasses all the 'sense-making' communication systems operative in and self-defining for a given culture. To avoid collapsing every problem into the catch-all category of 'culture', we can say that logological studies are particularly concerned with discursive formations in their self-reflexive aspects or with 'know-ledge' practices where individuals, communities, and institutions take an interest in their epistemic procedures, critically monitoring and assessing their own modes of perception. Whatever enables a person, organization, or culture to gain 'a sense of self' by recoiling upon operative presuppositions can be regarded as a reflexive practice. As we have seen above this may take the form of individual self-reflection upon self (whether in silent thought, dialogue with others or through the expressive media of ritual, art, poetry, literature, etc. – hence the subworlds of 'ritual reflex-ivity, 'aesthetic reflexivity', 'literary reflexivity', 'scientific reflexivity', etc.) or of those collective genres and public forms of self-reflection and self-definition we call ideologies – *modes of thought, belief systems*, and *world-views* promulgating a distinctive perspective upon selfhood and the world. Second, by stressing the generative dynamics of rhetoric we commend the idea that logological disciplines excavate the metaphoric grounds and principles of reflexive phenomena across the full array of their diverse manifestations, institutional displays and political mo-dalities – indexed most sensitively by the heterogeneous and contestable vocabularies of self, identity, mind, embodiment, will, consciousness, emotion, and so forth which either appear with these practices or are elaborated by them. Third, *'knowledge'* is commensurately defined very broadly as culturally coded, stored, and disseminated 'universes of meaning'. Fourth, *'culture'* is respecified in the light of the technopoiesis hypothesis as a dynamic configuration of materially embodied meaning *processes* and knowledge systems. The focus upon ideas, words, *lexis*, information, discourses, ideologies, rhetorics, and other symbolically-mediated representations (*knowledge systems*) should not be understood as a reduction of the adventure of thought to the structure and workings of language narrowly conceived as 'speech', 'writing', or 'discourse'. We distinguish 'discourse' in the narrower, linguistic sense from the wider arenas and contested practices of *semio-praxis* (in the sense of a culture's differential repertoires of articulation in the fields

427

of religion, art, law, science, popular culture, and so on). Emphasis is placed upon the processual, conflictual, transformative, and event-character of meaningful praxis as cultural production is socially organized and controlled. We have no wish to critique 'mindless' materialism only to fall into a 'higher' cognitive, linguistic, or cultural reductionism. To avoid all trace of linguistic idealism at the outset we stress the reciprocal interrelationships between discursive and non-discursive 'phenomena' and the complex articulations of objects, societal practices, and self-formations as the contingent achievements of specific historical epochs, powerful groups, and agencies. The accent is upon transactional relationships rather than upon words or language as autonomous structures. Said in another way, we commend a reflexive framework of configurational 'realism' which triangulates the societal constitution of *objectual meaning*, the historical processes of *self-formation* centred upon the genesis of *self-representations* and *universes of understanding*, and the changing constellations of *social power*. If these material configurations can be described as 'language-games' then logological researches are reflexive inquiries into language-games in the full-bodied institutional, cultural, and praxical senses folded into this expression.

2 The logosphere of incarnate rhetorics, representations, language-games, narratives, ideologies, life-world praxis, modes of communication, and social discourses *as semiopraxis* has not been 'colonized' in any coherent or systematic way by existing rhetorical disciplines; the field of social communication and cultural production displays the characteristically anomic features of our own contingent history and disciplinary fragmentation. There is still no reflexive science of the dialectics of knowledge in society, no comprehensive 'informatics' defining the dynamic role of meaning, information, and communication throughout the practices and institutions of social and economic life. With notable exceptions 'knowledge' is still implicitly understood in ahistorical and socially epiphenomenal terms. At one extreme we have the humanist notion of the speaking subject (or subjects) as a sovereign 'first-person' agent; while at the other extreme, it is the work of abstract structures, modes of production, disembodied economies of desire, and social forces which inscribe the body of the speaking subject in sovereign neglect of the dialectics of concrete agency, everyday interaction, and the mediating systems of communication (exemplified by the texts of such luminaries as Claude Lévi-Strauss, Louis Althusser, Michel Foucault, Jean-François Lyotard, and Jean Baudrillard). Extant semiotic, linguistic, Marxist, psychoanalytic, and hermeneutic codes represent one-sided definitions of the cultural field, reflecting their limited awareness of the social processes of self-in-society. For our purposes, existing approaches to 'signification' and 'communication' cannot be used as uncritical resources in blocking out fields for logological investigation. As influential discourses in the human sciences today these conceptual frameworks should themselves be questioned and examined as persuasive rhetorics from a more radical genealogical standpoint. Existing approaches to the 'philosophy of the self', for example, still lack an explicit awareness of the historical and cultural complexity of communicative praxis and thereby, in their various reductionist modes, fail to theorize the multiple, configurational mediations and social interdependence of meaning, media, and instruments of communication on the one hand, and societal institutions and power relations on the other. They thus split into either humanist 'defences' of the isolated 'actor' or equally extreme pronouncements of the 'death of the subject'. Foucault has claimed that 'man would be erased, like a face drawn in sand at the edge of the sea' in *The Order of Things* – 'Taking a relatively short chronological sample within a restricted area – European culture since the sixteenth century – one can be certain that man is a recent invention within it ... As the archaeology of our thought easily shows, man is an invention of recent date. And

one perhaps nearing its end' (1970: 386–7; see also Part II, Ch. 7, 217–49); Derrida's seminal essay on similar topics is 'The ends of Man' (1968), in *Margins of Philosophy* (1982: 109–36). Structural Marxism in the influential form given to this framework by Louis Althusser and his students in the late 1960s and early 1970s is one striking instance of the limited utility of an unreflexive vocabulary of structuration in understanding cultural praxis. Psychoanalytic reflection during the same period is another case in point: the psychoanalytic paradigm for example commends itself as a 'science' of meaning constructed through the careful study of the *loss* of significance and its systematic recovery through dialogic therapy, but the basic orientation, conceptual orientation, and institutional implementation of classical psychoanalysis remains locked into individualistic, egocentric, objectivist, and unreflexive ontological assumptions (the heterodox writings of Jacques Lacan, Henri Ey, and their students are exceptions which confirm the general picture – see Lacan's *Ecrits* (1977)). Analogous criticism can be made of the diverse attempts to reconstitute structuralist methodology by internally deconstructing its basic epistemological and ontological presuppositions – for example, in the work of Roland Barthes, Paul Ricoeur, Michel Serres, René Girard, Michel Foucault (the 'Foucault' who wrote *The Order of Things: An Archaeology of the Human Sciences* (1970) and the *Archaeology of Knowledge* (1972), if not the Foucault of *Discipline and Punish: The Birth of the Prison* (1977), the *History of Sexuality* (*The History of Sexuality, Volume 1* (1979), *Volume 2: An Introduction The Uses of Pleasure* (1987) and 'Nietzsche, genealogy, history', in *Language, Counter-Memory, Practice* (1977)), Gilles Deleuze, Jacques Derrida, and others. We require, in other words, a richer *logological* framework of procedures to facilitate the reflexive exploration of the *social* genesis of self, imagination, communication, self-representations and their associated rhetorics, practices, and institutions as cultural formations. We need, in other words, a reflexive *sociology of the processes, structures, and fields of semiopraxis*. For directives toward such a generative 'sociology of culture' see: Bakhtin, 1986; Benjamin, 1973; De Certeau, 1984; Bourdieu, 1984; Hélène Cixous, 'The laugh of the Medusa', in Elaine Marks and Isabelle De Courtivron, eds, *New French Feminisms* (Brighton: Harvester, 1976): 245–64; Diana Crane, ed., *The Sociology of Culture* (Oxford: Blackwell, 1994); Michel Foucault, 'Orders of Discourse', *Social Science Information*, 10 (2), 1971: 7–30; Foucault, 1987, 1977; Linda Hutcheon, 'Discourse, power, ideology: humanism and postmodernism', in Edmund J. Smyth, ed., *Postmodernism and Contemporary Fiction* (London: B.T. Batsford, 1991): 105–22; Michael J. Shapiro, *Reading the Postmodern Polity: Political Theory as Textual Practice* (Minneapolis: University of Minnesota Press, 1991); Meir Sternberg, 'How indirect discourse means: syntax, semantics, poetics, pragmatics', in Roger D. Sell, ed., *Literary Pragmatics* (London: Routledge, 1991): 62–93; Robert Weimann, 'Text, author-function and society: towards a sociology of representation and appropriation in modern narrative', in Peter Collier and Helga Geyer-Ryan, eds, *Literary Theory Today* (Cambridge: Polity Press, 1990: 91–106.

3 On the generalized importance of 'actor-networks' in social analysis see Callon, 1991: Michel Callon, 132–61; 'Society in the making: the study of technology as a tool for sociological analysis', in Bijker, *et al.*, eds, 1987: 83–103; and Callon and Latour, 1981: 277–303.

4 This would be the place for a detailed historical sociology of the techniques and instruments of reflection available to different societies and historical epochs. We can imagine a subdiscipline of logological investigations concerned purely with the semantic and pragmatic properties of the diverse 'arts of self-invention' in different cultures and civilizations. Approaching 'reflection' and 'self-reflection' as an embodied, material technology leads to specific sociological hypotheses interrelating

analyses of the 'instruments of intellectual production' to wider social patterns of cultural production. As one writer has recently expressed this:

> Such a sociology of cultural production illuminates the making of the social world that goes on in the practices through which culture producers inscribe intention in artifacts, and social actors, generally, make sense *with* things.

> (David Brain, 'Cultural production as "society in the making"', in Diana Crane, ed., *The Sociology of Culture* (Oxford: Blackwell, 1994): 191–220)

5 In the above paragraphs and the chapters which follow we commend a generically social view of rhetoric as constructive semiopraxis. This might be compared with Gadamer's conception of the rhetorical in human life: 'Rhetoric is the universal form of human communication, which even today determines our social life in an incomparably more profound fashion than does science' (1986: 17).

2 THE EPOCH OF REPRESENTATION

1 Volumes 2 and 3 will present a detailed analysis of the cultural origins and unintended consequences of this *quest for order and reason* in ancient Greece. See also Arendt, 1958; Auerbach, 1957; Castoriadis, 1984; Curtius, 1973; Euben, 1990; Feyerabend, 1987; Goody, 1968, 1986; Misch, 1950; Paglia, 1990; Havelock, 1978; Hegel, 1956; Holton, 1973, 1978; MacIntyre, 1985; Nussbaum, 1986, 1990; Shibles, 1971; Webster, 1974; and Weber, 1968. The fascination with 'order' and the 'ordering' properties of modern theories, sciences, and technologies becomes one of the central characteristics of the phenomenology of modernity (cf. Leiss, 1972; Plumwood, 1993: ch. 5; Gouldner, 1976; Harvey, 1989; Jordanova, 1989: chs 1–3; Sturrock, 1993).
2 Bakhtin/Volosinov, 1973, 1976; and of course Weber's thesis concerning the general rationalization of the conduct of life in the West (1968: 92–3).
3 Weber's theory of the progressive rationalization of economic and social ethics in Western Europe (Weber, 1968); cf. Freud, 1962; Elias, 1978b. The sociological implications of Weber's theorizing is explored in the contributions to Scott Lash and Sam Whimster, eds, *Max Weber, Rationality and Modernity* (London: Allen and Unwin, 1987). For an introduction to Weber's comparative sociology of rationalization and bureaucratization see Stephen Kalberg, *Max Weber's Comparative-Historical Sociology* (Cambridge: Polity Press, 1994).
4 Bourdieu, 1990: Book I; Elias, 1978b, 1982, 1987. The most explicit and speculative version of this idea of embodied rationality lies in the political thought of Hegel and more particularly, in Hegelian state theory where the *Logos* is interpreted quite literally as the incarnation of Reason in the practices and institutions of the State. The central text is Hegel, 1952. It should be said, however, that the ideal of a transcendent 'state' (city, republic, constitution, etc.) as the 'carrier' of rationality dates back to the political metaphysics of antiquity. See Z.A. Pelcynski, ed., *The State and Civil Society: Studies in Hegel's Political Philosophy* (Cambridge: Cambridge University Press, 1984) and G.E. McCarthy, ed., *Marx and Aristotle: Nineteenth-Century German Social Theory and Classical Antiquity* (Savage, Maryland: Rowman and Littlefield Publishers, 1992).
5 Cf. Collingwood:

> Deep down beneath the surface of their [historians of the Enlightenment] work lay a conception of the historical process as a process developing neither by the will of enlightened despots nor by rigid plans of a transcen-

dent God, but by a necessity of its own, an immanent necessity in which unreason itself is only a disguised form of reason.

(1993: 81)

The 'ordering' mythology of progressive Enlightenment rationality is a central theme of Adorno and Horkheimer's *Dialectic of Enlightenment* and Foucault's *Madness and Civilization*. The theory of the institutionalization of instrumental rationality as the essential dynamic of modernity forms one of the targets of the Frankfurt School of critical theory. It has been reformulated as a critique of scientific rationalism and objectivism by Paul Feyerabend in his *Farewell to Reason* (1987).

6 See Dumézil's *L'Ideologie Tripartite des Indo-Européens* (1958); cf. Dumont, 1980. Gellner makes an analogous classification into a sociological scheme of interpretation in his *Plough, Sword and Book: The Structure of Human History* (London: Collins Harvill, 1988). A purely structuralist analysis of social divisions obviously ignores historical context and the institutional elaboration of these generative *codes*; for the analysis of the actual institutional workings of such 'imaginary formations' see Cornelius Castoriadis, *The Imagination Institution of Society* (Cambridge, Mass.: MIT Press, 1987) and Castoriadis, 1984.

7 Freud, 1962, 114; cited by Bell, 1991: 209. For the historical background to the study of European patriarchal power systems see Mann, 1986; John Keane, *Democracy and Civil Society* (London: Verso, 1988); Anthony Giddens, *The Nation-State and Violence* (Cambridge: Polity Press, 1985).

8 For a critical analysis of the social impact of literacy on European conceptions of civilization and order see Harvey J. Graff, *The Legacies of Literacy: Continuities and Contradictions in Western Culture and Society* (Bloomington and Indianapolis: Indiana University Press, 1987), esp. Parts 2 and 3 on the Middle Ages and early modern period; also: Diringer, 1968; Castoriadis, 1984; Dodds, 1951; Fränkel, 1975; Gouldner, 1965; Glacken, 1967; Illich and Sanders, 1988; Ong, 1982; and Lobkowicz, 1967.

9 On the use of particular technologies as tropes of the self and social life see Cipolla, 1969; Clanchy, 1979; Diringer, 1968; Eisenstein, 1979; Gelb, 1963a; Goody, ed. 1968, 1977, 1986; Havelock, 1963; Harris, 1989; Ifrah, 1985; Illich and Sanders, 1988; Jensen, 1970; Lowe, 1982; Mukerji, 1983; Ong, 1982; Poster, 1990; Street, 1984; Thomas, 1989; and Williams, 1981.

10 Jameson, 1988b: 151.

11 Marx, 1973; Weber, 1968; cf. Holton and Turner, 1989: ch. 4; Jameson, 1988: ch.1; Marcuse, 1968; Mommsen, 1989, chs 9, 11; Schluchter, 1989: Part 1; Habermas, 1985, 1987b, 1992.

12 Bury, 1921; Berger, 1987; Fukuyama, 1989, 1992; Habermas, 1989; Nisbet, 1980; Vattimo, 1992.

13 Baudrillard, 1981, 1983; Benjamin, 1969, 1973; Habermas, 1987b; Haraway, 1989, 1991; Harvey, 1989; Lyotard, 1984, 1989; Vattimo, 1992.

14 Lefebvre, 1974, 1991a, b; Baudrillard, 1983; Soja, 1989; Giddens, 1992; Vattimo, 1992; Virilio, 1994; Virilio and Lotringer, 1983.

15 Sloterdijk, 1988: 535; cf. Lyotard, 1984.

16 Related reflections on similar issues can be found in Bauman, 1991; Buci-Glucksmann, 1986, trans. as *Baroque Reason: the Aesthetics of Modernity* (London: Sage, 1994); Lévinas, 1994.

3 GENERIC REFLECTION

1 Hegel, 1955: I, 302–3.
2 For the concept of 'essentially contested concepts', see W.B. Gallie, 'Essentially contested concepts', *Proceedings of the Aristotelian Society*, 56, 1955–6: 167–98; the influential essay is also included in Gallie's *Philosophy and Historical Understanding* (New York: Schocken Books, 1964), and reprinted in Max Black, ed., *The Importance of Language* (Englewood Cliffs: Prentice-Hall, 1962). We can also think of terms such as 'consciousness', 'self-consciousness', 'mind', 'the mental', and 'reflexivity' as essentially polysemic, multifunctional, multifaceted concepts or, if you prefer, words encompassing a range of 'vague', 'gerrymandered' classes or 'fuzzy' sets – almost impossible to define in the traditional Aristotelian manner of *genus* and specific *differentiae* yet indispensable for reflecting upon and understanding human experience (see Zadeh on 'approximate reasoning' in everyday life, 1975, 1977); yet precisely because of their complex everyday usage and functional 'family resemblance' logic, such 'unbounded' concepts encourage further *dialectical* reflection of both a first-order and second-order character. To 'problematize' the natural way of thinking of words in abstraction from their ideological contexts and multiple uses we might adopt techniques popularized by Ludwig Wittgenstein and John Austin. Attention to the complexity of family resemblances facilitating our everyday use of concepts is one antidote to what Wittgenstein once described as 'our craving for generality' (1969a: 17, 18; on the cultural basis of this attitude as a reductionism of the spirit see Wittgenstein, 1980, 1969), and *Remarks on Colour* (Berkeley: University of California Press, 1977)). Wittgenstein reminds the theoretical generalist of the difference and multiplicity intrinsic to ordinary usage: 'But how many kinds of sentence are there? Say assertion, question, and command? – There are *countless* kinds: countless different kinds of use of what we call "symbols", "words", "sentences". And their multiplicity is not something fixed, given once for all; but new types of language, new language-games, as we may say, come into existence, and others become obsolete and get forgotten. (We can get a *rough picture* of this from the changes in mathematics)' (1968: I.23 and §§90–133); cf. the complementary thought of George Herbert Mead: 'Language is a part of social behavior. There are an indefinite number of signs or symbols which may serve the purpose of what we term "language" ' (1934: 13–14). A case can also be made for the thesis that all words and utterances are in principle 'contestable' and 'open textured' not because they shelter multiple *concepts* or are used with varying semantic inflections in different situations, but by virtue of the context-bound or indexical character of communication and conversational language as situated, inventive human accomplishments (cf. Russell on egocentric particulars or token-reflexives in *An Inquiry into Meaning and Truth* (London: Allen and Unwin, 1940 ch.7); Gilbert Ryle on 'index words' like the 'systematically elusive' word 'I' (1949: 177–89); Bronislaw Malinowski (1884–1942) on the way utterances are tied to the 'context of situation', and J.R. Firth (1890–1960) on embedded utterances in ongoing ways of life – *Selected Papers of J.R. Firth 1952–59* (London: Longman, 1968)). Ordinary language with its changing vocabularies and shifting idioms is chronically 'indexical', saturated with context-specific meanings, particularized usages, imprecise expressions, metaphors, creative extensions, and so forth; 'meaning' is thus tied to communicative occasions of semantic implicature and entailment without complete formal rules or axiomatic interpretive procedures. The linguist – whether lay or professional – is thus faced with the same translation problems as the anthropologist – not merely of making sense of isolated words and sequences of utterances, but of reconstructing the 'contexts', 'possible worlds', or 'form of life' in which words and texts function. For a sociological assessment of the radical

implications of the indexical properties of natural language for any constructive activity of formal reasoning or theorizing see Garfinkel and Sacks (1970: 337–66). For Garfinkel and Sacks, Wittgenstein's explication of language-games consists of 'a sustained, extensive, and penetrating corpus of observations of indexical phenomena' (1970: 337–66). They are referring, of course, to the author of the *Philosophical Investigations* (and perhaps, more precisely to the famous discussion of language-games and family resemblances at 1968: §§66–7). In practice, individuals and communities negotiate the sense of terms and utterances by drawing temporary boundaries around the range of meanings of concepts and language-games. We might term this the process of *ethnodefinition* – the routine methods by which the indexicality of language is managed 'for all intents and purposes'. The study of implicit *definitions*, being closely linked with everyday *description* and *framing* practices (argument, contestation, modification, respecification, restatement, interpretation, etc.) should be treated as more than a brief chapter in the history of classification; in fact it is one of the royal roads into the interpretive practices of everyday reasoning in social life. The concepts, categorial definitions, and descriptive predicates subscribed to by theorists in their accounts are, for example, frequently invaluable clues to their background frames of reference, ideological assumptions, and presuppositional orientations. In logological terminology, they are *dialogical traces of their generative forms of life*. See also Harold Garfinkel, 'Evidence for locally produced, naturally accountable phenomena of order', *Sociological Theory*, 6, 1988: 131–58. Establishing what counts as an accepted 'premise' or 'framework' for practical reasoning in a given community is a fruitful way of beginning a dialogical analysis of a social practice.

3   On nature's reflexivity as *autopoiesis* (or as we would now say, on nature figured through the symbolic imagery of *autopoiesis*), 'nature *is* the very history of its evolutionary differentiation. If we think of nature as a development, we discern the presence of this tendency towards self-consciousness and, ultimately, toward freedom' (Bookchin, 1989: 41–2). To paraphase Bookchin, if we think of 'nature' as developmental we prepare further stories concerning nature's potential for emergence complexity, synthetic processes, symbiotic interdependence, and emergent self-consciousness. Experience is the armature of nature's reflexivity in the sense that the emergence of psychophysical organisms, natural knowledge, and life represents 'a growing self-disclosure of nature itself' (Dewey, 1958: x). Some physicists have also been impressed by nature's proclivity toward increasing differentiation, relational interdependence, and reflexive complexity – formulating an 'anthropic cosmology' to explain how anything like consciousness and a cognizing, theorizing species – the human species – could be produced through natural evolution (see John D. Barrow and Frank J. Tipler, *The Anthropic Cosmological Principle* (Oxford: Oxford University Press, 1988)); the anthropic theory also resonates with recent feminist attempts to refigure knowledge of nature as a holistic relationship between knower and known, an active exchange and cooperation between human praxis and natural possibilities; James E. Lovelock defines the Gaia Hypothesis in analogous terms:

> This postulates that the physical and chemical condition of the surfaces of the Earth, of the atmosphere, and of the oceans has been and is actively made fit and comfortable by the presence of life itself. This is in contrast to the conventional wisdom which held that life adapted to the planetary conditions as it and they evolved their separate ways.
>
> (Lovelock, 1979: 152; see also Lovelock, 1991)

Philosophy, as Mead observed, is

concerned ... with the import of the appearance and presence in the universe of human reflective intelligence – that intelligence which transforms causes and effects into means and consequences, reactions into responses, and termini of natural processes into ends-in-view.

(1938: 517)

The anthropic principle leads some scientists to the kind of teleological story familiar to readers of Hegel ('the evolution of *homo sapiens*, with his technological inventiveness and his increasingly subtle communications network, has vastly increased Gaia's range of perception. She is now through us awake and aware of herself. She has seen the reflection of her fair face through the eyes of astronauts and the television cameras of orbiting spacecraft' (Lovelock, 1979: 148)). Consider the more ecological imagery of Mead and Dewey: 'All living organisms are bound up in a general social environment or situation, in a complex of social interrelations and interactions upon which their continued existence depends' (Mead, 1934. 228); 'because when nature is viewed as consisting of events rather than substances, it is characterized by *histories*, that is, by continuity of change proceeding from beginnings to endings' (Dewey, 1958: xi-xii). But Mead and Dewey draw back from Hegelian teleology: 'changes are simply explained by variations and adaptation to the situations that arise. There is no necessity of bringing in an end toward which all creation moves' (Mead, 1934: 251) and 'Owing to the presence of uncertain and precarious factors in these histories, attainment of ends, of goods, is unstable and evanescent' (Dewey, 1958: xii). The dynamics and structures of societal organization and self-consciousness are implicit within the processes of natural evolution – 'mind' or 'reflexiveness' is a natural emergent of evolutionary complexity.

4 I use the term 'relevant ecology' or 'environing world' in a way roughly synonymous with Jakob von Uexküll's *Umwelt* (pl. *Umwelten*), George Herbert Mead's concept of *'environment'* (1959: esp ch. 2, 32–46), and the more structural and sociological concept of *'milieu'*. See von Uexküll, 1957: 5–80; von Uexküll's major work (*Theoretische Biologie* (1970), an early statement for a phenomenological or subject-relative approach to the constitution of 'appearances' or 'relative worlds'. The true philosophical precursor of this idea for both Mead and von Uexküll, however, is undoubtedly Gottfried Wilhelm Leibniz (1646–1716) with his relativistic idea that each 'monad' mirrors and perceives the universe – the natural order – from its own particular perspective; this 'world perspectivism' entails that there are as many 'possible worlds' or different universes (*Innenwelt*, in von Uexküll's terminology) as there are perspectives. The geography of the natural world is intrinsically polymodal: 'Since every mind [or *monad*] is like a world apart, self-sufficient, independent of any other creature, containing infinity, and expressing the universe, it is as durable, subsistent, and absolute as the universe of creatures itself' (Leibniz, 1989: 144–5). Each form of species life introduces a different mode of reflexive relation toward reality, and with this relation a different 'definition' of the universe as the correlate of its transformational behaviour: 'Just as the same city viewed from different directions appears entirely different and, as it were, multiplied perspectively, in just the same way it happens that, because of the infinite multitude of simple substances, there are, as it were, just as many different universes, which are, nevertheless, only perspectives on a single one, corresponding to the different points of view of each monad' (*Monadology*, para. 57; see Leibniz, *The Principles of Philosophy, or the Monadology* paras 7, 56, 57, 61, 157 (in Leibniz, 1989: 213–34); *Principles of Nature and Grace, Based on Reason*, paras 1, 3, 4, 7, 8, 17 (in Leibniz, 1989: 206–13); *Die Philosophischen Schriften von G.W. Leibniz*, ed. C.I. Gerhardt, 7 vols (Hildesheim: Georg Olms 1965); *Opuscules et fragments inédits de Leibniz*, ed. Louis Couturat (Hildesheim: Georg Olms 1961); *G.W.*

Leibniz: Philosophical Essays, ed. Roger Ariew and Daniel Garber (Indianapolis and Cambridge: Hackett Publishing Company, 1989); L.E. Loemker, ed., *Leibniz: Philosophical Papers and Letters*, 2nd edn (Dordrecht-Holland: Reidel, 1969); P. Weiner, ed., *Leibniz: Selections*, New York: Charles Scribner's Sons, 1951); and G.H.R. Parkinson, *Leibniz: Philosophical Writings* (London: Dent, 1973). For the concept of 'milieu' see Georges Canguilhem, *La Connaissance de la vie*, second edition (Paris: Librairie philosophique J. Vrin, 1965) and *Le Normal et le pathologique* (Paris: PUF, 1966)).

5 In the context of emergent, non-linear, hierarchical evolutionism the application of categories such as 'sensing', 'feeling', 'sensibility', 'suffering', 'intelligence', 'self-monitoring', 'reflexivity', and so forth to animal species is interwoven with complex ethical questions about the epistemological status of animal 'existence' and the 'rights' of animals. Consider for example the proposition which, according to Karl Popper, would 'completely revolutionize' the theory of knowledge as it is still widely taught: that *animals can know something* (Popper, 1990: 30). Popper elaborates: 'it implies the hypothesis that some organ of the dog, in this case presumably the brain, has a function that corresponds not in some vague sense to the biological function of human knowledge, but is homologous with it' (30–1). In particular, animals 'know' in the sense of operating with 'hypotheses' or conjectural expectations relevant to their environment. Typically the attribution of 'consciousness' to animals is (i) socially accomplished from the perspective of particular practical and disciplinary interests and (ii) logically and empirically dependent upon preheld views of the nature, organization, and structure of 'consciousness' (or its equivalent such as 'intelligent behaviour', 'knowledge', etc.), and (iii) subject to historical variation and change. Attributions of reflexivity are frequently direct projections of an anthropocentric frame or folk-taxonomy in which the more a species resembles human life the more ready we are to ascribe reflexive predicates to it (in this schema the so-called higher mammals stand out as almost literal bearers of human modes of consciousness while other species and genera take on these predicates 'merely metaphorically'). Anthropocentric projection is strengthened where the species in question is also regarded as a 'social' or 'communicative species', concepts which are also 'essentially contested'. For example, consider Mead's description of 'feeling' as the 'lowest form of consciousness': 'what is implied is that when living forms enter such a systematic process they react purposively and as wholes to their own conditions, consciousness as feeling arises within life ... Into this situation there now comes a form that not only lives but makes its own organic conditions, favorable or unfavorable to life, part of the field to which it reacts or within which it lives. A conscious form is one that can make phases of its own life-process parts of its environment ... Feeling is the term we use for this added element in life, when the animal enters in some degree into its own environment' (Mead, 1959: 70; Mead warns against the anthropocentric fallacy in the following terms: 'All communication, all conversations of gestures, among the lower animals, and even among the members of the more highly developed insect societies, is presumably unconscious. Hence, it is only in human society – only within the peculiarly complex context of social relations and interactions which the human central nervous system makes physiologically possible – that minds arise or can arise; and thus also human beings are evidently the only biological organisms which are or can be self-conscious or possessed of selves' (1934: 235, n. 3; see §§31–3)). Cf. Wittgenstein, *Philosophical Investigations*, Part II, 223e and Popper's thesis: 'All adaptations to environmental and to internal regularities, to long-term situations and to short-term situations, are kinds of knowledge – kinds of knowledge whose great importance we can learn from evolutionary biology' (1990: 38). The psychological and cultural grounds for these forms of projection, their histori-

cal evolution and transformation forms an important topic in the history of reflexivity – which would begin by exploring the logological properties of rhetorics of attribution (classification, practical projection, ascriptive criteria for consciousness, the role of cultural prejudices, ethnobiologies, metaphors, and so forth). Such a history (or histories) would undoubtedly demonstrate that major changes have occurred in our views of and attitude toward the reflexivities of animate life. Problems in the sociocultural construction of 'animal existence' and questions about the phylogenesis of consciousness have been forced into prominence not only by constructivist sociology and evolutionary biology, but also by developments in cognitive science and artificial intelligence research which have been forced to abandon mechanistic models and inert concepts of natural processes and mind by virtue of their own discoveries about the active, intentional, information-processing nature of the mind. Literature in these areas is as follows: artificial intelligence: M. Boden, *Purposive Explanation in Psychology* (Cambridge, Mass.: Harvard University Press, 1972); M. Boden, *Artificial Intelligence and Natural Man* (New York: Basic Books/Brighton: Harvester, 1979); M. Boden, *Minds and Mechanisms: Philosophical Psychology and Computational Models* (Brighton: Harvester, 1981); J.D. Bolter, *Turing's Man* (Harmondsworth: Penguin, 1986); H.L. Dreyfus, *What Computers Can't Do: A Critique of Artificial Reason* (New York: Harper and Row, 1979); H. Gardner, *The Mind's New Science: A History of the Cognitive Revolution* (New York: Basic Books, 1985); Hofstadter, 1980. Philosophical psychology and neurophysiology: Hofstadter and Dennett, eds, 1981: esp. Section II P. Johnson-Laird, *The Computer and the Mind* (London: Fontana, 1988); cf. J.-P. Changeux, *Neuronal Man* (Oxford: Oxford University Press, 1986); Patricia Churchland's *Neurophilosophy* (Cambridge, Mass.: MIT Press, 1986); Ray Jackendorff, *Consciousness and the Computational Mind* (Cambridge, Mass.: MIT Press, 1987); Karl Pribram, *Languages of the Brain* (Englewood Cliffs: Prentice-Hall, 1971), Peter Russell, *The Brain Book* (London: Routledge & Kegan Paul, 1979). Linguistics: the speculations of Noam Chomsky and others on the innate neurological basis of language acquisition (for example, his *Language and Mind* (New York: Harcourt Brace Jovanovich, 1972) and *Reflections on Language* (New York: Pantheon, 1975); cf. Richard Langacker, *Language and its Structure* (New York: Harcourt Brace Jovanovich, 1967)), and recent work on the communicative-semiotic organization of animal life *(zoösemiotics* – currently a thriving area of contemporary semiology). For a stimulating attempt at a synthesis in these fields see G. Harman, ed., *On Noam Chomsky: Critical Essays* (Amherst: University of Massachusetts Press, 1982); R. Hoage and L. Goldman, eds, *Animal Intelligence: Insights into the Animal Mind* (Washington, DC: Smithsonian Press, 1986); Edward M. Hundert, *Philosophy, Psychiatry and Neuroscience: Three Approaches to the Mind: A Synthetic Analysis of the Varieties of Human Experience* (Oxford: Clarendon Press, 1989): esp. 187–275, 307–13; and M. Piattelli-Palmarini, ed., *Language and Learning: The Debate Between Jean Piaget and Noam Chomsky* (Cambridge, Mass.: Harvard University Press, 1980).

For an introduction to the literature on animal rights, ascriptions of sentience, and 'consciousness' in animals see: Mary Midgley, *Beast and Man: The Roots of Human Nature* (London: Methuen, 1979); *Animals and Why They Matter: A Journey Around the Species Barrier* (Athens: University of Georgia Press/Harmondsworth: Penguin, 1983): esp. 125–33, 134–43, and her essay 'Gene-juggling and rival fatalisms', in A. Montague, ed., *Sociobiology Re-examined* (Oxford: Oxford University Press, 1980); Patrick Bateson, 'Animal communication', in D.H. Mellor, ed., *Ways of Communicating* (Cambridge: Cambridge University Press, 1990): 35–55; Steven Rose, R.C. Lewontin, and Leon J. Kamin, *Not in Our Genes: Biology, Ideology and Human Nature* (Harmondsworth: Penguin, 1984); for the cultural history of attitudes toward animals in premodern England: Keith Thomas, *Man and the Natural World. Changing Attitudes in England 1500–1800* (London: Allen Lane, 1983); also R. Bleier, *Feminist Approaches to Science* (Oxford: Pergamon, 1986); B. Eastlea, *Fathering the Unthinkable* (London: Pluto Press, 1983); Haraway, 1989; Carolyn Merchant, *The Death of Nature: Woman, Ecology and the Scientific Revolution* (New York: Harper and Row, 1980); John Passmore, *The Perfectibility of Man* (London: Duckworth, 1970); and Peter Singer, *Animal Liberation* (New York: Random House, 1975).

On the phylogenesis of consciousness and its relation to the origins of speech and language: Derek Bickerton, *Roots of Language* (Ann Arbor: Karoma, 1981); J. Campbell, *Grammatical Man* (Harmondsworth: Penguin, 1984); Stevan R. Harnad, R. Stelkis and H.D. and Jane Lancaster, eds, *Origins and Evolution of Language and Speech* (New York: Academy of Sciences, 1976); H. and I. Jerison, eds, *Intelligence and Evolutionary Biology* (Berlin: Springer, 1988); Philip Lieberman, *On the Origins of Language: An Introduction to the Evolution of Human Speech* (New York: Macmillan, 1975); Philip Lieberman, *The Biology and Evolution of Language* (Cambridge, Mass.: Harvard University Press, 1984), and his earlier book, *The Speech of Primates* (The Hague: Mouton, 1972) and summary article 'Voice in the wilderness', *The Sciences*, 28 (4), 1988: 23–9; Andrew J. Lock, ed., *Action, Gesture and Symbol: The Emergence of Language* (New York: Academic Press, 1978); E.M. Macphail, *Brain and Intelligence in Vertebrates* (Oxford: Clarendon Press, 1986); A.R. Luria, *Higher Cortical Functions in Man* (New York: Basic Books, 1966); A.R. Luria, *Basic Problems of Neurolinguistics* (The Hague: Mouton, 1976); A.R. Luria, *Cognitive Development* (Cambridge, Mass.: Harvard University Press, 1976); John Lyons, 'Origins of language', in A.C. Fabian, ed., *Origins: The Darwin College Lectures* (Cambridge: Cambridge University Press, 1988): 141–66; Kirsten Malmkjær, 'Origin of language', in K. Malmkjær, ed., *The Linguistics Encyclopedia* (London: Routledge, 1991): 324–9; Mead, 1934; Tran duc Thao, *Investigations into the Origin of Language and Consciousness* (Dordrecht: Reidel, 1984); F. von Schilcher and N. Tennant, *Philosophy, Evolution and Human Nature* (London: Routledge and Kegan Paul, 1984).

On animal communication and the zoösemiotic perspective: Charles Darwin, *The Expression of Emotions in Man and the Animals* (Chicago: Chicago University Press, 1965); D. Griffin, *The Question of Animal Awareness* (New York: Rockefeller Press, 1976); Haraway, 1989; Eugene Linden, *Apes, Men and Language* (Harmondsworth: Penguin, 1976); T.A. Sebeok, ed., *How Animals Communicate* (Bloomington: Indiana University Press, 1977); E. Linden, *Apes, Men and Language* (Harmondsworth: Penguin, 1976); Konrad Lorenz, *On Aggression* (London: Methuen, 1966); Konrad Lorenz, *Studies in Animal and Human Behaviour*, 2 vols (London: Methuen, 1970, 1971); T.A. Sebeok and J.U. Umiker-Sebeok, eds *Speaking of Apes: A Critical Anthology of Two-Way Communication with Man* (New York: Plenum Press, 1980); Claire F. Schiller, ed., *Instinctive Behavior: The development of a modern concept* (New York: International Universities Press, 1957); H. Terrace, *Nim: A Chimpanzee Who Learned Sign Language* (New York: Knopf, 1979); N. Tinbergen, *The Study of Instinct* (Oxford: Oxford University Press, 1953); N. Tinbergen, *Social Behaviour in Animals* (London: Methuen, 1953); W. Koehler, *The Mentality of Apes* (London: Routledge and Kegan Paul, 1956); R.M. Yerkes, *The Social Behavior of Chimpanzees* (Washington, DC: American Psychological Association, 1940); G.C. Gallup Jr, 'Self-recognition in primates: a comparative approach to the bi-directional properties of consciousness', *American Psychologist*, 32, 1977: 329–38; Karl von Frisch, *Bees: Their Vision, Chemical Senses and Language* (Ithaca: Cornell University Press, 1950); Karl von Frisch, *The Dancing Bees* (London: Methuen, 1954); Karl von Frisch, *The Dance and Orienta-*

tion of Bees (Cambridge, Mass: Harvard University Press, 1967); M. Lindauer, *Communication Among Social Bees* (Cambridge, Mass.: Harvard University Press, 1960); T. Nagel, 'What is it like to be a bat?', *The Philosophical Review*, LXXXIII, 1974: 435–51 (also reprinted in Nagel's *Mortal Questions* (Cambridge: Cambridge University Press, 1986); Edward O. Wilson, *The Insect Societies* (Cambridge, Mass.: Belknap, Harvard University Press, 1971); Edward O. Wilson, *Sociobiology: The New Synthesis* (Cambridge, Mass.: Harvard University Press, 1975); Edward O. Wilson, *On Human Nature* (Cambridge, Mass.: Harvard University Press, 1978).

6 Among the relevant modern literature on *autopoiesis* see: Maturana and Varela, 1980; H.R. Maturana and F.J. Varela, *The Tree of Knowledge* (Boston, Mass.: New Science Library, 1985); G. Nicolis and I. Prigogine, *Exploring Complexity* (San Francisco: Freeman, 1986); Francisco J. Varela, *Principles of Biological Autonomy* (New York: North Holland, 1979); W. Krohn, *et al.*, eds, *Selforganization: Portrait of a Scientific Revolution* (Dordrecht: Kluwer, 1990).

7 The 'social' theory of cellular structure is quite common in evolutionary biology: 'I prefer to think of the body as a colony of *genes*, and of the cell as a convenient working unit for the chemical industries of the genes' (Dawkins, 1976).

> Our bodies are formed of cell co-operatives. Each nucleus-containing body cell is an association of lesser entities in symbiosis. If the product of all this co-operative effort, a human being, seems beautiful when correctly and expertly assembled, is it too much to suggest that we may recognize by the same instinct the beauty and fittingness of an environment created by an assembly of creatures, including man, and by other forms of life?
>
> (Lovelock, 1979: 143)

Perhaps this is also another way of approaching Dawkins' idea of the evolution of 'survival machines' as organic 'replicators' competing for living-space: 'The first survival machines probably consisted of nothing more than a protective coat. But making a living got steadily harder as new rivals arose with better and more effective survival machines. Survival machines got bigger and more elaborate, and the process was cumulative and progressive' (1976). The end point of this evolutionary process is the fabrication of centrally coordinated networks of cells – individuated bodies – and the 'use' of such bodies as a survival machine for the replicator Dawkins'calls the 'selfish gene':

> We, the individual survival machines in the world, can expect to live a few more decades. But the genes in the world have an expectation of life which must be measured not in decades but in thousands and millions of years.

On the logic of self-differentiating, self-organizing and self-replicating systems: Erich Jantsch, *The Self-Organising Universe: Scientific and Human Implications of the Emerging Paradigm of Evolution* (Oxford: Pergamon Press, 1980); Ernst Mayr, 'Teleological and teleonomic: a new analysis', in *Evolution and the Diversity of Life: Selected Essays* (Cambridge, Mass.: Harvard University Press, 1976); E. Mayr, 'How biology differs from the physical sciences', in D. Depew and B. Weber, eds, *Evolution at a Crossroads: The New Biology and the New Philosophy of Science* (Cambridge, Mass.: MIT Press, 1985); G. Nicolis and I. Prigogine, *Self-Organization in Nonequilibrium Systems* (New York: John Wiley, 1977); W. Poundstone, *The Recursive Universe* (New York: Morrow, 1985); I. Prigogine, *From Being to Becoming: Time and Complexity in the Physical Sciences* (San Francisco: Freeman, 1980); I. Prigogine, 'Origins of complexity', in A.C. Fabian, ed., *Origins: The Darwin College Lectures* (Cambridge: Cambridge University Press, 1988): 69–88;

M.C. Yovits, G.T. Jacobi and G.D. Goldstein, eds, *Self-Organising Systems* (Washington: Spartan Books, 1959); also: Francisco J. Varela, *Principles of Biological Autonomy* (New York: North Holland, 1979 and Maturana and Varela, 1980.

8 For example, J.J. Gibson, *The Senses Considered as Perceptual Systems* (Boston: Houghton Mifflin, 1966); J.J. Gibson, *The Ecological Approach to Visual Perception* (Boston: Houghton Mifflin, 1979); R. H. Whittaker, *Communities and Ecosystems*, 2nd edn (New York: Collier-Macmillan, 1975). Also P. Shepard, ed., *The Subversive Science: Essays Toward an Ecology of Man* (Boston: Houghton Mifflin, 1969). For introductions to the basic perspective of the new ecology: Gregory Bateson, *Mind and Nature* (London: Fontana, 1985); Johan Galtung, 'On the last 2,500 years in Western history, and some remarks on the coming 500', in Peter Burke, ed., *The New Cambridge Modern History, XIII Companion Volume* (Cambridge: Cambridge University Press, 1979): 318–61; Alison Jaggar, *Feminist Politics and Human Nature* (Totowa: Rowman and Allanheld, 1983); A. Koestler and J.T. Smythies, eds, *Beyond Reductionism* (Boston: Beacon Press, 1969); Peter Russell, *The Awakening Earth* (London: Routledge and Kegan Paul, 1982); Jonathan Schell, *The Fate of the Earth* (New York: Knopf, 1982); Rupert Sheldrake, *A New Science of Life* (London: Paladin, 1983); and, more speculatively, Rupert Sheldrake, *The Presence of the Past: Morphic Resonance and the Habits of Nature* (London: Collins, 1988). The ecological paradigm as a logic of living systems and processes has obvious affinities with the more 'philosophical' idiom of Dialectics with its central recommendation contained in the maxim that 'the true is the whole' (cf. Niklas Luhmann, *Soziale Systeme: Grundriss einer allgemeinen Theorie*, Frankfurt: Suhrkamp, 1984). The basic model of the 'organism-in-relation-to-the-universe' (in Alan Watts' phrase, 1992: 112) shares the dialectical intuition that 'change', 'development', or 'evolution' are not linear, uni-directional and monocausal sequences, but reflexive, multidirectional and multidimensional 'histories' (discontinuities, heterogeneous event systems, the 'simultaneity of the non-simultaneous', and so forth); it also embraces the naturalistic possibility of *discontinuity* and *qualitative transformation* as a normal aspect of organic life, and accepts the recurrence of chaotic periods of destructuration and catastrophic singularities in living systems. Non-linear Evolutionists, Open-System Theorists and Dialecticians, for historical reasons, choose to describe the self-reflexive characteristics of evolutionary self-differentiation in different idioms and language-games. But the emerging view of nature as 'experience-in-process', a reflexive, 'reason-engendering' universe is substantially the same (ecological metaphysics operates with an analogous concept of integral knowledge of the ecosphere as a creative self-awareness of the whole). The developmental inquiry into the 'truth of the whole' is also integrally connected with the self-development of the whole (this might be described as the reflexive root of both ecological and dialectical paradigms of inquiry). After Aristotle, Hegel is the first European philosopher who was completely at home in the reflexive idioms of ecological thought; witness the centrality of the following speculative concepts to his conception of rational inquiry: totality (the systematic interconnectedness of the life of the absolute idea), wholeness, process as dynamic change, self-differentiation, creative contradiction, the 'unity of opposites', 'the transformation of opposites', the 'subjective' in the object and the 'objective' in the subject, the unity of subject and substance, the dialectical growth of self-awareness through conflict, organic reflexivity, the self-moving concept (*Begriff*), concrete universality, consciousness-in-and-of-itself, and so forth.

4 CONSCIOUSNESS AND LIFE-WORLD

1 Julian Jaynes has written a book with the title *The Origin of Consciousness in the Breakdown of the Bicameral Mind* (Boston: Houghton Mifflin, 1976) where rather than view 'consciousness' as an innate capacity or predisposition of the human mind he claims that reflective awareness emerged relatively recently – the axial period dating from the second millennium BC (between 1400 BC and 600 BC); prior to this crucial 'splitting' human beings were not controlled from 'within' but by externalized, collective voices. Only the 'breakdown' or 'bicameralization' of mind produces the idea of an internal monitor and with this the beginnings of conscience. Jaynes links this speculation to a neurological argument concerning the growing dominance of the verbal, linguistic, and symbolic functions of the left-brain hemisphere, suggesting a long-term cultural shift from right- to left-brain specialization, from synthetic-analogue operations to analytic-digital functions. For discussion of Jayne's theory see Jaynes, in Kolak and Martin, eds, 1991: 16–39. For an ironical deconstruction of these quasi-scientific theses see Margolis, 1989: 3–34. Also of interest in this context: P.M. Churchland, *Neurophilosophy: Toward a Unified Science of the Mind/Brain* (Cambridge, Mass.: Harvard University Press, 1987); P.M. Churchland, *Matter and Consciousness* (Cambridge, Mass.: MIT Press, 1988); N. Humphrey, *Consciousness Regained: Chapters in the Development of Mind* (Oxford: Clarendon Press, 1983); N. Humphrey, *The Inner Eye* (London: Faber and Faber, 1986); N. Humphrey, *A History of the Mind* (London: Chatto and Windus, 1992); Charles Landesman, 'Consciousness', *The Encyclopedia of Philosophy* (London: Collier-Macmillan, 1967): vol. II; Ervin Laszlo, *Cosmic Connections: Evolution in the Whole-Field Universe* (New York: Bantam Books, 1990); William G. Lycan, *Consciousness* (Cambridge, Mass.: MIT Press, 1987); Joseph O'Connor and John Seymour, *Introducing Neuro-linguistic Programming: The New Psychology of Personal Excellence* (Bodmin, Cornwall: Crucible, 1990); G.S. Rousseau, ed., *Languages of the Psyche* (Los Angeles: University of California Press, 1990); D. Wiggins, *Sameness and Substance* (Oxford: Blackwell, 1980); B. Williams, *Problems of the Self* (Cambridge: Cambridge University Press, 1973).

2 For example:

> When I speak of intuition, I by no means exclude intellect and feeling, or even sense-perception. The total state of consciousness always contains all these elements. As the focus of attention shifts, it seems as if energy were gathered into some one of these elements at the expense of the rest.
>
> (Cornford, 1950: 25)

An influential tradition theorizes the self as a theme or 'object' of consciousness. The act of attentional thematization constitutes the distinction between consciousness and object-consciousness: 'What is known through consciousness must be something; mediation aims at the mediated ... The object's primacy is the *intentio obliqua*' (Adorno, 1978: 502); for the non-egological variant of this view of immanent self-awareness see Jean-Paul Sartre, *The Transcendence of the Ego: An Existentialist Theory of Consciousness* (New York: Noonday Press, 1957)); Wilhelm Dilthey's historicist account of the possibility of selfhood: 'When we reflect, turning the "I" upon itself, the "I" can become an object to itself; it becomes capable of enjoying itself and being an object of enjoyment to others ... when we, as sensitive beings, become objects to ourselves and thus aware of ourselves, our actions and the enjoyment we derive from them, the unique concept of the intrinsic value of the person arises – distinguishing him from everything which, as far as we know, does not enjoy itself. In this sense, the Renaissance formed the idea of the monad in which "thinghood", enjoyment, value and perfection were united. Leibniz enriched German philosophy and literature with this concept and the strong emotions contained in it' (Dilthey, in Rickman, ed., 1976: 243); Dilthey's account is still in the same Lockean-Kantian-Leibnizian tradition of reflection as introspective, immanent self-awareness (cf. Hans-Georg Gadamer, *Wahrheit und Methode* (Tübingen: Mohr, 1960); Taylor, 1989).

The risk to radical reflection in this process is not discussed by Dilthey; it has, however, been pointed out by Maurice Merleau-Ponty in terms of the manner in which philosophy – the vocation of radical questioning – may lose its orientation and aim in the very success of its formal and technical achievements. This is particularly true of the Eurocentric dream of a totally transparent, self-grounded knowledge (or what I refer to in the text as the videological form of life). Merleau-Ponty phrases the point as follows: 'While it is an acknowledged fact that all major philosophies seek to consider the human mind both in itself *and in its various aspects* (ideas and their development, understanding and sense-perception), there is a certain myth which presents philosophy as the authoritarian assertion of the mind's absolute autonomy. In this interpretation philosophy is no longer a process of questioning. It is rather a fixed body of doctrines, set up in order to ensure an absolutely *unbounded* mind the enjoyment of itself and its ideas' (Merleau-Ponty, 'The philosopher and sociology', in 1964b); reprinted in Thomas Luckmann, ed., 1978: 142–60, 143). See also Merleau-Ponty, 1968.

3 Talcott Parsons, 'Consciousness and symbolic processes', in Abramson, ed., 1954: 47–135, 47–8; also Parsons' metatheory of 'normative' or culturally determined social action in *The Structure of Social Action* (New York: Free Press, 1937); see also J.A.C. Brown, *Freud and the Post-Freudians* (Harmondsworth: Penguin, 1964); Jerome Bruner, *Actual Minds, Possible Worlds* (Cambridge, Mass.: Harvard University Press, 1986); Sigmund Freud, *The Ego and the Id*, in *The Standard Edition of the Complete Psychological Works*, vol. 19 (London: Hogarth Press, 1962); Harold Garfinkel, *The Perception of the Other: A Study in Social Order*, unpublished doctoral dissertation (Department of Sociology, Harvard University, 1952); Lawrence Kohlberg, *Essays on Moral Development*, vol. 1, and *The Psychology of Moral Development*, vol. 2 (San Francisco: Harper & Row, 1984); Hans Kohut, *The Analysis of the Self* (New York: International Universities Press, 1971) and *The Restoration of the Self* (New York: International University Press, 1977); Jacques Lacan, *Ecrits: A Selection* (New York: W.W. Norton, 1977); John Shotter and K. Gergen, eds, *Texts of Identity* (Newbury Park, Sage, 1989); Gregory P. Stone and H. Faberman, eds, *Social Psychology through Symbolic Interaction* (Waltham: Ginn-Blaisdell, 1970); Richard Wollheim and J. Hopkins, eds, *Philosophical Essays on Freud* (Cambridge: Cambridge University Press, 1982). Cf. Habermas, 1985b, 1987a; J. Habermas, *Moralbewusstsein und kommunikatives Handeln* (Frankfurt: Suhrkamp, 1983): ch. 4; Taylor, 1989: 3–107.

4 See C. McGinn, *The Problem of Consciousness* (Oxford: Blackwell 1991); W.G. Lycan, *Consciousness* (Cambridge, Mass: MIT Press, 1987) and J.R. Searle, *The Rediscovery of the Mind* (Cambridge, Mass: MIT Press, 1972). For general discussions of identity, self, and mind in recent philosophical literature see Hookaway and Peterson, eds, 1993; Kolak and Martin, eds, 1991: esp. Parts II, III; Michael E. Levin, *Metaphysics and the Mind-Body Problem* (New York: Oxford University Press, 1979); and Norman Malcolm, *Problems of Mind: Descartes to Wittgenstein* (New York: Harper and Row, 1971); H. Noonan, ed., *Personal Identity* (Aldershot: Dartmouth, 1993); and S. Shoemaker, *Self-Knowledge and Self-identity* (Ithaca: Cornell University Press, 1963).

5 The idea that consciousness has its origins in linguistic capacities is a common feature of contemporary thought. It was particularly important to the American pragmatists; but is today defended by a wide spectrum of 'naturalizing' philo-

sophers, psychologists, and critical social theorists (e.g. C. Altieri, *Subjective Agency: A Theory of First Person Expressivity and Its Social Implications* (Oxford: Blackwell, 1994); G. Globus, ed., *Consciousness and the Brain* (New York: Plenum, 1976); William Lyons, *The Disappearance of Introspection* (Cambridge, Mass.: MIT Press, 1987); Derek Parfit, *Reasons and Persons* (Oxford: Oxford University Press, 1984), A.O. Rorty, ed., *The Identities of Persons* (Berkeley: University of California Press, 1976). Julian Jaynes (in Kolak and Martin, eds, 1991: 16–39) speaks of consciousness or the mind-space of spatialized time as a product of verbal metaphors or analogues of behaviour in the physical world (esp. 20–3, 27–9 and the 'Discussion', 29–39).

6 For example, G.S. Rousseau, 'Psychology', in G.S. Rousseau and R. Porter, eds, *The Ferment of Knowledge: Studies in the Historiography of Eighteenth-Century Science* (Cambridge: Cambridge University Press, 1980): 143–210; and G.S. Rousseau, ed., *The Languages of Psyche: Mind and Body in Enlightenment Thought* (Berkeley: University of California Press, 1990), especially the introductory essay, G.S. Rousseau and R. Porter, 'Introduction: toward a natural history of mind and body', 3–44. For more sociological contributions see S. Lash and J. Friedman, eds, *Modernity and Identity* (Oxford: Blackwell, 1992).

7 The systematic 'excavation' of these prereflective forms of valuation, reflexivity and human relatedness form an overlapping field for a wide range of contemporary philosophers and theorists, including Julian Jaynes, Charles Taylor, Stanley Cavell, Bernard Williams, Martha Nussbaum, Alastair MacIntyre, Agnes Heller, Hannah Arendt, Seyla Benhabib, and others (see bibliography for detailed references).

5 REFLECTION AS SPECULATIVE THOUGHT

1 Hence the categorical imperative: 'Treat other people as ends in themselves, never as means to an end.' Compare: 'A person can refer to himself by pointing to himself only if he can conceive of himself as a totality' (Johnstone 1970, 50). Mead writes: 'The reflexive character of self-consciousness enables the individual to contemplate himself as a whole; his ability to take the social attitudes of other individuals and also of the generalized other toward himself, within the given organized society of which he is a member, makes possible his bringing himself, as an objective whole, within his own experiential purview; and thus he can consciously integrate and unify the various aspects of his self, to form a single consistent and coherent and organized personality. Moreover, by the same means, he can undertake and effect intelligent reconstruction of that self or personality in terms of its relations to the given social order, whenever the exigencies of adaptation to his social environment demand such reconstructions' (1934: 309, n. 19); see also: James, 1912, 1950; Mead, 1934; S. Collins, *Selfless Persons* (Cambridge: Cambridge University Press, 1982); P. Caruthers, *Introducing Persons: Theories and Arguments in the Philosophy of Mind* (London: Croom Helm, 1986); Roderick M. Chisholm, *The First Person* (Minneapolis: University of Minnesota Press, 1981); John Macmurray, *The Self as Agent* (London: Faber, 1957) and *Persons in Relation* (London: Faber, 1961); Jonathan Dancy, *Introduction to Contemporary Epistemology* (Oxford: Blackwell, 1985); Hampshire 1959; Hywel Lewis, *The Elusive Self* (Philadelphia: Westminster, 1982); Catherine McCall, *Concepts of Person: An Analysis of Concepts of Person, Self and Human Being* (Aldershot: Avebury, 1990); Thomas Nagel, *The View from Nowhere* (Oxford: Oxford University Press, 1986); Derek Parfit, *Reasons and Persons* (Oxford: Clarendon Press, 1984): Part III; J. Perry, ed., *Personal Identity* (Berkeley: Hackett, 1975); J. Perry, *A Dialogue on Personal Identity and Immortality* (Indianapolis: Hackett, 1978); K.S. Pope and J.L. Singer,

eds, *The Stream of Consciousness* (New York: Plenum, 1978); Shoemaker, 1963; P. Smith and O.R. Jones, *The Philosophy of Mind* (Cambridge: Cambridge University Press, 1986); Peter Strawson, *Individuals* (London: Methuen, 1959); Taylor, 1989; Ernst Tugendhat, *Self-Consciousness and Self-Determination* (London: MIT Press, 1986); J. Teichman, *Philosophy and the Mind* (Oxford: Blackwell, 1988); Peter Unger, *Identity, Consciousness and Value* (New York and Oxford: Oxford University Press, 1990); D.W. Winnicott, *Playing and Reality* (London: Tavistock, 1971); D.W. Winnicott, *Human Nature* (London: Free Association Books, 1988); Andrew Woodfield, *Thought and Object: Essays on Intentionality* (Oxford: Oxford University Press, 1982).

Accepting the historicity of selves cannot avoid the problem of human invariance, which can be formulated in terms of what invariant conditions we would accept in ascribing 'personhood' or 'humanity' to the individuals who populate different forms of life, historical societies, and civilizations. Charles Taylor notes the problem:

> The really difficult thing is distinguishing the human universals from the historical constellations and not eliding the second into the first so that one particular way seems somehow inescapable for humans as such, as we are always tempted to do.
>
> (1989: 112)

Joseph Margolis has recently stated the essential point: 'Paradigmatically, man is a cogniscent or cognizing being distinguished by his linguistic aptitude and by his aptitude for perception and action indissolubly joined to, and informed by, that linguistic ability. To admit such abilities *is* to admit both the historically contingent personae of different civilizations and different ages and the projection, within the limits of our familiarity with these, of a universalized or provisionally invariant notion of what it is, generically, to be a human person' (Margolis, 1989: 8–9. See also his related volume, *Science without Unity: Reconciling the Human and Natural Sciences* (Oxford: Blackwell, 1987): esp Part II chs 11, 12. Also McCall, 1990: esp. chs 10, 13–15.

Important articles on the topic of self and ascriptions of consciousness can be found in: G. Globus, *et al.*, eds, *Consciousness and Brain: A Scientific and Philosophical Inquiry* (New York: Plenum, 1976); G. Underwood and R. Stevens, eds, *Aspects of Consciousness, Vol. 1 Psychological Issues* (London: Academic Press, 1979); G. Underwood and R. Stevens, eds, *Aspects of Consciousness, Vol. 2 Structural Issues* (London: Academic Press, 1981); G. Underwood, ed., *Aspects of Consciousness, Vol. 3 Awareness and Self-awareness* (London: Academic Press, 1982); J. Perry, ed., *Personal Identity* (Berkeley: University of California Press, 1975); Kenneth Pope and Jerome Singer, eds, *The Stream of Consciousness* (New York: Plenum, 1978) Ronald S. Valle and Rolf von Eckatsberg, eds, *The Metaphors of Consciousness* (New York: Plenum, 1981); R. Wollheim, *The Thread of Life* (Cambridge: Cambridge University Press, 1984); Andrew Whiten, ed., *Natural Theories of Mind. Evolution, Development and Simulation of Everyday Mindreading* (Oxford: Blackwell, 1991).

2 Margolis, 1989: 301; cf. Heidegger, 1967b, 1982: esp. Part 1, ch. 1, §9 and Part 2, ch. 1, §§20–2; 1992: Preliminary Part, ch. 2, §5; Gadamer, 1960, 1979: Part III.

6 THE REFLEXIVE SELF

1 The key texts for this reorientation in contemporary philosophy are Wittgenstein's *Philosophical Investigations* (1968): §§243ff., 246, 261, 271, 289, 315–17, 339, 351,

411–15, 580, and Part II, i-ii, v, vi, xi, xiii, *passim*) and Heidegger, 1967b: Introduction, and Part I ('The interpretation of Dasein in terms of temporality, and the explication of time as the transcendental horizon for the question of Being', especially the chapters of Division One ('Preparatory fundamental analysis of Dasein').

2 This would be the place for a comprehensive historical and comparative logological investigation of the evolution of the rhetorics of thought and thinking presupposed by a wide range of everyday practices, intellectual disciplines, and cultural practices.

3 For the history of mechanical paradigms of thinking see Elie Halevy, *The Growth of Philosophic Radicalism* (London: Faber, 1928); Fritjhof Capra, *The Turning Point: Science, Society and the Rising Culture* (New York and London: Wildwood, 1982); Ryle, 1954 and his *Collected Papers* (London: Hutchinson, 1971); Will Wright, *Wild Knowledge: Science, Language, and Social Life in a Fragile Environment* (Minneapolis: University of Minnesota Press, 1992).

7 BEING-IN-THE-WORLD AS INCARNATE REFLEXIVITY

1 Marjorie Grene, 1968: 93 and her later books *The Understanding of Nature* (Dordrecht: D. Reidel, 1974) and Grene, 1984; the whole of Chapter 2 on Helmuth Plessner's philosophical anthropology is relevant to this discussion; Plessner's major work, *Die Stufen des Organischen und der Mensch* (1928) is profoundly influenced by the phenomenological tradition, particularly by the ontological turn given to this tradition by Martin Heidegger's *Sein und Zeit* (1927, esp. the chapters of the first division) and the 'philosophical anthropology' of Max Scheler (see for example the studies in his *Selected Philosophical Essays* (Evanston: Northwestern University Press, 1973); particular studies of eccentric positionality can be found in Plessner's *Lachen und Weinen* (1941), recently translated as *Laughing and Crying: A Study of the Limits of Human Behavior* (Evanston: Northwestern University Press, 1970); other relevant texts include: Adolph Portmann, *New Paths in Biology* (New York: Harper and Row, 1964); Scheler, Kurt Goldstein, *The Organism: A Holistic Approach to Biology* (Boston: Beacon Press, 1963);Kurt Goldstein, *A Kurt Goldstein Reader: The Shaping of Neurophysiology* (New York: AMS Press, 1986); Maurice Merleau-Ponty, *La Structure du comportement* (Paris: PUF, 1953); Wolfgang Kohler, *Gestalt Psychology* (London: G. Bell & Sons, 1930); Maurice Merleau-Ponty, *La Phénoménologie de la perception* (Paris: Gallimard, 1945); Paul Schilder, *The Image and Appearance of the Human Body* (New York: International Universities Press, 1950); Schutz, 1967a: Part II, 'Phenomenology and the social sciences', esp. 'Scheler's Theory of Intersubjectivity and the general thesis of the alter ego' and 'Sartre's theory of the alter ego'; Herbert Spiegelberg, *Phenomenology in Psychology and Psychiatry* (Evanston: Northwestern University Press, 1972); Erwin W. Straus, *The Primary World of Senses* (New York: Free Press of Glencoe, 1963); Erwin W. Straus, *Selected Papers: Phenomenological Psychology* (London: Tavistock, 1966); Edmund Husserl, *Krisis* (1937/8) (*The Crisis of European Sciences and Transcendental Phenomenology* (Evanston: Northwestern University Press, 1970); Arnold Gehlen, *Der Mensch: Seine Natur und Seine Stellung in der Welt* (Frankfurt: Athenäum Verlag, 1940).

For a general overview of the whole tradition of philosophical anthropology see H.O. Pappe, 'Philosophical anthropology', in Paul Edwards, ed., *Encyclopedia of Philosophy* (New York: Macmillan, 1967): vol. 6. Also see Charles Guignon's *Heidegger and the Problem of Knowledge* (Indianapolis: Hackett, 1983) and Paul

Tillich, *The System of the Sciences according to Objects and Methods* (London and Toronto: Associated University Presses, 1981).

2 For the contrast between 'knowing-how' and 'knowing that' see Ryle, 1949: Ch. 2, 26–60; Ryle uses the distinction to criticize the 'category mistakes' that lead to Cartesian dualism (see ch. 1, 'Descartes' myth' and 'The origin of the category mistake'); see also John L. Austin, *Philosophical Papers* (Oxford: Oxford University Press, 1979): 76–116; Phenomenology also speaks of the distinction between *operative* awareness and *thematic* consciousness. The distinction overlaps with the hermeneutic tradition's separation of understanding (*Verstehen*) which is closer to 'understanding' or 'comprehending' the other (*qua* other person) and *Erklaren*, which is often translated as explanation or explanatory understanding; we might also mention the distinction between 'knowledge-by-acquaintance' and 'knowing-that' (*knowing something* and *knowing-about* something). For both the analytic and the phenomenological traditions, 'knowing-that' presupposes prior configurations of 'knowing-how' (in the language of this chapter reflective knowledge is founded upon an infrastructure of reflexive knowledge), just as all technical, instrumental, methodic inquiry takes for granted a richer field of tacit skills, capacities, and embodied 'know-how' (the relationship between the two types of knowledge forms the central topic of Polanyi 1973. Polanyi has restated the thesis in a later book explicitly devoted to the topic of the tacit structure of our everyday reflexive skills (Polanyi, 1976). The topic has been most acutely decribed by the anthropologist Clifford Geertz (in his *Local Knowledge*, New York: Basic Books, 1983). For background discussion to the debate as it applies to the human sciences see the essays in R. Wilson, ed., 1974.

8 PRAXICAL REFLEXIVITY

1 Bohm, 1980; more technical discussion can be found in Bohm's *Causality and Chance in Modern Physics* (Philadelphia: University of Pennsylvania Press, 1957); also see B. Hiley and F. David, eds, *Quantum Implications: Essays in Honor of David Bohm* (London: Routledge and Kegan Paul, 1987); cf. Capra, 1975, 1982; R. Sheldrake, *A New Science of Life* (London: Paladin, 1983); Zukav, 1979; R. Weber, *Dialogues with Scientists and Sages* (London: Routledge and Kegan Paul, 1986); O'Malley, 1972; Margolis, 1989: chs 3, 4. Bohm utilizes the Gestalt idea of 'implicate order' as a primary perspective upon objects, description, and inquiry, whether this occurs in everyday life or in science:

> our notions of order are pervasive, for not only do they involve our thinking but also our senses, our feelings, our intuitions, our physical environment, our relationships with other people and with society as a whole and, indeed, every phase of our lives. It is thus difficult to 'step back' from our old notions of order sufficiently to be able seriously to consider new notions of order.
>
> (1980: 176)

On the fundamental importance of 'holistic' contextuality or 'Gestalt contextures' and the study of the 'lived body' (*le corps propre*) within the referential field of consciousness see Maurice Merleau-Ponty, *The Phenomenology of Perception* (London: Routledge and Kegan Paul, 1962); A. Gurwitsch, *The Field of Consciousness* (Pittsburgh: Duquesne University Press, 1964): 309–75; A. Gurwitsch, *Marginal Consciousness*, ed. L. Embree (Athens: Ohio University Press, 1985). The 'field' terminology of 'contexture' has been recently appropriated and used by Harold Garfinkel and his students (see M. Lynch, E. Livingstone and H. Garfinkel, 'Temporal order in laboratory work', in Knorr-Cetina and Mulkay, eds, 1983), and the literature included in n. 2 below. The extensive literature on the history of embodiment includes: M. Feher, ed., *Fragments for a History of the Human Body*, 3 vols (New York: Zone, 1989); M.M. Bakhtin, *Rabelais and His World* (Cambridge, Mass.: MIT Press, 1968); Piero Camporesi, *Bread of Dreams: Food and Fantasy in Early Modern Europe* (Cambridge: Polity Press, 1989); Piero Camporesi, *The Incorruptible Flesh: Bodily Mutation and Mortification in Religion and Folklore* (Cambridge: Cambridge University Press, 1988); Piero Camporesi, *The Body in the Cosmos: Natural Symbols in Medieval and Early Modern Italy* (Cambridge: Polity Press, 1992).

2   A great deal of contemporary phenomenological writing cuts across the topic of praxical reflexivity (and more broadly of the praxical-embodied, *configurational* nature of the constructed world, selfhood, commonsense knowledge, informal rationality, consciousness, and historicity). For 'thinking' as constitutive praxis see Martin Heidegger, 1968 and Hannah Arendt, *The Life of the Mind, Vol. 1: Thinking* (New York: Harcourt Brace Jovanovich, 1977); Kosík, 1976. For the tacit dimensions of embodied perception, rational observation, and theorizing see the work of Michael Polanyi, especially *Personal Knowledge* (London: Routledge and Kegan Paul, 1958 and *The Tacit Dimension* (New York: Doubleday, 1966). Accenting the involvement of subjects with worlds of material objects see: Csikszentmihalyi and Rochberg-Halton, 1981; Peter Burke, *The Historical Anthropology of Early Modern Italy: Essays on Perception and Communication* (Cambridge: Cambridge University Press, 1987); Pirsig, 1974; D. Miller, *Material Culture and Mass Consumption* (Oxford: Blackwell, 1987).

Important sociological work on 'embodied/incarnate reflexivity' is available in the writings of the following: Gregory Bateson, Herbert Blumer, Alfred Schutz, Jean-Paul Sartre, Aron Gurwitsch, Harold Garfinkel, Aaron Cicourel, Harvey Sacks, Erving Goffman, George Herbert Mead, Stephan Strasser, David Sudnow, Michael Polanyi, Pierre Bourdieu, and Maurice Merleau-Ponty; ethnomethodology, in particular, has come to treat situationally embodied 'practical reflexivity' as its central programmatic theme – as indicated by the citation to Schutz's work which frames Harold Garfinkel and Harvey Sacks' paper 'On formal structures of practical actions' (1970); also Melvin Pollner's essay 'Mundane Reasoning', *Philosophy of Social Science*, 4, 1974: 35–54; in this context we should also mention phenomenology's concern with the 'prereflective' *Lebenswelt*, the world of mundane *doxa*, the natural attitude or prepredicative world and, of course, in more recent Marxian traditions the topics of everyday life, 'material' experience and praxis (for example in the early writings of Georg Lukács, 1971b), the writings of Henri Lefebvre – his *Everyday Life in the Modern World* (London: Harper & Row, 1971); and 1991a: esp. ch.2, 'The knowledge of everyday life' and ch. 3, 'Marxism as critical knowledge of everyday life'; Agnes Heller, *Everyday Life* (London: Routledge, 1984); Pierre Bourdieu, Outline of a Theory of Practice (Cambridge: Cambridge University Press, 1977); 1990, and the seminal work of the Italian Marxist, Enzo Paci, 1972, the project to reconstruct historical materialism around a 'quasi-transcendental' philosophy of intersubjective communication in the later work of Jürgen Habermas, and in the extensive explorations contained in the last sections of Gerd Brand's *Die Lebenswelt: Eine Philosophie des konkreten Apriori* (Berlin: de Gruyter, 1971). On these latter topics see the work of Calvin O. Schrag, *Radical Reflection and the Origin of the Human Sciences*, 1980; and his later book, *Communication, Praxis, and the Space of Subjectivity* (Bloomington: Indiana University Press, 1986); in *Radical Reflection* Schrag advocates a radical 'return' to questions of the origin of the sciences, 'the establishment of a reflexivity whereby the originative questioning of man about himself, within a precategorial and prescientific matrix of human experience, is recovered' (1980: 9); and Fred R.

Dallmayr, 'Phenomenology and Marxism: a Salute to Enzo Paci', in Psathas, ed., 1973. The common thread of the 'meaning genesis' or meaning derivation of the sciences as an idealizing abstraction from the *Lebenswelt*, and the salutary dereifying self-reflection upon the occluded origins of the sociocultural *Lebenswelt* runs through these perspectives: 'the concept of the life-world is revealed in its entire and central significance as the basis of meaning of all sciences, including natural sciences and including also philosophy in so far as it wishes to appear as an exact science. Thus, every reflection finds its evidence only in the process of recurring to its originally founding experience within this life-world, and it remains the endless task of thought to make intelligible the intentional constitution of the contributive subjectivity in reference to this its basis of meaning' (Alfred Schutz, 'Phenomenology and the social sciences', in 1967a; Schutz and Luckmann, 1973; cf. Gurwitsch, 1966: 397–447: in Calvin Schrag's terms:

> We furrowed the path to this world of prephilosophical and prescientific comprehension by way of a deconstruction of the transcendental-empirical framework of inquiry, which has determined the development of philosophical anthropology from its beginnings. This led to a radical critique of the metaphor of philosophical foundations and a replacement of the quest for unification and integration of the methods and results of the special human sciences with a quest for the origin or scientific and philosophical knowledge of man.
>
> (Schrag, 1980:78)

The difference-in-continuity between the genetic phenomenology of the life-world (in the writings of Maurice Merleau-Ponty, Aron Gurwitsch, and Alfred Schutz) and the genealogical motif of ethnomethodology concerns the role of the 'constitutional matrix' disclosed by phenomenological reduction (or ethnomethodological indifference) in the Husserlian and Garfinkelian projects; the latter resolutely abandons the Cartesian premises of Husserl in favour of a richer understanding of incarnate praxical reflexivity, and situated reasoning *in situ*: by abandoning the terminological apparatus of the Cartesian philosophy of consciousness (even where radicalized in Husserl's later transcendental phenomenology), ethnomethodology embraces the fundamental linguisticality of its domain of problems – evident in the early definition given to his inquiries by Garfinkel: ethnomethodology as the principaled sociological analysis of the rational properties, methods, and uses of indexical expressions embedded in the concrete and ordinary features of everyday communication (cf. Schrag, 1980: 5 and his more 'sociological' version of radical reflexivity which closely parallels the motivation of Garfinkel's pragmatic turn to everyday sense-making constellations: 'the reflexivity of radical anthropological reflection marks out a return not to an epistemological ego but to a precategorial world of prephilosophical and prescientific comprehension. A reflexivity upon the world as experienced replaces the interiorized self-reflexivity of a transcendental, epistemological subject attempting to establish the foundations of all knowledge' (Schrag, 1980: 72–3)).

See also Husserl, 1965, 1970, 1973; Schutz, 1970b: 272; Merleau-Ponty, 1962, 1964c, 1968; Gurwitsch, 1964; cf. David Carr, *Phenomenology and the Problem of History* (Evanston: Northwestern University Press, 1974); F.A. Elliston and P. McCormick, eds, *Husserl: Expositions and Appraisals* (Notre Dame: University of Notre Dame Press, 1977); Ludwig Landgrebe, *The Phenomenology of Edmund Husserl: Six Essays* (Ithaca and London: Cornell University Press, 1981); Edward N. Lee and Maurice Mandelbaum, eds, *Phenomenology and Existentialism* (Baltimore: Johns Hopkins University Press, 1967); Werner Marx, 'The life-world and the particular subworlds', in Maurice Natanson, ed., *Phenomenology and Social Real-*

ity: Essays in Memory of Alfred Schutz (The Hague: Martinus Nijhoff, 1970); Berger and Luckmann, 1967; Erving Goffman, *Relations in Public: Microstudies of the Public Order* (New York: Harper and Row, 1971); Michael Hammond, Jane Howarth, and Russell Keat, *Understanding Phenomenology* (Oxford: Blackwell, 1991); Burkhart Holzner, *Reality Construction in Society* (Cambridge: Schenkmann Publishing Company, 1968); W. Outhwaite, *Understanding Social Life*, 2nd edn (Lewes: Jean Stroud, 1986); Schrag, 1980: esp. ch. 5, 'Understanding and reason: towards a hermeneutic of everyday life'; Laurie Spurling, *Phenomenology and the Social World* (London: Routledge and Kegan Paul, 1977); M. Theunissen, *The Other: Studies in the Social Ontology of Husserl, Heidegger, Sartre and Buber* (Cambridge, Mass.: MIT Press, 1984); Zaner, 1971. See also Habermas, 1987a; Joseph Margolis, 1989: 101–43.

On the situated, routine organization of talk as an artful accomplishment see Garfinkel, 1967, Garfinkel and Sacks, 1970, Sacks, 1972, Sacks, 1974 in R. Bauman and J. Sherzer, eds, 1974, Schegloff, 1972, Sacks, Schegloff, and Jefferson, 1974, Turner, 1974, Schenkein, ed, 1978, Psathas, ed, 1979. For a critical historical-semiotic introduction to the whole ethnomethodological tradition see Pierce J. Flynn, *The Ethnomethodological Movement: Sociosemiotic Interpretations* (Berlin and New York: Mouton de Gruyter, 1991).

David Sudnow's study of the acquisition of the 'incarnate skills' required to become a jazz pianist, *Ways of the Hand* (1978) offers a practical demonstration of the deconstructive potential of a detailed ethnomethodological study of a skilled cultural practice (also David Sudnow, ed., 1972, 1978).

For the concepts of 'mundane reason' and 'informal reasoning': Schutz, 1967a, Garfinkel, 1967; McHugh, 1968; Zimmerman, 1971; Zimmerman and Pollner, 1971; Cicourel, 1973, Pollner, 1974, 1979; M. Pollner prescribes that 'the assumption of an intersubjective world taken together with the inferential operations for which it provides comprises what we shall term an idiom of *mundane reason*' (1974: 35). Schutz's phenomenology of the 'natural attitude', building upon Husserl's painstaking and exhaustive studies of the life-world, begins the seminal project of a radical sociology of *mundanity* and *mundane reason*:

> we can speak of fundamental assumptions characteristic of the natural attitude in the life-world, which themselves are accepted as unquestionably given; namely the assumptions of the constancy of the structure of the world, of the constancy of the validity of our experience of the world, and of the constancy of our ability to act upon the world and within the world.
>
> (1970c: 116)

In practice Schutz's phenomenology of mundanity concentrates on the following relatively 'static' structures: (1) the spatiotemporal zonal stratification of everyday experience organized around normative 'relevance systems'; (2) the prepredicative logic of typification in mundane knowledge (everyday reason's thematic, horizonal, and marginal fields, the assumption of the natural attitude, the reciprocity of perspectives, the congruency of relevance systems, and so on); (3) the social structuration and distribution of the stock of everyday knowledge in terms of pragmatic relevance motives and norms; (4) the cultural symbolization of experience into 'finite provinces of meaning' (science, dreaming, theatre, etc.) which define the sociocultural horizons of social action; (5) the central role of the biographical situation of human agency and action; (6) the projective-anticipational motivational character of social action; and (7) the transformations of mundane reason introduced by the 'disinterested attitude' of scientific observation and scientific rationalities (for adumbrations of all of these themes see Schutz, 1967). The importance of 'everyday experience', 'the world of everyday life', and the cultural construction of 'fictional worlds' as a shared concern of documentary cinema, the novel, ethnography, ethnomethodology, and visual sociology should also be noted in this context. See: Paul Atkinson, *The Ethnographic Imagination: Textual Constructions of Reality* (London: Routledge, 1990); Richard Harvey Brown, *A Poetic for Sociology: Toward a Logic of Discovery for the Human Sciences* (Chicago: University of Chicago Press, 1989); Richard Harvey Brown, *Society as Text: Essays on Rhetoric, Reason, and Reality* (Chicago: University of Chicago Press, 1987); Edward S. Casey, *Imagining: A Phenomenological Study* (Bloomington, Indiana University Press, 1976); De Certeau, 1984; John Fiske, *Understanding Popular Culture* (London: Unwin Hyman, 1989); Ann Game, *Undoing the Social: Towards a Deconstructive Sociology* (Milton Keynes: Open University Press, 1991); Erving Goffman, *Behavior in Public Places* (New York: Free Press, 1963); Erving Goffman, *Interaction Ritual* (London: Allen Lane, 1967); Erving Goffman, *Relations in Public: Microstudies of the Public Order* (New York: Harper and Row, 1971); Erving Goffman, *Frame Analysis* (New York: Harper and Row, 1974); Garfinkel, 1967; Doreen Maitre, *Literature and Possible Worlds* (London: Middlesex Polytechnic Press, 1983); Thomas Pavel, *Fictional Worlds* (Cambridge, Mass.: Harvard University Press, 1986); Michael Riffaterre, *Fictional Truth* (Baltimore and London: Johns Hopkins University Press, 1990); Maurice Roche, *Phenomenology, Language and the Social Sciences* (London: Routledge and Kegan Paul, 1973); Rorty, 1989; Stephen Tyler, ed., *Cognitive Anthropology* (New York: Aldine Publishing Company, 1970); Becker, 1982; Richard M. Barsam, *Nonfiction Film Theory and Criticism* (New York, Dutton and Co., 1976); D. Bordwell, *Narration in the Fiction Film* (Madison University of Wisconsin Press, 1985).

3   For variations on the repetitive thematics of social order see Harold Garfinkel, *The Perception of the Other: A Study in Social Order* (unpublished doctoral dissertation, Department of Sociology, Harvard University, 1952); Harold Garfinkel, 1967, where ethnomethodology's programme is presented as 'the investigation into the rational properties of indexical expressions and other practical actions as contingent accomplishments of organised, artful practices of everyday life' (1967: 11); Alan Blum and Peter McHugh, 'The social ascription of motives', *American Sociological Review*, 36, 1971: 98–109; McHugh, 1968; Zimmerman and Pollner, 1971; Atkinson, 1981: 201–23; Atkinson bases his account of the uniqueness of the ethnomethodological perspective on its resolution of the problem of social order: 'the ethnomethodological interest in the methods of reasoning routinely used by societal members, both lay and professional, in finding *practical* solutions to the basic dilemmas that divide positivist and interpretivist sociologies is informed by the quest for just such a model of social order'; and further, 'Garfinkel's stress on the importance for social organization of taken-for-granted methods of practical reasoning meant that empirical research should be directed towards an examination of the ways in which tacit rules, background expectancies and common-sense theories were used by members in achieving orderliness in particular contexts').

4   Harold Garfinkel and D. Lawrence Wieder, 'Two incommensurable, asymmetrically alternate technologies of social analysis', in Graham Watson and Robert M. Seiler, eds, *Texts in Context: Contributions to Ethnomethodology* (London: Sage Publications, 1992): 175–206, the cited texts occur on pages 177 and 202. Compare Garfinkel's description of the earlier programme as investigations of members' reflexive methods for producing social order: 'Members know, require, count on, and make use of this reflexivity to produce, accomplish, recognize, or demonstrate rational-adequacy-for-all-practical-purposes of their procedures and findings' (1967: 8).

5   Simmel, 1986: 15. The classical Marxist texts are, of course, the *Economic and*

Philosophical Manuscripts of 1844, the *Communist Manifesto*, the Preface to the Introduction to a *Critique of Political Economy*, the *Grundrisse* (1973) and *Capital*, vols. I, II and III (1961a, 1961b and 1966). For the other works see McLellan, ed., 1977: 1–127, 219–47, 388–92. For a creative extension of these arguments see D. Noble, *Forces of Production* (New York: Knopf, 1984).

9 PHRONETIC REFLEXIVITY: BETWEEN MORALITY AND PRAXIS

1 Charles Horton Cooley, 1902: 184; also his *Social Organization* (New York: Schocken Books, 1962), and *Social Process* (Carbondale: Southern Illinois University Press, 1929); cf. William James, 'The stream of thought', in 1890, 1912, 1977; Mead, 1938; Dewey, 1958. The religious tradition of American Puritanism and Transcendentalism should be examined as the cultural template for many of these 'communitarian' beliefs and practices. Consider the actual history of social regulation implicit in Cooley's definition of the subject matter of sociology: 'the imaginations which people have of one another are the solid facts of society, and to observe and interpret these must be the chief aim of sociology' (1902: 121). For background see Ross, 1991: Parts II, III.
2 For illuminating discussion of these phenomena see Garfinkel, 1956: 420–4, 1967; Goffman, 1959; H. Fingarette, *Self-Deception* (New York: Humanities Press, 1969); M. Johnston, 'Self-deception and the nature of mind', in Kolak and Martin, eds, 1991: 422–35; Lévinas, 1969, 1987, 1994; and Sartre, 1957a).

10 GENEALOGICAL SELF-REFLEXIVITY

1 Husserl, 1960: 152–3; the classic statement is still Husserl, 1931; cf. Heidegger, 1982. Cf. Schutz's gloss on the rigour of transcendental phenomenology's method 'concerned with the demonstration and explanation of the activities of consciousness (*Bewusstseinsleistungen*) of the transcendental subjectivity within which this life-world is constituted. Since transcendental phenomenology accepts nothing as self-evident, but undertakes to bring everything to self-evidence, it escapes all naive positivism and may expect to be the true science of mind (*Geist*) in true rationality, in the proper meaning of this term' Schutz, 1967a: 118–39); also his 'Concept and theory formation in the social sciences', in 1967a: 48–66 and 'some structures of the life-world', in 1970c: 118–39. Schutz's own most systematic presentation of the implications of phenomenological reduction and meaning reactivation for the foundational problems of the social science is presented in Schutz, 1967. See also Herbert Spiegelberg, *The Phenomenological Movement: A Historical Introduction* (The Hague: Martinus Nijhoff, 1965). For a systematic re-evaluation of Schutz's 'pragmatic life-world theory' see Ilja Srubar, *Kosmion: Die Genese der pragmatischen Lebenswelttheorie von Alfred Schutz und ihr anthropologischer Hintergrund* (Frankfurt: Suhrkamp, 1988): esp. Section III, 'Der sinnhafte Aufbau der sozialen Welt' on the reflexive 'anthropology' at work in Schutz's theory of meaning-constitution (Sinnkonstitution), esp. 97–131. I am grateful to Scott Lash for drawing Srubar's work to my attention.
2 I have been influenced in this critique by the work of Maurice Merleau-Ponty, Paul Ricoeur, Karel Kosík, and Jan Patocka. For a sample of the latter's work in phenomenology, see *Jan Patocka, Philosophy and Selected Writings*, ed. Erazim Kohak (Chicago: University of Chicago Press, 1989) esp. the essays, 'The "Natural" world and phenomenology', 'The movement of human existence: a selection

from Body, community, language, world', and 'Cartesianism and phenomeno-logy'.

11 TRANSACTIONAL REFLEXIVITY

1 Gouldner, 1970; also his essays in 1973, 1965. One of the most-read essays on the theme of value-neutrality is Gouldner's 'Anti-minotaur: the myth of a value-free sociology', *Social Problems*, 9, 1962: 199–213; the essay can also be found in Jack Douglas, ed., *The Relevance of Sociology* (New York: Appleton-Century Crofts, 1970): 64–84. Other writings that are symptomatic of the climate at the end of the 1960s and prefigure the growth of more reflexive perspectives in sociology and political theory are Gunnar Myrdal, *Values in Social Theory* (New York: Harpers, 1959); Robert Friedrichs, *A Sociology of Sociology* (New York: Free Press, 1970); N. Mullins, *Theories and Theory Groups in Contemporary American Sociology* (New York: Harper and Row, 1973); O'Neill, 1972; also *Perception, Expression and History: The Social Phenomenology of Maurice Merleau-Ponty* (Evanston: Northwestern University Press, 1970); J.E. Curtis and J.W. Petras, eds, *The Sociology of Knowledge* (New York: Praeger, 1970); W. Pope, J. Cohen, and L. Hazelrigg, 'On the divergence of Weber and Durkheim: a critique of Parsons' convergence thesis', *American Sociological Review* 40, 1975: 412–27; G. Radnitzky, *Contemporary Schools of Metascience* (Chicago: Henry Regnery, 1973); J.D. Douglas and J.M. Johnson, eds, *Existential Sociology* (Cambridge: Cambridge University Press, 1977). O'Neill has interesting things to say on the implications of limited reflexivity for our understanding of the project of *critique*:

> The notion of *critique* which we may derive from the concept of reflexivity as institution is one which is grounded in a contextual environment which lies open horizontally to the corpus of social science knowledges rather than through any transcendental reflection. This notion of critique is the result of abandoning Husserl's attempt to construct an eidetic of any possible corpus of knowledge as the correlative of a universal and timeless constitut-ing reflexivity and the problems it raises for intersubjectivity, rationality, and philosophy itself. The corpus of the historical and social sciences is not, properly speaking, constituted through any object or act of reflection. It arises from a continual production or verification (*reprise*) which each individual undertakes according to his situation and times. Thus each one's work must be continually reviewed to unearth its own auspices sedimented in the archaeology of human sciences. This is not a simplistic argument for eternal starts, any more than a crude rejection of the accumulation of human knowledge. It is rather an attempt to interpret the *rhetorical* nature of the appeal of knowledge and criticism through which tradition and rebellion are made.
>
> (O'Neill, 1972: 231–2)

2 Work in this area includes: Alan Blum, 'Theorizing', in J.D. Douglas, ed., 1971; Alan Blum, 'Rereading Marx', in *Sociological Inquiry*, 43, 1971: 23–34; Blum, 1974, 1978; Alan Blum and Peter McHugh, 'The social ascription of motives', in *Ameri-can Sociological Review*, 36, 1971: 98–109; Peter McHugh, 'On the failure of positivism', in Douglas, ed., 1971: 320–35; Peter McHugh, Stanley Raffel, Daniel C. Foss, and Alan F. Blum, *On the Beginning of Social Inquiry* (London: Routledge and Kegan Paul, 1974); Blum and McHugh, eds, 1979, Blum and McHugh, 1984; Stanley Raffel, *Habermas, Lyotard and the Concept of Justice* (London: Macmillan, 1992): 8–12; Sandywell, *et. al.*, 1975. We might also mention the sociologically

informed critique of philosophy in the work of Paci, 1972, Stanley Rosen (particularly 1969, 1980), and W. Marx, 1971.

3 For related work see Bourdieu, 1990, 1991, 1992, 1993; C. Calhoun, E. LiPuma, and M. Postone, eds, *Bourdieu: Critical Perspectives* (Cambridge: Polity Press, 1993); S. Aronowitz, *Science as Power* (Minneapolis: University of Minnesota Press, 1988); A. Feenberg, *Critical Theory of Technology* (New York: Oxford University Press, 1991); A. Ross, *No Respect* (London: Routledge, 1989); D. Hoy and T. McCarthy, *Critical Theory* (Oxford: Blackwell, 1994); S.E. Bronner, *Of Critical Theory and Its Theorists* (Oxford: Blackwell, 1994).

12 DIALOGICAL REFLEXIVITY

1 It follows from this premise that the ontogenesis of consciousness, self-awareness, and reflection should be formulated in strict correlation with the social ontogenesis of language as a many-dimensional stratification of semiopraxical articulation:

> The connection of consciousness with symbolic process is also in accord with certain known facts about the development of consciousness in the child. It has often been hypothesized, on the basis of careful observations, that the development of consciousness is correlative with that of language, so that only when the child has learned to talk with others can he talk to himself and thus become fully conscious. We suggest that this 'talk to himself' is internal communication between internalized objects (meaning matrices), and that these internalizations derive from the child's integration into a sufficiently complex social interaction system. Furthermore, this 'talk to himself' is the very prototype of consciousness as we have discussed it above.
>
> (Talcott Parsons, in Abramson, ed., 1954: 54)

Cf. Karl-Otto Apel, *Analytical Philosophy of Language and the Geisteswissenschaften* (Dodrecht, D. Reidel, 1967); Church, 1961; Aaron V. Cicourel, 'The acquisition of social structure: toward a developmental sociology of language and meaning', in J. Douglas, ed., 1971; Ralf Dahrendorf, *Essays in the Theory of Society* (Stanford: Stanford University Press, 1968); Gendlin, 1962; Garfinkel, 1967; Luckmann, ed., 1978; A.R. Luria, *The Man with a Shattered World* (Cambridge, Mass.: Harvard University Press, 1987); Merleau-Ponty, 1963; Miller, 1973; G.A. Miller, E. Gallanter, and K.H. Pribram, *Plans and the Structure of Behaviour* (New York: Holt Rhinehart, 1960); Paul Pfeutze, *Self, Society and Existence* (New York: Harper and Row, 1954); Jean Piaget, *Structuralism* (New York: Basic Books, 1970); Sacks, 1985; Scarry, 1985; Schutz, 1967; Vygotsky, 1962, 1978, 1987.

2 We might compare the logological concepts of *articulation* and *configuration* with the hermeneutic-phenomenological concepts of 'meaning', 'meaningfulness', 'provinces of meaning', or 'orders of existence'. The common root of both vocabularies is, of course, the configurational phenomenology of Gestalt psychology. Meaningfulness as the constitutive being-of-the-world for beings-in-the-world is the ultimate context for these categories. Aron Gurwitsch helpfully clarifies the concept of 'experiential order' as follows:

> For an object – of any description whatever – to exist means that it is inserted into a context based upon and, therefore, dominated by, a specific relevancy principle. *Existence means existence within a system* at a certain place in the latter and, hence, in well-defined relationships with other objects pertaining to the same systematic context. To illustrate, one may refer to mathematical

existence and, more specifically, to the system of natural numbers ... one might even go so far as to say that a number is nothing but a certain place within that systematic context. In any event, the number has its existence among, with reference to, and *only* with reference to, other members of the system in question.

(Gurwitsch, 1966: 123)

Gurwitsch's conceptualization is examined in greater detail in his systematic work, *The Field of Consciousness* (1964) and in his more dynamic phenomenology of the field-organization of experience in *Marginal Consciousness* (1985). The notion of 'referential context' (including equipmental contexts, lived spatiotemporal comportments in everyday life, structures of concern, and so forth is basic to Heidegger's hermeneutic analysis of everyday Dasein (see Heidegger, 1967b) and the more accessible lectures for *Being and Time, History of the Concept of Time* (1992, esp. §§19–31)). Alfred Schutz's development of the idea of 'finite provinces of meaning' and their social organization in terms of relevance systems can be found in his *Collected Papers*, 3 vols, 1964, 1967a, 1970c and in 1970a). For the role of provinces of meaning as a central 'structure of the life-world' see Schutz and Luckmann, 1973. See also Gurwitsch, 1966. The logological concepts of 'articulation' and 'field of articulation' might be approached as a generalization and radicalization of these seminal phenomenological and hermeneutical ideas. As we have seen in the chapters above the same train of thought can be found in the writings of George Herbert Mead and John Dewey. Mead writes:

> Experience, even that of the individual, must start with some whole. It must involve some whole in order that we may get the elements we are after. What is of peculiar importance to us is this recognition of an element which is common in the perception of the individual and that which is regarded as a condition under which that perception arises – a position in opposition to an analysis of experience which proceeds on the assumption that the whole we have in our perception is simply an organization of these separate elements. *Gestalt* psychology gives us another element which is common to the experience of the individual and the world which determines the conditions under which that experience arises ... we have a certain structure that has to be recognized both in the experience of the individual and the conditioning world.

> (1934: 37–8)

For Mead – as for Dewey and Marx – the ultimate 'Gestalt' in understanding experience and discourse is the antecedent social framework of ongoing institutions and social practices. The latter determines the categorial positions and discourses of individuals who enter the interactional order of social life. All of these orientations converge – at least tacitly – on the logological category of 'life-in-the-world'.

3 We have seen that classical phenomenology tends to treat the 'life-world' (*Lebenswelt*) as the uniquely privileged foundation of all semiopraxis, forgetting that the life-world has a genesis and constructed history – and, more tellingly, that 'life-world' structures and activities are practically accomplished, situation-specific formations (or what we have termed 'articulations'). Gurwitsch writes, for example:

> Though orders of existence other than the life-world preserve their specific nature and also their autonomy with respect to the life-world, they can be understood only on the basis of the latter. In accounting for them, one has to start from the life-world. Because of the privileged status of the life-world, the theory of perception plays a prominent role in the writings of Husserl as well as other phenomenological authors.

(1966: 121)

See also Lester E. Embree, ed., *Life-World and Consciousness: Essays for Aron Gurwitsch* (Evanston: Northwestern University Press, 1972); Eugen Fink, *Studien zur Phaenomenologie: 1930–1939* (The Hague: Martinus Nijhoff, 1966). To counter this egological bias theorists like Giddens propose a social theory of world constitution: 'By the *duality of structure* I mean that social structure is both constituted *by* human agency and yet is at the same time the very *medium* of this constitution' (1993: 128–9). With respect to classical phenomenological theory our emphasis differs in concentrating upon the material origins and institutional specification of life-worlds as mutable structures of social interaction. More recent examples of phenomenological practice have avoided these strictures; see for example W.S. Hamrick, ed., *Phenomenology in Practice and Theory* (The Hague: Martinus Nijhoff, 1985), E.S. Casey, *Remembering: A Phenomenological Study* (Bloomington: Indiana University Press, 1987).

4 On 'people's history', see Peter Burke, *Popular Culture in Early Modern Europe* (London: Temple Smith/New York: Harper and Row, 1978); Peter Burke, 'We, the people: popular culture and popular identity in modern Europe', in Scott Lash and Jonathan Friedman, eds, *Modernity and Identity* (Oxford: Blackwell, 1992): 293–308; E.P. Thompson, *The Making of the English Working Class* (London: Gollancz, 1963); E. P. Thompson, 'Time, work-discipline, and industrial capitalism', *Past and Present*, 38, 1967: 56–97; H.J. Kaye and K. McLelland, eds, *E.P. Thompson: Critical Perspectives* (Cambridge: Cambridge University Press, 1990); G. Stedman Jones, *Languages of Class* (Cambridge: Cambridge University Press, 1983); Jan Vansina's *The Oral Tradition: A Study in Historical Methodology* (Chicago: Aldine, 1965); Eric Wolf, *Europe and the People Without History* (Berkeley: University of California Press, 1982). The collection of important articles edited by Chandra Mukerji and Michael Schudson, *Rethinking Popular Culture: Contemporary Perspectives in Cultural Studies* (Berkeley: University of California Press, 1991), is a good place to start – especially the essays in Part 1, 'Popular culture in historical studies', 63–235. Cf. the project of cultural hermeneutics which

> attempts to correlate the deep archaeology of *subjectivity* and its surface, *objective* counterpart, that is, to analyze the underlying deep structures of culture called 'meanings' as they are embodied, expressed, and institutionalized in the actual life of men in their 'natural attitude' and to understand them as the people of a particular culture understand them. Thus cultural hermeneutics is an attempt to understand the experiential topography of meanings and values by which people themselves live. This deep sedimentation of cultural meanings and values is the essence of what we have called the life-world

> Hermeneutic autonomy means that to get at the deep structures that underlie surface phenomena in culture, we must come to grips with the structure of intersubjective meanings that are embodied in the common practices and institutions of a particular culture. For culture is a calculus of intersubjective meanings. The fundamental underlying principle of hermeneutic autonomy is the notion that man is a self-interpreting animal.

> The *nexus* of intersubjective meanings is the way of experiencing thought and action (both individual and institutional) which is the very original stuff of practices and institutions in society at a given period of time. To put it differently, cultural 'mentality' or 'orientation' is *a system of intersubjective*

meanings commonly shared by a group of people that has persisted throughout the ages within a given geographical area.

(Jung, 1979: 77, 78, 79 respectively)

Also Ricoeur, 1981, 1984–7.

5 For example, George Duby's archaeology of marriage patterns in medieval France as an excavation of the everyday theory and practice of the institution traced through influential theological texts: George Duby, *The Knight, the Lady and the Priest: The Making of Modern Marriage in Medieval France* (London: Allen Lane, 1984), or his study of the discourses of status order in medieval culture 1980. On the historiographical problems of studying popular ideas, attitudes, values, and *mentalités*: Peter Burke, *The Historical Anthropology of Early Modern Italy: Essays on Perception and Communication* (Cambridge: Cambridge University Press, 1987), Robert Darnton, *The Great Cat Massacre and Other Episodes in French Cultural History* (New York: Basic Books, 1984), Ginzburg, 1980; E. Hobsbawm and T. Ringer, eds, *The Invention of Tradition* (Cambridge: Cambridge University Press, 1983); Natalie Davis, *Society and Culture in Early Modern France* (Stanford: Stanford University Press, 1975); Natalie Davis, *The Return of Martin Guerre* (Cambridge, Mass.: Harvard University Press, 1983). For *Annales* historiography of *la vie quotidienne*: Ginzburg, 1980; Emmanuel Le Roy Ladurie, *Peasants of Languedoc* (Urbana: University of Illinois Press, 1974); Le Roy Ladurie, 1979; Jacques Le Goff, *The Medieval Imagination* (Chicago: University of Chicago Press, 1985); On 'long-durational' historiography: Philip Abrams, *Historical Sociology* (Ithaca: Cornell University Press, 1982); F. Braudel, *Capitalism and Material Life: 1400–1800* (London: Weidenfeld and Nicolson, 1973); F. Braudel, *The Mediterranean and the Mediterranean World in the Age of Philip II* (London: Collins, 1973); F. Braudel, *The Structures of Everyday Life: The Limits of the Possible* (London: Collins, 1981); F. Braudel, *The Wheels of Commerce* (London: Collins, 1982); F. Braudel, *Afterthoughts on Material Civilization and Capitalism* (Baltimore: Johns Hopkins University Press, 1977); F. Braudel, *On History* (Chicago: University of Chicago Press, 1980); R. Chartier, ed., *A History of Private Life*, vol. 3 (Cambridge, Mass.: Belknap Press, 1989); N. Elias, *The Civilising Process*, 2 vols (Oxford: Blackwell, 1982 and 1987); N. Elias, *An Essay on Time* (Oxford: Blackwell, 1990); Lynn Hunt, ed., *The New Cultural History* (Berkeley: University of California Press, 1989); G.C. Iggers, *New Directions in European Historiography* (Middletown: Wesleyan University Press, 1975); Michael Mann, *The Sources of Social Power*, vol. 1 (Cambridge: Cambridge University Press, 1986); Brian Stock, *Listening for the Text: On the Uses of the Past* (Baltimore and London: Johns Hopkins University Press, 1990); Lawrence Stone, *The Family, Sex and Marriage in England 1500–1800* (New York: Harper and Row, 1977); Charles Tilly, *As Sociology Meets History* (New York: Academic Press, 1981); Charles Tilly, *Big Structures, Large Processes, Huge Comparisons* (New York: Sage, 1984).

6 As an example of this dialectic of interpretation consider the unanticipated ways in which psychoanalytic vocabularies have now permeated Anglo-American culture, becoming everyday logological frames for very different groups and strata, or the more general phenomenon of the emergence of hyperconscious social strata actively assuming the role of moral, ethical, or religious interpreters for their societies. Cf. Daniel Boorstin, *The Image: A Guide to Pseudo-events in America* (New York: Harper Colophon, 1964); E.G. Boring, *A History of Experimental Psychology*, 2nd edn (New York: Appleton-Century-Crofts, 1950): 707; Frank Cioffi, ed., *Freud: Modern Judgments* (London: Macmillan, 1973); Martin L. Gross, *The Psychological Society: A Critical Analysis of Psychiatry, Psychotherapy, and the Psychological Revolution* (New York: Touchstone, 1978); Philip Rieff, *The Triumph of the*

Therapeutic (New York: Norton, 1966); Philip Rieff, *Freud: The Mind of the Moralist* (New York: Viking, 1969); Christopher Lasch, *The Culture of Narcissism* (New York: Norton, 1979): 80ff.; Christopher Lasch, *The Minimal Self* (New York: Norton, 1984). Also Richard Wollheim, ed., *Freud: A Collection of Critical Essays* (New York: Anchor Doubleday, 1974). On the dialectics of anticipated and unanticipated consequences of social action see the classic article of Robert K. Merton, 'The unanticipated consequences of social action' in *Sociological Ambivalence* (New York: Free Press, 1976): 145–55; also Raymond Boudon, *The Unintended Consequences of Social Action* (London: Macmillan, 1982). The theme is central to the metatheoretical debate between structuralist and agency theorists in contemporary social science. See Giddens, 1979, 1987, 1993; Halfpenny, 1982; Sahlins, 1976, 1981; Swingewood, 1991; Therborn, 1976.

7 The 'long-durational' character of such 'epochal formations' presents analysis with difficult problems. For instance, what began as a ritual, myth, or particularistic ideology may sediment as the basic materials of a logological space; the difference between logological structure and ideologies blurs in practice; the 'longevity' of deep structures makes them difficult 'objects' to isolate and analyze (given that the analyst, like the agent, tends to take them for granted as the context of her own question-frames and interpretations). These problems are implicit in Michel Foucault's positivistic conception of an archaeology of knowledge as

> an attempt to reveal discursive practices in their complexity and density; to show that to speak is to do something – something other than to express what one thinks ... to show that a change in the order of discourse does not presuppose 'new ideas', a little invention and creativity, a different mentality, but transformations in a practice, perhaps also in neighbouring practices, and in their common articulation. I have not denied – far from it – the possibility of changing discourse: I have deprived the sovereignty of the subject of the exclusive and instantaneous right to it.

Moreover:

> the positivities that I have tried to establish must not be understood as a set of determinations imposed from the outside on the thought of individuals, or inhabiting it from the inside, in advance as it were; they constitute rather the set of conditions in accordance with which a practice is exercised, in accordance with which that practice gives rise to partially or totally new statements, and in accordance with which it can be modified. These positivities are not so much limitations imposed on the initiative of subjects as the field in which that initiative is articulated (without, however, constituting its centre), rules that it puts into operation (without it having invented or formulated them), relations that provide it with a support (without it being either their final result or their point of convergence).
>
> (1972: 208–9)

See the related discussion of the reflexive processes by which the 'habitus' of a society is transmitted and reproduced in Bourdieu, 1990 and more particularly in his essay 'Cultural reproduction and social reproduction', in Richard Brown, ed., *Knowledge, Education, and Cultural Change* (London: Tavistock, 1973). His most extensive empirical application of the concept of cultural habitus can be found in Bourdieu, 1984. Also of relevance is Reiner Schürmann's reconstruction of Heidegger's analysis of the closure of Western metaphysics in terms of a genealogy of epochal principles (1987: esp. Part 1, chs 1–3 for discussion of the difficult methodological issues in this kind of deconstructive analysis).

8

> That individual philosophical concepts are not anything capricious or autonomously evolving, but grow up in connection and with each other; that, however suddenly and arbitrarily they seem to appear in the history of thought, they nevertheless belong just as much to a system as all the members of the fauna of a continent – is betrayed ... by the fact that the most diverse philosophers keep filling in a definite fundamental scheme of possible philosophies.
>
> (Nietzsche, 1978: §20)

See also Nietzsche, 1968: §481; *Basic Writings of Nietzsche*, trans. Walter Kaufmann (New York: Random House, 1968); Nietzsche, 1969); *Untimely Meditations* (Cambridge: Cambridge University Press, 1983); *Twilight of the Idols and The Anti-Christ* (Harmondsworth: Penguin, 1968), *A Nietzsche Reader*, trans. R.J. Hollingdale (Harmondsworth: Penguin, 1977) and the review and self-interpretation of his own literary production in Nietzsche, 1979. Cf. Wittgenstein's suggestion in *Philosophical Investigations*: 'These philosophical problems are, of course, not empirical problems; they are solved, rather, by looking into the workings of our language, and that in such a way as to make us recognize those workings' (1968: §109). Cf. Wittgenstein, 1969. And, from within a different problematic, Jacques Derrida's Heideggerian 'derivation' of the language of Western metaphysics from a 'matrix' based on the Indo-European concern for 'being-as-presence':

> the entire history of the concept of structure ... must be thought of as a series of substitutions of center for center, as a linked chain of determinations of the center. Successively, and in a regulated fashion, the center receives different forms or names. The history of metaphysics like the history of the West is the history of these metaphors and metonymies. Its matrix ... is the determination of Being as *presence* in all senses of this word. It could be shown that all names related to fundamentals, to principles, or to the center have always designated an invariable presence – *eidos, arche, telos, energeia, ousia* (essence, existence, substance, subject), *aletheia*, transcendentality, consciousness, God, man, and so forth.
>
> (1978a: 277–8)

Nietzsche also observed that:

> Under an invisible spell, they always revolve once more in the same orbit; however independent of each other they may feel themselves with their critical or systematic wills, something within them leads them, something impels them in a definite order, to wit, the innate systematic structure and relationship of their concepts. Their thinking is, in fact, far less a discovery than a recognition, a remembering, a return and homecoming to a remote, primordial, and inclusive household of the soul, out of which those concepts grew originally: philosophizing is to this extent a kind of atavism of the highest order
>
> (1978: §20)

Finally Nietzsche, Wittgenstein, and Derrida concur that by excavating the 'workings of language' we reach back into the occluded history of a society, that the intellectual praxis of millennia is deposited and sedimented in language's differential practices. But these thinkers also formulate the crucial point that this 'back-tracking' does not take the genealogist to a pristine 'starting point' or unmediated *origin*. The 'bracketing' of a cultural practice (a language-game) and its

genealogical explication leads to a realm of interpretive transformations and mis-
prisions (as it were, 'revisionism' is an inherent vector in the sphere of culture):

> There is no set of maxims more important for an historian than this: that
> the actual causes of a thing's origin and its eventual uses, the manner of its
> incorporation into a system of purposes, are worlds apart; that everything
> that exists no matter what its origin, is periodically reinterpreted by those
> in power in terms of fresh intentions ... in the course of which the earlier
> meaning and purpose are necessarily either lost or obscured.
>
> (1969: Essay II, xii)

This can also be compared to Husserl's notion of phenomenology as an archaeology of the primordial structures of the *Lebenswelt*, of philosophical reflection as a
'grounding' or 'digging' praxis (*Philosophie von unten*). Genealogy corrects the
unreflexive idea of the 'primordial *Lebenswelt*' as an interpretation-free 'layer'
upon which the superstructures of science, technology, art, and theoretical praxis
are constituted. It also avoids the extreme form of linguistic determinism which
contends that the grammatical structures of empirical languages prestructure what
can be thought, thus determining the basic language of belief and interpretation for
members of that speech community: the world (or 'life-worlds') of a given society
are *linguistically* constructed; 'linguistic relativity' is usually referred to as the
'Sapir-Whorf' hypothesis (see Sapir, 1921, and Whorf, 1956). In keeping with the
spirit of Nietzsche's genealogical prospectus, later genealogists view the field of
language and discourse more generally as text matrices continuously subject to
radical acts of reinterpretation – this, *in nuce*, is what Derrida calls a system of
difference(s): the dispersal of the 'transcendental signified' opens the field of infinite
signification.

9   Nietzsche, 1968:§ 409. Also see 1984: §§11, 19; 1978: §20; 1974: §§354, 355.
'Against positivism, which halts at phenomena – "There are only *facts*" – I would
say: No, facts is precisely what there is not, only interpretations ... "Everything is
subjective", you say; but even this is interpretation. The "subject" is not something
given, it is something added and invented and projected behind what there is. –
Finally, is it necessary to posit an interpreter behind the interpretation? Even this
is invention, hypothesis. In so far as the word "knowledge" has any meaning, the
world is knowable; but it is *interpretable*. "Perspectivism". It is our needs that
interpret the world' (1968: §481; cf. 'there are *no eternal facts*, just as there are no
absolute truths. Consequently what is needed from now on is historical philosophizing, and with it the virtue of modesty' (1984: 2)). For recent interpretations
of Nietzsche's thought on radical interpretivism, perspectivism, and related matters
see: David B. Allinson, ed., *The New Nietzsche: Contemporary Styles of Interpretation* (Cambridge, Mass.: MIT Press, 1985); Keith Ansell-Pearson, ed., *Nietzsche
and Modern German Thought* (London and New York: Routledge, 1991); Roy
Boyne, *Foucault and Derrida: The Other Side of Reason* (London: Unwin Hyman,
1990); Maudemarie Clark, *Nietzsche on Truth and Philosophy* (Cambridge: Cambridge University Press, 1990); R.J. Hollingdale, *Nietzsche: The Man and His
Philosophy* (London: Routledge and Kegan Paul, 1973); Walter Kaufmann,
Nietzsche: Philosopher, Psychologist, Anti-Christ (Princeton: Princeton University
Press, 1968); Nancy Love, *Marx, Nietzsche and Modernity* (Columbia: Columbia
University Press, 1986); B. Magnus, *Nietzsche's Existential Imperative* (Bloom-
ington: Indiana University Press, 1978); J. Minson, *Genealogies of Morals* (London:
Macmillan, 1985); Alexander Nehamas, *Nietzsche: Life as Literature* (Cambridge,
Mass.: Harvard University Press, 1985); A. Schrift, *Nietzsche and the Question of
Interpretation* (London: Routledge, 1990); Georg Stauth and Bryan S. Turner,
Nietzsche's Dance: Resentment, Reciprocity and Resistance in Social Life (Oxford:

Blackwell, 1988); J.P. Stern and M. Silk, *Nietzsche on Tragedy* (Cambridge: Cambridge University Press, 1981); J.P. Stern, *Nietzsche* (London: Fontana, 1990); Gianni Vattimo, *The End of Modernity* (Cambridge: Polity Press, 1988).

10 Thus even as a heuristic framework it is difficult to separate 'the political' from other spheres of modern society. The model of society which divides institutions into three axial principles – for example economic, political, and cultural – may even be symptomatic of the very ideology of postmodernism with its inflated conception of the role of theoretical knowledge systems:

> In capitalist society the axial institution has been private property and in the post-industrial society it is the centrality of theoretical knowledge. In Western culture in the last one hundred years the axial thread has been 'modernism' with its onslaught on tradition and established institutions. In the Western political system the axial problem is the relation between the desire for popular participation and bureaucracy.
>
> (Bell, 1974: 115; also cf. Lyotard, 1984)

Bell's conceptualization has the effect of separating 'knowledge' and 'knowledge systems' from structural issues of power, eliding the ways in which the dynamics of 'postindustrial' knowledge systems actually flow from older systems of economic and political power. Failing to connect 'discourse' and 'power' leads to a definite 'cognitivist' conception of modern societies: 'In the post-industrial society, the chief problem is the organization of science, and the primary institution the university or the research institute where such work is carried out' (1974: 116); 'the control of society is no longer primarily economic but political' (1974: 373); and 'What the concept of a post-industrial society suggests is that there is a common core of problems, hinging largely on the relation of science to public policy, which will have to be solved by these societies' (1974: 119). For ways of thinking 'the political' which avoids either the traditional schema of 'private life and the public sphere' or the sociologist's axial typology see the work of Antonio Gramsci, Hannah Arendt, and Agnes Heller. There is also a growing body of work on the active role of ethical-political discourses and practices in shaping the cultural conditions of knowledge, selfhood, public space, and communality. Among the most useful texts I have found are Arendt, 1958; Hannah Arendt, *On Revolution* (New York: Viking, 1963); Hannah Arendt, *The Life of the Mind, Part 1, Thinking* (London: Secker and Warburg, 1978), Hannah Arendt, *Lectures on Kant's Political Philosophy* (Brighton: Harvester, 1982); Bauman, 1992; Kenelm Burridge, *Someone, No One: An Essay on Individuality* (Princeton: Princeton University Press, 1979); Richard J. Bernstein, *The New Constellation: The Ethical-Political Horizons of Modernity/Postmodernity* (Cambridge: Polity Press, 1991); Heller and Fehér, 1988; Eugene Kamenka, ed., *Community as a Social Ideal* (London: Arnold, 1982) and his book *Justice* (London: Arnold, 1979); W. Kymlicka, *Liberalism, Community and Culture* (Oxford: Clarendon Press, 1989); Michael J. Sandel, *Liberalism and the Limits of Justice* (Cambridge: Cambridge University Press, 1982); Taylor, 1989; M. Walzer, *Spheres of Justice* (Oxford: Martin Robertson, 1983); James Boyd White, *When Words Lose Their Meaning* (Chicago: University of Chicago Press, 1984); R. Wollheim, *The Thread of Life* (Cambridge: Cambridge University Press, 1984).

11 For example, of reflexive social sciences subject to 'new rules of sociological method': 'the primary tasks of sociological analysis are the following: (a) the hermeneutic explication and mediation of divergent forms of life within descriptive metalanguages of social science; (b) explication of the production and reproduction of society as the accomplished outcome of human agency' (Giddens, 1993: 170).

12 For exemplary explorations of the alterities of reflexive experience see: B. Ashcroft,

et al., *The Empire Writes Back: Theory and Practice in Post-colonial Literatures* (London: Routledge, 1989); U. Beck, A. Giddens and S. Lash, *Reflexive Modernization: Politics, Tradition and Aesthetics in the Modern Social Order* (Cambridge: Polity Press, 1994); G. Bock and S. James, eds, *Beyond Equality and Difference: Citizenship, Feminist Politics and Female Subjectivity* (London: Routledge, 1992); Rosi Braidotti, *Patterns of Dissonance: A Study of Women in Contemporary Philosophy* (Cambridge: Polity Press, 1991): esp. chs 7, 8; De Certeau, 1984; Critchley, 1992; D.R. Dickens and A. Fontana, eds, *Postmodernism and Social Inquiry* (London: UCL Press, 1994: Part 1, 'Postmodern theories of society'; Anthony Elliott, *Social Theory and Psychoanalysis in Transition: Self and Society from Freud to Kristeva* (Oxford: Blackwell, 1992): ch. 7; Luce Irigaray, *An Ethics of Sexual Difference* (London: Athlone Press, 1993); John Llewelyn, *Beyond Metaphysics?: The Hermeneutic Circle in Contemporary Continental Philosophy* (New Jersey: Humanities Press, 1985): chs 9, 10; Ricoeur, 1994: esp. Sixth to Tenth Studies, 140–356; John Shotter, *Cultural Politics of Everyday Life* (Buckingham: Open University Press, 1993): Part 3.

BIBLIOGRAPHY

Abramson, H., ed., *Problems of Consciousness* (New York: Corlies, Macy and Co., 1954).

Adorno, T.W., 'Subject and object', in A. Arato and E. Gebhardt, eds, *The Essential Frankfurt School Reader* (Oxford: Blackwell, 1978).

Adorno, T.W., *Notes to Literature, Volume 1* (New York: Columbia University Press, 1991a).

Adorno, T.W., *The Culture Industry: Selected Essays on Mass Culture* (London: Routledge, 1991b).

Adorno, T.W. and Horkheimer, M., *Dialectic of Enlightenment* (London: Verso, 1979).

Althusser, L., 'Ideology and ideological state apparatuses (notes toward an investigation)', in *Lenin and Philosophy and Other Essays* (London: New Left Books, 1971).

Anderson, B., *Imagined Communities: Reflections on the Origin and Spread of Nationalism* (London: Verso, 1983).

Anderson, P., *Considerations on Western Marxism* (London: Verso, 1976).

Arato, A. and Gebhardt, E., eds, *The Essential Frankfurt School Reader* (Oxford: Blackwell, 1978).

Arendt, H., *The Human Condition* (Chicago: University of Chicago Press, 1958).

Aristotle, *Physics, De Anima, De Interpretatione*, in Aristotle, *The Basic Works of Aristotle* (New York: Random House, 1941).

Aristotle, *Art of Rhetoric*, trans. John Henry Freese (London: Heinemann/Loeb Classical Library, 1947).

Aristotle, *The Clarendon Aristotle*, ed. J. Ackrill (Oxford: Oxford University Press, 1961–73).

Aristotle, *Metaphysics*, trans. Hippocrates G. Apostle (Bloomington, Ind.: Indiana University Press, 1966).

Aristotle, *Politics*, trans. T.A. Sinclair, revised by Trevor J. Saunders (Harmondsworth: Penguin, 1981a).

Aristotle *et al.*, *Classical Literary Criticism*, trans. T.S. Dorsch (Harmondsworth: Penguin, 1981b).

Ariès, P., *L'homme devant la mort* (Paris: Seuil, 1979).

Ashmore, M., *The Reflexive Thesis: Wrighting the Sociology of Scientific Knowledge* (Chicago: University of Chicago Press, 1989).

Atkinson, J.M., 'Ethnomethodological approaches to socio-legal studies', in A. Podgorecki and C.J. Whelan, eds, *Sociological Approaches to Law* (London: Croom Helm, 1981).

Atkinson, J.M. and Drew, P., *Order in Court: The Organization of Verbal Interaction in Judicial Settings* (London: Macmillan, 1979).

Auden, W.H., *The Dyer's Hand* (London: Faber, 1963).

Auerbach, E., *Mimesis: The Representation of Reality in Western Literature* (1946) (Garden City: Doubleday Anchor Books, 1957).

Augustine, St, *The City of God (De Civitate Dei)* (London: Dent/Everyman's Library, 1945).

Austin, J.L., *Philosophical Papers* 2nd edn (London: Oxford University Press, 1970).

Bachelard, G., *The Psychoanalysis of Fire* (London: Quartet Books, 1987).

Bader, F., *Die Ursprünge der Transzendental-philosophie bei Descartes*, 2 vols (Bonn: Bouvier Verlag H. Grundman, 1979–83).

Bakan, D., *Disease, Pain and Sacrifice: Towards a Psychology of Suffering* (Chicago: University of Chicago Press, 1968).

Bakhtin, M.M., *The Dialogic Imagination: Four Essays by M.M. Bakhtin* (Austin: University of Texas Press, 1981).

Bakhtin, M.M., *Rabelais and His World* (Bloomington: Indiana University Press, 1984).

Bakhtin, M.M., *Speech Genres and Other Late Essays* (Austin: University of Texas Press, 1986).

Bakhtin, M.M. and Volosinov, V.N., *Marxism and the Philosophy of Language* (London: Academic Press, 1973).

Bakhtin, M.M. and Volosinov, V.N., *Freudianism: A Marxist Critique* (New York and London: Academic Press, 1976).

Barnes, B., *Scientific Knowledge and Sociological Theory* (London: Routledge and Kegan Paul, 1974).

Barnes, B. and Shapin, S., eds, *Natural Order: Historical Studies of Scientific Culture* (London: Sage, 1979).

Barraclough, G., *An Introduction to Contemporary History* (1964) (Harmondsworth: Penguin, 1990).

Barrow, J.D. and Tipler, F.J., *The Anthropic Cosmological Principle* (Oxford: Oxford University Press, 1986).

Barthes, R., *Essais critiques* (Paris: Editions du Seuil, 1964a).

Barthes, R., *On Racine* (New York: Hill and Wang 1964b).

Barthes, R., *Elements of Semiology* (London: Jonathan Cape, 1967).

Barthes, R., *Writing Degree Zero* (London: Jonathan Cape, 1968).

Barthes, R., *Le Plaisir du texte* (Paris: Editions de Seuil, 1973).

Barthes, R., *S/Z* (New York: Hill and Wang, 1974).

Barthes, R., *The Pleasure of the Text* (New York: Hill and Wang, 1975).

Barthes, R., 'From work to text', in Josué V. Harari, ed., *Textual Strategies: Perspectives in Post-Structuralist Criticism* (London: Methuen, 1979): 73–81.

Bataille, G., *Visions of Excess: Selected Writings 1927–1939* (Minneapolis: University of Minnesota/Manchester: University of Manchester Press, 1985).

Bateson, G., *Steps to an Ecology of Mind* (London: Paladin, 1972).

Bateson, G., *Mind and Nature* (London: Fontana, 1985).

Baudrillard, J., *La Société de consommation* (Paris: Gallimard, 1970).

Baudrillard, J., *The Mirror of Production* (St Louis: Telos Press, 1973).

Baudrillard, J., *For a Critique of the Political Economy of Signs* (St Louis: Telos Press, 1981).

Baudrillard, J., *Simulations* (New York: Semiotext(e), 1983).

Baudrillard, J., 'On nihilism', *On the Beach*, 6, 1984.

Baudrillard, J., *Selected Writings* (Cambridge: Polity Press, 1988a).

Baudrillard, J., *America* (London: Verso, 1988b).

Baudrillard, J., *Revenge of the Crystal: Selected Writing on the Modern Object and its Destiny, 1968–1983* (London: Pluto Press, 1990).

Bauman, R. and Sherzer, J. eds, *Explorations in the Ethnography of Speaking* (Cambridge: Cambridge University Press, 1974).

Bauman, Z., *Modernity and Ambivalence* (Cambridge: Polity Press, 1991).

Bauman, Z., *Intimations of Postmodernity* (London: Routledge, 1992).

Bazerman, C., *Shaping Written Knowledge: The Genre and Activity of the Experimental Article in Science* (Madison: University of Wisconsin Press, 1988).

Beck, U., *Risikogesellschaft* (Frankfurt: Suhrkamp, 1986).

Beck, U., *Risk Society: Towards Another Modernity* (London: Sage, 1992).

Beck, U., Giddens, A., and Lash, S., *Reflexive Modernization: Politics, Tradition and Aesthetics in the Modern Social Order* (Cambridge: Polity Press, 1994).

Becker, H.S., *Art Worlds* (Berkeley: University of California Press, 1982).

Bell, D., *The Coming of Post-Industrial Society: A Venture in Social Forecasting* (London: Heinemann, 1974).

Bell, D., *The Cultural Contradictions of Capitalism* (New York: Basic Books/London: Heinemann, 1976).

Bell, D., *Sociological Journeys: Essays 1960–1980* (London: Heinemann, 1980).

Bell, D., *The Winding Passage: Sociological Essays and Journeys* (New Brunswick and London: Transaction Publishers, 1991).

Bellamy, R., *Liberalism and Modern Society* (Cambridge: Polity Press, 1992).

Benhabib, S., *Critique, Norm, and Utopia* (New York: Columbia University Press, 1986).

Benjamin, W., *Charles Baudelaire: A Lyric Poet in the Era of High Capitalism* (London: New Left Books, 1973).

Benjamin, W., *The Origin of German Tragic Drama* (London: New Left Books, 1977).

Benjamin, W., *Reflections: Essays, Aphorisms, Autobiographical Writings* (New York: Harcourt Brace Jovanovich, 1978).

Benjamin, W., *One-way Street and Other Writings* (London: New Left Books, 1979).

Benjamin, W., *Das Passagen-Werk* (Frankfurt: Suhrkamp, 1982).

Benjamin, W., *Moscow Diary* (Cambridge, Mass.: Harvard University Press, 1986).

Benjamin, W., *Illuminations: Essays and Reflections* (London: Fontana, 1992).

Benner, P., ed., *Interpretive Phenomenology: Embodiment, Caring, and Ethics in Health and Illness* (London: Sage, 1994).

Bensman J. and Lilienfeld, R., *Craft and Consciousness: Occupational Technique and the Development of World Images* (New York: John Wiley, 1973).

Benthall, J. and Polhemus, T., eds, *The Body as a Medium of Expression* (London: Allen Lane, 1975).

Benveniste, E., *Problems in General Linguistics* (Miami: University of Miami Press, 1971).

Benveniste, E., *Indo-European Language and Society* (London: Faber 1973).

Benveniste, E., *Problèmes de linguistique générale* (Paris: Gallimard, 1974).

Berger, J., *Ways of Seeing* (Harmondsworth: Penguin, 1972).

Berger, P. and Luckmann, T., *The Social Construction of Reality: A Treatise in the Sociology of Knowledge* (Garden City: Doubleday Anchor, 1967).

Berger, P.L., *The Capitalist Revolution: Fifty Propositions About Prosperity, Equality, and Liberty* (Aldershot: Gower, 1987).

Bergson, H., *Duration and Simultaneity* (New York: Bobbs-Merrill, 1965).

Bergson, H., *Time and Free Will: An Essay on the Immediate Data of Consciousness* (London: George Allen and Unwin, 1971).

Berman, M., *All That is Solid Melts into Air: The Experience of Modernity* (London: Verso, 1982).

Bernstein, R.J., *The New Constellation: The Ethical-political Horizons of Modernity/Postmodernity* (Cambridge: Polity Press, 1991).

Bhaskar, R., *Philosophy and the Idea of Freedom* (Oxford: Blackwell, 1991).

Bijker, W. and Law, J., eds, *Shaping Technology, Building Society: Studies in Sociotechnical Change* (Cambridge, Mass.: MIT Press, 1991).

BIBLIOGRAPHY

Bijker, W., *et al.*, eds, *The Social Construction of Technological Systems: New Directions in the Sociology and History of Technology* (Cambridge, Mass.: MIT Press, 1987).

Binswanger, L., *Being-in-the-World: Selected Papers of Ludwig Binswanger* (New York: Basic Books, 1963).

Bittner, E., 'The police on skid-row: a study of peace keeping', *American Sociological Review*, 32, 1967: 699–715.

Blau, P., *Bureaucracy in Modern Society* (New York: Random House, 1956).

Bloch, E., *et al.*, *Aesthetics and Politics* (London: New Left Review, 1977).

Bloor, D., *Knowledge and Social Imagery* (London: Routledge and Kegan Paul, 1976).

Bloor, D., *Wittgenstein: A Social Theory of Knowledge* (New York: Columbia University Press, 1983).

Blum, A., *Theorizing* (London: Routledge and Kegan Paul, 1974).

Blum, A., *Socrates: The Original and Its Images* (London: Routledge and Kegan Paul, 1978).

Blum, A. and McHugh, P., eds, *Friends, Enemies, and Strangers: Theorizing in Art, Science, and Everyday Life* (Norwood: Ablex Publishing Corporation, 1979).

Blum, A. and McHugh, P., *Self-reflection in the Arts and Sciences* (Atlantic Highlands: Humanities Press, 1984).

Bohm, D., *Wholeness and the Implicate Order* (London: Routledge and Kegan Paul, 1980).

Böll, H., 'An approach to the rationality of poetry' (Nobel address delivered on 2 May 1973), reprinted in Heinrich Böll, *On his Death: Selected Obituaries and the Last Interview* (Bonn: Inter Nationes, 1985): 32–46.

Bookchin, M., *Toward an Ecological Society* (Montreal: Black Rose Books, 1980).

Bookchin, M., *The Ecology of Freedom: The Emergence of Hierarchy* (Palo Alto: Cheshire Books, 1982).

Bookchin, M., *Remaking Society* (Montreal: Black Rose Books, 1989).

Bourdieu, P. *Outline of a Theory of Practice* (Cambridge: Cambridge University Press, 1977).

Bourdieu, P., *Le Sens practique* (Paris: Editions de Minuit, 1980).

Bourdieu, P., *Distinction: A Social Critique of the Judgement of Taste* (London: Routledge and Kegan Paul, 1984).

Bourdieu, P., *The Logic of Practice* (Stanford: Stanford University Press, 1990).

Bourdieu, P., *The Political Ontology of Martin Heidegger* (Cambridge: Polity Press, 1991).

Bourdieu, P., *Language and Symbolic Power* (Cambridge: Polity Press, 1992).

Bourdieu, P., *The Field of Cultural Production: Essays on Art and Literature* (Cambridge: Polity Press, 1993).

Bourdieu, P. and Darbel, A., *The Love of Art: European Art Museums and their Public* (Cambridge: Polity Press, 1991).

Bourdieu, P., and Wacquant, L.J.D., *An Invitation to Reflexive Sociology* (Cambridge: Polity Press, 1992).

Bourdieu, P., Chamboredon, J.-C. and Passeron, J.-C., *The Craft of Sociology: Epistemological Preliminaries* (Berlin and New York: Walter de Gruyter, 1991).

Bowles, S. and Gintis, H., *Schooling in Capitalist America* (New York: Basic Books, 1976).

Boyd White, J., *When Words Lose Their Meaning: Constitutions and Reconstitutions of Language, Character, and Community* (Chicago: University of Chicago Press, 1984).

Bradley, F.H., *Appearance and Reality: A Metaphysical Essay*, 2nd edn (Oxford: Clarendon Press, 1930).

Braudel, F., *Afterthoughts on Material Civilization and Capitalism* (Baltimore and London: Johns Hopkins University Press, 1977).

464

Braudel, F., *On History* (Chicago: University of Chicago Press, 1980).

Brennan, J.F., *History and Systems of Psychology*, 3rd edn (Englewood Cliffs: Prentice-Hall, 1991).

Brentano, F., *Psychology from an Empirical Standpoint* (London: Routledge and Kegan Paul, 1973).

Bronner, S. and Kellner, D., eds, Critical Theory and Society: A Reader (London: Routledge, 1989).

Buber, M., *I and Thou* (New York: Scribner/Edinburgh: T. & T. Clark, 1970).

Buber, M., *Between Man and Man* (New York: Macmillan, 1972).

Buber, M., *On Intersubjectivity and Cultural Creativity* (Chicago and London: University of Chicago Press, 1992).

Buci-Glucksmann, C., *La Folie du voir: de l'esthétique baroque* (Paris: Editions Galilée, 1986).

Burke, K., *Language as Symbolic Action: Essays on Life, Literature, and Method* (Berkeley: University of California Press, 1966).

Burke, K., *A Grammar of Motives* (Berkeley: University of California Press, 1969).

Burwick, F. and Douglass, P., eds, *The Crisis of Modernism: Bergson and the Vitalist Tradition* (Cambridge: Cambridge University Press, 1990).

Bury, J.B., *The Idea of Progress: An Inquiry into its Origin and Growth* (London: Macmillan, 1921).

Butterfield, H., *The Whig Interpretation of History* (1931) (New York: W.W. Norton, 1965).

Callon, M., 'Techno-economic networks and irreversibility', in John Law, ed., *A Sociology of Monsters: Essays on Power, Technology and Domination* (London: Routledge, 1991): 132–61.

Callon, M. and Latour, B., 'Unscrewing the big Leviathan: how actors macro-structure reality and sociologists help them to do so', in K. Knorr-Cetina and A. V. Cicourel, eds, *Advances in Social Theory and Methodology: Toward an Integration of Micro and Macro Sociologies* (London: Routledge and Kegan Paul, 1981): 277–303.

Campbell, J., ed., *Papers From the Eranos Yearbooks* Volume 1 and 3 (London: Routledge and Kegan Paul, 1955 (Volume 1) and 1958 (Volume 3)).

Campbell, J., *Myths to Live By* (London: Souvenir Press, 1973).

Capra, F., *The Tao of Physics: An Exploration of the Parallels between Modern Physics and Eastern Mysticism* (London: Wildwood House, 1975).

Capra, F., *The Turning Point: Science, Society, and the Rising Culture* (London: Wildwood House, 1982).

Carroll, J.B., ed., *Language, Thought and Reality: Selected Writings of Benjamin Lee Whorf* (New York: Wiley/Cambridge, Mass: MIT Press, 1956).

Castoriadis, C., *Crossroads in the Labyrinth* (Brighton: Harvester Press, 1984).

Cavell, S., *The Claim of Reason* (Oxford: Clarendon Press, 1979).

Chomsky, N., *Toward a New Cold War: Essays on the Current Crisis and How We Got There* (London: Sinclair Browne, 1982).

Christensen, S.M. and Turner, D.R., eds, *Folk Psychology and the Philosophy of Mind* (Hove: Lawrence Erlbaum, 1993).

Church, J., *Language and the Discovery of Reality: A Developmental Psychology of Cognition* (New York: Vintage Books, 1961).

Cicourel, A.V., *Method and Measurement in Sociology* (New York: Free Press, 1964).

Cicourel, A.V., *The Social Organization of Juvenile Justice* (New York: Wiley, 1968).

Cicourel, A.V., *Cognitive Sociology: Language and Meaning in Social Interaction* (Harmondsworth: Penguin, 1973).

Cipolla, C.M., *Literacy and Development in the West* (Harmondsworth: Penguin, 1969).

BIBLIOGRAPHY

Clanchy, M.T., *From Memory to Written Record, England 1066–1307* (Cambridge: Cambridge University Press, 1979).

Clifford, J. and Marcus, G.E., eds, *Writing Culture: The Poetics and Politics of Ethnography* (Berkeley: University of California Press, 1986).

Collingwood, R.G., *An Essay on Philosophical Method* (Oxford: Clarendon Press, 1933).

Collingwood, R.G., *The Principles of Art* (Oxford: Clarendon Press, 1938).

Collingwood, R.G., *An Autobiography* (Oxford: Clarendon Press, 1939).

Collingwood, R.G., *An Essay on Metaphysics* (Oxford: Clarendon Press, 1940).

Collingwood, R.G., *Speculum Mentis or The Map of Knowledge* (1924) (Oxford: Clarendon Press, 1970).

Collingwood, R.G., *The Idea of History* (1946) (Oxford: Oxford University Press, 1983).

Collingwood, R.G., *The Idea of History*, revised edn (Oxford: Clarendon Press, 1993).

Collins, H. and Pinch, T., *Frames of Meaning: The Social Construction of Extraordinary Science* (London: Routledge and Kegan Paul, 1982).

Connolly, W.E., *Identity/Difference: Democratic Negotiations of Political Paradox* (Ithaca and London: Cornell University Press, 1991).

Cooley, C.H., *Human Nature and the Social Order* (New York: Charles Scribner's, 1902).

Cornford, F.M., *The Unwritten Philosophy and Other Essays* (Cambridge University Press, 1950).

Craib, I., *Modern Social Theory: From Parsons to Habermas* (London: Harvester Wheatsheaf, 1992).

Crapanzano, V., 'Text, transference, and indexicality', in *Hermes' Dilemma and Hamlet's Dream: On the Epistemology of Interpretation* (Cambridge, Mass.: Harvard University Press, 1992): 115–35.

Crary, J., *Techniques of the Observer: On Vision and Modernity in the Nineteenth Century* (Cambridge, Mass.: MIT Press, 1990).

Critchley, S., *The Ethics of Deconstruction: Derrida and Lévinas* (Oxford: Blackwell, 1992).

Crook, J.A., *Law and Life of Rome* (London: Thames and Hudson, 1967).

Crook, S., Pakulski, J. and Waters, M., *Postmodernization: Change in Advanced Society* (London: Sage, 1992).

Csikszentmihalyi, M. and Rochberg-Halton, E., *The Meaning of Things* (New York: Cambridge University Press, 1981).

Curtius, E.R., *European Literature and the Latin Middle Ages* (1948) (Princeton: Princeton University Press, 1973).

Dallmayr, F., *Life-world, Modernity and Critique: Paths between Heidegger and the Frankfurt School* (Cambridge: Polity Press, 1991).

Dallmayr, F. and McCarthy, T., eds, *Understanding and Social Inquiry* (Notre Dame: Notre Dame University Press, 1977).

Dawkins, R., *The Selfish Gene* (Oxford: Oxford University Press, 1976).

Certeau, M. de, *The Practice of Everyday Life* (Berkeley: University of California Press, 1984).

Deleuze, G., *Nietzsche and Philosophy* (London: Athlone Press, 1983).

Deleuze, G., *Foucault* (Minneapolis: University of Minnesota Press, 1988).

Deleuze, G., *The Logic of Sense* (New York: Columbia University Press, 1990).

Deleuze, G., *Difference and Repetition* (London: Athlone Press, 1994).

Deleuze, G. and Guattari, F., *Anti-Oedipus: Capitalism and Schizophrenia* (London: Athlone Press, 1983).

Deleuze, G. and Guattari, F., *A Thousand Plateaus: Capitalism and Schizophrenia* (London: Athlone Press, 1988).

466

Deleuze, G. and Guattari, F., *What is Philosophy?* (London: Verso, 1994).

Deleuze, G. and Parnet, C., *Dialogues* (London: Athlone Press, 1987).

Derrida, J., *La Voix et le phénomène: introduction au problème du signe dans la phénoménologie de Husserl* (Paris: Presses Universitaires de France, 1967).

Derrida, J., *Margins of Philosophy* (Chicago: University of Chicago Press, 1972a).

Derrida, J., 'Freud and the scene of writing', *Yale French Studies*, 48, 1972b: 74–117.

Derrida, J., *Speech and Phenomena: And Other Essays on Husserl's Theory of Signs* (Evanston: Northwestern University Press, 1973).

Derrida, J., 'White mythology: metaphor in the text of philosophy', *New Literary History*, 6 (1), 1974: 5–74.

Derrida, J., *Of Grammatology* (Baltimore: Johns Hopkins University Press, 1976).

Derrida, J., *Writing and Difference* (London: Routledge and Kegan Paul, 1978a).

Derrida, J., *Edmund Husserl's 'Origins of Geometry': An Introduction* (Boulder: Great Eastern Press, 1978b).

Derrida, J. *La Carte postale: De Socrate à Freud et au-delà* (Paris: Aubier-Flammarion, 1980).

Derrida, J., *Positions* (Chicago: University of Chicago Press, 1981).

Derrida, J., *Margins of Philosophy* (Chicago: University of Chicago Press, 1982).

Descartes, R., *The Philosophical Works of Descartes*, trans. E.S. Haldane and G.R.T. Ross (Cambridge: Cambridge University Press, 1911).

Descartes, R., *Oeuvres de Descartes*, ed. C. Adam and P. Tannery (Paris: Vrin, 1964–76).

Descartes, R., *Discourse on Method and the Meditations* (Harmondsworth: Penguin, 1968).

Descartes, R., *Le Monde, our Traité de la lumière* (New York: Abaris Books, 1979).

Descartes, R., *The Philosophical Writings of Descartes*, ed. and trans. J. Cottingham, R. Stoothoff, and D. Murdoch (Cambridge: Cambridge University Press, 1985).

Descombes, V., *Modern French Philosophy* (Cambridge: Cambridge University Press, 1980).

Dewey, J., *Human Nature and Conduct* (New York: Modern Library, 1922).

Dewey, J., *How We Think: A Restatement of the Relation of Reflective Thinking to the Educative Process* (New York: D.C. Heath and Company, 1933).

Dewey, J., *Art as Experience* (New York: Minton, Balch and Co., 1934).

Dewey, J., *Logic: The Theory of Inquiry* (London: Allen and Unwin, 1939).

Dewey, J., *Reconstruction in Philosophy* (New York: New American Library, 1952).

Dewey, J., *Experience and Nature* (New York: Dover Publications, 1958).

Dilthey, W., *Selected Writings*, ed. H.P. Rickman (Cambridge: Cambridge University Press, 1976).

Diringer, D., *The Alphabet: A Key to the History of Mankind*, 2nd edn (New York: Philosophical Library, 1968).

Dobbin, F.R., 'Cultural models of organization: the social construction of rational organizing principles', in D. Crane, ed., *The Sociology of Culture* (Oxford: Blackwell, 1994): 117–41.

Dodds, E.R., *The Greeks and the Irrational* (Berkeley and Los Angeles: University of California Press, 1951).

Douglas, J.D., *The Social Meaning of Suicide* (Princeton: Princeton University Press, 1967).

Douglas, J.D., ed., *Understanding Everyday Life: Towards the Reconstruction of Sociological Knowledge* (London: Routledge and Kegan Paul, 1971).

Duby, G., *The Three Orders* (Chicago: University of Chicago Press, 1980).

Dumézil, G., *L'Ideologie des Indo-Européens* (Brussels: Latonus, 1958).

Dumont, L., *Homo Hierarchicus: The Caste System and Its Implications* (Chicago: University of Chicago Press, 1980).

Durkheim, E., *Suicide: A Study in Sociology* (New York: Free Press, 1951).

Durkheim, E., *The Elementary Forms of the Religious Life* (Glencoe: The Free Press, 1954a).

Durkheim, E., *The Division of Labour in Society* (New York: The Free Press, 1954b).

Durkheim, E., *The Rules of Sociological Method and Selected Texts on Sociology and its Method* (London: Macmillan, 1982).

Durkheim, E., *Pragmatism and Sociology* (Cambridge: Cambridge University Press, 1983).

Dutton, D., ed., *The Forger's Art* (Berkeley: University of California Press, 1983).

Eco, U., *Travels in Hyperreality* (London: Picador, 1986).

Ehrenreich, B. and Ehrenreich, J., 'The professional-managerial class', in P. Walker, ed., *Between Capital and Labour* (Boston: South End Press, 1979): 5–45.

Eisenstein, E., *The Printing Press as an Agent of Change: Communications and Cultural Transformations in Early-modern Europe* (Cambridge: Cambridge University Press, 1979).

Elias, N., *What is Sociology?* (London: Hutchinson, 1978a).

Elias, N., *The Civilizing Process: The History of Manners* (Oxford: Basil Blackwell, 1978b).

Elias, N., *The Civilizing Process: State Formation and Civilisation* (Oxford: Blackwell, 1982).

Elias, N., *The Court Society* (Oxford: Blackwell, 1983).

Elias, N., *Involvement and Detachment* (Oxford: Blackwell, 1987).

Elias, N., *The Symbol Theory* (Oxford: Blackwell, 1990).

Elias, N., *Time: An Essay* (Oxford: Blackwell, 1992).

Ellenberger, H.P., *The Discovery of the Unconscious: The History and Evolution of Dynamic Psychiatry* (New York: Basic Books, 1970).

Erikson, E., *The Life Cycle Completed: A Review* (New York and London: W.W. Norton, 1985).

Euben, J.P., *The Tragedy of Political Theory* (Princeton: Princeton University Press, 1990).

Eucken, R., *The Life of the Spirit: An Introduction to Philosophy* (London: Williams and Norgate, 1909).

Eucken, R., *Main Currents of Modern Thought: A Study of the Spiritual and Intellectual Movements of the Present Day* (London: T. Fisher Unwin, 1912).

Ey, H., *Consciousness: A Phenomenological Study of Being Conscious and Becoming Conscious* (1963) (Bloomington: Indiana University Press, 1978).

Fairley, P., *The Conquest of Pain* (1978) (New York: Charles Scribner's Sons, 1980).

Fanon, F., *The Wretched of the Earth* (Harmondsworth: Penguin, 1967).

Feyerabend, P., *Farewell to Reason* (London: Verso, 1987).

Fichte, J.G., *The Vocation of Man* (La Salle: Open Court, 1965).

Fichte, J.G., *Science of Knowledge (Wissenschaftslehre)* (New York: Appleton-Century Crofts, 1970).

Foucault, M., *Madness and Civilization: A History of Insanity in the Age of Reason* (London: Tavistock, 1967).

Foucault, M., *The Order of Things: An Archaeology of the Human Sciences* (London: Tavistock/New York: Pantheon, 1970).

Foucault, M., *The Archaeology of Knowledge and the Discourse on Language* (London: Tavistock/New York: Pantheon/Colophon, 1972).

Foucault, M., *The Birth of the Clinic* (London: Tavistock, 1973).

Foucault, M., *Language, Counter-Memory, Practice; Selected Essays and Interviews* (Oxford: Blackwell/Ithaca: Cornell University Press, 1977a).

Foucault, M., *Discipline and Punish: The Birth of the Prison* (New York: Pantheon Books, 1977b).

Foucault, M., *Power/Knowledge: Selected Interviews and Other Writings 1972–1977* (Brighton: Harvester Press, 1980a).

Foucault, M., *History of Sexuality, Volume I: An Introduction* (New York: Vintage, 1980b).

Foucault, M., *The Foucault Reader*, ed. P. Rabinow (New York: Pantheon Books, 1984).

Foucault, M., *History of Sexuality, Volume II: The Uses of Pleasure* (Harmondsworth: Penguin/Viking, 1987).

Foucault, M., *History of Sexuality, Volume III: The Care of the Self* (London: Allen Lane, 1988a).

Foucault, M., *Michel Foucault: Politics, Philosophy, Culture: Interviews and Other Writings 1977–1984*, ed. Lawrence D. Kritzman (New York and London: Routledge, 1988b).

Fraser, N., *Unruly Practices: Power, Discourse and Gender in Contemporary Social Theory* (Minneapolis: University of Minnesota Press, 1989).

Fränkel, H., *Early Greek Poetry and Philosophy* (Oxford and New York: Blackwell, 1975).

Freud, S., *The Standard Edition of the Complete Psychological Works of Sigmund Freud*, ed. J. Strachey (London: Hogarth Press, 1953–74).

Freud, S., *Civilization and Its Discontents* (New York: W.W. Norton, 1962).

Freud, S., *An Outline of Psycho-Analysis* (London: Hogarth Press and the Institute of Psycho-Analysis, 1969).

Freud, S., *The Interpretation of Dreams* (Harmondsworth: Penguin, 1976).

Freud, S., *Introductory Lectures on Psychoanalysis* (Harmondsworth: Penguin, 1987).

Fukuyama, F., 'The end of history?', *The National Interest*, 16 (Summer), 1989: 3–18.

Fukuyama, F., *The End of History and the Last Man* (London: Hamish Hamilton, 1992).

Gadamer, H.-G., *Wahrheit und Methode: Grundzüge einer philosophischen Hermeneutik* (Tübingen: Mohr, 1960).

Gadamer, H.-G., *Philosophical Hermeneutics* (Berkeley: University of California Press, 1976).

Gadamer, H.-G., *Dialogue and Dialectic: Eight Hermeneutical Studies on Plato* (New Haven and London: Yale University Press, 1980).

Gadamer, H.-G., *Reason in the Age of Science* (Cambridge, Mass.: MIT Press, 1982).

Gadamer, H.-G., *The Idea of the Good in Platonic-Aristotelian Philosophy* (New Haven and London: Yale University Press, 1986a).

Gadamer, H.-G., *The Relevance of the Beautiful and Other Essays* (Cambridge: Cambridge University Press, 1986b).

Gadamer, H.-G., *Truth and Method*, 2nd revised edn. (New York: Crossroad, 1989).

Gardiner, M., *The Dialogics of Critique: M.M. Bakhtin and the Theory of Ideology* (London: Routledge, 1992).

Gardner, H., *The Shattered Mind: The Patient After Brain Damage* (New York: Knopf, 1974).

Garfinkel, H., 'Conditions of successful degradation ceremonies', *American Journal of Sociology*, 61, 1956: 420–4.

Garfinkel, H., *Studies in Ethnomethodology* (Englewood Cliffs: Prentice-Hall, 1967).

Garfinkel, H., 'The origins of the term "ethnomethodology"', in R. Turner, ed., *Ethnomethodology* (Harmondsworth: Penguin, 1974): 15–18.

Garfinkel, H. and Sacks, H., 'On formal structures of practical actions', in J.C. McKinney and E.A. Tiryakian, eds, *Theoretical Sociology* (New York: Appleton-Century Crofts, 1970).

Garfinkel, H., Lynch, M. and Livingstone, E., 'The work of a discovering science construed with materials from the optically discovered pulsar', *Philosophy of the Social Sciences*, 11, 1981: 131–58.

Geertz, C., *Works and Lives: The Anthropologist as Author* (Stanford: Stanford University Press, 1987).

Gehlen, A., *Man, His Nature and Place in the World* (New York: Columbia University Press, 1988).

Gelb, I.J., *A Study of Writing* (Chicago: University of Chicago Press, 1969).

Gendin, E.T., *Experiencing and the Creation of Meaning* (New York: The Free Press, 1962).

Genette, G., *Figures III* (Paris: Seuil, 1972).

Gibson, H.B., *Pain and Its Conquest* (London: Peter Owen, 1982).

Giddens, A., *Central Problems in Social Theory* (London: Macmillan, 1979).

Giddens, A., *Sociology: A Brief but Critical Introduction*, 2nd edn (London: Macmillan, 1986).

Giddens, A., *Social Theory and Modern Sociology* (Cambridge: Polity Press, 1987).

Giddens, A., *The Consequences of Modernity* (Cambridge: Polity Press, 1990).

Giddens, A., *Modernity and Self-identity: Self and Society in the Late Modern Age* (Cambridge: Polity Press, 1991).

Giddens, A., *The Transformation of Intimacy* (Cambridge: Polity Press, 1992).

Giddens, A., *New Rules of Sociological Method: A Positive Critique of Interpretative Sociologies*, 2nd edn (Cambridge: Polity Press, 1993).

Gilbert, N. and Mulkay, M.J., *Opening Pandora's Box: A Sociological Analysis of Scientists' Discourse* (Cambridge: Cambridge University Press, 1984).

Gillan, G., *From Sign to Symbol* (Brighton: Harvester Press, 1982).

Ginszurg, C., *The Cheese and the Worms: the Cosmos of a Sixteenth-Century Miller* (London: Routledge and Kegan Paul, 1980).

Girard, R., *To Double Business Bound: Essays on Literature, Mimesis, and Anthropology* (London: Athlone Press, 1988).

Glacken, G.C., *Traces on the Rhodian Shore: Nature and Culture in Western Thought from Ancient Times to the End of the Eighteenth Century* (Berkeley: University of California Press, 1967).

Gleick, J., *Chaos* (London: Heinemann, 1987).

Glucksmann, A., *Les Maîtres Penseurs* (Paris: Bernard Grasset, 1977).

Goethe, J.W., *Faust, Part One* (Harmondsworth: Penguin, 1949).

Goethe, J.W., *Faust Der Tragödie Erster Teil* (Stuttgart: Philipp Reclam, 1969).

Goffman, E., *The Presentation of Self in Everyday Life* (New York: Doubleday, 1959).

Goffman, E., *Frame Analysis: An Essay on the Organization of Experience* (Cambridge, Mass.: Harvard University Press, 1974).

Goldmann, L., *The Human Sciences and Philosophy* (London: Jonathan Cape, 1969).

Goldthorpe, J., 'On the service class, its formation and future', in A. Giddens and G. Mackenzie, eds, *Social Class and the Division of Labour: Essays in honour of Ilya Neustadt* (Cambridge: Cambridge University Press, 1982): 162–85.

Gonzalez-Crussi, F., *Notes of An Anatomist* (London: Picador/Pan, 1985).

Gonzalez-Crussi, F., *Three Forms of Sudden Death, And Other Reflections on the Grandeur and Misery of the Body* (London: Picador/Pan, 1986).

Goody, J., ed., *Literacy in Traditional Societies* (Cambridge: Cambridge University Press, 1968).

Goody, J., *The Domestication of the Savage Mind* (Cambridge: Cambridge University Press, 1977).

Goody, J., *The Interface Between the Written and the Oral* (Cambridge: Cambridge University Press, 1986).

Goody, J. and Watt, I., *Literacy in Traditional Societies* (Cambridge: Cambridge University Press, 1988).

470

Gouldner, A.W., *Enter Plato: Classical Greece and the Origins of Social Theory* (New York: Basic Books, 1965).

Gouldner, A.W., *The Coming Crisis of Western Sociology* (London: Heinemann, 1970).

Gouldner, A.W., *For Sociology* (London: Allen Lane, 1973).

Gouldner, A.W., *The Dialectic of Ideology and Technology: The Origins, Grammar, and Future of Ideology* (London: Macmillan, 1976).

Gouldner, A.W., *The Future of Intellectuals and the Rise of the New Class* (New York: Seabury, 1979).

Gouldner, A.W., *The Two Marxisms* (London: Macmillan, 1980).

Graff, H., *The Labyrinths of Literacy* (London: Falmer, 1987).

Gramsci, A., *Selections from the Prison Notebooks* (New York: Lawrence and Wishart, 1971).

Gramsci, A., *The Modern Prince and Other Writings* (New York: International Publishers, 1972).

Gramsci, A., *Selections from the Political Writings* (London: Lawrence and Wishart, 1978).

Gramsci, A., 'Notes on language', *Telos*, LIX, 1984: 127–50.

Gramsci, A., *Selections from Cultural Writings* (London: Lawrence and Wishart, 1985).

Gregory, D. and Urry, J., eds, *Social Relations and Spatial Structures* (New York: St. Martin's Press, 1985).

Grene, M., *Approaches to a Philosophical Biology* (New York: Basic Books, 1968).

Grene, M., *The Knower and the Known* (London: Faber/New York: Basic Books, 1984).

Grice, P., 'Meaning', *Philosophical Review*, 66, 1957: 377–88.

Grice, P., *Studies in the Way of Words* (Cambridge, Mass.: Harvard University Press, 1989).

Gumperz, J.J. and Hymes, D., eds, *Directions in Sociolinguistics* (New York: Holt, Rinehart and Winston, 1972).

Gurwitsch, A., *The Field of Consciousness* (Pittsburgh: Duquesne University Press, 1964).

Gurwitsch, A., *Studies in Phenomenology and Psychology* (Evanston: Northwestern University Press, 1966).

Gurwitsch, A., *Phenomenology and the Theory of Science* (Evanston: Northwestern University Press, 1974).

Gurwitsch, A., *Marginal Consciousness* (Athens: Ohio University Press, 1985).

Habermas, J., *Knowledge and Human Interests* (Boston: Beacon Press, 1972).

Habermas, J., *Theory and Practice* (London: Heinemann, 1974).

Habermas, J., 'Modernity – an incomplete project', in H. Foster, ed., *Postmodern Culture* (London: Pluto Press, 1985a): 3–15.

Habermas, J., *The Theory of Communicative Action, Volume 1: Reason and the Rationalization of Society* (Boston: Beacon Press, 1985b).

Habermas, J., *The Theory of Communicative Action, Volume 2: Lifeworld and System* (Boston: Beacon Press, 1987a).

Habermas, J., *The Philosophical Discourse of Modernity* (Cambridge: Polity Press, 1987b).

Habermas, J., *The Structural Transformation of the Public Sphere: An Inquiry into a Category of Bourgeois Society* (Cambridge, Mass.: MIT Press, 1989).

Habermas, J., *Philosophical-Political Profiles* (Cambridge, Mass: MIT Press, 1992).

Habermas, J., *Autonomy and Solidarity* (London: Verso, 1992a).

Halfpenny, P., *Positivism and Sociology* (London: George Allen and Unwin, 1982).

Hamann, J.G., *Socratic Memorabilia* (Baltimore: Johns Hopkins University Press, 1967).

Hampshire, S., *Thought and Action* (London: Chatto and Windus, 1959).

Haraway, D., *Primate Visions: Race, Gender, and Nature in the World of Modern Science* (London: Routledge and Kegan Paul, 1989).

Haraway, D., 'A manifesto for cyborgs: science, technology, and socialist feminism in the 1980s', in Haraway, *Simians, Cyborgs, and Women: The Reinvention of Nature* (London: Free Association, 1991): 149–81.

Harper, D., 'Portraying *bricolage*', *Knowledge and Society: Studies in the Sociology of Culture Past and Present*, 6, 1986: 209–31.

Harris, R. and Taylor, T.J., *Landmarks in Linguistic Thought: The Western Tradition from Socrates to Saussure* (London: Routledge, 1989).

Harris, W.V., *Ancient Literacy* (Cambridge Mass: Harvard University Press, 1989).

Hartman, G.H., *Minor Prophecies: The Literary Essay in the Culture Wars* (Cambridge, Mass.: Harvard University Press, 1991).

Harvey, D., *The Condition of Postmodernity: An Enquiry into the Origins of Cultural Change* (Oxford: Blackwell, 1989).

Havelock, E.A., *Preface to Plato* (Cambridge Mass: Harvard University Press, 1963).

Havelock, E.A., *The Greek Concept of Justice: From Its Shadow in Homer to its Substance in Plato* (Cambridge, Mass.: Harvard University Press, 1978).

Hegel, G.W.F., *The Philosophy of Right* (Oxford: Oxford University Press, 1952).

Hegel, G.W.F., *Lectures on the History of Philosophy* (1892) (London: Routledge and Kegan Paul, 1955).

Hegel, G.W.F., *The Philosophy of History* (New York: Dover Publications, 1956).

Hegel, G.W.F., *The Logic of Hegel* (trans. from *Enzyklopädie* by William Wallace, 1873), 2nd revised edn (London: Oxford University Press, 1959).

Hegel, G.W.F., *The Phenomenology of Mind* (New York: Harper and Row, 1967).

Hegel, G.W.F., *Hegel's Science of Logic* (London: George Allen and Unwin, 1969).

Hegel, G.W.F., *Philosophy of Nature* (London: George Allen and Unwin, 1970).

Hegel, G.W.F., *Encyclopaedia of the Philosophical Sciences*, 3 vols (Oxford: Oxford University Press, 1971).

Hegel, G.W.F., *Sämtliche Werke*, ed. H. Glockner (Stuttgart: Jubiläumausgabe, 1972–).

Hegel, G.W.F., *Lectures on the Philosophy of World History: Introduction: Reason in History* (Cambridge: Cambridge University Press, 1975).

Hegel, G.W.F., *Faith and Knowledge* (1802) (Albany: State University of New York, 1977a).

Hegel, G.W.F., *The Phenomenology of Spirit* (Oxford: Clarendon Press, 1977b).

Hegel, G.W.F., *The Difference Between Fichte's and Schelling's System of Philosophy* (Albany: State University of New York Press, 1977c).

Hegel, G.W.F., *Philosophy of Subjective Spirit* (Dordrecht: D. Reidel, 1978).

Hegel, G.W.F., *Philosophical Propaedeutic* (Oxford: Blackwell, 1986).

Heidegger, M., *Sein und Zeit* (Tübingen: Max Niemeyer, 1927).

Heidegger, M., *What is Philosophy?* (London: Vision Press, 1956).

Heidegger, M., *The Question of Being* (London: Vision Press, 1959).

Heidegger, M., *Vorträge und Aufsätze* (Pfüllingen: Günter Neske, 1961).

Heidegger, M., *Discourse on Thinking* (a translation of *Gelassenheit*) (New York: Harper Torchbooks, 1966).

Heidegger, M., *What is a Thing?* (Chicago: Henry Regnery Company, 1967a).

Heidegger, M., *Being and Time* (Oxford: Blackwell, 1967b).

Heidegger, M., *What is called Thinking?* (New York: Harper and Row 1968).

Heidegger, M., *Kant and the Problem of Metaphysics* (Bloomington: Indiana University Press, 1969).

Heidegger, M., *Poetry, Language, Thought* (New York: Harper and Row, 1971a).

Heidegger, M., *On the Way to Language* (New York: Harper and Row, 1971b).

Heidegger, M., 'The turning', trans. Kenneth Maly, in *Research in Phenomenology*, vol. 1, ed. John Sallis (Pittsburgh: Duquesne University Press, 1971c).

Heidegger, M., *An Introduction to Metaphysics* (New Haven and London: Yale University Press, 1973a).

Heidegger, M., *The End of Philosophy* (New York: Harper and Row, 1973b).

Heidegger, M., *The Piety of Thinking* (Bloomington: Indiana University Press, 1976).

Heidegger, M., *The Question Concerning Technology and Other Essays* (New York: Harper and Row, 1977).

Heidegger, M., *The Basic Problems of Phenomenology* (Bloomington: Indiana University Press, 1982).

Heidegger, M., *History of the Concept of Time* (Bloomington: Indiana University Press, 1992).

Heidegger, M., *Basic Writings* (London: Routledge and Kegan Paul, 1978).

Heim, M., *The Metaphysics of Virtual Reality* (New York: Oxford University Press, 1993).

Held, D., *Models of Democracy* (Cambridge: Polity Press, 1987).

Heller, A. and Fehér, F., *The Postmodern Political Condition* (Cambridge: Polity Press, 1988).

Heller, E., *The Disinherited Mind: Essays in Modern German Literature and Thought* (London: Bowes and Bowes, 1975).

Heraclitus, trans. T.M. Robinson, *Heraclitus: Fragments: A Text and Translation with a Commentary* (Toronto: University of Toronto Press, 1987).

von Herder, J.G., *Essay on the Origin of Language* (New York: Frederick Ungar, 1966).

von Herder, J.G., *Reflections on the Philosophy of the History of Mankind* (Chicago and London: University of Chicago Press, 1968).

von Herder, J.G., *J.G. Herder on Social and Political Culture*, trans. F.M. Barnard (Cambridge: Cambridge University Press, 1969).

Heritage, J., *Garfinkel and Ethnomethodology* (Cambridge: Polity Press, 1984).

Herrigel, E., *Zen in the Art of Archery* (London: Routledge and Kegan Paul, 1953).

Herrigel, E., *The Method of Zen* (London: Routledge and Kegan Paul, 1960).

Hesiod and Theognis, *Theogony and Works and Days* (Harmondsworth: Penguin, 1985).

Hodgson, D., *The Mind Matters: Consciousness and Choice in a Quantum World* (Oxford: Clarendon Press, 1991).

Hofstadter, D.R., *Gödel, Escher, Bach: An Eternal Golden Braid* (Harmondsworth: Penguin, 1980).

Hofstadter, D.R., *Metamagical Themas* (Harmondsworth: Penguin, 1986).

Hofstadter, D.R. and Dennett, D.C., eds, *The Mind's I: Fantasies and Reflections on Self and Soul* (Harmondsworth: Penguin, 1982).

Hollis, M. and Lukes, S., eds, *Rationality and Relativism* (Oxford: Blackwell, 1982).

Holton, G., *Thematic Origins of Scientific Thought* (Cambridge, Mass.: Harvard University Press, 1973).

Holton, G., *The Scientific Imagination: Case Studies* (Cambridge: Cambridge University Press, 1978).

Holton, R.J. and Turner, B.S., *Max Weber on Economy and Society* (London: Routledge, 1989).

Hookway, C. and Peterson, D., eds, *Philosophy and Cognitive Science* (Cambridge: Cambridge University Press, 1993).

Horkheimer, M., *Critical Theory* (New York: Herder and Herder, 1972).

Horkheimer, M., *Eclipse of Reason* (New York: Seabury Press, 1974a).

Horkheimer, M., *Critique of Instrumental Reason: Lectures and Essays Since the End of World War II* (New York: Seabury Press, 1974b).

Horkheimer, M. and Adorno, T.W., *Dialectic of Enlightenment* (New York: Herder and Herder, 1972).

Hume, D., *Enquiry concerning Human Understanding*, 3rd edn, ed. L.A. Selby-Bigge (Oxford: Clarendon/Oxford University Press 1975).

Hume, D., *A Treatise of Human Nature*, ed. L.A. Selby-Bigge (Oxford: Oxford University Press, 1988).

Humphrey, N., *Consciousness Regained: Chapters in the Development of Mind* (Oxford: Clarendon Press, 1983).

Humphrey, N., *The Inner Eye* (London: Faber, 1986).

Humphrey, N., *A History of the Mind* (London: Chatto and Windus, 1992).

Husserl, E., *Ideas: General Introduction to Pure Phenomenology*, trans. W.R. Boyce (New York: Macmillan, 1931).

Husserl, E., *Cartesian Meditations* (The Hague: Martinus Nijhoff, 1960).

Husserl, E., *The Phenomenology of Internal Time Consciousness* (Bloomington: Indiana University Press, 1964a).

Husserl, E., *The Paris Lectures* (The Hague: Martinus Nijhoff, 1964b).

Husserl, E., *Phenomenology and the Crisis of Philosophy: Philosophy as Rigorous Science and Philosophy and the Crisis of European Man* (New York: Harper Torchbooks, 1965).

Husserl, E., *Formal and Transcendental Logic* (The Hague: Martinus Nijhoff, 1969).

Husserl, E., *The Crisis of European Science and Transcendental Phenomenology: An Introduction to Phenomenological Philosophy* (Evanston: Northwestern University Press, 1970).

Husserl, E., *The Idea of Phenomenology* (The Hague: Martinus Nijhoff, 1970a).

Husserl, E., *Logical Investigations*, (1900–1) 2vols (London: Routledge and Kegan Paul, 1970b).

Husserl, E., 'Inaugural Lecture at Freiburg im Bresgau (1917)', trans. Robert Welsh Jordan, in Lester E. Embree, ed., *Life-World and Consciousness: Essays for Aron Gurwitsch* (Evanston: Northwestern University Press, 1972).

Husserl, E., *Experience and Judgment: Investigations in a Genealogy of Logic* (London: Routledge and Kegan Paul, 1973).

Husserl, E., *Logische Untersuchungen*, 3 vols (The Hague: Martinus Nijhoff, 1975 (Volume 1), 1984 (Volumes 2, 3)).

Husserl, E., *Ideas Pertaining to a Pure Phenomenology and to a Phenomenological Philosophy: Third Book: Phenomenology and the Foundations of the Sciences (Ideen III)* (The Hague: Martinus Nijhoff, 1980).

Husserl, E., *Ideas Pertaining to a Pure Phenomenology and to a Phenomenological Philosophy: Second Book: Studies in the Phenomenology of Constitution (Ideen II)* (Dordrecht: Kluwer Academic Publishers, 1989).

Husserl, E., *Ideas Pertaining to a Pure Phenomenology and to a Phenomenological Philosophy: First Book: General Introduction to a Pure Phenomenology (Ideen I)* (The Hague: Martinus Nijhoff, 1982).

Ifrah, G., *From One to Zero: A Universal History of Numbers* (New York: Viking, 1985).

Illich, I. and Sanders, B., *ABC: The Alphabetization of the Popular Mind* (London: Marion Boyars, 1988).

James, W., *Psychology (Briefer Course)* (London: Macmillan, 1892).

James, W., W., *Essays in Radical Empiricism* (London: Longmans, Green and Co., 1912).

James, W., *The Varieties of Religious Experience: A Study in Human Nature* (London: Longmans, Green and Co., 1928).

James, W., *The Principles of Psychology* (1890) (New York: Dover, 1950).

James, W., *William James: The Essential Writings*, ed. Bruce W. Wilshire (New York: Harper Torchbooks, 1971).

James, W., *The Meaning of Truth* (Cambridge, Mass.: Harvard University Press, 1975).

James, W., *A Pluralist Universe* (Cambridge, Mass.: Harvard University Press, 1977).

James, W., *Pragmatism: A New Name for Some Old Ways of Thinking and The Meaning of Truth: A Sequel to Pragmatism* (Cambridge, Mass.: Harvard University Press, 1978).

James, W., *The Principles of Psychology* (Cambridge, Mass: Harvard University Press, 1981).

Jameson, F., *The Ideologies of Theory: Essays 1971–1986: Volume 1: Situations of Theory* (London: Routledge, 1988a).

Jameson, F., *The Ideologies of Theory: Essays 1971–1986: Volume 2: The Syntax of History* (London: Routledge, 1988b).

Jameson, F., *Postmodernism, or The Cultural Logic of Late Capitalism* (London: Verso, 1991).

Jay, M., *Marxism and Totality: The Adventures of a Concept from Lucács to Habermas* (Berkeley: University of California Press, 1984).

Jensen, H., *Sign, Symbol and Script: An Account of Man's Efforts to Write* (London: George Allen and Unwin, 1970).

Jerusalem, W., *Introduction to Philosophy* (New York: Macmillan Company, 1920).

Johnstone, H.W., Jr, *The Problem of the Self* (University Park: Pennsylvania State University Press, 1970).

Jordanova, L., *Sexual Visions: Images of Gender in Science and Medicine between the 18th and 20th Centuries* (Hemel Hempstead: Harvester Wheatsheaf, 1989).

Jung, H.Y., *The Crisis of Political Understanding: A Phenomenological Perspective in the Conduct of Political Inquiry* (Pittsburgh: Duquesne University Press, 1979).

Kant, I., *Critique of Pure Reason*, trans. N. Kemp Smith (London: Macmillan, 1929).

Kant, I., *Prolegomena to any Future Metaphysics* (Indianapolis, and New York: Bobbs-Merrill, 1950).

Kant, I., *Kant: Selected Pre-critical Writings and Correspondence with Beck* (Manchester: Manchester University Press, 1968).

Kant, I., *Logic* (New York: Bobbs-Merrill, 1974).

Kant, I., *Critique of Practical Reason: And Other Writings in Moral Philosophy* (Chicago: University of Chicago Press, 1976).

Kant, I., *Kant, Political Writings*, ed. H.S. Reiss (Cambridge: Cambridge University Press, 1977).

Kant, I., *Anthropology from a Pragmatic Point of View* (1976) (Carbondale and Edwardsville: Southern Illinois University Press, 1978).

Kant, I., *Lectures on Logic* (Cambridge: Cambridge University Press, 1992).

Kant, I., *Opus Postumum* (Cambridge: Cambridge University Press, 1993).

Kelly, M., ed., *Hermeneutics and Critical Theory in Ethics and Politics* (Cambridge, Mass.: MIT Press, 1990).

Kern, S., *The Culture of Time and Space, 1880–1918* (Cambridge, Mass.: Harvard University Press, 1983).

Kierkegaard, S., *Repetition* (Princeton: Princeton University Press, 1946).

Kierkegaard, S., *The Journals of Søren Kierkegaard* (London: Oxford University Press, 1951).

Kierkegaard, S., *The Point of View For My Work as an Author: A Report to History and Related Writings* (New York: Harper Torchbooks, 1962).

Kierkegaard, S., *The Concept of Irony* (London: Collins, 1966).

Kierkegaard, S., *Two Ages. The Age of Revolution and the Present Age: A Literary Review* (Princeton: Princeton University Press, 1978).

Kierkegaard, S. *Fear and Trembling, Repetition* (1843), in Kierkegaard's *Writings, VI*, ed. and trans. H.V. Hong and E.H. Hong (Princeton: University Press, 1983).

Klein, D.B., *The Unconscious: Invention or Discovery?* (Santa Monica: Goodyear, 1977).

Kleinman, A., *Social Origins of Distress and Disease* (New Haven: Yale University Press, 1986).

Knorr-Cetina, K.D., *The Manufacture of Knowledge: An Essay on the Constructivist and Contextual Nature of Science* (Oxford: Pergamon Press, 1981).

Knorr-Cetina, K.D. and Mulkay, M.J. eds, *Science Observed: Perspectives on the Social Study of Science* (London: Sage, 1983).

Kolak, D. and Martin, R., eds, *Self and Identity: Contemporary Philosophical Issues* (New York: Macmillan, 1991).

Konrad, G. and Szelényi, I., *The Intellectuals on the Road to Class Power* (Brighton: Harvester Press, 1979).

Koselleck, R., *Futures Past: On the Semantics of Historical Time* (Cambridge, Mass.: MIT Press, 1985).

Koselleck, R., *Critique and Crisis: Enlightenment and the Pathogenesis of Modern Society* (Cambridge, Mass.: MIT Press, 1988).

Kosík, K., *Dialectics of the Concrete: A Study on Problems of Man and World* (Dordrecht: D. Reidel, 1976).

Kristeva, J., *Desire in Language: A Semiotic Approach to Literature and Art* (Oxford: Blackwell, 1980).

Kristeva, J., *Powers of Horror* (New York: Columbia University Press, 1982).

Kristeva, J., *Revolution in Poetic Language* (New York: Columbia University Press, 1984).

Kristeva, J., *The Kristeva Reader*, ed., T. Moi (Oxford: Blackwell, 1986).

Kristeva, J., *Language: The Unknown* (Brighton: Harvester Wheatsheaf, 1989).

Kroker, A. and Cook, D., *The Postmodern Scene: Excremental Culture and Hyper-Aesthetics*, 2nd edn. (London: Macmillan, 1991).

Kuhn, T.S., *The Structure of Scientific Revolutions* (Chicago: University of Chicago Press, 1970).

Lacan, J., *Écrits*, 2 vols (Paris: Editions du Seuil, 1966).

Lacan, J., *Speech and Language in Psychoanalysis* (Baltimore and London: Johns Hopkins University Press, 1968).

Lacan, J., 'Seminar on 'The purloined letter', in *French Freud: Structural Studies in Psychoanalysis, Yale French Studies*, 48, 1972: 38–72.

Lacan, J., *Écrits: A Selection* (London: Tavistock, 1977).

Lacan, J., *The Four Fundamental Concepts of Psycho-Analysis* (New York: W.W. Norton, 1978).

Ladurie, E. Le Roy, *Carnival in Romans: A People's Uprising at Romans 1579–1580* (Harmonsworth: Penguin, 1979).

Lakoff, G. and Johnson, M., *Metaphors We Live By* (Chicago: University of Chicago Press, 1980).

Lasch, C., *The Culture of Narcissism* (New York: W.W. Norton, 1979).

Lash, S. and Urry, J., *The End of Organized Capitalism* (Cambridge: Polity Press, 1987).

Lash, S. and Urry, J., *Economies of Signs and Space* (London: Sage, 1993).

Latour, B., *Science in Action: How to Follow Scientists and Engineers through Society* (Cambridge, Mass.: Harvard University Press, 1987).

Latour, B., *The Pasteurization of France* (Cambridge, Mass.: Harvard University Press, 1988).

Latour, B., 'Drawing things together', in M. Lynch and S. Woolgar, eds, *Representation in Scientific Practice* (Cambridge, Mass.: MIT Press, 1990).

Latour, B., 'Technology is society made durable', in John Law, ed., *A Sociology of Monsters: Essays on Power, Technology and Domination* (London: Routledge, 1991): 103–31.

Latour, B., *We Have Never Been Modern* (Hemel Hempstead: Harvester Wheatsheaf, 1993).

Latour, B. and Woolgar, S., *Laboratory Life: The Social Construction of Scientific Facts* (Beverly Hills: Sage Publications, 1979).

Law, J., ed., *Power, Action and Belief: A New Sociology of Knowledge?* (London: Routledge and Kegan Paul, 1986).

Law, J., *Organizing Modernity* (Oxford: Blackwell, 1994).

Lefebvre, H., *La Production de l'espace* (Paris: Editions Anthropos, 1974).

Lefebvre, H., *Critique of Everyday Life, Volume 1* (London: Verso, 1991a).

Lefebvre, H., *The Production of Space* (Oxford: Blackwell, 1991b).

Le Guin, U.K., *Dancing at the Edge of the World: Thoughts on Words, Women, Places* (London: Paladin, 1992).

Leibniz, G.W., *New Essays Concerning Human Understanding* (La Salle: Open Court Publishing Co., 1949).

Leibniz, G.W., *Selections*, ed. P. Weiner (New York: Charles Scribner's Sons, 1951).

Leibniz, G.W., *Opuscules et Fragments Inédits de Leibniz*, ed. L. Couturat (Hildesheim: Georg Olms Verlagsnuchhandlung, 1961).

Leibniz, G.W., *Monadology and Other Philosophical Essays* (Indianapolis: Bobbs-Merill, 1965).

Leibniz, G.W., *New Essays on Human Understanding* (Cambridge: Cambridge University Press, 1981).

Leibniz, G.W., 'New essays on the human understanding', *Leibniz: Philosophical Writings* (London: Dent/Everyman's Library, 1968: 141–91).

Leibniz, G.W., *Philosophical Papers and Letters* (Dordrecht: D. Reidel, 1969).

Leibniz, G.W., *Philosophical Writings* (London: J.M. Dent, 1973).

Leibniz, G.W., *G.W. Leibniz: Philosophical Essays* (Indianapolis and Cambridge: Hackett Publishing Company, 1989).

Leiss, W., *The Domination of Nature* (New York: George Braziller, 1972).

Lentricchia, F., ed., *Critical Terms* (Chicago: University of Chicago Press, 1992).

Levin, D.M., *The Opening of Vision: Nihilism and the Postmodern Situation* (London: Routledge, 1985).

Lévinas, E., *Totality and Infinity* (Pittsburgh: Duquesne University Press, 1969).

Lévinas, E., *The Theory of Intuition in Husserl's Phenomenology* (Evanston: Northwestern University Press, 1973).

Lévinas, E., *Existence and Existents* (The Hague: Martinus Nijhoff, 1978).

Lévinas, E., *Otherwise than Being, or beyond Essence* (The Hague: Martinus Nijhoff, 1981).

Lévinas, E., *Time and the Other* (Pittsburgh: Duquesne University Press, 1987).

Lévinas, E., *Outside the Subject* (London: Athlone Press, 1994).

Levins, R. and Lewontin, R., *The Dialectical Biologist* (Cambridge, Mass.: Harvard University Press, 1985).

Lévi-Strauss, C., *Tristes Tropiques* (Paris: Plon, 1955).

Lévi-Strauss, C., *Anthropologie structurale* (Paris: Plon, 1958).

Lévi-Strauss, C., *Structural Anthropology* (New York: Basic Books, 1963).

Lévi-Strauss, C., *The Savage Mind* (London: Weidenfeld, 1966).

Lévi-Strauss, C., *The Scope of Anthropology* (London: Jonathan Cape, 1967).

Lévi-Strauss, C., *The Naked Man: Introduction to a Science of Mythology – IV* (London: Jonathan Cape, 1981).

Lévi-Strauss, C., *The View From Afar* (Oxford: Blackwell, 1985).

Liddell H.G. and Scott, R., *An Intermediate Greek-English Lexicon* (Oxford: Clarendon Press, 1964).

Lloyd, G., *Being in Time: Selves and Narrators in Philosophy and Literature* (London: Routledge, 1993).

Lobkowicz, N., *Theory and Practice: History of a Concept from Aristotle to Marx* (Notre Dame: University of Notre Dame Press, 1967).

Locke, J., *Essay Concerning Human Understanding* (Oxford: Clarendon Press, 1975).

Lovelock, J.E., *Gaia: A New Look at Life on Earth* (Oxford: Oxford University Press, 1979).

Lovelock, J.E., *The Ages of Gaia: A Biography of Our Living Earth* (New York: W.W. Norton 1988).

Lovelock, J.E., *Gaia: The Practical Science of Planetary Medicine* (London: Gaia Books, 1991).

Lowe, D.M., *History of Bourgeois Perception* (Chicago: Chicago University Press/Brighton: Harvester Press, 1982).

Luckmann, T., ed., *Phenomenology and Sociology: Selected Readings* (Harmondsworth: Penguin, 1978).

Luckmann, T., *Life-World and Social Realities* (London: Heinemann, 1983).

Luft, D.S., *Robert Musil and the Crisis of European Culture 1880–1942* (Berkeley: University of California Press, 1980).

Luhmann, N., *The Differentiation of Society* (New York: Columbia University Press, 1982).

Luhmann, N., *Ecological Communication* (Cambridge: Polity Press, 1989).

Lukács, G., *The Historical Novel* (London: Merlin Press, 1962).

Lukács, G., *Studies in European Realism* (New York: Grosset and Dunlap, 1964).

Lukács, G., *Writer and Critic and Other Essays* (London: Merlin Press, 1970).

Lukács, G., *The Theory of the Novel: A Historico-philosophical Essay on the Form of the Great Epic Literature* (1920) (Cambridge, Mass.: MIT Press, 1971a).

Lukács, G., *History and Class Consciousness: Studies in Marxist Dialectics* (Cambridge, Mass.: MIT Press/London: Merlin Press, 1971b).

Lukes, S., *Emile Durkheim: His Life and Work* (London: Allen Lane, 1975).

Lynch, M., *Art and Artifact in Laboratory Science: A Study of Shop Work and Shop Talk in a Research Laboratory* (London: Routledge and Kegan Paul, 1985).

Lynch, M. and Woolgar, S., *Representation in Scientific Practice* (Cambridge, Mass.: MIT Press, 1990).

Lyon, D., *The Electronic Eye: The Rise of Surveillance Society* (Cambridge: Polity Press, 1994).

Lyon, D., *The Information Society* (Cambridge: Polity Press, 1988).

Lyotard, J.-F., *Le Différend* (Paris: Editions de Minuit, 1983).

Lyotard, J.-F., *The Postmodern Condition: A Report on Knowledge* (Manchester: Manchester University Press, 1984).

Lyotard, J.-F., *The Differend: Phrases in Dispute* (1983) (Minneapolis: University of Minnesota Press, 1989).

Lyotard, J.-F., *Libidinal Economy* (Bloomington: Indiana University Press, 1993).

McCall, C., *Concepts of Person: An Analysis of Concepts of Persons, Self and Human Being* (Aldershot: Avebury, 1990).

McCarthy, T., *The Critical Theory of Jürgen Habermas* (Cambridge, Mass.: MIT Press, 1978).

McCloskey, D.N., *The Rhetoric of Economics* (Brighton: Harvester, 1986).

McGinn, C., *The Character of Mind* (Oxford: Oxford University Press, 1982).

McHale, B., *Postmodernist Fiction* (London: Methuen, 1987).

McHugh, P., *Defining the Situation: The Organization of Meaning in Social Interaction* (Indianapolis, New York: Bobbs-Merrill, 1968).

MacIntyre, A., *After Virtue: A Study in Moral Theory* (London: Duckworth, 1985).

MacKenzie, D. and Wajcman, J., eds, *The Social Shaping of Technology: How the Refrigerator Got Its Hum* (Milton Keynes: Open University Press, 1985).

McLellan, D., ed., *Karl Marx: Selected Writings* (Oxford: Oxford University Press, 1977).

McNeill, W., *The Pursuit of Power* (Chicago: University of Chicago Press, 1982).

McNeill, J.H., *A History of the Cure of Souls* (London: SCM Press, 1952).

McRobbie, A., *Postmodernism and Popular Culture* (London: Routledge, 1994).

Malcolm, N., *Ludwig Wittgenstein: A Memoir* (London: Oxford University Press, 1958).

Mandelbrot, B., *The Fractal Geometry of Nature* (New York: Freeman and Company, 1983).

Mann, M., *The Sources of Social Power*, Volume 1: *A history of Power from the Beginning to A.D. 1760* (Cambridge: Cambridge University Press, 1986).

Mann, M., *States, War, and Capitalism* (Oxford: Blackwell, 1988).

Mannheim, K., *Essays on the Sociology of Knowledge* (London: Routledge and Kegan Paul, 1952).

Mannheim, K., *Essays in Sociology and Social Psychology* (London: Routledge and Kegan Paul, 1953).

Mannheim, K., *Structures of Thinking* (London: Routledge and Kegan Paul, 1982).

Mannheim, K., *Conservatism: A Contribution to the Sociology of Knowledge* (London: Routledge and Kegan Paul, 1986).

Mannheim, K., *Ideology and Utopia* (London: Routledge and Kegan Paul, 1991).

Mannheim, K., *Essays on the Sociology of Culture* (1956) (London: Routledge 1992).

Marcus, G.E. and Fisher, M.M.J., *Anthropology as Cultural Critique: An Experimental Moment in the Human Sciences* (Chicago and London: University of Chicago Press, 1986).

Marcuse, H., *One-Dimensional Man* (Boston: Beacon Press, 1966).

Marcuse, H., *Negations: Essays in Critical Theory* (Boston: Beacon Press, 1968).

Marcuse, H., *The Aesthetic Dimension: Toward a Critique of Marxist Aesthetics* (London: Macmillan, 1979).

Marglin, S.A. and Schor, J.B., eds, *The Golden Age of Capitalism: Reinterpreting the Postwar Experience* (Oxford: Clarendon Press, 1990).

Margolis, J., *The Persistence of Reality – Texts without Referents: Reconciling Science and Narrative* (Oxford: Blackwell, 1989).

Marias, J., *Philosophy as Dramatic Theory* (University Park: Pennsylvania State Press, 1971).

Marx, K., *Grundrisse der Kritik der Politischen Oekonomie (Rohentwurf 1857–1858)* (Berlin: Dietz Verlag, 1953).

Marx, K., *Capital*, Volume 1, *A Critical Analysis of Capitalist Production* (Moscow: Foreign Languages Publishing House, 1961a).

Marx, K., *Capital*, Volume 2, *A Critique of Political Economy* (Moscow: Foreign Languages Publishing House, 1961b).

Marx, K., *Pre-capitalist Economic Formations* (London: Lawrence and Wishart, 1964).

Marx, K., *Capital*, Volume 3, *A Critique of Political Economy* (Moscow: Foreign Languages Publishing House, 1966).

Marx, K., *Selected Works* (London: Lawrence and Wishart, 1968).

Marx, K., *Grundrisse: Foundations of the Critique of Political Economy:* (Harmondsworth: Penguin, 1973).

Marx, K., *Early Writings* (Harmondsworth: Penguin, 1975).

Marx, K. and Engels, F., *The German Ideology* (London: Lawrence and Wishart, 1970).

Marx, W., *Heidegger and the Tradition* (Evanston: Northwestern University Press, 1971).

Massey, D., *Spatial Divions of Labour* (London: Macmillan, 1984).

Maturana, H.R. and Varela, F.J., *Autopoiesis and Cognition: The Realization of the Living* (Dordrecht: D. Reidel, 1980).

Mauss, M., 'Techniques of the body', *Economy and Society*, 2, 1972: 70–88.

Mauss, M., *Sociologie et anthropologie* (Paris: Presses Universitaires de France, 1973).

Mayr, O., *Liberty and Automatic Machines in Early Modern Europe* (Baltimore: Johns Hopkins University Press, 1986).

Mead, G.H., 'What social objects must psychology presuppose?', *Journal of Philosophy*, VII, 1910: 174–80.

Mead, G.H., *Mind, Self, and Society: From the Standpoint of a Social Behaviourist* (Chicago: University of Chicago Press, 1934).

Mead, G.H., *Movements of Thought in the Nineteenth Century* (Chicago: University of Chicago Press, 1936).

Mead, G.H., *The Philosophy of the Act* (Chicago: University of Chicago Press, 1938).

Mead, G.H., *The Philosophy of the Present* (La Salle: Open Court, 1959).

Mead, G.H., 'The social self', in *Selected Writings of George Herbert Mead*, ed. A.J. Reck (Indianapolis: Bobbs-Merrill, 1964a): 146–7.

Mead, G.H., *On Social Psychology* (Chicago: University of Chicago Press, 1964b).

Mehan, H., *Learning Lessons: Social Organization in the Classroom* (Harvard: Harvard University Press, 1979).

Mehan, H. and Wood, H., *The Reality of Ethnomethodology* (New York: John Wiley, 1975).

Mellor, D.H., ed., *Ways of Communicating* (Cambridge: Cambridge University Press, 1990).

Melzack, R. and Wall, P.D., *The Challenge of Pain* (New York: Basic Books, 1983).

Merchant, C., *The Death of Nature: Women, Ecology, and the Scientific Spirit* (New York: Harper and Row, 1980).

Merleau-Ponty, M., *Phénoménologie de la perception* (Paris: Gallimard, 1945).

Merleau-Ponty, M., *Signes* (Paris: Gallimard, 1960).

Merleau-Ponty, M., *The Phenomenology of Perception* (London: Routledge and Kegan Paul, 1962).

Merleau-Ponty, M., *The Structure of Behavior* (Boston: Beacon Press, 1963).

Merleau-Ponty, M., *Sense and Non-Sense* (Evanston: Northwestern University Press, 1964a).

Merleau-Ponty, M., *Signs* (Evanston: Northwestern University Press, 1964b).

Merleau-Ponty, M., *The Primacy of Perception* (Evanston: Northwestern University Press, 1964c).

Merleau-Ponty, M., *The Visible and the Invisible* (Evanston: Northwestern University Press, 1968).

Merleau-Ponty, M., *Themes from the Lectures at the Collège de France 1952–1960* (Evanston: Northwestern University Press, 1970).

Merleau-Ponty, M., *Consciousness and the Acquisition of Language* (Evanston: Northwestern University Press, 1973a).

Merleau-Ponty, M., *The Prose of the World* (Evanston: Northwestern University Press, 1973b).

Merleau-Ponty, M., *Adventures of the Dialectic* (London: Heinemann, 1974).

Merquior, J.G., *Western Marxism* (London: Granada, 1986).

Merton, R.K., *On the Shoulders of Giants: A Shandean Postscript* (New York: Free Press, 1965).

Meyrowitz, J., *No Sense of Place: The Impact of Electronic Media on Social Behaviour* (New York: Oxford University Press, 1985).

Miller, D.L., *George Herbert Mead: Self, Language and the World* (Austin: University of Texas Press, 1973).

Milner, A., *Contemporary Cultural Theory* (London: UCL Press, 1994).

Misch, G., *A History of Autobiography in Antiquity*, 2 vols (London: Routledge and Kegan Paul, 1950).

Mommsen, W.J., *The Political and Social Theory of Max Weber: Collected Essays* (Cambridge: Polity Press, 1989).

Morgan, G., *Organizations in Society* (London: Macmillan, 1990).

Mortley, R., *French Philosophers in Conversation: Lévinas, Schneider, Serres, Irigaray, Le Doeuff, Derrida* (London: Routledge, 1991).

Mukerji, C., *From Graven Images* (New York: Columbia University Press 1983).

Mulkay, M.J.M., *Science and the Sociology of Knowledge* (London: George Allen and Unwin, 1979).

Mulkay, M.J.M., *The Word and the World: Explorations in the Form of Sociological Analysis* (London: George Allen and Unwin, 1985).

Mumford, L., *Technics and Civilization* (New York: Harcourt, Brace and World, 1963).

Mumford, L., *The Condition of Man* (London: Warburg Institute, 1944).

Murray, D.J., *A History of Western Psychology* (Englewood Cliffs: Prentice-Hall, 1983).

Murray, G., *The Classical Tradition in Poetry* (London: Oxford University Press, 1927).

Nagel, T., *Mortal Questions* (Cambridge: Cambridge University Press, 1979).

Niethammer, L., *Posthistoire: Has History Come to an End?* (London: Verso, 1992).

Nietzsche, F., *Thus Spake Zarathustra* (New York: Viking Press, 1954).

Nietzsche, F., *The Use and Abuse of History* (New York: Library of Liberal Arts Press, 1957).

Nietzsche, F., *Die Geburt der Tragödie aus dem Geiste der Musik (Griechentum und Pessimismus)* (München: Wilhelm Goldmann Verlag, 1959).

Nietzsche, F., *Philosophy in the Tragic Age of the Greeks* (Chicago: Henry Regnery, 1962).

Nietzsche, F., *The Birth of Tragedy and the Case of Wagner* (New York: Vintage Press, 1967).

Nietzsche, F., *The Will to Power* (New York: Vintage Books, 1968).

Nietzsche, F., *Twilight of the Idols and The Anti-Christ* (Harmondsworth: Penguin, 1968a).

Nietzsche, F., *On the Genealogy of Morals and Ecce Homo* (New York: Vintage Books, 1969).

Nietzsche, F., *The Gay Science* (New York: Random House, 1974).

Nietzsche, F., *Beyond Good and Evil: Prelude to a Philosophy of the Future* (Harmondsworth: Penguin, 1978).

Nietzsche, F., *Ecce Homo* (Harmondsworth: Penguin, 1979).

Nietzsche, F., *On the Advantage and Disadvantage of History for Life* (Indianapolis: Hackett Publishing, 1980).

Nietzsche, F., *Human, All Too Human* (Lincoln and London: University of Nebraska Press, 1984).

Nietzsche, F., 'On truth and lying in an extra-moral sense', in *Friedrich Nietzsche on Rhetoric and Language*, ed. Gilman, *et al.* (New York: Oxford University Press, 1989).

Nin, A., *A Woman Speaks: The Lectures, Seminars, and Interviews of Anaïs Nin* (London: W.H. Allen, 1978).

Nisbet, R.A., *A History of the Idea of Progress* (New York: Basic Books, 1980).

Noble, D.F., *America by Design: Science, Technology, and the Rise of Corporate Capitalism* (New York: Knopf, 1977).

Nozick, R., *Philosophical Explanations* (Cambridge, Mass.: Harvard University Press, 1981).

Nussbaum, M., *The Fragility of Goodness: Luck and Ethics in Greek Tragedy and Philosophy* (Cambridge: Cambridge University Press, 1986).

Nussbaum, M., *Love's Knowledge: Essays on Philosophy and Literature* (New York and Oxford: Oxford University Press, 1990).

Nye, D.E., *Electrifying America: Social Meanings of a New Technology* (Cambridge Mass: MIT Press, 1990).

Offe, C., *Disorganized Capitalism* (Cambridge: Polity Press, 1985).

Oliver, K., *Reading Kristeva: Unraveling the Double-bind* (Bloomington: Indiana University Press, 1993).

O'Malley, J.B., *Sociology of Meaning* (London: Human Context Books, 1972).

O'Neill, J., *Sociology as a Skin Trade: Essays Towards A Reflexive Sociology* (London: Heinemann, 1972).

O'Neill, J., *Five Bodies: The Human Shape of Modern Society* (Ithaca: Cornell University Press, 1985).

Ong, W.J., *Orality and Literature: The Technologizing of the Word* (London: Methuen, 1982).

Ornstein, R., *The Psychology of Consciousness* (1972) (Harmondsworth: Penguin, 1986).

Paci, E., *The Function of the Sciences and the Meaning of Man* (Evanston: Northwestern University Press, 1972).

Paglia, C., *Sexual Personae: Art and Decadence from Nefertiti to Emily Dickinson* (New Haven and London: Yale University Press, 1990).

Parain, B., *A Metaphysics of Language* (Garden City: Doubleday/Anchor, 1971).

Parfit, D., *Reasons and Persons* (Oxford: Oxford University Press, 1984).

Parsons, T., *The Structure of Social Action* (New York: Free Press, 1937).

Pateman, C., *The Disorder of Women: Democracy, Feminism, and Political Theory* (Cambridge: Polity Press, 1989).

Patocka, J., *Jan Patocka: Philosophy and Selected Writings* (Chicago: University of Chicago Press, 1989).

Peirce, C.S., *The Collected Papers of Charles Sanders Peirce* (1931–58) (Cambridge, Mass.: Harvard University Press, 1960).

Perrow, C., *Normal Accidents* (New York: Basic Books, 1984).

Perrow, C., *Complex Organizations: A Critical Essay*, 3rd edn (New York: Random House, 1987).

Perry, R.B., *The New Realism* (Cambridge, Mass.: Harvard University Press, 1912).

Pickering, A., *Constructing Quarks: A Sociological History of Particle Physics* (Chicago: University of Chicago Press, 1984).

Pinch, T. and Pinch, T., 'Reservations about reflexivity and new literary forms or why let the devil have all the good tunes?', in S. Woolgar, ed., *Knowledge and Reflexivity* (London: Sage, 1988).

Pirsig, R.M., *Zen and the Art of Motorcycle Maintenance: An Inquiry into Values* (London: The Bodley Head, 1974).

Plato, *Dialogues* (Oxford: Clarendon Press, 1953) and Penguin editions of individual dialogues).

Plato, *Epistles*, trans. Glenn R. Morrow (Indianapolis: Bobbs-Merrill, 1962).

Plessner, H., *Die Stufen des Organischen und der Mensch* (Berlin: de Gruyter, 1928).

Plessner, H., *Laughing and Crying: A Study of the Limits of Human Behaviour* (Evanston: Northwestern University Press, 1970).

Plumwood, V., *Feminism and the Mastery of Nature* (London: Routledge, 1993).

Polanyi, M., *The Tacit Dimension* London: Routledge and Kegan Paul, 1967).

Polanyi, M., *Personal Knowledge: Towards Post-Critical Philosophy* (London: Routledge and Kegan Paul, 1973).

Polanyi, M. and Prosch, H., *Meaning* (Chicago: University of Chicago Press, 1975).

Polhemus, T., ed., *Social Aspects of the Human Body* (Harmondsworth: Penguin, 1978).

Pollner, M., 'Mundane reasoning', *Philosophy of the Social Sciences*, 4, 1974: 35–54.

482

Pollner, M., *Mundane Reason: Reality in Everyday and Sociological Discourse* (Cambridge: Cambridge University Press, 1987).

Pope, A., *An Essay on Criticism*, 3 vols. (London: Bell, 1878): vol. 2.

Popper, K.R., *A World of Propensities* (Brighton: Thoemmes, 1990).

Portmann, A., 'Biology and the phenomenon of the spiritual', in J. Campbell, ed., *Spirit and Nature, Papers from the Eranos Yearbook* (London: Routledge and Kegan Paul, 1955): 342–70.

Portmann, A., 'Time in the life of the organism', in J. Campbell, ed., *Man and Time, Papers from the Eranos Yearbook* (London: Routledge and Kegan Paul, 1958): 308–23.

Poster, M., *The Mode of Information: Poststructuralism and Social Context* (Cambridge: Polity Press, 1990).

Prigogine, I., *From Being to Becoming: Time and Complexity in the Physical Sciences* (San Francisco: Freeman, 1980).

Prigogine, I. and Sengers, I., *Order Out of Chaos: Man's New Dialogue with Nature* (London: Heinemann/New York: Bantam Books, 1984).

Prigogine, I., 'Origins of complexity', in A.C. Fabian, ed., *Origins: The Darwin College Lectures* (Cambridge: Cambridge University Press, 1988): 69–88.

Proust, M., *Remembrance of Things Past* (Harmondsworth: Penguin, 1984).

Prufer, T., 'Martin Heidegger: Dasein and the ontological status of the speaker in philosophical discourse', in John K. Ryan, ed., *Twentieth-Century Thinkers* (Staten Island: Alba House, 1965): 159–73.

Psathas, G., ed., *Everyday Language: Studies in Ethnomethodology* (New York: Irvington Press, 1979).

Psathas, G., ed., *Phenomenological Sociology: Issues and Applications* (New York: John Wiley, 1973).

Ragland-Sullivan, E., *Jacques Lacan and the Philosophy of Psychoanalysis* (Urbana: University of Illinois Press, 1986).

Ray, L., ed., *Critical Sociology* (London: Edward Arnold, 1990).

Restivo, S., *The Social Relations of Physics, Mysticism, and Mathematics: Studies in Social Structure, Interests, and Ideas* (Dordrecht: D. Reidel, 1983).

Rickman, H.P., ed., *Dilthey: Selected Writings* (Cambridge: Cambridge University Press, 1976).

Ricoeur, P., *Freedom and Nature: The Voluntary and the Involuntary* (Evanston: Northwestern University Press, 1966).

Ricoeur, P., *Freud and Philosophy: An Essay on Interpretation* (New Haven and London: Yale University Press, 1970).

Ricoeur, P., 'The model of the text: meaningful action considered as a text', *Social Research*, 38, 1971: 529–62.

Ricoeur, P., *The Conflict of Interpretations: Essays in Hermeneutics* (Evanston: Northwestern University Press, 1974).

Ricoeur, P., *Interpretation Theory: Discourse and the Surplus of Meaning* (Fort Worth: Texas Christian University Press, 1976).

Ricoeur, P., *The Rule of Metaphor: Multi-disciplinary Studies of the Creation of Meaning in Language* (London: Routledge and Kegan Paul, 1978).

Ricoeur, P., *Hermeneutics and the Human Sciences* (Cambridge: Cambridge University Press, 1981).

Ricoeur, P., *Time and Narrative* (Chicago: University of Chicago Press, 1984–7).

Ricoeur, P., *Lectures on Ideology and Utopia* (New York: Columbia University Press, 1986).

Ricoeur, P., *Oneself as Another* (Chicago: The University of Chicago Press, 1994).

Rieber, R.W., ed., *Wilhelm Wundt and the Making of a Scientific Psychology* (New York: Plenum Press, 1980).

Robbins, D., *The Work of Pierre Bourdieu: Recognizing Society* (Milton Keynes: Open University Press, 1991).

Rorty, R., *Philosophy and the Mirror of Nature* (Princeton: Princeton University Press, 1979).

Rorty, R., *Contingency, Irony and Solidarity* (Cambridge: Cambridge University Press, 1989).

Rosaldo, M.Z., *Knowledge and Passion: Ilongot Notions of Self and Social Life* (Cambridge: Cambridge University Press, 1980).

Rosaldo, R., *Culture and Truth: The Remaking of Social Analysis* (Boston: Beacon Press, 1989).

Rosen, S., *Nihilism: A Philosophical Essay* (New Haven and London: Yale University Press, 1969).

Rosen, S., *The Limits of Analysis* (New York: Basic Books, 1980).

Ross, D., *The Origins of American Social Science* (Cambridge: Cambridge University Press, 1991).

Rousseau, G.S., ed., *The Languages of Psyche: Mind and Body in Enlightenment Thought* (Berkeley: University of California Press, 1990).

Rousseau, J.-J., *The Confessions of Jean-Jacques Rousseau*, trans. W. Conyngham Mallory (New York: Tudor Publishing Company, 1928).

Rousseau, J.-J., *Les Rêveries du promeneur solitaire* (Paris: Librairie Jules Tallandier, 1969).

Rousseau, J.-J., *Reveries of the Solitary Walker* (Harmondsworth: Penguin, 1979).

Ryave, A.L. and Schenkein, J.N., 'Notes on the art of walking', in R. Turner, ed., *Ethnomethodology* (Harmondsworth: Penguin, 1974): 265–74.

Rycroft, C., *The Innocence of Dreams* (London: The Hogarth Press, 1991).

Ryle, G., *The Concept of Mind* (London: Hutchinson, 1949).

Ryle, G., *Dilemmas* (Cambridge: Cambridge University Press, 1954).

Sacks, H., 'Sociological description', *Berkeley Journal of Sociology*, 8, 1963: 1–16.

Sacks, H., *The Search for Help: No One To Turn To* (unpublished doctoral dissertation, Department of Sociology, University of California at Berkeley, 1966).

Sacks, H., 'On the analysability of stories by children', in J.J. Gumperz and D. Hymes, eds, *Directions in Sociolinguistics* (New York: Holt, Rinehart and Winston, 1972).

Sacks, H., Schegloff, E.A. and Jefferson, G., 'A simplest systematics for the organization of turn-taking for conversation', *Language*, 50, 1974.

Sacks, O.W., *Awakenings* (Harmondsworth: Penguin, 1976).

Sacks, O.W., *A Leg to Stand On* (London: Duckworth, 1984).

Sacks, O.W., *The Man Who Mistook His Wife for a Hat* (London: Duckworth, 1985).

Sacks, O.W., *Seeing Voices: A Journey into the World of the Deaf* (London: Picador/Pan Books, 1989).

Sahlins, M., *Culture and Practical Reason* (Chicago: University of Chicago Press, 1976).

Sahlins, M., *Historical Metaphors and Mythical Realities* (Ann Arbor: University of Michigan Press, 1981).

Sandel, M.J., 'The procedural republic and the unencumbered self', *Political Theory* 12 (1), February, 1984: 81–96.

Sandywell, B., *et al.*, *Problems of Reflexivity and Dialectics in Sociological Inquiry: Language Theorizing Difference* (London: Routledge and Kegan Paul, 1975).

Sapir, E., *Selected Writings of Edward Sapir in Language, Culture and Personality* (Berkeley and Los Angeles: University of California Press, 1961).

Sapir, E., *Language: An Introduction to the Study of Speech* (London: Rupert Hart-Davis, 1971).

Sartre, J.-P., *What is Literature?* (New York: Philosophical Library, 1949).

Sartre, J.-P., *Being and Nothingness* (London: Methuen, 1957a).

Sartre, J.-P., *The Transcendence of the Ego: An Existentialist Theory of Consciousness* (New York: Noonday Press, 1957b).

Sartre, J.-P., *Critique de la raison dialectique* (Paris: Gallimard, 1960).

Sartre, J.-P., *The Problem of Method* (London: Methuen, 1964).

Sartre, J.-P., *Nausea* (Harmondsworth: Penguin, 1965).

Sartre, J.-P., *The Psychology of Imagination* (London: Methuen, 1972).

Sartre, J.-P., *The Writings of Jean-Paul Sartre. Volume 2: Selected Prose* (Evanston: Northwestern University Press, 1974).

Sartre, J.-P., *Critique of Dialectical Reason, Volume 1: Theory of Practical Ensembles* (London: New Left Books, 1976).

Saussure, de, F., *Course in General Linguistics*, trans. Roy Harris (London: Duckworth, 1983).

Scarry, E., *The Body in Pain: The Making and Unmaking of the World* (Oxford: Oxford University Press, 1985).

Schegloff, E.A., 'Notes on conversational practice: formulating place', in Sudnow, D., ed., *Studies in Social Interaction* (New York: Free Press, 1972): 75–119.

Scheler, M., *Philosophical Perspectives* (Boston: Beacon Press, 1958).

Scheler, M., *Ressentiment* (New York: Free Press, 1961).

Scheler, M., *The Nature of Sympathy* (London: Routledge and Kegan Paul, 1970).

Scheler, M., *On the Eternal in Man* (Hamden, Connecticut: Archon Books, 1972).

Scheler, M., *Formalism in Ethics and Non-Formal Ethics of Value: A New Attempt Toward the Foundation of an Ethical Personalism* (Evanston: Northwestern University Press, 1973).

Scheler, M., *On Feeling, Knowing, and Valuing: Selected Writings* (Chicago: University of Chicago Press, 1992).

Schelling, F.W.J., *Of Human Freedom* (1809) (Chicago: Open Court Publishing Company, 1936).

Schelling, F.W.J., *On University Studies* (Athens: Ohio University Press, 1966).

Schelling, F.W.J., *The Ages of the World* (New York: AMS Press, 1967).

Schelling, F.W.J., *System of Transcendental Idealism* (1800) (Charlottesville: University Press of Virginia, 1978).

Schelling, F.W.J., *The Unconditional in Human Knowledge: Four Early Essays (1794–1796)* (Lewisburg: Bucknell University Press, 1980).

Schenkein, J.N., ed., *Studies in the Organization of Conversational Interaction* (New York: Academic Press, 1978).

Schilder, P., *Brain and Personality: Studies in the Psychological Aspects of Cerebral Neuropathology and the Neuropsychiatric Aspects of the Motility of Schizophrenics* (New York: International Universities Press, 1951).

Schiller, H.I., *Mass Communications and American Empire* (New York: Kelley, 1970).

Schivelbusch, W., *The Railway Journey: The Industrialization of Time and Space in the 19th Century* (Leamington Spa/Hamburg/New York: Berg, 1986).

Schivelbusch, W., *Disenchanted Night: The Industrialisation of Light in the Nineteenth Century* (Oxford: Berg, 1988).

Schluchter, W., *The Rise of Western Rationalism: Max Weber's Developmental History* (Berkeley: University of California Press, 1981).

Schluchter, W., *Rationalism, Religion, and Domination: A Weberian Perspective* (Berkeley: University of California Press, 1989).

Schopenhauer, A., *The World as Will and Representation*, 2 vols (New York: Dover, 1958, 1966).

Schopenhauer, A., *Parerga and Paralipomena: Short Philosophical Essays*, 2 vols (Oxford: Clarendon Press, 1974).

Schopenhauer, A., *Manuscript Remains in Four Volumes, Volume III: Berlin Manuscripts (1818–1830)* (Oxford: Berg Publishers, 1989).

Schopenhauer, A., *Manuscript Remains in Four Volumes, Volume I: Early Manuscripts (1808–1818)* (Oxford: Berg Publishers, 1988).

Schorske, C.E., *Fin-de-siècle Vienna: Politics and Culture* (New York: Alfred A. Knopf, 1980).

Schrag, C.O., *Radical Reflection and the Origin of the Human Sciences* (West Lafayette: Purdue University Press, 1980).

Schürmann, R., *Heidegger on Being and Acting: From Principles to Anarchy* (Bloomington: Indiana University Press, 1987).

Schutz, A., 'William James' concept of the stream of thought phenomenologically interpreted', *Philosophy and Phenomenological Research*, 1, June 1941: 442–52; reprinted in *Collected Papers*, vol. III, 1966.

Schutz, A., *The Phenomenology of the Social World* (1932) (Evanston: Northwestern University Press, 1967).

Schutz, A., *Reflections on the Problem of Relevance* (New Haven and London: Yale University Press, 1970a).

Schutz, A., *On Phenomenology and Social Relations* (Chicago: University of Chicago Press, 1970b).

Schutz, A., *Collected Papers* (The Hague: Martinus Nijhoff, Volume 1, *The Problem of Social Reality*, 1967a; Volume 2, *Studies in Social Theory*, 1964; Volume 3, *Studies in Phenomenological Philosophy*, 1970c).

Schutz, A., *Life Forms and Meaning Structure* (London: Routledge and Kegan Paul, 1982).

Schutz, A., and Luckman, T., *The Structures of the Life-World* (Evanston: Northwestern University Press, 1973).

Shapin, S. and Shaffer, S., *The Leviathan and the Air Pump* (Princeton: Princeton University Press, 1985).

Shibles, W.A., *Models of Ancient Greek Philosophy* (London: Vision Press, 1971).

Shoemaker, S., *Self-Knowledge and Self-Identity* (Ithaca: Cornell University Press, 1963).

Simmel, G., *The Conflict in Modern Culture and Other Essays* (New York: Teachers College Press, 1968).

Simmel, G., *On Individuality and Social Forms* (Chicago: University of Chicago Press, 1971).

Simmel, G., *Schopenhauer and Nietzsche* (Amherst: University of Massachusetts Press, 1986).

Simmel, G., *The Philosophy of Money* (London: Routledge and Kegan Paul, 1990).

Singer, J.L., 'Experimental studies of ongoing conscious experience', in CIBA, *Experimental and Theoretical Studies of Consciousness* (New York: Wiley and Sons, 1993): 100–22.

Sloterdijk, P., *Critique of Cynical Reason* (London: Verso, 1988).

Smith, A., *The Theory of Moral Sentiments*, in *The Works of Adam Smith Volume 1* (Aalen: Otto Zeller, 1963).

Smith, A., *An Inquiry Into the Nature and Causes of the Wealth of Nations*, eds Campbell, R.H., and Skinner, A.S. (Oxford: Clarendon Press, 1976).

Soja, E.W., *Postmodern Geographies: The Reassertion of Space in Critical Social Theory* (London: Verso, 1989).

Sokolowski, R., *The Formation of Husserl's Concept of Constitution* (The Hague: Martinus Nijhoff, 1970).

Solomon, R.C., *History and Human Nature: A Philosophical Review of European Philsophy and Culture, 1750–1850* (Brighton: Harvester Press, 1980).

Solomon, R.C., *Continental Philosophy since 1750: the Rise and Fall of the Subject* (Oxford: Oxford University Press, 1988).

Spinoza, B., *Opera*, ed. C. Gebhardt (Heidelberg: Carl Winters Universitätsbuchhandlung, 1925).

Spinoza, B., *The Chief Works of Benedict de Spinoza*, ed. R.H.M. Elwes (New York: Dover, 1955).

Spinoza, B., *Ethics and On the Correction of the Understanding* (London: Dent/Everyman's Library, 1986).

Sprigge, T.L.S., *Theories of Existence* (Harmondsworth: Penguin, 1985).

Stonier, T., *The Wealth of Information: A Profile of the Post-Industrial Economy* (London: Thames Matheson, 1983).

Straus, E., *The Primary World of the Senses: A Vindication of Sensory Experience* (New York: Free Press of Glencoe, 1963).

Strawson, P.F., *Analysis and Metaphysics: An Introduction to Philosophy* (Oxford: Oxford University Press, 1992).

Street, B., *Literacy in Theory and Practice* (Cambridge: Cambridge University Press, 1984).

Stuart Hughes, H., *Consciousness and Society: The Reorientation of European Social Thought 1890–1930* (London: Macgibbon and Kee, 1959).

Sturrock, J., *Structuralism* (London: Fontana, 1993).

Styron, W., *Darkness Visible: A Memoir of Madness* (London: Jonathan Cape, 1991).

Sudnow, D., ed., *Studies in Social Interaction* (New York: Free Press, 1972).

Sudnow, D., *Ways of the Hand* (Cambridge, Mass.: Harvard University Press, 1978).

Sulloway, F.J., *Freud, Biologist of the Mind: Beyond the Psychoanalytic Legend* (London: Burnett Books/André Deutsch, 1979).

Swingewood, A., *A Short History of Sociological Thought*, 2nd edn (London: Macmillan, 1991).

Sylvester, C., *Feminist Theory and International Relations in a Postmodern Era* (Cambridge: Cambridge University Press, 1994).

Szasz, T., *Pain and Pleasure: A Study of Bodily Feelings* (London: Tavistock Publications, 1957).

Tagg, J., 'Globalization, totalization and the discursive field', in Anthony D. King, ed., *Culture, Globalization and the World-System* (London: Macmillan, 1991): 155–60.

Taussig, M., *Mimesis and Alterity: A Particular History of the Senses* (London: Routledge, 1993).

Taylor, C., *Sources of the Self: The Making of the Modern Identity* (Cambridge: Cambridge University Press, 1989).

Thayer, H.S., *Meaning and Action: A Critical History of Pragmatism* (Indianapolis: Hackett, 1981).

Thayer, H.S., *Pragmatism: The Classical Writings* (Indianapolis: Hackett, 1982).

Therborn, G., *Science, Class and Society* (London: New Left Books, 1976).

Thomas, R., *Oral Tradition and Written Record in Classical Athens* (Cambridge: Cambridge University Press, 1989).

Thompson, E.P., *et al.*, eds, *Exterminism and Cold War* (London: Verso, 1982).

Thompson, J.B., *Critical Hermeneutics: A Study in the Thought of Paul Ricoeur and Jürgen Habermas* (Cambridge: Cambridge University Press, 1981).

Thompson, J.B., *Studies in the Theory of Ideology* (Cambridge: Polity Press, 1984).

Tillich, P., *The System of the Sciences according to Objects and Methods* (Lewisburg: Bicknell University Press/London and Toronto: Associated University Presses, 1981).

Turner, R., ed., *Ethnomethodology: Selected Readings* (Harmondsworth: Penguin, 1974).

Tye, M., 'Blindsight, the absent qualita hypothesis, and the mystery of consciousness', in C. Hookaway and D. Peterson, eds, *Philosophy and Cognitive Science* (Cambridge: Cambridge University Press, 1993): 19–40.

von Uexküll, J., *Theoretische Biologie* (Frankfurt: Suhrkamp, 1970).
von Uexküll, J., 'A stroll through the world of animals and men', in C.H. Schiller, ed., *Instinctive Behavior* (New York: International Universities Press, 1957): 5–80.
Vaihinger, H., *The Philosophy of 'As If'. A System of the Theoretical, Practical and Religious Fictions of Mankind* (London: Routledge and Kegan Paul, 1924).
Vattimo, G., *The End of Modernity: Nihilism and Hermeneutics in Postmodern Culture* (Cambridge: Polity Press, 1988).
Vattimo, G., *The Transparent Society* (Oxford: Blackwell, 1992).
Vattimo, H. and Rovatti, P.A., eds, *Il pensiero debole* (Milan: Feltrinelli, 1983).
Veyne, P., *Bread and Circuses: Historical Sociology and Political Pluralism* (London: Harmondsworth, 1990).
Virilio, P., *The Vision Machine* (London: British Film Institute, 1994).
Virilio, P. and Lotringer, S., *Pure War* (New York: Semiotext(e), 1983).
Vygotsky, L.S., *Thought and Language* (Cambridge, Mass.: MIT Press, 1962).
Vygotsky, L.S., *Mind in Society: The Development of Higher Psychological Processes* (Cambridge, Mass.: Harvard University Press, 1978).
Vygotsky, L.S., *The Collected Works of L.S. Vygotsky, Volume 1: Problems of General Psychology* (New York and London: Plenum Press, 1987).
Wagner, P., *A Sociology of Modernity: Liberty and Discipline* (London: Routledge, 1994).
Walby, S., *Theorizing Patriarchy* (Oxford: Blackwell, 1989).
Warnke, G., *Gadamer: Hermeneutics, Tradition and Reason* (Cambridge: Polity Press, 1987).
Watts, A., *The Wisdom of Insecurity: A Message for an Age of Anxiety* (London: Rider Books, 1992).
Weber, A., *Farewell to European History or The Conquest of Nihilism* (London: Kegan Paul, Trench, Trubner, 1947).
Weber, M., *From Max Weber*, trans. H. Gerth and C. Wright Mills (London: Routledge and Kegan Paul, 1948).
Weber, M., *The Methodology of the Social Sciences* (New York: Free Press, 1949).
Weber, M., 'Objectivity' in social science and social policy', in *The Methodology of the Social Sciences* (New York: Free Press, 1949): 50–112.
Weber, M., *The Theory of Social and Economic Organization* (New York: The Free Press, 1964).
Weber, M., *The Sociology of Religion* (London: Methuen, 1966).
Weber, M., *Ancient Judaism* (New York: Free Press, 1967).
Weber, M., *Economy and Society: An Outline of Interpretive Sociology*, 2 vols (Berkeley: University of California Press, 1968).
Weber, M., *The Interpretation of Social Reality*, ed., J.E.T. Eldridge (London: Michael Joseph, 1971).
Webster, C., ed., *The Intellectual Revolution of the Seventeenth Century* (London: Routledge and Kegan Paul, 1974).
Weizenbaum, J., *Computer Power and Human Reason* (San Francisco: Freeman, 1976; Harmondsworth: Penguin, 1984).
Wellmer, A., *Critical Theory of Society* (New York: Herder and Herder, 1971).
Wellmer, A., 'Reason, utopia, and the dialectic of Enlightenment', *Praxis International*, 3, 1983: 83–107.
White, H., *Tropics of Discourse: Essays in Cultural Criticism* (Baltimore and London: Johns Hopkins University Press, 1985).
Whorf, B.L., *Language, Thought, and Reality: Selected Essays of Benjamin Lee Whorf*, ed. J.B. Carroll (Cambridge, Mass.: MIT Press, 1956).
Whyte, L.L., *The Unconscious Before Freud* (New York: Doubleday, 1962).
Wieder, D.L., *Language and Social Reality* (The Hague: Mouton, 1974a).

Wieder, D.L., 'Telling the code', in Turner, R., ed., *Ethnomethodology* (Harmondsworth: Penguin, 1974b): 144–72.

Wiggershaus, R., *The Frankfurt School: Its History, Theories, and Political Significance* (Cambridge: Polity Press, 1993).

Wilder, C. and Weakland, J.H., eds, *Rigor and Imagination: Essays from the Legacy of Gregory Bateson* (New York: Praeger Publishers, 1981).

Williams, R., *Modern Tragedy* (Stanford: Stanford University Press, 1966).

Williams, R., *Contact: Human Communication and its History* (London: Thames and Hudson, 1981).

Williams, R., *Towards 2000* (London: Chatto and Windus/The Hogarth Press, 1983).

Williams, R., *Notes on the Underground: An Essay on Technology, Society, and the Imagination* (Cambridge, Mass.: MIT Press, 1990).

Wilson, B., ed., *Rationality* (Oxford: Blackwell, 1974).

Wittgenstein, L., *Remarks on the Foundations of Mathematics* (Oxford: Blackwell, 1956).

Wittgenstein, L., *Zettel* (Oxford: Blackwell, 1967).

Wittgenstein, L., *Philosophical Investigations* (Oxford: Blackwell, 1968).

Wittgenstein, L., *On Certainty* (Oxford: Blackwell, 1969).

Wittgenstein, L., *The Blue and Brown Books* (Oxford: Blackwell, 1969a).

Wittgenstein, L., *Notebooks 1914–1916* (Oxford: Blackwell, 1969b).

Wittgenstein, L., *Lectures and Conversations on Aesthetics, Psychology and Religious Belief* (Oxford: Blackwell, 1970).

Wittgenstein, L., *Tractatus Logico-Philosophicus* (London: Routledge and Kegan Paul, 1971).

Wittgenstein, L., *Wittgenstein's Lectures: Cambridge, 1932–1935* (Oxford: Blackwell, 1979).

Wittgenstein, L., *Wittgenstein's Lectures. Cambridge 1930–1932*, ed. Desmond Lee (Oxford: Blackwell, 1980a).

Wittgenstein, L., *Culture and Value* (Oxford: Blackwell, 1980b).

Wittgenstein, L., *Wittgenstein's Lectures on Philosophical Psychology 1946–47*, ed. Peter Geach (London: Harvester Wheatsheaf, 1988).

Woodward, K., ed., *The Myths of Information: Technology and Post-Industrial Culture* (London: Routledge and Kegan Paul, 1980).

Woolgar, S., *Science: The Very Idea* (London: Tavistock Publications, 1988).

Woolgar, S., ed., *Knowledge and Reflexivity: New Frontiers in the Sociology of Knowledge* (London: Sage Publications, 1988).

Wright Mills, C., *The Sociological Imagination* (Harmondsworth: Penguin, 1970).

Wundt, W., *The Elements of Folk Psychology (Völkerpsychologie)* 1900–1920) (London: Allen and Unwin, 1916).

Wundt, W., *The Language of Gestures* (from *Völkerpsychologie*) (The Hague: Mouton, 1973).

Zadeh, L.A., 'Fuzzy logic and approximate reasoning', *Synthese*, 30(3–4), 1975: 407–28.

Zadeh, L.A., 'Theory of fuzzy sets', in Belzer, J., et al., eds, *Encyclopedia of Computer Science and Technology* (New York: Dekker, 1977): vol. VII.

Zaner, R., *The Problem of Embodiment: Some Contributions to a Phenomenology of the Body* (The Hague: Martinus Nijhoff, 1971).

Zborowski, M., 'Cultural components in responses to pain', *Journal of Social Issues* 8, 1952: 16–30.

Zimmerman, D., 'The practicalities of rule use', in J. Douglas, ed., *Understanding Everyday Life* (London: Routledge and Kegan Paul, 1971): 221–38.

Zimmerman, D. and Pollner, M., 'The everyday world as a phenomenon', in J. Douglas, ed., *Understanding Everyday Life* (London: Routledge and Kegan Paul, 1971): 80–103.

Zimmerman, D. and Weider, L., 'Ethnomethodology and the problem of order: comment on Denizen', in J. Douglas, ed., *Understanding Everyday Life* (London: Routledge and Kegan Paul, 1971): 285–98.

Zizek, S., *The Sublime Object of Ideology* (London: Verso, 1989).

Zukav, W.H., *The Dancing Wu Li Masters* (London: Fontana, 1979).

NAME INDEX

SUBJECT INDEX

absolute knowledge 97, 102, 214–15

absolutism: of classical philosophy
292–3; of prescriptive moral systems
329–30; of principles 288–90; of
videology 123

account: accounting practices (as topic
of ethnomethodological
investigation) 299–300;
accountings-of-social-action 308;
agents' accounts of action 390–3;
members' accounting procedures 300,
389; *see* discourse, ethnomethodology

accountability 38, 67, 244–5, 299–300;
institutional systems of 299–300, 301

action: Aristotle's explanation of in
terms of chance, nature, and
compulsion 245, 272–3; Aristotle's
explanation of in terms of habit,
reason, anger, and desire 245;
attentive 172–83, 202–7; cooperative
237, 272–3; as central theme of
reflexive social theory 293, 298–9;
criteria for 208, 223, 244–5, 273–4;
definition 177, 208, 311; deliberate
208, 244–5; deliberative 319, 320 and
whole of Chapter 9; Austin on
deliberate, purposeful, and
intentional action 244–5, 280–1;
end-oriented 177, 244; free/voluntary
223, 244–5; meaningful 177, 189; as
practical syllogism, 244–5, 320; as
praxis 207–8, 237, 320–4; human 244,
311–13; intentional 189–90, 243–7,
244–8; distinguished from voluntary
action 244–5, 280–1; involuntary
244–5; purposive 177, 244–5; social
177, 244–8; teleological 177, 243–5;
thoughtful 272–3; unintentional 190,

244–5; voluntary 245

aesthetic (*aisthesis*): 67–8, 184, 188–93;
discourse 67–8; experience 67, 188–9,
315

affectivity 126–8, 350–6; as central
theme of logological research 127–8,
188–93, 193–4; and others 275–6; and
preontological relation to Being 243,
246–7, 275, 284–5, 353–4

Aletheia, alethic (truth, truthlike) 138,
140–1, 143, 239, 242–3; presupposed
by concepts of truth as correctness,
adequation, coherence,
correspondence, etc. 242–3;
world-openness 246–7

alienation xix; of absolute Spirit 216–22;
central theme of all critical theory
370–3; of everyday life 363–4;
problematic 360; of science from its
sustaining life-world 359, 360

alterity: in analytic sociology 395–6; as
dialogue 5, 345ff.; discourses of the
Other 5; excluded other of Reflection
249; in Heideggerian phenomenology
228; of all other forms of life 164–5;
of language 247–8; irreducible 352;
orders of alterity (discourse,
embodiment, historicity, practical
judgement) 249; of nature 219; of
other subjects 219; powers of alterity
defining *reflexivity* 4; self-and-other
xiii, 38; symbolized xii–xiii; xix–xx

anima (soul, source of animation) 170

animal (*zoion*) 132, absence of conscious
will 175; attitudes toward 437n5; as
complex of entelechial substances
159; as colony of interdependent
monads 159; creativity of 161;

498

ontological 275, 377–8; and praxial experience 276, 296; as transactional process 276, 343, 377;

information 13–14; markets (graphic specialization) 23; in modern capitalist mode of production 15, 24–32; organisms as information processing 152–6; in reflexive modernization 18–19, 24–5, 26; in reflexive systems 161–5; technology 27, 33

institution(s): buffer 21; bureaucratized 18–22; as an organization of social attitudes (in Mead) 261, 262; micro and macro 278, 302; and the microphysics of power 308; modern corporate 14, 15; social xi, 4, 94; technocratic 18–22

intention, intentional 85–6, 225–6; intentional directedness 224–5, 226–7, 245–6; intentional inexistence 175; intention to communicate 86; as synonymous with 'the cultural' 247–8; as teleology 244

intentionality 202–7, 222–7; act intentionality (Brentano) 175, 245; the concept explicated 243–48;defined by Hegel, 233–4; as dialogical relation 235; dimensions of 248; family of terms associated with the word 244; founded in Dasein's transcendence 236–7; functioning 236; in Heidegger's description 228 as a mode of existential comportment; of Dasein 228–33, 230–1, 245–6; in Husserlian phenomenology 202–6, 223–7, 231, 245–6; incarnate 231; misinterpretations of intentionality 246–7; as plan or project 244–5; as semantic property (intension of a concept) 245; as teleology 244; as transcendence or world-openness 246–7

internalization 252; of the discourse of the Other 268; of language and its worlds 258; of normative voices of others 258, 264–5, 268; of social objects and relations 255

interpersonal communication 127, 210; relationships 252, 267–9, 269–74, 296–7, 376; worlds 341–2

intrapersonal communication 353; the unconscious as 350, 353, 354–6

intersubjective recognition 205, 221–22, 235–6; moral character 253; ontological primacy of 253

intersubjectivity 118, 127, 128, 186, 205, 221–22, 226, 228, 230–1, 249, 303–4, 341–3; deconstruction of the term 380–1; displaced by the concept of transactional configuration 380; ethical 376–7; theories of 259; transcendental 231, 235–6, 267–9, 348, 359

intertextuality 49–50, 65, in deconstruction 373–5; in Kristevan semiotics 91; of the Other and Unconsciousness 353–6

judgement: in action (the practical syllogism) 320; Aristotle on 318; and 'appraisal praxis' 325; concept of 324–6; critical/discriminatory 318, 324–5; as cultural faculty/competence 323; everyday 185, 228, 270, 300, 319–24; and decision-making 320–1; forensic 300, 321–4; forms of; practical 270–4; non-dilemmatic 310, 318; moral 310, 326–32; moral situations 310, 318, 320; practical art 320; prepredicative 228; rules of 323; as a spectrum of judgemental processes and activities 325–6; styles of 323–4; toward a sociological theory of judgement 325–6; types of 319; warranted (warranted assertability) 323–4; without explicit rules 319–20, 322–4; see phronesis

judgement form(s): aesthetic, ethical, and epistemic 318–19, 321; moral, aesthetic, religious, scientific and philosophical 324–5; and forms of life 319; political 319; styles 324

kinaesthesia; kinaesthetic intentionalities 202; motility 201–2; mutually coordinated kinaesthetic systems 311–12; mutual movement 382; practical 'kinaesthetic maps' 310; of the lived-body 311–13

knowledge and power xviii, 14–15, 18–22, 117

knowledge: apodictic 79; *a priori* 42, 174, 213; embodied 5, 185ff., 226–7, 272–4, 275, 276–7 ('thought-in-practice'); everyday

18–19, 36–7, 185, 299–302;
commonsense 37–8, 270–1; forms of
27–8, 357–8; immediate 186; interests
370–1; intuitive 271, 272–3, 287–90,
290; mediate 186–7, 296; as organon
of action (pragmatism) 297;
perceptual 184–6, 187–93;
philosophical (as topics for the
sociology of knowledge) 385;
production xviii, 384–5, 385–9;
prereflective 208–11, 225–6; as
revelation/disclosure 408–10, 410–22;
scientific 229, 385–9; sensory 148–51,
184–93; social 288–90; sociology of
384–9, 389–93; tacit 288–90;
technologies 14; transcendental 173.
174. 175
knowledgeable activities xviii, 18–19,
269–74, 279–82, 296
language: as act/activity 88–92; as
ancient city (Wittgenstein) 94–5; as
channel 85; as communicative vehicle,
73, 85–8; as conventional code 86; as
description 77–8, 79; as dialogical
texture of semiotic praxis 353–4,
377–8, 400–22 and throughout
Chapter 12; as discourse of
discourses 404–5 and throughout
Chapter 12; as domain of
articulations 365–7, 400ff.; as energy
73, 88–92; as expression 73, 88–92,
93–4; as 'the house of Being'
(Heidegger) 91; as information 85; as
instrument 39–40, 73; as lamp 93,
173; as language-games (*Sprachspiele*)
93–4, 95, 257–8, 275; as machine
82–4; as matrix of mind and self
255–62, 400ff.; as means of
communication 85–8; as medium
85–8, 94; as mirror 13, 39, 57, 73–2,
84, 93, 107–8; as nascent science 75;
as object 80; as organon of organons
82, 297, 314; as picture 75–6, 79–80;
as play/game 365–7; as practical
consciousness 403–8; as primal
thinking 269; as prior field of
articulations 404–5; as prior
ontological site of human action
404–8; as power (*energeia*) 88–9; as
productivity 88–92; as reality 80; as
reflective 73–82; as reflector 80; as
resource 7; as screen 80; as
self-revising machine 82; as sign

system 85, 364–7; as *speculum mentis*
84; as surface 80; as swamp (Popper)
95; as symbolic communication
264–5, 265–74; as system of
differences 364–7; as topic 7; as
transparent medium 34; as vehicle
85–8, 93–4; world-disclosure 88–90;
formal 12, 87, 364–5; functions 82;
'has no essence' 91–4; private 86; pure
289–90; of things 75–6; and the
unconscious 352–6, 365
Lebenswelt 151, 226, 236
life: as being-addressed 377; as
configured time 147; concept of
140–1; continuum of 145–6; horizon
of 141; life-forms 143, 145–7, 152–3,
153–6 (see *forms of life*); life-orders
(*Lebensordnungen*) 27; life-*driven* as
against life-*experiencing* organisms
142, 143, 148–51, 160–5; life-tasks
(sensing, digesting, perceiving, etc.)
150–1; pre-understanding of; sentient
155–6; sciences, Chapter 3, esp.
158–65
life-in-the-world x, 141, 205, 261–2,
275–6, 278–8, 286–7; dialectical
nature of 376–84, 452–3n2, 453n3; *see*
life-world
life-with-others 281–2, 286–7, 376–84
life-world 7, 147, 151, 359–64; *a priori*
structures of 305; colonization of
22–3; commonality as necessary
fiction 187; in Husserl's later
phenomenology 305, 453n3;
life-worlds 38; loss/occlusion of 124,
359–64; of organisms 143–156,
158–65, 259; prepredicative
intentionalities 225–7;
intersubjectively shared 255, 275–6;
literature on 446–9n2; pretheoretical
177, 208, 226; and rationalized
systems 22; primary world of
perception 185, 226; reflexive 'return'
to the life-world 236; in Schutzian
phenomenology 304–5; sociocultural
nature 205, 376–84; temporal 225–6,
227;
light 40; of consciousness 168; as food
150–1; as metaphor 40; light-sensitive
organisms 150–1, 153; light-writing
(inscription, *Lichtbild*) 63;
ontological image (*Licht*) 139
limit(s): four concepts of limit 6–13